Contemporary Linguistics
An Introduction

Learning About Language

General Editors:

Geoffrey Leech and Mick Short, *Lancaster University*
Guy Cook, *Institute of Education, University of London*

For a full list see page xiii

Contemporary Linguistics

An Introduction

Edited by
WILLIAM O'GRADY
MICHAEL DOBROVOLSKY
FRANCIS KATAMBA

LONGMAN
London and New York

Addison Wesley Longman Limited
Edinburgh Gate
Harlow, Essex CM20 2JE
United Kingdom
and Associated Companies throughout the world

First edition © Copp Clark Pitman Ltd., 1987
Second edition © Copp Clark Pitman Ltd., 1992
Third edition © Copp Clark Pitman Ltd., 1996

First published by Copp Clark Pitman Ltd., 1987 under the title of Contemporary
Linguistic Analysis: An Introduction
This adapted edition © Addison Wesley Longman Limited 1997 except the chapter on
Computational Linguistics © St Martin's Press Inc.

ISBN 0 582 24691 1 Ppr

British Library Cataloguing-in-Publication Data

A catalogue record for this book is
available from the British Library

Library of Congress Cataloging-in-Publication Data

Contemporary linguistics : an introduction / edited by William
   O'Grady, Michael Dobrovolsky, Francis Katamba.
       p.   cm. – (Learning about language)
     Adaptation of: Contemporary linguistics analysis.
     Includes bibliographical references and index.
     ISBN 0-582-24691-1 (pbk.)
     1. Linguistics.   I. O'Grady, William D. (William Delaney), 1952– .
II. Dobrovolsky, Michael, 1942–.   III. Katamba, Francis, 1947– .
IV. Title: Contemporary linguistics analysis.   V. Series.
P121.C5854   1997
410–dc20   96-23860
                                          CIP

Set by 33 in 10/12pt Times
Produced by Longman Asia Limited, Hong Kong
NPCC/01

To the memory of our friend and colleague
Ewa Iwanicka
1950–1986

Convinced at once that, in order to break loose from the beaten paths of opinions and systems, it was necessary to proceed in my study of man and society by scientific methods, and in a rigorous manner, I devoted one year to philology and grammar; linguistics, or the natural history of speech, being, of all the sciences, that which best suited the researches which I was about to commence.

* Pierre-Joseph Proudhon, *What is Property?* (1840)

Table of contents

Learning About Language

General Editors:
Geoffrey Leech and Mick Short, *Lancaster University*
Guy Cook, *Institute of Education, University of London*

Already published:

Acknowledgements

We are grateful to the following for permission to reproduce copyright material:

Faber & Faber Ltd for an extract from the poem *East Coker* by T.S. Eliot in *Four Quartets*; the author Dr Judith Klavans, for an updated version of the chapter 'Computational Linguistics' by Dr Judith L. Klavans from *Contemporary Linguistic Analysis* by William O'Grady and Michael Dobrovolsky © (1996) St Martin's Press Inc.; International Phonetic Association for the use of the International Phonetic Alphabet on the inside back cover and Table 2.35; Harcourt Brace & Company for maps from *Problems in the Origins and Development of the English Language*, Third Edition, by John Algeo, copyright © 1982 by Harcourt Brace & Company, reproduced by permission of the publisher; Stanford University Press and Hodder Headline plc (Edward Arnold Publishers Ltd) for the map (our Figure 9.10) based on map 6.4 from *A guide to the world's languages Vol I: Classification* by Merritt Ruhlen (1990); American Psychological Association and the author Professor Elizabeth Stine-Morrow for our Figure 11.3 'Bar-pressing times in sentence reading' from 'On-line Processing of Written Text by Younger and Older Adults' *Psychology and Aging*, 1990, **5**, 68–78; Holt, Rinehart and Winston, Inc. (HRWC) for our Figure 11.10, being Figure 7.6, 'Levelt's Model', on page 296 of *Psycholinguistics* by Jean B. Gleason and Nan B. Ratner (1993); Blackwell Publishers for our Figure 14.3 'A Portion of the Clonard network, showing density of 100 per cent' being Figure 3.2 on page 58 in *Language and Social Networks* by Lesley Milroy (1987); Sage Publications and Louise Peronnet for our Figure 14.4 'Words for "Fishhook" [Standard French *hamecon*] in French dialects of Atlantic Canada and western France' from Louise Peronnet and Paul-Andre Arsenault 'Linguistic Atlas of French Maritime Terminology: Computerized Maps' in *Journal of English Linguistics* **22** (1): 25–29 (1990); The Athlone Press Limited for our Figure 14.5 'Map showing the distribution of words for *Cow-house*' from Martin Wakelin/*English Dialects: An Introduction* (1972); the Sports Council for our Figure 15.4 'Contemporary pictograms: British Sports Council signs for sporting events'; The University of Nebraska Press for our Figures 15.9 'Changes in cuneiform writing' and 15.17 'Development of writing systems' from pages 45 and 89 of *The Origins of Writing* edited by Wayne M. Senner (1989); Charles E. Tuttle Publishing Co., Inc. for our Figure 15.19 'Hiragana and katakana syllabaries and their phonetic values' from *Read Japanese Today* by Len Walsh (1971); Springer-Verlag GmbH & Co. KG for our Figure 16.7 'The graded continuum from sobbing to screaming' from D. Todt's 'Serial Calling as a Mediator of Interaction Processes: Crying' pp. 88–107 in *Primate Vocal Communication*, edited by D. Todt, D.P. Goedeking and D. Symmes (1988); Harvard University Press for our Figure 16.8 'Bee dancing' from page 57 of *The Dance Language An Orientation of Bees* by K. Von Frische © 1967, 1993 by the President and Fellows of Harvard College; Cambridge University Press for our Figure 16.9 'Spectrogram of a robin song' from *Bird Song* by W.H. Thorpe; Harcourt Brace & Company (HBC) for the spectrograms in our Figures 17.1 and 17.2, being Figures 8.6 and 8.9 on pages 177 and 182 of the second edition of *A Course in Phonetics* edited by Peter Ladefoged (1982); The Institute of Education, University of London for our Table 14.15 from The Linguistic Minorities Project Report *Linguistic Minorities in England* (1983).

There is a 'Source' section at the end of each chapter.

Whilst every effort has been made to trace the owners of copyright material, in a few cases this has proved impossible and we take this opportunity to offer our apologies to any copyright holders whose rights we may have unwittingly infringed.

Preface

Linguistics as a discipline has both blossomed and fragmented in recent years. To some extent, this has been reflected in the fact that many authors of up-to-date introductions to the subject have preferred to write separate introductions to phonetics, syntax, semantics, psycholinguistics, sociolinguistics, and so on, rather than general surveys of the entire field.

I suspect that there are quite a few teachers of introductory linguistic classes who, like me, have been frustrated by the lack of a single book that can give their students a self-contained overview of the subject reflecting today's linguistic theory and practice. There have been books like Hockett's *A Course in Modern Linguistics*, Gleason's *An Introduction to Descriptive Linguistics* and Robins' *General Linguistics: An Introductory Survey* which provide a comprehensive grounding in the linguistics of their time. There is a need for a comparable integrated survey of today's linguistics. For, undoubtedly, it is still important for beginning students to get a panoramic view of the vast landscape of human language before delving deep into the nooks and crannies of the various linguistics specialisms. So, a while ago, I began writing an introductory linguistics textbook which was intended to provide students with a solid grounding in current linguistics.

Soon after the project got underway, while on a visit to America, I went browsing in a bookshop and picked up a copy of William O'Grady, Michael Dobrovolsky and Mark Aronoff's book *Contemporary Linguistics: An Introduction* which had been adapted from *Contemporary Linguistic Analysis: An Introduction* published by Copp Clark Pitman Ltd, Canada. It was the most fortunate browsing I have ever done. Here was a book that does extremely well what my embryonic book was attempting to do.

It treats in considerable detail the core areas of theoretical linguistics as well as many branches of applied linguistics. Just as important, it is both accessible and unstuffy without being patronizing; it is critical without being unduly polemical. I bought myself a copy and as I read through it, I realized why this book had become a standard introduction to linguistics in North America.

I therefore agreed with Addison Wesley Longman in the UK that rather than try to replicate what *Contemporary Linguistic Analysis: An Introduction* does so well, it would be more sensible for me to team up with William O'Grady and Michael Dobrovolsky (who were just about to start work on a revised third Canadian edition of the book) and produce a non-North American edition of *Contemporary Linguistic Analysis*. That is what happened. The result of our collaboration is the product you have before you.

This text is in many respects the same as that of the third Canadian edition, however, it differs from it (and from the US edition prepared by Mark Aronoff) in a number of important ways. Specifically Canadian material has been omitted. Thus, virtually all of the chapter on the Amerindian languages of Canada has been left out – only a short extract from it has been included in the chapter on 'The classification of languages'. Furthermore, the discussion of the English sound system in the phonetics and phonology chapters focuses on British rather than North American English. Also, throughout the book, where a British example can illustrate a point just as well as a Canadian example, Canadian material has been replaced with British material. This is especially true of sections dealing with the social aspects of language in both the opening chapter and in the chapter on sociolinguistics, which have both been extensively revised. However, where Canadian data illustrate a point of general interest, they have been left unchanged.

Linguistics is a fast-developing discipline. To make sure that the book is up-to-date, there are extensive revisions of the previous edition, most of them shared with the Canadian third edition, especially in the core areas of the phonology, morphology, syntax, interfaces and semantics. As well, new chapters on psycholinguistics and second language acquisition that appear for the first time in the third Canadian edition are included here, as is an updated version of the chapter on computational linguistics which was originally commissioned for the American edition.

An important feature of this book is that the text is graded in order to cater for the different needs and expectations of its readers – some students begin studying linguistics at university while others have already encountered it, having read books previously used on first-year university courses, as part of the Advanced Level English language syllabus. Most of the material is suitable for all readers. But certain sections are signposted as 'advanced' and are intended for those who are ready to pursue a particular topic in greater depth.

Another feature of the book is the inclusion in some chapters of appendices which take the student step by step through the production of a particular type of linguistic analysis. This reflects our belief that students learn linguistics by *doing* it themselves.

There are many people I must thank for their assistance in preparing this volume. First and foremost, I must acknowledge my sincere debt of gratitude to William O'Grady, Michael Dobrovolsky and Hui-hua Hwang who enthusiastically read and commented on alterations and additions I introduced. As well, this book has benefited from the extensive comments of Geoff Leech and the advice and support of Mark Aronoff.

Thanks also go to a number of people at Addison Wesley Longman in the UK and Canada who were always eager to help and whose assistance helped to make the preparation of the book both smooth and pleasant.

Lancaster, December 1996   Francis Katamba

Preface to the original edition

published by Copp Clark Pitman Ltd, Canada

Thanks to the application of rigorous analysis to familiar subject matter, linguistics provides students with an ideal introduction to the kind of thinking we call 'scientific'. Such thinking proceeds from an appreciation of problems arising from bodies of data, to hypotheses that attempt to account for those problems, to the careful testing and extension of these hypotheses. But science is more than a formal activity. One of the great pleasures offered to introductory students of linguistics is the discovery of the impressive body of subconscious knowledge that underlies language use. This book attempts to emphasize the extent of this knowledge as well as to introduce the scientific methodology used in linguistic analysis.

Although this is the first linguistics textbook designed primarily for a Canadian readership, we have tried to do much more than simply provide coverage of linguistic phenomena peculiar to Canada. As the title suggests, we have attempted an introduction to linguistic analysis as it is practised at this stage in the development of our discipline. While we do not ignore or reject other fruitful approaches to linguistics, we have taken the generative paradigm as basic for two reasons. First, generative linguistics provides a relatively coherent and integrated approach to basic linguistic phenomena. Phonetics, phonology, morphology, syntax, and semantics are viewed within this framework as perhaps in no other as fully integrated and interrelated. Secondly, the generative approach has been widely influential in its application to a broad range of other linguistic phenomena over the past twenty years.

The extent of our 'contemporariness' has been limited by the inevitable compromise between the need to present basic concepts and the demands of sophisticated and competing recent approaches. In many cases, early versions of our chapters were judged 'too contemporary' by instructors who were not specialists in the subfields in question. This led to substantial revisions and a somewhat more traditional approach to certain issues (especially in the area of syntax) than was originally intended. Where possible, however, later sections of the chapters are used to present more contemporary material. In this way, we have attempted to provide what is promised by the title – an introductory text that provides a solid grounding in basic linguistic concepts, but one that also prepares the student to go on to current work in the discipline. For this reason, the student is introduced to multi-levelled phonology (in preparation for further tiered analyses), allophonic/ morphophonemic distinctions (in preparation for lexical phonology), inter- action among components of the grammar (in preparation for a more extended modular approach), word formation rules in morphology, and examples of parametric variation in syntax.

To the extent possible, we have attempted to integrate the basic mechanisms outlined in the first five chapters of the book into our discussion of phenomena in later chapters. Thus, our discussion of semantics, historical linguistics, first and second language acquisition, and neurolinguistics draws to some degree on the notions presented in our introduction to generative grammar.

No textbook can be all things to all users. We hope that this book will provide students not only with a springboard to the realm of scientific linguistic analysis, but with a greater appreciation for the wonder of human language, the variety and complexity of its structure, and the subtlety of its use.

William O'Grady
Michael Dobrovolsky

List of technical abbreviations

*	(in rules) one or more	Det	determiner
*	(in front of words or sentences) unacceptable	DR	delayed release
		EEG	Electroencephalogram
#	word boundary	EA	error analysis
1	first person	Erg	ergative case
1	primary stress	ERP	event-related potential
2	second person	ESL	English as a second language
2	secondary stress		
3	third person	FN	first name
A	adjective	Fut	future tense
Abl	ablative case	Gen	genitive case
Abs	absolutive case	go	goal
Ac	accusative case	H	high tone
Adv	adverb	IA	inflectional affix
AdvP	adverb phrase	IL	interlanguage
Af	affix	indic	indicative
ag	agent	inf	infinitive
AP	adjective phrase	Infl	Inflection
ATR	advanced tongue root	IPA	International Phonetic Alphabet
Aux	auxiliary verb		
B	bound root	KT	kinterm
C	coda	L	low tone
C	complementizer	L1	first language
C	consonant	L2	second language
CA	contrastive analysis	LN	last name
caus	cause	Loc	locative case
CG	constricted glottis	Loc	location
CLT	communicative language teaching	M	man
		M	mid tone
C_0	any number of consonants	MRD	machine-readable dictionary
Con	conjunction	μ	mora
CP	complementizer phrase	N	noun
CT	computerized axial tomography	N	nucleus
		Nom	nominative case
CYC	Cape York Creole	num	number
DA	derivational affix	NP	noun phrase
Dat	dative case	O	(direct) object
Deg	degree word	O	onset

Obl	oblique	S	sentence
OE	Old English	S	subject
P	preposition	σ	syllable
Pass	passive	SES	socio-economic status
PC	Principal Component	SG	spread glottis
PCA	Principal Components Analysis	sg	singular
		SLA	second language acquisition
PET	Positron Emission Tomography	Spec	specifier
		th	theme
PIE	Proto-Indo-European	T	title alone
pl	plural	TLN	title + last name
PP	prepositional phrase	Top	topic
PR	phonetic representation	UG	Universal Grammar
Prs	present tense	UR	underlying representation
Pst	past tense	UR	unrounded
R	rhyme	V	verb
R	rounded	V	vowel
RC	relative clause	VP	verb phrase
REA	right ear advantage	W	woman
recip	recipient	Wd	word
RP	Received Pronunciation		

Language: a preview

William O'Grady, Michael Dobrovolsky and Francis Katamba

The gift of language is the single human trait that marks us all genetically, setting us apart from the rest of life.

≈ Lewis Thomas, *The Lives of a Cell*

Language is many things – a system of communication, a medium for thought, a vehicle for literary expression, a social institution, a matter for political controversy, a catalyst for nation building. All human beings normally speak at least one language and it is hard to imagine much significant social, intellectual, or artistic activity taking place in its absence. Each of us, then, has a stake in understanding something about the nature and use of language. This book provides a basic introduction to linguistics, the discipline that studies these matters.

A CREATIVE SYSTEM

What is human language? What does it mean to know a language? To answer these questions, it is first necessary to understand the resources that a language makes available to its **native speakers**, those who have acquired it as children in a natural setting.

The scope and diversity of human thought and experience place great demands on language. Because communication is not restricted to a fixed set of topics, language must do something more than provide a package of ready-made messages. It must enable us to produce and understand new words, phrases, and sentences as the need arises. In short, human language must be **creative** – allowing novelty and innovation in response to new thoughts, experiences, and situations.

Underlying the creative aspect of language is an intricate mental system that defines the boundaries within which innovation can take place. The operation of this system can be illustrated by a relatively simple phenomenon in English (see Table 1.1): the process that creates verbs (roughly, words naming actions) from nouns (roughly, words naming things).

Table 1.1 Nouns used as verbs

Noun use	*Verb use*
leave the boat on the *beach*	*beach* the boat
keep the aeroplane on the *ground*	*ground* the aeroplane
crush the aspirin into *powder*	*powder* the aspirin
stab the man with a *knife*	*knife* the man
catch the fish with a *spear*	*spear* the fish
make the child an *orphan*	*orphan* the child

As the following sentences show, there is a great deal of freedom to innovate in the formation of such verbs.

1)

a. I *wristed* the ball over the net.

b. He would try to *stiff-upper-lip* it through.

c. She *Houdini'd* her way out of the locked closet.

There are also limits on this freedom, however. For instance, a new verb is rarely coined if a word with the intended meaning already exists. Although we say *jail the robber* to mean 'put the robber in jail', we do not say *prison the robber* to mean 'put the robber in prison'. This is because the well-established verb *imprison* already has the meaning that the new form would have.

There are also special constraints on the meaning and use of particular subclasses of these verbs. One such constraint involves verbs that are created from time expressions such as *summer*, *holiday*, and so on.

2)

a. Julia *summered* in Paris.

b. Harry *wintered* in Mexico.

c. Bob *holidayed* in France.

d. They *honeymooned* in Hawaii.

Although the sentences in *2)* are all natural-sounding, not all time expressions can be used in this way. (Throughout this book, an asterisk is used to indicate that a linguistic form or utterance is unacceptable.)

3)

a. *Jerome *midnighted* in the streets.

b. *Andrea *nooned* at the restaurant.

c. *Philip *one o'clocked* at the airport.

These examples show that when a verb is created from a time expression, it must be given a very specific interpretation – roughly paraphrasable as 'to be somewhere for the period of time X'. Thus, *to summer in Paris* is 'to be in Paris for the summer', *to holiday in France* is 'to be in France for the holidays', and so on. Since *noon* and *midnight* express points in time rather than extended periods of time, they cannot be used to create new verbs of this type.[1]

Systematic constraints are essential to the viability of the creative process. If well-established words were constantly being replaced by new creations, the vocabulary of English would be so unstable that communication could be jeopardized. A similar danger would arise if there were no constraints on the meaning of new words. If *They winter in Hawaii* could mean 'They make it snow in Hawaii' or 'They wish it were winter in Hawaii' or any other arbitrary thing, the production and interpretation of language would be chaotic and unsystematic, undermining the role of language communication.

Some other examples

Creative systems are found in all aspects of language, including the way in which sounds are combined to form words. The forms in *4)*, for instance, are recognizable as possible English words (which might be used as names for new products or processes).

4)

a.   prasp

b.   flib

c.   traf

Such forms contrast with the patterns in *5)*, which simply do not have the shape of English words.

5)

a.   *psapr

b.   *bfli

c.   *ftra

The contrast between the forms in *4)* and *5)* illustrates that the set of possible sound patterns reflects considerations that permit certain novel sound combinations, but prohibit others.

Still other considerations determine how new words can be created from already existing forms with the help of special endings. Imagine, for example, that the word *soleme* entered the English language (used perhaps for a newly discovered atomic particle). As a speaker of English, you then automatically know that something with the properties of a soleme could be called *solemic*. You also know that to make something solemic is to *solemicize* it, and you would call this process *solemicization*. Further, you know that the *c* is pronounced as *s* in *solemicize* but as *k* in *solemic*. Without hesitation, you also recognize that *solemicize* is pronounced with the stress on the second syllable. (You would say *soLEmicize*, not *SOlemicize* or *solemiCIZE*.)

Nowhere is the ability to deal with novel utterances more obvious than in the production and comprehension of sentences. Apart from a few fixed expressions and greetings, much of what you say, hear, and read in the course of a day consists of sentences that are new to you. In conversations, lectures, newscasts, and textbooks you are regularly exposed to novel combinations of words, the expression of unfamiliar ideas, and the presentation of new information. Consider, for instance, the paragraph that you are currently reading. While each of these sentences is no doubt perfectly comprehensible to you, it is extremely unlikely that you have ever seen any of them before.

This ability to produce and understand unfamiliar utterances does not ensure that you can understand or use any imaginable combination of words. For example, you doubtlessly find it difficult (if not impossible) to interpret the utterance in *6)*. Even though all the words used here are familiar ones, they are simply not arranged in the right way to be a sentence of English.

6)

*Frightened dog the cat that the chased mouse a.

Moreover, even though you can probably understand a sentence such as *7a)*, by analogy perhaps with *7b)*, there is something about it that makes it sound less than acceptable.

7)

a.   *He brought a chair in order to sit on.

b.   He brought a chair to sit on.

As with other aspects of language, the ability to form and interpret sentences is subject to systematic limitations.

2

GRAMMAR AND LINGUISTIC COMPETENCE

As we have seen, speakers of a language are able to produce and understand an unlimited number of utterances, including many that are novel and unfamiliar. This ability, which is often called **linguistic competence**, constitutes the central subject matter of linguistics and of this book.

In investigating linguistic competence, linguists focus on the mental system that allows human beings to form and interpret the words and sentences of their language. This system is called a **grammar**. For the purposes of this book, we will divide the grammar into the components shown in Table 1.2.

Table 1.2   The components of a grammar

Component	Responsibility
Phonetics	the articulation and perception of speech sounds
Phonology	the patterning of speech sounds
Morphology	word formation
Syntax	sentence formation
Semantics	the interpretation of words and sentences

Linguists use the term *grammar* in a rather special and technical way.

Because this usage may be unfamiliar to the average university student, we will devote some time to considering several fundamental properties of the system that linguists call a grammar.

2.1

Generality: all languages have a grammar

One of the most fundamental claims of modern linguistic analysis is that all languages have a grammar. This can be verified by considering a few simple facts. Since all languages are spoken, they must have phonetic and phonological systems; since they all have words and sentences, they also must have a morphology and a syntax; and since these words and sentences have systematic meanings, there obviously must be semantic principles as well. As these are the very things that make up a grammar, it follows that all human languages have this type of system.

It is not unusual to hear the remark that some language – Acadian French, Cree, or Swahili – 'has no grammar'. (This is especially common in the case of languages that are not written or have not yet been analysed by Western scholars.) Unfamiliar languages sometimes appear to an untrained observer to have no grammar simply because their grammatical systems are different from those of better-known languages. In Walbiri (an aboriginal language of Australia), for example, the relative ordering of words is so free that the English sentence *The two dogs now see several kangaroos* could be translated by the equivalent of any of the following sentences.

8)

a.   Dogs two now see kangaroos several.

b.   See now dogs two kangaroos several.

c.   See now kangaroos several dogs two.

d.   Kangaroos several now dogs two see.

e.   Kangaroos several now see dogs two.

Whereas Walbiri may not restrict the order of words in the way English does, its grammar imposes other types of requirements. For example, in the sentence types we are considering, Walbiri speakers must place the ending *lu* on the word for 'dogs' to indicate that it names the animals that do the seeing rather than the animals that are seen. In English, by contrast, this information is conveyed by placing *two dogs* in front of the verb and *several kangaroos* after it.

Rather than showing that Walbiri has no grammar, such differences simply demonstrate that it has a grammar unlike that of English in certain respects. This important point is applicable to all differences among languages: although no two languages have exactly the same grammar, there are no languages without a grammar.

A similar point can be made about different varieties of the same language. As you are probably already aware, English is the language of many different communities around the world. The particular variety of English found within each of these communities has its own characteristic pronunciation, vocabulary, and sentence patterns. This is just another way of saying that each variety of English has its own grammar. Just as it is impossible to have a language without a grammar, so no variety of a language could exist if it did not have a grammar.

2.2

Equality: all grammars are equal

Whenever there is more than one variety of a particular language, questions arise as to whether one is somehow better or more correct than another. From the point of view of modern linguistics, it makes no more sense to say that one variety of English is better than another than it does to say that the grammar of English is better (or worse) than the grammar of Thai.

All languages and all varieties of a particular language have grammars that enable their speakers to express any proposition that the human mind can produce. In terms of this all-important criterion, then, all varieties of language are absolutely equal as instruments of communication and thought. The goal of contemporary linguistic analysis is not to rank languages on some imaginary scale of superiority. Rather, linguists seek to understand the nature of the grammatical systems that allow people to speak and understand a language.

This same point is sometimes made by noting that linguistics is **descriptive**, not **prescriptive**. This means that linguists seek to *describe* human linguistic ability and knowledge, not to *prescribe* one system in preference to another. A parallel point of view is adopted in other scientific disciplines as well. The first concern of all scientists is to describe and explain the facts they observe, not to change them.

Even though it rejects prescriptivism, modern linguistic analysis does not deny the importance of clear expression in writing and speech. Such skills are quite rightly an object of concern among educators. However, the difficulties that arise in these areas typically result from the inconsistent or careless use of one's linguistic knowledge, not from any inherent flaw in the grammar itself.

Linguists also acknowledge that certain patterns (*I seen that*, *They was there*, *He didn't do nothing*, *He ain't here*) may be restricted to particular socio-economic groups within the English-speaking community. As discussed in more detail in Chapter 14, the use of these patterns may therefore have negative social consequences: it may be harder to win a scholarship, to get a job, to be accepted in certain circles, and so forth. From a purely linguistic point of view, however, there is absolutely nothing wrong with grammars that permit such structures. Like grammars for other variants of English (and other languages), they permit their users to express and understand the same unlimited range of thoughts and ideas.

2.3

Universality: grammars are alike in basic ways

There are many differences among languages, as even a superficial examination of their sound patterns, vocabularies, and word order reveals. But this does not mean that there are no limits on the type of grammars that human beings can acquire and use. Quite to the contrary, current research suggests that there are important grammatical principles and tendencies shared by all human languages.

One such principle involves the manner in which sentences are negated. With unlimited variation, one would expect the equivalent of English *not* to occur in different positions within the sentence in different languages. Thus, we might predict that each of the following possibilities should occur with roughly equal frequency.

9)

a.   Not Pat is here.

b.   Pat not is here.

c.   Pat is not here.

d.   Pat is here not.

As it happens, the first and fourth patterns are very rare. In virtually all languages, negative elements such as *not* either immediately precede or immediately follow the verb.

The relative ordering of other elements is also subject to constraints. To see this, we need only consider the six logically possible orders for a simple three-word statement such as *Australians like cricket*.

10)

a.   Australians like cricket.

b.   Australians cricket like.

c.   Like Australians cricket.

d.   Like cricket Australians.

e.   Cricket like Australians.

f.   Cricket Australians like.

Interestingly, the overwhelming majority of the world's languages adopt one of the first three orders for basic statements. Only a handful of languages use any of the last three orders as basic. This once again reflects the existence of constraints and preferences that limit variation among languages.

These are not isolated examples. As later chapters will show, some grammatical categories and principles are universal. And where there is variation (as in the case of word order), there is typically a very limited set of options. Contrary to first appearances, then, the set of grammars learned and used by human beings is limited in significant ways.

2.4

Tacitness

Because the use of language to communicate presupposes a grammar, it follows that all speakers of a language must have knowledge of its grammar. However, this knowledge differs from knowledge of arithmetic, road safety, and other subjects that are taught at home or in school. Unlike these other types of knowledge, grammatical knowledge is acquired without the help of instruction when one is still a child and it remains largely subconscious throughout life. As an example of this, consider your pronunciation of the past tense ending written as *ed* in the following words.

11)

a. hunted

b. slipped

c. buzzed

Notice that whereas you say *id* in *hunted*, you say *t* in *slipped* and *d* in *buzzed*. Moreover, if you heard the new verb *flib*, you would form the past tense as *flibbed* and pronounce the ending as *d*. Although it is unlikely that you have ever been aware of this phenomenon before now, you make these distinctions automatically if you are a native speaker of English. This is because you acquired the grammatical subsystem regulating this aspect of speech when you were a child and it now exists subconsciously in your mind.

Even more subtle phonological patterning can be found in language, as the following contrasts help illustrate.

12)

pint	*paynk
fiend	*fiemp
locked	*lockf
wronged	*wrongv
next	*nexk
glimpse	*glimpk

The words in the left-hand column obey an obscure constraint on the selection of consonant sequences in word-final position: when a vowel is long and followed by two consonants (*pint*) or when a vowel is short and followed by three consonant sounds (*next*, pronounced 'nekst'), the final consonant must always be one made with the tongue tip raised. (The consonants *t*, *d*, *s*, and *z* are made in this manner, but consonants such as *p*, *f*, *v*, and *k* are not.) Words that violate this phonological constraint (the right-hand column) are unacceptable to speakers of English. Even linguists have to dig deeply to uncover such patterning, but in everyday language use, we routinely make decisions about the acceptability of forms based on subconscious knowledge of such constraints.

Consider one final example. Speakers of English know that there are certain structures in which the word *he* can refer to each member of a group or to a single individual outside that group.

13)

Each boy who(m) the woman interviewed thinks that he is a genius.

Sentence *13)* can mean either that each boy in the group that the woman interviewed thinks that he himself is a genius or that each boy thinks that a particular person not mentioned in the sentence (say, the teacher) is a genius.

However, only one of these interpretations is possible in the following sentence.

14)
The woman who interviewed each boy thinks that he is a genius.

In *14)*, *he* can refer only to someone not mentioned in the sentence. In contrast with what happens in sentence *13)*, *he* cannot refer to each individual in the group designated by the phrase *each boy*. Since speakers are able to make this contrast, they must have knowledge of the relevant grammatical principle even though they are not consciously aware of it.

2.5

Grammar

Linguists use the term *grammar* to refer to a subconscious linguistic system of a particular type. Consisting of several components (phonetics, phonology, morphology, syntax, and semantics), a grammar makes possible the production and comprehension of a potentially unlimited number of utterances. Because no language can exist without a grammar and no one can use a language without knowledge of its grammar, the study of grammatical systems has come to be the focus of contemporary linguistic analysis.

As noted above, the grammatical knowledge needed to use and understand language is acquired without the benefit of instruction and is for the most part subconscious. Since we therefore cannot investigate grammar by simply recalling prior training or by self-consultation, the study of human linguistic systems requires considerable effort and ingenuity. As is the case in all science, information about facts that can be observed (the pronunciation of words, the interpretation of sentences, and so on) must be used to draw inferences about the sometimes invisible mechanisms (atoms, cells, or grammars, as the case may be) that are ultimately responsible for these phenomena. A good deal of this book is concerned with the findings of this research and with what they tell us about the nature and use of human language.

3

CHANGEABILITY: GRAMMARS CHANGE OVER TIME

It is a well-established fact that the grammars of all languages are constantly changing. Some of these changes are relatively minor and occur very quickly (for example, the addition of new words such as *ethnic cleansing*, *spin doctor*, *yuppie*, *glasnost*, *yobbocracy*, *able-bodism*, *chunnel*, *internet*, *autocrime*, *nukemare*, *vegeburger*, *grunge* and *acid house* to the vocabulary of English). Other changes have a more dramatic effect on the overall form of the language and typically take place over a long period of time. The formation of negative structures in English has undergone this type of change. Prior to 1200, English formed negative constructions by placing *ne* before the verb and *not* (sometimes spelled *nawt*) after it.

15)

a. Ic ne seye not. ('I don't say.')

b. He ne speketh nawt. ('He does not speak.')

By 1400 or thereabouts, *ne* was used infrequently and *not* (or *nawt*) typically occurred by itself after the verb.

16)

a. I seye not the wordes.

b. We saw nawt the knyghtes.

It was not until about two centuries later that English developed its current practice of allowing *not* to occur after only certain types of verbs (such as *do*, *have*, *will*, and so on).

17)

a. I will not say the words. (versus *I will say not the words.)

b. He did not see the knights. (versus *He saw not the knights.)

These modifications illustrate the extent to which grammars can change over time. The structures exemplified in *16)* are archaic by today's standards and those in *15)* sound completely foreign to most speakers of modern English.

3.1

Purists view change as decay

Through the centuries, individuals and organizations who believe that certain varieties of language are better than others have frequently expressed concern over what they perceive to be the deterioration of English. Today, the lamentations of these purists can be found in books like J. Simon's *Paradigms Lost: Reflections on Literacy and its Decline* published in America in 1980 and J. Honey's *The Language Trap: Race, Class and the 'Standard English' Issue in British Schools*, which appeared in England in 1983.

'Diseased English'

Some of the denunciations of decline have taken the form of dictionaries in which the ailments of the language are catalogued. A good example of such a book is an annotated dictionary which was compiled by Kenneth Hudson, and suitably entitled *The Dictionary of Diseased English*. It was published in 1977. In the foreword to this dictionary, Richard Hoggart writes:

The last half-century has seen some powerful, and abundantly justified, criticisms of the increasing corruption of the English language. T.S. Eliot, F.R. Leavis, George Orwell and W.H. Auden come to mind at once. Earlier still, there was Ezra Pound's passionate assertion that when a language goes rotten the very substance of our thoughts and feelings goes rotten too.

Hudson's dictionary is intended to stem the rot by exposing the cancer that afflicts the English language. His selection of examples of diseased English runs to nearly 260 pages. A sample of entries will give you a flavour of the book:

Great
Very good. The Americans have nearly, but not quite, worked this poor word to death, in their need to avoid using the word 'good'.

Less able
Stupid, not gifted, idle. The brutal words do not accord with today's educational theory, by which all pupils are categorised as 'able' or 'less able' etc.

Staff
Servants. 'Servants' is now an obscene word, anyone who advertised in these terms would get no replies etc.

Hudson stands in a long line of purists who have lambasted and ridiculed change as evidence of culpable slovenliness, or worse. Similar concerns have been expressed about the state of English in other English-speaking countries and in other historical periods. Thus, in 1857, members of the Canadian Institute in Toronto heard a speech describing Canadian English as 'a corrupt dialect growing up amongst our population'. The speaker objected to the use of words such as *lot* (for 'a division of land'), *boss* (for 'master'), *store* (for 'shop'), *fix* (for 'mend'), and *guess* (for 'think', as in *I guess I'll go*). Judging by current usage, he objected in vain.

Eighteenth-century reformers

The feeling that the language is tottering at the edge of the abyss was particularly strong in the eighteenth century. In 1712, for example, Jonathan Swift (the author of *Gulliver's Travels*) addressed a famous pamphlet entitled 'A Proposal for Correcting, Improving and Ascertaining the English Tongue' to the Lord High Treasurer, Robert the Earl of Oxford and Mortimer. He wrote:

My lord, I do here, in the name of all the learned and polite persons of the nation, complain to your lordship, as *First Minister*, that our language is extremely imperfect; that its daily improvements are by no means in proportion to its daily corruptions; that the pretenders to polish and refine it, have chiefly multiplied abuses and absurdities; and, that in many instances, it offends against every part of grammar.

One of the many imperfections that troubled Swift was the 'perpetual disposition to shorten our words by retrenching the vowels' (and indeed entire syllables) as in the abbreviation of *reputation* to *rep* or the use of contracted forms of verbs such as *can't* for *cannot* and *he's* for *he is*, although he had no objection to *Tis* for *It is*.

Purists have always been eager to identify the culprits responsible for the degeneration of the language. Swift denounced 'illiterate Court-Fops, half-witted-Poets, and the University-Boys' for the decay of English in his time. In our day, the characters in the rogues' gallery have changed. They usually include modern linguists and the liberal education establishment. Linguists are singled out because modern linguistic science insists, as we have seen, that its task is to describe language in all its variety rather than to dictate and police 'correct' usage. Unfortunately, this descriptivist stance has been mistaken by critics for the espousal of the principle of 'Anything Goes', which is said to have had a disastrous effect on the standards of English language teaching.

English-speaking people were (and are) by no means unique in considering their language imperilled. The anxiety about plummeting linguistic standards has always been shared by many in the rest of Western Europe. A century after Swift, the German philologist Jacob Grimm (better known for the folktales) bemoaned the degeneration of his language:

In reading carefully the old Gothonic (altdeutschen) sources, I was every day discovering forms and perfections which we generally envy the Greeks and Romans when we consider the present condition of our language.... Six hundred years ago every rustic knew, that is to say, practised daily, perfections and niceties in the German language of which the best grammarians nowadays do not even dream....

3.2

Language standardization

The French and Italians had already confronted, a few centuries before, the apparent problem of linguistic decline by setting up language academies. The Italian *Accademia della Crusca* was founded in 1582 and the *Académie française* in 1635. These academies provided the model which Swift urged the English to emulate when he proposed the establishment of a society to 'ascertain' (i.e., standardize) the English language and stop it from changing by prescribing and proscribing usage.

Although the call for an academy was never taken up by the state, certain concerned citizens took it upon themselves to safeguard the purity of the language. Before the eighteenth century was out, the English language was codified and standardized by lexicographers and grammarians.

Dr Johnson's dictionary

The most notable of these standardizers was Dr Samuel Johnson who, in 1755, published *A Dictionary of the English Language*. In the preface, he made the purpose of his dictionary very clear:

Tongues, like governments, have a natural tendency to degeneration: we have long preserved our constitution, let us make some struggle for our language.

Clearly, the dictionary was not intended by Dr Johnson to serve merely as a listing of English vocabulary. Rather, it was meant to be a vital weapon in the defence of the language against decay. As he put it, 'every language has its improprieties and absurdities, which it is the duty of the lexicographer to correct or proscribe'.

Grammars

Grammarians too set about the task of preserving the purity of the language with equal determination and enthusiasm. In 1762 Robert Lowth, a scholar who later became Bishop of London, published his very influential manual entitled *A Short Introduction to English Grammar*. Lowth complained in the preface that 'the English Language as it is spoken by the politest part of the nation and as it stands in the writings of our most approved authors, offends against every part of Grammar...'. He showed how even classics like the King James Bible and the works of eminent writers like Dryden, Pope, and even Swift himself, were contaminated by 'error'. For instance, on page 116, Lowth explains that 'If the sentence be Negative, the Adverb *not* is placed after the Auxiliary: as "it *did not* touch him;" or, "it *touched* him *not*"'. He then chides Dryden for 'the impropriety of placing the Adverb *not* before the verb' in 'I hope, my Lord, said he, I *not offend*' (Dryden, *Fables*).

Many of the prescriptive rules of English grammar that have been handed down over the last 250 years or so can be traced back to Lowth. Thanks to him, successive generations of pupils have been taught, for example, that 'When the Qualities of different things are compared, the latter Noun is governed, not by the conjunction *than* or *as*, (for a Conjunction has no government of Cases,) but by the verb or the Preposition, expressed or understood.' Hence, according to Lowth, one should say 'You are not so tall as *I*' (not *You are not so tall as *me*). So, he criticizes Swift for writing 'You are a much greater loser than *me* by his death' (Swift to Pope, *Letter* 63). Present-day usage shows that the efforts of the purists to save the language from such 'errors' have not been particularly successful.

Linguists reject the view that languages attain a state of perfection at some point in their history and that subsequent changes lead to deterioration and corruption. As noted above, there are simply no grounds for claiming that one system of grammar is somehow superior to another. There is therefore no reason to think that language change can or will undermine the adequacy of English (or any other language) as a medium of communication.

4

BIOLOGICAL SPECIALIZATION FOR LANGUAGE

As far as can be determined, the languages spoken in the world today cannot be traced to a common source. Rather, they seem to belong to a number of distinct families whose histories can be traced back no more than a few thousand years. Archaeological evidence suggests that language existed prior to that time for perhaps as long as 100,000 years, but virtually nothing is known about this period of linguistic prehistory or about how language originated in the first place.

Nonetheless, there is every reason to believe that humans have a special capacity for language that is not shared by other creatures. The evolutionary adaptation of certain physiological mechanisms for linguistic ends has occurred only in humans. The so-called speech organs (the lungs, larynx, tongue, teeth, lips, soft palate, and nasal passages) were – and still are – directly concerned with ensuring the survival of the organism. Table 1.3 compares the linguistic uses of the major speech organs with their primary survival functions in humans and other mammals.

In humans, these organs have all become highly specialized for linguistic ends. The vocal folds, for example, are more muscular and less fatty in humans than in non-human primates such as chimpanzees and gorillas. Because of a very highly developed network of neural pathways, they also respond more precisely to commands from the brain. The same extensive set of neural pathways allows a high degree of control over other speech organs, such as the tongue, palate, and lips. Such control exceeds anything found in even our closest primate relatives.

Table 1.3 Dual functions of the speech organs

Organ	Survival function	Speech function
Lungs	to exchange CO_2, oxygen	to supply air for speech
Vocal cords	to create seal over passage to lungs	to produce voice for speech sounds
Tongue	to move food back to throat	to articulate vowels and consonants
Teeth	to break up food	to provide place of articulation for consonants
Lips	to seal oral cavity	to articulate vowels and consonants
Nasal cavities	breathing	to provide nasal resonance

There are additional indications of the evolution of linguistic vocalization. Unlike the breathing of survival respiration, speech breathing shows higher lung pressure and a longer exhalation time than respiration. Abdominal muscles that are not normally employed for respiration are brought into play in a systematic and refined manner in order to maintain the air pressure needed for speech. Again, a specialized, extensive set of neurological controls exclusive to humans makes this type of breathing possible.

The preceding facts suggest that the human capacity for speech is superimposed on already existing biological structures. Evolution has produced a refinement both in degree and in kind through a long interplay between the demands of language and the development of the human speech-producing apparatus.

There is also evidence that humans are specialized for the perception of speech. It has been suggested, for example, that we have special neural mechanisms that enable us to perceive distinctions among consonants and that these mechanisms are not found in other mammals.

We know considerably less about the evolutionary specialization for non-vocal and non-auditory aspects of language such as word formation, sentence formation, and the interpretation of meaning. Nonetheless, it is clear that some sort of evolutionary specialization must have occurred. As we will see in Chapter 11, specific parts of the brain are associated with each of these linguistic activities. This suggests that the human brain is specially structured for language, and that species with different types of brains will not be able to acquire or use the types of grammars associated with human language. We will return to this point in the penultimate chapter of this book.

Summing up

Human language is characterized by **creativity**. Speakers of a language have access to a **grammar**, a mental system that allows them to form and interpret familiar and novel utterances. The grammar governs the articulation, perception, and patterning of speech sounds, the formation of words and sentences, and the interpretation of utterances. All languages have grammars that are equal in their expressive capacity, and all speakers of a language have (subconscious) knowledge of its grammar. The existence of such linguistic systems in humans is the product of unique anatomical and cognitive specialization.

Note

1   Not all nouns naming periods of time can be converted into verbs, however. Thus, for reasons that are still not understood, the nouns *autumn* and *week* do not make very good verbs.
*They autumned/weeked in Scotland.

Sources

The discussion of word creation is based on an article by Eve Clark and Herb Clark, 'When nouns surface as verbs', in *Language* 55: 767–811 (1979). The Walbiri data are based on K. Hale's article 'Person marking in Walbiri', in *A Festschrift for Morris Halle*, edited by S. Anderson and P. Kiparsky (New York: Holt, Rinehart & Winston, 1973). The quotation from Grimm is taken from Otto Jespersen *Language: its Nature, Development and Origin* (London: Allen & Unwin, 1922) (page 42). Jonathan Swift's 'A proposal for correcting, improving and ascertaining the English tongue' is from W.F. Bolton (ed.) *The English Language; Essays by English and American Men of Letters* 1490–1839 (Cambridge, Cambridge University Press, 1966). The discussion of Lowth is based on Robert Lowth, *A Short Introduction to English Grammar* (London: Millar & Dodsley , 1762). The 1857 speech on the status of Canadian English is cited in Mark Orkin's *Speaking Canadian English* (Toronto: General Publishing Company, 1970). The data on the positioning of negative elements within sentences in human language come from an article by O. Dahl, 'Typology of sentence negation', *Linguistics* 17: 79-106 (1979). The book by Bickerton, cited below, provides a fresh look at the emergence of language in the human species.

The exercises for this chapter were prepared by Joyce Hildebrand.

Recommended reading

Aitchison, Jean. 1989. *The Articulate Mammal: An Introduction to Psycholinguistics.* 3rd edn. London: Routledge.

Aitchison, Jean. 1987. *Linguistics.* 3rd edn. Teach Yourself Books. Sevenoaks, Kent: Hodder & Stoughton.

Aitchison, Jean. 1991. *Language Change: Progress or Decay?* 2nd edn. Cambridge: Cambridge University Press.

Bickerton, Derek. 1990. *Language and Species.* Chicago: University of Chicago Press.

Clark, Eve and Clark, Herb. 1979. 'When nouns surface as verbs.' *Language* 55: 767-811.

Crystal, David. 1987. *The Cambridge Encyclopedia of Language.* Cambridge: Cambridge University Press.

Jackendoff, Ray. 1993. *Patterns in the Mind.* Harvester Wheatsheaf: Hemel Hempstead, Herts.

Milroy, James and Milroy, Leslie. 1991. *Authority in Language.* 2nd edn. London: Routledge.

Pinker, Steve. 1994. *The Language Instinct: The New Science of Language and Mind.* London: Allen Lane.

Questions

1. The following sentences contain verbs created from nouns in accordance with the process described in section 1 of the chapter. Describe the meaning of each of these new verbs.
   a) We punk-rocked the night away.
   b) She dog-teamed her way across the arctic.
   c) We MG'd to Perth.
   d) We Concorded to London.
   e) He Maradonna'd the ball into the net.
   f) I microwaved the parsnips.
   g) She Robinson Crusoed in the Galapagos.
   h) We'll have to Ajax the sink.
   i) He Windolened the windows.
   j) You should Clairol your hair.
   k) Let's carton the eggs.

2. Using the examples in the preceding exercise as a model, create five new verbs from nouns. Build a sentence around each of these new verbs to show its meaning.

3. Which of the following forms are possible words of English? Solicit the help of an acquaintance and see if you agree on your judgements.
   a) mbood   c) coofp   e) sproke   g) worpz
   b) frall   d) ktleem   f) flube   h) bsarn

4. Imagine that you are an advertising executive and that your job involves inventing new names for products. Create four new forms that are possible words of English and four that are not.

5. Part of linguistic competence involves the ability to recognize whether novel utterances are acceptable. Consider the following sentences and determine which are possible sentences in English. For each unacceptable sentence, change the sentence to make it acceptable, and compare the two.
   a) Jason's mother left himself with nothing to eat.
   b) Miriam is eager to talk to.
   c) This is the man who I took a picture of.
   d) Colin made Jane a sandwich.
   e) Is the dog sleeping the bone again?
   f) Chris prepared Robin a cake.
   g) Max cleaned the garden up.
   h) Max cleaned up the garden.
   i) Max cleaned up it.
   j) I desire you to leave.
   k) That you likes liver surprises me.

6. Consider the following sentences, each of which is acceptable to some speakers of English. Try to identify the prescriptive rules that are violated in each case.

a) He don't know about the race.
b) You was out when I called.
c) Did you send one yet?
d) There's twenty horses registered in the show.
e) That window's broke, so be careful.
f) Jim and me are gonna go campin' this weekend.
g) I seen the parade last week.
h) He been lost in the woods for ten days.
i) My car needs cleaned 'cause of all the rain.
j) Julie ain't got none.
k) Somebody left their book on the train.
m) Murray hurt hisself in the game.
n) They've went to town.
o) She very kind.
p) Ah hink . . . mibbe she wouldnae ov came if youse'd telt her.
q) We sees her every day in the pub.
r) Did him give you de knife you a-look for?
s) Paddy does be drinking.

Phonetics: the sounds of language

Michael Dobrovolsky and Francis Katamba

Heavenly labials in a world of gutturals.

• Wallace Stevens

We do not need to speak in order to use language. Language can be written, recorded mechanically, and even produced by computers in limited ways, but nevertheless, speech remains the primary way we encode it. Our species spoke long before we began to write language down, and, as we saw in the first chapter of this book, this long history of spoken language is reflected in our anatomical specialization for it. Humans also appear to have specialized neural mechanisms for the perception of speech sounds. Because language and speech are so closely linked, we begin our study of language by examining the inventory and structure of the sounds of language. This branch of linguistics is called **phonetics**.

Human languages display a wide variety of sounds, called **phones** or **speech sounds**. There are a great many speech sounds, but not an infinite number of them – the class of possible speech sounds is finite, and a portion of the total set will be found in the inventory of any human language. Certain sounds that humans are capable of producing with the vocal tract do not occur in speech, such as the sound made by inhaling through one corner of the mouth, or the 'raspberry' produced by sticking out the tongue and blowing hard across it. Nonetheless, a very wide range of sounds is found in human language, including such sounds as the click made by drawing the tongue hard away from the upper molars on one side of the mouth, or the sound made by constricting the insides of the throat as you breathe out. The class of possible speech sounds is also universal. Any human, child or adult, can learn how to pronounce these sounds.

There are two ways of approaching phonetics. One approach studies the physiological mechanisms of speech production. This is known as **articulatory phonetics**. The other, known as **acoustic phonetics**, deals with speech sounds in terms of how we hear them. To this end, it is concerned with measuring and analysing the physical properties of sound waves we produce when we speak. Both approaches are indispensable to an understanding of phonetics. This chapter focuses on articulatory phonetics, but also makes some reference to the acoustic properties of sounds and to acoustic analysis. More detailed discussion of acoustic phonetics will be presented in Chapter 17.

1

PHONETIC
TRANSCRIPTION

Since the sixteenth century, efforts have been made to devise a universal system for transcribing the sounds of speech. The best-known system, the **International Phonetic Alphabet (IPA)**, has been developing since 1888. This system of transcription attempts to represent each sound of human speech with a single symbol. These symbols are enclosed in brackets [ ] to indicate that the transcription is phonetic and does not represent the spelling system of a particular language. For example, the sound spelled *th* in English *this* is transcribed as [ð] (pronounced *eth*, as in *wea__th__er*). IPA uses this symbol to represent the sound in whichever language it is heard (see Table 2.1), whether it is English, Spanish, Turkmen (a Turkic language spoken in Central Asia and written with the Cyrillic alphabet), or any other.

Table 2.1 Use of [ð] in the International Phonetic Alphabet

Language	Spelling	IPA	Meaning
English	__this__	[ðɪs]	'this'
Spanish	bo__d__a	[boða]	'wedding'
Turkmen	a__д__ak	[aðak]	'foot'

The use of a standardized phonetic alphabet enables linguists to transcribe languages consistently and accurately. In North American usage, however, some phonetic symbols differ from those employed by IPA transcription. For example, the sound heard at the beginning of the English word __shark__ is transcribed as [ʃ] in IPA, but usually as [š] in North America. This book employs IPA variants, but notes North American symbols where relevant.

If you wish to start practising the phonetic transcription of English, turn to Tables 2.16 and 2.17, pages 42 to 43, for examples.

1.1

Units of
representation

Anyone who hears a language spoken for the first time finds it hard to break up the flow of speech into individual units of production. Even when hearing our own language spoken, we do not focus attention on individual sounds as much as we do on the meanings of words, phrases, and sentences. Many alphabets, including the IPA, represent speech in the form of **segments**, or individual speech sounds like [a], [o], [p], or [m]. Using segments, however, is only one way to represent speech. The **syllable**, presented in Chapter 3, is also represented in some writing systems (see Chapter 15, sections 1.2, 3.2, and 4.2). In one form of Japanese writing, for example, signs such as か

[ka], と [to], and み [mi] represent syllables without recourse to segmental transcription.

Segments are composed of smaller subunits called **features** such as 'nasal', which characterizes consonants like [m] and [n] as opposed to [b] and [d]. Even though features are not usually represented in writing systems, they are important elements of linguistic representation. Features reflect individual aspects of articulatory control or acoustic effects produced by articulation. This chapter presents segmental transcription, since it is the most widely used way of representing speech. Features and syllables are introduced in the following chapter.

1.2

Segments

We have defined the segment as an individual speech sound. There are several kinds of evidence that suggest that speakers have the linguistic knowledge that makes it possible to break down a stream of speech into sound segments.

Errors in speech production provide one kind of evidence for the existence of segments. Slips of the tongue such as *Kolacodor* for *Kodacolor* and *melcome wat* for *welcome mat* show segments shifting and reversing position within words. This suggests that segments are individual units of linguistic structure and should be represented individually in a system of transcription.

The relative invariance of speech sounds in human language also suggests that segmental phonetic transcription is a well-motivated way of transcribing speech. It is impossible to represent all variants of human speech sounds, since no one says the same sound in exactly the same way twice. Nonetheless, the sounds of speech remain invariant enough from language to language for us to transcribe them consistently. A *p* sound is much the same in English, Russian, or Uzbek. The fact that when producing a *p* sound, English speakers press their lips together but Russian speakers draw theirs slightly inward does not make the sounds different enough to warrant separate symbols. But the sounds *p* and *t* are distinct enough from each other in languages the world over to be consistently transcribed with separate symbols.

2

THE SOUND-PRODUCING SYSTEM

Sound is produced when air is set in motion. Think of the speech production mechanism as consisting of an air supply, a sound source that sets the air in motion in ways specifically relevant to speech production, and a set of filters that modifies the sound in various ways. The air supply is provided by the lungs. The sound source is in the **larynx**, where a set of muscles called the **vocal folds** (or **vocal cords**) are located. The filters are the organs above the larynx: the tube of the throat between the oral cavity and the larynx, which is called the **pharynx**, the oral cavity, and the nasal cavity (Figure 2.1). These passages are collectively known as the **vocal tract**.

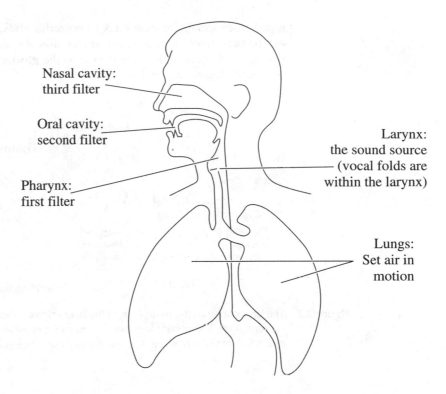

Nasal cavity:
third filter

Oral cavity:
second filter

Pharynx:
first filter

Larynx:
the sound source
(vocal folds are
within the larynx)

Lungs:
Set air in
motion

Figure 2.1 The sound-producing system.

2.1

The lungs

In order to produce the majority of sounds in the world's languages, we take air into the lungs and then expel it during speech. (A small number of sounds are made with air as it flows into the vocal tract as we will see in section 10.2 below.) A certain level of air pressure is needed to keep the speech mechanism functioning steadily. The pressure is maintained by the action of various sets of muscles coming into play during the course of an utterance. The muscles are primarily the **intercostals** (the muscles between the ribs) and the **diaphragm** (the large sheet of muscle that separates the chest cavity from the abdomen).

2.2

The larynx

As air flows out of the lungs up the **trachea** (windpipe), it passes through a box-like structure made of cartilage and muscle, the larynx (commonly known as the voice box or Adam's apple; Figure 2.2). The main portion of the larynx is formed by the **thyroid cartilage**, which spreads outward like the head of a plough. The thyroid cartilage rests on the ring-shaped **cricoid cartilage**. Fine sheets of muscle flare from the inner sides of the larynx, forming the paired vocal folds (vocal cords). The vocal folds are each attached to the thyroid cartilage at the front of the larynx, and to the **arytenoid** cartilages at the back. The vocal folds can be pulled apart or drawn closer together, especially at their back or posterior ends, where each is attached to one of two small cartilages, the **arytenoids**. As air passes through the space between the vocal folds, which is called the **glottis**, different glottal states are produced, depending on their positioning.

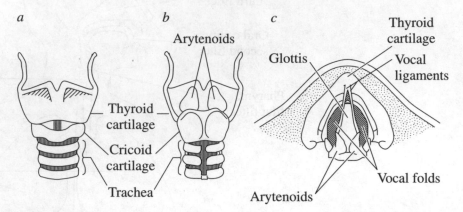

Figure 2.2   The larynx: *a*, from the front; *b*, from the back; *c*, from above, with the vocal folds in the open position. The striated lines indicate muscles, a number of which have been eliminated from the drawings to show the cartilages more clearly.

2.3
Glottal states

The vocal folds may be positioned in a number of ways to produce different glottal states. The first two glottal states presented in Figure 2.3 are commonly encountered in most of the world's languages. The third describes the glottal state that underlies a common speech phenomenon, and the fourth illustrates one of a number of glottal states not encountered in English.

Voicelessness

When the vocal folds are pulled apart as illustrated in Figure 2.3, air passes directly through the glottis. Any sound made with the vocal folds in this position is said to be **voiceless**. You can confirm a sound's voicelessness by touching your fingers to the larynx as you produce it. You will not feel any vibration from the vocal folds being transmitted to your fingertips. The initial sounds of *fish*, *sing*, and *house* are all voiceless.

Voicing

When the vocal folds are brought close together, but not tightly closed, air passing between them causes them to vibrate, producing sounds that are said to be **voiced**. (See Figure 2.3, where the movement of the vocal folds during voicing is indicated by the wavy line.) You can determine whether a sound is voiced in the same way you determined voicelessness. By lightly touching the fingers to the larynx as you produce an extended version of the initial sounds of the words *zip* or *vow*, or any vowel, you can sense the vibration of the vocal folds within the larynx.

Whisper

Another glottal state produces a **whisper**. Whispering is voiceless, but, as shown in Figure 2.3, the vocal folds are adjusted so that the anterior (front) portions are pulled close together, while the posterior (back) portions are apart.

Murmur

Yet another glottal state produces a **murmur**, also known as **whispery voice**. Sounds produced with this glottal configuration are voiced, but the vocal folds are relaxed to allow enough air to escape to produce a simultaneous whispery effect.

These four glottal states represent only some of the possibilities of sound production at the glottis. Combined with various articulations made above the larynx, they produce a wide range of phones. Before examining these in more detail, we will first consider the three major classes of phone.

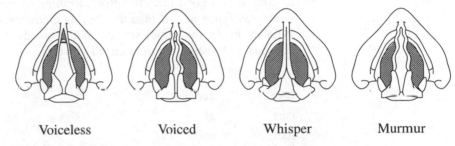

Voiceless   Voiced   Whisper   Murmur

Figure 2.3 Four glottal states: the stylized drawing represents the vocal folds and glottis from above; its anterior position is towards the top. The small triangles represent the arytenoid cartilages which help spread or close the vocal folds.

3

SOUND CLASSES

The sounds of language can be grouped into **classes**, based on the phonetic properties that they share. You have already seen what some of these properties can be. All voiced sounds, for example, form a class, as do all voiceless sounds. Sounds fall into two major classes, **vowels** and **consonants**. Another class, the **glides**, shares properties of both vowels and consonants.

3.1

Vowels, consonants, and glides (syllabic and non-syllabic elements)

Vowels, consonants and glides can be distinguished on the basis of differences in articulation, or by their acoustic properties. We can also distinguish among these elements with respect to whether they function as syllabic or non-syllabic elements.

The articulatory difference

Consonantal sounds, which may be voiced or voiceless, are made with a narrow or complete closure in the vocal tract. The airflow is either blocked momentarily or restricted so much that noise is produced as air flows past the constriction. Vowels are produced with little obstruction in the vocal tract and are generally voiced.

The acoustic difference

As a result of the difference in articulation, consonants and vowels differ in the way they sound. Vowels are more sonorous than consonants, and so we perceive them as louder and longer lasting. (You can observe this if you compare the consonant and vowel sounds in your pronunciation of words like *pet* and *bad*.)

Syllabic and non-syllabic

The greater sonority of vowels allows them to form the basis of **syllables**. A syllable can be defined phonetically as a peak of sonority surrounded by less sonorous segments. For example, the words *a* and *go* each contain one syllable, the word *laughing* two syllables, and the word *telephone* three syllables. In counting the syllables in these words, we are in effect counting the vowels. A vowel is thus said to form the **nucleus** of a syllable. In section 5.7 it will be shown that certain types of consonants can form syllabic nuclei as well. It is a good idea, therefore, to think of vowels and consonants not simply as types of articulations, but as elements that may or may not be syllabic. In *1)*, the initial sounds of the words in the left column are all consonants; those on the right are all vowels.

1)

take	above
cart	at
feel	eel
jump	it
think	ugly
bell	open

Table 2.2 sums up the differences between the two classes presented so far.

Table 2.2   The major diferences between consonants and vowels

Vowels *(and other syllabic elements)*	Consonants *(non-syllabic elements)*
• are produced with relatively little obstruction in the vocal tract	• are produced with a narrow or complete closure in the vocal tract
• are more sonorous	• are less sonorous
• are syllabic	• are not syllabic

Glides

A type of sound that shows properties of both consonants and vowels is called a **glide**. Glides may be thought of as rapidly articulated vowels. This is the auditory impression they produce. Glides are produced with an articulation like that of a vowel. However, they move quickly to another articulation, as do the initial glides in *yet* or *wet*.

Even though they are vowel-like in articulation, glides pattern or function as consonants. For example, glides can never form the nucleus of a syllable. Since glides show properties of both consonants and vowels, the terms *semivowel* and *semiconsonant* may be used interchangeably with the term *glide*.

4

CONSONANT ARTICULATION

Airflow is modified in the oral cavity by the placement of the tongue and the positioning of the lips. These modifications occur at specific places or points of articulation. The major places of articulation used in speech production are outlined in this section. Figure 2.4 provides a **midsagittal section**, or cutaway view, of the vocal tract on which each place of articulation has been indicated.

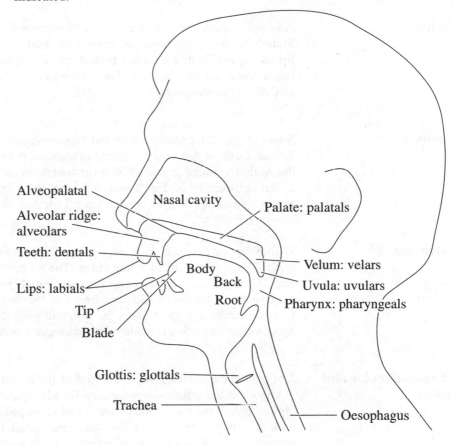

Figure 2.4 The vocal tract.

4.1

The tongue

The primary articulating organ is the tongue, which is very agile. It can be raised, lowered, thrust forward or drawn back, and even rolled back. The sides of the tongue can also be raised or lowered.

Phonetic description refers to five areas of the tongue. The **tip** is the narrow area at the front. Just behind the tip lies the **blade**. The main mass of the tongue is called the **body**, and the hindmost part of the tongue that lies in the mouth is called the **back**. The body and back of the tongue can also be referred to jointly as the **dorsum**. The **root** of the tongue is contained in the upper part of the throat (pharynx).

4.2

Places of articulation

Each point at which the airstream can be modified to produce a different sound is called a **place** (or **point**) of **articulation**. Places of articulation are found at the lips, within the oral cavity, in the pharynx, and at the glottis.

Labial

Any sound made with closure or near closure of the lips is said to be **labial**. Sounds involving both lips are termed **bilabial**; sounds involving the lower lip and upper teeth are called **labiodentals**. English includes the bilabials heard word-initially in *peer*, *bin*, and *month*, and the labiodentals heard initially in *fire* and *vow*.

Dental

Some phones are produced with the tongue placed against or near the teeth. Sounds made in this way are called **dentals**. If the tongue is placed between the teeth, the sound is said to be **interdental**. Interdentals in English are the initial consonants of the words *this* and *thing*. (Some English speakers produce *s* and *z* as dentals; see section 5.3 for more details.)

Alveolar

Within the oral cavity, a small ridge protrudes from just behind the upper front teeth. This is called the **alveolar ridge**. The tongue may touch or be brought near this ridge in the production of certain sounds which are hence described as **alveolar**. Alveolar sounds are heard at the beginning of the following English words: *top*, *deer*, *soap*, *zip*, *lip*, and *neck*. Some languages, such as Spanish, have an *r* that is made with the tongue touching the alveolar ridge.

Palato-alveolar and palatal

Just behind the alveolar ridge, the roof of the mouth rises sharply. This area is known as the **palato-alveolar** area (or **alveopalatal** in some books). The highest part of the roof of the mouth is called the **palate**, and sounds produced with the tongue on or near this area are called **palatals**. Palato-alveolar consonants are heard in the following English words: *show*, *measure*, *chip*, and *judge*. The word-initial phone in *yes* is a palatal glide.

Velar

The soft area towards the rear of the roof of the mouth is called the **velum**. Sounds made with the tongue touching or near this position are called **velars**. Velars are heard in English at the beginning of the words *call* and *go*, and at the end of the word *hang*. The glide heard word-initially in *wet* is called a

labiovelar, since the tongue is raised near the velum and the lips are rounded at the same time.

Uvulars

The small fleshy flap of tissue known as the **uvula** hangs down from the velum. Sounds made with the tongue near or touching this area are called **uvulars**. English has no uvulars, but the *r* sound of standard European (Parisian) French is uvular.

Pharyngeals

The area of the throat between the uvula and the larynx is known as the **pharynx**. Sounds made through the modification of airflow in this region by retracting the tongue or constricting the pharynx are called **pharyngeals**. Pharyngeals can be found in many dialects of Arabic, but not in English.

Glottal

Sounds produced by using the vocal folds as the primary articulators are called **glottals**. The sound at the beginning of the English words <u>h</u>eave and <u>h</u>ug is made at the glottis.

5

MANNERS OF ARTICULATION

The lips, tongue, velum, and glottis can be positioned in different ways to produce different sound types. These various configurations are called the **manners of articulation**.

5.1

Oral versus nasal phones

A basic distinction in manner of articulation is between **oral** and **nasal** phones. When the velum is raised, cutting off the airflow through the nasal passages, oral sounds are produced. The velum, however, can be lowered to allow air to pass through the nasal passages, producing a sound that is nasal. Both consonants and vowels can be nasal, in which case they are generally voiced. (Unless otherwise noted, all nasals represented in this chapter are voiced.) The consonants at the end of the English words *su<u>n</u>*, *su<u>m</u>*, and *su<u>ng</u>* are nasal. For speakers of North American English, the vowels of words such as *ba<u>n</u>k* and *wi<u>n</u>k* are also nasal.

5.2

Stops

Stops are made with a complete and momentary closure of airflow through the vocal tract. In the world's languages, stops are found at bilabial, dental, alveolar, palatal, velar, uvular, and glottal points of articulation.

The glottal stop is commonly heard in many popular British dialects (instead of the [t] in the Queen's English) in words like *butter, water* and *bottle*. This glottal stop is often spelled with an apostrophe (*bu'er, wa'er* and *bo'l*).

In English, bilabial, alveolar, and velar oral and nasal stops occur in the words listed in Table 2.3. Note that [ŋ] does not occur word-initially in English.

Table 2.3   English stops and their transcription

Bilabial	Transcription	
Voiceless	s<u>p</u>an	[p]
Voiced	<u>b</u>an	[b]
Nasal	<u>m</u>an	[m]
Alveolar		
Voiceless	s<u>t</u>un	[t]
Voiced	<u>d</u>ot	[d]
Nasal	<u>n</u>ot	[n]
Velar		
Voiceless	s<u>k</u>ill	[k]
Voiced	<u>g</u>ap	[g]
Nasal	wi<u>ng</u>	[ŋ]
Glottal		
Voiceless	(see below)	[ʔ]

A grid for stops

Table 2.4 presents a phonetic grid on which the stop consonants of English are ranged horizontally according to place of articulation. As you can see, each stop, with one exception, has voiced and voiceless counterparts. The glottal stop is always voiceless. It is produced with the vocal folds drawn firmly together, and since no air can pass through the glottis, the vocal folds cannot be set in motion.

Table 2.4   English stops and their transcription

	Bilabial	Alveolar	Velar	Glottal
Voiceless	[p]	[t]	[k]	[ʔ]
Voiced	[b]	[d]	[g]	
Nasal	[m]	[n]	[ŋ]	

5.3

Fricative

Fricatives are consonants produced with a continuous airflow through the mouth. They belong to a large class of sounds called **continuants** (a class that also includes vowels and glides), all of which share this property. The fricatives form a special class of continuants; during their production, they are accompanied by a continuous audible noise because the air used in their production passes through a very narrow opening (Table 2.5, below).

English fricatives

English has voiceless and voiced labiodental fricatives at the beginnings of the words *fat* and *vat*, voiceless and voiced interdental fricatives word-initially in the words *thin* and *those*, alveolar fricatives word-initially in *sing* and *zip*, and a voiceless palato-alveolar fricative word-initially in *ship*. The voiced palato-alveolar fricative is rare in English. It is the first consonant in the word *azure*, and is also heard in the words *pleasure* and *rouge*. The voiceless glottal fricative of English is heard in *hole* and *hat*.

Table 2.5   The transcription of English fricatives

Glottal state	Place of articulation	Transcription
	Labiodental	
Voiceless	fat	[f]
Voiced	vat	[v]
	Interdental	
Voiceless	thin	[θ]
Voiced	those	[ð]
	Alveolar	
Voiceless	sing	[s]
Voiced	zip	[z]
	Palato-alveolar	
Voiceless	ship	[ʃ]
Voiced	azure	[ʒ]
	Glottal	
Voiceless	hat	[h]

Special note must be taken of the alveolar fricatives [s] and [z]. There are two ways that English speakers commonly produce these sounds. Some speakers raise the tongue tip to the alveolar ridge (or to just behind the upper front teeth) and allow the air to pass through a grooved channel in the tongue. Other speakers form this same channel using the blade of the tongue; the tip is placed behind the lower front teeth.

A grid for fricatives

Table 2.6 presents a grid on which the fricative consonants of English are ranged according to place of articulation. As in Table 2.5, dentals are not distinguished from alveolars, since most languages have sounds with either one or the other place of articulation, but not both. Note that IPA [ʃ] and [ʒ] correspond respectively to North American [š] and [ž].

Table 2.6 English fricatives

	Labiodental	Interdental	Alveolar	Palato-alveolar	Glottal
Voiceless	[f]	[θ]	[s]	[ʃ]	[h]
Voiced	[v]	[ð]	[z]	[ʒ]	

5.4

Affricates

When a stop articulation is released, the tongue moves rapidly away from the place of articulation. Some non-continuant consonants show a slow release of the closure; these sounds are called **affricates**. English has only two affricates, both of which are palato-alveolar. They are heard word-initially in _church_ and _jump_, and are transcribed as [tʃ] and [dʒ], respectively. (The IPA transcription of an affricate using a symbol for a stop, such as [t] or [d], followed by a symbol for a fricative like [ʃ] or [ʒ] is meant to reflect the fact that an affricate is a stop that is released gradually so that in its final phase it is a fricative.)

A grid for affricates

Table 2.7 presents a grid showing the two English affricates. Note that IPA [tʃ] and [dʒ] correspond to North American [č] and [ǰ] respectively.

Table 2.7 English affricates

	Palato-alveolar
Voiceless	[tʃ]
Voiced	[dʒ]

Stridents and sibilants

At the beginning of this chapter, it was noted that acoustic as well as articulatory criteria are sometimes used in describing speech sounds. An acoustic criterion comes into play to describe fricatives and affricates. These sounds are subdivided into two types, some of which are distinctly louder than others. These noisier fricatives and affricates are called **stridents** (Table 2.8). Their quieter counterparts, which have the same or nearly same place of articulation, are considered non-strident. All these 'hissing' stridents are also known as **sibilants**.

Table 2.8 Strident fricatives and affricates in English

Place of Articulation	Voiceless	Voiced
Alveolar	[s]	[z]
Palato-alveolar	[ʃ]	[ʒ]
	[tʃ]	[dʒ]

5.5

Voice lag and aspiration

After the release of certain voiceless stops in English, you can sometimes perceive a lag or brief delay before the voicing of a following vowel. Since the lag in the onset of vocalic voicing is accompanied by the release of air, the traditional term for this phenomenon is **aspiration**. It is transcribed with a small raised 'h' after the aspirated consonant. Table 2.9 provides some examples of aspirated and unaspirated consonants in English (some vowel symbols are introduced here as well). Notice that the sounds that have both aspirated and unaspirated varieties are all voiceless stops. In other languages, voiceless fricatives and affricates may also be aspirated or unaspirated.

Table 2.9 Aspirated and unaspirated consonants in English

Aspirated		*Unaspirated*	
[pʰæt]	pat	[spæt]	spat
[tʰʌb]	tub	[stʌb]	stub
[kʰɪd]	kid	[skɪd]	skid

Figure 2.5 shows how aspiration of a voiceless consonant takes place, using the aspirated consonant [pʰ] as an example. Though the sequence of articulations takes places continuously, the figure illustrates only certain moments.

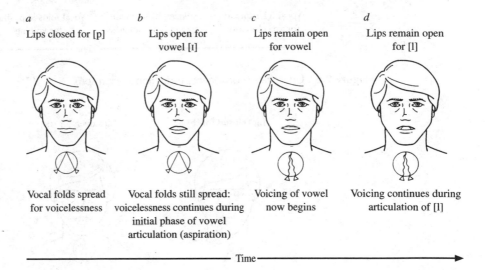

a	*b*	*c*	*d*
Lips closed for [p]	Lips open for vowel [ɪ]	Lips remain open for vowel	Lips remain open for [l]
Vocal folds spread for voicelessness	Vocal folds still spread: voicelessness continues during initial phase of vowel articulation (aspiration)	Voicing of vowel now begins	Voicing continues during articulation of [l]

Time ⟶

Figure 2.5 Aspirated consonant production (English *pill*).

a) As articulation of the voiceless consonant is begun, the glottis is open.

b) The closure for the consonant is released and the vowel articulation begins; however, the glottis is not yet closed enough to permit voicing to begin. Because of this, the vowel is briefly voiceless, giving the impression of an extra release of air that we call *aspiration*.

c) After a short delay, measurable in milliseconds, voicing of the vowel begins.

d) The lips remain open and voicing continues during the articulation of the final consonant of the word.

Figures 2.6 and 2.7 show the relation between articulation and voicing for unaspirated and voiced consonants. The unaspirated consonant, such as the [p] of English **spill**, shows voicing of the vowel starting very soon after release of the consonant articulation. The voiced initial [b] of English **bill** shows voicing starting just before the release of the bilabial articulators.

a	b	c	d
Lips open for [s]	Lips closed for [p]	Lips open for [ɪ]	Lips remain open during articulation of [l]
Vocal folds spread for voicelessness	Vocal folds remain spread (voicelessness)	Vocal folds in position for voicing	Voicing continues

⸻ Time ⟶

Figure 2.6 Unaspirated consonant production (English *spill*).

a	b	c
Lips closed for [b]	Lips open for [ɪ]	Lips remain open during articulation of [l]
Vocal folds in position for voicing, which starts slightly after lip closure	Voicing continues	Voicing continues

⸻ Time ⟶

Figure 2.7 Voiced consonant release (English *bill*).

5.6

Liquids

Among the sounds commonly found in the world's languages are *l* and *r* and their numerous variants. They form a special class of consonants known as **liquids**.

Laterals

Varieties of *l* are called **laterals**. As laterals are articulated, air escapes through the mouth along the lowered sides of the tongue. When the tongue tip is raised to the dental or alveolar position, the dental or alveolar laterals are produced. Both may be transcribed as [l].

Because laterals are generally voiced, the term *lateral* used alone usually means 'voiced lateral'. Still, there are instances of voiceless laterals in speech. The voiceless dental or alveolar lateral is written with an additional phonetic symbol, called a **diacritic**. In this case, the diacritic is a circle beneath the symbol: [l̥]. Voiceless laterals can be heard in the pronunciation of the English words *please* and *clear* and also in the Welsh pronunciation of '*ll*' in such names as *Llandaff*.

English *r* sounds

Numerous varieties of *r* are also heard in the world's languages. This section describes some of the types found in English.

In **received pronunciation** (RP for short), the generally accepted variety of spoken standard southern British English, *r* is a **post-alveolar approximant**. The term **approximant** (or **frictionless continuant**) describes a consonant with a manner of articulation that involves bringing the articulators quite close together while at the same time leaving a sufficiently large gap between them for air to escape without causing audible turbulence. Typically, in the RP articulation of *r* (as in *reed* and *raw*), the tip of the tongue is brought close to the area just past the alveolar ridge (hence the label post-alveolar) without making firm contact with the roof of the mouth. The IPA symbol for this sound is [ɹ], but for convenience the symbol [r] is normally used.

The *r* of English as it is spoken in Canada and the United States as well as in southwest England is also an approximant. But its place of articulation is slightly farther back. This *r* (symbolized by [ɻ] in IPA) is made by curling the tongue tip back so that the underside of the tongue tip makes contact with the back of the alveolar ridge (or by bunching the tongue upwards and back in the mouth). It is known as a **retroflex** *r* and is heard in *ride* and *car*. It is also often transcribed as [r] (following a common convention of using non-Roman alphabet symbols like [ɻ] sparingly).

Another sound commonly identified with *r* is the **flap**. The flap is produced when the tongue tip strikes the alveolar ridge as it passes across it. It is heard in the North American English pronunciation of *bitter* and *butter*, and in some British pronunciations of *very* (as in Scouse, the dialect of Liverpool). It is commonly transcribed as [ɾ] and is generally voiced. Table 2.10 presents the laterals, *r*, and flap in different varieties of English.

Table 2.10   English liquids

	Alveolar		Post-alveolar	Retroflex
	Voiced	Voiceless	Voiced	Voiced
Laterals	[l]	[l̥]		
r-sounds				
Approximant	[r]	[r̥]	[ɹ]	[ɽ]
Flap	[ɾ]			

5.7

Syllabic liquids and nasals

Liquids and nasals are more sonorous than other consonants and in this respect are more like vowels than are the other consonants. In fact, they are so sonorous that they may function as syllabic nuclei. When they do so, they are called **syllabic liquids** and **syllabic nasals**. Syllabic liquids and nasals (Table 2.11) are found in many of the world's languages, including English. In transcription, they are usually marked with a short vertical line underneath. Thus, for example, the syllabic *l* at the end of *kettle* ([ketl]) is transcribed as [l̩]. Unfortunately for beginning linguistics students, North American transcription is not always consistent here. The syllabic *r* sound heard in words like *bird* and *her* is transcribed as a vowel-*r* sequence: [ər]. (The vowel symbol is presented in section 6.2 of this chapter.) The IPA symbol for this sound is [ɚ].

Table 2.11   Syllabic liquids and nasals in English

Syllabic		Non-syllabic	
bottle	[bɒtl̩]	lift	[lɪft]
funnel	[fʌnl̩]	pill	[pɪl]
sudden	[sʌdn̩]	net	[net]
button	[bʌtn̩]	tent	[tent]

5.8

Glides

Recall that a glide is a very rapidly articulated non-syllabic segment. The two RP English glides are the y-glide [y] or [j] of *yes* and *yell*, and the w-glide [w] of *wet*, and *wing*. The [j] of IPA transcription corresponds to [y] in North American transcription. (In British transcription too, [y] is sometimes used instead of [j] to represent this sound.)

The [j] is a palatal glide (often cited as palato-alveolar as well) whose articulation is virtually identical to that of the vowel [i] of *see*. You can verify this by pronouncing a [j] in an extended manner; it will sound very close to an [i]. The glide [w] is made with the tongue raised and pulled back near the velum and with the lips protruding, or **rounded**. For this reason, it is sometimes called a **labiovelar**. The [w] corresponds closely in articulation to the vowel [u] of *who*. This can be verified by extending the pronunciation of a [w]. We will consider [w] a rounded velar glide for purposes of description. Some speakers of English also have a voiceless labiovelar glide, transcribed [ʍ], in the words *when, where,* and *which* (but not in *witch*). The [ʍ] pronunciation is common in Scotland and North America, but it is increasingly rare elsewhere (except in contexts where [w] is preceded by a voiceless stop as in Table 2.17 on page 43 below). In word-initial position it derives from a historical [hw] consonant cluster which has been simplified to [w] by dropping [h] in most dialects (Table 2.12).

Table 2.12   English consonants: places and manners of articulation

Manners of articulation		*Labial*	*Labio-dental*	*Inter-dental*	*Alveolar*	*Palato-alveolar*	*Velar*	*Glottal*
Stop	voiceless	p			t		k	ʔ
	voiced	b			d		g	
Nasal	voiced	m			n		ŋ	
Fricative	voiceless		f	θ	s	ʃ		h
	voiced		v	ð	z	ʒ		
Affricate	voiceless					tʃ		
	voiced					dʒ		
Liquid	voiced lateral				l			
	voiced post-alveolar approximant/ retroflex				r			
Glide	voiced						j	w
	(voiceless)							(ʍ)

Above "Places of articulation" spans the place columns.

6

VOWELS

Vowels are sonorous, syllabic sounds made with the vocal tract more open than it is for consonant and glide articulations. Different vowel sounds (also called vowel *qualities*) are produced by varying the placement of the body of the tongue and shaping the lips. The shape of the cavity can be further altered by protruding the lips to produce rounded vowels, or by lowering the velum to produce a nasal vowel. Finally, vowels may be tense or lax, depending on the degree of vocal tract constriction during their articulation.

In the following section on vowels you are introduced to most of the basic vowels of English. Some phonetic detail is omitted that will be introduced in the following chapter.

6.1

Simple vowels and diphthongs

English vowels are divided into two major types, **simple vowels** (also called **pure vowels** or **monophthongs**) and **diphthongs** (Table 2.13). Simple vowels do not show a noticeable change in quality. The vowels of *pit*, *set*, *cat*, *dog*, *but*, *put*, and the first vowel of *suppose* are all simple vowels. Diphthongs are vowels that exhibit a change in quality within a single syllable. English diphthongs show changes in quality that are due to tongue movement away from the initial vowel articulation towards another vowel position. This change in vowel quality is clearly perceptible in words such as *say*, *buy*, *cow*, *ice*, *lout*, *go*, and *boy*. The first part of a diphthong is much longer and perceptually more salient than the second.

In standard British English, there are nine diphthongs and they fall into two classes: **centring diphthongs** and **rising diphthongs** (also called **closing diphthongs**). In a centring diphthong, during the final phase of the vowel articulation, the highest point of the tongue moves quickly towards the centre of the mouth – the typical position it assumes for the articulation of schwa ([ə]), the vowel at the beginning of the word *address*. There are four centring diphthongs, namely [ɪə], as in *dear*, *cheer*, and *clear*; [eə] as in *rare*, *wear*, and *air*; [ʊə] as *boor*, *sure*, and *dour*; and [ɔə] as in *oar*, *shore*, and *roar*. Nowadays, [ɔə] and [ʊə] are disappearing from RP and many other varieties of British English. They are being replaced by [ɔ:]. As a result, words like *paw*, *pore*, and *poor* rhyme with each other. They all come out as [pɔ:].

In rising diphthongs, the tongue starts in a relatively low position and ends up in a high position either in the palatal area at the front of the mouth in the region where the glide [j] is articulated, or at the back of the mouth in the velar area where the glide [w] is produced. There are three rising diphthongs that end in [ɪ]. They are [eɪ] which is found in *way*, *weight*, and *tail*; [aɪ] which is found in *tie*, *buy*, and *my*; and [ɔɪ] which is found in *oil*, *boy*, and *coin*. There are only two diphthongs rising to [ʊ], namely [əʊ] as in *no*, *go*, and *slow* and [aʊ] which occurs in *proud*, *town*, and *round*.

Table 2.13   Some simple vowels and diphthongs of British (RP) English

Simple vowel		Diphthong	
pit	[ɪ]	bite	[aɪ]
pet	[e]	say	[eɪ]
port	[ɔ:]	air	[eə]
pot	[ɒ]	beer	[ɪə]
pat	[æ]	toy	[ɔɪ]
putt	[ʌ]	oar	[ɔə]
part	[ɑ:]	poor	[ʊə]
		now	[aʊ]
		grow	[əʊ]

Note: The colon indicates length. (See section 6.3 below.)

In all cases, the diphthongs are somewhat longer than the short simple vowels.[1]

6.2

Basic parameters for describing vowels

Vowel articulations are not as easy to feel as consonant articulations at first, since the vocal tract is not narrowed as much. To become acquainted with vowel articulation, alternately pronounce the vowels of *he* and *pot*. You will feel the tongue move from a **high front** to a **low back** position. Once you feel this tongue movement, alternate between the vowels of *pot* and *pat*. You will feel the tongue moving from the **low back** (and the lips will be rounded at the same time) to **low front** position (with the lips unrounded). Finally, alternate between the vowels of *he* and *who*. You will notice that in addition to a tongue movement between the high front and high back position, you are also pursing your lips for the [u:].

Figure 2.8 shows a midsagittal view of the tongue position for the vowels [i:], [ɑ], and [u:] based on X-ray studies of Canadian English. These Canadian vowels are very similar to the British RP English vowels described above. The only vowel in the figure that needs special comment is [ɑ]. This is like the British vowel [ɒ] in *pot*. The only significant difference is that Canadian [ɑ] is formed with the lips in a fairly neutral position while RP [ɒ] is made with the lips pursed. The position of the tongue is virtually the same.

Figure 2.8   Tongue position and transcription for three English vowels.

Vowels for which the tongue is neither raised nor lowered are called **mid** vowels. In some cases, the relative height of the tongue in the general mid zone results in vowels that are perceptibly different. So, it may be necessary to distinguish between **mid**, **mid-high** and **mid-low** vowels. Thus, in RP, [e] the front vowel of *set* is said to be mid-high, front, and unrounded while [ɔ:], the vowel of *storm*, is mid-low, back, and rounded. Schwa ([ə]), the first and the last vowels of *Madonna* is a mid, central vowel. Similar to schwa is the long unrounded central vowel [ɜ:] found in words like *bird*, and *word*. (See section 6.3 below for further discussion .)

Unfortunately, there are no clear cutoff points between various tongue height positions. Hence it is not always obvious whether a sound should be classified, say, as mid-high rather than mid, or as mid rather than mid-low. That is why there is some variation in the symbols chosen by phoneticians to represent the vowel sound in words like *pet* and *tell* in RP. Those in whose judgement the tongue is in a relatively high position use the symbol [e], which represents a fairly mid-high articulation, while those who think the tongue is relatively low use the symbol [ɛ], which represents a more open, mid-lowish vowel.

The motivation for the distinction between mid-high and mid-low vowels is much clearer in Scottish English where a contrast normally exists between the mid-high front unrounded vowel [e] of *tail* and the mid-low front unrounded vowel [ɛ] found in *tell*. A similar contrast exists between the mid-high back rounded vowel [o] of *boat* and the mid-low back rounded vowel [ɔ] found in *bought*.

The RP vowels presented so far in this section are summed up in Table 2.14. Note that in describing the vowels, the articulatory parameters are presented in the order *height*, *backness*, *rounding*.

Table 2.14   Basic phonetic parameters for describing RP English vowels

sh<u>ee</u>t	[iː]	high front unrounded
s<u>e</u>t	[e]	mid-high front unrounded
sh<u>oo</u>t	[uː]	high back rounded
m<u>a</u>d	[æ]	low front unrounded
p<u>ur</u>r	[ɜː]	central (i.e., mid and neither front nor back) unrounded
c<u>au</u>ght	[ɔː]	mid-low back rounded
c<u>o</u>t	[ɒ]	low back rounded
c<u>ar</u>t	[ɑː]	low back unrounded

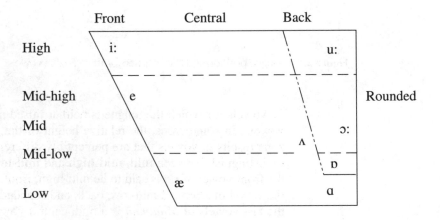

Figure 2.9   Basic positions for RP vowels.

Tongue positions for these vowels are illustrated in Figure 2.9 on page 38. The trapezoid diagram corresponds roughly to the space within which the tongue moves, which is wider at the top of the oral cavity and more restricted at the bottom.

Before leaving this section, there is a lack of terminological uniformity about which you should be warned. The terms high, high-mid, low-mid and low used in this book correspond respectively to **close**, **close-mid**, **open-mid** and **open** which are used by some other linguists. (See the IPA vowel chart on page 63.)

6.3

Tense and lax vowels

All of the vowels illustrated in Figure 2.9, except [æ] and [ɒ], are tense; they are produced with a placement of the tongue that results in greater vocal tract constriction than that of non-tense vowels; in addition, tense vowels are longer than non-tense vowels. Some vowels of English are made with roughly the same tongue position as the tense vowels, but with a less constricted articulation; they are called **lax** vowels. Table 2.15 provides examples from RP comparing tense and lax simple vowels. Note that not all the vowels come in tense/lax pairs.

Table 2.15 Tense and lax vowels in RP

	Tense		Lax
a) *Pure vowels*			
f<u>ee</u>t	[iː]	f<u>i</u>t	[ɪ]
—	—	m<u>e</u>t	[ɛ]
—	—	m<u>a</u>t	[æ]
b<u>a</u>rd	[ɑː]	—	—
p<u>oo</u>l	[uː]	p<u>u</u>ll	[ʊ]
c<u>augh</u>t	[ɔː]	—	—
—	—	c<u>o</u>t	[ɒ]
w<u>or</u>d	[ɜː]	cobr<u>a</u>	[ə]
b) *Diphthongs*			
m<u>a</u>ke	[eɪ]		
b<u>i</u>ke	[aɪ]		
b<u>oi</u>l	[ɔɪ]		
n<u>o</u>te	[əʊ]		
sh<u>ou</u>t	[aʊ]		
r<u>a</u>re	[eə]		
d<u>ee</u>r	[ɪə]		
b<u>oo</u>r	[ʊə]		
r<u>oa</u>r	[ɔə] (marginal		

The difference between two of the vowels illustrated in Table 2.15 is often not easy to hear at first. The vowel [ʌ] in c<u>u</u>t, d<u>u</u>d, pl<u>u</u>ck, and r<u>u</u>n is back, unrounded, mid-low and lax while the vowel [ə] of b<u>a</u>nana, <u>a</u>bout, tom<u>a</u>hawk, and *sofa* is mid, central, unrounded, and lax. The vowel [ʌ] is derived historically from [ʊ]. The change of [ʊ] to [ʌ] affected some words like *cut*, *dud*, *pluck*, and *run*, but not others like *pull*, *push*, *butcher*, and *bull* which retained the [ʊ] pronunciation. Furthermore, the change did not affect all regions. Most speakers of north of England dialects do not have the vowel [ʌ]. In this area the change from [ʊ] to [ʌ] did not take place. So, northern dialects have retained the original pronunciation of *cut*, *dull*, and *pluck* as [kʊt], [dʊl], and [plʊk]. The vowel of the second set of examples, labelled **schwa**, is called a reduced vowel. In addition to being lax, it is characterized by very brief duration.

In English the tense vowels tend to be longer than their lax counterparts. For this reason, some phoneticians refer to them as **long** and **short** vowels respectively. As we saw above, diphthongs are longer than simple vowels. In many cases they display the same behaviour as tense simple vowels. So, they are also classified as tense. Indeed, in some dialects, the same vowel may be realized as a tense simple vowel or as a diphthong in different contexts. For instance, in RP, when tense [i:] and [u:] occur at the end of a word they are often pronounced not as pure vowels, but as the diphthongs [ij] and [uw].

The vowel [ɜː] of *word*, *bird*, *nerve*, *church*, and *journal* is mid, central, unrounded, and tense. In other words, it is just like schwa in all things but tenseness (or length). The spelling gives a clue to its origins. In most cases [ɜː] is derived from a vowel followed by [r]. In most varieties of British English the [r] following a vowel was lost, leaving behind a lengthened, tense vowel. In North America, the southwest of England, and parts of Lancashire in the northwest of England the [r] was not entirely lost. There is still a residual [r] which 'colours' the preceding vowel. The *r*-colouring of a vowel is referred to as **rhotacization**. A rhotacized schwa is represented by the symbol [ɚ] in IPA. (See also the discussion of centring diphthongs in section 6.1 above.)

There is a simple test that helps determine whether vowels are tense or lax. In English, monosyllabic words spoken in isolation do not end in lax vowels. We find *see* [siː], *say* [seɪ], *Sue* [suː], *so* [səʊ], and *saw* [sɔː], but not *[sɪ], *[se], *[sæ], *[sʊ], or *[sʌ]. Schwa, however, frequently appears in unstressed position in polysyllabic words like *sof*[ə] and *Canad*[ə]. It should be pointed out – especially for those who think their ears are deceiving them – that many speakers produce the final vowel in the last two examples not as [ə] but as [ʌ].

The representation of vowels and their articulatory positions (Figure 2.9) is expanded in Figure 2.10 to include both tense and lax vowels.

This rather formidable crowd of vowels should not intimidate you. If you are a native speaker of RP, you have been using these vowels (and others, some of which you will be introduced to in the next chapter) most of your life. Learning to hear them consciously and transcribe them is not a difficult task. The next section provides more examples of the transcription of English consonants and vowels.

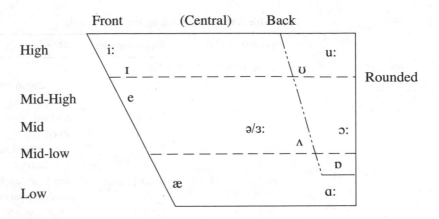

Figure 2.10 Basic positions for RP.

7

PHONETIC TRANSCRIPTION OF RP VOWELS AND CONSONANTS

Tables 2.16 and 2.17 (shown overleaf on pages 42 and 43) show the phonetic symbols for vowels and consonants commonly used to transcribe RP. To show how each symbol is used, one word is transcribed completely, and then other words in which the same sound is found are given. Notice that, in the example words, the spelling of the sound may vary. Be careful of this when you transcribe words phonetically – the sound of a word, not its spelling, is what is transcribed!

8

SUPRASEGMENTALS

All phones have certain inherent **suprasegmental** or **prosodic** properties that form part of their makeup no matter what their place or manner of articulation. These properties are pitch, loudness, and length.

Pitch is the auditory property of a sound that enables us to place it on a scale that ranges from low to high. All sounds give us a subjective impression of being relatively higher or lower in pitch. Pitch is especially noticeable in sonorous sounds like vowels, glides, liquids, and nasals. Even stop and fricative consonants convey different pitches. This is particularly noticeable among the fricatives, as you can hear by extending the pronunciation of [s] and then of [ʃ]; the [s] is clearly higher pitched. All sounds have some degree of intrinsic loudness as well or they could not be heard. Moreover, all sounds occupy a certain stretch of time – they give the subjective impression of length.

8.1

Pitch: tone and intonation

Speakers of any language have the ability to control the level of pitch they speak on. This is accomplished by controlling the tension of the vocal folds and the amount of air that passes through the glottis. The combination of tensed vocal folds and greater air pressure results in higher voice pitch on

Table 2.16 Transcribing English vowels

Symbol	Word	Transcription	More examples
TENSE PURE VOWELS			
[i:]	fee	[fi:]	she, cream, believe, receive, serene, amoeba, ski
[u:]	boot	[bu:t]	to, two, loose, brew, Louise, Lucy, through, Peru
[ɑ:]	cart	[kɑ:t]	card, guard, master, laugh, aunt, heart, sergeant
[ɜ:]	firm	[fɜ:m]	herd, prefer, Hurd, err, heard, worm, connoisseur, myrrh, colonel
[ɔ:]	saw	[sɔ:w]	court, caught, port, walk, decor, dinosaur, Auckland
(TENSE) DIPHTHONGS			
[eɪ]	fate	[feɪt]	they, clay, grain, gauge, escape, way, engage, great, sleigh
[aɪ]	rice	[raɪs]	I, eye, my, try, tide, thigh, byte, buy, dye, die
[ɔɪ]	boy	[bɔɪ]	voice, boil, toy, royal
[əʊ]	note	[nəʊt]	no, toe, sumo, throat, though, slow, oaf, Toronto, O'Connor
[aʊ]	crowd	[kraʊd]	out, house, plough, town, now, glaucoma, Faust
[ɪə]	cheer	[tʃɪə]	clear, idea, criteria, weird, here, mere
[eə]	chair	[tʃeə]	flare, flair, parent, where, heir, mayor
[ʊə]	poor	[pʊə]	sure, moor, tour, velour, paramour
[ɔə]	oar	[ɔə]	door, ore, roar, shore, more, pour
LAX VOWELS			
[ɪ]	fit	[fɪt]	hit, income, definition, pity, (for some speakers)
[e]	let	[let]	led, head, says, said, sever, guest, friend, wet
[æ]	bat	[bæt]	panic, van, marry, racket, gas, planet, plastic
[ɒ]	cod	[kɒd]	dog, rock, holly, yacht, watch, what, cough
[ʊ]	put	[pʊt]	bush, hook, foot, book, hood, woman, wolf
[ʌ]	shut	[ʃʌt]	cut, putt, other, udder, lucky, son, tough, flood, supper
[ə]	letter	[letə]	about, abbot, woman, splendor, Canberra, canary, support, colour

vowels and sonorant consonants, while less tense vocal folds and lower air pressure result in lower voice pitch. Two kinds of controlled pitch movement found in human language are called **tone** and **intonation**.

Table 2.17 Transcribing English consonants

Symbol	Word	Transcription	More examples
[pʰ]	pit	[pʰɪt]	pain, upon, apart
[p]	spit	[spɪt]	spar, crispy, up, culprit, bumper
[tʰ]	tick	[tʰɪk]	tell, attire, terror, tutu
[t]	stuck	[stʌk]	stem, hunt, nasty, mostly
[kʰ]	keep	[kʰiːp]	cow, kernel, chaos
[k]	skip	[skɪp]	scatter, uncle, blacklist, likely
[tʃ]	chip	[tʃʰɪp]	lunch, lecher, ditch, belch
[dʒ]	judge	[dʒʌdʒ]	germ, journal, budgie, wedge
[b]	bib	[bɪb]	boat, liberate, rob, blast
[ʔ]	atlas	[æʔtləs]	witness, top, rich (glottal reinforcement of a following stop or affricate)
[g]	get	[get]	gape, mugger, twig, gleam
[f]	fit	[fɪt]	flash, coughing, proof, phlegmatic, gopher, office
[v]	vat	[væt]	vote, oven, prove
[θ]	thick	[θɪk]	thought, ether, teeth, three, bathroom
[ð]	though	[ðəʊ]	then, bother, teethe, bathe
[s]	sip	[sɪp]	psychology, fasten, fancy, bass, curse, science
[z]	zap	[zæp]	Xerox, scissors, desire, zipper, fuzzy
[ʃ]	ship	[ʃɪp]	shock, nation, mission, vicious, wish, chivalry
[ʒ]	azure	[eɪʒə]	measure, rouge, visual, garage (for some speakers), Taj Mahal
[h]	hat	[hæt]	who, ahoy, forehead, behind
[j]	yet	[jet]	use, few, yes
[w]	witch	[wɪtʃ]	wait, weird, when
[ʍ]	twit	[tʍɪt]	twelve, squeak, quit
[l]	huddle	[hʌdl]	bottle, needle, medal
[r]	reef	[riːf]	prod, arrive
[m]	moat	[məʊt]	mind, humour, shimmer, sum, thumb, lamb
[m̩]	bottom	[bɒtm̩]	atom, random, Adam, rhythm, anthem
[n]	note	[nəʊt]	now, winner, angel, sign, wind
[n̩]	button	[bʌtn̩]	cotton, mutton, happen, sudden
[ŋ]	sing	[sɪŋ]	singer, longer, bank, twinkle

Tone

A language is said to have tone or be a **tone language** when differences in word meaning are signalled by differences in pitch. Pitch on forms in tone languages functions very differently from the movement of pitch in a non-tone language. When a speaker of English says *a car*? with a rising pitch, the word *car* does not mean anything different from the same form pronounced on a different pitch level or with a different pitch contour. In contrast, when a speaker of a tone language such as Mandarin Chinese pronounces the form *ma* [mà] with a falling pitch, it means 'scold', but when the same form (*ma*) is pronounced with a rising pitch, as [má], the meaning is 'hemp' (see Figure 2.13). There is no parallel to anything like this in non-tone languages such as English and French.

Some tone languages show tones at only certain pitch levels. Sarcee, an Athapaskan language spoken in the Canadian province of Alberta, has tones heard at high, mid, and low pitch levels. In Figure 2.11, the upper-case letters H, M, and L stand for high, mid, and low tones, respectively. A line called an **association line** drawn from the letters to the vowel links the segments with their respective tones.

Figure 2.11   Sarcee level tones.

This type of notation is known as **autosegmental** notation.

Level tones that signal meaning differences are called **register tones**: two or three register tones are the norm in most of the world's register tone languages, though four have been reported for Mazatec, a language spoken in Mexico.

A single tone may be associated with more than one syllabic element. In Mende, a language spoken in West Africa (Table 2.18), there are certain polysyllabic forms that show the same tone on each syllable (here, the diacritic ´ indicates a high tone and the diacritic ` indicates a low tone).

Table 2.18   High-tone and low-tone words in Mende

pélé	'house'
háwámá	'waistline'
kpàkàlì	'tripod chair'

Autosegmental notation allows us to represent the tone as characteristic of an entire form. The single underlying tone unit is associated with all vowels (Figure 2.12).

Figure 2.12   Tone as a word feature.

In some languages, tones change pitch on single syllabic elements. Moving pitches that signal meaning differences are called **contour tones**. In Mandarin, both register and contour tones are heard. Contour tones are shown by association lines that converge above the vowel, as shown in Figure 2.13.

[ma]	'mother'	high tone
[ma]	'hemp'	mid rise
[ma]	'horse'	fall rise
[ma]	'scold'	high fall

Figure 2.13 Register and contour tones in Mandarin.

In Figure 2.13, there is one (high) register tone. The other tones are all contour tones.

In other languages, tone can have an even more extended function. In Bini, a language spoken in Nigeria, tone can signal differences in the tense of a verb (such as past versus present), as Figure 2.14 shows.

Timeless	ima	'I show'
Continuous	ima	'I am showing'
Past	ima	'I showed'

Figure 2.14 Tense and tone in Bini.

Although tones may seem exotic to native speakers of Western European languages, they are very widespread. Tone languages are found throughout North and South America, sub-Saharan Africa, and East Asia.

Intonation

Pitch movement in spoken utterances that is not related to differences in word meaning is called intonation. It makes no difference to the meaning of the word *seven*, for example, whether it is pronounced with a rising pitch or a falling pitch. However, intonation does serve to convey information of a broadly meaningful nature. For example, the falling pitch we hear at the end of a statement in English such as *Fred parked the car* signals that the utterance is complete. For this reason, falling intonation at the end of an utterance is called a **terminal (intonation) contour**. Conversely, a rising or level intonation, called a **non-terminal (intonation) contour**, often signals incompleteness. Non-terminal contours are often heard in the non-final forms found in lists and telephone numbers (Figure 2.15).

Sally Fred Helen and J_{oe}

two eight four two five one three

Figure 2.15 Rising non-terminal intonations in a list and a telephone number.

In questions, final rising intonations also signal a kind of incompleteness in that they indicate that a conversational exchange is not finished.

Did you have a nice time

Figure 2.16 Rising non-terminal intonation in a question.

However, English sentences that contain question words like *who*, *what*, *when*, and *how* (for example, *What did you buy?*) ordinarily do not have rising intonation. It is as if the question word itself is enough to indicate that an answer is expected.

Intonation can be represented graphically as in Figures 2.15 and 2.16. A more formal way of representing intonation is shown in Figure 2.17. Here, as in tonal representation, L and H are relative terms for differences in pitch. The letters HL are placed above the syllabic elements on which the pitch change occurs. The dotted lines indicate that the lowering pitch spreads across the remaining pitch-bearing elements.

Figure 2.17   A terminal contour.

Rising intonation on names or requests is commonly heard in addressing people. Its use indicates that the speaker is opening a conversation or that some further action is expected from the listener (Figure 2.18).

Figure 2.18   Two non-terminal contours.

The complex uses of intonation have just been touched on here. Consider, for example, that rising intonation is often used to express politeness, as in *Please sit down*. Some linguists think that this use is an extension of the 'open-ended mode' of intonation, and that since a rising intonation indicates that further response is expected (but not demanded) of the hearer, a sentence uttered with a rising intonation sounds less like an order and so is more polite.

Intonation and tone   Tone and intonation are not mutually exclusive. Tone languages show intonation of all types. This is possible since the tones are not absolute but

'He is trying to ride a bicycle.'

Figure 2.19   Tone and intonation: downdrift in Igbo.

relative pitches. A tone is perceived as high if it is high relative to the pitches around it. As long as this relative difference is maintained, the pitch distinctions will also be maintained. Figure 2.19 shows this graphically. It represents the overall pitch of a declarative sentence in Igbo, a West African language with register tones. Note how an Igbo speaker clearly maintains the distinction among the pitch registers even as the overall pitch of the utterance falls. Each high tone is always lower than the preceding high tone, but higher than the low tone that immediately precedes it. This phenomenon is known as **downdrift**.

8.2
Length

In many languages there are both vowels and consonants whose articulation is held longer relative to that of other vowels and consonants. This phenomenon, known as length, is widespread in the world's languages. As mentioned above, length is indicated in phonetic transcription by the use of a colon [:] (IPA [ː]) placed after the long segment.

Italian, Hungarian, German, Cree, and Finnish are a few of the many languages that show long and short vowels. Yap, a language spoken on the island of Yap in the Western Pacific, shows short and long vowels in pairs of words, such as those shown in Table 2.19.

Table 2.19   Short and long vowels in Yap

[θis]	'to topple'	[θiːs]	'(a) post'
[pul]	'to gather'	[puːl]	'moon'
[ʔer]	'near you'	[ʔeːr]	'part of a lagoon'

Italian shows short and long consonants in pairs of words, such as those shown in Table 2.20.

Table 2.20   Short and long consonants in Italian

fato	[fatɔ]	'fate'	fatto	[fatːɔ]	'fact'
fano	[fanɔ]	'grove'	fanno	[fanːɔ]	'they do'
casa	[kasa]	'house'	cassa	[kasːa]	'box'

Long and short consonants are also found in many other languages, including Finnish, Turkish, and Hungarian.

8.3
Stress

In any utterance, some vowels are perceived as more prominent than others. In a word such as *telegraphic* [tʰèləgræfɪk], the two vowel nuclei that are more prominent than the others are [e] and [æ]. Syllabic segments perceived as relatively more prominent are **stressed**.

Stress is a cover term for the combined effects of pitch, loudness, and length – the result of which is syllabic segment prominence. In each language, the effect of these prosodic features varies. In general, English stressed vowels are higher in pitch, longer, and louder than unstressed ones. But this is not always the case. The example word *telegraphic* could just as well be pronounced with the stressed syllables lower than the unstressed ones. The important thing is that they be prominent with respect to the syllables around them, and this is usually accomplished by a relatively large shift in one, two, or all of the three parameters of pitch, loudness, and length.

In some languages, the impression of vowel prominence results from an interaction of the prosodic parameters that is different from that found in English. In Modern Greek, for example, syllables tend to be of equal length. Stress, therefore, is manifested by a change only in pitch and loudness and not in syllable length. Tone languages do not change the pitch level or contour of tones to mark stress. In many of these languages, relative prominence is marked by exaggerating the vowel length or pitch contour.

There are various ways to mark stress in phonetic transcription. A commonly used convention is to employ an acute accent [´] placed over the vowel nucleus in question to mark the most prominent or **primary** stress, and a grave accent [`] to mark the second most prominent or **secondary** stress or stresses. (This should not be confused with the use of the same diacritics to mark tone in tone languages.) Stress can also be marked by placing numbers above the stressed vowels, usually ^{1} for a primary stress and ^{2} for a secondary stress. The word *telegraphic* is transcribed as either of the following:

2)

$$[t^h\grave{e}l\partial gr\acute{æ}fɪk] \quad \text{or} \quad [t^h\overset{2}{e}l\partial gr\overset{1}{æ}fɪk]$$

The examples in Table 2.21 show some differences in English stress placement.

Table 2.21   Differing stress placement in English

(an) éxport	[ékspɔ̀:t]	(to) expórt	[ekspɔ́:t]
(a) présent	[prézənt]	(to) presént	[prɪzént]
télegràph	[tʰéləgræ̀f]		
telégraphy	[tʰəlégrəfɪ]		
tèlegráphic	[tʰèləgræfɪk]		

In the last four examples in the table, you can also see that the quality of certain vowels varies depending on whether they are stressed or unstressed. This phenomenon is common in English, Russian, Palauan, and many other languages, but is not universal.

9

PROCESSES

Speech production is not a series of isolated events. The process of articulation is a complex one. The articulatory organs are operating independently of each other, and many fine adjustments are carried out very rapidly as we speak. As a consequence, speech production often results in the articulation of one sound affecting that of another.

9.1

Co-articulation

The accommodation between overlapping articulatory gestures used in the production of adjacent segments is referred to as **co-articulation**. Figures 2.5 to 2.7 showed how aspiration results from co-articulation. Figure 2.20 shows some more complex aspects of co-articulation. It presents some of the articulatory organs involved in the production of the word *pan* in North American English or in Cockney. Reading from top to bottom, the actions of the lips, tongue, velum, and larynx are shown. The bold black line in each box represents the state of articulation listed to the right of the box.

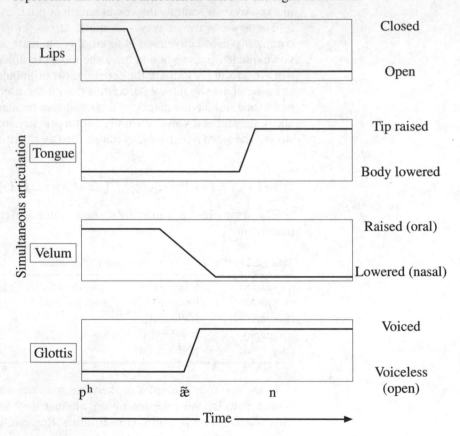

Figure 2.20   Coarticulation among several articulatory parameters.

Lips

The raised line in the upper box indicates that the lips are closed for the articulation of the initial [p] of *pan*. In order to articulate the vowel, the lips are opened – represented by the change in the position of the line – and they stay open during the articulation of the [n].

Tongue	The tongue body is lowered in anticipation of the low front vowel [æ] during articulation of the word-initial consonant. As the vowel articulation ends, the tongue tip is raised to articulate the final [n] of the word.
Velum	You have seen how nasal consonants are produced with the velum lowered to allow air to pass through the nasal cavities. The raising and lowering of the velum is not always precisely co-ordinated with other speech production activity. Speakers often anticipate lowering the velum for nasal consonants and, consequently, produce a nasal vowel before a nasal consonant. Speakers of North American English as well as speakers of some other dialects like Cockney do this consistently in fluent speech when they pronounce words like *pan* [pʰæ̃n] or *bank* [bæ̃ŋk] (the tilde [˜] over the vowel indicates nasality). This is reflected in Figure 2.20. The line representing the velum closure changes to the open (lowered) position during the articulation of the vowel, before the tongue tip is raised to articulate the word-final [n].
Glottis	You have already seen in section 5.5 how aspiration results from a delay in voicing after the release of a voiced stop. Aspiration is shown in Figure 2.20 by the black line remaining in the voiceless position even after the lips have opened and the vowel articulation is in place.
Consonant co-articulation with vowels	All speech is characterized by the kind of complex **co-articulation** among the articulatory organs illustrated in Figure 2.20. Another typical co-articulation phenomenon occurs when we pronounce the sound [k] before the vowel [iː] in English in words such as *keys* and *keel*. The [k] we articulate before [iː] is pronounced with the back of the tongue so far forward it nearly touches the palate (and is transcribed as [k̟]). It is scarcely a velar articulation at all for many speakers. The [k] we pronounce before the vowels [ɒ] and [ɔː] in words such as *cot* and *caught* is articulated further back, and is a true velar. These adjustments are made in anticipation of the tongue position that will be needed for the vowel in question: front for the [iː] and back for the [ɒ] and [ɔː]. The [k] pronounced before the vowel [uː] in a word such as *cool* also shows lip rounding in anticipation of the following (back) rounded vowel and is transcribed as [kʷ].

9.2

Processes and efficiency	Articulatory adjustments that occur during the production of speech are called **processes**. Their cumulative effect often results in making words easier to articulate, and in this sense they are said to make speech more efficient. When speakers of North American English nasalize the vowel of *bank* they do not delay lowering the velum until the exact moment the nasal consonant articulation is reached. Most North American English speakers begin lowering the velum for a nasal consonant almost as soon as they articulate the vowel that precedes it.

In a parallel manner, when speakers pronounce [k̟] as more palatal in a word such as *key*, they are speaking more efficiently from the point of view of articulation since they are making a less drastic adjustment in moving from the articulation of a more palatal [k̟] to that of a high front vowel than they would make in moving from a velar [k] to a high front vowel. Even more drastically, a speaker of English who says [pɹ̥eɪd] for *parade* is making a major adjustment that results in a more efficient articulation: the two syllables of a careful pronunciation of *parade* are reduced to one by dropping the unstressed vowel of the first syllable; the tongue position for [r] can be anticipated during pronunciation of the [p]; finally, the voicelessness of the initial stop is carried on through the [ɹ̥].

9.3

Processes and clarity

Some processes appear to make articulation less, not more efficient. For example, English speakers often lengthen consonants and vowels when they are asked to repeat a word that someone has not heard clearly. The following kind of exchange is typical.

3)

'It's Fred.'

'Did you say, "It's red"?'

'No, I said, "Fffreeed!"'

Lengthening segments results in a greater articulatory effort, but the process results in a form being more distinct and therefore easier to perceive.

Another process that results in more easily perceivable speech adds a segment under certain conditions. When speaking slowly and carefully in a noisy environment, for example, English speakers often insert a vowel between groups of consonants. This breaks up the sequence of consonants into separate syllables. To judge from the use people often make of this process when they wish to be clearly understood, it may well make words easier to perceive.

4)

'Stop screaming!'

'What?'

'I said, "Stop sc [ə] reaming."'

These examples show that there are two basic reasons for the existence of articulatory processes. Some processes result in a more efficient articulation of a series of sounds in that precise timing and co-ordination of speech is relaxed to various degrees. Other processes result in a more distinct output, which is easier to perceive than fluent or rapid everyday speech. Although these two types of processes might at first appear to be contradictory, each serves a particular end in speech production.

9.4

Articulatory processes

Only a finite number of processes operate in language, though their end result is to produce a great deal of linguistic variability. In this section, we survey some of the most common of these processes.

Assimilation

A number of different processes, collectively known as **assimilation**, result from the influence of one segment on another. Assimilation always results from a sound becoming more like another nearby sound in terms of one or more of its phonetic characteristics.

Nasalization of a vowel before a nasal consonant (as in Figure 2.20 above) is caused by speakers anticipating the lowering of the velum in advance of a nasal segment. The result is that the preceding segment takes on the nasality of the following consonant. This type of assimilation is known as **regressive assimilation**, since the nasalization is, in effect, moving *backwards* to a preceding segment.

The nasalization of vowels following nasal consonants in Scots Gaelic is an example of **progressive assimilation**, since the nasality moves *forward* from the nasal consonant onto the vowel (Table 2.22). It results from not immediately raising the velum after the production of a nasal stop. (No nasalization is found where a vowel is preceded by an oral consonant, as in *glé thoilichte* [kle:`hɔliçt̪e] 'very pleased'.)

Table 2.22   Progressive nasalization of vowels in Scots Gaelic

[mõ:r]	'big'
[nĩ]	'cattle'
[mũ]	'about'
[nẽ:l]	'cloud'

Voicing assimilation is also widespread. For many speakers of English, voiceless liquids and glides occur after voiceless stops in words such as *please* [pl̥i:z], *proud* [pr̥aʊd], and *pure* [pj̥ʊə]. These sounds are said to be devoiced in this environment. **Devoicing** is a kind of assimilation. Here, the vocal folds are not set in motion immediately after the release of the voiceless consonant closure.

The opposite of devoicing is **voicing**. In Dutch, fricatives assimilate to the voicing of the stops that follow them, in anticipation of the voiced consonant. For example, the word *af* [ɑf] 'off, over' is pronounced with a [v] in the words *afbelen* 'to ring off', and *afdeken* 'to cover over'.

Assimilation for place of articulation is also widespread in the world's languages. Nasal consonants are very likely to undergo this type of assimilation, as shown in Table 2.23 on the next page.

The negative form of each of these words is made with either *im* or *in*. In both cases, the form shows a nasal consonant that has the same place of articulation as the stop consonant that follows it: labial in the case of *possible*

Table 2.23 Assimilation for place of articulation in English

possible	impossible
potent	impotent
tolerable	intolerable
tangible	intangible

and *potent*, and alveolar in the case of *tolerable* and *tangible*. In informal speech, many English speakers pronounce words like *incomplete* and *inconsiderate* with an [ŋ] where the spelling shows *n*. Assimilation can also be heard in pronunciations such as *La*[ŋ]*caster* and *Ba*[ɱ]*ff* (the symbol [ɱ] represents a labiodental nasal). Assimilation may even cross the boundaries between words. In rapid speech, it is not uncommon to hear people pronounce phrases such as *in code* as [ɪŋkʰəʊd].

The preceding English example shows regressive assimilation to place of articulation. The example in Table 2.24, taken from German, shows progressive assimilation that again affects nasal consonants. In careful speech, certain German verb forms are pronounced with a final [ən], as in *laden* 'to invite', *loben* 'to praise', and *backen* 'to bake'. In informal speech, the final [ən] is reduced to a syllabic nasal, which takes on the point of articulation of the preceding consonant. The diacritic line under the phonetically transcribed nasals indicates that they are syllabic.

Table 2.24 Progressive assimilation in German

Careful speech		Informal speech	
laden	[la:dən]	[la:dn̩]	'to invite'
loben	[lo:bən]	[lo:bm̩]	'to praise'
backen	[bakən]	[bakŋ̩]	'to bake'

Flapping is a process in which a dental or alveolar stop articulation changes to a flap [ɾ] articulation. This process normally applies in North American English, and less often in Cockney. It affects both [t] and [d] if they occur between vowels, the first of which is stressed. Flaps are heard in casual North American pronunciations of words such as *butter*, *fatter*, *wader*, and *waiter*, and even in phrases such as *I bought it* [aɪbáɾɪt]. The alveolar flap is always voiced.

Flapping is considered a type of assimilation since it changes a non-continuant segment (a stop) to a continuant segment in the environment of other continuants (vowels). In addition, we may note that voicing assimilation also occurs in the change of the voiceless [t] to the voiced [ɾ].

Dissimilation

Dissimilation, the opposite of assimilation, results in two sounds becoming less alike in articulatory or acoustic terms. The resulting sequence of sounds is easier to articulate and distinguish. It is a much rarer process than assimilation. One commonly heard example of dissimilation in English occurs in words ending with three consecutive fricatives, such as *fifths*. Many speakers dissimilate the final [fθs] sequence to [fts], apparently to break up the sequence of three fricatives with a stop.

More transparent cases of dissimilation are found in some of the Bantu languages spoken in east and central Africa. The dissimilation typically involves voicing in prefixes. For instance, in Kirundi (spoken in Burundi), if a prefix has a voiceless stop like *k* (followed by a vowel), that stop alternates with a voiced stop made at the same place of articulation when the form to which it is prefixed starts with a voiceless consonant. Thus, for example, the marker of the infinitive form of the verb has two forms *ku-* and *gu-*. The form chosen to appear in a particular word is the one that has a consonant in the prefix which has the opposite specification for voicing to that of the first sound of the verb root. So, where the verb root begins with a voiced sound like _r-_ or _b-_, _ku-_ is selected as in _ku-rora_ 'to look at' or _ku-baríira_ 'to sew'. But where the verb root starts with a voiceless sound like _s-_ or _t-_, _gu-_ is selected as in _gu-seka_ 'to laugh' or _gu-túma_ 'to send' (the diacritic ´ indicates a high tone).

Deletion

Deletion is a process that removes a segment from certain phonetic contexts. Deletion occurs in everyday rapid speech in many languages. In English, a schwa [ə] is often deleted when the next vowel in the word is stressed (Table 2.25).

Table 2.25   Deletion of [ə] in English

Slow speech	Rapid speech	
[pəréɪd]	[pɹéɪd]	parade
[kəɹə́ʊd]	[kɹə́ʊd]	corrode
[səpə́ʊz]	[spə́ʊz]	suppose

Deletion also occurs as an alternative to dissimilation in words such as *fifths*. Many speakers delete the [θ] of the final consonant cluster and say [fɪfs]. In very rapid speech, both the second [f] and [θ] are sometimes deleted, resulting in [fɪs].

Epenthesis

Epenthesis is a process that inserts a syllabic or a non-syllabic segment within an existing string of segments. For example, in careful speech, the words *warmth* and *something* are pronounced [wɔ:rmθ] and [sʌmθɪŋ]. It is common in casual speech for speakers to insert a [p] between the *m* and the *th* and pronounce the words [wɔ:rmpθ] and [sʌmpθɪŋ]. Consonant epenthesis of this type is another example of a co-articulation phenomenon (Table 2.26). In English, the articulatory transition from a sonorant consonant to a non-sonorant appears to be eased by the insertion of a consonant that shares properties of both segments. Notice that the epenthesized consonants are all

Table 2.26   Some examples of English consonant epenthesis

Word	Non-epenthesized pronunciation	Epenthesized pronunciation
something	[sʌmθɪŋ]	[sʌmpθɪŋ]
warmth	[wɔːmθ]	[wɔːmpθ]
length	[leŋθ]	[leŋkθ]
prince	[prɪns]	[prɪnts]
tenth	[tenθ]	[tentθ]

non-sonorant, have the same place of articulation as the sonorant consonant to their left, and all have the same voicing as the non-sonorant consonant to their right.

Vowels may also be epenthesized. In Turkish, a word may not begin with two consonants. When words are borrowed into Turkish, an epenthetic vowel is inserted between certain sequences of two initial consonants, creating a new and permissible sequence (Table 2.27). (The reason for the differences among the vowels need not concern us here; note, though, that the vowel is always high; see section 10.1 for further presentation of [ɯ] and other unfamiliar symbols.)

Table 2.27   Vowel epenthesis in Turkish

Source word	Turkish form
train	tiren
club	kulyp
sport	sɯpor

Metathesis

Metathesis is a process that reorders a sequence of segments. Metathesis often results in a sequence of phones that is easier to articulate. It is common to hear metathesis in the speech of children, who often cannot pronounce all the consonant sequences that adults can. For example, English-speaking children may pronounce *spaghetti* as *pesghetti* [pəsketiː]. In this form, the initial sequence [spə], which is often difficult for children to pronounce, is metathesized to [pəs].

The pronunciations of *prescribe* and *prescription* as *perscribe* and *perscription* in dialects such as American English, where *r* is pronounced following a vowel, are often-cited examples of metathesis in adult speech. In these cases, metathesis facilitates the pronunciation of two successive consonant-*r* sequences in each word.

Vowel reduction

In many languages, the articulation of vowels may move to a more central position when the vowels are unstressed. This process is known as (**vowel**) **reduction**. Typically, the outcome of vowel reduction is schwa; this can be observed in pairs of related words that show different stress placement such as *considerate* [kʰənsídərət] versus *consideration* [kʰənsɪdəréɪʃən]. Note that the fourth vowel, which is unstressed in the word *considerate*, is pronounced [ə]. But when that same vowel is stressed, as in *consideration*, it is pronounced as [eɪ]. Likewise, in *photograph* [fə́ʊtəgɹɑːf] versus *photography* [fətˈgɹəfɪ], the first vowel is pronounced [əʊ] when stressed and [ə] when unstressed. Since we cannot predict which vowel schwa may 'turn into' when stressed, we assume that the fourth vowel basic to both words in the first pair is [eɪ] while in the second pair, the first vowel basic to both words is [ə́ʊ].

10

OTHER VOWELS AND CONSONANTS (ADVANCED)

This chapter has considered only the vowels and consonants of English, many of which are found in other languages. There are also many speech sounds found in the world's languages that are not heard in English. Since phonetic descriptions are universally valid, once the basic articulatory parameters have been mastered, it is not too difficult to describe and even to pronounce less familiar sounds. This section presents a number of speech sounds found in other languages.

10.1

Vowels

Front vowels, which in English are always unrounded, can also be rounded. A high front tense rounded vowel is heard in French *pur* 'pure', German *Bücher* 'books', and Turkish *düğme* 'button'. It is transcribed as [y] in IPA, but as [ü] in North American transcription – a difference that sometimes leads to confusion. A rounded high front lax vowel, transcribed as in IPA [ʏ] (and as [ʊ] in North America) is heard in Canadian French *lune* 'moon' and *duc* 'duke'. A rounded mid-high front tense vowel, often transcribed [ö] ([ø] in IPA), is found in French *peu* 'few' and German *schön* 'beautiful'. A rounded mid-low front lax vowel, transcribed [œ], is heard in French *oeuf* 'egg' and *peur* 'fear', German *örtlich* 'local', and Turkish *göl* 'lake'. Finally, back vowels may be unrounded. For instance, a high back unrounded vowel, transcribed as [ɯ], is heard in Russian words like *byl* 'was', and Rumanian *mînǎ* 'hand'. These vowels, as well as other 'exotic' ones, are found in many other languages as well. Table 2.28 illustrates the vowels presented in this chapter (UR = unrounded; R = rounded).

Table 2.28 Articulatory grid of vowels presented in this chapter

	Front		Central		Back	
	UR	R	UR	R	UR	R
High	i	y (ü)			ɯ	u tense
	ɪ	ʏ (ʊ)				ʊ lax
Mid	e	ø (ö)	ə (reduced)			o tense
	ɛ	œ	ʌ			ɔ lax
Low	æ (lax)		a (lax)		ɑ (tense)	

Nasal vowels

Nasal vowels, like nasal consonants, are produced with a lowered velum. Air passes simultaneously through the oral and nasal cavities. Nasal vowels can be heard in North American English, French, Portuguese, Hindi, and a wide variety of other languages (Table 2.29). They are often transcribed with a tilde [˜] over the vowel symbol.

Table 2.29 Some nasal vowels

American English	win	[wĩn]	'win'
French	pain	[pɛ̃]	'bread'
Portuguese	sento	[sẽntu]	'one hundred'
Polish	ząb	[zɔ̃p]	'tooth'

Consonants

Consonants are described with reference to six parameters.
a) the source of the airstream that is modified within the production of the sound
b) the direction in which the airstream flows
c) the state of the vocal cords (resulting in *voiced*, *voiceless* or *murmured* sounds)
d) the positioning of the soft palate – whether it is raised so that air only escapes through the mouth to produce an *oral* sound or lowered to allow air to escape through the nose resulting in a *nasal* sound
e) the place of articulation (e.g., *labial*, *alveolar*, *velar*, etc.)
f) the manner of articulation (e.g., *stop*, *fricative*, *affricate*, etc.)

All but the first two criteria have been described already in some detail in the preceding pages. What remains to be elaborated are the notions **airstream mechanisms** and the **direction of airflow**. We will explore these in the next section, which explores stop consonants further.

Stops

The same stop consonants found in English are widespread in other languages. A few additional stops are introduced in this section.

In many European languages, we find not the alveolar stops [t], [d], and [n], but dental stops [t̪], [d̪] and [n̪]. Although this seems like a very slight difference in articulation, it can readily be observed in the speech of French, Spanish, or Italian speakers.

Some languages also have retroflex stops (as well as fricatives and liquids) which are made by curling the tip of the tongue right back so that the underside of the tongue makes contact with the roof of the mouth just past the alveolar ridge. Such post-alveolar sounds (symbolized as [ɳ], [ʈ], [ɖ], [ɽ], etc.) are common in the languages of Australia and in those of the Indian subcontinent (cf. [ɖuguɽ] 'yam' (Dyribal, Australia) and [kuʈʈi] 'child' (Malayalam, India)). In order to distinguish between retroflex sounds and palato-alveolar ones like [ʃ] and [ʒ], which are also post-alveolar, phoneticians use the terms **apical** and **laminal** to indicate precisely the part of the tongue used in the production of these sounds. Consonants made with the tip of the tongue are described as apical and those made with the tongue blade are called laminal. Retroflex sounds are then described as apical post-alveolar while palato-alveolar sounds are designated as laminal post-alveolar.

A number of other stop positions are also common in the world's languages. Serbo-Croatian has both a voiceless and a voiced palatal stop in words like *ćaśa* 'dish' and *đak* 'pupil'. These are transcribed as [c] and [ɟ], respectively. Inuktitut dialects spoken in Canada show a voiceless and voiced uvular stop pair in words like *imaq* 'sea', and *ugsik* 'cow'. These are transcribed as [q] and [G], respectively. A nasal stop is also made at the palatal point of articulation, as in Spanish *año* 'year' (transcribed as [ɲ] in IPA and as [ñ] in non-IPA notation), and at the uvula as well, where it is transcribed as [N].

We now return to the glottal state known as *whispery voice* or *murmur* that was introduced in section 2.3. In Hindi there is a series of stops sometimes incorrectly referred to as voiced aspirated stops that make use of whispery voice (murmur). These stops are represented with double underdots.

In Table 2.30, examples of stop articulations and glottal states are laid out. Sounds found in some, if not all, varieties of English are set off in boxes.

Table 2.30 Stops

	Bilabial	Dental	Alveolar	Retroflex	Palatal	Velar	Ulvular	Glottal
Voiceless	[p]	[t̪]	[t]	[ʈ]	[c]	[k]	[q]	[ʔ]
Voiced (oral)	[b]	[d̪]	[d]	[ɖ]	[ɟ]	[g]	[G]	
Voiced (nasal)	[m]	[n̪]	[n]	[ɳ]	[ɲ]	[ŋ]	[N]	
Murmured	[b̤]	[d̪̈]	[d̈]	[ɖ̈]	[ɟ̈]	[g̈]		

Airstream mechanisms

The production of speech sounds always involves modifying in some way a body of moving air. All the speech sounds described until now are produced by modifying air pushed out of the lungs, up the windpipe and into the vocal tract as the speaker breathes out in a subconsciously controlled way. This method of setting in motion a body of air is called the **pulmonic** (i.e., lung) **airstream mechanism** and, as we have mentioned before, the direction of the airflow is **egressive** (i.e., outward).

The stops of English and other languages that we have seen up to this point are all produced using the pulmonic egressive airstream. Such stops are called **plosives**. The pulmonic egressive airstream mechanism is by far the commonest mechanism employed in the production of speech. But it is not the only method that is available. There are consonants that are not produced with the pulmonic airstream but rather with the **glottalic** or **velaric** one.

To produce a glottalic sound (so-called because the movement of the air is initiated in the glottis), the vocal cords are brought firmly together and then they are moved apart pulling upwards or downwards with them the entire larynx which, as a result, acts as a piston in pushing air up and outwards or down and inwards. At the same time, the air is obstructed at some place in the oral cavity like the lips or the alveolar ridge. When the larynx is pushed up, the air trapped in the mouth is compressed. It is then released and flows outwards once the forward closure is removed. Consonants produced with this **egressive** airstream mechanism are called **ejectives**. Normally, they are voiceless. An example of an ejective is the alveolar stop [t′] in the word [t′oqok] 'to throw' (*vs.* [toqok] 'to break') in K′ekchi, a language of Guatemala. (The diacritic ′ after a consonant symbol indicates that it is an ejective.)

There is an alternative way of producing glottalic consonants. If the vocal cords are brought together tightly and the larynx is pulled down while maintaining an obstruction made at some place forward in the mouth, the air trapped between the place where the articulators form the obstruction and the larynx is rarefied. When the obstruction is released, the air flows inwards, making the vocal cords vibrate. Consonants produced with this **ingressive** airstream mechanism are called **implosives**. Examples include [ɓ] and [ɗ] as in Hausa (Nigeria) [ɓa:ɓe:] 'to estrange' (*vs.* [ba:be] 'type of locust') and [faɗa] 'quarrel' (*vs.* [fa:da:] 'chief's residence').

Stops can also be produced using the **velaric** airstream mechanism. To do this, the back of the tongue is brought firmly against the velum, effecting a complete closure. Simultaneously, another closure is made at a point in the front of that closure, say at the lips or the alveolar ridge. The air trapped in the mouth is then rarefied when the tongue moves backwards and down. If, at the same time, the forward closure is released, air is sucked in with a popping noise. Stops produced using the **velaric ingressive** airstream mechanism are called **clicks**. An example of a click is the dental click [ǀ] (not to be confused with [l]) found in the Zulu word [ǀaǀa] 'climb'.

Fricatives

Fricatives other than those of English are found in the world's languages. A bilabial fricative, produced by drawing the lips almost together and forcing the airstream through the narrow opening, is found in many languages. The voiceless bilabial fricative [ɸ] is heard word-initially in the Japanese word *Fuji* (the mountain). The voiced bilabial fricative [β] is found in Spanish words like *deber* 'to owe'. A voiceless palatal fricative [ç] is found in Standard German; the word *ich* 'I' contains this sound. Velar fricatives are not found in English but are widespread in the world's languages. The voiceless velar fricative [x] is common in German and Russian. The composer Bach's name, pronounced in German, has a final voiceless velar fricative. A voiced velar fricative [ɣ] is commonly heard in Spanish words like *agua* 'water'.

Table 2.31 presents a grid on which some common fricative consonants are ranged according to point and manner of articulation. As in Table 2.30, dentals are not distinguished from alveolars, as most languages have sounds with either one or the other point of articulation, but not both. Sounds found in English are set off in boxes.

Table 2.31 Fricatives

	Bilabial	Labio-dental	Inter-dental	Alveolar	Alveo-palatal	Palatal	Velar	Glottal
Voiceless	[ɸ]	[f]	[θ]	[s]	[ʃ]	[ç]	[x]	[h]
Voiced	[β]	[v]	[ð]	[z]	[ʒ]	[ʝ]	[ɣ]	

Affricates

Affricates are found at most points of articulation. In German, a voiceless labiodental affricate, transcribed as [pᶠ], is heard at the beginning of the word *pferd* 'horse'. Many dialects of Canadian French have voiceless and voiced dental (or alveolar) affricates, [tˢ] and [dᶻ], in words like *tu* 'you' and *dire* 'to say'.

Table 2.32 presents a grid including the two English affricates and some others commonly found in other languages. The English sounds are again set off in a box.

Table 2.32 Affricates

	Labiodental	Alveolar	Palato-alveolar	Velar
Voiceless	[pᶠ]	[tˢ]	[tʃ]	[kˣ]
Voiced	[bᵛ]	[dᶻ]	[dʒ]	[gˠ]

Liquids

As with the stops, laterals may be dental as well as alveolar. Laterals can also be made with the tongue body raised to the palate. Such a sound is called a palatal lateral, and is transcribed with the symbol [ʎ]. It is heard in some pronunciations of the Spanish words *caballo* 'horse' and *calle* 'street', and in the Serbo-Croatian words *dalje* 'farther' and *ljudi* 'people'. The palatal lateral may also be voiceless, in which case it is transcribed as [ʎ̥].

Lateral fricatives are produced when a lateral is made with a narrow enough closure to be classified as a fricative. This sound is transcribed as [ɮ] when voiced and [ɬ] when voiceless. Lateral fricatives can be heard in many American Indian languages, in Zulu, in Welsh, and in the languages spoken in the Caucasus. Table 2.33 shows some examples of voiceless alveolar lateral fricatives from Welsh.

Table 2.33 Voiceless lateral fricatives in Welsh

llan	[ɬan]	'clan'
ambell	[ambeɬ]	'some'

Other *r*-like sounds are widely heard in the world's languages. A common one is the **trill**, which is made by passing air over the raised tongue tip and allowing it to vibrate. Trills are commonly transcribed as [r̃] (IPA [r]). They can be heard in the Spanish words *perro* 'dog' and *río* 'river', and the Italian words *carro* 'wagon' and *birra* 'beer'. A similar trilling effect can be made with the uvula, and is called a uvular trill. Its IPA symbol is [R].

A uvular r made without trilling is more commonly heard, however. This is the voiced *r* of Standard French, and is also widespread in German. IPA transcription classifies this sound along with the fricatives. It is transcribed as [χ] when voiceless and as [ʁ] when voiced.

Table 2.34 presents the liquids. As before, sounds found in English are set off in boxes.

Table 2.34 Liquids

		Dental/alveolar	Palatal	Uvular
Laterals	Voiced	[l]	[ʎ]	
	Voiceless	[l̥]	[ʎ̥]	
Lateral fricatives	Voiced	[ɮ]		
	Voiceless	[ɬ]		
r's	Retroflex	[ɽ]		
	Approximant	[ɹ]		
	Flap	[ɾ]		
	Trill	[r̃]		[R]

Flaps and trills can be voiceless as well. Voicelessness for these sounds is usually indicated by a small open circle beneath the symbol, as in [r̥̃] or [R̥].

Other glides are found in the world's languages. A commonly heard one is made with the tongue position of [j] but with the lips rounded. It is transcribed as [ɥ] and can be heard in French words such as [ɥit] *huit* 'eight', [ɥil] *huile* 'oil', and [ɥitχ] *huitre* 'oyster'.

A complete list of all IPA symbols and diacritics can be seen in Table 2.35.

Glides

Summing up

The study of the sounds of human language is called **phonetics**. These sounds are widely transcribed by means of the **International Phonetic Alphabet**.

The sounds of language are commonly described in **articulatory** and **acoustic terms**, and fall into two major types: **syllabic sounds** (**vowels**, **syllabic liquids**, and **nasals**) and **non-syllabic sounds** (**consonants** and **glides**). Sounds may be **voiced** or **voiceless**, and **oral** or **nasal**. Consonants are produced at various **places of articulation**: **labial**, **dental**, **alveolar**, **palato-alveolar**, **palatal**, **velar**, **uvular**, **glottal**, and **pharyngeal**. At the places of articulation, the airstream is modified by different **manners of articulation** and the resulting sounds are **stops**, **fricatives**, or **affricates**. Vowels are produced with less drastic closure and are described with reference to tongue position (**high**, **low**, **back**, and **front**), tension (**tense** or **lax**), and lip rounding (**rounded** or **unrounded**). Language also shows **suprasegmental** phenomena such as **tone**, **intonation**, and **stress**.

The International Phonetic Alphabet (revised to 1993, corrected 1996)

CONSONANTS (PULMONIC)

	Bilabial	Labiodental	Dental	Alveolar	Postalveolar	Retroflex	Palatal	Velar	Uvular	Pharyngeal	Glottal
Plosive	p b			t d		ʈ ɖ	c ɟ	k ɡ	q ɢ		ʔ
Nasal	m	ɱ		n		ɳ	ɲ	ŋ	N		
Trill	ʙ			r					ʀ		
Tap or Flap				ɾ		ɽ					
Fricative	ɸ β	f v	θ ð	s z	ʃ ʒ	ʂ ʐ	ç ʝ	x ɣ	χ ʁ	ħ ʕ	h ɦ
Lateral fricative				ɬ ɮ							
Approximant		ʋ		ɹ		ɻ	j	ɰ			
Lateral approximant				l		ɭ	ʎ	ʟ			

Where symbols appear in pairs, the one to the right represents a voiced consonant. Shaded areas denote articulations judged impossible.

CONSONANTS (NON-PULMONIC)

Clicks		Voiced implosives		Ejectives	
ʘ	Bilabial	ɓ	Bilabial	ʼ	Examples:
ǀ	Dental	ɗ	Dental/alveolar	pʼ	Bilabial
ǃ	(Post)alveolar	ʄ	Palatal	tʼ	Dental/alveolar
ǂ	Palatoalveolar	ɠ	Velar	kʼ	Velar
ǁ	Alveolar lateral	ʛ	Uvular	sʼ	Alveolar fricative

OTHER SYMBOLS

ʍ Voiceless labial-velar fricative
w Voiced labial-velar approximant
ɥ Voiced labial-palatal approximant
ʜ Voiceless epiglottal fricative
ʢ Voiced epiglottal fricative
ʡ Epiglottal plosive

ɕ ʑ Alveolo-palatal fricatives
ɺ Alveolar lateral flap
ɧ Simultaneous ʃ and x

Affricates and double articulations can be represented by two symbols joined by a tie bar if necessary.   k͡p t͡s

VOWELS

Where symbols appear in pairs, the one to the right represents a rounded vowel.

SUPRASEGMENTALS

ˈ	Primary stress
ˌ	Secondary stress
ː	Long
ˑ	Half-long
˘	Extra-short
ǀ	Minor (foot) group
‖	Major (intonation) group
.	Syllable break
‿	Linking (absence of a break)

ˌfoʊnəˈtɪʃən
eː
eˑ
ě
ɹi.ækt

DIACRITICS
Diacritics may be placed above a symbol with a descender, e.g. ŋ̊

̥	Voiceless	n̥ d̥	̤	Breathy voiced	b̤ a̤	̪	Dental	t̪ d̪
̬	Voiced	s̬ t̬	̰	Creaky voiced	b̰ a̰	̺	Apical	t̺ d̺
ʰ	Aspirated	tʰ dʰ	̼	Linguolabial	t̼ d̼	̻	Laminal	t̻ d̻
̹	More rounded	ɔ̹	ʷ	Labialized	tʷ dʷ	̃	Nasalized	ẽ
̜	Less rounded	ɔ̜	ʲ	Palatalized	tʲ dʲ	ⁿ	Nasal release	dⁿ
̟	Advanced	u̟	ˠ	Velarized	tˠ dˠ	ˡ	Lateral release	dˡ
̠	Retracted	e̠	ˤ	Pharyngealized	tˤ dˤ	̚	No audible release	d̚
̈	Centralized	ë	̃	Velarized or pharyngealized	ɫ			
̽	Mid-centralized	e̽	̝	Raised	e̝ (ɹ̝ = voiced alveolar fricative)			
̩	Syllabic	n̩	̞	Lowered	e̞ (β̞ = voiced bilabial approximant)			
̯	Non-syllabic	e̯	̘	Advanced Tongue Root	e̘			
˞	Rhoticity	ɚ a˞	̙	Retracted Tongue Root	e̙			

TONES AND WORD ACCENTS

LEVEL			CONTOUR		
e̋ or ꜛ	Extra high		ě or ꜛ	Rising	
é	˥ High		ê	˥ Falling	
ē	˧ Mid		e᷄	High rising	
è	˨ Low		e᷅	Low rising	
ȅ	˩ Extra low		e᷈	Rising-falling	
ꜜ	Downstep		↗	Global rise	
ꜛ	Upstep		↘	Global fall	

Table 2.35 The International Phonetic Alphabet (revised to 1993, corrected 1996)

Notes

1   There is still a great deal of discussion among linguists on the subject of diphthongs. English vowels that show a change in quality are considered diphthongs as long as the change in quality follows the vowel nucleus. Words such as *yes* and *yak* are considered to begin with a glide that is not an integral part of the vocalic nucleus. However, in transcribing other languages (Finnish, for example), sounds like [jɛ] and [wo] are considered to be diphthongs. For now, treat the diphthongs presented in Table 2.15 as unit vowels, and the initial two sounds of words like *yes* and *yak* as distinct segments. This approach will be revised somewhat in Chapter 3.

2   In RP as we have seen, as well as in many other dialects of English worldwide, the vowel of *caught* (and certain other words such as *law*) is the mid-low back rounded lax vowel [ɔ:], which is distinct from the low back rounded vowel [ɒ] of *pot* and *cot*. However, in standard Canadian English, and in, for example, the Pittsburgh area in the United States, there is no difference between the vowels of a pair of words like *cot* and *caught*, whose vowels are both [ɑ]. For a good exposition of issues in the analysis and transcription of English vowels we recommend that you read especially Chapters 2 and 3 of Giegerich (1992), which is cited below.

Sources

Information on the International Phonetic Alphabet can be obtained from the International Phonetic Association, University College, Gower Street, London, WC1E 6BT, England. Sarcee data are taken from E.-D. Cook, 'Vowels and tones in Sarcee', *Language* 47: 164–79; Gaelic data are courtesy of James Galbraith. Bini data are adapted from Ladefoged (cited below). More detailed reading on the phonetics of English and other languages is reported below. The Kirundi data are from A.E. Meussen, 1959, *Essai de Grammaire Rundi*, Annales du Musée Royal du Congo Belge, Tervuren, Série numéro 8. (Sciences de l'Homme: Linguistique. Volume 24.)

Some of the questions in this chapter were prepared by Joyce Hildebrand.

Recommended reading

Catford, J.C. 1977. *Fundamental Problems in Phonetics*. Edinburgh: Edinburgh University Press.

Cruttenden, Alan. 1986. *Intonation*. Cambridge: Cambridge University Press.

Fromkin, V.A. ed. 1978. *Tone: A Linguistic Survey*. New York: Academic Press.

Giegerich, H.J. 1992. *English Phonology: An Introduction*. Cambridge: Cambridge University Press.

Gimson, A.C. 1994. *Pronunciation of English*. London: Arnold (5th edn, revised by A. Cruttenden).

Ladefoged, P. 1993. *A Course in Phonetics*. 3rd edn. New York: Harcourt Brace Jovanovich.

Ladefoged, P., and Maddieson, I. 1996. *The Sounds of the World's Languages*. Oxford: Blackwell.

Laver, J. 1994. *Principles of Phonetics*. Cambridge: Cambridge University Press.

Pullum, G.K., and Ladusaw, W.A. 1986. *Phonetic Symbol Guide*. Chicago: University of Chicago Press.

Rogers, H. 1991. *Theoretical and Practical Phonetics*. Toronto: Copp Clark Pitman Ltd.

Shearer, William M. 1968. *Illustrated Speech Anatomy*. Springfield, Illinois: Charles C. Thomas.

Questions

1. In order to become more aware of the differences between spelling and pronunciation, answer the following questions about English spelling.
   a) Find four words that show four alternate spellings of the sound [f].
   b) Find six words that have the letter *a* pronounced differently.
   c) Find four words in which different groups of letters represent only one sound.
   d) Find two words in which two different sounds are pronounced but not spelled out.

2. How many segments are there in the following words?
   a) at
   b) maths
   c) cure
   d) hopping
   e) psychology
   f) knowledge
   g) mailbox
   h) awesome

3. Is the first sound in each of the following words voiced or voiceless?

though	zoom	huge	when
thought	silk	choose	ghetto
form	pan	judge	pneumatic
view	boat	buns	winced

4. Using the words presented in question 3, state whether the last sound of each word is voiced or voiceless.

5. For each of the following pairs of sounds, state whether they have the same or different place of articulation. Then identify the place of articulation for each sound.
   a) [s] : [l]
   b) [k] : [ŋ]
   c) [p] : [g]
   d) [l] : [r]
   e) [m] : [n]
   f) [dʒ] : [ʃ]
   g) [f] : [h]
   h) [w] : [j]
   i) [b] : [f]
   j) [tʃ] : [dʒ]
   k) [s] : [v]
   l) [θ] : [t]

6. For each of the following pairs of sounds, state whether they have the same or different manner of articulation. Then identify the manner of articulation for each sound.
   a) [s] : [θ]
   b) [k] : [g]
   c) [w] : [j]
   d) [f] : [ʃ]
   e) [l] : [t]
   f) [ð] : [v]
   g) [tʃ] : [ʃ]
   h) [m] : [ŋ]
   i) [r] : [w]
   j) [tʃ]:[dʒ]
   k) [h] : [ʔ]
   l) [z] : [ʒ]

7. After each of the following articulatory descriptions, write in phonetic brackets the sound described.
   a) voiceless velar stop
   b) voiced labiodental fricative
   c) voiced palato-alveolar affricate
   d) voiced palatal glide
   e) voiced velar nasal
   f) voiceless interdental fricative

g) high back rounded lax vowel

h) low front unrounded vowel

8. Which of the following pairs of words show the same vowel quality? Mark each pair as *same* or *different*. Then transcribe each word.

a)	back	sat	h) hide	height
b)	cot	caught	i) least	heed
c)	bid	key	j) drug	cook
d)	luck	flick	k) sink	fit
e)	ooze	deuce	l) oak	own
f)	cot	court	m) pour	port
g)	fell	fail	n) mouse	cow

9. Using descriptive phonetic terms like sibilant, fricative, and so on, provide a single phonetic characteristic that all the segments in each group share. Try to avoid over-obvious answers such as 'consonant', or 'vowel'.

Example: [b d g œ m y] are all voiced.

a) [p t k g ʔ]   f) [h ʔ]

b) [i e ɛ æ]   g) [u o e]

c) [tʃ ʒ ʃ dʒ]   h) [s z tʃ dʒ ʃ ʒ]

d) [p b m f v]   i) [l r m n ŋ j w]

e) [ʌ ə ʊ a]   j) [t d l r n s z]

10. Transcribe the following sets of words. You may use these words to practise transcribing aspiration.

a) tug	i) peel	q) spell
b) kid	j) stun	r) cord
c) attain	k) Oscar	s) accord
d) despise	l) cooler	t) astound
e) elbow	m) sigh	u) pure
f) haul	n) hulk	v) wheeze
g) juice	o) explode	w) remove
h) thimble	p) tube	x) clinical

11. Using H, L, and association lines, transcribe the intonation of the following English phrases. Compare your results with the transcriptions of several classmates. Are they the same? If they are not, discuss what aspects of intonation (such as emotion or speech context) might account for the differences in transcription.

a) 'Hi, Alice.'

b) 'Allen got a trumpet and a flute for Christmas.'

c) 'Soccer and swimming are Judy's favourite sports.'

12. Mark primary and secondary (where present) stresses on the following words. It is not necessary to transcribe them.

a) sunny	f) arrive	k) secret
b) banana	g) defy	l) exceed
c) blackboard	h) summary	m) summery

d)	Canada	i)	Canadian	n)	Canadianize
e)	(to) reject	j)	(a) reject	o)	difficult

13. Find a fluent speaker of a language other than English and transcribe phonetically ten words of that language. In the unlikely event of your encountering any sounds for which symbols are not found in this chapter (including section 10 and the IPA chart on page 63), attempt to describe them in phonetic terms and then invent diacritics to help you transcribe them.

14. Using Figure 2.20 as your model, provide co-articulation diagrams for the following words. Be sure that your diagrams capture the movement of the lips, tongue, velum, and glottis as in the model.
    a) had   b) snap   c) please   d) dome

15. Compare the following careful speech and rapid speech pronunciations of the following English words and phrases. Then, name the process or processes that make the rapid speech pronunciation different from the careful speech. (Stress is omitted here.)

		Careful speech	*Rapid speech*
a)	in my room	[ɪn maɪ ruːm]	[ɪm maɪ ruːm]
b)	I see him	[aɪ siː hɪm]	[aɪ siː jɪm]
c)	shall we	[ʃəl wɪ]	[ʃwɪ]
d)	balloons	[bəluːnz]	[bluːnz]
e)	once	[wʌns]	[wʌnts]
f)	my advice	[maɪ ədvaɪs]	[maɪ əvaɪs]
g)	best book	[best bʊk]	[bes bʊk]
h)	protection	[prətekʃən]	[pərtekʃən]
i)	hand me that	[hænd miː ðæt]	[hæmiː ðæt]
j)	Pam will miss you	[pæm wɪl mɪs juː]	[pæm̩mɪʃjə]

Phonology: the function and patterning of sounds

Michael Dobrovolsky and Francis Katamba

A person's tongue is a twisty thing, there are plenty of words there of every kind, and the range of words is wide, and their variation.

❧ Homer, *The Illiad, 20*

We saw in Chapter 2 that there is a large number of speech sounds that human beings can produce and perceive. But no human language exploits all these possibilities. Furthermore, the sounds of all languages are patterned and organized in such ways that linguists can discover some system that underlies their appearance. Linguists generally assume that speakers have (at least) some subconscious or implicit knowledge of this system. For example, we saw in Chapter 1 that English speakers know that forms like *slish* and *screnk* are acceptable, while forms like *srish* and *screpk* are not. In fact, speakers can do more than note that some forms are unnatural in their system; they can also correct such forms to make them acceptable. Most English speakers would pronounce a form like *srish* as [sərɪʃ] rather than [srɪʃ], [rɪʃ] or [sɪʃ] without knowing exactly why. It is this largely subconscious knowledge of sound patterns that phonologists are interested in uncovering.

This chapter is about **phonology**, the component of a grammar made up of the elements and principles that determine how sounds pattern in a language. Phonologists attempt to make explicit statements about the sound patterns of individual languages in order to discover something about the linguistic knowledge that people must have in order to use these patterns. Even more broadly, the study of phonology attempts to discover general principles that underlie the patterning of sounds in human language.

The existence of patterns in language depends on the organization of certain basic elements or units that combine to make up these patterns. Three major units of analysis will be presented in this chapter. We are already acquainted with the idea that the flow of speech can be divided into segments. In this chapter, we investigate the patterned variation of segments. We will also investigate the properties of the **syllable**, the basic unit in which segments are grouped. A syllable is a unit of linguistic structure that consists of a syllabic element – normally a vowel – and any segments that are associated with it. To illustrate, the word *segment* can be divided into two syllables: *seg* and *ment*. A third unit of phonological analysis is the **feature**.

Features may be thought of as the smallest building blocks of phonological structure, corresponding as they do to articulatory or acoustic categories such as [voice] or [strident]. We will learn how segments are built up from features and how this fact affects phonological patterning. These units – feature, segment, and syllable – interact with the processes we investigated in the previous chapter, and with certain general principles, to produce the sound pattern of language.

The existence of patterned elements implies that there must be some principles of organization. Features, segments, and syllables are organized into hierarchical levels: each level is composed of elements at the level beneath it. In Figure 3.1, the word-level unit *segment* is represented by the abbreviation *Wd*. This word consists of two syllables, each of which is represented with the Greek letter σ *(sigma)*. Each syllable is made up of a number of segments (the internal structure of syllables is also hierarchical, as we will see in sections 4 and 9 of this chapter where the syllable is treated more elaborately). Each segment, in turn, is composed of features. A representation of *segment* is given in Figure 3.1. (For purposes of illustration, only a few features are provided for each segment.)

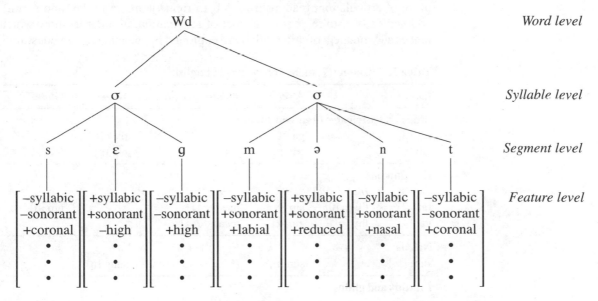

Figure 3.1 Partial phonological representation of *segment*.

In the next sections, we look at the phonological knowledge that enables speakers to distinguish among forms and to deal with the considerable phonetic variation found in the pronunciation of speech segments.

1

All speakers know which segments of their language **contrast**. Segments are said to contrast (or to be **distinctive** or be in **opposition**) when their presence alone may distinguish forms with different meanings from each other. The segments [s] and [z] contrast in the words *sip* and *zip*, as do the vowels of *hit*, *hate*, and *ho*.

1.1

Minimal pairs

A basic test for a sound's distinctiveness is called a **minimal pair** test. A **minimal pair** consists of two forms with distinct meanings that differ by only one segment found in the same position in each form. The examples [sɪp] *sip* and [zɪp] *zip* given previously form a minimal pair and show that the sounds [s] and [z] contrast in English.

A number of minimal pairs that demonstrate consonant contrasts for English are given in Table 3.1 – remember it is on the basis of sound and not spelling that minimal pairs are established. In displaying contrasts, the relevant words are often placed along the horizontal axis with respect to their place of articulation, reading from left to right (labial, alveolar, and so on), and vertically with respect to manner of articulation, in order to show which places and manners of articulation are exploited by the language in question.[1]

Table 3.1   Contrasts among consonants in English

Labial		*Alveolar*	*Palato-alveolar*	*Velar*	*Glottal*
Stops and affricates (non-continuants)					
tap [p]		pat [t]	chug [tʃ]	pick [k]	
tab [b]		pad [d]	jug [dʒ]	pig [g]	
Continuants					
	Interdental				
fat [f]	thigh [θ]	sip [s]	mesher [ʃ]		hip [h]
vat [v]	thy [ð]	zip [z]	measure [ʒ]		
Nasals					
sum [m]		sun [n]		sung [ŋ]	
Liquids and glides					
wet [w]			yet [j]		
		leer [l]			
		rear [r]			

The phonetic context in which a sound occurs is called its **environment**. Pairs that show segments in nearly identical environments, such as *shoulder* ([ʃəʊldə])/*soldier* ([səʊldʒə]) or *author* ([ɔ:θə])/*either* ([i:ðə]) are called near-minimal pairs. They help to establish contrasts where no minimal pairs can be found.

You may assume that two segments contrast once a minimal pair or a near-minimal pair has been established. It is in fact rare to find minimal pairs for all distinctive sounds in all environments in a language, since the historical evolution of every language has led to some sounds being utilized more frequently than others, or being eliminated from some environments. For example, you will find no minimal pairs involving [h] and [ŋ] in word-initial or word-final position in English, because there are no words that begin with [ŋ] or end in [h]. It is also difficult to find minimal pairs in English that involve the sound [ʒ], which occurs for the most part in words borrowed from French such as *azure* and *mirage*.

Vowel contrasts in English

Contrasts among English vowels can be established with a few sets of examples (Table 3.2). For now, we will assume that English tense vowels like [i:] and [u:], and diphthongs like [eɪ], [aʊ], [əʊ], and so on are single vowels. From this perspective, we can say that the vowels [i:] and [ɪ], [eɪ] and [e], and so on, contrast.

Table 3.2 Vowel contrasts in English

beet	[biːt]	[iː]
bit	[bɪt]	[ɪ]
bait	[beɪt]	[eɪ]
bet	[bet]	[e]
bat	[bæt]	[æ]
cooed	[kʰuːd]	[uː]
could	[kʰʊd]	[ʊ]
code	[kʰəʊd]	[əʊ]
cod	[kʰɒd]	[ɒ][2]
cud	[kʰʌd]	[ʌ]
lewd	[luːd]	[uː]
loud	[laʊd]	[aʊ]
lied	[laɪd]	[aɪ]
Lloyd	[lɔɪd]	[ɔɪ]

1.2

Language-specific contrasts

Contrasts are language-specific: sounds that are distinctive in one language will not necessarily be distinctive in another. For example, the difference between the two vowels [e] and [æ] is crucial to English, as we can see from minimal pairs like *Ben* [ben] and *ban* [bæn]. But in Turkish, this difference in pronunciation is not distinctive. A Turkish speaker may pronounce the word for 'I' as [ben] or [bæn] (Table 3.3, overleaf), and it will make no difference to the meaning.

Conversely, sounds that do not contrast in English, such as long and short vowels, may be distinctive in another language. There are no minimal pairs of the type [hæt]:[hæːt] or [lʊs]:[lʊːs] in English. But in Japanese and Finnish, short and long vowels contrast, as the examples in Table 3.4 on the next page show.

Table 3.3 Language-specific vowel contrasts: English versus Turkish

English		*Turkish*	
[ben]	Ben	[ben]	I
[bæn]	ban	[bæn]	I

Table 3.4 Short/long vowel contrasts in Japanese and Finnish

Japanese			
[tori]	'bird'	[tori:]	'shrine gate'
[kibo]	'scale'	[kibo:]	'hope'
Finnish			
[tuli]	'fire'	[tu:li]	'wind'
[hætæ]	'distress'	[hæ:tæ:]	'to evict'

Establishing the contrasting segments in a language is a first step in phonological analysis. But in any language, there are many sounds that never contrast. The following section deals with this major subject of phonological analysis.

2

PHONETICALLY CONDITIONED VARIATION: PHONEMES AND ALLOPHONES

Everyday speech contains a great deal of phonetic variation. Some of it is due to variation in articulation that arises from extralinguistic factors such as orthodontic work, fatigue, excitement, gum chewing, and the like. Such variation is not part of the domain of phonology. Much phonetic variation, however, is systematic. It occurs most often among phonetically similar segments and is conditioned by the phonetic context (environment) in which the segments are found. This variation occurs because segments are affected and altered by the phonetic characteristics of neighbouring elements or the larger phonological context in which they occur. Every speaker has the ability to factor out this variation in order to focus attention on only the relevant contrasts of the language.

2.1

Complementary distribution

When first learning phonetic transcription, English speakers are often surprised that all the *l*s they pronounce are not identical. In Table 3.5, the *l*s in column A are voiced, while those in column B are voiceless (indicated here by a subscript ₒ). Many speakers of English are unaware that they routinely produce this difference in articulation, which can be heard clearly when the words in column B are pronounced slowly.

The voicelessness of the *l* sounds in column B is an automatic consequence of their phonetic environment. Voiced and voiceless *l*s vary systematically in that all of the voiceless *l*s occur predictably after the class of voiceless stops.

Table 3.5   Voiced and voiceless *l* in English

A		B	
blue	[blu:]	plough	[pl̥aʊ]
gleam	[gli:m]	clap	[kl̥æp]
slip	[slɪp]	clear	[kl̥ɪə]
flog	[flɒg]	play	[pl̥eɪ]
leaf	[li:f]		

Since no voiced [l] ever occurs in the same phonetic environment as a voiceless one (and vice versa), we say that the two variants of *l* are in **complementary distribution**.

Table 3.6   Complementary distribution of [l] and [l̥] in English

	[l]	[l̥]
After voiceless stops	no	yes
Elsewhere	yes	no

The term *elsewhere* is used in Table 3.6 to indicate the wider distribution (occurrence in a greater number of different phonetic environments) of voiced [l]. It occurs after voiced stops, voiceless fricatives, and in word-initial position.

In spite of these phonetic differences, native speakers consider the two English *l*s to be instances of the same sound, since they are phonetically similar and the differences between them are systematic and predictable. This perception of sameness is supported by the fact that the two *l*s never contrast in English. There are no minimal pairs like [pleɪ] and [pl̥eɪ]. We can sum up the relationship that the two *l*s bear to each other by stating that, for speakers of English, the two *l*s are *phonetically* different but in the sound system of English, given their phonetic similarity, predictable distribution, and non-contrastiveness, they are *phonologically* the same.

2.2

Phonemes and allophones

The ability to group phonetically different sounds together into one class is shared by all speakers of all languages. This phonological knowledge is represented formally on a level of phonological representation that is distinct from phonetic representation. Predictable sounds that are phonetically similar, and that do not contrast with each other, are grouped together into a phonological unit called a **phoneme**. These variants, which are referred to as **allophones**, are in complementary distribution. A representation of this relationship is shown in Figure 3.2 overleaf. The phonemic symbol for the class – generally the same symbol as the elsewhere variant – is placed between slashes, and the symbols for allophones are enclosed in phonetic brackets.

Allophonic variation is found throughout language. In fact, every speech sound we utter is an allophone of some phoneme and can be grouped together with other phonetically similar sounds into a class which is represented by a

(Phoneme →) /l/

(Allophones →) [l̥] [l]

After voiceless stops Elsewhere

Figure 3.2 The phoneme /l/ and its allophones [l] and [l̥] in English.

phoneme on a phonological level of representation. An important part of phonological analysis deals with discovering the phonemes of languages and accounting for allophonic variation.

Some other considerations

Before we go on to examine in more detail the patterning of phonemes and allophones, some other considerations in determining their status in a language must be taken into account. So far, we have seen that a minimal pair test is a quick and direct way of establishing that two sounds belong to separate phonemes in a language. If the sounds contrast, they are members of different phonemes. We have also seen that if certain phonetically similar sounds are non-contrastive and in complementary distribution, they may be considered allophones of one phoneme. In some cases, however, we must go beyond these procedures to discover the phonological inventory of a language.

As noted in section 1.1, certain patterns of distribution prevent some sounds in a language from ever contrasting with each other. In cases like these, we can establish the phonemic status of a sound by default. The following data from English help to illustrate this point.

1)

*[ŋəʊp]   (does not exist)   [həʊp]   'hope'
*[ŋeɪt]   (does not exist)   [heɪt]   'hate'

We can see here that [h] and [ŋ] do not contrast in initial position in English. The following examples show that they do not contrast in final position either.

2)

[lɒŋ]   'long'   *[lɒh]   (does not exist)
[sɪŋ]   'sing'   *[sɪh]   (does not exist)
[klæŋ]   'clang' *[klæh] (does not exist)

These lists could be extended for pages, but a minimal pair involving [h] and [ŋ] could never be found in English. This is because the two sounds are in complementary distribution: [h] occurs only syllable-initially, followed by a vowel, and [ŋ] occurs elsewhere (i.e., syllable-finally or before a syllable-final consonant). Nevertheless, these facts taken together do not lead us to conclude that [h] and [ŋ] are allophones of one phoneme. Since they are so different phonetically, we assume that each one is a member of a separate phoneme.

Minimal pairs or near-minimal pairs help us establish which sounds contrast in a language and therefore belong to different phonemes. Phonetic similarity and complementary distribution help us decide which sounds are allophones of one phoneme. But not all examples of variation among sounds can be dealt with through these approaches.

In some cases, phonetically similar sounds are neither in complementary distribution nor found to contrast. It is still possible, nevertheless, to determine the phonemes to which these sounds belong. A case in point is the variation in English voiceless stops when they are found in word-final position, as in the word *stop*. Sometimes an English speaker releases the articulation of these sounds rather forcefully. Let us represent this with a diacritic sign [!]. At other times, the same speaker may keep the articulators closed for a moment after the articulation; the diacritic [˺] can represent this. Some speakers may even co-articulate a glottal closure (represented here with the symbol for a glottal stop preceding the consonant in question) and produce the word as [stɑʔp]. Thus we can find at least three pronunciations of *stop*: [stɑp!], [stɑp˺], and [stɑʔp]. Since there is no difference in the meaning of these forms, and since the final consonants are phonetically similar, we say that these sounds are in **free variation**, and that they are all allophones of the phoneme /p/. The same pattern holds for the other voiceless stops of English.

2.3

The reality of phonemes

Phonemes are more than convenient symbols for groups of allophones. Phonemes represent a form of linguistic knowledge. Even though we never pronounce a phoneme, only its allophones, there is evidence that speakers mentally store the phonological system of their language in terms of phonemes. It is not surprising, for example, that English spelling uses only one letter for both [l] and [ḻ], since there is only one /l/ phoneme. Generally, spelling systems all over the world ignore phonetic variation that is non-distinctive.

Another demonstration of the reality of phonological versus phonetic distinctions lies in speech perception. Speakers of English often have a hard time hearing the phonetic difference between the voiced and voiceless allophones of /l/, because the difference is not contrastive. Allophonic differences are easily ignored in perception, even though they are systematically produced in the appropriate context. Phonologically relevant distinctions, such as that between /l/ and /r/ in the English words *lift* and *rift*, are never missed. Speakers of languages other than English sometimes find it difficult to distinguish between [r] and [l] when learning English if these two sounds are not contrastive in their language. In Korean, for example, [l] and [r] are allophones of the same phoneme. It is not surprising that speakers of Japanese sometimes have difficulty making this distinction in English. Conversely, English speakers may have a difficult time perceiving and producing the long versus short vowel contrasts of Japanese, since length by itself is not used to distinguish vowels in English (with the possible exception of [ə] and [ɜ:] as in *a* versus *err* in those dialects that have the vowel [ɜ:], length differences between vowels like [iː] and [ɪ] or [uː] and [ʊ] also involve quality differences).

Classes and generalization in phonology

Phonological analysis permits us to account for the great amount of phonetic variation in everyday speech. This systematic variation is widespread within languages. Compare the English data in Table 3.5 with those in Table 3.7.

Table 3.7   Voiced and voiceless allophones of English /r/

A		B	
brew	[bruː]	prow	[pr̥aʊ]
green	[griːn]	creep	[kr̥iːp]
drip	[drɪp]	trip	[tr̥ɪp]
frog	[frɒg]	pray	[pr̥eɪ]
shrimp	[ʃrɪmp]		

The data show that the allophones of English /r/ pattern like those of English /l/. Based on this information, we can state that there is an /r/ phoneme in English with (at least) two allophones – one voiced, the other voiceless. But if we were to stop there, we would overlook an important point. The phonemes /r/ and /l/ belong to the same class of sounds: both are *liquids*. By taking this information into account, we can state a general fact about English.

3)

In English, liquids have voiceless allophones after voiceless stops and voiced allophones elsewhere.

A major goal of phonological description is the formulation of the most general statements possible about sound patterns. Reference to classes of segments helps accomplish this. In Tables 3.8 and 3.9, additional data from English illustrate this point.

Table 3.8   Voiced allophones of English glides

beauty	[bjuːtɪ]	dwell	[dwel]	Gwen	[gwen]
view	[vjuː]	swim	[swɪm]	thwack	[θwæk]

Table 3.9   Voiceless allophones of English glides

putrid	[pj̥uːtrɪd]	twin	[tw̥ɪn]
quick	[kw̥ɪk]	cute	[kj̥uːt]

These forms demonstrate that the contrasting glides /j/ and /w/ each pattern like the liquids. We can now extend our general statement even further.

4)

In English, liquids and glides have voiceless allophones after voiceless stops, and voiced allophones elsewhere.

Clearly, allophones do not pattern piecemeal, but rather according to their class membership.

2.5

English vowels and glides

We will now consider an example of phonological patterning that again refers to classes of segments, but which unlike the data in the previous section, is not due to allophonic variation. Our example involves **liaison** or **linking** in British English where having two distinct vowel phonemes next to each other tends to be avoided. Usually, one of the approximants [r], [j] or [w] is inserted to link the vowels. If the first vowel is not high, a *linking r* is used. However, if the first vowel is high, a glide is inserted between the two vowels. Such a glide tends to be very short. It is conventionally represented by a superscript [ʲ] or [ʷ]. These facts are illustrated in Table 3.10.

Table 3.10 English liaison

Linking r

star	[stɑː]	starring	[stɑːrɪŋ]	star in	[stɑːr ɪn]
roar	[rɔː] (or [rɔə])	roaring	[rɔːrɪŋ]	roar again	[rɔːr əgeɪn]
purr	[pɜː]	purring	[pɜːrɪŋ]	purr aloud	[pɜːr əlaʊd]
stir	[stɜː]	stirring	[stɜːrɪŋ]	stir up	[stɜːr ʌp]
near	[nɪə]	nearing	[nɪərɪŋ]	near and far	[nɪər ən fɑː]
stare	[steə]	staring	[steərɪŋ]	stare at	[steər æt]

Linking j

see	[siː]	seeing	[siːʲɪŋ]	see in	[siːʲɪn]
weigh	[weɪ]	weighing	[weɪʲɪŋ]	weigh all	[weɪʲɔːl]
tie	[taɪ]	tying	[taɪʲɪŋ]	tie up	[taɪʲ ʌp]

Linking w

sue	[suː]	suing	[suːʷɪŋ]	sue Arthur	[suːʷɑːθə]
show	[ʃəʊ]	showing	[ʃəʊʷɪŋ]	show it	[ʃəʊʷɪt]
allow	[əlaʊ]	allowing	[əlaʊʷɪŋ]	allow us	[əlaʊʷʌs]

The behaviour of *linking r* requires further discussion because it is more complex than that of the linking glides [w] and [j]. In our account, we are assuming that a *linking r* is inserted in order to separate the vowels that would otherwise abut. Of course, we could have proposed an alternative analysis where an underlying *post-vocalic r* is posited in the words in Table 3.10 and a deletion rule is used to remove that *post-vocalic r* in environments where it is not followed by a vowel.

Although the idea of positing an underlying /r/ which is subject to deletion in the words in Table 3.10 is historically correct, it is not the best way of describing *linking r* in contemporary English. This is because the appearance of *linking r* is not restricted to words that historically contained a *post-vocalic r* for which an underlying /r/ can be motivated. As seen in *5)* below, *linking r* is used productively in present-day English – even in contexts where no plausible source of a historical or underlying /r/ exists. The epenthetic *r* observed here is normally referred to as an *intrusive r*. The appropriateness of this label is especially obvious in borrowed and foreign words.

5)

[emər ætkɪnz]	'Emma Atkins'
[spɑːr ænəks]	'spa annex'
[vənɪlər ən bənænər aɪskriːm]	'vanilla and banana ice-cream'
[mɪstə jamæʃitər ən mɪ]	'Mr Yamashita and me'
[ʃɪ vɪzɪtɪd gəʊər ən delɪ]	'She visited Goa and Delhi'
[əkrɑːr ən dækɑː]	'Accra and Dakar'

If we assume, as we have done in this book, that the liaison rule inserts a *linking r* in the appropriate environments (stated below in *6)*), all cases of liaison involving [r] can be treated simply and in a uniform way, regardless of whether there was an underlying word-final /r/ at some point in the past.

6)

a. When two vowels are adjacent, if the first is high, it is predictably linked to the vowel that follows it by an epenthetic glide that has the same backness and roundedness. So, after [iː] and [ɪ] we find [ʲ] and after [uː] or [ʊ] we find [ʷ].

b. In similar contexts, non-high vowels are linked by [r] to the following vowel. (This [r] may either be a vestige of the historical [r] which has survived in the spelling long after being dropped in English accents like RP when they introduced a rule that deletes *post-vocalic r* as in Table 3.10 or an *intrusive r* as in *5)*.)

The data in *5)* and in Table 3.10 which we have been examining show parallels with the allophonic distribution that we have considered so far: certain elements are predictable under certain systematically statable phonetic conditions. Here, however, instead of a number of variants of a phoneme, we have sounds whose distribution is statable in a specific environment once we know they belong to a certain class of sounds. We can thus draw from the data in Table 3.10 the generalizations stated in *6)* above which apply equally to a monophthong and to the closing part of a diphthong.

Tense and lax sets

We will conclude the discussion of phonological classes with a brief examination of **tense** and **lax** vowels. As we saw in section 6.3 of Chapter 2, English vowels can be classified as tense or lax. Vowels belonging to these two sets show different types of phonological distribution. Though they can be shown to be separate phonemes since they contrast in some environments, nonetheless their distribution is predictable in certain contexts. Figure 3.3 sums up the distributional patterns of the vowels of English in stressed syllables and these patterns are illustrated in Figure 3.4 (overleaf).

Figure 3.3 The distribution of tense and lax vowels.

First, whereas any kind of vowel except schwa (see section 6.3 of Chapter 2) can occur in a stressed **closed syllable**, i.e., one that ends in a consonant, only tense vowels are allowed in stressed **open syllables**, i.e., ones that end in a vowel. Thus, whereas minimal pairs showing the contrast between tense and lax vowels can be found in the third column of Figure 3.4 (overleaf) which has closed syllables, no minimal pairs can be listed in the fourth column which contains open syllables. There only tense vowels occur.

Second, as seen in the fifth column, any lax vowel except [ə] can occur in a syllable closed by [ŋ]. But tense vowels are excluded from this environment and, as a result, there is no possibility of contrast between tense and lax vowels in this context.

2.6

Language-specific patterns

Although the phenomenon of allophonic variation is universal, the patterning of phonemes and allophones is language-specific. What we discover for one language may not hold true for another.

Language-specific variation in allophonic nasalization

It is not unusual for nasal vowel allophones to occur near a nasal consonant, but, as Table 3.11 shows, the patterning may vary from language to language.

Table 3.11 Nasal vowels in Scots Gaelic

[mõːr]	'big'
[ni]	'cattle'
[nẽːl]	'cloud'
[mũ]	'about'
[rũn]	'secret'

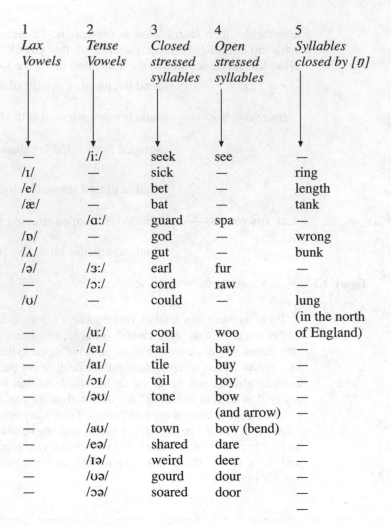

1 *Lax Vowels*	2 *Tense Vowels*	3 *Closed stressed syllables*	4 *Open stressed syllables*	5 *Syllables closed by [ŋ]*
—	/iː/	seek	see	—
/ɪ/	—	sick	—	ring
/e/	—	bet	—	length
/æ/	—	bat	—	tank
—	/ɑː/	guard	spa	—
/ɒ/	—	god	—	wrong
/ʌ/	—	gut	—	bunk
/ə/	/ɜː/	earl	fur	—
—	/ɔː/	cord	raw	—
/ʊ/	—	could	—	lung (in the north of England)
—	/uː/	cool	woo	—
—	/eɪ/	tail	bay	—
—	/aɪ/	tile	buy	—
—	/ɔɪ/	toil	boy	—
—	/əʊ/	tone	bow (and arrow)	—
—	/aʊ/	town	bow (bend)	—
—	/eə/	shared	dare	—
—	/ɪə/	weird	deer	—
—	/ʊə/	gourd	dour	—
—	/ɔə/	soared	door	—
				—

Figure 3.4 The distribution of tense and lax vowels.

Note: For convenience, the transcription oFRP vowels used in this book follows the very widespread practice in British books on linguistics of employing symbols that (redundantly) reflect both quality (tense/lax) and length differences, e.g., /ɪ/ *vs.* /iː/, /ʊ/ *vs.* /uː/ etc. rather than those that only distinguish length /i/ *vs.* /iː/, ʊ/ *vs*/ /uː/, etc. or just quality, e.g., /ɪ/ *vs.* /i/, /ʊ/ *vs.* /u/ which are more economical but are used by a minority oFauthors.

Scots Gaelic has oral and nasal vowel allophones. Here we can state the following.

7)

Vowels are nasal in Scots Gaelic when preceded or followed by a nasal consonant.

As Table 3.12 below helps to illustrate, Malay, a language spoken in Malaysia and Singapore, presents another variation on the theme of nasal allophones.

Table 3.12   Nasalization in Malay

[mẽw̃ãh]	'luxurious'
[mãj̃ãŋ]	'stalk'
[mãrah]	'scold'
[nãẽʔ]	'ascend'
[mə̃laraŋ]	'forbid'
[mãkan]	'eat'
[rumãh]	'house'
[kəreta]	'car'

Here, all vowels and glides following a nasal are predictably nasalized until an obstruent, liquid, or glottal ([h], [ʔ]) is reached. For Malay the generalization is as follows.

8)

In Malay, all vowels and glides following a nasal consonant and not separated from it by a non-nasal consonant are nasalized.

Language-specific variation in allophonic distribution

As was shown in section 1.2, a phonemic contrast in one language may not prove to be a phonemic contrast in another. This means that the relationship of phonemes to allophones may vary. A comparison of the contrasts among stops in English and Khmer (Cambodian) illustrates this point (Table 3.13). In both languages, aspirated and unaspirated phones can be heard.

Table 3.13   Stop phones in English and Khmer

English		Khmer	
[p]	[pʰ]	[p]	[pʰ]
[t]	[tʰ]	[t]	[tʰ]
[k]	[kʰ]	[k]	[kʰ]

In English, aspirated and unaspirated stops are allophonic; there are no contrasting forms like [pɪk] and [pʰɪk]. In Khmer, unaspirated and aspirated voiceless stops contrast, as shown in Table 3.14.

Table 3.14   Khmer contrastive voiceless stops

[pɔːŋ]	'to wish'	[pʰɔːŋ]	'also'
[tɔp]	'to support'	[tʰɔp]	'be suffocated'
[kat]	'to cut'	[kʰat]	'to polish'

The phonological contrasts in the two languages are different, even though the phones are not (Figure 3.5 overleaf). (The other voiceless stops in the two languages have the same distributional patterns.)

Figure 3.5 English and Khmer voiceless bilabial stop phonemes and allophones.

3

PHONETIC AND PHONEMIC TRANSCRIPTION

Having seen how non-distinctive properties of segments are factored out by phonological analysis, we can now compare the type of transcription used for segmental phonological representation with phonetic transcription. The examples given in Table 3.15 show this difference for the classes of sounds in English that we have examined so far.

Table 3.15 Phonetic and phonemic transcription

Phonetic transcription	Phonemic transcription	Word	Predictable property(s) not represented in phonemic transcription
[pl̥aʊ]	/plaʊ/	plough	voicelessness of liquid
[kr̥iːp]	/kriːp/	creep	voicelessness of liquid
[kw̥ik]	/kwɪk/	quick	voicelessness of glide
[let]	/let/	let	—
[tʰaɪd]	/taɪd/	tied	aspiration

The contrast between phonetic and phonemic representation is even more striking for the Malay forms given earlier, as shown in Table 3.16, where nasalization on all vowel and glide segments is predictable and is therefore omitted from the phonological representation.

Table 3.16 Phonetic and phonemic transcription of Malay nasal vowels

Phonetic transcription	Phonemic transcription	Word	Predictable property(s) not represented in phonemic transcription
[mẽw̃ãh]	/mewah/	'luxurious'	nasalization
[mãj̃ãn]	/majan/	'stalk'	nasalization
[nãɛ̃ʔ]	/naɛʔ/	'ascend'	nasalization

4

We have established a segmental unit of phonological analysis called the phoneme. The examples of allophonic variation used thus far all result from conditioning by neighbouring segments. The examples of allophonic variation in this section depend on conditioning that involves another level of phonological representation, the **syllable**.

4.1

Defining the syllable

The syllable is composed of a nucleus (usually a vowel) and its associated non-syllabic segments. Native speakers of a language demonstrate their awareness of this unit of phonological structure whenever they count syllables in a word. No English speaker would hesitate to say that the word *accident* has three syllables, and most speakers would feel confident that it could be broken up into the syllables /æk . sɪ . dənt/ (the ' . ' marks syllable divisions informally). As we will see later on in this chapter, speakers also demonstrate knowledge that syllables have internal structure as well. The organization of a syllable is shown in Figure 3.6 with the monosyllabic English word *sprint*.

Figure 3.6   Internal structure of a syllable.

A complete description of the internal structure of a syllable requires four subsyllabic units. The **nucleus** (abbreviated N) is the syllable's only obligatory member; it is a syllabic element that forms the core of a syllable. The **coda** (C) consists of those elements that follow the nucleus in the same syllable. Th **rhyme** (R) is made up of the nucleus and the coda. The **onset** (O) is made up of those elements that precede the rhyme in the same syllable.

We assume the existence of subsyllabic units for a number of reasons. One of them is the fact that speakers do not syllabify words in random or variable ways. The word extreme /ekstriːm/ would never be syllabified as /e . kstriːm/. Instead, syllables comply with certain constraints that prohibit them (in English) from beginning with a sequence like *kstr* and so result in the syllabification /ek . striːm/.

Table 3.17   Some syllable-initial sequences in English

/ə.plɔːd/	applaud
/di.klaɪn/	decline
/ek.spleɪn/	explain
/ɪm.prə.vaɪz/	improvise

Constraints can be stated for each of the terminal subsyllabic units O, N, and C. To illustrate this, we turn to the constraints that govern the phonological shape of onsets in English.

4.2

Onset constraints and phonotactics

Native speakers of any language intuitively know that certain words that come from other languages sound unusual and they often adjust the segment sequences of these words to conform with the pronunciation requirements of their own language. These intuitions are based on a tacit knowledge of the permissible syllable structures of the speaker's own language. For example, English-speaking students learning Russian have difficulty pronouncing a word like *vprog* [fprɔk] 'value, good', since the sequence [fpr] is never found in English onsets. Since speakers typically adjust an impermissible sequence by altering it to a permissible one, many English speakers would pronounce the Russian word [fprɔk] as [fəprɔk], or even delete the initial /f/ and say [prɔk] in order to adjust the impermissible sequence *fpr* to a permissible English onset. **Phonotactics**, the set of constraints on how sequences of segments pattern, forms part of a speaker's knowledge of the phonology of his or her language.

Some English onsets

Table 3.18 contains examples of the possible syllable-initial consonant sequences of English that contain a voiceless stop consonant. These sequences are all illustrated in word-initial position to make them easier to pick out. (Stress marking and phonetic details such as liquid–glide devoicing which are not relevant to the present discussion are omitted here.)

Table 3.18 Initial consonant clusters in English containing a voiceless stop

Labial + sonorant		Coronal + sonorant		Velar + sonorant	
[pl]	please	[tl]	—	[kl]	clean
[pr]	proud	[tr]	trade	[kr]	cream
[pw]	—	[tw]	twin	[kw]	queen
[pj]	pure	[tj]	tune	[kj]	cute
[spl]	splat	[stl]	—	[skl]	sclerosis
[spr]	spring	[str]	strip	[skr]	scrap
[spw]	—	[stw]	—	[skw]	squeak
[spj]	spew	[stj]	stew	[skj]	skewer

The examples in Table 3.18 show that the first segment of a word-initial three-consonant cluster in English is always *s*, the second consonant in the series is always a voiceless stop, and the third is either a liquid or a glide. These sound patterns can be formally represented as shown in Figure 3.7.

In this formalization, σ indicates the boundary of a syllable, and the

$$\sigma \,[\,s \quad \begin{Bmatrix} p \\ t \\ k \end{Bmatrix} \quad \begin{Bmatrix} (l) \\ r \\ (w) \\ j \end{Bmatrix} \quad \text{Nucleus}$$

Figure 3.7   Possible initial three-consonant clusters in English.

curly braces designate 'either/or'. The sounds in parentheses are not found in all combinations. Although there are twenty-four possible two- and three-consonant syllable-initial sequences in English containing a voiceless stop, not all of these combinations are exploited in the vocabulary of the language.

4.3

Accidental and systematic gaps

Some gaps in the inventory of possible English words include *snool*, *splick*, *sklop*, *flis*, *trok*, and *criff*, none of which violates any constraints on onset combinations found in English. Gaps in a language's inventory of forms that correspond to non-occurring but possible forms are called **accidental gaps**. Occasionally, an accidental gap will be filled in by the invention of a new word. The word *Kodak* is one such invented word. Borrowed words such as *perestroika* (from Russian), *taco* (from Spanish), and *Zen* (from Japanese) are readily accepted by English speakers as long as their syllable structures conform to the phonotactic patterns of the language.

Table 3.18 has shown which syllable-initial consonant clusters involving voiceless stops are permissible in English. Gaps in the occurring syllable structures of a language that result from the exclusion of certain sequences are called **systematic gaps**. For instance, certain onset sequences like /bz/, /pt/, and /fp/ are systematic gaps in the pattern of English and are outright unacceptable to English speakers. Such sequences will ordinarily be adjusted phonologically when they are pronounced in spontaneous speech. This can be seen in the case of borrowings from other languages into English. Many Greek words beginning with *ps-* and *pt-* have been absorbed into English, as the spellings of *psychology*, *psoriasis*, and *pterodactyl* attest. In these words, the impermissible onset clusters $*_\sigma ps$- and $*_\sigma pt$- have been reduced to $_\sigma s$- or $_\sigma t$- in onsets. However, when these same forms occur word-internally, where their syllabification is different, the 'lost' segments may resurface. For example, the *pter* of *pterodactyl* means 'wing'; both consonants are heard in the word *helicopter*, where English syllabification has resulted in the structure *heli*$_\sigma$*cop*$_\sigma$*ter*$_\sigma$.

There are many other words that violate phonotactic conditions and that nonetheless do commonly appear in spoken English, such as *pueblo* [pwebləʊ], Tlingit [tlɪŋɪt], and the common pronunciation in young children's speech of 'street' as *stweet* [stwi:t] (which results from a replacement of /r/ by /w/). The British pronunciation of 'Tuesday' as [tju:zdeɪ] is also not difficult for North American speakers who normally say [tu:zdeɪ], as in their system [j] cannot occur immediately after an alveolar consonant. This appears to be the case because these sequences are not absolutely excluded from the onset phonotactics of English as are such sequences as *$_σ$ps- and *$_σ$bz-. As Figure 3.7 shows, onsets like *$_σ$pw- and *$_σ$stw- are possibilities that are not exploited due to language-specific restrictions on the sequencing of certain features. For example, a labiovelar glide does not usually occur in an onset after a labial consonant, and an alveolar stop such as /t/ is not followed by /l/; in both cases there is a restriction (in English) on stop-sonorant onset sequences with the same place of articulation. Such restrictions are nonetheless relatively easy to overcome in pronunciation.

Language-specific phonotactics

It is important to emphasize that certain aspects of the particular constraints discussed in the previous section are universal (form part of human linguistic ability), whereas others are language-specific. An onset like *pl* is found in many languages besides English (for example, in Russian, Thai, and French), while an onset sequence like *lp* is rarely if ever found. We may therefore say that no restrictions against an onset like *pl* appear to exist as part of human linguistic capacity, while the virtual non-existence of onsets like *lp* suggest that something in their articulatory makeup normally disqualifies them from occurring in language.

Language-specific constraints, on the other hand, hold true for individual languages such as English, and they may or may not be found in other languages. Each language has its own set of restrictions on the phonological shapes of its syllable constituents. Speakers of Russian, for example, are quite accustomed to pronouncing onset sequences such as $_σ$pt-, $_σ$ps-, and $_σ$fsl-, which are not found in English.

Table 3.19 Some onset sequences in Russian

[psa]	'dog's'
[fslux]	'aloud'
[ptʲitsə]	'bird'

Phonotactic constraints represent one kind of phonological knowledge. You might wonder what prevents English words like *extreme*, *applaud*, *decline*, *explain*, and *improvise* from being syllabified as /eks.tri:m/, /əp.lɒd/, /dɪk.laɪn/, /eks.pleɪn/, and /ɪmp.rəv.aɪz/, since these divisions do not violate any phonotactic constraints either. The next section answers this question by providing a procedure for establishing the association of consonants and vowels in syllables.

4.4

Setting up syllables

Each language defines its own syllable structure, although there are universal principles that interact with language-specific factors. The process for setting up syllables in a given language involves the following steps.

- **Step a** (Figure 3.8) Since the syllabic nucleus is the only obligatory constituent of a syllable, it is constructed first. Each vowel segment in a word makes up a syllabic nucleus. To represent this, link a vowel to an N above it by drawing an association line. Above each nucleus symbol, place an R (for rhyme), which is filled out in step c below. Above each R, place a σ symbol; link all with association lines.

Figure 3.8

- **Step b** (Figure 3.9) Onsets before codas: the longest sequence of consonants to the left of each nucleus that does not violate the phonotactic constraints of the language in question is called the **onset** of the syllable. Link these consonants to an O and join it to the same syllable as the vowel to the right. Note that there is no onset in the first syllable of *extreme*.

Figure 3.9

- **Step c** (Figure 3.10) Any remaining consonants to the right of each nucleus form the **coda** and are linked to a C above them. This C is associated with the syllable nucleus to its left in the rhyme. A syllable with a coda is called a **closed syllable**.

Figure 3.10

- **Step d** (Figure 3.11) Syllables that make up a single form (usually a word) branch out from the representation *Wd* (this step is frequently omitted from phonological representations to save space; the complete representation is understood even when *Wd* is not written out).

Figure 3.11

Given this procedure, it is clear why words such as *applaud* and *explain* in Table 3.17 are syllabified the way they are. In accordance with step b, 'build onsets before codas', the permissible consonant clusters make up the onset of the second syllable, and not the coda of the first syllable.

Some further syllabification

This procedure is used to syllabify forms in any language. An example from Turkish demonstrates in more detail how this universal syllabification procedure works. Turkish has different syllable structure constraints than English. As in English, onsets are optional in Turkish, but when present, may consist of no more than one segment – a constraint not found in English. A nucleus may consist of a long vowel (which is equivalent to two short vowels in length) or a short vowel. Codas can be no more than two segments long, and are largely limited to the following combinations: fricative-stop (for example, $-ft_\sigma$), or sonorant-obstruent (for example, $-rp_\sigma$).

The words in Figure 3.12 can be syllabified in the steps given above (steps c

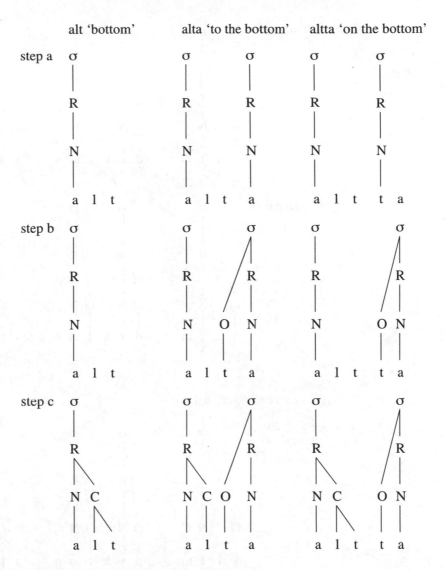

Figure 3.12 Examples of syllabification in Turkish.

and d have been collapsed here). Note how the procedure leads to a different syllabification of the morpheme *alt*, 'bottom' in steps b and c of the examples.

In these examples, both the *l* and *t* of *alt* 'bottom' are assigned to the coda of the first syllable, since there is no syllable with an available onset position following it. However, the same phoneme *t* in *alta* 'to the bottom' is assigned to the second syllable, since onsets are filled first and *t* is available to fill the position. In *altta* 'on the bottom', the two *t*s fill the available coda and onset positions of their respective syllables.

As a final example of the procedure, Figure 3.13 demonstrates the syllabification of the English words *slim*, *decline*, and *scrimp* (again steps c and d have been collapsed).

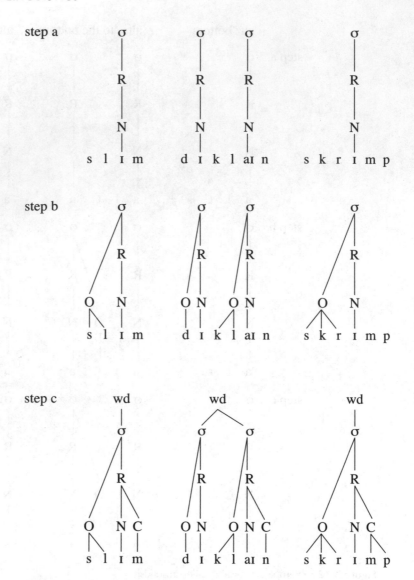

Figure 3.13 Examples of syllabification in English.

With this method in mind, we can now consider the relevance of syllables to phonological description.

4.5

Syllabic phonology

One reason for treating syllables as units of phonological structure is that they are relevant to stating generalizations about the distribution of allophonic features. The next sections provide examples of the role of syllables in phonological analysis.

Aspiration in English

As Table 3.20 shows, the voiceless stops of English each have an aspirated and an unaspirated allophone.

Table 3.20 English aspiration

A		B		C		D	
[pʰǽn]	pan	[nʌtɪ]	nutty	[spǽn]	span	[slǽp]	slap
[pʰéɪn]	pain	[təmáːtə]	tomato	[spéɪn]	Spain	[slɑ́t]	slot
[pʰóʊk]	poke	[təkʰíːlə]	tequila	[spóʊk]	spoke	[blɑ́k]	block
[tʰóʊn]	tone	[kʰənúː]	canoe	[stóʊn]	stone		
[kʰín]	kin	[pəspáɪə]	perspire	[skín]	skin		
[ətʰénd]	attend			[splǽt]	splat		
[əpʰń]	upon			[ʌpsét]	upset		

The distribution of aspiration can be stated generally by referring to syllable structure (Table 3.21).

Table 3.21 Distribution of aspirated stops in English

Aspirated stops	*Unaspirated stops*
• At the start of a stressed syllable	Elsewhere: • in a syllable onset preceded by *s* (whether another C follows or not) • before a consonant • initially in an unstressed syllable • in a syllable coda

The phonemic representations of the three English stops are unaspirated, since aspiration is a predictable feature. The environments where aspiration occurs can be stated very generally by referring to syllable structure.

9)

English voiceless stops are aspirated when initial in a stressed syllable.

This statement accounts for all the data in Table 3.20. In column A, where voiceless stops appear syllable-initially in stressed syllables, they are aspirated. But in column B voiceless stops are unaspirated because, although they are at the start of a syllable, that syllable is unstressed. (Note especially how in *tequila* the [kʰ] which is initial in a stressed syllable is aspirated and the [t] which is initial in an unstressed syllable is unaspirated.) Likewise, no aspiration is found in the forms in columns C and D since the voiceless stops appear either as the second member of the syllable onset (in *span*, *Spain*, *spoke*, *stone*, and *skin*), or in a coda, as in *upset*.[3]

Ambisyllabicity (advanced)

Some English words, such as *upper*, *happy*, and *walking*, do not show aspiration where it is expected, given that the syllabification procedure results in the following: /ʌ . pə/, /hæ . pɪ/, and /wɔː . kɪŋ/. This fact is accounted for by assuming that the voiceless stops in these forms are simultaneously in both syllables, a phenomenon known as **ambisyllabicity**. These consonants are all preceded by a stressed syllable; in contrast, the aspirated stops in words like *upon* [əpʰ́n] and *attack* [ətʰǽk] (Table 3.20, column A) show aspiration, but are all found as the onset of a stressed syllable. In words with ambisyllabic voiceless stops, it is assumed that the stress attracts the voiceless stop into the preceding syllable. This requires us to assume further that a word is resyllabified after stress has been applied to the appropriate syllable. Figure 3.14 shows this process in stages. Figure 3.14*a* shows initial syllabification of the word *happy*; Figure 3.14*b* shows stress placement on the first syllable; in Figure 3.14*c*, the dotted line shows the ambisyllabicity of the voiceless stop that is caused by the stress. The now ambisyllabic consonant cannot undergo aspiration since it is (at least partly) in the preceding syllable.

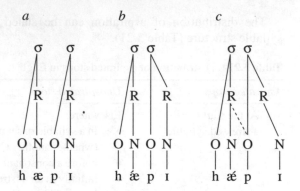

Figure 3.14   Ambisyllabicity in English: *a*, initial syllabification; *b*, stress; *c*, resyllabification with ambisyllabic consonant.

Ambisyllabicity is not as arbitrary as it might appear at first. Its presence not only accounts for the lack of aspiration in these forms, but also helps explain why the first syllables of *upper*, *happy*, and *kicking* might otherwise appear to end in stressed lax vowels, a distribution which is otherwise not normally allowed in English (except in expressive/onomatopoeic words like *baa* /bæ/). The simultaneous presence of the voiceless stop in the coda of the first syllable and the onset of the second means not only that we do not expect aspiration, but also that the first syllable is closed and so the presence of a lax vowel is normal.

Phonetic length in English vowels

English offers a second example of the phonological relevance of syllables. Phonetic length (here shown using a macron '¯' over a vowel, e.g., *ē*) is predictable in English vowels, as Table 3.22 on page 93 shows.

Whatever their inherent length (or, to put it another way, regardless of whether they are phonologically tense or lax) English vowels are phonetically somewhat shorter than they would normally be, when they occur before voiceless consonants, before sonorant consonants, and in word-final position.

Table 3.22   Phonetic length in English

A		B	
bad	[bǣd]	bat	[bæt]
wed	[wēd]	wet	[wet]
Abe	[ēɪb]	ape	[eɪp]
phase	[fēɪz]	face	[feɪs]
pod	[pōd]	pot	[pɒt]
tag	[tʰǣg]	tack	[tʰæk]
brogue	[brə̄ūg]	broke	[brəʊk]
		tame	[tʰeɪm]
		can	[kʰæn]
		sell	[sel]

Conversely, the vowels are relatively longer than they would normally be, when they occur before voiced non-sonorant consonants. As Table 3.23 shows, the phonetic duration of vowels is determined by syllable structure. The first-syllable vowels all precede voiced, non-sonorant consonants, but they are not lengthened since the voiced consonant is in the following syllable.

Table 3.23   Vowels shorter before voiced consonants in English

adept	[æ.dept]	/ædɛpt/
negate	[ne.geɪt]	/negeɪt/
revise	[rɪ.vaɪz]	/rɪ vaɪz/
sadist	[seɪ.dɪst]	/seɪdɪst/

The following generalization can now be made.

10)

English vowels are lengthened when followed by a voiced obstruent in the same syllable.

As the analyses of the distribution of aspiration and vowel length in English have shown, the use of syllabic representations in phonology permits us in some cases to make more general statements about allophonic patterns in language than if we use only statements that do not make reference to syllable structure.

Syllables and stress in English

English provides a final example of the relevance of syllabic units to phonological analysis. Recall (from Chapter 2, section 8.3) that stress is defined as the perceived prominence of one or more syllabic elements over others in a word. In some languages – English among them – the structure of individual syllables plays a role in determining which vowel is stressed. Consider the data in Table 3.24.

Table 3.24   English noun stress

A	B	C
synópsis	aróma	cábinet
veránda	archipélago	América
agénda	hiátus	cínema
consénsus	horízon	aspáragus
amálgam	thrombósis	metrópolis
uténsil	coróna	jávelin
asbéstos	aréna	vénison
phlogíston	Minnesóta	ásterisk
appéndix	angína	lábyrinth
placénta	factótum	análysis

The words in columns A and B are all stressed on the **penultimate** (next-to-last) syllable, while those in column C are all stressed on the third syllable from the end of the word (the **antepenultimate** syllable), as the form *cabinet* makes clear. Although the stressing of the words may seem arbitrary at first, reference to syllable structure makes clear that there is some system underlying the assignment of stress here.

Syllabification of examples from Table 3.24 reveals what stress assignment is based on. Figure 3.15 provides the syllabification of one representative word (shown in phonetic transcription) from each column.

Figure 3.15   Syllable-based stress in English.

All the words in column A share a correlation between their syllabification and their stress: the stressed penultimate syllable has a coda (a syllable with a coda is said to be *closed*, as we saw on page 83). All the words in column B also share a syllable structure characteristic: their nucleus contains a tense vowel. Although the syllable is not closed, the nucleus vowel with two elements in it (the [ə] and [ʊ] of the diphthong [əʊ]) is now represented as branching. In other words, tense vowels have the same effect on stress assignment as consonants in closed syllables. So, closed syllables as well as open syllables with two rhythmic elements in the rhyme are referred to as

heavy while syllables with just a short vowel are said to be **light**. To put it differently, syllables with one **rhythmic beat** or **mora** are light and those with two are heavy. Note that the onset contributes nothing to **syllable weight**.

Now compare these words with the representative item in column C. We see that the final syllable in column C is not heavy: it is neither closed nor does it contain a branching nucleus. With these facts before us, we can state our generalization. We will be careful to limit it to English *nouns*.

11)

English nouns are stressed on the penultimate syllable when it is heavy; otherwise, they are stressed on the antepenultimate syllable.

We have limited our generalization to English nouns because the stress patterns of English are rather elaborate. Nevertheless, there is no doubt that syllabification plays a central role in determining stress placement in English.

Although the phonetic and phonemic transcriptions up to this point have employed segments, segmental notation is itself a kind of shorthand, since segments are ultimately composed of features. The next section takes up this aspect of phonology.

5

FEATURES

Current linguistic practice does not assume that segments are the ultimate units of phonological structure. Instead, linguists take segments to be composed of smaller elements. This section deals with **features** – the units of phonological structure that make up segments.

5.1

Why we use features

There are a number of reasons why linguists have settled on features as the most basic phonological unit.

Features as independent and coordinated elements

We have already seen in Chapter 2 that speech is produced by a number of coordinated articulatory activities such as voicing, tongue position, lip rounding, and so on. Features such as [voice], [high], [round] – note that features are written in square brackets – directly reflect this activity, in that each feature is rooted in an independently controllable aspect of speech production. The representation of a segment by features captures this coordinated activity by placing features in an array called a **matrix**. Each feature or group of features defines a specific property of the segment. This representation is in binary terms: [+] means that a feature is present, and [–] means that it is absent. Figure 3.16 shows a feature matrix for the English vowel [ɑ:].

[ɑ:]

$$\begin{bmatrix} +\text{syllabic} \\ -\text{consonantal} \\ +\text{sonorant} \\ -\text{high} \\ +\text{low} \\ +\text{back} \\ -\text{round} \\ +\text{tense} \end{bmatrix}$$

These features define the segment as consonant, vowel, or glide (here, a vowel)

These features define the placement of the tongue (here, a low back vowel)

→ This feature defines lip rounding (here, unrounded)
→ This feature defines tenseness/laxness (here, tense)

Figure 3.16 Feature matrix for the English vowel / :/.

Features and natural causes

A second reason for viewing segments as composed of features is that each feature may represent a phonologically relevant characteristic of segments. To understand what is meant by this, we first examine how features enable us to distinguish among classes of sounds with many members. For example, the set of sounds /p/, /t/, /tʃ/, and /s/ can be readily distinguished from the set /b/, /d/, /dʒ/, and /z/ by the feature [voice] alone. In phonological terms, features capture **natural classes**, which are classes of sounds that share a feature or features, such as voiceless stops, glides, high vowels, nasal consonants, and so on. Any natural class requires fewer features to define it than to define any one of its members. In Table 3.25, for example, more features are needed to define any of the segments in the class of English front vowels than to capture the entire class: it takes seven features to characterize the vowel /æ/, but only four features suffice to specify the natural class of front vowels.

Table 3.25 Two natural classes: front and back vowels in English

$$\begin{bmatrix} -\text{consonantal} \\ +\text{syllabic} \\ +\text{sonorant} \\ -\text{back} \end{bmatrix} \quad \begin{bmatrix} -\text{consonantal} \\ +\text{syllabic} \\ +\text{sonorant} \\ +\text{back} \end{bmatrix} \quad \begin{bmatrix} -\text{consonantal} \\ +\text{syllabic} \\ +\text{sonorant} \\ -\text{back} \\ -\text{high} \\ +\text{low} \\ -\text{round} \end{bmatrix}$$

/i:/	/u:/	
/ɪ/	/ʊ/	
/eɪ/	/əʊ/	
/e/	/ʌ/	
/æ/	/ɑ:/	/æ/

Because features define natural classes, we can now see their relevance to phonological analysis. It is not individual phonemes such as /p/, /b/, /k/, and /g/ that contrast in English; rather, the entire class of voiced stops contrasts with the class of voiceless stops. It is the feature [voice] that is contrastive, not the individual segments, since we can define the contrast between each pair of segments with otherwise identical articulations as residing in the feature [voice]. Since this single feature is employed in all voiced–voiceless contrasts, we say that [voice] is a **distinctive feature** of English.

Other features provide for other contrasts. For example, we can capture the contrast between /t/ and /s/ in English with the feature [continuant]. Both /t/ and /s/ are voiceless and have an alveolar point of articulation. (The fact that the tongue tip is used in the production of one sound and the tongue blade is used in the other is not relevant to this phonological distinction in English, and can therefore be ignored.) By viewing the relevant distinctive feature as [continuant], we can use the same feature to distinguish between /p/ and /f/, /b/ and /v/, and /d/ and /z/.

Table 3.26   Stop-fricative contrasts as a feature

[–continuant]	[+continuant]
p	f
b	v
t	s
d	z

By systematically examining the phonemic contrasts of a language, we can extract the phonologically distinctive features and state the phonemic inventory in terms of these irreducible linguistic elements.

Features, processes, and allophonic variation

Reference to features also enables us to understand the nature of allophonic variation more exactly. Viewed from the perspective of features, allophonic variation is not simply the substitution of one sound for another, but rather the environmentally conditioned change or specification of a feature or features. Processes like those presented in Chapter 2 are the primary factors in the changing of features. Liquid-glide devoicing in English, for example, is the change of the value of the feature [voice] from [+voice] to [–voice] after voiceless consonants. Vowel nasalization in Malay is the change of the value of the nasal feature from [–nasal] to [+nasal] under just the conditions stated in 8) on page 81.

Certain features capture classes of sounds that are not always reflected in traditional descriptive terminology but which are also relevant to phonological patterning. The feature [coronal], for example, refers to the class of sounds made with the tongue tip or blade raised. It turns out that just this feature is required to state the constraint on the selection of consonant sequences in coda position (i.e., following a vowel in the same syllable) in English presented in Chapter 1: when a vowel is tense and followed by two consonants (*pint*), or when a vowel is lax and followed by three consonants (*next*), the final consonant must always be [+coronal] (t, d, s, z, θ, ð, ʃ, ʒ, tʃ or dʒ). Features are thus more than phonetic descriptions in a different guise.

Since features are considered to be the ultimate building blocks of phonology, linguists have attempted to state all possible phonological facts about language with the fewest number of features possible. Only a limited number of features – currently around twenty-four – have been proposed. Features thus constitute an important part of a theory of what is possible (and what is not possible) in the phonological behaviour of human beings.

Table 3.27 Feature matrix for English consonants

		p	pʰ	b	t	tʰ	d	k	kʰ	g	f	v	s	z	θ	ð	ʃ	ʒ	tʃ	dʒ	m	n	ŋ	l	r	j	w	ʍ	h	ʔ
Major class features	[consonantal]	+	+	+	+	+	+	+	+	+	+	+	+	+	+	+	+	+	+	+	+	+	+	+	+	−	−	−	−	−
	[sonorant]	−	−	−	−	−	−	−	−	−	−	−	−	−	−	−	−	−	−	−	+	+	+	+	+	+	+	−	−	−
	[syllabic]	−	−	−	−	−	−	−	−	−	−	−	−	−	−	−	−	−	−	−	−	−	−	−	−	−	−	−	−	−
Laryngeal features	[voice]	−	−	+	−	−	+	−	−	+	−	+	−	+	−	+	−	+	−	+	+	+	+	+	+	+	+	−	−	−
	[CG]	−	−	−	−	−	−	−	−	−	−	−	−	−	−	−	−	−	−	−	−	−	−	−	−	−	−	−	−	+
	[SG]	−	+	−	−	+	−	−	+	−	−	−	−	−	−	−	−	−	−	−	−	−	−	−	−	−	−	−	+	−
Place features	[labial]	+	+	+	−	−	−	−	−	−	+	+	−	−	−	−	−	−	−	−	+	−	−	−	−	−	+	+	−	−
	[round]	−	−	−	−	−	−	−	−	−	−	−	−	−	−	−	−	−	−	−	−	−	−	−	−	−	+	+	−	−
	[coronal]	−	−	−	+	+	+	−	−	−	−	−	+	+	+	+	+	+	+	+	−	+	−	+	+	−	−	−	−	−
	[anterior]	−	−	−	+	+	+	−	−	−	−	−	+	+	+	+	−	−	−	−	−	+	−	+	−	−	−	−	−	−
	[strident]	−	−	−	−	−	−	−	−	−	+	+	+	+	−	−	+	+	+	+	−	−	−	−	−	−	−	−	−	−
Dorsal	[high]	−	−	−	−	−	−	+	+	+	−	−	−	−	−	−	−	−	−	−	−	−	+	−	−	+	+	+	−	−
	[back]	−	−	−	−	−	−	+	+	+	−	−	−	−	−	−	−	−	−	−	−	−	+	−	−	−	+	+	−	−
Manner	[nasal]	−	−	−	−	−	−	−	−	−	−	−	−	−	−	−	−	−	−	−	+	+	+	−	−	−	−	−	−	−
	[continuant]	−	−	−	−	−	−	−	−	−	+	+	+	+	+	+	+	+	−	−	−	−	−	−	+	+	+	+	+	−
	[lateral]	−	−	−	−	−	−	−	−	−	−	−	−	−	−	−	−	−	−	−	−	−	−	+	−	−	−	−	−	−
	[delayed release]	−	−	−	−	−	−	−	−	−	−	−	−	−	−	−	−	−	+	+	−	−	−	−	−	−	−	−	−	−

Table 3.28   Feature matrix for some English vowels

		iː	ɪ	e	æ	ʌ	ə	ɜː	ɑː	ɒ	ɔː	ʊ	uː
Major class features	[consonantal]	−	−	−	−	−	−	−	−	−	−	−	−
	[sonorant]	+	+	+	+	+	+	+	+	+	+	+	+
	[syllabic]	+	+	+	+	+	+	+	+	+	+	+	+
Laryngeal features	[voice]	+	+	+	+	+	+	+	+	+	+	+	+
Place features	[round]	−	−	−	−	−	−	−	−	+	+	+	+
Dorsal features	[high]	+	+	−	−	−	−	−	−	−	−	+	+
	[low]	−	−	−	+	−	−	−	+	−	−	−	−
	[back]	−	−	−	−	+	+	+	+	+	+	+	+
	[tense]	+	−	−	−	−	−	+	+	−	+	−	−
	[reduced]	−	−	−	−	−	+	−	−	−	−	−	−
Manner features	[continuant]	+	+	+	+	+	+	+	+	+	+	+	+

The next section presents the features of English. Tables 3.27 and 3.28 present the consonant and vowel segments of English along with the features needed to represent them in matrix form. It is a good idea to look these tables over before going on to read about individual features.

5.2

The features of English

Most features have labels that reflect traditional articulatory terms such as [voice], [consonantal], and [nasal]. These features require little further description. A few features have less familiar labels, such as [coronal] and [anterior]. From this point on, features will be used to describe classes of sounds. At the same time, we will continue throughout the book to use time-honoured terms such as *consonant*, *glide*, and *obstruent* (a fricative, affricate, or non-nasal stop) in phonetic description. The traditional terminology will be maintained because it is still widely used in phonetic description.

Features are not ranged haphazardly in a matrix. Rather, they are organized into groups that reflect natural classes. The following headings indicate what these classes are and how the features represent them.

- **Major class features** (Table 3.29) *Features that represent the classes consonant, obstruent, and sonorant (nasal, liquid, glide, and vowel).*

  [consonantal] Produced with a major obstruction in the vocal tract. All non-sonorant consonants are [+consonantal]. *Examples*: [p b s z ʃ ʒ tʃ dʒ].

  [syllabic] Vowels and syllabic liquids and nasals. *Examples*: [iː e ɑː l̩ r̩ m̩ n̩].

  [sonorant] All and only the 'singables': vowels, glides, liquids, and nasals (even when they are voiceless).

Table 3.29 Use of major class features

	Obstruents	Vowels	Glides	Liquids	Nasals
[consonantal]	+	–	–	+	+
[syllabic]	–	+	–	+	–
[sonorant]	–	+	+	+	+
Examples:	p b z θ	iː ɑː	j w	l r	m n

- **Laryngeal features** *Features that represent laryngeal states.*

  [voice] All voiced sounds are [+voice]; all voiceless sounds are [–voice].

  [spread glottis] (**[SG]**) This feature distinguishes unaspirated from aspirated consonants. Aspirated consonants are [+SG].

  [constricted glottis] (**[CG]**) Made with the glottis closed. In English, only the glottal stop [ʔ] is [+CG].

- **Place features** (Table 3.30) *Features that represent place of articulation.*

  [labial] Any sound articulated with one or both lips is [+labial]. In English: [p] [b] [f] [v] [w]. See [round].

  [round] Rounded vowels and the rounded labiovelar glide [w]. Sounds that are [+round] are made by protruding the lips; therefore, all [+round] sounds are also [+labial]. Sounds that are [+labial], however, are not necessarily [+round], since sounds like [p] or [f] can be produced without necessarily rounding the lips.

  [coronal] Any sound articulated with the tongue tip or blade raised is [+coronal]. *Examples*: [t] [d] [θ] [ð] [s] [z] [tʃ] [dʒ] [n] [l] [r].

  [anterior] Any sound articulated in front of the palato-alveolar region is considered to be [+anterior]. *Examples*: [p] [b] [t] [d] [s] [z] [θ] [ð].

  [strident] The 'noisy' fricatives and affricates only. In English, [s] [z] [ʃ] [ʒ] [tʃ] and [dʒ] are [+strident].

Table 3.30 Use of place of articulation features

	Labials	Dentals/ alveolars	Palato- alveolars	Palatals/ velars
[anterior]	+	+	–	–
[coronal]	–	+	+	–
Examples:	p b m	t d ð θ s z n l r	ʃ ʒ tʃ dʒ	k g ŋ

- **Dorsal features** *Features that represent placement of the body of the tongue.*

  [high] Sounds produced with the tongue body raised are considered [+high]. This applies to both vowels and consonants. *Examples*: [i:] [u:] [j] [k] [g].

  [low] Vowels made with the tongue body distinctly lowered from a central position in the oral cavity are [+low]. *Examples*: [æ] [ɑ:]; but [h] and [ʔ] are *not* [+low] since they are not made in the oral cavity.

  [back] Any sound articulated behind the palatal region in the oral cavity. *Examples*: [u:] [əʊ] [ɑ:] [k] [g].

  [tense] Captures the tense-lax distinctions among vowels.

  [reduced] Only the schwa ([ə]) is [+reduced].

- **Manner features** *Features that represent manner of articulation.*

  [nasal] Any sound made with the velum lowered is [+nasal].

  [continuant] Free or nearly free airflow though the oral cavity: vowels, fricatives, glides, and liquids. *Examples*: [e] [j] [r].

  [lateral] All and only varieties of *l* are [+lateral]. (See page 33.)

  [delayed release] All and only affricate consonants such as [tʃ] and [dʒ] are [+delayed release].

Feature notation does not provide a convenient way to distinguish diphthongs like [aɪ], [aʊ], and [ɔɪ] from the other vowels. These diphthongs may be treated as vowel–vowel sequences when using features. For example, [aɪ] can be regarded as [aɪ] ([a] + [ɪ]), [aʊ] as [aʊ] ([a] + [ʊ]), and so on.

5.3

Representation and the feature hierarchy

We have seen that segments are composed of smaller elements called features. We have also seen that features are organized into groupings that reflect natural classes. Figure 3.17 (overleaf) presents the grouping of features into a **feature hierarchy**, which is a representation of how features are related to each other.

Reading the feature hierarchy: nodes and tiers

Each feature grouping in the feature hierarchy is represented by a label called a **class node** or simply **node** (the node symbol is a small circle: o). Beneath each node are grouped the feature or features that make up that subclass.

Nodes and features are ranked on levels or **tiers** that reflect their relation to each other. For example, all major class features are grouped together at the highest node, called the **root node**. The root node thus defines whether a segment is a vowel, consonant, or glide.

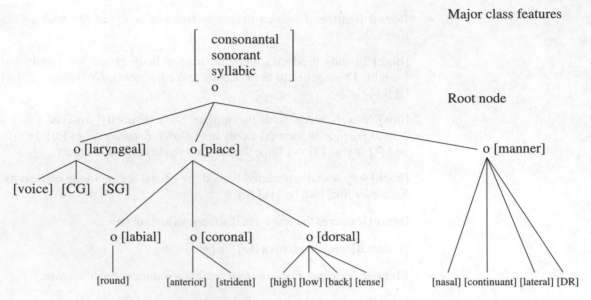

Figure 3.17   The feature hierarchy.

On the first tier under the root node are placed the nodes and features that specify all the remaining articulatory properties of a segment. From the **laryngeal node** branch out the features that capture voicing states. The **place node** branches out into the major place features. The **manner node** branches out into features that relate to general manner of articulation.

Nodes serve a dual purpose in the hierarchy. First, they function as labels for natural classes of features – hence labels like *laryngeal node*, *place node*, and *manner node*. At the same time, nodes, like features themselves, may be referred to directly when making statements about processes.

While feature representation may at first look more complex and clumsy than strictly segmental representation, it is in the long run very advantageous. Instead of listing individual sets of contrastive phonemes, we can capture contrasts at the level of the feature as in English, where we can say that the feature [voice] is contrastive. Much allophonic variation can now be represented as the addition, loss, or change of a few features. The influence of the conditioning environment is also made more obvious with this type of representation, as shown in section 7 of this chapter.[4]

6

DERIVATIONS AND RULE ORDERING

At this point, we have established the existence of three hierarchically related levels of phonological structure. In this model, phonological elements from a lower level are organized and grouped into higher-level elements. Thus, *features* are grouped into (segmental) *phonemes*, which in turn are organized into *syllables*. We have also seen how general statements that refer to natural classes and syllable structure account for the presence of non-contrastive elements. Current linguistics also provides a way to link phonological and phonetic representations in a formal manner.

The relationship between phonological and phonetic representation is formalized by assuming that the unpredictable features of the phonemic segment are basic or **underlying**. For our present purposes, the terms *phonemic* and *underlying* mean the same thing. Phonetic representations are then **derived** by the use of **phonological rules**. (For now, we will refer to general statements such as *8)* on page 81 and *9)* on page 91 as rules; in section 7 we will see how these statements are formalized.) In order to keep the presentation simple, underlying and derived representations are given in segmental transcription; nevertheless, keep in mind that all segments are understood to be composed of features.

6.1

Derivations

Phonetic forms are derived by setting up the underlying representation (also called an *underlying form*) and then allowing the rule or rules in question to operate in those contexts where they are relevant.

The derivation of three phonetic representations (PRs) from underlying representations (URs) is presented in Figure 3.18. Here, the underlying representation is on the top line (the cross hatch [#] symbolizes a word boundary); reading downward, each rule applies if the appropriate input is present, and the underlying representation is adjusted as required. Where a rule fails to apply, the form remains unchanged; this information is conveyed by dashes. The resulting output then serves as the input to the following rule. Finally, when all rules relevant to the derivation in question have applied, a phonetic representation is provided. The two rules presented in the following example are aspiration and vowel lengthening (see section 4.5).

UR	#slæp# 'slap'	#tæp# 'tap'	#pæd# 'pad'
Aspiration	—	#tʰæp#	#pʰæd#
V-length	—	—	#pʰǣd#
PR	[slæp]	[tʰæp]	[pʰǣd]

Figure 3.18 The phonological derivation of three English words.

In this example, two rules are applied (since the words being derived are all monosyllabic, the syllable boundaries are equivalent to word boundaries and so are not indicated here). The first accounts for aspiration. Since the initial consonant of the URs #tæp# and #pæd# are voiceless stops found in onset position, they fulfil the conditions under which English stops become aspirated. We therefore indicate that aspiration occurs by providing an intermediate form on a new line.

We have also seen that, in English, vowels are predictably long when they occur before a voiced stop in the same syllable. In Figure 3.18, the /æ/'s of *slap* and *tap* occur before voiceless stops and so are not lengthened. The vowel of *pad*, however, occurs in just the environment associated with long vowels and so is predictably lengthened.

The use of such derivations underscores the fact that allophonic variation is the result of processes that apply in the course of language use. Underlying representations capture the knowledge that speakers have about the nature of their phonological system, rules reflect the application of allophonic processes, and the phonetic representation reflects the speech output.

6.2

Rule application

We have seen that more than one rule may be employed in a derivation. Consequently, we must now ask how several rules are applied to a given underlying form when these rules interact.

Unordered and feeding rule application

In Figure 3.18, we saw the application of the rules of English aspiration and vowel lengthening, which apply to voiceless stops and vowels, respectively. Note that the environments in which each of these rules apply (onset and pre-coda position, respectively) are entirely different. Therefore, these rules do not interact or affect each other in any way; the order in which they are applied makes no difference to the outcome of a derivation. Figure 3.19 shows the same rules applied in reverse order; there is no difference in the outcome.

UR	#slæp# slap	#tæp# tap	#pæd# pad
V-length	—	—	#pǣd#
Aspiration	—	#tʰæp#	#pʰǣd#
PR	[slæp]	[tʰæp]	[pʰǣd]

Figure 3.19 Unordered rule application.

We therefore say that the rules of aspiration and vowel lengthening are *unordered* with respect to each other.

A second type of rule ordering is called **feeding**. Rules are said to be in a feeding order when the application of one rule creates an environment that makes possible the application of another rule that could otherwise not apply. The rules of English stress and schwa-deletion (Figure 3.20) are in a feeding relationship in the pronunciation of a word like *parade*. Since the presence of stress is a crucial condition of the schwa-deletion rule, stress must first be applied to an underlying form so that the schwa-deletion rule can work. The stress rule, therefore, feeds the schwa-deletion rule.

The rules of English schwa-deletion, which is optional, and liquid–glide devoicing, given in example *4)*, are also in a feeding relation in the casual speech pronunciation of a word like *parade*. After a schwa has been lost through schwa-deletion, a liquid or glide that follows the schwa in the underlying representation is now directly after a voiceless stop, and therefore subject to liquid-glide devoicing, as Figure 3.20 shows. The arrows, which are

UR	#pəréɪd# parade
Stress	#pəréɪd#
Schwa-deletion	#préɪd#
Liquid–glide devoicing	#pr̥éɪd#
Vowel lengthening	#pr̥éːɪd#
PR	#pr̥éːɪd#

Figure 3.20 Feeding order in a derivation.

normally not written in derivations, here indicate feeding relationships.

Notice now that no incorrect forms would result if, say, the schwa-deletion rule attempted to apply before the stress rule. Because its environment is not present, the schwa-deletion rule would simply fail to apply. However, once the stress rule was applied, the schwa-deletion rule could then follow in its turn, ultimately leading to a correct phonetic representation. What these facts suggest is that rules in a feeding relation may apply in *free order*, each attempting to apply wherever the required conditions are met, with no need to stipulate which rule applies first. The result will be the desired phonetic output.

6.3

The form and notation of rules

General statements about allophonic distribution are formalized as rules, which reflect the dynamic nature of processes (Chapter 2, section 9.4).

Rules

Rules take the following form.

12)

$A \rightarrow B / X \_\_\_ Y$

In this notation, A stands for an element in the underlying representation, B for the change it undergoes, and X and Y for the conditioning environment. Either of the elements X or Y may be absent (null) if the conditioning environment is found only on one side of the allophone. Also, as we will soon see below, the element A may be null (in the case of epenthesis) and the element B may be null (in the case of a deletion rule). The ___ (focus bar) indicates the position of the segment undergoing the rule. The slash separates the statement of the change from the statement of the conditioning environment. This rule is read as *A becomes B between X and Y*.

As an example of rule writing, we return to the distribution of liquid–glide devoicing in English (section 2.4): in English, liquids and glides have voiceless allophones after syllable-initial voiceless stops, voiced allophones elsewhere. The rule statement operates on the voiced allophones of liquids and glides as basic (underlying) and changes the feature [+voice] to [–voice] in the appropriate environment.

Figure 3.21 Liquid–glide devoicing in English expressed as a rule.

The rule in Figure 3.21 is read as follows.

13)

Liquids and glides become voiceless after syllable-initial voiceless stops.

Rule and feature notation formally represents the origin of allophones in phonetic processes that arise in the course of speech. For example, the devoicing of liquids and glides in English is a typical process of assimilation. The rule notation in Figure 3.21 shows explicitly how this change of [+voice] to [–voice] occurs in a specific class of sounds following the class of stops that is [–voice].

Deletion as a rule

We have already seen that English speakers (optionally) drop a schwa [ə] in an open syllable when it is followed by a stressed syllable, as in *police* [pl̥i:s] and *parade* [pr̥eɪd]. The rule can be formalized as shown in Figure 3.22. Here, Cø is an abbreviation for any number of successive consonants from zero up and σ represents a syllable boundary.

$$[\text{B}] \rightarrow \varnothing \ / \ C\varnothing \underline{\qquad} \sigma C\varnothing \quad \begin{matrix} V \\ [+\text{stress}] \end{matrix}$$

Figure 3.22 Schwa-deletion in English.

The English schwa-deletion rule interacts with the constraint on possible consonant sequences. It automatically fails to apply when an impermissible sequence would result. Since σ[ptʰ and σ[dl are impermissible onsets in English, there are no forms like *[ptʰéɪtəʊ] *potato* or *[dlí:t] *delete* (except in extremely fast speech).

Epenthesis and alpha rules

Recall that epenthesis involves the insertion of a segment into a sequence of other segments (cf. Chapter 2, section 9.4). In section 2.5 of this chapter we saw that, in liaison, the glides inserted after English tense non-low vowels are predictable by a general rule: the tense non-low [–back] vowels /i/ and /ɪ/ are followed by the [–back], glide /j/; the tense non-low [+back] vowels /u/ and /ʊ/ are followed by the [+back] glide /w/.

In order to represent this epenthesis, we can make use of a type of notation called *alpha notation*. Here, the Greek letter *a* is a variable (like *x* in algebra) that can stand for either feature value. For example, a feature statement like [a round] can be read as either [+round] or [−round], but an alpha variable must have the same value wherever it occurs. For example, if an alpha is read as '+', all other alphas in the same rule are to be read as '+'.

With alpha notation (Figure 3.23), we can capture the variability of glide insertion in English.

$$\varnothing \rightarrow \begin{bmatrix} -\text{consonantal} \\ -\text{syllabic} \\ +\text{sonorant} \\ \alpha \text{ back} \end{bmatrix} / \begin{bmatrix} -\text{consonantal} \\ +\text{syllabic} \\ +\text{sonorant} \\ -\text{low} \\ \alpha \text{ back} \end{bmatrix} \underline{\quad\quad}$$

Figure 3.23 Alpha notation in English glide epenthesis.

Remember: in reading an alpha, you are reading a rule twice, once with the plus value for the alpha feature, and once with the minus value. The rule in Figure 3.23 states that a [+back] glide is inserted after a [+back] non-low vowel and that a [−back] glide is inserted after a [−back] non-low vowel. Since there are only two glides in the phonological inventory of English, [+back] /w/ and [−back] /j/, the correct glide will be inserted by the rule.

Rules that refer to syllable structure

Recall the rule of vowel lengthening in English. This rule makes reference to syllable structure.

14)

English vowels are long when followed by a voiced obstruent consonant in the same syllable.

Presented as a rule, an underlying short vowel is lengthened in the appropriate context. The boundary of the syllable may be represented by a bracket and a subscript σ, as in Figure 3.24.

$$\begin{bmatrix} +\text{syllabic} \\ -\text{consonantal} \\ +\text{sonorant} \end{bmatrix} \rightarrow [+\text{long}] / \underline{\quad\quad} \begin{bmatrix} -\text{syllabic} \\ +\text{consonantal} \\ -\text{sonorant} \\ +\text{voice} \\ -\text{nasal} \end{bmatrix} \sigma$$

Figure 3.24 Vowel lengthening in English.

Notice here that the onset of the syllable is irrelevant to the statement of the rule and so is not included in the formalization.

Vowel epenthesis

Vowel epenthesis is frequently triggered when an impermissible phonotactic structure is encountered in a borrowed word, as in the English pronunciation of the name *Dmitri*. It is also the case that, in some dialects of English, a coda consisting of *l* and another consonant is not permitted. In these dialects, *milk* is pronounced [mɪlək] and *film* [fɪləm]. This change can be represented in rule format as follows.

$$\varnothing \rightarrow [\text{ə}] \ / \ [\ +\text{lateral}] \underline{\hspace{2cm}} \begin{bmatrix} -\text{syllabic} \\ +\text{consonantal} \end{bmatrix} \sigma$$

Figure 3.25 Schwa epenthesis in English as a rule.

A more complete representation of this process requires showing the change of syllable structure, as in Figure 3.26.

Figure 3.26 Syllabic representation of schwa epenthesis in English.

7

REPRESENTATIONS (ADVANCED)

In recent years, the formalization of rules has become more graphic. This change has taken place because certain types of processes have been viewed as the spreading of features from one segment (represented as a feature matrix) to another one. It has also been claimed that a simple set of principles governs the way in which features spread.

These graphic presentations of feature changes are referred to as **representations**. The features themselves are referred to as **autosegments** – the label suggests that each feature has a certain degree of autonomy in its operation.

7.1

Assimilation and the feature hierarchy

Assimilation processes are particularly amenable to autosegmental representation using the feature hierarchy. This is the case because the overlapping production typical of co-articulation (see Chapter 2, section 9.1) is neatly represented by the spread of individual features from one segment to another.

Nasal assimilation

In North American English, a vowel nasalizes when it is immediately followed by a nasal consonant in the same syllable. One or more consonants may follow the nasal consonant. (For some speakers, the vowels must also be stressed for nasalization to occur.) The words *banks*, *shunted*, and *nimble*, for example, are pronounced [bæ̃ŋks], [ʃʌ̃ntəd], and [nĩmbl̩]. This regressive nasalization in English is represented in Figure 3.27 (the subscript σ following the square bracket indicates the boundary of the syllable, that is, that the nasal consonant is in the coda; the change undergone by the word *bank* is provided in phonetic transcription below the representation).

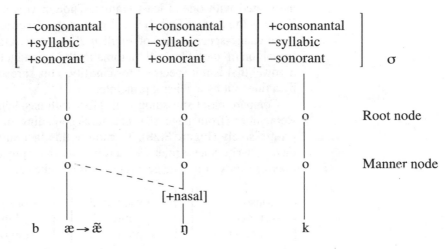

Figure 3.27   Vowel nasalization in American English (regressive assimilation).

Note that the English non-nasal vowel is represented as having no feature [nasal]. This fact will be very important in our discussion of representations below. With autosegmental representation, there is no need to list individual segments or even to write a rule. Why not? The next section outlines the principles that govern the spreading of features.

7.2

Autosegmental principles

Most linguists agree that it is preferable to describe languages using general principles of universal grammar wherever possible and to use language-specific rules sparingly – resorting to them only in those cases where there are wrinkles in the grammar of a particular language that are not covered by universal principles.

In this spirit, it is claimed that only three principles account for the many processes that can be represented with autosegmental notation.

- **Association: feature-to-segment** Each autosegment (feature) is associated with at least one segment by an association line.
- **Association: segment-feature** Each segment is associated with at least one autosegment (feature) by an association line.
- **No crossing** Association lines do not cross. This is a formal way of indicating the fact that one entire segment cannot be inserted inside another distinct segment. (See section 1.6 of Chapter 6.)

Feature spreading

We are now in a position to understand how English nasalization can be viewed as a form of spreading. The notion of **underspecification** plays a vital role here. Since English vowels never contrast the feature [nasal], they can be underspecified (i.e., left unspecified) for nasality. Our principles require each feature to be associated with at least one segment, and each segment to be associated with one at least feature. Though vowels are capable of bearing nasality, the feature [nasal] is not part of the specification of English vowels. A language-specific rule of English allows leftward spreading. The feature [nasal] on /n/ therefore will 'automatically' spread leftwards whenever it finds a vowel that is not specified for nasality. This spreading is not accomplished by a rule, but by a general principle.

Compare nasal spreading in English with nasal spreading in Scots Gaelic. Remember (from page 80) that nasal spreading in Scots Gaelic can occur progressively (Figure 3.28). To capture this fact autosegmentally, we do not have to write a new rule; we merely state that spreading in Scots Gaelic can operate rightwards. The general principles take care of the rest.

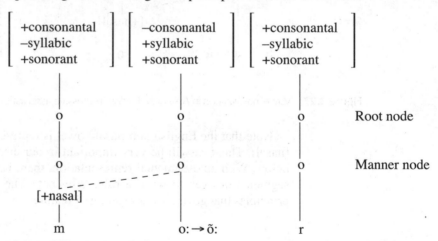

Figure 3.28 Nasal spreading in Scots Gaelic.

The spreading of autosegments need not only apply to the feature [+nasal]. In theory, just about any feature should follow the same principles. The next section shows how spreading can apply to voicing features.

Laryngeal assimilation: English liquid–glide devoicing revisited

We have already seen (Figure 3.21) how English liquid–glide devoicing is stated in rule format. Since this particular variation is in fact assimilatory, it lends itself well to statement as a representation (Figure 3.29).

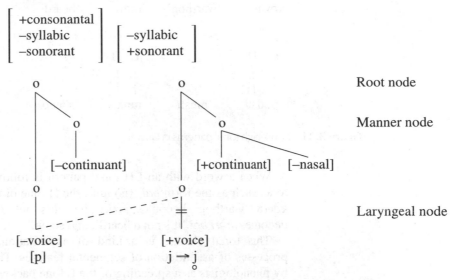

Figure 3.29 Liquid–glide devoicing in English as a representation.

The root and manner node features represent the leftmost class as stops and the class to its right as liquids or glides. The place node is not represented since the place of articulation of both the stops and the liquids and glides is irrelevant to the process in question here. The dotted line represents the spreading of the laryngeal node feature [–voice] from the voiceless stop to the liquid or glide, and the breaking of the association line that links the [+voice] feature of the liquid or glide to the laryngeal node indicates its disassociation.

7.3

Tonal assimilation as a representation

In Chapter 2, you saw how tone is represented on separate levels or tiers of phonological description. Association lines link the tone to the appropriate vowel. A representation of the word *tunko* 'sheep' from Duwai, a language spoken in West Africa, is as follows, where L indicates low tone, and H high.

Figure 3.30 Representing tone.

This type of representation has the advantage of being able to show explicitly certain facts about tone languages. Tones, like other phonological phenomena, are subject to contextually conditioned variation. Figure 3.31 shows a good example of this from Duwai, where many words show the tonal pattern LH (low–high).

Figure 3.31 Low–high tonal patterns in Duwai.

When a word with an LH tonal pattern is followed by a word with an L tone, such as the form *bài* '(is) not', the H tone of the first word becomes L: *kə̀vús* 'warthog' becomes *kə̀vùs bài* 'it's not a warthog'; *mə̀rí* 'beard' becomes *mə̀rì bài* 'it's not a beard', and so on.

This tonal change is a kind of assimilation, and parallels common processes of assimilation of segmental features. This assimilation is viewed by phonologists as a spreading of the L tone backwards from the word *bài* to the final vowel of the preceding word, and is shown in Figure 3.32 by drawing a dotted association line (which represents the change in tone) and breaking the original association line from the vowel to the former tone value (the short double lines indicate the loss of association).

Figure 3.32 Tone assimilation in Duwai.

Thus, both features and tonal material are handled by the same type of representation and the same principles.

7.4

Processes, rules and representations: a last word

The combined use of features and processes in phonological description reflects the dynamic nature of linguistic behaviour. First, the use of features reflects a basic level of phonological activity – contrasts take place on the feature level, not on the level where segments are represented. Second, the use of process notation and rule formalization reflects the realities of linguistic production, in which sounds are affected by the context in which they are pronounced as we speak.

Overall, the patterning of phonological units is seen to be based on the interaction between a universal set of features, universal and language-specific phonotactic constraints and syllabification procedures, and the use of rules and representations. This current theory of phonology is based on principles that are applicable to the study of any human language.

8

STRESS AND METRICS (ADVANCED)

Many languages exhibit stress, which is defined as the perceived prominence of one or more syllabic elements over others in a word (Chapter 2, section 8.3). Recall that stress is easily perceived in English in pairs of semantically related words such as the contrasting noun and verb pairs présent/presént, and éxport/expórt (see Chapter 2, section 8.3).

This section is concerned with stress whose placement can be predicted by general linguistic principles. The study of stress placement is referred to as **metrics**. Properly speaking, it is the rhyme of a syllable that bears stress; however, current notation refers directly to syllables in representing stress.

8.1

Unbounded feet

The formalization of stress in much current analysis rests on the use of units called **metrical feet** (often referred to simply as *feet*), which are elements of metrical structure consisting of a stressed syllable and an associated unstressed syllable (or syllables). To see how this works, Table 3.31 shows an example from French.

Table 3.31 Stress placement in French

pás	'step'
amí	'friend'
emportér	'carry off'
amicalemént	'amicably'
hospitalisatión	'hospitalization'

In French, the last vowel of a word receives primary stress. Metrical feet capture this final stress by placing an x directly over the rightmost (final) syllable nucleus of a word at a level of representation called the **foot level**. Unstressed syllables within the foot are represented by dots; the foot is enclosed in parentheses. Details of syllable structure are not given unless it is necessary.

The x in Figure 3.33 on page 114 represents the stressed element, or **head**, of the metrical foot (students will have to forgive linguists for employing terminology in which a foot has a head). The head is the obligatory element of a metrical foot – no foot can be without a stress. Since there is only one primary stress in each French word, only one foot is represented. We can also see from the data provided that any number of unstressed syllables may be a part of a metrical foot in French. This type of foot, consisting of a head and any number of unstressed syllables, is called an **unbounded foot**. French specifically requires a **right-headed unbounded foot** in each word – a foot in which the head is located over the rightmost syllable. We can also see that monosyllabic words have only the obligatory element of a foot (the head). A metrical foot that consists only of a head is called a **minimal foot** (because it is the smallest foot possible) or a **degenerate foot** (because, compared to the ideal foot with a head accompanied by a dependent syllable, it is imperfect, as it were.)

Figure 3.33   French stress: right-headed unbounded foot.

Some languages predictably stress the initial syllable of each word. Figure 3.34 shows a **left-headed unbounded foot** (a foot in which the head is located over the leftmost syllable), which is needed to represent the initial stressing pattern of the Hungarian words for 'mixed', 'keep stirring', and 'unstirred'.

```
(x   .)          (x   .   .)          (x   .   .   .)   Foot level
 σ   σ            σ   σ   σ            σ   σ   σ   σ
kevert          keverget          keveretlen
```

Figure 3.34   Hungarian stress: left-headed unbounded foot.

8.2

Bounded feet

Frequently, more than one stress is heard in a word. In many languages, words with multiple stresses fall on alternating syllables. Alternating stresses can be heard in English words like *ànecdótal* and *pròvidéntial* In Chemehuevi (an Amerindian language spoken in California), the word *ha ʔɨsutùivì* 's/he likes' is a typical example of alternating stress. In alternating stress languages, the stresses fall exactly two syllables apart (degenerate feet excepted), and only one stress is primary in each word. Alternating stress is captured by employing a constituent called a **bounded foot**, which is a unit of metrical representation that consists of a stressed syllable and no more than one unstressed syllable.

Bounded feet can be left-headed or right-headed. You may already be familiar with such traditional terms in poetic metre as **trochaic** and **iambic** which capture this insight (Figure 3.35). A trochaic foot is equivalent to a bounded, left-headed foot. An iambic foot is equivalent to a bounded, right-headed foot.

Trochaic foot	Iambic foot
(bounded, left-headed)	(bounded, right-headed)
(x .)	(. x) Foot level
σ σ	σ σ
promise	collect

Figure 3.35   Two traditional bounded foot types and their metrical representations.

Building in either direction

Since alternating stress languages show more than one foot on each word, we have to assign feet to the words in some systematic manner. It seems reasonable to assume that feet are assigned to a word by starting at the beginning of the word, and working through it from left to right. Figure 3.36 shows both left-headed and right-headed bounded feet built from left-to-right over words in two different languages. Note the presence of degenerate feet in two of the examples; remember that these result because a head is required on each foot, and whenever binary feet are constructed over an odd number of syllables, one syllable will be left over at the end of the procedure. In the example, words are given with primary stresses only; how secondary stresses are represented is shown later on in this section. The arrows are placed before the feet simply as a reminder of directionality of application; they are not ordinarily written. The syllable numbers are also provided for the sake of clarity and are also not usually written.

Left-headed bounded foot, left-to-right application Language: Maranungku (Australia)	Right-headed bounded foot, left-to-right application Language: Chemehuevi (California)
→ (x .) (x .)(x)	→ (. x) (. x)(x) Foot level
σ₁ σ₂ σ₃ σ₄σ₅	σ₁ σ₂ σ₃ σ₄ σ₅
l a 0 k a r a t e t i 'prawn'	u n i n u p 4 r u 'make'
→ (x .) (x .) (x .)	→ (. x) (. x) (. x) Foot level
σ₁σ₂σ₃σ₄ σ₅ σ₆	σ₁ σ₂ σ₃ σ₄σ₅ σ₆
w e l e p e l e m a n t a 'kind of duck'	h a + 4 s u t u i v 4 's/he liked'

Figure 3.36   Two types of alternating stress, left-to-right application.

As these examples show, left-headed bounded feet ordinarily result in stresses on odd-numbered syllables, while right-headed bounded feet result in stresses on even-numbered syllables.

A curious fact about the assigning of bounded feet is that in some languages it appears to start at the ends of words and work its way 'backwards' from right to left. Figure 3.37 provides examples of right-to-left foot building in two languages. Here again, the bounded, left-headed foot results in stress on odd-numbered syllables, and the bounded, right-headed foot assigns stress to even numbered syllables.

Left-headed bounded foot, right-to-left application Language: Warao (Venezuela)	Right-headed bounded foot, *correct* right-to-left application Language: Weri (New Guinea)
(x .) (x .) ←	(. x) (. x) ← Foot level
$\sigma_1\ \sigma_2\ \ \sigma_3\ \sigma_4$	$\sigma_1\ \sigma_2\ \sigma_3\ \ \sigma_4$
w a r a w a r a 'kind of fish'	u l u a m i t 'mist'

Figure 3.37 Two types of alternating stress, right-to-left application.

At first glance, however, there seems to be no reason to assume that stressing was applied from right to left, since the same results can be obtained by building the appropriate bounded feet from left to right. Stress on the word *warawara*, for example, will also fall on the first and third syllables with left-to-right application. How can we tell that stress is applied right to left in these languages?

The answer to this question lies in the fact that the words in Figure 3.37 above all consist of an even number of syllables. The stress pattern of words in these same languages with odd numbers of syllables will not work out unless stress is applied right to left. Figure 3.38 shows the correct stressing for two forms with an odd number of syllables.

Left-headed bounded foot, *correct* right-to-left application Language: Warao	Right-headed bounded foot, *correct* right-to-left application Language: Weri
(x) (x .) (x .) ←	(x) (. x) (. x) ← Foot level
$\sigma_1\ \ \sigma_2\ \sigma_3\ \sigma_4\ \sigma_5$	$\sigma_1\ \sigma_2\ \ \sigma_3\ \sigma_4\ \sigma_5$
j i w a r a n a e 'he found it'	a k u n e t e p a l 'times'

Figure 3.38 Right-to-left application in words with an odd number of syllables. The result is the correct stress pattern required in these languages.

However, if we try to apply stress from left to right in these forms, incorrect patterns result, as Figure 3.39 shows.

Therefore, in order to know whether alternating stresses are being applied left to right or right to left in a language, we must be sure to compare words with both odd- and even-numbered syllables.

Left-headed bounded foot, *incorrect* left-to-right application Language: Warao	Right-headed bounded foot, *incorrect* left-to-right application Language: Weri
→ (x .) (x .) (x) σ_1 σ_2 σ_3 σ_4 σ_5 *j i w a r a n a e	→ (x .) (x .) (x) Foot level σ_1 σ_2 σ_3 σ_4 σ_5 *a k u n e t e p a l

Figure 3.39   Incorrectly applied left-to-right application. Compare this figure with the required correct result shown in Figure 3.38.

It is important to note that it is rare to find a pure alternating stress language, since other factors (see section 8.5 for an example of one of them) may intervene to complicate the stress pattern. Nevertheless, the basic principle of alternating stress assignment holds in a great many of the world's languages.

8.3

Primary and secondary stress

To understand the basis of secondary stress assignment, we return briefly to the stressing of the words *promise* and *collect* in Figure 3.35, where we were left with the appearance that stress had been assigned to the words. In fact, this was not the case. Stress had only been assigned to feet. The placement of stress on the word is represented by assigning an x on a new level, not unsurprisingly called the **word level**, over the existing stress on the foot level. Two word-level feet are illustrated in Figure 3.40.

(x)	(x)	Word level
(x .)	(. x)	Foot level
σ σ	σ σ	
promise	collect	

Figure 3.40   Foot- and word-level stress representation.

This same principle accounts for the placement of secondary stresses, which are derived from the initial placement of stresses by the basic metrical pattern. On the word level, we build another foot (usually an unbounded one) over the syllable-level foot that takes the primary word stress. The result will be that one of the stresses initially assigned by foot building will be the head of the word-level foot and will be interpreted as the primary stress. The remaining stresses are considered to be secondary stresses.

As an example, let us take the Chemehuevi word *ha ʔɨsutuivɨ* 's/he liked' from Figure 3.36. Its complete stress pattern is *ha ʔɨsutùivɨ*. To represent this pattern, we begin as above by building right-headed bounded feet from left to right over the word form at the foot level (Figure 3.41).

(.   x) (.   x) (. x) Foot level

σ σ σ σ σ   σ

ha?ɨ sutu i v ɨ

Figure 3.41   Initial foot building in Chemehuevi: right-headed bounded feet, left-to-right application.

On the word level (Figure 3.42), we build (for Chemehuevi) a left-headed unbounded foot over the leftmost foot-level stress. This captures the fact that the first stress in a Chemehuevi word is the primary one. In this way, we represent both primary and secondary stresses: the syllable with the greatest number of x's over it is taken to be the most prominent, or primary stressed syllable; the syllables with only one x have secondary stress; the remaining syllables are unstressed.

(x   ) Word level: left-headed unbounded foot

(.   x) (.   x)(.   x) Foot level: right-headed bounded feet, L→R

σσ   σ σ σ σ

ha?ɨ   su tu i vɨ

Figure 3.42   Word-level foot building in Chemeheuvi. Both primary and secondary stresses are now represented.

The formal generalization for Chemehuevi stress is as follows – foot level: right-headed bounded feet, applying from left to right; word level: left-headed unbounded foot.

8.4

Complexity from simplicity: stress parameters

Stress patterns in language can be highly intricate, but linguists believe that their complexity, like so much other linguistic complexity, arises from interaction among a set of universally available options. These options are called **parameters**. Table 3.32 lists the stress parameters we have explored in this chapter.

Table 3.32   Some stress parameters

1.   bounded/unbounded feet
2.   left-/right-headed feet
3.   directionality: left-to-right/right-to-left

Interaction among the setting of these three parameters, along with a fourth parameter, extrametricality (see section 8.5), accounts for a wide variety of the stress patterns found in human language. All of the examples of stress patterning that have been presented in this section resulted from the setting of just these three parameters, as Table 3.33 shows. Note that the directionality parameter is not relevant for languages with unbounded feet. Primary stress is excluded from the table.

Table 3.33 Stress parameter setting for languages presented in this section

Language	Bounded/unbounded feet	Headedness	Directionality
French	unbounded	right	
Hungarian	unbounded	left	
Maranungku	bounded	left	left to right
Chemehuevi	bounded	right	left to right
Warao	bounded	left	right to left
Weri	bounded	right	right to left

8.5

Extrametricality

There are exceptions to the requirement that all syllables are associated with some foot for the purposes of stress assignment. In some languages, we find that a single syllable at the beginning or end of a word is never stressed. Because it falls outside the effects of stress rules, such a syllable is said to be **extrametrical**. To represent this fact formally, an extrametrical syllable is formally excluded from the foot-building procedure. To see how extrametricality interacts with foot structure, Table 3.34 shows some data from Kusaiean, a language spoken in the Caroline Islands.

Table 3.34 Penultimate stress in Kusaiean

kʌ́ta:	'some'
kókɔ:	'to lead'
pʌlákfɔːn	'stupid'
mɨníni:	'thin'
mʌlǽlæ	'light'
mʌlælǽjak	'become light'

In Kusaiean, stress always falls on the penultimate (next-to-last) syllable of a word. The data in the table show this clearly; stress may be found on first, second, third, and even fourth syllables, since stress is always on the penultimate syllable of polysyllabic words. The final syllable, however, is never stressed. This regularity is captured by representing word-final syllables as extrametrical, as in Figure 3.43. The angled brackets represent the fact that final syllables are invisible to stress assignment, which otherwise proceeds as usual, here building a right-headed unbounded foot over the word.

You may wonder what happens to extrametrical syllables after stress has been assigned. Since all syllables must belong to a foot, it is assumed that extrametrical syllables are joined to the metrical foot after stress placement.

Figure 3.43 Kusaiean stress assignment using extrametricality.

This process is called **stray syllable adjunction**.

Stress universally falls towards the margins (beginning or end) of words. Since stress falls towards the left or right margin of a word, it is rare to find a primary stress landing more than one syllable from the margin of a form. Extrametrical syllables capture this fact in that they are limited to a single occurrence as the initial or final syllable of words; they are not found word-internally. The careful use of extrametricality allows us to adhere to the basic principles that account for all stressing in terms of either unbounded or bounded feet. The next section provides additional justification for the use of extrametricality in stress assignment, and shows how it interacts with the building of bounded feet.

Bounded feet and extrametricality

In Swahili, stress falls on alternating syllables; the penultimate (next-to-last) syllable receives the strongest stress.

Table 3.35   Stress in Swahili

tʃúra	'toad'
tʃakúla	'food'
kàratási	'paper'
uʃikamáno	'adhesion'

To assign primary and secondary stresses in Swahili, we first tentatively assume that final syllables are extrametrical, since they are never stressed. Since stresses are alternating, we know that they must be assigned using bounded feet. Applying the principles presented in section 8.2, we can arrive at a decision about the headedness of the bounded feet. Left-headed feet, whether formed from left to right or right to left, are excluded, since they would result in the first syllable of a word like uʃikamano being stressed. Given that the bounded feet needed to assign stress in Swahili are right-headed, we must then decide on the direction of application. The words tʃakúla and uʃikamáno provide no definitive answer, since their stresses would be correct (still assuming extrametricality) whether the right-headed feet were assigned from left to right or from right to left. The word kàratási is crucial. Its final syllable is unavailable to the stress rule because it is extrametrical. So, forming bounded, right-headed feet from left to right will produce the wrong pattern of stresses. The first stress will fall incorrectly on the second syllable *ra* which is the head of the first foot. Since all feet, unless extrametrical, must be stressed, the third syllable *(ta)*, which constitutes a degenerate foot, receives stress. The result is the incorrect form **karátási.*

However, by employing extrametricality and building from right to left, we can come up with the right stress pattern (see Figure 3.44). We therefore employ bounded, right-headed feet assigned from right to left in conjunction with extrametricality since these settings will provide all and only correct stresses.

Figure 3.44 Swahili stress assignment using right-headed bounded feet and right-to-left application.

On a second line of the metrical representation we build a right-headed unbounded foot. Since primary stress assignment on the word level is sensitive only to the x's on the foot level (Figure 3.45), the result will be main stress on the penultimate syllable and secondary stresses on any preceding stressed syllables.

Figure 3.45 Swahili word-level stress assignment.

Summing up

Phonology deals with the sequential and phonetically conditioned patterning of sounds in language. To account for this patterning, three units of phonological representation have been established: the **feature**, the **phoneme**, and the **syllable**. Phonemes are contrastive segmental units composed of distinctive features. Phonetically conditioned variants of phonemes are called **allophones**.

Phonology makes use of **underlying forms**, **derivations**, **phonological rules**, and **representations** in its formal notation. Rules apply in **free** or **feeding** order to guarantee that correct phonetic representations are derived from underlying representation.

The chapter also reviews the **processes** that are the basis of this patterned variation, and shows how the patterning of phonological units is based upon general elements and principles that are applicable to the study of any human language. Interacting with features and segmental processes, a limited set of **parameters** accounts for the phenomenon of **stress** in human language.

Notes

1   Of course, words can differ in meaning without contrasting phonetically. In every language, there are words (called *homophones*) that are identical in pronunciation but that differ in meaning, such as English *well* 'spring' and *well* 'all right'. The following French words provide a more dramatic example of homophones.

vert	[vɛ:ʁ]	'green'
vers	[vɛ:ʁ]	'towards'
vers	[vɛ:ʁ]	'verse'
verre	[vɛ:ʁ]	'glass'
ver	[vɛ:ʁ]	'worm'

2   In most dialects of English there is a contrast between [ɒ] and [ɔ:] in words like *cot* [kʰɒt] and *caught* [kʰɔ:t]. In North American English, these words and other analogous ones are usually both pronounced [kʰat] but in Canada they say [kʰɒt].

3   Perhaps you have noticed that voiceless sonorant allophones occur in the same context as aspiration: in syllable onsets. Both types of voicelessness are indeed a manifestation of voice lag. It would not be inappropriate to represent aspiration as [pɪ̥n] 'pin' or liquid–glide devoicing as [pl̥ʰʌk] 'pluck'. This book, however, will stick to the traditional distinct representations.

4   In the course of this chapter, you will note that a complete set of features is not given for every phoneme. In some cases, we can dispense with certain features that are inherently predictable. For example, vowels that are [+high] are not specified as [–low], since the two tongue positions are mutually exclusive. Conversely, vowels that are [+low] are not specified as [–high]. The phoneme /l/ can be captured with just the feature [+lateral], since it is the only lateral in the language. English vowels are not specified for nasality, since they are not contrastively nasal. English glides need only be specified as [–back] or [+back], since there are only two of them, /j/ and /w/. You may assume that all predictable features are carried along with the abbreviated notation.

Sources

A classic and still valuable presentation of phonemic analysis is found in H.A. Gleason Jr's *An Introduction to Descriptive Linguistics* (New York: Holt, Rinehart & Winston, 1961). Tone data on Mende are from W.R. Leben's 'The representation of tone' and on Duwai from R.G. Schuh's 'Tone rules', both in *Tone: A Linguistic Survey*, edited by V.A. Fromkin (New York: Academic Press, 1978). Syllabification, tone, and autosegmental analysis are drawn from numerous sources, all summarized recently in Goldsmith (cited below). The approach to stress is inspired by Hayes 1987 (cited below), whereas the representations used follow both the direction of M. Halle and J.-R. Vergnaud, *An Essay on Stress* (Cambridge, Mass.: MIT Press, 1987) and B. Hayes, 'A revised parametric metrical theory', *Proceedings of NELS* 17(1): 1987. The Malay data are adapted from Kenstowicz and Kisseberth (cited below); additional examples were provided by S.L. Lee (personal communication). The English data in

Table 3.24 come from N. Chomsky and M. Halle, *The Sound Pattern of English*, p. 71 (New York: Harper and Row, 1968).

Data sources for questions are as follows: for Inuktitut, B. Harnum (personal communication); for Gascon, R.C. Kelley's *A Descriptive Analysis of Gascon* (Amsterdam: Mouton, 1978); for Tamil, R. Radhakrishnan (personal communication); for Mende, W.R. Leben, 'The representation of tone', in *Tone: A Linguistic Survey*, edited by V.A. Fromkin (New York: Academic Press, 1978); for Moru, A.N. Tucker, *The Eastern Sudanic Languages*, pp. 112, 271 (London: Dawsons, 1967/1940); for Tzutujil, John R. Dayley, *Tzutujil Grammar* (Berkeley, Calif.: University of California Press, 1985); for Huallaga Quechua, David John Weber, *A Grammar of Huallaga (Huñuco) Quechua* (Berkeley, Calif.: University of California Press, 1989); for Maung, A. Capell and H.E. Hinch, *Maung Grammar, Texts and Vocabulary* (The Hague: Mouton, 1970).

Recommended reading

Anderson, Stephen R. 1985. *Phonology in the Twentieth Century*. Chicago: University of Chicago Press.

Carr, Philip, 1993. *Phonology*. London: Macmillan.

Clements, George N. and Keyser, Samuel Jay. 1983. *CV Phonology*. Cambridge, Mass.: MIT Press.

Durand, Jacques and Katamba, Francis. eds. 1995. *Frontiers of Phonology*. London: Longman.

Goldsmith, John. 1990. *Autosegmental and Metrical Phonology*. Oxford: Blackwell.

Goldsmith, John. 1990 *The Handbook of Phonological Theory*. Oxford: Blackwell.

Hayes, Bruce. 1995. *Metrical Stress Theory: Principles and Case Studies*. Chicago: University of Chicago Press.

Hogg, Richard, and McCully, C.B. 1987. *Metrical Phonology: A Coursebook*. Cambridge: Cambridge University Press.

Hyman, Larry M. 1975. *Phonology: Theory and Analysis*. New York: Holt, Rinehart & Winston.

Katamba, Francis. 1989. *An Introduction to Phonology*. London: Longman.

Kaye, Jonathan. 1989. *Phonology: A Cognitive View*. Hillsdale, NJ: Lawrence Erlbaum Associates.

Keating, Patricia. 1988. 'The phonology–phonetics interface.' In *Linguistics: The Cambridge Survey*. Vol. 1. Edited by F. Newmeyer, pp. 281–302. Cambridge: Cambridge University Press.

Kenstowicz, Michael. 1994. *Phonology in Generative Grammar*. Oxford: Blackwell.

Kenstowicz, Michael and Kisseberth, Charles. 1979. *Generative Phonology*. New York: Academic Press.

Spencer, Andrew. 1996. *Phonology*. Oxford: Blackwell.

Stampe, David. 1980. *A Dissertation on Natural Phonology*. New York: Garland.

Appendix: Hints for solving phonology problems

The task of solving a phonology problem is made easier if certain facts presented in this chapter and summarized here are kept in mind.

1. Begin by looking for minimal pairs. These establish which segments are contrastive. For example, in the following data from Tagalog (Philippines), minimal pairs in items a) and e) and c) and f), and the near minimal pair b) and d) show that the phones [h] and [?] contrast and therefore belong to separate phonemes, /h/ and /?/, respectively.

a)	kahon	'box'	d)	ʔari	'property'
b)	hariʔ	'king'	e)	kaʔon	'to fetch'
c)	ʔumagos	'to flow'	f)	humagos	'to paint'

2. Allophones of a given phoneme are usually phonetically similar. Look for sounds that are phonetically similar, and check to see whether they are in complementary distribution. The best way to do this is to list the environments. In the following data, also from Tagalog, [d] and [r], both voiced alveolars, should be considered as possible allophones. List the environments in which these sounds are found. Are they in complementary distribution?

a)	datiŋ	'to arrive'	f)	daraʔiŋ	'will complain'
b	dami	'amount'	g)	marumi	'dirty'
c)	dumi	'dirt'	h)	marami	'many'
d)	daratiŋ	'will arrive'	i)	daʔiŋ	'to complain'
e)	mandurukot	'pickpocket'	j)	mandukot	'to go pickpocketing'

3. If two potential allophones of one phoneme are in complementary distribution, you can be reasonably sure they are allophones of the same phoneme. Try to make a general statement about their distribution in terms of some natural phonological class. For example:

> Tagalog [d] and [r] are in complementary distribution and are allophones of one phoneme. The allophone [r] occurs between vowels; [d] occurs elsewhere – here, word-initially, as in items a), b), c), f), and so on, and after nasal consonants, as in items e) and j).

4. Select one allophone as basic. This is usually the allophone with the widest distribution (the elsewhere variant). It may be helpful to set up a traditional phoneme–allophone diagram. (See Figure 3.3.)

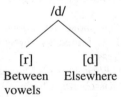

5. Write a phonological rule or provide a representation that accounts for the predictable features of the other allophones. Your rule (or representation) is probably correct if it describes a common linguistic process in terms of natural classes of sounds interacting with neighbouring segments and/ or syllable structure.

  For example, for the above: d →r / V __ V

  Here, the process that leads to allophony is a form of assimilation, in that an underlying stop consonant becomes a continuant when found between two continuants (the vowels).

6. You can assume that any segments are phonemic if they cannot be shown to be allophones of a phoneme. The data simply did not provide minimal

pairs. (For instance, though /ʃ/ and /ʒ/ are separate phonemes in English, it is difficult to find minimal pairs proving their phonemic status.)

Questions

Assume phonetic transcription of the data in all exercises.

1. *Inuktitut* (Eastern) (Native Canadian)

a)	iglumut	'to a house'	h)	pinna	'that one up there'
b)	ukiaq	'late fall'	i)	ani	'female's brother'
c)	aiviq	'walrus'	j)	iglu	'(snow)house'
d)	aniguvit	'if you leave'	k)	panna	'that place up there'
e)	aglu	'seal's breathing hole'	l)	aivuq	'she goes home'
f)	iglumit	'from a house'	m)	ini	'place, spot'
g)	anigavit	'because you leave'	n)	ukiuq	'winter'

i) List all the minimal pairs in these data. Based on the minimal pairs you have found, list all the contrastive pairs of vowels.

ii) Using the vowel charts in Figures 2.9 and 2.10 as your models, make a chart of Inuktitut vowel phonemes.

iii) Now consider the data again; here they are transcribed in more phonetic detail. In the data there are phonetically similar segments that are in complementary distribution. Look for them and answer the questions that follow the data.

aa)	iglumut	'to a house'	hh)	pinna	'that one up there'
bb)	ukiaq	'late fall'	ii)	anɪ	'female's brother'
cc)	aivɪq	'walrus'	jj)	iglɪu	'(snow)house'
dd)	aniguvit	'if you leave'	kk)	panna	'that place up there'
ee)	aglʊ	'seal's breathing hole'	ll)	aivʊq	'she goes home'
ff)	iglumit	'from a house'	mm)	inɪ	'place, spot'
gg)	anigavit	'because you leave'	nn)	ukiʊq	'winter'

2. *Gascon* (Gascon is spoken in southwest France) The phones [b], [β], [d], [ð], [g], and [ɣ] are all found in Gascon, as the following examples show.

a)	brẽn	'endanger'	n)	gat	'cat'
b)	bako	'cow'	o)	lũŋg	'long'
c)	ũmbro	'shadow'	p)	saliβo	'saliva'
d)	krãmbo	'room'	q)	noβi	'husband'
e)	dilys	'Monday'	r)	aβe	'to have'
f)	dũŋko	'until'	s)	ʃiβaw	'horse'
g)	duso	'sweet'	t)	byðɛt	'gut'
h)	taldepãn	'leftover bread'	u)	eʃaðo	'hoe'
i)	pũnde	'to lay eggs'	v)	biɣar	'mosquito'
j)	dudze	'twelve'	w)	riɣut	'he laughed'
k)	guteʒa	'flow'	x)	agro	'sour'
l)	ẽŋgwãn	'this year'	y)	ʒuɣɛt	'he played'
m)	puðe	'to be able'			

i) Which pairs among the phones [b], [β], [d], [ð], [g], and [ɣ] are the most phonetically similar? Support your claim with phonetic descriptions of the similar pairs.

ii) List the environments in which the phones [b], [β], [d], [ð], [g], and [ɣ] are found. You may ignore word-final position in your consideration.

iii) Is there any evidence for grouping these pairs of sounds into phonemes? State the evidence for each pair.

iv) Make a general statement about the patterning of the phonemes you have established.

v) Following your analysis, write the following forms in phonemic transcription.

    a) [puɣo]   b) [deðat]   c) [ʃiβaw]   d) [krãmbo]

vi) Using Figure 3.19 as your model, provide complete derivations of the forms for k) *hand*, m) *axe*, and o) *tooth*.

3. *Hindi* (Hindi is a language of the Indo-European family spoken in India) Consider the segments [b] and b̤ in the data below and answer the questions that follow. The segment transcribed [b̤] is a murmured voiced stop; it was presented in Chapter 2, section 10.2.

a)	[bara]	'large'	f)	[b̤ɛd]	'disagreement'
b)	[b̤ari]	'heavy'	g)	[bais]	'twenty-two'
c)	[bina]	'without'	h)	[b̤əs]	'buffalo'
d)	[b̤ir]	'crowd'	i)	[bap]	'father'
e)	[bori]	'sackcloth'	j)	[b̤ag]	'part'

Are the segments [b] and [b̤] allophones of the same phoneme or do they belong to separate phonemes? If you believe they belong to separate phonemes, give evidence from the data to support your analysis. If you believe they are allophones of the same phoneme, list the conditioning environments.

4. Name the single feature that distinguishes the following pairs of sounds.

a)	[θ] : [ð]	e)	[b] : [m]	i)	[ʌ] : [ə]
b)	[p] : [f]	f)	[s] : [ʃ]	j)	[s] : [θ]
c)	[u] : [ʊ]	g)	[ɪ] : [i]	k)	[l] : [r]
d)	[i] : [e]	h)	[k] : [x]	l)	[u] : [o]

5. There are a number of natural classes in the vowel and consonant data below. Circle three natural classes in each set of data. Indicate which feature or features define the class, as in the example.

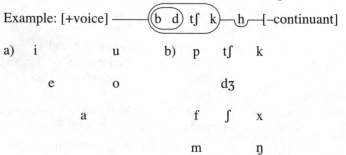

Example: [+voice] ⎯⎯⎯ (b d) tʃ k ⎯ h ⎯ [–continuant]

a) i   u   b) p tʃ   k

       e   o   dʒ

            a   f ʃ   x

                        m   ŋ

6. Complete the feature matrix for each of the sounds indicated. The V abbreviates the features [+syllabic, –consonantal], and the C abbreviates the features [–syllabic, +consonantal].

a) [e] V

+sonorant
–high
–low

b) [tʃ] C

–sonorant
–voice

c) [m] C

+sonorant
+anterior
+nasal

d) [s] C

–sonorant
+strident
+coronal

e) [l] C

[+sonorant]

f) [j]

–syllabic
–consonantal
+high

Using the appropriate features from Figure 3.30, represent each segment on a feature hierarchy tree.

7. *English*

Many speakers of English have two types of [l]. One, called *clear l*, is transcribed as [l] in the following data. The other, called *dark l*, is transcribed with [ɫ]. Examine the data, and answer the questions that follow.

a) [laɪf]   life
b) [li:p]   leap
c) [lu: z]   lose
d) [ɪləʊp]   elope
e) [dɪlaɪt]   delight
f) [sli:p]   sleep

g) [pʰɪɫ]   pill
h) [fi:ɫ]   feel
i) [heɫp]   help
j) [bʌɫk]   bulk
k) [səʊɫd]   sold
l) [fʊɫ]   full

Do [l] and [ɫ] belong to separate phonemes or are they allophones of the same phoneme? If you believe they belong to separate phonemes, answer question *i*). If you believe they are allophones of the same phoneme, answer question *ii*).

i)   List the evidence that makes your case for considering [l] and [ɫ] as separate phonemes.

ii) State the distribution of [l] and [ɫ] in words.

iii) Which variant makes the best underlying form? Why?

iv) Can you make reference to syllable structure in your distribution statement? If you can, do so in rule form.

8. *Turkish*

As you saw in section 4.4, Turkish syllables have the following structure:

- maximum number of consonants in an onset: 1
- maximum number of vowels in a nucleus: 1
- maximum number of consonants in a coda: 2, of which the first is a fricative or sonorant.

With these stipulations in mind, syllabify the following forms:

a) kurttɛn   b) kelɛptʃɛ   c) kemɛnd   d) kemɛndɛ

In these further data from Turkish, the phones [i] and [ɪ] are in complementary distribution and form one phoneme, and the phones [e] and [ɛ] are also in complementary distribution and form another (separate) phoneme. Examine the data and answer the questions that follow.

a) gɛldɪk 'we arrived' f) tʃitʃɛk 'flower'   k) liman 'harbour'
b) ɪʃ 'work'   g) tʃɪft 'plough'   l) emɪn 'sure'
c) elɪm 'your hand'   h) ɛl 'hand'   m) didɪk 'shredded'
d) ɪp 'thread'   i) memɛr 'passage'   n) bɪt 'louse'
e) sɛs 'voice'   j) sɛksɛn 'eighty'   o) silah 'weapon'

i) Provide a statement of the distribution of [i] and [ɪ] and [e] and [ɛ] in words. Make your statement as general as possible, but be precise!

ii) Write a rule that derives the allophones of both phonemes from the underlying form. Use features! Remember to give your rule a mnemonic name; use this name in the answer to question *iii)*.

iii) Provide derivations for the following underlying forms.

UR	#	# 'cord' #	# 'lasso'
PR	[sidʒɪm]	[kemɛnd]	

9. State each of the following rules in plain ordinary English, making reference to natural classes and common linguistic processes.

Example:
$$\begin{bmatrix} -\text{syllabic} \\ +\text{consonantal} \\ -\text{sonorant} \end{bmatrix} \rightarrow \emptyset\, /\, \underline{\quad}\, \#\ (\textit{an obstruent is deleted word-finally})$$

a) $\emptyset \rightarrow \begin{bmatrix} +\text{syllabic} \\ -\text{consonantal} \\ +\text{sonorant} \\ -\text{high} \\ -\text{low} \\ -\text{round} \\ -\text{back} \\ +\text{tense} \end{bmatrix} /\, \#\, \underline{\quad} \begin{bmatrix} -\text{syllabic} \\ +\text{consonantal} \\ -\text{sonorant} \end{bmatrix} \begin{bmatrix} -\text{syllabic} \\ +\text{consonantal} \\ -\text{sonorant} \end{bmatrix}$

b) $\begin{bmatrix} +\text{syllabic} \\ -\text{consonantal} \\ +\text{sonorant} \\ -\text{round} \end{bmatrix} \rightarrow [+\text{round}] /\, \begin{bmatrix} -\text{syllabic} \\ +\text{consonantal} \\ +\text{anterior} \\ -\text{coronal} \end{bmatrix} \underline{\quad} \begin{bmatrix} -\text{syllabic} \\ +\text{consonantal} \\ +\text{anterior} \\ -\text{coronal} \end{bmatrix}$

10. Change the following statements into rule notation. Give a name to the process in question in each case.
   a) Voiceless stops become corresponding fricatives between vowels.
   b) A schwa is inserted after a voiced stop word-finally.
   c) Low unrounded vowels become rounded before *m*.

11. *Tamil* (Tamil is a Dravidian language spoken in South India and Sri Lanka)

In the following Tamil data, some words begin with glides while others do not. The symbol [ɖ] represents a voiced retroflex stop and the diacritic [̪] indicates dentals.

Initial j-glide		*Initial w-glide*		*No initial glide*	
a) jeli	'rat'	f) woɖi	'break'	k) arivu	'knowledge'
b) ji:	'fly'	g) wo:laj	'palm leaf'	l) ai̪n̪tu	'five'
c) jilaj	'leaf'	h) wu:si	'needle'	m) a:saj	'desire'
d) jeŋge:	'where'	i) wujir	'life'	n) a:ru	'river'
e) jiɖuppu	'waist'	j) wo:ram	'edge'	o) a:di	'origin'

i) The occurrence of these glides is predictable. Using your knowledge of natural classes, make a general statement about the distribution of the glides.

ii) Assuming the glides are not present in the underlying representations, name the process that accounts for their presence in the phonetic forms.

iii) Using features, write a rule using alpha notation that formalizes this process. Show the derivation of the forms for *fly* and *break*.

12. *Mende* (Mende is spoken in Liberia and Sierra Leone)

In Mende, the forms that mean 'on' (*ma*) and 'in' (*hu*) are suffixes (they are attached to a preceding word; see Chapter 4, section 1.3). Notice in the data below that suffixes all bear tone, but that the tone varies on different words. In the examples, ´ indicates a high tone, ` a low tone, and ^ a falling (high-to-low) tone.

a) kɔ́ 'war'   kɔ́má 'on war'   kɔ́hú 'in war'
b) pélé 'house'   pélémá 'on (the) house'   péléhú 'in (the) house'
c) bèlè 'trousers'   bèlèmà 'on trousers'   bèlèhù 'in trousers'
d) ngílà 'dog'   ngílàmà 'on (the) dog'   ngílàhù 'in (the) dog'

i) Can you account for the differences in tone on the suffixes for 'on' and 'in' in Mende? State your solution with autosegmental notation such as that illustrated in Figures 3.31 to 3.33. (*Hint*: Assume that the suffixes have no tone to begin with, but that the words to which they are attached do have tone.)

ii) Assuming that you have answered question *i*) successfully, account for the tones of the suffixes meaning 'on' and 'in' in the additional examples below.

e) mbû 'owl'   mbúmà 'on (the) owl'   mbúhù 'in (the) owl'
f) ɲàhâ 'woman'   ɲàhámà 'on (the) woman'   ɲàháhù 'in (the) woman'

13. *Moru* (Miza dialect; Moru is a Sudanic language)

In Moru, contour tones are not found on short vowels in underlying representations. However, phonetic forms of combined lexical items do show contour tones. Can you represent this using autosegmental notation? (*Hint*: A segmental process is involved as well as a typical suprasegmental process and the two processes must be ordered.) In the data provided, ´ indicates a high tone, ` a low tone, and ^ a falling (high-to-low) tone. Vowels with no tone mark need not be considered.

a) màá   →   [mǎ]
    'we'   'we'

b) ká ùmu   →   [kûmu]
    'he runs'   'he runs'

c) ká ɔ̀ŋga   →   [kɔ̂ŋga]
    'he jumps'   'he jumps'

d) njá àdì ùzi ja →   [njâdùzi ja]
    'you call who?'   'who are you calling?'

14. The English data below provide examples of stress placement on certain verbs.

A	B	C
appéar	adápt	astónish
collíde	collápse	consíder
eráse	eléct	imágine
caróuse	obsérve	detérmine
corróde	tormént	prómise

i)   Describe in words the stress placement on these verbs. Make sure you refer to syllable structure in your statement.

ii) Provide syllabified representations of the words *collíde, eléct*, and *consíder* in order to illustrate your conclusion about stress placement in these forms.

15. Consider the stress patterns in the language data below. Using Table 3.32 as your model, state which parameters are necessary to account for stress placement and what the settings for the necessary parameters are for each set of data.

Latvian (Latvia)
a) víens   'I'
b) mázga:t   'to wash'
c) mázga:ties   'to wash oneself'
d) némazga:ties   'not to wash oneself'
e) pá:rka:rtoʃana:s   'reorganization'

Maung (Goulburn Islands, Australia)
a) ŋábi   'I'
b) bàládʒi   'bag'
c) wùɣíba   'mangrove worm'
d) jìniwúnjan   'he cooked it'
e) àwùniláŋuŋ   'he was eating them'
f) gùniɣába   'you must give it to him'

Tzutujil (Guatemala)
a) sá   'white'
b) waʔnáq   'eaten'
c) ʃwaʔí   'he ate'
d) ʃtʃʔɛjo:ní   'he hit'
e) tatʃʔejáʔ   'hit it'

f) atʃaxiló:m   'husband'

Hiligaynon (Philippines): not all Hiligaynon words are assigned stress in the same way; only one class of words is represented here. (*Hint*: Note that in this language foot building is limited to a maximum of two feet. You need not formalize this fact in your answer.)

a) pamàŋkután   'problem'
b) kàwatán   'thief'
c) bulág   'blind'
d) palaŋìtaʔún   'highly sought after'
e) nagapaŋìtaʔáj   'to look for each other'

Huallaga Quechua (Peru) (*Hint*: This answer will require reference to section 8.5.)

a) umá:ta   'to my head'
b) uma:píta   'from my head'
c) uma:pitámi   'from my head (assertive)'
d) tʃajlláraq   'just a moment ago'
e) ajwajkánmi   'they are going'
f) ajwashajkikáma   'hit it'
g) ájwaj   'go'

Morphology: the analysis of word structure

William O'Grady and Videa P. de Guzman

Carve every word before you let it fall.

&Oliver Wendell Holmes, Sr

Part of linguistic competence involves the ability to construct and interpret words. The average high school student knows about 60,000 words whose form and meaning are not derived from those of other words. Such words – including *read*, *language*, *on*, *cold*, and *if*, to name but a few – must be learned and stored as separate items in the **lexicon** (or mental dictionary). However, countless other words can be constructed and comprehended by the application of quite general rules to more basic words. For example, any speaker of English who knows the meaning of the noun *fax* – and the verb derived from it – could form and interpret words such as *faxable* (for things that can be faxed) and *fax machine* (for the device that sends and receives faxes).

The system of categories and rules involved in word formation and interpretation is called **morphology**. This chapter presents an introduction to the study of morphology, beginning with the inventory of notions relevant to the analysis of word structure.

1

WORDS AND WORD STRUCTURE

Of all the units of linguistic analysis, the **word** is the most familiar. As literate speakers of English, we rarely have difficulty segmenting a stream of speech sounds into words or deciding where to leave spaces when writing a sentence. What, though, is a word?

The most reliable defining property of words is that they are the smallest **free forms** found in language. A free form is an element that can occur in isolation and/or whose position with respect to neighbouring elements is not entirely fixed. Consider in this regard the first two words in the following sentence.

1)

The birds left.

The plural marker *-s* cannot be a word (a free form) since it must always be attached to the end of a noun. (Elements that must be attached to another form are written here with a hyphen.)

2)
*The bird left -s.

In contrast, *birds* is a word since it can occur in isolation, as in the following exchange.

3)
Speaker A: What are those things in the tree?
Speaker B: Birds.

Moreover, even when *birds* occurs as part of a larger sentence, it is not attached to anything else. This is why it can occur in different positions within a sentence, as illustrated in *4)*.

4)

a.   *birds* occurring in front of a verb:
     Birds avoid cats.

b.   *birds* occurring after a verb:
     Cats chase birds.

Some words, such as *the* in sentence *1)*, do not normally occur in isolation. However, they are still free forms since their positioning with respect to neighbouring categories is not entirely fixed. Thus, as shown by the following sentence, *the* does not always have to occur immediately in front of a noun.

5)
The young birds remained in the nest.

1.1

Morphemes

Like syllables and sentences, words have an internal structure consisting of smaller units organized with respect to each other in a particular way. The most important component of word structure is the **morpheme**, the smallest unit of language that carries information about meaning or function. The word *builder*, for example, consists of two morphemes: *build* (with the meaning of 'construct') and *-er* (which indicates that the entire word functions as a noun with the meaning 'one who builds'). Similarly, the word *houses* is made up of the morphemes *house* (with the meaning of 'dwelling') and *-s* (with the meaning 'more than one').

Some words consist of a single morpheme. For example, the word *train* cannot be divided into smaller parts (say, *tr* and *ain*) that carry information about its meaning or function. Such words are said to be **simple**. However, Table 4.1 shows that many words are **complex** in that they contain two or more morphemes.

Table 4.1 Words consisting of one or more morphemes

One	Two	Three	More than three
and			
boy	boy-s		
hunt	hunt-er	hunt-er-s	
act	act-ive	act-iv-ate	re-act-iv-ate
man	gentle-man	gentle-man-ly	gentle-man-li-ness

Free and bound

A morpheme that can be a word by itself is called **free** while a morpheme that must be attached to another element is said to be **bound**. The morpheme *house*, for example, is free since it can be used as a word on its own; plural *-s*, on the other hand, is bound.

Concepts that are expressed by free morphemes in English do not necessarily have the same status in other languages. For example, in Hare (an Athapaskan language spoken in Canada's Northwest Territories), morphemes that indicate body parts (Table 4.2) must always be attached to a morpheme designating a possessor. (A high tone is marked by the diacritic ´.)

Table 4.2 Some body part names in Hare

Without possessor		With possessor	
*fí	'head'	sefí	'my head'
*bé	'belly'	nebé	'your belly'
*dzé	'heart'	ʔedzé	'someone's heart/a heart'

In English, of course, these body part names are free morphemes and do not have to be attached to another element.

Conversely, there are also some bound forms in English whose counterparts in other languages are free. For example, the notion 'past' or 'completed' is expressed by a bound morpheme (usually spelled *-ed*) in English, but by the free morpheme *lɛɛw* in Thai. As the following sentence shows, this morpheme can even be separated from the verb by an intervening word. (Tone is not marked here.)

6)

Boon huŋ   khaaw lɛɛw.
Boon cook rice   past
'Boon cooked rice.'

Allomorphs

Morphemes do not always have an invariant form. The morpheme used to express indefiniteness in English, for instance, has two forms – *a* and *an*.

7)

an orange	a building
an accent	a car
an eel	a girl

The form *a* is used before words beginning with a consonant and the form *an* before words beginning with a vowel.[1] The variant forms of a morpheme are called its **allomorphs**.

Another example of allomorphic variation is found in the pronunciation of the plural morpheme *-s* in the following words.

8)

cats

dogs

judges

Whereas the plural is pronounced as /s/ in the first case, it is realized as /z/ in the second, and as /ɪz/ (or perhaps /əz/) in the third. Here again, selection of the proper allomorph is dependent on phonological facts. We will examine this phenomenon in more detail in Chapter 6.

Other examples of patterns in which a morpheme's form changes when it combines with another element are easy to find in English. The final segment in *invent* and *assert*, for instance, is realized as /t/ when these morphemes stand alone as separate words but as /ʃ/ when they combine with the morpheme *-ion* in the words *invention* and *assertion*. Comparable alternations are found in words such as *permit/permiss-ive* ([t]~[s]), *electric/electric-ity* ([k]~[s]), *divide/divis-ion* ([d]~[ʒ]), *impress/impress-ion* ([s]~[ʃ]), and so on. In all these cases, we are dealing with variant forms of a single morpheme.

Beginning students can also be confused by changes in spelling found in some morphological patterns even when there are no corresponding changes in pronunciation. Thus, the final *e* in the words *create* and *write* is lost when they combine with a morpheme beginning with a vowel (*creat-ive*, *writ-er*). These spelling modifications do not change a morpheme's identity, of course, and should simply be ignored when doing morphological analysis.

1.2

Representing word structure

In order to represent the internal structure of words, it is necessary not only to identify each of the component morphemes but also to classify these elements in terms of their contribution to the meaning and function of the larger word.

Roots and affixes

Complex words typically consist of a **root** and one or more **affixes**. The root morpheme carries the major component of the word's meaning and belongs to a **lexical category** – noun (N), verb (V), adjective (A), or preposition (P). These categories will be discussed in more detail in Chapter 5, section 1.1. For now it suffices to note that nouns typically refer to concrete and abstract 'things' (*tree*, *treatment*) while verbs (*treat*, *teach*) tend to denote actions, adjectives usually name properties (*kind*, *red*), and prepositions (*in*, *near*) encode spatial relations. In general, nouns can occur with *the* (*the car*), verbs with *will* (*will go*), and adjectives with *very* (*very kind*).

Unlike roots, affixes do not belong to a lexical category and are always bound morphemes. A straightforward illustration of this contrast is found in the word *teacher*, which consists of the root *teach*, a verb, and the affix *-er*, a bound morpheme that combines with the root and gives a noun with the meaning 'one who teaches'. The internal structure of this word can be represented in diagram form, as shown in Figure 4.1. (The symbol 'Af' stands for affix.)

Figure 4.1   The internal structure of the word *teacher.*

The internal structure of some other complex words is depicted in Figure 4.2.

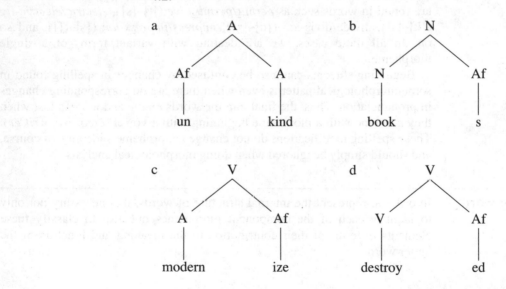

Figure 4.2   Some other words with an internal structure consisting of a root and an affix.

These diagrams, which are often called **tree structures**, represent the details of a word's internal organization. Where these details are irrelevant to the point being considered, it is traditional to use a much simpler system of representation that indicates only the location of the morpheme boundaries: *un-kind*, *modern-ize*, and so on.

Bases

A **base** is the form to which an affix is added. In many cases, the base is also the root. In *books*, for example, the element to which the affix *-s* is added corresponds to the word's root. In other cases, however, an affix can be added to a unit larger than a root. This happens in words such as *blackened*, in which the past tense affix *-ed* is added to the verbal base *blacken* –a unit consisting of the root morpheme *black* and the suffix *-en*.

In Figure 4.3, *black* is not only the root for the entire word but also the base for *-en*. The unit *blacken*, on the other hand, is simply the base for *-ed*.

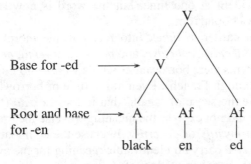

Figure 4.3   A word illustrating the difference between a root and a base.

Problematic cases (advanced)

The vast majority of complex words in English are built from roots that are free morphemes in that they can be used in other contexts as independent words. In the words *re-do* and *treat-ment*, for example, the root (*do* and *treat*, respectively) is a V that can appear elsewhere in the language without an affix. Because most complex words are formed from a root that can itself be a word, English morphology is said to be **word-based**.

This notwithstanding, English contains a significant number of words in which the root is not free. For example, *unkempt* seems to consist of the prefix *un-* (with the meaning 'not') and the root *kempt* (meaning 'groomed'), even though *kempt* cannot be used as an independent word. Other common words of this type include *horr-ify*, *venge-ance*, *in-ept*, and *salv-ation*, to name but a few. We will assign morphemes such as *kempt*, *horr*, *venge*, *ept*, and *salv* to the special category 'bound root' (B in Figure 4.4 overleaf), which we will reserve for root morphemes that cannot be used as words and therefore do not belong to a conventional lexical category such as noun or verb.

The origin of most bound roots in words such as these is the result of specific events in the history of English. For example, there was once a word *kempt* in English (with the meaning 'combed'), and it was to this base that the affix *un-* was originally attached. At a later point, however, *kempt* disappeared from the language, leaving behind the word *unkempt* in which an affix appears with a bound root. The form *inept* (from the Latin *ineptus* 'unsuited'),

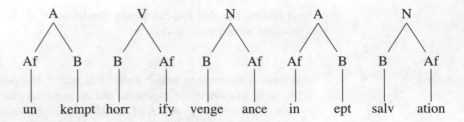

Figure 4.4 The internal structure of words built around a bound root.

on the other hand, was borrowed into English as a whole word. The relationship of its root, *-ept*, to the word *apt* (from the same source) may have been evident at one time, but the word is now seen by most speakers to involve a bound root.

Even harder to break into recognizable morphemes are words such as *receive*, *deceive*, *conceive*, and *perceive* or *remit*, *permit*, *submit*, and *commit*. These items were borrowed as whole words into English (many of them from Latin through French). Even at the time of borrowing, the *re-* of *receive* did not have the sense of 'again' that it does in *redo* ('do again') and the *de-* of *deceive* did not express the meaning 'reverse the process' associated with the *de-* in *demystify* or *decertify*. Because the components of words like *receive* and *deceive* carry no identifiable meaning for the average speaker of English (who has no knowledge of Latin), we will not treat them as separate morphemes in this book.[2] Thus, we take the word *receive* to consist of a single morpheme.

1.3

Some common morphological phenomena

Human language makes use of a variety of operations or processes that can modify the structure of a word, either by adding some element to it or by making an internal change in order to express a new meaning or to mark a grammatical contrast (such as past versus non-past, N versus V, and so on).

Affixation

The addition of an **affix**, a process known as **affixation**, is an extremely common morphological process in language. Normally, linguists distinguish among three types of affixes. An affix that is attached to the front of its base is called a **prefix** while an affix that is attached to the end of its base is termed a **suffix**. Both types of affix occur in English, as Table 4.3 shows.

Table 4.3 Some English prefixes and suffixes

Prefixes	*Suffixes*
<u>de</u>-activate	vivid-<u>ly</u>
<u>re</u>-play	govern-<u>ment</u>
<u>inter</u>-marry	hunt-<u>er</u>
<u>in</u>-accurate	kind-<u>ness</u>

We will consider the nature and properties of English affixes in more detail in sections 2.1 and 5.

Far less common than prefixes and suffixes are **infixes**, a type of affix that occurs within a base. Table 4.4 shows data from the Philippine language Tagalog. The data contain two infixes, -*um*- and -*in*-, which are inserted after the first consonant of the base to mark a completed event.

Table 4.4   Some Tagalog infixes

Base		Infixed form	
takbuh	'run'	t-<u>um</u>-akbuh	'ran'
lakad	'walk'	l-<u>um</u>-akad	'walked'
pili?	'choose'	p-<u>in</u>-ili?	'chose'

Beginning students sometimes think that a morpheme such as -*ish* in *boy-ish-ness* is an infix since it occurs between two other morphemes (*boy* and -*ness*), but this is not so. To be an infix, an affix must occur inside its base (as when -*um*- in Tagalog occurs inside *takbuh* 'run'). Nothing of this sort happens in the case of -*ish*, since its base is *boy*, not the impossible **boyness*.

A very special type of infixing system is found in Arabic, in which a typical root consists simply of three consonants. Affixes consisting of two vowels are then inserted into this root in a manner that intersperses the vowels among the consonants. (In the examples that follow, the segments of the root are written in bold face.)

9)

katab   kutib   **aktub   uktb**
'write' 'have been written'   'be writing' 'being written'

One way to represent the structure of such words is as follows, with the root and affix assigned to different **tiers**, or levels of structure, that are intercalated in the actual pronunciation of the word. (See the discussion of templatic morphology in section 1.6 of Chapter 6.)

10)

a   Af (present)   b   Af (passive perfective)

k a t a b   k u t i b

Root ('write')   Root ('write')

'write'   'have been written'

Cliticization   Some words are unable to stand alone as independent forms for phonological reasons. Such elements, called **clitics**, must be attached to another word in the sentence. A good example of this can be found in English, where certain verb forms have reduced variants (*'m* for *am*, *'s* for *is*, and *'re* for *are*) that cannot stand alone since they no longer constitute a syllable – a word must minimally contain at least one syllable. Cliticization occurs, attaching these elements to the preceding word.

11)

a.   I'<u>m</u> leaving now.

b.   Mary'**s** going to succeed.

c.   They'<u>re</u> here now.

Cliticization is also common in French, which includes a set of unstressed clitic pronouns that must be attached to the verb. (Although not evident in the written language, the clitic and the verb are pronounced as if they formed a single word.)

12)

Suzanne les voit.

Suzanne them-sees

Suzanne sees them.

Clitics that attach to the end of a preceding word (as in the English examples) are called **enclitics**; those that attach to the beginning of a following word (as in the French example) are known as **proclitics**.

The effects of cliticization can bear a superficial resemblance to affixation since in both cases an element that cannot stand alone is attached to a base. The key difference is that – unlike affixes – all the clitics discussed so far are members of a lexical category such as verb, noun (or pronoun), or preposition.

In fact, there is another type of clitic which is not a contracted form of any self-standing lexical category, but which nevertheless is incapable of occurring in isolation. The genitive -*'s* in English is regarded in many current grammars of English as a good example of such a clitic. Although it is a bound morpheme, the genitive -*'s* is not a suffix. The crucial difference is this: whereas a suffix gets fully integrated phonologically, semantically, and syntactically with the base to which it is attached, and cannot be torn away from it and attached to another constituent of the sentence, a clitic has a much looser association with its host. Thus, the phonological host may be different from the syntactic and semantic host of a clitic. This can be seen in the contrasting placement of the genitive *'s* in the following:

13)

a.   The President's eloquence

b.   The President of India's eloquence

Whereas in *13a)* the genitive *'s* is appended to the noun *President* to indicate the fact that the President has the property of being eloquent, in *13b)* the genitive *'s* is appended to *India* although it is still the President, and not India, that is eloquent.

Unlike clitics, suffixes must always be attached phonologically to the word to which they belong in terms of grammar and meaning. So, below in *14)* since it is just the noun *Presidents* that is plural in meaning, only the first of the two sentences is well-formed:

14)

a. Several Presidents of India have been members of the Congress Party.

b. *Several President of Indias have been members of the Congress Party.

The plural suffix cannot be attached to any noun other than the noun that is plural. Hence the ungrammaticality of *14b)*.

Internal change

Internal change is a process that substitutes one non-morphemic segment for another, as illustrated in the pairs of words in Table 4.5.

Table 4.5 Internal change in English

sing (present)	sang (past)
sink (present)	sank (past)
drive (present)	drove (past)
foot (singular)	feet (plural)
goose (singular)	geese (plural

Verbs such as *sing*, *sink*, and *drive* form their past tense by changing the vowel (e.g., from *i* to *a* in the first two examples). The term **ablaut** is often used for vowel alternations that mark grammatical contrasts in this way.

Ablaut can be distinguished from **umlaut**, which involves the fronting of a vowel under the influence of a front vowel in the following syllable. Historically, this is what is responsible for the use of *feet* and *geese* as the plural forms of *foot* and *goose*, respectively: the back vowel in the root (originally /o:/) was fronted in anticipation of the front vowel in the old plural suffix /iz/, which was subsequently dropped.

The internal changes just considered are not examples of infixing for two reasons. First, there is no reason to think that English has root morphemes such as **ft* (meaning 'lower extremity of the leg') or **sng* (meaning 'produce words in a musical tone'). As shown by the Tagalog examples in Table 4.4, the base into which an infix is inserted must exist as a separate form. Second, there is no independent reason to think that there is a morpheme *oo* in English that means 'singular' or a morpheme *ee* that means 'plural' in the *foot/feet* example any more than there is a morpheme *i* meaning 'present' or a morpheme *a* meaning 'past' in the *sing/sang* case. Since infixes are by definition morphemes, we can conclude that these examples involve internal change (the substitution of non-morphemic segments) rather than infixing.

Suppletion

Internal change must also be distinguished from **suppletion**, a morphological process whereby a root morpheme is replaced by a phonologically unrelated form in order to indicate a grammatical contrast (Table 4.6). A simple example of this phenomenon in English is the use of *went* as the past tense form of the verb *go* or *was* and *were* as the past tense forms of *be*.

Table 4.6   Suppletion in other languages

Language	Basic form		Suppletive form	
French	avoir	'to have'	eu	'had'
Spanish	ir	'to go'	fue	'(he) went'
German	ist	'is'	sind	'are'
Russian	xoroʃo	'good'	lutʃʃe	'better' ('more good')

In some cases, it is hard to distinguish between suppletion and internal change. For example, are the past tenses of *think* (*thought*) and *seek* (*sought*) the result of suppletion or internal change? Because the initial phoneme of these verbs remains unchanged, we will consider this alternation to involve an extreme form of internal change rather than true suppletion. (However, the term **partial suppletion** is used by some linguists for these cases.)

Stress and tone placement

Sometimes, a base can undergo a change in the placement of stress or tone to reflect a change in its category. In English, for example, there are pairs of words such as those in Table 4.7 in which the verb has stress on the final syllable while the corresponding noun is stressed on the first syllable. (Stress is represented here by ´.)

Table 4.7   Stress placement in English

Verb	Noun
implánt	ímplant
impórt	ímport
presént	présent
subjéct	súbject
contést	cóntest

In the language Mono-Bili (spoken in the African country of Zaïre), tone is used to make the distinction between past and future tense (Table 4.8). (A high tone is marked by ´ and a low tone is marked by `.)

Table 4.8   Past verus future in Mono-Bili

Past		Future	
dá	'spanked'	dà	'will spank'
zɨ́	'ate'	zɨ̀	'will eat'
wó	'killed'	wò	'will kill'

As can easily be observed here, high tone is associated with the past tense and low tone with the future. (The use of tone to mark tense contrasts was also exemplifed in Chapter 2; see Figure 2.14.)

Reduplication

Yet another common morphological process in certain languages (but not English) is **reduplication**, which duplicates all or part of the base to which it applies to mark a grammatical or semantic contrast. **Full reduplication** is the repetition of the entire word, as in the data from Turkish and Indonesian, respectively, shown in Table 4.9.

Table 4.9   Some examples of full reduplication

Base		Reduplicated form	
Turkish			
tʃabuk	'quickly'	tʃabuk tʃabuk	'very quickly'
javaʃ	'slowly'	javaʃ javaʃ	'very slowly'
iji	'well'	iji iji	'very well'
gyzel	'beautifully'	gyzel gyzel	'very beautifully'
Indonesian			
oraŋ	'man'	oraŋ oraŋ	'all sorts of men'
anak	'child'	anak anak	'all sorts of children'
maŋga	'mango'	maŋga maŋga	'all sorts of mangoes'

In contrast, **partial reduplication** copies only part of the word. In the following data from Tagalog, for instance (Table 4.10), reduplication affects only the first consonant–vowel sequence of the base.

Table 4.10   Reduplication in Tagalog

Base		Reduplicated form	
takbuh	'run'	tatakbuh	'will run'
lakad	'walk'	lalakad	'will walk'
piliʔ	'choose'	pipiliʔ	'will choose'

Compounding

Still another common morphological process in human language involves **compounding**, the combination of lexical categories (nouns, adjectives, verbs, or prepositions) to create a larger word. There are countless compounds in English, some of which are shown in Table 4.11.

Table 4.11   Some examples of English compounds

Noun + Noun	Adjective + Noun	Verb + Noun	Preposition + Noun
street light	bluebird	swear word	overlord
campsite	happy hour	washcloth	outhouse
bookcase	high chair	scrub lady	in-group

As these examples show, the elements making up a compound can all typically occur as independent words elsewhere in the language. In this, compounds differ from words created by either affixation or cliticization. We will consider the properties of compounds in much more detail in section 4.

Cranberry morphemes (advanced)

If a word contains elements whose morphological status is ambiguous, as in the case of *cranberry* and *huckleberry*, determining its internal structure can be a tricky business. Although *berry* is clearly a morpheme, one is not sure what to make of *cran-* and *huckle-*. Comparable words like *elderberry* and *waxberry* can be analysed uncontroversially as Noun+Noun compounds – *elder* denotes the elder tree which produces elderberries and *wax* is short for wax-myrtle, the shrub which produces waxberries. However, similar treatment of *cranberry* and *huckleberry* is untenable because there is no **cran* or **huckle* tree or shrub that produces *cranberry* or *huckleberry* fruits. The forms *cran-* and *huckle-* never occur elsewhere in the language as independent words, or even as bound morphemes (cf. the discussion of words like *unkempt* on page 137 above.)

Notwithstanding this complication, because of the obvious parallelism between the problematic cases like *cranberry* and *huckleberry* on the one hand, and the unproblematic cases like *elderberry* and *waxberry* on the other, *cran-* and *huckle-* are treated as bound (noun) root morphemes whose distribution is restricted to just one (compound) word. Such marginal morphemes are normally referred to, after their most famous exemplar, as **cranberry morphemes**. Let us hasten to add that cranberry morphemes are relatively rare. Normally, the morphological status of elements and the internal structure of words can be established in a straightforward manner.

As first noted in Chapter 1, speakers of English and other languages are able to form and interpret an unlimited number of utterances. An important part of this ability involves the formation and interpretation of words, including forms that may not have been encountered before. Of the morphological operations just outlined, two deserve special attention because of the crucial role they play in the formation of new words in English and other languages – a type of affixation known as derivation and compounding. We will consider these two processes in turn in the next sections of this chapter.

2

DERIVATION

Derivation forms a word with a meaning and/or category distinct from that of its base through the addition of an affix. Table 4.12 contains words formed by adding the suffix *-er* to a verb to form a noun with the meaning 'one who does X'. (Do not confuse this suffix with the *-er* that applies to an N in cases such as *Londoner* and *islander* or the *-er* that combines with an adjective in cases such as *taller and smarter*.)

Table 4.12   The *-er* affix

Verb base	Resulting noun
sell	sell-er
write	writ-er
teach	teach-er
sing	sing-er
discover	discover-er

Once formed, derived words become independent lexical items that receive their own entry in a speaker's mental dictionary. As time goes by, they often take on a special sense that is not entirely predictable from the component morphemes: *writer* usually refers to someone who writes for a living; *comparable* (with stress on the first syllable) means 'similar' rather than 'able to be compared'; *profession* usually denotes a career rather than the act of professing, and so on.

The remainder of this section focuses on the role of derivation in English word formation.

2.1

English derivational affixes

Table 4.13 lists some examples of English derivational affixes, along with information about the category of their base (ignoring bound roots) and of the resulting new word. The first entry states that the affix *-able* applies to a verb base and converts it into an adjective. Thus, if we add the affix *-able* to the verb *fix*, we get an adjective (with the meaning 'able to be fixed').

Table 4.13   Some English derivational affixes

Affix	Change	Examples
Suffixes		
-able	V → A	fix-able, do-able, understand-able
-(at)ion	V → N	realiz-ation, assert-ion, protect-ion
-er	V → N	teach-er, work-er
-ing$_1$	V → N	the shoot-ing, the danc-ing
-ing$_2$	V → A	the sleep-ing giant, a blaz-ing fire
-ive	V → A	assert-ive, impress-ive, restrict-ive
-al	V → N	refusal, disposal
-ment	V → N	adjourn-ment, treat-ment, amaze-ment
-ful	N → A	faith-ful, hope-ful, dread-ful
-(i)al	N → A	president-ial, nation-al, medic-al
-(i)an$_1$	N → A	Arab-ian, Singapore-an, Mali-an
-(i)an$_2$	N → A	Einstein-ian, Newton-ian, Chomsky-an
-ic	N → A	cub-ic, optimist-ic, moron-ic

Table 4.13 Continued

Affix	Change	Examples
-ize$_1$	N → V	hospital-ize, crystal-ize
-less	N → A	penni-less, brain-less
-ous	N → A	poison-ous, lecher-ous
-ate	A → V	activ-ate, captiv-ate
-en	A → V	dead-en, black-en, hard-en
-ity	A → N	stupid-ity, prior-ity
-ize$_2$	A → V	modern-ize, familiar-ize
-ly	A → Adv	quiet-ly, slow-ly, careful-ly
-ness	A → N	happi-ness, sad-ness
Prefixes		
anti-	N → N	anti-abortion, anti-pollution
de-	V → V	de-activate, de-mystify
dis-	V → V	dis-continue, dis-obey
ex-	N → N	ex-president, ex-wife, ex-friend
in-	A → A	in-competent, in-complete
mis-	V → V	mis-identify, mis-place
un$_1$-	A → A	un-happy, un-fair, un-intelligent
un$_2$-	V → V	un-tie, un-lock, un-do
re-	V → V	re-think, re-do, re-state

Sometimes beginning students have trouble determining the category of the base to which an affix is added. In the case of *worker*, for instance, the base (*work*) is sometimes used as a verb (as in *they work hard*) and sometimes as a noun (as in *the work is time-consuming*). This may then make it difficult to know which category occurs with the suffix *-er* in the word *worker*. The solution to this problem is to consider the use of *-er* (in the sense of 'one who X's') with bases whose category can be unequivocally determined. In the words *teacher* and *writer*, for instance, we see this affix used with bases (*teach* and *write*) that are clearly verbs. Moreover, we know that *-er* can combine with the verb *sell* (*seller*) but not the noun *sale* (**saler*). These facts allow us to conclude that the base with which it combines in the word *worker* must be a verb rather than a noun.

2.2

Derivation at work

The information contained in Table 4.13 allows us to build word structures such as those shown in Figure 4.5.

In each of these structures, an affix combines with a base of a particular type to give a new word, in accordance with the properties listed in Table 4.13. In the case of *treatment*, for instance, the affix *-ment* combines with the V *treat* to give the N *treatment*.

These examples illustrate an important property of English complex words: the rightmost morpheme is generally the one that determines the

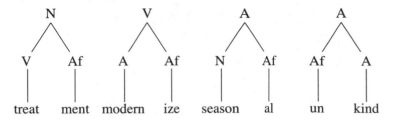

Figure 4.5 Some words formed by derivation.

category of the entire word. Thus, the word *unkind* is an adjective because *kind* (the rightmost morpheme) is an adjective. In contrast, the word *treatment* is a noun since the rightmost element is the affix *-ment*, which combines with a V to give an N (see Table 4.13).[3]

Of course, in some languages the morpheme that determines the category of the entire word can appear on the left rather than the right. In the Philippine language Tagalog, for example (Figure 4.6), the prefix *ma-* combines with a noun base to form an adjective.

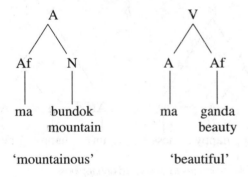

Figure 4.6 Tagalog words with a category-changing prefix.

In these examples, it is the prefix – the morpheme to the left – that determines that the entire word will be an adjective.

Complex derivations

Since derivation can apply more than once, it is possible to create multiple levels of word structure, as shown in Figure 4.7 (overleaf).

The word *activation* is built in several layers, each of which reflects the attachment of an affix to a base of the appropriate type. In the first layer, the affix *-ive* combines with the V base *act* to give an A. (As noted in Table 4.13, *-ive* is the type of affix that converts a V into an A.) In the next layer, the affix *-ate* combines with this A and converts it into a V (*activate*). At this point, the affix *-ion* is added, converting the V into a N and giving the word *activation*. (Mute *e* is deleted in the spelling.)

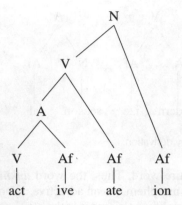

Figure 4.7 A word with a multi-layered internal structure.

In some cases, the internal structure of a complex word is not obvious. The word *unhappiness*, for instance, could apparently be analysed in either of the ways indicated in Figure 4.8.

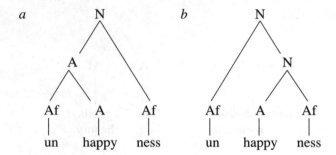

Figure 4.8 Two possible structures for the word *unhappiness*.

By considering the properties of the affixes *un-* and *-ness*, however, it is possible to find an argument that favours Figure 4.8*a* over 4.8*b*. The key observation here is that the prefix *un-* combines quite freely with adjectives, but not with nouns (Table 4.14). (*Uncola* in the old slogans advertising *7-Up* is an interesting exception to this rule and therefore attracts the attention of the reader or listener.)

Table 4.14 The prefix *un-*

un + *Adj*	un + *N*
unable	*unknowledge
unkind	*unhealth
unhurt	*uninjury

This suggests that *un-* must combine with the adjective *happy* before it is converted into a noun by the suffix *-ness*, exactly as depicted in Figure 4.8*a*.

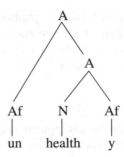

Figure 4.9 The internal structure of the word *unhealthy.*

By contrast, in a word such as *unhealthy* (Figure 4.9), the prefix *un-* can be attached only *after* the suffix *-y* has been added to the root. Otherwise, there would be no adjective category to which it could attach.

The important point to remember here is that even in the case of quite complex words, derivation involves the same steps found in simpler words. In all cases, a derivational affix combines with the appropriate type of base (which may itself have been formed by derivation) and yields a new word of a particular type.

Constraints on derivation	Derivation often does not apply freely to the members of a given category. For instance, the suffix *-ant* (see Table 4.13) can combine only with **Latinate** bases (i.e., bases borrowed from Latin or Romance languages which are traceable back to Latin) – as in *defendant, assailant, contestant, servant,* and so forth. This is why it cannot occur with bases such as *fight* and *teach* (**fightant, *teachant*), which are of native English origin.

Sometimes, a derivational affix is able to attach only to bases with particular phonological properties. A good example of this involves the English suffix *-en* (see Table 4.13), which combines with adjectives to create verbs with a causative meaning ('cause to become x'). As Table 4.15 illustrates, however, there are many adjectives with which *-en* cannot combine.

Table 4.15   Restrictions on the use of *-en*

Acceptable	Unacceptable
whiten	*abstracten
soften	*bluen
madden	*angryen
quicken	*slowen
liven	*greenen

The suffix *-en* is subject to this phonological constraint: it can only combine with a monosyllabic base that ends in an obstruent. Hence it can be added to *white*, which is both monosyllabic and ends in an obstruent, but not to *abstract*, which has two syllables, or to *blue*, which does not end in an obstruent.

Two classes derivational affixes (advanced)

In English, it is common to distinguish between two sets of derivational affixes which we will call class 1 and class 2 (see Tables 4.16 and 4.17). **Class 1** affixes – most of which are Latinate – normally trigger changes in the consonant or vowel segments of the base with which they occur. In addition, they usually also affect the assignment of stress. (As the final two examples help to show, Class 1 affixes often combine with bound roots.)

Table 4.16   Typical effects of Class 1 affixes

Affix	Sample word	Change triggered by affix
-ity	san-ity	vowel in the base changes from /eɪ/ to /æ/ (cf. *sane*)
	public-ity	final consonant of the base changes from /k/ to /s/, stress shifts to second syllable (cf. *públic* vs *publícity.*)
-y	democrac-y	final consonant of the base changes from /t/ to /s/, stress shifts to second syllable (cf. *démocrat* vs *demócracy.*)
-ive	product-ive	stress shifts to second syllable (cf. *próduct*)
-(i)al	part-ial	final consonant of the base changes from /t/ to /ʃ/ (cf. *part*)
-ize	public-ize	final consonant of the base changes from /k/ to /s/ (cf. *public*)
-ious	audac-ious	final consonant of the base changes from /s/ to /ʃ/ (cf. *audac-ity*)
-ion	nat-ion	final consonant of the base changes from /t/ to /ʃ/ (cf. *native*)

Table 4.17   Some typical Class 2 affixes

Affix	Sample word	Change triggered by the affix
-ness	prompt-ness	none
-less	hair-less	none
-ful	hope-ful	none
-ly	quiet-ly	none
-er	defend-er	none
-ish	self-ish	none
-able	commend-able	none

In contrast, **Class 2** affixes (which are mostly native) tend to be phonologically neutral, having no effect on the segmental makeup of the base or on stress assignment.

When Class 1 and Class 2 affixes appear in the same word, the former type of morpheme normally occurs closer to the root than the latter. Thus, while a Class 1 affix can follow another Class 1 affix and while a Class 2 affix can follow a Class 1 or another Class 2 affix, a Class 2 affix does not normally come before a Class 1 affix. The various possibilities are illustrated below in *15)*.

15)

domest-ic-ity	spac-ious-ness	fear-less-ness	*humour-less-ity
root 1 1	root 1 2	root 2 2	root 2 1

Notice that in the form that is ruled out *(*humourlessity)* a Class 1 affix follows a Class 2 affix.

However, the requirement that Class 1 affixes be closer to the root than Class 2 affixes is not an inviolable, cast iron rule. There are a few cases where Class 2 affixes are paradoxically found next to the root, and Class 1 affixes on the periphery of the word, as the examples in *16)* show. (We have already established in Tables 4.16 and 4.17 that *-ity* is a Class 1 affix and *-able* is a Class 2 affix – the latter may be realised as *-abil-* when followed by another suffix).

16)

like-abil-ity	read-abil-ity	accept-abil-ity
root 2 1	root 2 1	root 2 1

(*like-ity-able	*read-ity-able	*accept-ity-able)
root 1 2	root 1 2	root 1 2

3

COMPOUNDING

Another common way to build words in English involves **compounding**, the combination of lexical categories (nouns, adjectives, verbs, or prepositions). With very few exceptions, the resulting compound word is a noun, a verb, or an adjective (Figure 4.10, overleaf). (Possible examples of compound prepositions include the words *into* and *onto*.)

In these and most other compounds, the rightmost morpheme determines the category of the entire word. Thus, *greenhouse* is an N because its rightmost component is an N, *spoon-feed* is a V because *feed* also belongs to this category, and *nationwide* is an A just as *wide* is. The morpheme that determines the category of the entire word is called the **head**.

Noun compounds

Verb compounds

Adjective compounds

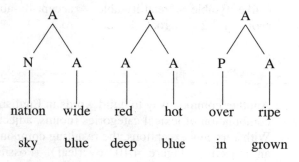

Figure 4.10 Some English compounds.

Once formed, compounds can be combined with other lexical categories to create still larger compounds, as in Figure 4.11.

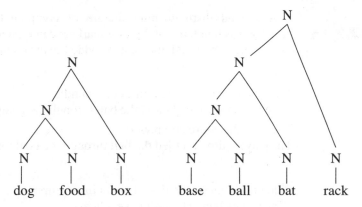

Figure 4.11 Compounds formed from smaller compounds.

In addition, the word formation processes responsible for derivation and compounding can interact with each other. In Figure 4.12, for instance, a compound is formed by combining a simple word (*debate*) with the derived word *abortion*.

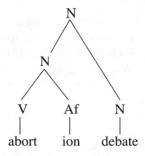

Figure 4.12 The interaction of derivation with compounding.

3.1

Properties of compounds

English orthography is not consistent in representing compounds since they are sometimes written as single words, sometimes with an intervening hyphen, and sometimes as separate words. In terms of pronunciation, however, there is an important generalization to be made. In particular, most A–N compounds are characterized by a more prominent stress on their first component. In non-compounds, the second element is generally stressed, as shown in Table 4.18.

Table 4.18 Compounds versus non-compounds

Compound word		Non-compound expression	
greénhoùse	'an indoor garden'	greèn hoúse	'a house painted green'
bláckboàrd	'a chalkboard	blàck boárd	'a board which is black'
wét suìt	'a diver's costume'	wèt suít	'a suit that is wet'

A second distinguishing feature of compounds in English and other languages is that tense and plural markers can typically not be attached to the first element, although they can be added to the compound as a whole.

17)

Tense on the first element in a compound:
*The player [dropp_ed_ kick] the ball through the goalposts.

Tense on the entire compound:
The player [drop kick]_ed_ the ball through the goalposts.

18)

Plural marking on the first element in a compound is usually disallowed:
*The [fox_es_ hunter] didn't have a licence.
*The [road_s_ map] are expensive.

(There a few exceptions such as *passers-by, parks supervisor* and mothers-in-law.)

Plural on the entire compound is the norm:
The [fox hunter]_s_ didn't have a licence.
The [road map]_s_ are expensive.

The preceding criteria are especially helpful for identifying compounds whose initial component is a verb or a noun. An A–N compound (*greenhouse, wet suit*) can be identified with the help of a different test. As illustrated in the following example, the A in a compound cannot be preceded by a word such as *very*.

19)

Compound with *very*:
*We live next to a very [greenhouse].

Of course, when it is not part of a compound, an adjective can typically be accompanied by this type of word.

20)

very with an adjective that is not part of a compound:
We live next to a very green fence.

3.2

Types of compounds

Compounds are used to express a wide range of semantic relationships in English. Table 4.19 contains examples of just some of the semantic patterns found in N-N compounds.

In most cases the rightmost component of the compound identifies the general class to which the meaning of the entire word belongs. Thus *dog food* is a type of food, a *cave man* is a type of man, and so on. Such compounds, which include all the examples in Table 4.19, are called **endocentric**.

In a smaller number of cases, however, the meaning of the compound does not follow from the meanings of its parts in this way. Thus, a *greenbottle* is not a type of bottle; rather, it is a fly of the genus lucilia. Similarly, a *redneck* is not a type of neck but an ultra conservative, white working-class person; and a *sugar-daddy* is not a type of sugar-coated father but a woman's lover – who is deemed to be both overgenerous and much too old for her. Such compounds are said to be **exocentric**.

Table 4.19 Some N–N compounds

Example	Meaning
steamboat	'a boat powered by steam'
airplane	'a conveyence that travels through the air'
air hose	'a hose that carries air'
air field	'a field where airplanes land'
fire truck	'a vehicle used to put out fires'
fire drill	'a practice in the event of a fire'
bath tub	'a place in which to bathe'
bath towel	'a towel used after bathing'

A very striking difference between endocentric and exocentric compounds shows up in English in those rare cases where the head of the compound has an irregular plural. Consider in this regard the examples in Table 4.20.

Table 4.20 Pluralization in English compounds

In endocentric compounds	In exocentric compounds
oak leaves	Maple Leafs (Toronto's NHL hockey team)
wisdom teeth	sabre tooths (extinct species of tiger)
club feet	bigfoots (members of an extinct tiger species)
policemen	Walkmans (a type of portable audio cassette player)

Notice that the exocentric compounds permit the plural suffix -*s* for words such as *leaf*, *tooth*, *foot*, and *man*, even though these forms require an irregular plural when used elsewhere in the language.

3.3

Compounds in other languages

Although the rules for forming compounds differ from language to language, the practice of combining lexical categories to build a word is very widespread. As Table 4.21 (overleaf), which shows examples from various languages, helps to illustrate, compound nouns are especially common.

With the exception of Tagalog, in which compounds are left-headed, these languages all have compounds in which the rightmost element is the head.

A special type of compounding process involves **incorporation**, the combination of a word (usually, but not always, a noun) with a verb to form a compound verb. Although English does not make use of incorporation, the process is common in other languages.

Table 4.21 Noun compounds in various languages

Korean

kot-elum	isul-pi	mwun-mwul
straight ice	dew rain	eye water
'icicle'	'drizzle'	'tears'

Tagalog

tanod bayan	anak araw	tubig ulan
guard town	child sun	water rain
'policeman'	'albino'	'rainwater'

German

Gast-hof	Wort-bedeutungs-lehre	Fern-seher
guest inn	word meaning theory	far seer
'hotel'	'semantics'	'television'

Finnish

lammas-nahka-turkki	elin-keino-tulo-vero-laki
sheep skin coat	life's means income tax law
'sheepskin coat'	'income tax law'

Tzotzil

piʃ-xól	méʔkʼínobal	ʔóra-tʃón
wrap-head	mother-mist	rightaway-snake
'hat'	'rainbow'	'deadly viper'

The examples in *21)* are from Chukchee, spoken in northeastern Siberia, and the Micronesian language Ponapean. As these examples help to illustrate, incorporation often involves phonological adjustments to the noun and/or the verb.

21)

a. Chukchee

Without incorporation	*With incorporation*
Tə-pelarkən qoraŋə	Tə-qora-pelarkən
I leave reindeer	I-reindeer-leave
'I'm leaving the reindeer'	'I am in the process of reindeer-leaving.'

b. Ponapean

Without incorporation	*With incorporation*
I pahn pereki lohs	I pahn perek-1os
I will unroll mat	I will unroll-mat
'I will unroll the mats.'	'I will engage in mat unrolling.'

4

<table>
<tr><td>

OTHER TYPES OF WORD FORMATION

</td><td>

Derivation and compounding are the two most common types of word formation in English, but they are not the only ones. As the examples presented in this section will show, there are various other ways to create new words.

</td></tr>
</table>

4.1

Conversion

Conversion is a process that assigns an already existing word to a new syntactic category. Even though it does not add an affix, conversion resembles derivation because of the change in category and meaning that it brings about. (For this reason, it is sometimes called **zero derivation**.)

Many examples of conversion involving the creation of a new verb from a noun were given in the first chapter of this book (*beach a boat*, *winter in Mexico*, and so on). Table 4.22 contains examples of the three most common types of conversion to have taken place in the history of English. (As noted in section 1.3 above, nouns derived from verbs sometimes undergo stress shift, which places the stress on the initial syllable. The effects of this phenomenon can be seen in the first three examples of the middle column.)

Table 4.22   Some examples of conversion

V derived from N	N derived from V	V derived from A
finger (a suspect)	(a building) pérmit	dirty (a shirt)
butter (the bread)	(an exciting) cóntest	empty (the box)
ship (the package)	(a new) súrvey	open (a door)
nail (the door shut)	(a brief) report	right (a wrong)
button (the shirt)	(a long) walk	dry (the clothes)

Less common types of conversion can yield an N from an A (*the poor, a gay*) and even a V from a P (*to down a beer, to up the price, to out gay bishops*).

Conversion is usually restricted to words containing a single morpheme, although there are a few exceptions such as *propos-ition* (noun and verb), *refer-ee* (noun and verb), and *dirt-y* (adjective and verb). In some cases, conversion can even apply to a compound, as when the compound N *grandstand* is used as a verb (*he likes to grandstand*) in the sense of 'show off'.

4.2

Clipping

Clipping is a process that shortens a polysyllabic word by deleting one or more syllables. Some of the most common products of clipping are names – *Liz, Ron, Rob, Sue*, and so on. Clipping is especially popular among students. It has yielded forms like *prof* for *professor*, *phys-ed* for *physical education*, *poli-sci* for *political science*, and *burger* for *hamburger*. A number of such abbreviations have been accepted in general usage: *doc, ad, auto, lab, sub, deli, porn, demo*, and *loco*. In some cases, speakers may not even realize that a particular word is a product of clipping: the word *zoo*, for instance, was formed from *zoological garden*. A more recent example of clipping that has rapidly become part of general English vocabulary is *fax*, from *facsimile* (meaning 'exact copy or reproduction').

4.3

Blends

Blends are words that are created from non-morphemic parts of two already existing items. Well-known examples of blends include *brunch* from *break-fast* and *lunch*, *smog* from *smoke* and *fog*, *spam* from *spiced* and *ham*, *telethon* from *telephone* and *marathon*, *aerobicise* from *aerobics* and *exercise*, *chunnel* (for the new underwater link between Britain and the continent) from *channel* and *tunnel*, and *infomercial* from *information* and *commercial*. As these examples show, a blend is usually formed from the first part of one word and the final part of a second one.

Some blends have become so integrated into the standard vocabulary of English that speakers are unaware of their status. For example, relatively few people know that blending has produced *chortle* (coined by author Lewis Carroll) from *chuckle* and *snort*, *motel* from *motor* and *hotel*, *bit* (in computer jargon) from *binary* and *digit*, and *modem* from *modulator* and *demodulator*.

Sometimes, a word is formed by a process that seems to be on the borderline between compounding and blending in that it combines all of one word with part of another. Examples of this in English include *perma-press* (for *permanent-press*), *workaholic*, *medicare*, and *guesstimate*. A more recent creation of this sort is the word *threepeat* in North American English, used to refer to the winning of a championship in three successive years (as in *Fans of the San Francisco 49ers were hoping for a threepeat in the Super Bowl*).

4.4

Backformation

Backformation is a process that creates a new word by removing a real or supposed affix from another word in the language. *Resurrect* was originally formed in this way from *resurrection*. Other backformations in English include *housekeep* from *housekeeper*, *enthuse* from *enthusiasm*, *donate* from *donation*, and *orient* or *orientate* from *orientation*. Sometimes, backformation involves an incorrect assumption about a word's form: for example, the word *pea* was derived from the earlier singular noun *pease* (sometimes written *peas*), whose final /z/ was incorrectly interpreted as the plural suffix.

A major source of backformations in English has been words that end with *-or* or *-er* and have meanings involving the notion of an agent, such as *editor*, *peddler*, *swindler*, and *stoker*. Because hundreds of words ending in these affixes are the result of affixation, it was assumed that these words too had been formed by adding *-or* or *-er* to a verb. By the process of backformation, the verbs *edit*, *peddle*, *swindle*, and *stoke* were formed. In the same manner, with the advent of the personal computer, from the compound noun *wordprocessor* the verb *wordprocess* was obtained. Yet another recent addition, but with a different source, is the verb *lase*, produced by backformation from *laser*, which itself originated as an acronym (see section 4.5).

Backformation continues to produce new words in modern English. Two relatively recent products of this process are the verbs *liaise* from *liaison* and *self-destruct* from *self-destruction*. The even more striking backformation *attrit*, from *attrition*, was often used by military officials during the recent Gulf War to refer to the decimation of Iraqi troops (as in *The enemy is 50 per cent attritted*). Among the backformations noticed recently by the authors are *liposuct* (from *liposuction*, seen in a magazine article) and *orate* (from *oration*, used in a newpaper editorial); the verb *tuit* (from *intuition*) was recently heard on Canadian Broadcasting Corporation radio!

4.5

Acronyms

Acronyms are formed by taking the initial letters of some or all of the words in a phrase or title and reading them as a word. This type of word formation is especially common in names of organizations and scientific terminology. Some examples of acronyms include UNICEF for United Nations International Children's Emergency Fund, NATO for North Atlantic Treaty Organization, ACAS for Advisory, Conciliation and Arbitration Service (in the UK), AIDS for Acquired Immune Deficiency Syndrome. But there are also examples, such as NIMBY, for Not In My Back Yard, that are found in everyday language.

In some cases, speakers may not know that a word in their vocabulary was originally formed as an acronym. Three commonly used words of this type are *radar* (from radio detecting and ranging), *scuba* (self-contained underwater breathing apparatus), and *laser* (light amplification by simulated emission of radiation). The name of the computer language BASIC is an acronym for Beginner's All-purpose Symbolic Instruction Code.

4.6

Onomatopoeia

All languages have words whose sound represents an aspect of the thing that they name. Examples of such **onomatopoeic** words in English include *buzz*, *hiss*, *sizzle*, and *cuckoo*.

Since onomatopoeic words are not exact phonetic copies of noises, their form can differ from language to language, as can be seen in Table 4.23.

Table 4.23 Onomatopoeia across languages

English	Japanese	Tagalog
cock-a-doodle-doo	kokekokko	kuk-kukauk
meow	nya	niyaw
chirp	pii-pii	tiririt
bow-wow	wan-wan	aw-aw

English does not always have an equivalent for the onomatopoeic words found in other languages. The Athapaskan language Slavey, for instance, has the onomatopoeic word *sah sah sah* for 'the sound of a bear walking unseen not far from camp', *ðik* for 'the sound of a knife hitting a tree', and *tɬóòtʃ* for 'the sound of an egg splattering'.

4.7

Other sources

In still other cases a word may be created from scratch, sometimes with the help of a computer. Called **word manufacture** or **coinage**, this phenomenon is especially common in cases where industry requires a new and attractive name for a product. *Kodak*, *Dacron*, *Orlon*, and *Teflon* are examples of product names that are the result of word manufacture. (Notice how the *-on* of the final three words makes them more scientific-sounding, perhaps because an affix of this form occurs in learned words of Greek origin such as *phenomenon* and *automaton*.)

Finally, it is sometimes possible to create new words from names. For example, brand names sometimes become so widely used that they are accepted as generic terms (*kleenex* for 'facial tissue' or *xerox* for 'photocopy'). Scientific terms such as *watt*, *curie*, and *fahrenheit* provide examples of words derived from the names of individuals (often the inventors or discoverers) associated with the things to which they refer.

5

INFLECTION

Virtually all languages have contrasts such as singular versus plural, and past versus non-past. These contrasts are often marked with the help of **inflection**, the modification of a word's form (through affixation, suppletion, internal change or one of the other processes described in section 1.3) to indicate the grammatical subclass to which it belongs. (The base to which an inflectional affix is added is sometimes called a **stem**.) In the case of English nouns, for instance, inflection normally marks the plural subclass by adding the affix *-s*. In the case of verbs, on the other hand, inflection can mark a distinction between the past and non-past subclasses – usually by adding the suffix *-ed* to indicate the past tense, as shown in Table 4.24.

Table 4.24   Inflection for number and tense

Number		Tense	
Singular	*Plural*	*Non-past*	*Past*
apple	apple-s	work	work-ed
car	car-s	jump	jump-ed
dog	dog-s	hunt	hunt-ed

Because inflection applies after the word formation processes discussed in section 4, the plural affix can be added to the output of derivation and compounding (Table 4.25), as well as to a simple noun.

Table 4.25   Number inflection of derived and compound nouns

Derived nouns	*Compound nouns*
[worker]-s	[football]-s
[creation]-s	[outlaw]-s
[kingdom]-s	[blackboard]-s

Similarly, tense affixes can be attached to the output of derivation and compounding, as well as to simple verbs (Table 4.26).

Table 4.26 Tense inflection of derived and compound verbs

Derived verbs	Compound verbs
[hospitalize]-d	[whitewash]-ed
[activate]-d	[off-load]-ed

5.1

Inflection versus derivation

As the preceding examples show, inflection is expressed primarily by means of affixation. Thus, in English the plural is marked by the suffix *-s* (barring a few exceptions such as *man/men*) while the past is generally marked by the suffix *-ed* (although a number of verbs use internal change, as in *sink/sank* and *ride/rode*).

Because inflection and derivation are both marked by affixation, the distinction between the two can be a subtle one and it is sometimes unclear which function a particular affix has. Three criteria are commonly used to help distinguish between inflectional and derivational affixes.

Category change

First, inflection does not change either the grammatical category or the type of meaning found in the word to which it applies.

Figure 4.13 The output of inflection: there is no change in either the category of the base or the type of meaning it denotes.

The form produced by adding the plural suffix *-s* in Figure 4.13*a* is still a noun and has the same type of meaning as the base. Even though *books* differs from *book* in referring to several things rather than just one, the type of thing(s) to which it refers remains the same. Similarly, a past tense suffix such as the one in Figure 4.13*b* indicates that the action took place in the past, but it does not change the word's category (which remains a V), nor does it modify the type of meaning. The verb continues to denote an action regardless of whether the tense is past or non-past.

In contrast, derivational affixes characteristically change the category and/or the type of meaning of the form to which they apply and are therefore said to create a new word. Consider the examples of derivation shown in Figure 4.14.

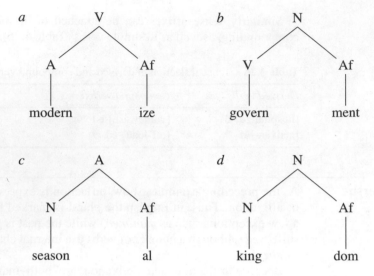

Figure 4.14 The output of derivation: there is a change in the category of the base and/or the type of meaning it denotes.

As Figure 4.14*a* shows, -*ize* makes a verb out of an adjective, changing the type of meaning it expresses from a property (*modern*) to an action (*modernize*). Parallel changes in category and type of meaning are brought about by -*ment* (V to N) and -*al* (N to A). Matters are a little different in the case of -*dom*, which does not bring about a category change (since both the base and the resulting word are N's). However, -*dom* does modify the type of meaning from 'person' (for *king*) to 'place' (for *kingdom*).

Order

A second property of inflectional affixes has to do with the order in which they are combined with a base relative to derivational affixes. As Figure 4.15 illustrates, a derivational affix must combine with the base before an inflectional affix does. (*IA* = inflectional affix; *DA* = derivational affix.)

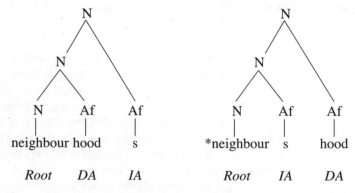

Figure 4.15 The relative positioning of derivational and inflectional affixes: the derivational affix must be closer to the root.

The positioning of inflectional affixes outside derivational affixes in these examples reflects the fact that inflection takes place after derivation.

Productivity

A third criterion for distinguishing between inflectional and derivational affixes has to do with **productivity**, the relative freedom with which they can combine with bases of the appropriate category. Inflectional affixes typically have relatively few exceptions. The suffix -*s*, for example, can combine with virtually any noun that allows a plural form (except for a few exceptions such as *oxen* and *feet*). In contrast, derivational affixes characteristically apply to restricted classes of bases. Thus, -*ize* can combine with only certain adjectives to form a verb.

22)

modern-ize	*new-ize
legal-ize	*lawful-ize
regular-ize	*straight-ize
priorit-ize	*first-ize

In the case of verbs, matters are somewhat more complicated, since many English verbs have irregular past tense forms (*saw*, *left*, *went*, and so on). Nonetheless, the distribution of the inflectional affix -*ed* is still considerably freer than that of a derivational affix such as -*ment*. In Table 4.27, for example, all the verbs can take the regular past tense ending, but only those in the first three rows are able to take the -*ment* suffix.

Table 4.27   Compatibility of bases with -*ed* and with -*ment*

Verb	With -ed	With -ment
confine	confined	confinement
align	aligned	alignment
treat	treated	treatment
arrest	arrested	*arrestment
straighten	straightened	*straightenment
cure	cured	*curement

5.2

English inflectional affixes

With only seven inflectional affixes (all suffixes), English is not a highly inflected language. Some languages have dozens of inflectional affixes and encode contrasts not represented in English (see section 6 for some examples). Table 4.28 (overleaf) gives a complete list of English inflectional affixes.[4]

Regular vs irregular inflection

Although the vast majority of inflection in English involves regular affixation, some words mark inflectional contrasts in less regular ways. This is most obvious in the case of verbs, a considerable number of which (actually, over two hundred) indicate past tense by internal changes of various sorts and even suppletion: *come–came, see–saw, fall–fell, eat–ate, drink–drank, lose–lost, think–thought, is–was, go–went*, and so on.

Table 4.28   English inflectional affixes

Nouns	
Plural -*s*	the books[5]
Verbs	
3rd person sg non-past -*s*	John reads well.
Progressive -*ing*	He is working.
Past tense -*ed*	He worked.
Past participle -*en*/-*ed*	He has eaten/studied.
Adjectives	
Comparative -*er*	the smaller one
Superlative -*est*	the smallest one

There is apparently a fundamental difference in the way in which regular and irregular inflection operates. In particular, it seems that whereas regular inflected forms are constructed as needed in accordance with a general morphological rule (such as 'Add -*ed* to mark the past tense'), irregular forms must be stored permanently in the language user's memory. Some evidence of this difference comes from studies of how long it takes speakers to utter the past tense form of a verb when presented with the base. For irregular forms, there is a correlation between response time and frequency of the verb: thus it takes less time to give the past form of frequent verbs such as *see* and *find* than it does for infrequent verbs such as *stride* and *bid* – presumably because it takes longer to locate infrequently used forms in one's memory. In the case of regular verbs, in contrast, response time is independent of frequency: because the past tense is formed by a regular rule, there is no need to 'look up' the word in the mental dictionary and all verbs can be handled with equal speed.

6

FURTHER EXAMPLES OF INFLECTION

6.1

Number

In this section, we will consider several types of grammatical information that are commonly expressed in human language with the help of inflectional affixes.

Number is the morphological category that expresses contrasts involving countable quantities. The simplest number contrast consists of a two-way distinction between **singular** (one) and **plural** (more than one). This is the contrast found in English, where a noun usually takes the suffix -*s* if it refers to two or more entities.

Even this basic distinction is not found in all languages, however. In Nancowry (spoken in India's Nicobarese Islands), for example, number is not marked on nouns at all. A sentence such as *23)* is therefore ambiguous since *nɔ̄t* 'pig' can refer to one or more pigs.

23)

sák   nɔ́t ʔin ciʔə́j.
spear pig the we
'We speared the pig(s).'

In Inuktitut (spoken in northern Canada), on the other hand, there is a three-way number contrast involving singular, dual (two and only two), and plural (more than two).

24)

iglu	'a house'
igluk	'two houses'
iglut	'three or more houses'

6.2

Noun class

Some languages divide nouns into two or more inflectional classes, based on shared phonological and/or semantic properties. The Bantu language SiSwati, for instance, makes use of prefixes to distinguish among more than a dozen noun classes, some of which are given in Table 4.29. (Tone is not represented in these examples.)

Table 4.29   Some noun classes in SiSwati

Prefix	Description of class	Example	
um(u)-	persons	um-fana	'boy'
li-	body parts, fruit	li-dvolo	'knee'
s(i)-	instruments	si-tja	'plate'
in-	animals	in-ja	'dog'
bu-	abstract properties	bu-bi	'evil'
pha-	locations	pha-ndle	'outside'

The gender contrasts of modern French also make up a type of noun classification system. Although the term *gender* is used by linguists to mean 'kind' rather than 'sex', there is a partial correlation between the French gender classes and the sex of the objects to which nouns can refer. Thus *frère* 'brother' is masculine while *soeur* 'sister' is feminine. However, most inanimate nouns are classified more or less arbitrarily: *lune* 'moon' is feminine, but *monde* 'world' is masculine. Even some nouns referring to animate entities seem to be classified arbitrarily since German *Mädchen* 'young girl' is neuter, not feminine, and French *victime* 'victim' is feminine regardless of whether the person referred to is male or female.

Noun class can be marked in a variety of ways. In some languages, the determiner is inflected to indicate the class of the noun. For example, French uses the definite determiner *le* for masculine, singular nouns and *la* for feminine, singular ones. In other languages, inflectional affixes rather than determiners can be used to indicate the gender class of the noun. Russian, for instance, uses one set of suffixes for nouns in the feminine, animate class and another set for nouns in the masculine, animate class. Table 4.30 shows the gender endings for nouns that function as subject of a sentence.

Table 4.30   Russian gender suffixes

Class	Suffix	Example	
Masculine	-ø	dom	'house'
Feminine	-a	ulic-a	'street'
Neuter	-o	tʃuvstv-o	'sensation'

6.3

Case

Still another type of inflectional contrast associated with nouns in many languages involves **case** – a category that encodes information about an element's grammatical role (subject, direct object, and so on). In Modern English, this information is expressed largely through word order and the use of prepositions.

25)

Anna composed a song on the bus.

In this sentence, the subject *Anna* occurs to the left of the verb and the direct object *a song* appears to the right, while the element expressing location (*the bus*) is preceded by the preposition *on*. In many languages, however, these distinctions are marked by inflectional affixes. As an illustration of this, consider the set of related nominal forms (called a **nominal paradigm** or **declension**) for the Turkish word *ev* 'house' given in Table 4.31.

Table 4.31   Turkish case

Case	Form	Type of element that it marks
Nominative	ev-ø	the subject
Accusative	ev-i	the direct object
Dative	ev-e	the recipient
Genitive	ev-in	a possessor
Locative	ev-de	a place or location
Ablative	ev-den	direction away from somewhere

The following sentences illustrate the uses of these case suffixes.

26)

a.   Adam-ø   ev-i   Ahmed-e   göster-di.
       Man-Nom house-Ac   Ahmed-Dat   show-past.
       'The man showed the house to Ahmed.'

b.   Ev-in   rengi-ø   māvidir
       house-Gen   colour-Nom   blue
       'The house's colour is blue.'

    c.   Adam-ø   ev-de   kaldɪ.
        man-Nom house-Loc stayed
        'The man stayed in the house.'

    d.   Adam-ø   ev-den   tʃikti.
        man-Nom house-Abl went
        'The man went from the house.'

Notice how in the final sentence, for example, *Adam* 'man' bears the zero ending of the nominative to indicate that it is subject while *ev* 'house' bears the ablative suffix indicating the place from which the man went.

The contrasts represented in the Turkish case system are intermediate in complexity compared to Finnish, which has fifteen distinct case categories, and Rumanian, which has only two contrasts.

Ergative case marking

Some languages make use of case marking to encode grammatical contrasts quite unlike those found in familiar European languages. In the Australian language Yidin[y], for instance, the case system groups together the subject of an **intransitive** verb and the direct object of a **transitive** verb (both of which receive a zero ending) while using a special marker (*-ngu*) for the subject of a transitive verb. (A verb is transitive if it takes a direct object and intransitive otherwise.)

27)

    a.   Yidin[y] sentence with a transitive verb:
        Wagudya-ngu dyugi-ø gundal.
        man-Erg   tree-Abs is-cutting.
        'The man is cutting the tree.'

    b.   Yidin[y] sentence with an intransitive verb:
        Wagudya-ø gundal
        man-Abs   is-cutting
        'The man is cutting.'

In this type of system, the case associated with the subject of the transitive verb, *wagudya* 'man' *27a)*, is called the **ergative**. The case associated with the direct object (*dyugi* 'tree' in the first sentence) and with the subject of an intransitive verb (*wagudya* 'man' in the second sentence) is called the **absolutive**.

Ergative case marking is found in a varied set of languages, including Basque (in north-west Spain and south-west France), Tagalog (in the Philippines), Georgian (in the Caucasus), Inuktitut (in northern Canada and Greenland), and Halkomelem (on the west coast of Canada). It is also found in many Australian languages such as Dyirbal, Warungu, and Yalarnnga.

Ergative case marking is far less common than the nominative–accusative pattern, which groups together the subjects of transitive and intransitive verbs, distinguishing them from direct objects. This is the pattern found in Turkish (as noted previously), German, Russian, Japanese, Korean, and many other languages.

English nouns and pronouns

At one time, English nouns and determiners (words such as *the*) were inflected for case (see discussion in Chapter 8). In modern English, however, the only remnant of this case system is the genitive -*'s*, used to mark possessors (*the man's book*). (Recall that in current treatments of English grammar this form is normally referred to as a clitic. See section 1.3 above.) Neither nouns nor determiners are inflected to distinguish grammatical roles such as subject and direct object.

28)

a.   the man in subject position
     The man smiled.
     The man took the book.

b.   the man in direct object position
     A noise frightened the man.

However, pronouns exhibit a more elaborate set of contrasts, distinguishing a nominative (*I*, *they*, *he*, *she*), an accusative (*me*, *them*, *him*, *her*), and a genitive (*my*, *their*, *his*, *hers*).

29)

Nominative: *He* smiled.
              He took the book.
Accusative: A noise frightened *him*.
Genitive: Sue took *his car*.

Since the same form of the pronoun is used for the subject of an intransitive verb (*smile*) and the subject of a transitive verb (*take*) and since this form differs from the one used for direct objects, these contrasts follow the nominative–accusative pattern.

6.4

Person and number agreement

A widely attested type of verbal inflection in human language involves **person** – a category that typically distinguishes among the first person (the speaker), the second person (the addressee), and the third person (anyone else). In many languages, the verb is marked for both the person and number (singular or plural) of the subject. When one category is inflected to mark properties (such as person and number) of another, the first category is said to **agree** with the second.

A very rich system of agreement is found in Italian, which exhibits certain contrasts in the present tense (see Table 4.32). (The set of inflected forms associated with a verb is called a **verbal paradigm** or a **conjugation**.)

Table 4.32   Italian present tense paradigm

	Singular		*Plural*	
1st person	parl-<u>o</u>	'I speak'	parl-<u>iamo</u>	'we speak'
2nd person	parl-<u>i</u>	'you speak'	parl-<u>ate</u>	'you speak'
3rd person	parl-<u>a</u>	'she, he speaks'	parl-<u>ano</u>	'they speak'

Because the inflectional markers provide so much information about the person and number of the subject phrase, this element need not be overtly present in Italian. Thus, *parla italiano* 'speaks Italian' can make up a complete sentence. The permissibility of 'understood subjects' in such sentences is a common feature of languages with rich verbal inflection.

Modern English has a much more impoverished system of person and number agreement in the verb, and Table 4.33 shows that an inflectional affix is used only for the third person singular in the non-past tense.

Table 4.33   English verbal paradigm

	Singular	*Plural*
1st person	I speak	we speak
2nd person	you speak	you speak
3rd person	she, he, or it speaks	they speak

Except for commands, formal English differs from Italian and many other languages with rich verbal inflection in requiring a complete sentence to have an overtly expressed subject.

30)
*Speaks English.

6.5

Tense

Tense is the category that encodes the time of an event with reference to the moment of speaking. Thus, the past tense is used with verbs denoting an action that occurs prior to the moment of speaking.

There are many different types of tense systems in the languages of the world. In terms of inflection, for example, English makes a two-way contrast between past (marked by the inflectional suffix *-ed* in regular verbs) and the non-past (unmarked). Figure 4.16 shows that the non-past form of the verb can be used, in certain circumstances, for both present and future events.

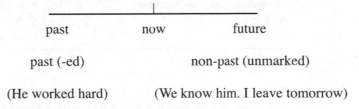

Figure 4.16   Tense in English.

In the Australian language Dyirbal, in contrast, there is a two-way distinction between future and non-future. As the following examples show, the latter form can be used for both present and past events.

31)

a. Future: *b.* Non-future:
   bani-ɲ   bani-ɲu
   'will come'   'came, is coming'

In Spanish and Lithuanian, on the other hand, inflectional endings are used to express a three-way past–present–future contrast.

32)

	Spanish:	Lithuanian:
a.	Juan habl-ó bien.	Dirb-au.
	'John spoke well.'	'I worked.'
b.	Juan habl-a bien.	Dirb-u.
	'John speaks well.'	'I work.'
c.	Juan habl-ar-á bien.	Dirb-siu.
	'John will speak well.'	'I will work.'

A still richer system of contrasts is found in ChiBemba (a Bantu language of Zambia) which uses its inflectional system to distinguish degrees of pastness and futurity. (In the examples in Table 4.34, the diacritics mark tone; affixes expressing tense contrasts are underlined.)

Table 4.34   Tense in ChiBemba

Past	Future
Remote past (before yesterday)	Remote future (after tomorrow)
ba-àlí-bomb-ele	ba-ká-bomba
'They worked.'	'They'll work.'
Removed past (yesterday)	Removed future (tomorrow)
ba-àlíí-bomba	ba-kà-bomba
'They worked.'	'They'll work.'
Near past (earlier today)	Near future (later today)
ba-àcí-bomba	ba-léé-bomba
'They worked.'	'They'll work.'
Immediate past (just happened)	Immediate future (very soon)
ba-á-bomba	ba-áláá-bomba
'They worked.'	'They'll work.'

Summing up

This chapter is concerned with the structure and formation of **words** in human language. Many words consist of smaller formative elements, called **morphemes**. These elements can be classified in a variety of ways (**free** versus **bound**, **root** versus **affix**, **prefix** versus **suffix**) and can be combined and modified under various conditions to build words. Operations that can combine and modify morphemes include **affixation**, **cliticization**, **internal change**, **suppletion**, and **reduplication**.

The two basic types of word formation in English are **derivation** and **compounding**. Less common types of word formation include **conversion**, **blending**, **clipping**, and **backformation**. Words may also be **inflected** to mark grammatical contrasts in **number**, **gender**, **case**, **person**, and **tense**.

Notes

1   In nonstandard English dialects like Cockney and the Lancashire dialect where word-initial *h* is dropped (leaving behind a vowel at the start of a word), people are likely to say and write [ən æt] *an hat* and [ən haʊs] *an house*.

2   An interesting fact about these forms is that although *ceive* and *mit* have no identifiable meaning, they undergo certain alternations that suggest that they have a special status in the grammar. Thus, the *ceive* in words like *receive* and *deceive* becomes *cept* in *receptive* and *deceptive* while the *mit* in words like *submit* and *permit* becomes *miss* in *submissive* and *permissive*. For further discussion of this point, see *Word Formation in Generative Grammar* by Mark Aronoff (Cambridge, Mass.: MIT Press, 1976).

3   There are some exceptions to this generalization, including *delouse* and *enrage*, in which the rightmost element is a noun but the prefix determines that the whole word is a verb.

4   There are three *-ing* affixes in English, one inflectional and two derivational. Inflectional *-ing* combines with a verb to give another verb, as in *He is breathing*. Derivational *-ing* combines with a verb to give a noun (*The breathing of the runners*) or an adjective (*the sleeping giant*) – see Table 4.13. There are also two types of *-en/-ed* suffix, one inflectional as noted in Table 4.28 and the other derivational. The latter suffix converts verbs into adjectives so that they can appear in structures such as the following.
a.   The *stolen* money
b.   The *escaped* convict

5   In traditional descriptions of English, normally the possessive *-'s* (as in *John's book*) is called a suffix. But for the reasons given on pages 140–1 above we are treating it as a clitic in this book. This is the standard practice today.

Sources

The estimate that the average high school student knows 60,000 'basic' words come from *The Language Instinct* by S. Pinker (London: Allen Lane: The Penguin Press), p. 150. The introduction to words and morphemes draws on the classic treatments found in L. Bloomfield's *Language* (New York: Holt, Rinehart & Winston, 1933), Gleason's *An Introduction to Descriptive Linguistics* (cited below), and C.F. Hockett's *A Course in Modern Linguistics* (New York: Macmillan, 1958). The discussion of word formation seeks to portray those aspects of recent and current work that represent widely accepted views and are appropriate for presentation in an introductory textbook. Much of this work is summarized in the books by Jensen, Katamba, and Spencer (cited below) and the many references cited therein.

The Arabic examples in section 1.3 are from p. 17 of the book by Spencer cited below. The tier-based analysis of Arabic word structure is based on work by John McCarthy, including his article 'A prosodic theory of nonconcatenative morphology', *Linguistic Inquiry* 12: 373–418 (1981). The facts concerning the requirement that *-ant* combine with a base of Latin origin (section 2.2) are noted on p. 71 of the book by Katamba cited below.

The example of Chukchee compounding in section 3.3 is from p. 15 of the book by Spencer, cited below. The Ponapean example is from p. 212 of *A Ponapean Reference Grammar* by Kenneth Rehg (Honolulu: University of Hawaii Press, 1981).

The examples of conversion given in section 4.1 come largely from the discussion in the books by Jensen (pp. 92–3) and Bauer (pp. 229–30) cited below. The data on Slavey onomatopoeia is from 'Slavey expressive terms' by M. Pepper, *Kansas Working Papers in Linguistics* 10(2): 85–100 (1985).

The definition of stem introduced in section 5 is from the article by S. Anderson cited below (p. 163). The discussion of the difference between regular and irregular inflection draws on information from 'Rules of language' by S. Pinker, *Science* 253: 530–35 (August 1991). The Nancowry example in the section on number was provided by R. Radhakrishnan. The data in the section on tense come principally from 'Tense, aspect and mood' by S. Chung and A. Timberlake in *Language Typology and Syntactic Description,* Vol. 3, edited by T. Shopen (Cambridge: Cambridge University Press, 1985), pp. 202–58.

The exercises for this chapter were prepared by Joyce Hildebrand. The data in problem 7 are from *Writing Transformational Grammars* by A. Koutsoudas (New York: McGraw-Hill, 1966).

Recommended reading

Anderson, Stephen. 1982. 'Where is morphology?', *Linguistic Inquiry* 13: 571–612.

Anderson, Stephen. 1988. 'Morphological theory.' In *Linguistics: The Cambridge Survey*. Vol. I. Edited by F. Newmeyer, pp. 145–91. Cambridge: Cambridge University Press.

Bauer, L. 1983. *English Word-Formation.* Cambridge: Cambridge University Press.

Gleason, H. 1955. *An Introduction to Descriptive Linguistics.* New York: Holt, Rinehart & Winston.

Jensen, John. 1990. *Morphology: Word Structure in Generative Grammar.* Amsterdam: John Benjamins Publishing Co.

Katamba, Francis. 1993. *Morphology.* London: Macmillan.

Spencer, Andrew. 1991. *Morphological Theory.* Oxford: Blackwell.

Appendix: How to identify morphemes in unfamiliar languages

One part of morphological analysis involves identifying morphemes in unfamiliar languages and determining the nature of the information they carry. (A number of the problems in the set of exercises at the end of this chapter will give you an opportunity to practise this type of analysis.) The key procedure to adopt in working on this sort of problem can be stated simply as follows:

- Identify recurring forms and match them with recurring meanings. Consider in this regard the small sample of data from Turkish, consisting of four words along with their English translations (Table 4.35). (In actual practice, of course, a data sample would also include sentences and it might well be unclear at first where the word boundaries should be placed.)

Table 4.35   Some Turkish words

/mumlar/	'candles'
/toplar/	'guns'
/adamlar/	'men'
/kitaplar/	'books'

You will note that the form /lar/ occurs in all four items in our sample. From the translations of these items, we can see that there is also a feature of meaning – namely, plurality – that is present in all four cases. Using the procedure just stated, we therefore hypothesize that /lar/ is the morpheme marking plurality in Turkish. Once this has been determined, we can then infer that /mum/ in /mumlar/ is also a morpheme (presumably with the meaning 'candle'), that /top/ in /toplar/ is a morpheme (with the meaning 'gun'), and so on. A larger sampling of Turkish data would confirm the correctness of these inferences.

In doing morphological analysis in unfamiliar languages, there are a number of pitfalls to avoid. For the type of exercise normally used at the introductory level, the following guidelines should prove especially useful.

- Do not assume that the morpheme order in the language you are analysing is the same as in English. In Korean, for example, morphemes indicating location (the rough equivalent of 'at', 'in', and so forth) follow rather than precede the noun (hence, *hakkyo-eyse* is literally 'school at').

- Do not assume that every semantic contrast expressed in English will also be manifested in the language you are analysing. In Turkish, for example, there is no equivalent for English *the* and *a*. In Mandarin Chinese, the same pronoun form can be used to refer to a male or a female (there is no *he–she* distinction).

- Do not assume that every contrast expressed in the language you are analysing is manifested in English. For example, some languages distinguish more than two number categories (Inuktitut distinguishes singular, dual, and plural; see section 6.1) and some languages make multiple tense contrasts (ChiBemba, discussed in section 6.5, has an eight-way distinction).

- Remember that a morpheme can have more than one form (allomorph). Just as the English plural suffix can be realized as /s/, /z/, or /ɪz/ (section 1.1), so morphemes in other languages can have more than one realization. For example, further study of Turkish would reveal that the plural suffix in this language can also be realized as /ler/, depending on the vowel in the base to which the suffix is attached. (This type of variation is discussed in more detail in Chapter 6.)

Questions

1. Consider the following words and answer the questions below.

a) fly	f) reuse	k) spiteful	p) preplan
b) desks	g) triumphed	l) suite	q) optionality
c) untie	h) delight	m) fastest	r) prettier
d) tree	i) justly	n) deform	s) mistreat
e) dislike	j) payment	o) disobey	t) premature

i) For each word, determine whether it is simple or complex.

ii) Circle all of the bound morphemes. Underline all of the roots.

2. All but one of the following Persian words consist of more than one

morpheme. (*Note*: *xar* means 'buy' and *-id* designates the past tense.)

a) xaridam   'I bought'
b) xaridi   'you (sg) bought'
c) xarid   '(he) bought'
d) naxaridam   'I did not buy'
e) namixaridand   'they were not buying'
f) naxaridim   'we did not buy'
g) mixarid   '(he) was buying'

i) Try to match each of the following notions with a morpheme in the Persian data.

a) I   e) they
b) you (sg)   f) not
c) we   g) was/were + -ing (continuos)
d) you (pl)

ii) How would you say the following in Persian?

a) They were buying.
b) You (sg) did not buy.
c) You (sg) were buying.

3. The following Turkish data involves allomorphic variation.

a) lokanta 'a restaurant'   lokantada 'in/at a restaurant'
b) kapɯ 'a door'   kapɯda 'in/at a door'
c) randevu 'an appointment'   randevuda 'in/at an appointment'
d) baʃ 'a head'   baʃta 'in/at a head'
e) kitap 'a book'   kitapta 'in/at a book'
f) koltuk 'an armchair'   koltukta 'in/at an armchair'
g) taraf 'a side'   tarafta 'in/at a side'

i) Does the Turkish morpheme meaning 'in/at' have more than one allomorph?

ii) If so, what are the allomorphs? Describe their distribution. Make your statement as general as possible.

4. Consider the following words.

a) desks   e) triumphed   i) preplan (V)   m) optionality
b) untie   f) ageless   j) fastest   n) prettier
c) invalid (A)   g) justice   k) reuse   o) mistreat
d) dislike (V)   h) payment   l) disobey   p) preview (V)

i) Draw a tree structure for each word.

ii) For the word *optionality*, what is the base for the affix *-ion*? What is the base for the suffix *-ity*? Are either of these bases also the root for the entire word? If so, which one?

5. Each of the following columns illustrates a different morphological process.

Column 1	*Column II*	*Column III*
a) mouse/mice	f) go/went	k) récord/recórd
b) ride/rode	g) is/was	l) ímport/impórt

c) take/took	h) good/better	m) cónvict/convíct
d) man/men	i) she/her	n) ímprint/imprínt
e) eat/ate	j) am/are	o) díspute/dispúte

i) What morphological process is at work in column I? column II? column III?

ii) Describe in your own words the difference between the process exemplified in column I versus that in column II.

iii) Think of at least one more English example to add to each column.

6. The following words can be either nouns or verbs.

a) record	f) outline	k) report
b) journey	g) convict	l) outrage
c) exchange	h) imprint	m) answer
d) remark	i) record	n) import
e) surprise	j) retreat	o) cripple

i) For each word, determine whether stress placement can be used to make the distinction between noun and verb.

ii) Think of two more English examples illustrating the process of stress shift to mark a category distinction.

7. The following Samoan data illustrate one of the morphological processes discussed in this chapter.

a) mate	'he dies'	mamate	'they die'
b) nofo	'he stays'	nonofo	'they stay'
c) galue	'he works'	galulue	'they work'
d) tanu	'he buries'	tatanu	'they bury'
e) alofa	'he loves'	alolofa	'they love'
f) taoto	'he lies'	taooto	'they lie'
g) atama?i	'he is intelligent'	atamama?i	'they are intelligent'

i) What morphological process is illustrated by these data?

ii) Describe how this process works.

iii) If 'he is strong' in Samoan is *malosi*, how would you say 'they are strong' in Samoan?

8. The following data from Agta (spoken in the Philippines) illustrate a specific type of affix.

a) dakal 'big'	dumakal 'grow big, grow up'
b) darág 'red'	dumarág 'redden'
c) furáw 'white'	fumuráw 'become white'

i) What is the affix in Agta meaning 'become X'?

ii) What type of affix is it?

iii) Describe its placement.

9. The following words from Chamorro, spoken in Guam and the Mariana Islands, illustrate some of the morphological processes described in this chapter.

I. *Root*	*Derived word*
a) adda 'mimic'	aadda 'mimicker'

b)   kanno 'eat'   kakanno 'eater'
c)   tuge 'write'   tutuge 'writer'

II.   *Root*   *Derived word*
d)   atan 'look at'   atanon 'nice to look at'
e)   sangan 'tell'   sanganon 'tellable'
f)   guaiya 'love'   guaiyayon 'lovable'
g)   tulaika 'exchange'   tulaikayon 'exchangeable'
h)   chalek 'laugh'   chalekon 'laughable'
i)   ngangas 'chew'   ngangason 'chewable'

III. *Root*   *Derived word*
j)   nalang 'hungry'   nalalang 'very hungry'
k)   dankolo 'big'   dankololo 'very big'
l)   metgot 'strong'   metgogot 'very strong'
m)   bunita 'pretty'   bunitata 'very pretty'

i)   What morphological process is involved in I? in II? in III?

ii) Do any changes in lexical category take place in I? in II? in III?

iii) Formulate a general statement as to how the derived words in I are formed. Do the same for III.

iv) Does the affix in II have more than one allomorph? If so, what are the allomorphs? What is their distribution?

10. In this chapter, an argument was presented in favour of the following structure for the word *unhappiness.*

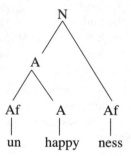

Using the same type of argument, justify tree structures for the words *incomprehensible*, *redisposal* and *disestablishment*. (*Hint*: This will involve determining the type of syntactic category with which the affixes in these words can combine; see Table 4.13.)

11. In English, the suffix *-er* can be added to a place name. Examine the words in the two columns below.

Column A	*Column B*
Londoner	*Glasgower
New Yorker	*Denverer
Berliner	*Sydneyer
Dubliner	*Australiaer
Newfoundlander	*Victoriaer

Winnipeger	*Calcuttaer
New Zealander	*Bristoler

a) In general terms, what does the suffix *-er* mean in these words?

b) How is this *-er* different in meaning from the *-er* found in the words *skater* and *walker*?

c) State the constraint on the distribution of *-er* illustrated above in your own words.

d) Does this constraint also apply to the type of *-er* used in the word *skater*? (*Hint*: What would you call 'one who discovers' or 'one who ploughs'?)

12. The following words have all been formed by compounding. Draw a tree structure for each word. (*Hint*: If you are in doubt as to the lexical category of the compound, remember that the category of the head determines the category of the word.)

a)	football	i)	tree trunk	q)	milestone
b)	yardstick	j)	lead free	r)	coffee table
c)	sunbather	k)	supermarkets	s)	flower-power
d)	in-crowd	l)	girlfriend	t)	blueprint
e)	fastfood	m)	city centre	u)	Greenpeace
f)	software	n)	failsafe	v)	space ship
g)	freeze-dry	o)	potato peel	w)	brain dead
h)	overbook	p)	bitter-sweet	x)	kill-joy

13. In this chapter, several ways of identifying compounds were discussed. Using the tests given in the left-hand column, verify the compound status of the compounds in the right-hand column.

	Test	*Compound*
a)	past tense	blowdry
b)	compatible with *very*	loudmouth
c)	plural	headlamp
d)	stress	poorhouse

14. Examine the following compounds and answer the questions below.

	A		B
a)	bigmouth	h)	cutthroat
b)	skinhead	i)	pickpocket
c)	kill-joy	j)	spoilsport
d)	bath towel	k)	crybaby
e)	death blow	l)	brain-dead
f)	bird-brain	m)	blow-dry
g)	Walkman	n)	armchair

i) For each of the compounds in column A, determine whether they are endocentric or exocentric.

ii) How do you form the plural of *Walkman* and *bigmouth*? (*Hint*: See Table 4.17. Also, pay special attention to the pronunciation of *mouth*. Is it any different here from what it is when it is used as an independent word?)

15. The words in column 2 have been created from the corresponding word in column 1. Indicate the morphological process responsible for the creation of each word in column 2.

Column 1		Column 2
a)	automation	→	automate
b)	humid	→	humidifier
c)	information, entertainment	→	infotainment
d)	love, seat	→	loveseat
e)	prógress	→	progréss
f)	typographical error	→	typo
g)	aerobics, marathon	→	aerobathon
h)	act	→	deactivate
i)	International, police	→	Interpol
j)	perambulator	→	pram
k)	(a) comb	→	comb (your hair)
l)	beef, buffalo	→	beefalo
m)	Action on Smoking and Health	→	ASH
n)	megabyte	→	meg
o)	teleprinter, exchange	→	telex
p)	influenza	→	flu
q)	They have finished	→	They've finished

16. Here are five instances where a new word is needed. Create a word for each of these definitions using the word formation process suggested. Fill in the blanks with your new words.
    a) Use an acronym . . . for your uncle's second oldest brother.
       'We visited my _____ at Christmas.'
    b) Use onomatopoeia . . . for the sound of a coffee percolator at work.
       'I can't concentrate because my perc is _____ing.'
    c) Use conversion . . . for wrapping something breakable in bubbles.
       'You'd better _____ that ornament or else it might break.'
    d) Use a compound . . . for the annoying string of cheese stretching from a slice of hot pizza to one's mouth.
       'As the _____ hung precariously from my lips, our eyes met!'
    e) Use backformation . . . for the action of backformation.
       'We had to _____ words in Linguistics today.'

17. Create new words for each of the following situations.
    a) Use a product name . . . for the act of scrubbing with Ajax.
       'I _____ed the tub after giving Fido a bath.'
    b) Use a proper name . . . for the act of breaking dishes, which Jonathan does regularly.
       'He's going to _____ all of my best dishes.'
    c) Use clipping . . . for a course in ovinology (the study of sheep).
       'Have you done your _____ assignment yet?'
    d) Use derivation . . . for being able to be contacted.
       'The counsellor is not very _____.'

e) Use a blend . . . for the name of a cafeteria that serves only chocolate beverages, cakes, icecreams etc.
   'Let's meet later at the _____ for a drink.'

18. Determine whether the words in each of the following groups are related to one another by processes of inflection or derivation.
    a) go, goes, going, gone
    b) discover, discovery, discoverer, discoverable, discoverability
    c) lovely, lovelier, loveliest
    d) inventor, inventor's, inventors, inventors'
    e) democracy, democrat, democratic, democratize

19. The following sentences contain both derivational and inflectional affixes. Underline all of the derivational affixes and circle the inflectional affixes.
    a) The farmer's cows escaped.
    b) It was raining.
    c) Those socks are inexpensive.
    d) Jill needs the newer copy.
    e) Fido has a broken leg.
    f) The strongest rower won.
    g) The pit bull has bitten the cyclist.
    h) She quickly closed the book.
    i) The dramatization went well.
    j) The dispute was eventually resolved after protracted negotiations.

20. (*Advanced.*) Each of the following corpora of data illustrates inflection of some type.

    I. GERMAN
    a) Der Mann ist krank.
       'The man is sick.'
    b) Die Frau ist krank.
       'The woman is sick.'

    II. GREEK
    c) o erɤatis fonazi ton andra
       'The worker calls the man.'
    d) o andras plironi ton erɤati
       'The man pays the worker.'
    e) o andras ine afstiros
       'The man is strict.'

    III. BASQUE
    f) Aitak bazuen fabrike aundi.
       father owned factory big
       'Father owned a big factory.'
    g) Aite izango da.
       'Father will be (there).'

    IV. ITALIAN
    h) le zíe sono amerikáne.
       'The aunts are American.'

i) gli zíi sono studiósi.
    'The uncles are studious.'
j) la zía e studiósa.
    'The aunt is studious.'
k) lo zío e amerikáno.
    'The uncle is American.'

V. ENGLISH
l) I am biting my tongue.
m) You are biting your tongue.
n) She is biting her tongue.

i) What type of nominal inflection do the German sentences illustrate?

ii) What type of nominal inflection is exemplified in the Greek data? It is marked morphologically in two ways. Identify both ways.

iii) Of the two patterns of case-marking discussed in the chapter, which does the Greek data show?

iv) How is the pattern of case-marking different in Basque from that of Greek?

v) In the Italian data, there are four different forms of the word meaning 'the'. Name two inflectional contrasts that are present in each of those four forms.

vi) What type of verbal inflection is illustrated in the Italian sentences?

vii) Examine the English data in V. What types of verbal inflection are present on the verb 'to be'? What types of nominal inflection are present on the six pronouns in these sentences?

Syntax: the analysis of sentence structure

William O'Grady

… the game is to say something new with old words.

Ralph Waldo Emerson (*Journals,* 1849)

One of the main themes of this book is that language use involves an intricate system of largely subconscious grammatical knowledge. Nowhere is this more obvious than in the study of how words are combined to form sentences. In this chapter we will consider the system of rules and categories that underlies sentence formation in human language. This component of the grammar is called **syntax**.

Like the other linguistic systems considered in this book, the syntactic component of the grammar is both creative and systematic. As noted in Chapter 1, speakers of a language are able to combine words in novel ways, forming sentences that they have neither heard nor seen before. However, not just any combination of words will give a well-formed sentence. English speakers recognize that the pattern in *1)* is not permissible even though the same words can be combined in a different way to form the acceptable structure in *2)*.

1)

*House painted student a the.

2)

A student painted the house.

We say that a sentence is **grammatical** if speakers judge it to be a possible sentence of their language. Thus, example *2)* is a grammatical sentence of English, but *1)* is not.

This chapter will focus on the 'architecture' of grammatical sentences, with an emphasis on the manner in which words are combined to form various types of sentences. Section 1 introduces some of the most common categories of words found in language as well as some simple rules that govern the organization of these categories into larger structural units. Subsequent sections describe other aspects of sentence structure, using examples and phenomena drawn from English and other languages.

Contemporary linguistic research has yet to reach a consensus about precisely how sentence structure should be analysed and a variety of quite different possibilities are currently being explored. This chapter will introduce a simple version of **transformational syntax**, currently the most popular and best known approach to syntactic analysis. Although many linguists disagree with various features of this approach, it is very widely used in linguistics and other disciplines concerned with language (especially cognitive science). For this reason, it is the usual point of departure for introductions to the study of sentence structure. Section 6 provides a brief discussion of some alternatives to transformational analysis.

1

CATEGORIES AND STRUCTURE

A fundamental fact about words in all human languages is that they can be grouped together into a relatively small number of classes, called **syntactic categories**. This classification refects a variety of factors, including the type of meaning that words express, the type of affixes that they take, and the type of structures in which they can occur.

1.1

Word-level categories

Table 5.1 provides examples of the word-level categories that are most central to the study of syntax.

Table 5.1 Syntactic categories

Lexical categories	Examples
Noun (N)	Harry, boy, wheat, policy, moisture, bravery
Verb (V)	arrive, discuss, melt, hear, remain, dislike
Adjective (A)	good, tall, old, intelligent, beautiful, fond
Preposition (P)	to, in, on, near, at, by
Adverb (Adv)	silently, slowly, quietly, quickly, now

Non-lexical categories	Examples
Determiner (Det)	the, a, this, these
Degree word (Deg)	too, so, very, more, quite
Qualifier (Qual)	always, perhaps, often, never, almost
Auxiliary (Aux)	will, can, may, must, should, could
Conjunction (Con)	and, or, but

The four most studied syntactic categories are **noun** (N), **verb** (V), **adjective** (A), and **preposition** (P). These elements, which are often called lexical categories, play a very important role in sentence formation, as we will soon see. A fifth and less studied lexical category consists of **adverbs** (Adv), most of which are derived from adjectives.

Languages may also contain **non-lexical** or **functional** categories, including **determiners** (Det), **auxiliary verbs** (Aux), **conjunctions** (Con) and

degree words (Deg). Such elements generally have meanings that are harder to define and paraphrase than those of lexical categories. For example, the meaning of the noun *hill* is easier to describe than the meaning of a determiner such as *the* or an auxiliary such as *would*.

A potential source of confusion in the area of word classification stems from the fact that some items can belong to more than one category.

3)

comb used as a noun:
The woman found a comb.

comb used as a verb:
The boy should comb his hair.

4)

near used as a preposition:
The child stood near the fence.

near used as a verb:
The runners neared the finishing line.

near used as an adjective:
The end is nearer than you might think.

How then can we determine a word's category?

Meaning

One criterion involves meaning. Nouns, for instance, typically name entities such as individuals (*Harry*, *Sue*) and objects (*book*, *desk*). Verbs, on the other hand, characteristically designate actions (*run*, *jump*), sensations (*feel*, *hurt*), and states (*be*, *remain*). Consistent with these tendencies, *comb* in *3)* refers to an object when used as a noun but to an action when used as a verb.

The meanings associated with nouns and verbs can be elaborated in various ways. The typical function of an adjective, for instance, is to designate a property or attribute of the entities denoted by nouns. Thus, when we say *That tall building*, we are attributing the property 'tall' to the building designated by the noun.

In a parallel way, adverbs typically denote properties and attributes of the actions, sensations, and states designated by verbs. In the following sentences, for example, the adverb *quickly* indicates the manner of Janet's leaving and the adverb *early* specifies its time.

5)

Janet left quickly.
Janet left early.

Unfortunately, a word's category membership does not always bear such a straightforward relationship to its meaning. For example, there are 'abstract' nouns such as *difficulty*, *truth*, and *likelihood*, which do not name entities in the strict sense. Moreover, even though words that name actions tend to be verbs, some action-naming words can also be used as nouns (*push* and *shove* are nouns in *give someone a push/shove*). Matters are further complicated by the fact that in some cases, words with very similar meanings belong to different categories. For instance, the words *like* and *fond* are very similar in meaning (as in *Mice like/are fond of cheese*), yet *like* is a verb and *fond* an adjective. As we will see later (section 4.1), this problem becomes even more acute when we consider the fact that languages can differ in terms of how they categorize words with particular types of meanings.

Inflection

Most linguists believe that meaning is only one of several criteria that enter into determining a word's category. A second criterion, compatibility with various types of inflection (see Chapter 4, section 5), is summarized in Table 5.2.

Table 5.2   Lexical categories and their inflectional affixes

Category	Inflectional affix	Examples
Noun	plural *-s*	books, chairs, doctors
Verb	past tense *-ed*	hunted, watched, judged
	progressive *-ing*	hunting, watching, judging
Adjective	comparative *-er*	taller, faster, smarter
	superlative *-est*	tallest, fastest, smartest

The omission of the genitive *-'s* from the list of inflectional affixes is deliberate. As you will recall, we pointed out in sections 1.3 and 6.3 of Chapter 4 that although traditionally the possessive *-'s* of *the king's horses* and *the man's clogs* is also regarded as an inflectional affix for nouns, in this book we are treating it as an enclitic rather than a suffix. This is because it is not strongly integrated in the word to which it belongs syntactically and semantically. It is common, especially in informal speech, for the genitive *-'s* to be separated from the word to which it relates (e.g., *the man's flowers* vs the *man next to him's flowers*; *the woman's neighbour* vs *the woman I used to work for's neighbour*). A true affix like the plural *-s* cannot occur at a distance from its base in this way.

Although helpful, inflection does not always provide the information needed to determine a word's category. In English, for example, not all adjectives can take the comparative and superlative affixes (**intelligenter*, **beautifulest*) and some nouns do not normally take the plural suffix (*moisture, bravery, knowledge*).

Distribution

A third and often more reliable criterion for determining a word's category involves the type of elements (especially functional categories) with which it can cooccur (its **distribution**). For example, nouns can typically appear with a determiner, verbs with an auxiliary, and adjectives with a degree word, as shown in Table 5.3.

Table 5.3   Distributional properties of Ns, Vs, and As

Category	Distributional property	Examples
Noun	ocurrence with a determiner	a car, the wheat
Verb	occurrence with an auxiliary	has gone, will stay
Adjective	occurrence with a degree word	very rich, too big

Put another way, a distributional property of nouns is that they can appear with a determiner but not an auxiliary, a distributional property of verbs is that they can appear with an auxiliary but not a determiner, and so forth.

6)

verb with a determiner:
*the destroy

noun with an auxiliary:
*will destruction

Together with information about a word's meaning and its inflectional capabilities, these distributional facts help identify its syntactic category.

1.2

Phrase structure

Sentences are not formed by simply stringing words together like beads on a necklace. Rather, sentences have a hierarchical design in which words are grouped together into successively larger structural units. This section will focus on the nature of syntactic units built around Ns, Vs, As, and Ps. Such units are called **phrases**.

Heads

Phrases are built around a 'skeleton' consisting of two levels, as depicted below. (The symbol P stands for 'phrase'.)

```
NP   VP   AP        PP      ← phrase level
|    |    |         |
N    V    A         P       ← word level
```

Figure 5.1   The organization of phrase structure.

Each level of phrase structure can be thought of as a sort of 'hook' (like a hook on a pole) to which elements of different types can be attached.

The lowest level is reserved for the word around which the phrase is built – an N in the case of NPs, a V in the case of VPs, and so on. This element is called the **head** of the phrase. As Figure 5.2 (overleaf) shows, it is possible to have a phrase in which only the head position is filled. (The material in parentheses provides a context in which these one-word phrases might occur; they are not part of the phrases themselves.)

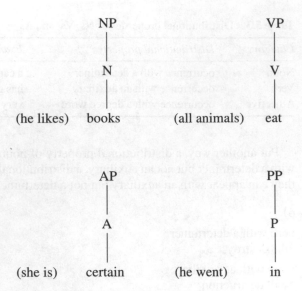

Figure 5.2 Phrases in which only the head position is filled.

Although phrases can consist of just one word, they often contain other elements as well. For example:

7)

a.   [NP the <u>books</u>]

b.   [VP never <u>eat</u>]

c.   [AP quite <u>certain</u>]

d.   [PP almost <u>in</u>]

In addition to a head (the underlined element), each of these phrases includes a second word that has a special semantic and syntactic role. Such words (determiners such as *the* and *a*, qualifiers such as *never* and *often*, and degree words such as *quite* or *almost*) are said to function as specifiers.

Specifiers

Semantically, **specifiers** help to make more precise the meaning of the head. Hence, the determiner (Det) *the* in *7a)* indicates that the speaker has in mind specific books, the qualifier (Qual) *never* in *7b)* indicates a non-occurring event, and the degree words (Deg) *quite* and *almost* in *7c, d)* indicate the extent to which a particular property or relation is manifested.

Syntactically, specifiers typically mark a phrase boundary. In English, specifiers occur at the left boundary (the beginning) of their respective phrases. They are attached to the top level of phrase structure, to the left of the head. Together, these two elements form the phrase structures depicted in the tree diagrams of Figure 5.3. As we will see in section 4, some languages (Thai, for example) place specifiers at the right boundary (the end) of phrases.

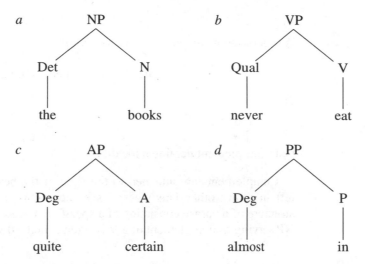

Figure 5.3 Phrases consisting of a head and a specifier.

The syntactic category of the specifier differs depending on the category of the head. As the examples in Figure 5.3 and Table 5.4 help to show, determiners serve as the specifiers of Ns while qualifiers typically function as the specifiers of Vs and degree words as the specifiers of As and (some) Ps. Question 3 at the end of the chapter provides practice in identifying specifiers and heads.

Table 5.4 Some specifiers

Category	Typical function	Examples
Determiner (Det)	specifier of N	the, a, this, those, no
Qualifier (Qual)	specifier of V	never, perhaps, often, always
Degree word (Deg)	specifier of A or P	very, quite, more, almost

Complements

Consider now some examples of slightly more complex phrases.

8)

a. [NP the <u>books</u> about the war]

b. [VP never <u>eat</u> a hamburger]

c. [AP quite <u>certain</u> about Mary]

d. [PP almost <u>in</u> the house]

In addition to a specifier and the underlined head, the phrases in 8) also contain a **complement**. These elements, which are themselves phrases, provide information about entities and locations whose existence is implied by the meaning of the head. For example, the meaning of *eat* implies an object that is eaten, the meaning of *in* implies a location, and so on.

9)

A vegetarian would never eat [a hamburger].

head   complement naming the thing eaten

10)

in   [the house]

head complement naming a location

Complements are attached to the right of the head in English (but to the left in many other languages – see section 4). Figure 5.4 illustrates the structure of a phrase consisting of a specifier, a head, and a complement. (The NP serving as complement of a V is often called a **direct object**.)

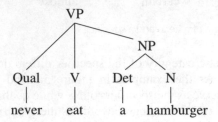

Figure 5.4   A VP consisting of a head, a specifier, and a complement.

As noted above, complements are themselves phrases. Thus, the complement of the V *eat* is an NP that itself consists of a determiner (*a*) and a head (*hamburger*). This phrase then combines with the verb and its specifier to form a still larger structural unit.

NPs, APs, and PPs can have a parallel internal structure, as the examples

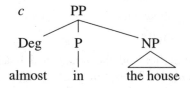

Figure 5.5   Other phrases consisting of a head, a specifier, and a complement.

in Figure 5.5 illustrate. (In order to save space, we do not depict the internal structure of the complement phrases in these examples.)

Question 4 at the end of the chapter provides practice in identifying complements.

The rules

How does the grammar ensure that specifiers, heads, and complements occupy the appropriate positions in phrase structure? The arrangement of the elements that make up a phrase is regulated by a special type of grammatical mechanism called a **phrase structure rule**. The following phrase structure rules stipulate the position of specifiers, heads, and complements in the various types of phrases that we have considered so far. (The arrow can be read as 'consists of' or 'branches into'. The three dots in each rule indicate that other complement options are available; these options will be discussed in section 2.)

11)

NP → (Det) N (PP) . . .
VP → (Qual) V (NP) . . .
AP → (Deg) A (PP) . . .
PP → (Deg) P (NP) . . .

The first of these rules states that an NP can consist of a determiner, an N head, and a PP complement (as in Figure 5.5*a*); the second rule captures the fact that a VP can be composed of a qualifier, a V, and an NP complement (as in Figure 5.4); and so on.

As the parentheses in our rules indicate, both specifiers and complements are optional. Thus, a phrase may consist of a specifier, a head, and a complement; a head and a complement; a specifier and a head; or just a head (Figure 5.6).

a

Phrase consisting of a specifier, a head, and a complement

b

Phrase consisting of a head and a complement

Figure 5.6   Some phrase types. Only the head is present in all patterns. (Continued overleaf)

c
Phrase consisting of a specifier and a head

d
Phrase consisting of just a head

Figure 5.6 continued

Generalizing the rules

By now, you will have noticed that there are very obvious structural similarities among the various phrase types exemplified in Figures 5.4 to 5.6. In all four phrases, the specifier is attached at the top level to the left of the head while the complement is attached to the right. These similarities can be summarized with the help of the template, or blueprint shown in Figure 5.7, in which X stands for N, V, A, or P.

Figure 5.7 The phrase structure template.

Instead of having four separate phrase structure rules to capture the placement of specifiers, heads, and complements, we now can formulate the single general rule in *12).*

12)

The XP Rule:
XP → (Specifier) X (Complement)

With the symbol X standing for N, V, A, or P, this rule is an abbreviation for the four separate phrase structure rules given in *11)* above.

The rule in *12)* is more abstract than the four more specific rules that were initially proposed since it makes use of the special symbol X. However, it is also more economical and is able to capture the structural properties shared by the four different phrase types. For these reasons, rules formulated in terms of the X notation are widely used in contemporary syntactic analysis.

Sentences

The largest unit of syntactic analysis is the sentence (S). Traditionally, sentences are taken to be the product of the rule in *13)*, which combines an NP (often called the **subject**) with a VP to yield structures such as the one in Figure 5.8.

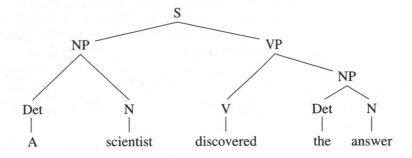

Figure 5.8   The structure of S (traditional view).

13)

The S Rule:
S → NP VP

This analysis assumes that S is special in the sense that, unlike other phrases, it does not have an internal structure (with a head, a complement and a specifier). However, many linguists now believe that S is essentially similar to other phrases and has the structure depicted in Figure 5.9.

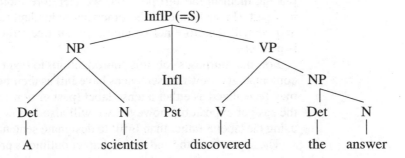

Figure 5.9   The structure of S (popular contemporary view).

According to this idea, sentences have as their head an abstract category dubbed 'Infl', short for 'inflection', which indicates the sentence's tense.[1] Because Infl, like all heads, is obligatory, this automatically accounts for the fact that all sentences of English have tense (e.g., they are either past or non-past). The rest of sentence structure follows from the fact that Infl takes a VP category as its complement and an NP (the subject) as its specifier. A further advantage of this analysis is that it gives sentences the same internal structure as other phrases and makes them consistent with the XP rule outlined earlier. There is therefore no need for the special S rule in *13)*.

Sometimes, an actual word can appear in the Infl position. As the next example in Figure 5.10 shows, auxiliary verbs can appear in the head position of sentences and are thus treated as an instance of the Infl category. For this reason, the Aux label is dispensed with. (Given the long-established meaning of the term *inflection* in morphology, the use of the label 'Infl' by syntacticians to include free forms such as *will* and *can* is unfortunate. However, we will follow this usage here in accordance with the current widespread practice.)

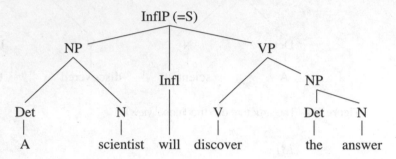

Figure 5.10   An S with an auxiliary in the Infl position.

A further justification for treating auxiliaries as a type of Infl is that many words of this type are inherently associated with a particular tense. For example, *will*, *can*, and *may* are necessarily non-past, as shown by the unacceptability of patterns such as **He will/can/may work yesterday*. By placing them in the Infl position, we therefore indicate that the sentence is non-past. (In such cases, it is somewhat redundant to also have a tense label, and we will therefore not include it in our tree structures when an auxiliary is present.)

For the purposes of this introduction to syntax, we will adopt the contemporary view that sentences have Infl as their head and that this element may be realized as either a tense label (past or non-past) or an auxiliary.[2] For the sake of exposition, however, we will also follow the common practice of using the label S rather than InflP to designate sentences.

The appendix at the end of the chapter outlines a procedure that should help you assign to sentences an appropriate tree structure. Question 5 provides an opportunity to practise this procedure.

A look ahead

Thus far in this chapter we have been concentrating on phrases that consist of specifiers, heads, and complements. In fact, however, human language contains other types of syntactic patterns as well. For example, some phrases – called **coordinate structures** – are formed by joining two (or more) elements of the same type with the help of a conjunction such as *and* or *or*.

14)

coordinate structures

a. [$_{NP}$ a pencil] and [$_{NP}$ a notebook]

b. [$_N$ hamburgers] or [$_N$ hotdogs]

Still another type of pattern includes a **modifier**, an optional element that describes a property of the head. The most common types of modifiers in English are adjectives (which modify noun heads) and adverbs (which modify verb heads).

15)

a. adjective modifying an N head
a *good* book

b. adverb modifying a V head
He slept *soundly*.

We can form sentences containing coordinate structures and modifiers by making relatively small and simple adjustments to our system of phrase structure rules. These adjustments are discussed in sections 5.1 and 5.2, which can be read now or later at the discretion of the course tutor. This textbook postpones discussion of these matters in favour of some topics in syntactic analysis that go beyond the simple modification of phrase structure rules.

1.4

Tests for phrase structure

According to the syntactic analysis being presented here, the words that make up a sentence form intermediate structural units called phrases. How do linguists using this approach to syntax determine which words should be grouped together into phrases? The existence of the syntactic units, or **constituents**, that make up tree structures can be independently verified with the help of special tests. Although we cannot consider all of these tests here, it is possible to give some examples.

The substitution test

Evidence that NPs are syntactic units comes from the fact that they can often be replaced by an element such as *they*, *it*, or *do so*. This is illustrated in *16)*, where *they* replaces the NP *the citizens* and *do so* replaces the VP *wear ties*. (This is called a **substitution test**.)

16)

a. [$_{NP}$The citizens] rebelled after *they* discovered the truth.
(they = the citizens)

b. The students will [$_{VP}$ wear ties] if the teachers will *do so*.
(do so = wear ties)

The substitution test also confirms that a PP such as *at the corner* is a unit since it can be replaced by a single word in sentences such as *17)*.

17)

They stopped [PP at the corner] and we stopped *there* too.
(there = at the corner)

The movement test

A second indication that *at the corner* forms a constituent is that it can be moved as a single unit to a different position within the sentence. (This is called a **movement test**.) In *18)*, for instance, *at the corner* can be moved from a position after the verb to the beginning of the sentence.

18)

They stopped [PP at the corner] → [PP At the corner], they stopped.

The coordination test

Finally, we can conclude that a group of words forms a constituent if it can be joined to another group of words by a conjunction such as *and*, *or*, or *but*. (This is labelled the **coordination test** since patterns built around a conjunction are called coordinate stuctures; see section 5.1 below.) Thus, we know that the VP *often sweep the floor* in *19)* is a constituent because it can be joined to another unit by *and* or *but*.

19)

The children [VP often sweep the floor] but [VP never make the bed].

1.5

X′ categories (advanced)

Thus far, we have been assuming that the architecture of phrase structure complies with the blueprint in Figure 5.11, which is identical to Figure 5.7 above.

Figure 5.11   The phrase structure template.

In fact, however, this is somewhat of a simplification since there is reason to believe that complements and heads may actually be attached to a level of phrase structure midway between the word level and the phrase level, as depicted in Figure 5.12. The intermediate level of structure is represented by the symbol X′ (pronounced 'X-bar').

According to this viewpoint, then, all phrases have the tri-level structures shown in Figure 5.13, in which the head and its complement form an X′-level constituent and the specifier is attached at the higher XP level. (The example illustrates the internal structure of an S, a VP, and an NP.)

The existence of X′ categories can be verified with the help of the same sort of syntactic tests discussed in the previous section. Consider, for example, the V′ *educate the public* in Figure 5.13. As the following sentence

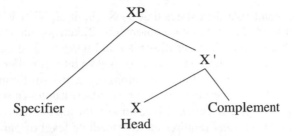

Figure 5.12   The phrase structure template (revised).

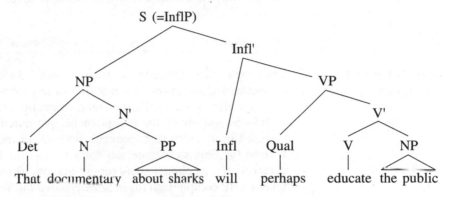

Figure 5.13   Phrase structure with the intermediate X' level.

shows, this unit can be replaced by *do so* and should therefore be a constituent according to the substitution test.

20)

That documentary about sharks will perhaps [$_{V'}$ educate the public], but media reports never *do so*. (*do so = educate the public*)

Now consider the N' *documentary about sharks* in Figure 5.13. As the next sentence shows, this unit can be replaced by the element *one*.

21)

That [$_{N'}$ documentary about sharks] is more informative than the previous *one*. (*one = documentary about sharks*)

The fact that *one* can replace *documentary about sharks* in this manner confirms that it is a syntactic unit, consistent with the structure in Figure 5.13.

In order to accommodate these new three-level structures, it is necessary to replace our original XP rule by the two phrase structure rules in *22)*.

22)

a.   XP → (Specifier) X'

b.   X' → X (Complement)

The first of these rules stipulates that XP categories such as NP and VP consist of an optional specifier (a determiner, a qualifier, and so forth) and an X'. The second rule then states that an X′ (be it an N′, a V′, or whatever) consists of a head, X, and any complements. Taken together, these two rules form the three-level structures illustrated in Figure 5.12, as desired.

Because three-level structures take up a considerable amount of space and can be tedious to draw, it is common practice to eliminate the intermediate level of phrase structure in most published work unless it is absolutely essential to the point being discussed. Since none of the phenomena that we will be considering in this chapter requires an intermediate level of phrase structure, we will not make further use of it here. In order to do more advanced syntactic analysis, though, you will need to be familiar with the X′ level.

2

COMPLEMENT OPTIONS

The simple rules outlined in sections 1.2 and 1.3 can form a very wide variety of phrases and sentences. Much of this variety stems from the fact that human language allows many different complement options.

Information about the complements permitted by a particular word is included in its entry in a speaker's **lexicon**, or mental dictionary. Thus, the lexicon for English includes an entry for *devour* that indicates its syntactic category (V), its phonological representation, its meaning, and the fact that it takes an NP complement (as in *She devoured the doughnut*).

23)

devour: category: V
phonological representation: /dɪvaʊə/
meaning: EAT HUNGRILY, . . .
complement: NP

The term **subcategorization** is used to refer to information about a word's complement options.

Subcategorization information interacts with the phrase structure rules to ensure that lexical items appear in the appropriate types of tree structures. Thus, because *devour* belongs to the subcategory of verbs that require an NP complement, it is permitted in the tree structure depicted in Figure 5.14*a* (where there is an NP complement) but not in the tree structure in Figure 5.14*b*.

Figure 5.14 Subcategorization determines the type of syntactic structure in which *devour* can occur.

Thanks to subcategorization information, heads occur only in tree structures where they have compatible complement phrases.

Complement options for verbs

Table 5.5 illustrates some of the more common complement options for verbs in English. The subscripted prepositions indicate the subtype of **verbs** PP complement, where this is relevant. *Loc* stands for any preposition expressing a location (such as *near*, *on*, *under*).

Table 5.5   Some examples of verb complements

Complement option	Sample heads	Example
$\emptyset$	vanish, arrive, die	The child vanished __.
NP	devour, cut, prove	The professor proved [$_{NP}$ *the theorem*].
AP	be, become	The man became [$_{AP}$ *very angry*].
PP$_{to}$	dash, talk, refer	The dog dashed [$_{PP}$ *to the door*].
NP NP	spare, hand, give	We handed [$_{NP}$ *the man*] [$_{NP}$ *a map*].
NP PP$_{to}$	hand, give, send	She gave [$_{NP}$ *a certificate*] [$_{PP}$ *to the student*].
NP PP$_{for}$	buy, cook, reserve	We bought [$_{NP}$ *a hat*] [$_{PP}$ *for Andy*].
NP PP$_{loc}$	put, place, stand	He put [$_{NP}$ *the silencer*] [$_{PP}$ *on the car*].
PP$_{to}$ PP$_{about}$	talk, speak	I talked [$_{PP}$ *to a doctor*] [$_{PP}$ *about Sue*].
NP PP$_{for}$ PP$_{with}$	open, repair, fix	We opened [$_{NP}$ *the door*] [$_{PP}$ *for Andy*] [$_{PP}$ *with a crowbar*].

According to this table, the verbs in the first line (*vanish*, *arrive*, and *die*) can occur without any complement, those in the second line occur with an NP complement, and so on.

A word can belong to more than one subcategory. The verb *eat*, for example, can occur either with or without an NP complement and therefore belongs to both of the first two subcategories in our table.

24)

After getting home, they ate (the sandwiches).

However, not all verbs exhibit this flexibility. Although *devour* is similar in meaning to *eat*, it requires an explicitly stated complement NP and therefore belongs only to the second subcategory in our table.

25)

a. *devour* without a complement:
    *After getting home, they devoured.

b. *devour* with a complement:
    After getting home, they devoured the sandwiches.

As the examples in Table 5.5 also show, some heads can take more than one complement. The verb *put* is a case in point, since it requires both an NP complement and a PP complement.

26)

put with an NP complement and a PP complement:
The librarian put [NP the book] [PP on the shelf].

27)

put without an NP complement:
*The librarian put [PP on the shelf].

28)

put without a PP complement:
*The librarian put [NP the book].

The VP *put the book on the shelf* has the structure depicted in Figure 5.15, in which the VP consists of the head *put* and its two complements – the NP *the book* and the PP *on the shelf*.

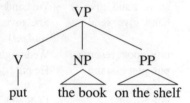

Figure 5.15   A verb with two complements.

We can therefore revise our earlier XP rule as follows, using an asterisk after the complement to indicate that one or more of these elements is permitted.

29)

The XP Rule (revised)
XP → (Specifier) X (Complement*)

This rule also captures the simple but important fact that complements (however many there are) occur to the right of the head in English.

2.2

Complement options for other categories

Various complement options are also available for Ns, As and Ps. Tables 5.6, 5.7 and 5.8 provide examples of various possibilities.

Table 5.6   Some examples of noun complements

Complement option	Sample heads	Example
Ø	car, boy, electricity	The car __
PP$_{of}$	memory, failure, death	the memory [PP *of a friend*]
PP$_{of}$ PP$_{to}$	presentation, description, donation	the presentation [PP *of a medal*] [PP *to the winner*]
PP$_{with}$ PP$_{about}$	argument, discussion, conversation	an argument [PP *with Stella*] [PP *about politics*]

Table 5.7   Some examples of adjective complements

Complement option	Sample heads	Example
Ø	tall, green, smart	very tall __
PP_about	curious, glad, angry	curious [PP *about China*]
PP_to	apparent, obvious	obvious [PP *to the student*]
PP_of	fond, full, tired	fond [PP *of chocolate*]

Table 5.8   Some examples of preposition complements

Complement option	Sample heads	Example
Ø	near, away, down	(he got) down __
NP	in, on, by, near	in [NP *the house*]
PP	down, up, out	down [PP *into the cellar*]

Here again, subcategorization ensures that particular heads can appear in tree structures only if there is an appropriate type of complement. Thus, in Figure 5.16, the adjective *curious* (Table 5.7) can occur with an '*about* PP', but the adjective *fond* cannot.

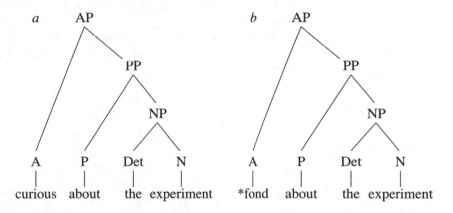

Figure 5.16   Subcategorization permits *curious,* but not *fond,* to take an '*about*-PP' as complement.

2.3

Complement clauses

In addition to the complement options considered to this point, all human languages allow sentence-like constructions to function as complements. A simple example of this from English is given in *30)*.

30)

[The psychic knows [that/whether/if the contestant will win]].

The smaller bracketed phrase in *30)* is called a **complement clause** while the larger phrase in which it occurs is called the **matrix clause**.

Words such as *that*, *if*, and *whether* are known as **complementizers** (Cs). They introduce an S complement, forming the CP (complementizer phrase) structure depicted in Figure 5.17.

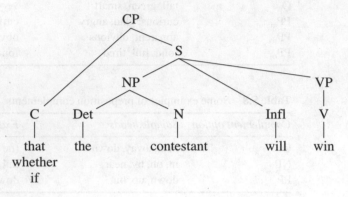

Figure 5.17 The structure of a CP.

Although Cs are non-lexical categories, they fit into structures parallel to those found with lexical categories. Thus, the head (C) and its complement (S) together make up an XP category (namely, CP). In section 3.4, we will see that there is even a type of element that can occur in the specifier position under CP.

When a CP occurs in a sentence such as *30)*, in which it serves as complement of the verb *know*, the entire sentence has the structure shown in Figure 5.18.

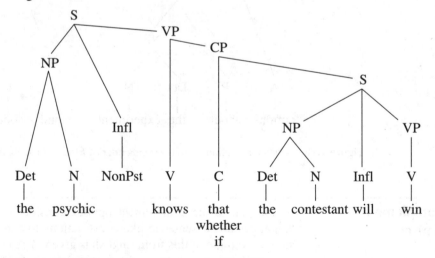

Figure 5.18 The structure of a sentence with an embedded CP.

Of course, not all verbs can take a CP complement. Table 5.9 provides examples of some of the verbs that are commonly found with a complement of this type.

Table 5.9   Some verbs permitting CP complements

Complement(s)	Sample heads	Example
CP	believe, know think, remember	They believe [CP *that Eric left*]
NP CP	persuade, tell	They told [NP *Mary*] [CP *that Eric had left*]
PP_to CP	convince, promise concede, admit	They admitted [PP *to Mary*] [CP *that Eric had left*]

There is no limit on the number of embedded clauses that can occur in a sentence, as Figure 5.19 helps to show.

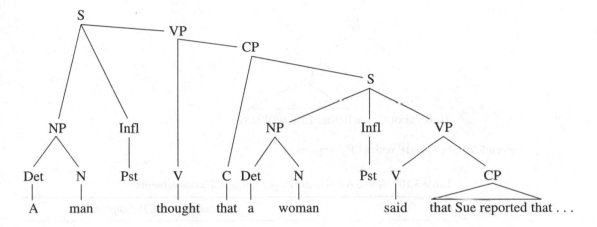

Figure 5.19   The structure of a sentence with more than one embedded CP.

This structure is made possible by the fact that each CP complement can contain a verb that itself permits a complement CP. Hence the topmost clause contains the verb *think*, whose complement clause contains the verb *say*, whose complement clause contains *report*, and so on.

Other categories with CP complements (advanced)

As the examples in Figure 5.20 (overleaf) show, a CP may serve as a complement to an N, an A, or a P in addition to a V.

Table 5.10 (overleaf) gives examples of some other adjectives, nouns, and prepositions that can take CP complements.

Although structures of this sort are common in English and other languages, we will restrict our attention in the remainder of this chapter to embedded clauses that are complements of Vs.

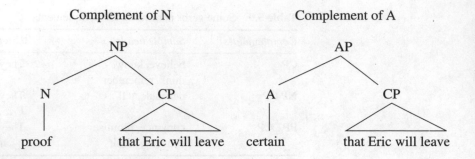

Complement of N   Complement of A

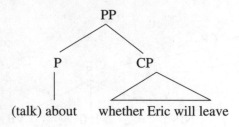

Complement of P

Figure 5.20   N, A, and P with a CP complement.

Table 5.10   Some As, Ns, and Ps permitting CP complements

Items	Example with CP complement
Adjectives afraid, certain, aware, confident	They are afraid [_CP_ *that Eric left*].
Nouns claim, belief, fact, knowledge, proof	They lack proof [_CP_ *that Eric left*].
Prepositions over, about	They argued over [_CP_ *whether Eric had left*].

3

TRANSFORMATIONS

Even though the phrase structure rule we have been using interacts with the set of complement options permitted by individual heads to form a very wide range of patterns, there are syntactic phenomena that this system cannot describe in an entirely satisfactory way. This section considers two such phenomena and discusses the changes that must be made in order to accommodate them.

3.1

Inversion in *yes–no* questions

To begin, let us consider the English *yes–no* questions exemplified in *31)*. (These structures are called *yes–no* questions because the expected response is usually 'yes' or 'no'.)

31)

a.   *Will* the boy leave?

b.   *Can* the cat climb this tree?

These sentences have an auxiliary verb to the left of the subject, in contrast to the more usual position illustrated in *32)*.

32)

a.   The boy *will* leave.

b.   The cat *can* climb this tree.

Our XP rule places the auxiliary in the appropriate position in *32)*, but not in *31)*. How does the word order found in *31)* come about?

The question structures that we are considering are built in two steps. In the first step, the usual XP rule is used to form a structure in which the auxiliary occupies its normal position in Infl, between the subject and the VP (Figure 5.21).

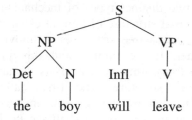

Figure 5.21   *Will* occurring in the head position between the subject (its specifier) and the VP (its complement).

The second step in the formation of question structures requires a **transformation**, a special type of rule that can move an element from one position to another. In the case we are considering, a transformation known as **inversion** moves the auxiliary from the Infl position to a position to the left of the subject. For now, we can formulate this transformation as follows.

33)

Inversion:

Move Infl to the left of the subject NP.

Inversion applies to the structure depicted in Figure 5.21, yielding the sentence in *34)* with the auxiliary verb to the left of the subject NP – the position appropriate for a question structure. (The arrow shows the movement brought about by inversion. For now, we will not try to draw a tree diagram for sentences that have undergone a transformation.)

34)

Will the boy ___ leave?

The transformational analysis has at least two advantages. First, we do not have to say that there are two types of auxiliary verbs in English: those that occur at the beginning of the sentence and those that occur in the usual Infl position between the subject and the VP. Rather, we can say that all auxiliaries occur under Infl, consistent with the analysis proposed in section 1.2. Those sentences that have an auxiliary verb to the left of the subject simply undergo an 'extra' process – the inversion transformation that moves Infl from its original position in order to signal a question.

Second, the transformational analysis automatically captures the fact – known to all speakers of English – that the sentence *Will the boy leave* is the question structure corresponding to *The boy will leave*. According to the analysis presented here, both sentences have exactly the same basic structure. They differ only in that inversion has applied to move the Infl category in the question structure.

3.2

Deep structure and surface structure

The preceding examples show that at least some sentences must be analysed with the help of two distinct types of mechanisms – the XP rule, which determines the internal structure of phrasal categories, and transformations, which can modify these tree structures by moving an element from one position to another. If we think about this in terms of a sentence's 'architecture', the transformational analysis is claiming that there are two levels of syntactic structure. The first, called **deep structure** (or **D-structure**), is formed by the XP rule in accordance with the head's subcategorization properties. As we shall see in the chapter on semantics, deep structure plays a special role in the interpretation of sentences.

The second level of syntactic structure corresponds to the final syntactic form of the sentence. Called **surface structure** (or **S-structure**), it results from applying whatever transformations are appropriate for the sentence in question.

The deep structure for the question *Will the boy leave?* is given in Figure 5.22.

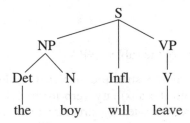

Figure 5.22   The deep structure for the question *Will the boy leave?*

The surface structure for the question pattern is then formed by applying the inversion transformation, yielding *35)*.

35)

Will the boy ___ leave?

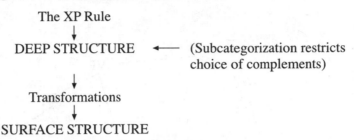

Figure 5.23 depicts the organization of the syntactic component of the grammar as it has just been outlined.

The XP Rule

↓

DEEP STRUCTURE   ⟵⟶   (Subcategorization restricts choice of complements)

↓

Transformations

↓

SURFACE STRUCTURE

Figure 5.23   The syntactic component of the grammar.

As this diagram shows, the grammar makes use of different syntactic mechanisms. Some of these mechanisms are responsible for the architecture of phrases (the XP rule), others for the determination of a head's possible complements (subcategorization), and still others for the movement of categories within syntactic structure (transformations).

3.3

Wh Movement

Consider now the set of question constructions exemplified in *36)*. These sentences are called ***wh* questions** because of the presence of a question word beginning with *wh*.

36)

a.   Which car should the man repair?

b.   What can the child sit on?

Do the deep structures associated with *36a)* and *36b)* resemble the surface form of these sentences or are they quite different? Within the system of syntactic analysis we are using, the sentences in *36)* have the deep structures illustrated in Figure 5.24 overleaf. (We treat the *wh* words *who* and *what* as simple nouns and *which* as a determiner.)

According to these deep structures, *which car* occurs as complement of the verb *repair* in Figure 5.24*a* while *what* appears as complement of the preposition *on* in Figure 5.24*b*. This captures an important fact about the meanings of these sentences since *which car* asks about the thing that was repaired in the first case while *what* asks about the location where the child can sit in the second case.

A second argument in favour of this analysis involves subcategorization.

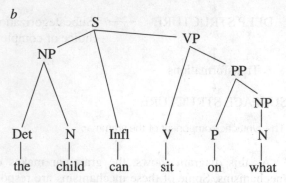

Figure 5.24 The deep structures for two *wh* questions.

Consider in this regard the following sentences.

37)

a. *The man should repair.

b. *The child can sit on.

Notice that these sentences are somehow incomplete without an NP after *repair* and *on*. However, there is no such problem with the *wh* questions in *36)*, which suggests that the *wh* phrases must be fulfilling the complement function in these sentences. The deep structures in Figure 5.24 capture this fact by treating the *wh* phrase as complement of the verb in the first pattern and complement of the preposition in the second.

In order to convert these deep structures into the corresponding surface structures, we need a transformation that will move the *wh* phrase from its position in deep structure to a position at the beginning of the sentence. The transformation in question, called **Wh Movement**, can be formulated as follows.

38)

Wh Movement:
Move the *wh* phrase to the beginning of the sentence.

By applying *Wh* Movement and inversion to the deep structure in Figure 5.24a, we can form the desired question structure.

39)

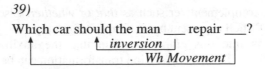

Which car should the man ___ repair ___?

Application of the same two transformations to the deep structure in Figure 5.24*b* yields the *wh* question in *40)*.

40)

What can the child ___ sit on ___?

3.4

A more detailed look at transformations (advanced)

Up until now, our discussion of transformations has left unsettled an important issue. Reconsider in this regard the simple *yes–no* question exemplified in *41)*.

41)

Will the boy ___ leave?

In what position does the auxiliary verb 'land' when it is moved by inversion to the left of the subject? If we assume that sentences such as *41)* are simple Ss, no position is available to the left of the subject, which is the specifier (and hence the first element in the S) according to our analysis.

Another look at inversion

This problem can be solved if we assume that all Ss occur within larger CPs, as depicted in Figure 5.25.

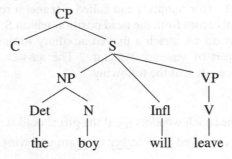

Figure 5.25 An S inside a CP 'shell'.

What lies behind the structure shown in Figure 5.25 is the assumption that *all* Ss occur within a CP, whether they are embedded or not. It may help to think of the CP category as a 'shell' that forms an outer layer of structure around an S. When embedded within a larger sentence, the CP can contain an overt complementizer such as *that* or *whether*. Elsewhere, the C position in the CP shell is present but is simply left empty.

It is into this empty position that the auxiliary is moved in *yes–no* questions. Thus, the inversion transformation can be reformulated as follows.

42)

Inversion (*revised*):
Move Infl to C.

According to this proposal, then, the sentence *Will the boy leave?* is formed by applying the inversion transformation to the deep structure in Figure 5.25 above to give the surface structure in Figure 5.26.

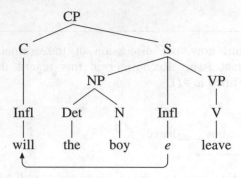

Figure 5.26   Movement of an auxiliary from Infl to C.

A transformation can do no more than change an element's position. It does not change the categories of any words and it cannot eliminate any part of the structural configuration created by the phrase structure rules. Thus, *will* retains its Infl label even though it is moved into the C position, and the position that it formerly occupied remains in the tree structure. Marked by the symbol *e* (for 'empty') and called a **trace**, it records the fact that the moved element comes from the head position within S.

Why do we attach a moved auxiliary to the C position rather than some other part of sentence structure? The answer lies in the embedded CPs in sentences such as the following.

43)

a.   The coach wonders [꜀ₚ if the girl should stay].

b.   A fan asked [꜀ₚ whether the team will win].

The underlined elements in these CPs are complementizers and therefore occur in the C position. Assuming that there can be only one element in each position in a tree structure, there should be no room for the moved auxiliary under the C label in the embedded CPs in *43)*. We therefore predict that inversion should not be able to apply in these cases. The ungrammaticality of the sentences in *44)* shows that this is correct.

44)

Inversion in embedded CPs that include complementizers:

a.   *The coach wonders [CP if-should the girl ___ stay].

b.   *A fan asked [CP whether-will the team ___ win].

Interestingly, the acceptability of inversion in embedded CPs improves quite dramatically when there is no complementizer (and the C position is therefore open to receive the moved auxiliary).

45)

Inversion in embedded CPs that do not have complementizers:

a.   The coach wondered [CP should the girl ___ stay].

b.   A fan asked [CP will the team ___ win].

Although some speakers prefer not to apply inversion in embedded clauses at all (especially in formal speech), most speakers of English find the sentences in *45)* to be much more natural than those in *44)*. This is just what we would expect if inversion must move the auxiliary to an empty C position, as required by our analysis.

To summarize before continuing, we have introduced two changes into the system of syntactic analysis used until now. First, we assume that all Ss occur inside CPs. Second, we assume that the inversion transformation moves the auxiliary from its position within S to an empty C position to the left of the subject NP. This not only gives the correct word order for question structures, it helps explain why inversion sounds so unnatural when the C position is already filled by another element, as in *44)*.

Do **insertion**

As we have just seen, formation of *yes–no* questions in English involves moving the Infl category, and the auxiliary verb that it contains, to the C position. How, then, do we form the questions corresponding to sentences such as those in *46)*, which contain no auxiliary?

46)

a.   The students liked the film.

b.   Those birds sing.

Since Infl in these sentences contains only an abstract (i.e., invisible) tense marker, there is nothing for the inversion transformation to move. English circumvents this problem by adding the special auxiliary verb *do*.

47)

a.   *Did* the students like the film?

b.   *Do* those birds sing?

As these examples show, *do* is inserted into sentences that do not already have an auxiliary verb, thereby making inversion possible. We can capture this fact by formulating an insertion rule, an operation that adds an element to a tree structure.

48)

Do Insertion
Insert interrogative *do* into an empty Infl position.

The sentence in *46b)* can now be analysed in the manner shown in Figure 5.27.

    a.   Deep Structure   *b.*   After *Do* Insertion

    c.   After Inversion

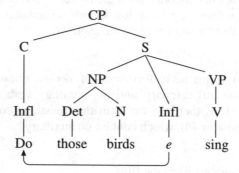

Figure 5.27 A sentence formed with the help of *Do* insertion.

As these tree structures show, the sentence *Do those birds sing?* is built in three steps. In the initial step, the usual XP rule gives the deep structure in Figure 5.27*a*, which contains no auxiliary verb in the Infl position. The transformation of *Do* insertion then inserts the special interrogative auxiliary *do* into this position. At this point, inversion applies, moving interrogative *do* to the C position and giving the desired surface structure.

Another look at *Wh* Movement

Now reconsider the *wh* question pattern in *49)*.

49)

Which car should the man ___ repair ___?

We have already seen that the transformation of *Wh* Movement moves the *wh* phrase to the beginning of the sentence to the left even of the fronted Aux, but we have not attempted to determine its precise place in the tree structure.

Given that the moved auxiliary is located in the C position (see above), it seems reasonable to conclude that the fronted *wh* phrase is in the specifier position of CP (this being the only position to the left of the C). Certainly, we know that this position is available to receive the moved *wh* phrase: because there is no class of words that serves as specifier of C, this position will always be empty in deep structure prior to the application of the *Wh* Movement.

We therefore reformulate the *Wh* Movement transformation as follows.

50)

Wh Movement (*revised*):
Move a *wh* phrase to the specifier position under CP.

The sentence *Which car should the man repair?* can now be analysed in steps, the first of which involves formation of the deep structure depicted in Figure 5.28. Consistent with our earlier assumption, the S here occurs within a CP shell.

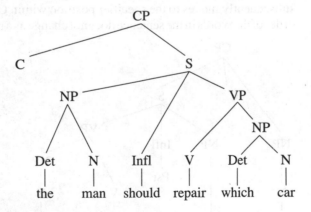

Figure 5.28   Deep structure for *Which car should the man repair?*

Wh Movement and Inversion then apply to this deep structure, yielding the surface structure in Figure 5.29.

Like other transformations, *Wh* Movement cannot eliminate any part of the structural configuration formed by the phrase structure rules. The position

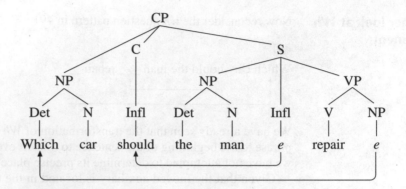

Figure 5.29 Surface structure for *Which car should the man repair?* Infl moves to the C position and the *wh* phrase moves to the specifier position under CP.

occupied by the *wh* phrase in deep structure is therefore not lost. Rather, it remains as a trace (an empty category), indicating that the moved element corresponds to the complement of the verb *repair*.

In the examples considered so far, the *wh* word originates as complement of a verb or preposition. In sentences such as the following, however, the *wh* word is the subject.

51)

Who criticized Maxwell?

In this sentence, the *wh* word asks about the person who does the criticizing (the subject), not about the person criticized (the direct object). Figure 5.30 shows that in such patterns the *wh* word originates in the subject position and subsequently moves to the specifier position within CP even though the actual order of the words in the sentence does not change as a result of this movement.

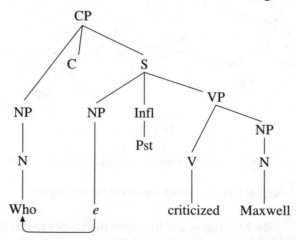

Figure 5.30 Movement of a subject *wh* word. Since there is nothing for the *wh* word to move over in such cases, there is no visible change in word order.

3.5

Constraints on transformations (advanced)

Transformations, like *Wh* Movement and inversion, are examples of movement rules: they move elements from one position within the sentence to another. Such rules are commonly referred to as instructions to '**Move α**', where 'alpha' is a cover term for any element that can be shifted from one location to another.

Movement is not unconstrained. In fact, much of the research undertaken in the field of syntax in recent years has been devoted to determining constraints on movement. It has been shown that only certain categories are targeted by movement rules, that only certain positions can serve as 'landing sites' for moved elements, and that there are limits on how far elements can be moved. For example, inversion can move an auxiliary from the Infl position only to the nearest C position.

52)

a. movement of an auxiliary to the nearest C position:

[CP [IP Harry should know [CP that the bottle might explode]]]. [Deep structure]
[CP should [IP Harry ___ know [CP whether the bottle might explode]]]. [Surface structure]

b. movement of an auxiliary to a more distant C position:

[CP [IP Harry should know [CP that the bottle might explode]]]. [Deep structure]
*[CP Might [IP Harry should know [CP that the bottle ___ explode]]]. [Surface structure]

There are also certain contexts in which transformations are unable to operate. As a preliminary illustration of this, consider the following two pairs of sentences.

53)

a. movement of a *wh* word from inside a complement phrase:

Carl should see [a picture of Dracula]. [Deep structure]
Who should Carl see [a picture of ___]? [Surface structure]

b. movement of a *wh* word from inside a subject phrase:

[A picture of Dracula] could frighten John. [Deep structure]
*Who could [a picture of ___] frighten John? [Surface structure]

In the first example, the *wh* word is extracted from a complement phrase and the result is acceptable. In *53b)*, in contrast, the *wh* word is extracted from the subject NP. The ungrammaticality of the resulting sentence suggests that it is not possible to move an element out of a subject phrase. We can capture this fact by formulating the following constraint on transformations.

54)

The Subject Constraint
No element may be removed from a subject phrase.

A constituent (such as the subject) that does not permit extraction of a component part is called an **island**.

Subject NPs are not the only type of island found in English. As the following examples show, it is also not possible to remove a *wh* word from a coordinate structure. (The coordinate structure is placed in brackets; as outlined in detail in section 5.1, a coordinate structure is a phrase in which a word such as *and* or *or* joins together categories of the same type.)

55)

a. The author might write [a story or a poem].

b. *What might the author write [a story or ___]?

56)

a. Sue will talk [to Tom and to Mary].
b. *Who will Sue talk [to Tom and to ___]?

We can account for these facts by formulating the following constraint.

57)

The Coordinate Structure Constraint:
No element may be removed from a coordinate structure.

There are many different types of islands in language, and a good deal of current research focuses on how they should be described, what properties they have in common, and how they differ from language to language. However, since most of this work is too complex to discuss in an introductory textbook, we can do no more than mention this important phenomenon here.

4

UNIVERSAL GRAMMAR AND PARAMETRIC VARIATION

Thus far, our discussion has focused on English. There are many other syntactic phenomena in our language that are worthy of consideration and we will examine some of them in section 5. First, though, it is important to extend the scope of our analysis to other languages.

The syntactic devices presented in earlier sections of this chapter are not found only in English. Indeed, recent work suggests that all languages share a small set of syntactic categories and that these categories can be combined to form phrases whose internal structure includes heads, complements, and specifiers. Moreover, it appears that transformational operations are subject to highly similar constraints in all languages. (For example, the prohibition against extraction from coordinate structures discussed in section 3.5 holds cross-linguistically, so that sentences like *55b)* and *56b)* in the previous section are not found in any language.) The system of categories, mechanisms and constraints shared by all human languages is called **Universal Grammar (UG**, for short).

The fact that certain syntactic properties are universal does not mean that languages must be alike in all respects. Universal Grammar leaves room for variation, allowing individual languages to differ with respect to certain parameters. (You can think of a **parameter** as the set of options that UG permits for a particular phenomenon.) In this section, we will consider a few examples of parametric variation, beginning with the inventory of syntactic categories. Some additional instances of cross-linguistic differences in syntax are considered in section 2.3 of Chapter 9.

4.1

Variation in syntactic categories

Of the syntactic categories considered in this chapter, only nouns and verbs are found in all human languages. The adjective category, while very common, is not universal. In many languages (such as Hausa, Korean, Telugu, Hua, and Bemba), there are no true adjectives and no direct translation for English sentences such as *58)*.

58)

The cat is hungry.

Instead, the concept 'hungry' is expressed with the help of a noun in structures such as *59a)* or a verb in structures such as *59b)*.

59)

a.   The cat has hunger.

b.   The cat hungers.

Some examples of this phenomenon in Korean follow. (Nom = nominative, the subject marker.)

60)

use of a noun where English uses an adjective:

a.   Ku chayk-i   *caymi* issta.
       that book-Nom interest exist
       'That book is interesting.'

b.   Ku pap-i   *mas* issta.
       that food-Nom taste exist
       'That food is tasty.'

61)

Use of a verb where English uses an adjective

a.   Ku pap-i   *maypta*.
       that food-Nom be-spicy
       'That food is spicy.'

b. Cip-i   *khuta.*
house-Nom be-big
'The house is big.'

Despite their English translation, the words *maypta* 'spicy' and *khuta* 'big' in the latter two examples are a type of verb in Korean, taking tense markers and other types of inflectional endings used for verbs in that language.

Still other languages seem to lack the P category. Where English has a preposition, the Mayan language Jacaltec, for example, either uses no morpheme at all (see *62a)*) or employs a noun (such as *s-wi'* 'head' for 'on', as in *62b)*).

62)

a. Xto   naj conob.
went he town
'He went to town.'

b. Ay naj *s-wi'* witz.
is he head hill
'He is on the hill.'

There are even languages that lack both As and Ps. For example, the Nootkan languages of Vancouver Island and northwest Washington State apparently have only two lexical categories – N and V.

Table 5.11 summarizes some of the variation in lexical categories found in human language.

Table 5.11   Parametric variation in lexical categories

Language	Categories used
Nootkan	N, V
Jacaltec	N, V, A
Korean	N, V, P
English	N, V, A, P

As you can see, the N and V categories are apparently universal, with languages differing from each other in terms of whether they use A and P.

4.2

Variation in phrase structure rules

Even where languages have the same categories, the precise rules for sentence formation may differ. But this variation is not random. For instance, there are significant patterns that recur in language after language in terms of the position of heads within their phrases. To account for these patterns, we can posit a Head Parameter that offers three options – head-initial, head-medial, and head-final. In Japanese, for example, heads consistently occur in the final position within their phrase (Figure 5.31). Thus, the noun comes at the end of the NP, the verb at the end of the VP, and so on. Because Ps occur at the end of the PP, they are called **postpositions** rather than prepositions. (Nom = nominative, the subject marker; CP is omitted to save space.)

Figure 5.31 Japanese phrase structure: the head is always final.

These word order differences reflect the positioning of heads with respect to the other elements in their phrases, not the presence of an entirely new type of syntactic system. We can account for these facts by formulating the following phrase structure rule for Japanese.

63)

XP → (Specifier) (Complement*) X

As this rule indicates, the head uniformly follows its specifier and complement(s) in Japanese. In English, on the other hand, the head follows its specifier but precedes any complements.

Matters are not always so simple, however. In Thai, for example, heads precede both complements and specifiers (the head-initial option) within phrases other than S. Thus, Ns appear at the beginning of NPs, Ps at the beginning of PPs, Vs at the beginning of VPs, and so on (Figure 5.32). (Tones have been omitted here.)

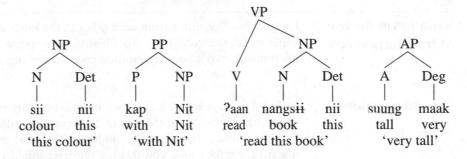

Figure 5.32 The phrase structure: the head is initial in phrases other than S.

Within S, however, as Figure 5.33 shows, the specifier (the subject NP) comes first, just as it does in English.

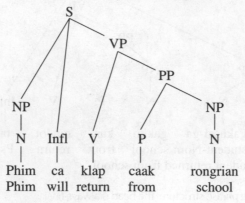

Figure 5.33 Thai sentence structure: the specifier (subject) precedes the head.

Thus, Thai uses one version of the XP rule for S and another version for phrases smaller than S.

64)

XP rule used in Thai for Ss:
XP → (Specifier) X (Complement*)

XP rule used in Thai for phrases smaller than S:
XP → X (Complement*) (Specifier)

The important thing to recognize here is that, despite the differences just noted, English, Japanese, and Thai all have phrases and these phrases include a head in addition to optional specifiers and complements. Beneath the obvious word order differences, then, there is a more fundamental similarity in the categories and rule types needed to build syntactic structure.

4.3

Variation in the use of transformations

Languages often differ from each other in the kinds of rules they use to form a particular sentence type. To illustrate this point we will consider three phenomena, two involving question patterns and one involving statements.

Yes–no questions

In Tamil (a language of India), *yes–no* questions are signalled by the presence of the morpheme -*ā* at the end of the sentence, rather than by an inversion transformation. (The diacritic ˳ indicates a dental point of articulation; the diacritic ¯ marks a long vowel; ḷ is a retroflex liquid.)

65)

a. Muttu paḷam parittān.
Muttu fruit picked
'Muttu picked the fruit.'

b. Muṭṭu paḷam pariṭṭān-ā.
Muttu fruit   picked -Ques
'Did Muttu pick the fruit?'

The morpheme *-ā* is treated as a type of complementizer whose sentence-final position follows from the fact that Tamil is a head-final language. As depicted in Figure 5.34, corresponding to sentence *65b)*, the V comes at the end of the VP, Infl at the end of S, and C (containing the question morpheme) at the end of CP.

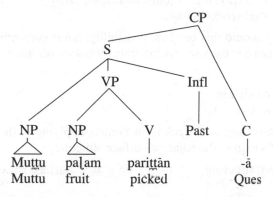

Figure 5.34   A question structure in Tamil.

Examples like this show that languages can use very different means to express the same type of meaning. Whereas English can use a movement transformation (inversion) to form *yes–no* questions, the corresponding sentence type in Tamil is formed by the phrase structure component of the grammar.

Wh questions

Just as many languages form *yes–no* questions without the help of the inversion transformation, many languages do not make use of *Wh* Movement in the formation of *wh* questions. Languages of this type include Japanese, Korean, Tamil, Chinese, and Thai. The following example is from Thai.

66)

Khun ʔaan ʔaray?
you read what
'What did you read?'

Notice that, unlike English, Thai does not front the question word in its *wh* questions.

Verb raising

Consider now the contrast between the following two English sentences.

67)

a.   Paul always works.

b.   *Paul works always.

This contrast is expected since the preverbal qualifier *always* functions as specifier of the verb and therefore should occur to its left, as in *67a*). Surprisingly, however, even though specifiers generally precede the head in French, qualifiers such as *toujours* 'always' must follow the verb in that language.

68)

a.   *Paul toujours travaille. (= English *67a*)
Paul always works

b.   Paul travaille toujours. (= English *67b*)
Paul works always

Why should this be? One possibility that is currently being considered is that French has the verb raising transformation outlined in *69*).

69)

Verb raising:
Move V to Infl

Verb raising is obligatory in French, applying to the deep structure in Figure 5.35*a* to give the adjacent surface structure.

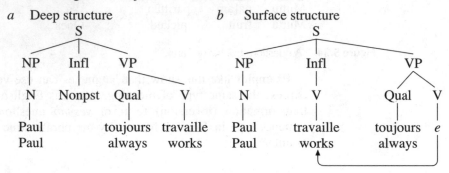

a   Deep structure   *b*   Surface structure

Figure 5.35   Verb raising in French.

By moving the verb to the Infl position in French, the verb raising transformation accounts for its occurrence to the left of its specifier in that language.

A fascinating piece of independent evidence for this proposal comes from the operation of the inversion transformation in French. As we have already seen (section 3.4), this transformation moves Infl to the C position. Now, in English only auxiliary verbs occur under Infl, which explains why only they can undergo inversion.

70)

a.   Inversion of an auxiliary verb in English:
Will you ___ know the answer?

b.   Inversion of a non-auxiliary verb in English:
*Know you ___ the answer?

However, in French non-auxiliary verbs can also occur under Infl, thanks to the operation of the verb raising transformation. This predicts that inversion should be able to apply to these Vs in French as well as to auxiliaries. This is correct. Like English, French can form a question by moving an auxiliary leftwards, as *71)* illustrates.

71)

Inversion of an auxiliary:
As-tu ___ essayé?

Have you tried?

However, unlike English, French also allows inversion of non-auxiliary Vs.

72)

Inversion of a non-auxiliary verb:
Vois-tu ___ le livre?

see you the book
'Do you see the book?'

Figure 5.36 depicts the interaction between verb raising and inversion needed to form this sentence. (We treat the pronoun *tu* 'you' as a type of NP.)

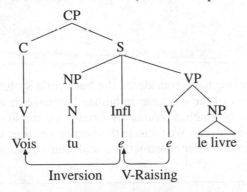

Figure 5.36   The interaction of verb raising and inversion in French.

Although English does not use the verb raising transformation in general, there is reason to believe that it applies to the 'copula' verb *be* as a special case. As shown by the following example, *be* sounds more natural when it occurs to the left of a qualifier such as *always*, which occurs in the specifier position within VP.

73)

a. *be* to the left of the specifier:
   Jonathan *is* always on time.

b. *be* to the right of the specifier:
   ?*Jonathan always *is* on time.

This suggests that *be* can be moved leftwards (Figure 5.37) to the Infl position by the verb raising transformation.

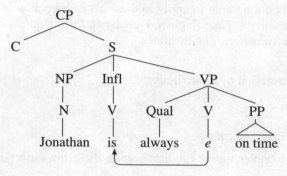

Figure 5.37   Raising of copula *be* in English.

As expected, *be* is also able to undergo subsequent movement to the C position (inversion) in *yes–no* questions, yielding sentences such as *74)*.

74)

Is Jonathan *e* always *e* on time?

5

SOME EXTENSIONS (ADVANCED)

Now that we have considered the basic rule systems used by the syntactic component of the grammar in human language, it is possible to broaden our treatment of English syntax by briefly examining a number of additional structural patterns. We focus in this section on three such patterns – coordinate structures, modifier constructions, and relative clauses.

5.1

Coordination

A common syntactic pattern in English and other languages is formed by grouping together two or more categories of the same type with the help of a conjunction such as *and* or *or*. This phenomenon is known as **coordination**.

75)

coordination of NPs:

a.   [NP the man] and [NP a child]

b   [NP a boy] or [NP a girl]

76)

coordination of VPs:

a   [VP go to the library] and [VP read a book]

b   [VP go to the library] or [VP read a book]

77)

coordination of PPs:

a.   [PP down the stairs] and [PP out the door]

b   [PP in the drawer] or [PP under the desk]

78)

coordination of APs:

a.   [AP quite beautiful] and [AP very expensive]

b.   [AP quite wealthy] but [AP very stingy]

79)

coordination of Ss:

a.   [S The man entered the building] and [S the woman waited in the car].

b.   [S The man entered the building] but [S the woman waited in the car].

Coordination exhibits four important properties. First, there is no limit on the number of coordinated categories that can appear prior to the conjunction. Thus, the grammar can form structures such as *80a)*, in which the subject NP contains four smaller NPs prior to the underlined conjunction and one after it. (When more than two NPs are conjoined with *and*, the conjunction is normally optionally omitted everywhere except before the last NP, as in the example *80b)*).

80)

a.   [NP A man, and a boy, and a cat, and a dog, <u>and</u> a hamster] got into the car.

b.   [NP A man, a boy, a cat, a dog, and a hamster] got into the car.

Second, a category at any level (a head or an entire XP) can be coordinated. The preceding examples illustrate coordination of XPs; the following are examples involving word-level categories.

81)

coordination of N:

The [N book] and [N magazine]

coordination of P:

[P up] and [P down] the stairs

coordination of V:

[V repair] and [V paint] the boat.

Third, coordinated categories must be of the same type. Thus, the coordinated categories are both NPs in *75)*, VPs in *76)*, and so on. As *82)* shows, coordination of different category types generally gives a quite unnatural result.

82)

coordination of an NP and a PP:

*He read [NP the book] and [PP in the library]

coordination of an NP and an AP:

*He left [NP the house] and [AP very angry]

Finally, the category type of the coordinate phrase is identical to the category type of the elements being conjoined (Figure 5.38). Hence, if VPs are coordinated, the coordinate structure is a VP; if NPs are coordinated, the coordinate structure is an NP; and so on.

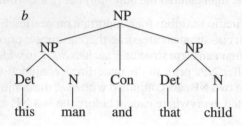

Figure 5.38 Some coordinate structures.

How does the grammar form coordinate structures? One possibility is that there is a separate rule for each coordinate structure. For N categories, for example, the following two rules could be formulated. (The * symbol indicates that one or more categories of that type can occur to the left of the conjunction, as in example *80)*; Con = conjunction.)

83)

a.   NP → NP* Con NP

b.   N → N* Con N

A set of parallel rules for verbal categories could also be formulated.

84)

a.   VP → VP* Con VP

b.   V → V* Con V

Similar rules can be devised for other categories (S, AP, PP, and so on) as well, but you can probably see that the result will be a rather long list of new rules.

Fortunately, we can avoid these complications by using the 'X notation' to formulate a single general statement that can take the place of the more specific rules exemplified above.

85)

The Coordination Rule:
$X^n \to X^{n*}$ Con X^n

The symbol X^n in this rule stands for 'a category at any structural level', indicating that either an X or an XP can be coordinated. As before, the asterisk (*) indicates that one or more categories can occur to the left of the conjunction. Thus, we can form not only structures such as *a man and a boy*, in which just two elements are coordinated, but also structures such as *a man, a boy, a cat, a dog, and a hamster*, in which a much larger number of items undergoes coordination. By adding just one more rule to the grammar, then, we can form a very broad range of coordination structures.

5.2

Modifiers

Thus far, our treatment of phrase structure has ignored **modifiers**, a class of elements that encode optionally expressible properties of heads. Although all lexical categories can have modifiers, we will focus here on the types of categories that can modify Ns and Vs.

Adjective phrases (APs) make up the single most commonly used class of modifiers in English. As the following examples show, APs serve as modifiers of Ns. (This is not the only function of APs: they can also function as complements of verbs such as *become* and *seem*, as in *He became/seemed [very angry]*; see Table 5.5.)

86)

APs serving as modifiers of N:
A *very tall* man walked into the room.
She made *exceptional* progress.

The most common modifiers of Vs are adverb phrases (AdvPs) and PPs that describe manner or time.

87)

AdvPs serving as modifiers of V:
describing manner: Helen proceeded *carefully*.
                       Helen *carefully* proceeded.
describing time: We arrived *early*.

88)

PPs serving as modifiers of V:
describing manner: Helen proceeded *with care*.
describing time: He stayed *for three days*.

As these examples show, English modifiers vary in terms of their position with respect to the head. Thus, APs precede the N while PPs follow the verb. Many AdvPs can occur either before or after the verb that they modify, as the first examples in *86)* and Table 5.12 illustrate.

Table 5.12   Modifier position in English

Modifier	Position
AP	precedes the head
PP	follows the head
AdvP	precedes or follows the head

A rule for modifiers   How do modifiers fit into phrase structure? For the purposes of this introduction to syntax, we will attach modifiers at the XP level of phrase structure, as depicted in Figure 5.39.

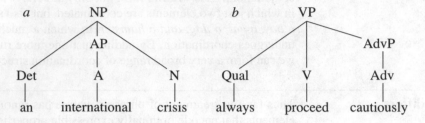

Figure 5.39   Phrases containing modifiers.

In order to account for the placement of modifiers, we must expand our original XP rule so that it allows the various options shown in *89)*.

89)

The Expanded XP Rule:
XP → (Spec) (Mod) X (Complement*) (Mod)

This rule allows a modifier to occur either before the head (as in Figure 5.39*a*) or after it (see Figure 5.39*b*). Where there is a complement, a modifier that occurs after the head will normally occur to the right of the complement as well. This is illustrated in Figure 5.40.

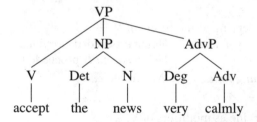

Figure 5.40   A phrase in which both the complement and the modifier occur after the head. In such cases, the modifier occurs after the complement.

In this example, the XP rule gives a phrase consisting of a head (the verb *accept*), a complement (the NP *the news*), and a modifier (the AdvP *very calmly*) – in that order.

5.3
___

Relative clauses (advanced)   Consider now the structure exemplified in *90)*.

90)

a.   Sue may know the man [whom Bob criticized ___].

b.   Harry visited the village [which Sue walked to ___].

The bracketed phrases in *90)* are **relative clauses**, CP-sized modifiers that provide information about the N head to their left. In sentence *90a)*, for example, the relative clause helps identify the man by indicating that he is the person criticized by Bob.

Like other modifiers, relative clauses occur within the same phrase as the head that they modify. Thus, the relative clause in *90a)* should be part of the NP headed by the N *man*. This can be verified with the help of the substitution test illustrated in *91)*, which shows that the sequence *the man who Bob criticized* is a syntactic unit since it can be replaced by the pronoun *him*.

91)

Sue may know [_{NP} the man [_{CP} whom Bob criticized ___]] and I know *him* too.
(*him = the man whom Bob criticized*)

Wh Movement again   Relative clause structures resemble embedded *wh* questions in two respects. First, they begin with a *wh* word such as *who* or *which*. Second, there is an empty position within the sentence from which the *wh* phrase has apparently been moved. In sentences *90a)* and *90b)*, for instance, the NP positions following the transitive verb *criticize* and the preposition *to* are unfilled in surface structure.

The first step in the formation of the relative clause in *90a)* involves the deep structure in Figure 5.41.

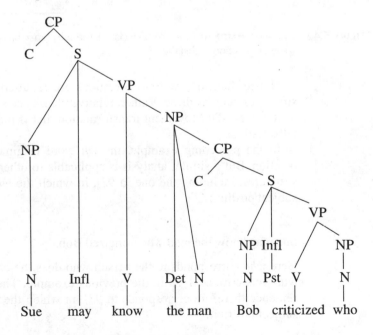

Figure 5.41   The deep structure for a relative clause.

Here, the *wh* word *who* occurs as complement of the verb *criticize* since it corresponds to the person who is criticized. (The relative clause itself is in the usual position for a posthead modifier; see the preceding section.)

The next step involves the application of the *Wh* Movement rule (as outlined in section 3.4) to give the structure in Figure 5.42.

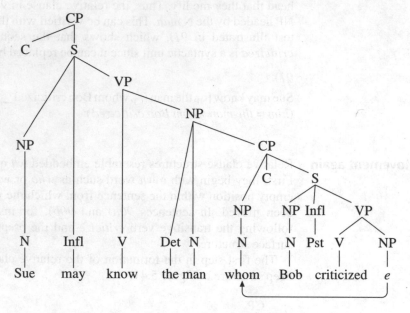

Figure 5.42 The surface structure for a relative clause: the *wh* phrase has moved to the specifier position within the CP.

Notice that no new transformations are required to form relative clause structures such as these. Rather, relative clauses can be formed with the help of the same *Wh* Movement transformation that is independently required for *wh* questions.

In the preceding example, the *wh* word originates in the direct object position. But a similar analysis is applicable to other types of relative clause structures, including the one in *92)*, in which the *wh* word originates in the subject position.

92)

Sue may know the man who criticized Bob.

Here *who* corresponds to the person who does the criticizing, not the person who gets criticized, as in the previous example. The deep structure for this sentence therefore corresponds to *93)*, in which the *wh* word appears in the subject position.

93)

Sue may know the man [CP [IP who criticized Bob]].

94)

Sue may know the man [CP **who** [IP ___ criticized Bob]].

Like other *wh* words, *who* subsequently moves to the specifier position within CP even though the actual order of the words in the sentence does not change as a result of this movement.

6

OTHER TYPES OF SYNTACTIC ANALYSIS

Thus far in this chapter, we have focused our attention on the analysis of sentence structure employed by practitioners of transformational syntax. As mentioned at the outset, however, this is not the only type of syntactic analysis used in contemporary linguistics. In this section, we will briefly consider two other types of syntactic analysis, one focusing on grammatical relations such as subject and direct object, and the other focusing on the way in which syntactic structure is used to communicate information. In order to illustrate how these analyses work, we will make use of a sentence type that has played a very important role in the development of syntactic theory over the last several decades.

6.1

Passive structures

Consider the pair of sentences in *95)*, which are virtually identical in meaning despite obvious structural differences.

95)

a. The thieves took the painting.

b. The painting was taken by the thieves.

In order to describe the differences and similarities between these two sentences, it is necessary to distinguish between the **agent** (the doer of the action designated by the verb) and the **theme** (the entity directly affected by that action). (These notions are discussed in more detail in Chapter 7.)

96)

a.   active sentence:
   The thieves took the painting.
   agent   *theme*

b.   passive sentence:
   The painting was taken (by the thieves).
   theme   *agent*

The *a)* sentence is called **active** because the agent is encoded as subject of the sentence while the *b)* sentence is called **passive** in recognition of the fact that the theme is encoded as subject. There are many other such pairs in English.

97)

a. The dog chased the truck.

b. The truck was chased by the dog.

98)

a. The teacher praised Ginette.

b. Ginette was praised by the teacher.

99)

a, The child broke the dishes.

b. The dishes were broken by the child.

The transformational analysis of passive sentences cannot be adequately discussed until we have considered some issues in the study of semantics (see section 2.3 of Chapter 7). However, it is possible to consider two other perspectives on the analysis of this important syntactic pattern.

6.2

Relational analysis

The key point of **relational analysis** is that at least some syntactic phenomena are best described in terms of grammatical relations such as subject and direct object rather than morphological patterns or the order of words. This can be seen by examining how the passive structure is formed in different languages.

In terms of morphology and word order, the English passive has two distinctive properties. First, a passive sentence contains some form of the auxiliary *be* (*was*, *is*, and so on) together with a verb in the so-called 'past participle form', which is normally marked by the suffix *-en* or *-ed* (as in *was taken*, *was chased*, and so on). Second, the relative order of the agent and theme in passive sentences is the reverse of that found in active sentences (Table 5.13). Thus, whereas the theme precedes the agent in passive sentences, the opposite order is found in active sentences, as sentence *96)* above demonstrated.

Table 5.13 Properties of the English passive

Morphology	Word order
some form of Aux *be* past participle form of the V	the theme comes before the agent

The general tendency in human language is to mark passivization both by a change in the relative order of the agent and the theme and by a modification to the form of the verb. The following example from Sre (a Mon-Khmer language spoken in Vietnam) provides another illustration of this.

100)

a. active sentence:
   Cal pa? mpon.
   wind open door
   'The wind opened the door.'

b. passive sentence:
   Mpon gə-pa?   mə cal.
   door Pass-opened by wind
   'The door was opened by the wind.'

However, it seems that passivization is not always signalled in this way. In Tzotzil (a Mayan language of Mexico), for instance, the relative order of the agent and the theme is the same in active and passive constructions.

101)

a. active sentence:
   Lá snákan ti vĩnike ti xpétule.
               theme   agent
   seated   the man the Peter
   'Peter seated the man.'

b. passive sentence:
   Inákanat   ti vĩnike yu?un ti xpétule.
            theme   agent
   was seated the man by   the Peter
   'The man was seated by Peter.'

Here the passive is signalled by a change in the form of the verb and the appearance of the preposition *yu?un* 'by' before the agent, but there is no change in the relative order of the agent and theme.
    Mandarin Chinese employs yet another option.

102)

a. active sentence:
   Zhu laoshi   piyue-le wode kaoshi.
   agent   theme
   Zhu professor marked my   test
   'Professor Zhu marked my test.'

b. passive sentence:
   Wode kaoshi bei Zhu laoshi   piyue-le.
       theme   agent
   my   test   by Zhu professor marked.
   'My test was marked by Professor Zhu.'

Here, the passive is marked by a change in word order and by the appearance of the preposition *bei* 'by' before the agent, but the verb has exactly the same form in both patterns.
    What then do the passive sentences of English, Tzotzil, Chinese, and other languages have in common? According to proponents of relational analysis,

the crucial facts involve a correspondence between the grammatical relations found in a passive sentence and those in its active counterpart.

103)

a.   active sentence: The thieves took the painting.
                 subject   *direct object*

                 subject   *oblique*

b.   passive sentence: The painting was taken (by the thieves).

Notice that the direct object in the active *103a)* (*the painting*) is the subject in the passive *103b)* while the subject in *103a)* (*the thieves*) occurs as part of a PP in *103b)*. (An NP that occurs with a preposition is said to be **oblique.**)

It is now possible to think of passive sentences as the product of the two changes shown in Table 5.14 to the corresponding active pattern.

Table 5.14   Properties of passive structures

Active pattern		*Passive pattern*
Subject	$\rightarrow$	oblique
Direct object	$\rightarrow$	subject

Since the criteria used to identify subjects and direct objects differ from language to language, these changes are compatible with a variety of different structural effects. In English, where the direct object appears after the verb and the subject before it, a change in an NP's grammatical relation will also involve a change in its linear position. Thus a theme NP that serves as subject (as in the passive) rather than direct object (as in the active) will appear to the left of the verb rather than to the right.

104)

a.   active sentence
     The thieves took the painting.
                        ↑
     theme serving as direct object

b.   passive sentence
     The painting was taken (by the thieves).
         ↑
     theme serving as subject

In other languages, changes in grammatical relations may be marked by something other than a change in word order. In the Tzotzil passive, for example, addition of the preposition *yuʔun* is enough to indicate that the agent is no longer the subject. Despite these differences, however, passive structures in both English and Tzotzil have in common the pair of relational changes stated in Table 5.14.

Many other syntactic phenomena can be analysed in terms of processes that affect subjects and direct objects. As our study of passivization illustrates, these concepts are especially useful when comparing syntactic phenomena in languages with different word order and/or morphological patterns. We will see some additional examples of this in section 2.3 of Chapter 9.

6.3

Functional analysis

Syntactic analysis can also focus on the way in which different syntactic structures are used to communicate information. Such analyses are often called **functional** since they seek to understand syntactic phenomena in terms of their communicative function. The contrast between active and passive sentences is especially instructive in this regard. Although both sentence types have the same basic meaning, they differ from each other in the way in which they present the situation that they describe. Put another way, they differ from each other in the way in which they 'package' the information to be communicated. Two differences can be noted here.

First, passive sentences tend to de-emphasize the role of the agent in the situation being described. In fact, the vast majority of passive sentences do not mention the agent at all. Hence, we can say simply *The painting was taken* or *The dishes were broken*, without attributing responsibility for these events to any particular person.

Second, passive sentences foreground the theme by making it the subject of the sentence. As a result, the situation is presented from the perspective of that individual. (As we will see in Chapter 7, the subject usually introduces the entity that the rest of the sentence is about.) Consider in this regard the following passage.

105)

MacGregor is a pretty lucky bloke. Last night, he went out, got drunk, and started rolling around in the street. Before too long, *he was hit by a car.* But he wasn't even injured. In fact, he got up and walked home.

The italicized passive sentence in this passage sounds completely natural since it brings to the foreground the pronoun *he*, which refers to the person (MacGregor) from whose perspective the entire series of events is being described. In contrast, the passive is not nearly so natural in the following context.

106)

MacGregor is a pretty lucky bloke. Last night, he went out, got drunk, and started rolling around in the street. Before too long, **a car was hit by him.* But his hand wasn't even injured . . .

Here the passive sentence seems quite out of place. This is because it foregrounds the car even though the rest of the passage is clearly about MacGregor. This in turn creates a discontinuity in the flow of information, making the passage quite unnatural.

In sum, then, the functional analysis of the passive pattern focuses on the way in which it packages information compared to active sentences. The key claim is that the function of this structure is to de-emphasize the agent (often deleting it entirely) and to draw attention to the theme NP.

By analysing syntactic structures functionally, it is often possible to gain insights into why human language has the particular syntactic patterns that it does and how these patterns contribute to the larger task of communication. For this reason, the functional method is being used by a growing number of linguists to analyse the sentence structures of human language.

Summing up

In this chapter we have been concerned with some of the fundamental devices involved in the analysis of sentence formation. As we have seen, these devices seem to be of different types: there are **phrase structure rules** (perhaps reducible to a single **XP rule**) that determine the architecture of a sentence's **deep structure**, **subcategorization** information that ensures a match between **heads** and the **complements** with which they appear in syntactic structure, and **transformations** that can modify deep structure in various ways to produce a **surface structure**. Taken together, these devices make up an important part of our overall linguistic competence in that they provide the means to combine words into sentences in endlessly novel ways.

Although the precise rules for sentence formation differ from language to language, **Universal Grammar** provides all languages with the same general types of devices (syntactic categories, phrase structure rules, and transformations). Many of the differences among languages can be traced to the existence of a small set of **parameters**, each of which makes available a variety of alternatives.

Notes

1   It is commonly assumed that the Infl node also contains information about subject–verb agreement, which – like tense – is often realized as verbal inflection (see Chapter 4, section 6.4). Thus, the tree in Figure 5.9 would actually look like Figure i, with the features under the Agr(eement) label matching those on the subject.

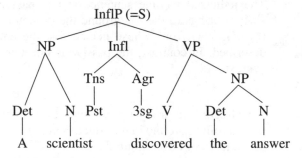

Figure i   The structure of S, with Infl containing information about tense and agreement.

Mechanisms not considered here ensure that the tense and agreement features under Infl are realized appropriately on the verb. In order to keep this introduction to syntax at a relatively simple level, we will not discuss agreement further in this chapter.

2   In this analysis, only the so-called 'modal' auxiliaries mentioned here count as instances of Infl. *Have* and *be* (traditionally called 'aspectual' auxiliaries) are treated as special verbs that take a VP as their complement. Figure ii shows that *should* (an instance of Infl) takes as its complement the VP headed by *be*, which in turn takes the VP *completing the assignment* as its complement.

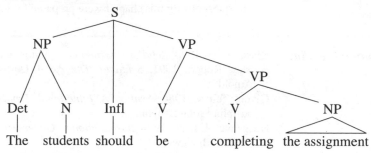

Figure ii   The structure of a sentence containing an aspectual auxiliary.

Sources

Transformational syntax is the most popular of the half dozen major syntactic theories used in contemporary linguistics. Normally, it is the theory taught in introductory linguistics courses, both because it is so widely used and because many of the other approaches that exist today have developed in response to it. The particular system outlined here involves a variety of simplifications to make it appropriate for presentation in an introductory course.

The treatment of auxiliary verbs involves a simplified version of the system proposed in *Barriers* by N. Chomsky (Cambridge, MA: MIT Press, 1986); see the book by Radford (cited below) for a more detailed introduction. The system of subcategorization employed here is loosely based on the one outlined in *Generalized Phrase Structure Grammar* by G. Gazdar, E. Klein, G. Pullum, and I. Sag (Cambridge, MA: Harvard University Press, 1985), which describes a non-transformational approach to syntax. The theory of transformations presented here is essentially the one employed throughout the 1980s by the vast majority of people working within transformational grammar.

The status of adjectives in Universal Grammar is discussed by R.M.W. Dixon in *Where Have All the Adjectives Gone?* (The Hague: Mouton, 1982). The data on Jacaltec (section 4.1) is from *The Jacaltec Language* by C. Day (Bloomington, IN: Indiana University Press, 1973). The claim that the Nootkan languages have only two lexical categories is based on the discussion in 'Noun and verb in Nootkan' by W. Jacobsen, Jr in *The Victoria Conference on Northwestern Languages* (Heritage Record No. 4. Vancouver: British Columbia Provincial Museum, 1979. Pp. 83-155). A similar system is described for the now extinct Yana by E. Sapir in *Language* (New York: Harcourt Brace, 1921).

The discussion of the relational analysis of passive sentences is intended to be neutral between Lexical Functional Grammar as outlined in *The Mental Representation of Grammatical Relations*, edited by Joan Bresnan (Cambridge, MA: MIT Press, 1982) and Relational Grammar as described in 'Toward a universal characterization of passivization' by D. Perlmutter and P. Postal in *Studies in Relational Grammar I*, edited by D. Perlmutter (Chicago: University of Chicago Press, 1983); the Chinese and Tzotzil examples cited in section 6.2 were taken from this paper. The Sre example is from 'Passive in the World's Languages' by E. Keenan in the first volume of the series edited by T. Shopen and recommended below. The functional analysis of passives draws on the discussion in *Functional Syntax* by Susumu Kuno (Chicago: University of Chicago Press, 1987) and *Functional Syntax and Universal Grammar* by W. Foley and R. Van Valin (Cambridge: Cambridge University Press, 1986).

The questions for this chapter were prepared by Joyce Hildebrand.

Recommended reading   Blake, Barry. 1990. *Relational Grammar.* London: Routledge.

Borsley, Robert. 1991. *Syntactic Theory: A Unified Approach.* London: Edward Arnold.

Givón, Talmy. 1984. *Syntax: A Functional Typological Approach.* Vol. 1. Philadelphia: John Benjamins.

Haegeman, Liliane. 1994. *Introduction to Government and Binding Theory.* 2nd edn. Oxford: Blackwell.

Radford, Andrew. 1988. *Transformational Grammar: A First Course.* Cambridge : Cambridge University Press.

Shopen, Timothy, ed. 1985. *Language Typology and Syntactic Description.* Vols 1–3. Cambridge : Cambridge University Press.

Appendix: How to build tree structures

Although it is relatively easy to check a tree structure to see if it complies with the XP rule, it is somewhat harder to build a tree structure from scratch when trying to analyse a new phrase or sentence. In such cases, you will probably find it easiest to proceed in steps, working from the bottom up and from right to left. As an illustration, let us first consider the phrase *near the door*.

The first step involves assigning each word to the appropriate lexical category, as depicted in Figure 5.43.

Figure 5.43   This first step: determining the word-level categories.

Then, working from right to left, the XP levels are added above each N, V, A, or P, as in Figure 5.44. Thus, we first add an NP label above the N *door*. There is clearly no complement here, but there is a specifier (the determiner *the*), which can be attached at the NP level in accordance with the XP rule.

Figure 5.44   Building the NP.

Next, as in Figure 5.45, we carry out the same procedure for the P *near*, adding the required PP level.

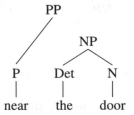

Figure 5.45   Adding the PP level above the P head.

The NP to the right of the P clearly functions as its complement (since it names the location entailed by the meaning of *near*). This element is therefore attached at the PP level in accordance with the XP rule, giving the complete structure depicted in Figure 5.46.

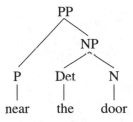

Figure 5.46   The complete PP.

A sentential example

Consider now how we proceed in the case of a complete sentence such as *The apple might hit the man*. Assignment of each word to the appropriate lexical category gives the structure depicted in Figure 5.47.

Figure 5.47   The categories for each word in the sentence.

Working from right to left, it is easy to see that the noun *man* heads an NP (Figure 5.48) that contains a specifier but no complement.

Figure 5.48   The structure of the rightmost NP.

Next, we focus on the V *hit*, adding the required VP level and attaching the complement NP *the man*, as in Figure 5.49.

Figure 5.49   Adding the VP level above the V head.

As an instance of Infl, the auxiliary *might* is the head of S, with the VP to the right serving as its complement and the NP to the left functioning as its specifier. This yields the complete sentence illustrated in Figure 5.50.

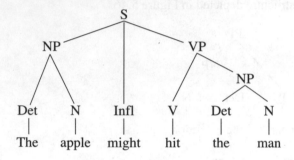

Figure 5.50   The complete sentence.

The entire sentence is then embedded in a CP 'shell', giving the tree in Figure 5.51.

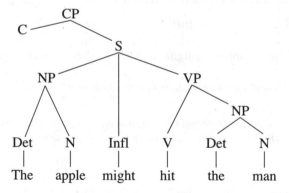

Figure 5.51   The sentence embedded in a CP shell.

Transformations   As explained in section 3, the syntactic analysis of some sentences involves transformations in addition to the usual phrase structure rules. It is simple to recognize if one of the transformations used in this chapter has applied: if a sentence contains an auxiliary verb to the left of the subject, then inversion has applied; if it begins with a *wh* word, then *Wh* Movement has applied. In the ecsentence *What should the farmers plant?*, then, both of these transformations have applied.

In order to determine the deep structure, we must 'return' the auxiliary verb to its position under Infl and we must determine the position from which the *wh* word has been moved. Since the *wh* word in the sentence *What should the farmers plant?* asks about the complement of the verb (the thing that is planted), we place *what* in the verbal complement position in deep structure. This gives the deep structure depicted in Figure 5.52.

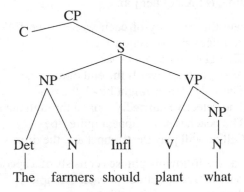

Figure 5.52 The deep structure for the sentence *what should the farmers plant?*

The auxiliary *should* then moves to the C position (inversion) and *what* to the specifier position under CP (*Wh* Movement), yielding the complete surface structure depicted in Figure 5.53.

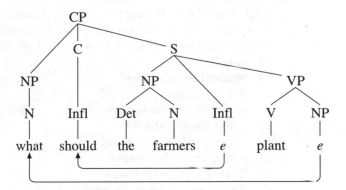

Figure 5.53 The surface structure.

Questions

1. Place an asterisk next to any of the sentences that are ungrammatical for you. Explain what makes these sentences ungrammatical?
   a) The tutor told the students to study.
   b) The tutor suggested the students to study.

c) The customer asked for a cold beer.
d) The customer requested for a cold beer.
e) He gave the Red Cross some money.
f) He donated the Red Cross some money.
g) The pilot landed the jet.
h) The jet landed.
i) A journalist wrote the article.
j) The article wrote.
k) Julie is bored of her job.
l) Julie is tired of her job.

2. Indicate the category of each word in the following sentences. (It may help to refer back to section 1.1.)
   a) That glass suddenly broke.
   b) A jogger ran towards the end of the lane.
   c) These dead trees might block the road.
   d) The detective hurriedly looked through the records.
   e) The peaches never appear quite ripe.
   f) Gillian will play the trumpet and the drums in the orchestra.

3. Each of the following phrases consists of a specifier and a head. Draw the appropriate tree structure for each example.
   a) the zoo   f) this house
   b) always try   g) very competent
   c) so witty   h) quite cheap
   d) perhaps pass   i) never surrender
   e) less bleak   j) those books

4. The following phrases include a head, a complement, and (in some cases) a specifier. Draw the appropriate tree structure for each example. For now, there is no need to depict the internal structure of complements. (See the tree diagrams in Figures 5.4 and 5.5 in the chapter.)
   a) into the house
   b) repaired the telephone
   c) full of mistakes
   d) more towards the window
   e) a film about pollution
   f) always study this material
   g) perhaps earn the money
   h) that argument with Owen
   i) the success of the programme

5. After carefully reading the first two sections of the appendix, draw phrase structure trees for each of the following sentences.
   a) Those guests should leave.
   b) Maria never ate the brownie.
   c) That shelf will fall.
   d) The glass broke.
   e) The student lost the debate.

    f)   The manager may offer an increment.
    g)   The judge often sentences shoplifters.
    h)   The teacher often organized a discussion.
    i)   A psychic will speak to this group.
    j)   Marianne could become quite fond of Larry.

6. Apply the substitution test to determine which of the bracketed sequences in the following sentences form constituents.
    a)   [The tragedy] upset the entire family.
    b)   They hid [in the cave].
    c)   The [computer was very] expensive.
    d)   [The town square and the civic building] will be rebuilt.
    e)   Jane [left town].
    f)   The goslings [swam across] the lake.

7. Apply the movement test to determine which of the bracketed sequences in the following sentences form constituents.
    a)   We ate our lunch [near the river bank].
    b)   Steve looked [up the number] in the book.
    c)   The [island has been] flooded.
    d)   I love [peanut butter and bacon sandwiches].
    e)   The environmental [movement is gaining momentum].

8. Lexical categories are divided into subcategories on the basis of their complements. For each of the following words, two potential complement options are given. For each of the words:
    i)   Determine which one of the two options better matches the subcategorization requirements of the verb, noun or adjective.
    ii)   Justify your choice by creating a sentence using that complement option.

	Verb	*Options*
a)	expire	∅ *or* NP NP
b)	destroy	NP *or* ∅
c)	observe	NP *or* PP_{to} PP_{about}
d)	discuss	NP *or* ∅
e)	clean	NP PP_{for} *or* NP NP
f)	mumble	NP *or* NP NP
g)	throw	∅ *or* NP PP_{loc}
h)	paint	NP PP_{to} *or* NP PP_{for}

	Noun	*Options*
a)	debate	PP_{of} PP_{to} *or* PP_{with} PP_{about}
b)	hammer	∅ *or* PP_{with} PP_{about}
c)	success	PP_{of} PP_{to} *or* PP_{of}
d)	transfer	PP_{with} PP_{about} *or* PP_{of} PP_{to}
e)	sickness	∅ *or* PP_{with} PP_{about}

	Adjective	*Options*
a)	strong	∅ *or* PP_{about}

   b) sick   NP *or* PP$_{of}$
   c) bored   PP$_{with}$ *or* PP$_{of}$
   d) knowledgeable PP$_{to}$ *or* PP$_{about}$
   e) small   PP$_{of}$ *or* ø

9. *i*) The following sentences all contain embedded clauses that function as complements of a verb. Draw a tree structure for each sentence.
   a) The reporter said that an accident injured a boy.
   b) The fishermen think that the company polluted the bay.
   c) Barbara reported that a student asked whether the eclipse would occur.

   ii) The following sentences all contain embedded clauses that function as complements of an adjective, a preposition or a noun. Draw a tree structure for each sentence.
   d) The police appeared happy that the criminal would surrender.
   e) That officer was sure that Gerry often speeds down the motorway.
   f) Anna wondered about whether the exam would cover that section.
   g) The jury will never believe the claim that the driver wrecked the Porsche.

10. The derivations of the following sentences involve the inversion transformation. Give the deep structure and the surface structure for each sentence.
   a) Will the boss hire Hilary?
   b) Can the dog fetch the frisbee?
   c) Should the student report the incident?
   d) Must the musician play that music?
   e) Is that player leaving the team?

11. The following sentences involve the rules of *Wh* Movement and inversion. Give the deep structure and the surface structure for each of these sentences.
   a) Who should the director call?
   b) Who should call the director?
   c) What is Joanne eating?
   d) Who will those immigrants live with?
   e) What might Chris bake for the party?
   f) What was Anne bringing to the gathering?

12. The following data is from Igbo, a language spoken in Nigeria.
   a) Nwáànyĩ áhừ   b) úlố   à
       woman   that   house this
       'that woman'   'this house'

   i) What is the relative order of the determiner and noun in Igbo?
   ii) Draw the phrase structure trees for the two Igbo phrases.

13. The following data are from Malagasy, spoken on the island of Madagascar.

a) Entin' kafe   izy.   b) Mankany amin' ny restauranta izy.
brings coffee he   goes   to   the restaurant he
'He brings coffee.'   'He goes to the restaurant.'

i) Based on these data, what are the phrase structure rules for Malagasy?

ii) Draw the tree structure for each of the Malagasy sentences.

14. Consider the following Selayarese data.

a) La?allei doe?   injo i-Baso.
took   money the Baso
'Baso took the money.'

b) nra?bai   sapon injo.
collapsed house the
'The house collapsed.'

c) Lataroi doe? injo ri lamari   injo i-Baso.
put   money the in cupboard the Baso
'Baso put the money in the cupboard.'

i) Write the XP rules required to form these sentences.

ii) How do they differ from English phrase structure rules?

15. The following data are from Korean. You may ignore the nominative (subject) and accusative (direct object) markers for the purposes of this exercise.

a) Terry-ka   ku yeca-lul coahanta.
Terry-Nom that girl-Ac likes
'Terry likes that girl.'

b) I   noin-i   hakkyo ey kassta.
this man-Nom school to went
'This man went to school.'

c) Sue-ka   chinkwu eykey chayk-ul ilkessta.
Sue-Nom friend to   book-Ac read
'Sue read the book to a friend.'

i) Based on these data, what is the XP rule for Korean?

ii) Draw the tree structure for each of the Korean sentences.

16. The following data illustrate the formation of *yes–no* questions in German.

a) Das Kind wird die Schwester lehren.
the child will the sister   teach
'The child will teach the sister.'

b) Wird das Kind die Schwester lehren?
will the child the sister   teach
'Will the child teach the sister?'

c) Der Mann liebt die Frau.
'The man loves the woman.'

d) Liebt der Mann die Frau?
loves the man   the woman
'Does the man love the woman?'

i) Assuming that German makes uses of the same inversion transformation as English (i.e., 'Move Infl to the C position'), does the above data tell us whether German employs the verb raising transformation? You must include the tree structures for b) and d) in your answer.

17. The following sentences all contain conjoined categories. Draw a tree structure for each of the sentences.
    a) The cyclist drank a gallon of water and a litre of Coke.
    b) The aeroplane will land at the airport and taxi to the terminal.
    c) The dog went down the stairs and out the door.
    d) Crusoe landed on an island and ate a goat.
    e) Jill should recycle that book and magazine.
    f) Hilary knows that spring will come and that the snow will melt.
    g) Mary is keen on calculus but tired of chemistry.

18. The following sentences contain modifiers of various types. For each sentence, first identify the modifier(s), then draw the tree structures.
    a) A large iguana suddenly appeared.
    b) The headteacher made an important announcement after the class.
    c) An unusual event occurred before the game.
    d) The very hazardous waste seeped into the ground quickly.
    e) A huge moon hung in the black sky.
    f) Timothy drew an enormous map during the afternoon.

19. Each of the following sentences contains a relative clause. Draw the deep structure and the surface structure trees for each of these sentences.
    a) The animals which Sam saw came from Kenya.
    b) Kyle likes the girl whom June befriended.
    c) The woman whom Keith lives with recycles plastic.
    d) Helen recited a poem which Wordsworth wrote.
    e) The canoe which Crusoe built was too heavy.

20. In each of the following sentences, indicate above each NP whether it is subject, direct object or oblique and indicate below each NP whether it is agent or theme.
    a) Marie purchased a present.
    b) The class was conducted by an expert.
    c) Those books were read by young children.
    d) An expert conducted the class.
    e) A present was purchased by Marie.

6

Interfaces

Michael Dobrovolsky, William O'Grady and Francis Katamba

...there is always some 'leakage' between the hierarchical levels of science...

୶ D. Hofstadter

Up to this point, the individual components of a grammar have each been presented in some detail. These components, however, do not function in isolation. Rules in one component may depend on or affect those in another component. In this chapter, we explore some ways in which the different components of a grammar are related to each other. These **interfaces**, as they are called in today's linguistic research, involve morphology and phonology, phonology and syntax, and morphology and syntax. (A fourth interface, between syntax and semantics, is considered in the next chapter as part of the discussion of semantics.)

1

MORPHOLOGY AND PHONOLOGY

Chapter 3 dealt with allophonic variation, which is represented by rules that derive allophones from underlying (phonemic) representations. A second type of variation in language involves morphemes and their allomorphs (first introduced in Chapter 4, section 1.1). An example of allomorphic variation can be seen in the English plural morpheme, which has different allomorphs in the words *cat*[s], *dog*[z], and *match*[ɪz]. Like allophonic variation, this phenomenon is analysed with the help of a single underlying representation from which the allomorphs can be derived. The rules that account for both allophonic and allomorphic variation make reference to phonetic environments, including syllable structure. There are, however, differences between allophonic and allomorphic variation, two of which are outlined in the following section.

1.1

Morphophonemic rules

Rules that account for alternations among allomorphs (morphophonemic alternations) are called **morphophonemic** rules. The major differences between allophonic and morphophonemic rules can be summed up under two major points.

- Allophonic rules are exceptionless – they apply in the appropriate environment to all classes and forms in a language. There are, for example, no exceptions to a rule such as aspiration in English of voiceless stops occurring syllable-initially in stressed syllables (see Chapter 3, section 5.5). In contrast, morphophonemic rules often show exceptions. They may, for example, apply to a limited class of forms, as in the case of the rule that changes final *f* to *v* in the plural of a few English words like *knife* and *thief* (but not in *cough, bluff, whiff, chief,* and so on); we will examine this rule in more detail in section 1.4.
- Morphophonemic rules often (but do not always) include affix boundaries in their environment. Such boundaries are not found in allophonic rules.

1.2

Deriving allomorphs

We analyse and derive allomorphs in much the same way we derive allophones. An underlying representation (UR) is set up, and rules apply to derive all phonetic variants from the same underlying representation. Often, the underlying representation of the morpheme is the elsewhere allomorph– the one that occurs with the widest distribution.

1.3

Conditioned allomorphs

The allomorphs of the English plural morpheme provide a typical example of phonologically conditioned allomorphs.

English plural

The plural morpheme in English shows three-way variation in its allomorphs. The three allomorphs, /-s/, /-z/, and /-ɪz/, are distributed in a systematic manner, as Table 6.1 illustrates.

Table 6.1   English plural allomorphs

Allomorph: /-s/		Environment
tops	/tɒps/	• bases end in a voiceless consonant that is not strident
twits	/twɪts/	
backs	/bæks/	
puffs	/pʌfs/	
months	/mʌnθs/	

Allomorph: /-z/		Environment
cobs	/kɒbz/	• bases end in a vowel or a voiced consonant that is not strident
lids	/lɪdz/	
lads	/lædz/	
doves	/dʌvz/	
lathes	/leɪðz/	
pins	/pɪnz/	
plums	/plʌmz/	
wings	/wɪŋz/	
knees	/ni:z/	
days	/deɪz/	

Table 6.1 English plural allomorphs (cont.)

Allomorph: /-ɪz/		Environment
hisses	/hɪsɪz/	• bases end in a consonant that is
buzzes	/bʌzɪz/	strident (s, z, ʃ, ʒ, tʃ, dʒ)
crutches	/krʌtʃɪz/	
judges	/dʒʌdʒɪz/	
wishes	/wɪʃɪz/	

The phonetic form of these allomorphs is determined by the segment that precedes them. Bases that end in a strident (sibilant) consonant always appear with the /-ɪz/ allomorph. Bases that end in a vowel or a voiced consonant that is not strident take the /-z/ allomorph, and bases that end in a voiceless consonant that is not strident take the /-s/ allomorph.

A fundamental strategy in selecting the underlying form (UF) of an allomorph is to choose the one with the widest distribution. Since the /-z/ allomorph occurs after all vowels as well as after most voiced consonants, it is chosen as basic. This choice results in underlying representations that show /-z/ after all bases (Table 6.2).

Table 6.2 Underlying representations of some English plurals

tops	/tɒp-z/	cobs	/kɒb-z/	hisses	/hɪs-z/
twits	/twɪt-z/	lids	/lɪd-z/	buzzes	/bʌz-z/
				judges	/dʒʌdʒ-z/

Derivation

Once the underlying representations have been set up, the phonetic forms can be derived. We can account for the allomorph /-ɪz/ by noting that whenever the underlying /-z/ appears after a base that ends in a strident coronal consonant, an /ɪ/ (or a schwa in the speech of those who pronounce this form as /əz/) is present. This reflects a phonotactic constraint of English that is expressible with reference to syllable structure: an English word cannot contain a sequence of strident consonants in the same coda. We can see that the reference to syllable structure is a necessary part of this statement by looking at other structures in which sequences of strident consonants occur. Such sequences are found across word boundaries in phrases and compounds, such as *bus shelter* /bʌs̠ ʃeltə/, *crash site* /kræʃ saɪt/ or *buzz saw* /bʌz̠ sɔː/. They may even occur word-internally across syllable boundaries, as in *posture* /pɒstʃə/ (/pɒʃtʃə/ for some speakers). But when a sequence of two coronal stridents occurs in a coda (Figure 6.1), it is broken up by the epenthesis of a somewhat centralized and reduced /ɪ/ (or a schwa). Since the coda sequence is impossible, a new syllable is created to accommodate it.

$$\varnothing \rightarrow \begin{bmatrix} +\text{syllabic} \\ +\text{reduced} \end{bmatrix} / \ [+\text{strident}] \ \underline{\hspace{1cm}} \ [+\text{strident}] \ \sigma$$

Figure 6.1 Strident coda epenthesis.

Given this process, we can derive forms such as *matches*, *judges*, and so on, as shown in Figure 6.2.

	N Coda
UR	#mætʃ-z#
Strident coda epenthesis	#mætʃ-ız#
PR	[mætʃız]

Figure 6.2   Derivation of English *matches*.

The appearance of [s] after voiceless consonants and [z] elsewhere is now representable as a case of voicing assimilation (laryngeal node spreading – Figure 6.3).

Figure 6.3   English coda voicing assimilation (laryngeal node spreading).

Figure 6.4 shows derivations of all three plural allomorphs. Note that the ordering of the rules is crucial here. If voicing assimilation applied first, the plural ending of forms such as *match* and *hiss* would incorrectly end up as */mætʃıs/ and */hısıs/, since the suffix would assimilate in voicing before epenthesis could apply.

	UF		
UF	#bʊk-z#	#fıb-z#	#mætʃ-z#
Strident coda epenthesis	—	—	#mætʃ-ız#
Voicing assimilation	#bʊk-s#	—	—
PF	[bʊks]	[fıbz]	[mætʃız]

Figure 6.4   Derivation of English plural forms.

In the next section we see how these same rules for determining the plural allomorphs of English interact with another type of morphophonemic rule.

1.4

Conditioning by morphological class

A second type of morphophonemic rule refers to a subclass of forms, rather than applying to all members of a class of forms. English plurals again provide the example.

Irregular English plurals

English includes a limited class of words that show an /f/ alternating with /v/ in their plural forms, and can be seen in Table 6.3.

Table 6.3   Alternating base-final /f/ and /v/ in English

The /f/-/v/ alternation (irregular forms)		No alteration (regular forms)	
wife	wives	whiff	whiffs
thief	thieves	chief	chiefs
leaf	leaves	fife	fifes
knife	knives	laugh	laughs

The alternating class is unproductive; new words with final /f/ entering English will not show this alternation. For example, speakers would pluralize a hypothetical new word *niff* as /nɪfs/, not */nɪvz/. This implies that each word in the unproductive class needs to be marked as undergoing a rule that voices its base-final segment when the form is pluralized. Such a rule takes the form shown in Figure 6.5, in which it is labelled *Rule PL*. Information about rules that a form must undergo is included in its entry in the lexicon. A form that undergoes Rule PL is marked as [+Rule PL]. Forms that are not so marked are automatically assumed to be [–Rule PL].

Rule PL: $f \rightarrow v /$ ____ $]$-$z_{plural]}$

Figure 6.5   The f → v alternation rule for English.

Following a base-changing rule such as Rule PL, the morphophonemic rule of voicing assimilation introduced in Figure 6.3 applies. (Stress is not shown in Figure 6.6. Nor is the allophonic rule that lengthens vowels before voiced obstruents.)

UR	#θiːf-z#[+Rule PL]	#tʃiːf-z#
Rule PL (f → v)	#θiːv-z#	—
Voicing assimilation	—	#tʃiːf-s#
PF	[θiːvz]	[tʃiːfs]

Figure 6.6   Derivation of English *thieves* and *chiefs*.

Many of the underlying forms presented so far in this chapter are distinct from their phonetic representations. For instance, we have seen that the regular plural suffix spelled as *-s* in the orthography, and represented as /-z/ in the underlying representation, is pronounced [-s], [-z] or [ɪz], depending on the phonetic context in which it occurs. Likewise, a form such as *thief* is pronounced with a [f] or [v], depending on whether it is singular or plural, with the voicing of the underlying /f/ being part of the marking of the plural. The next section takes up the implications of this kind of representation in more detail.

1.5

Abstract underlying representations

Underlying representations (URs) generally show some degree of difference from phonetic representations. There are no phonetic forms like *[mɪtz], *[pæθz], or *[waɪfz] in English, although such forms are found as URs. Underlying representations are therefore said to be **abstract**. By an abstract representation, we mean one that is to a greater or lesser degree distinct from its phonetic realization. The greater the difference between a phonological representation and its phonetic realization, the more abstract the phonological representation is said to be.

Although the URs that enable us to account for morphophonemic variation can be very abstract, there is an advantage to this kind of representation. Employing abstract URs enables us to make greater generalizations about the relationship among allomorphs. For example, we have just seen how two phonetically distinct forms of the root morpheme *thief* are derived from the same UR.

Abstraction and English bases

In English, we can derive the root of both *electri*[k] and *electri*[s]*ity* from one underlying form. This approach captures the fact that English speakers recognize the two forms as variants of the same morpheme. Assuming that the UR ends in *k*, Figure 6.7 depicts how we can write a morphophonemic rule that changes *k* to *s* before the suffix *-ity*.

k → s / ___ + ɪtɪ[1]

Figure 6.7   English *k* to *s* fronting.

The variant of the base that ends in *k* is chosen as underlying for two reasons. First, the base *electri*[k] has a wider distribution than the allomorph *electri*[s]; it occurs in words such as *electrical* as well as in the unsuffixed form. Second, our proposed rule has the advantage of reflecting a natural process of fronting of final /k/ to [s] before the high front vowel of the suffix. It would be more difficult to find phonetic motivation for a rule that changes an /s/ to [k] in final position or before the suffix *-al*.

It is also significant that the rule must include morphological information – the identity of the suffix that triggers the change – since /k/ is not pronounced as [s] whenever it appears before the vowel [ɪ] in English. If it were, English speakers would automatically pronounce *kill* as *sill*, and *kick* as *sick.* Since they do not, we assume that the morphological information is a crucial determining factor in this rule.

Derivations of *electric* and *electricity* are given in Figure 6.8. (The stress rule is also involved in this derivation but is not formalized here. Also omitted is the allophonic rule of flapping in North American English and in fast Cockney speech which yields a flap in words like [bʌɾə] 'butter' and [léɾə] 'letter'.)

UR	#ɪlektrɪk#	#ɪlektrɪk-ɪtɪ#
Stress k → s rule	#ɪléktrɪk# —	#ɪlektrík-ɪtɪ# #ɪlektrís-ɪtɪ#
PR	[ɪléktrɪk]	[ɪlektrís-ɪtɪ]

Figure 6.8 Derivation of *electric* and *electricity* in English.

The underlying form is abstract in the case of #ɪlektrɪk-ɪtɪ# but our rule has allowed us to represent an English speaker's knowledge that the bases *electri*[k] and *electri*[s] are allomorphs of the same morpheme.

The next section examines some of the interactions between phonology and syntax.

1.6

Prosodic morphology (advanced)

An aspect of the phonology–morphology interface that has received considerable attention recently in the model called **prosodic morphology**, is the way in which the application of some morphological rules is subject to phonological constraints which relate to prosodic structure. It is common to find morphological rules that only apply to bases that have a certain number of syllables or a particular metrical foot structure. As well, affix morphemes in some languages may be represented by forms that have no fixed, canonical segmental makeup but instead borrow whatever segments are present in the base to which they are attached. Such affixes can vary enormously in their phonological manifestation. The only requirement that has to be met is that the borrowed segments must satisfy a pre-specified prosodic configuration – i.e., the copied segments must fit in a particular syllable or metrical foot template.

English comparative degree adjectives

Let us take the first case first. We will illustrate it with a simple example from English. As Table 6.4 on page 252 shows, the comparative degree of adjectives is formed either by suffixing *-er* or by placing the word *more* before the basic degree form. The choice is dependent on prosodic factors which can be stated in terms of the number and internal structure of syllables.

We can formulate the following rules of thumb: normally, monosyllabic adjectives are inflected with *-er*, and so are disyllabic adjectives whose second syllable ends in a light rhyme containing an unstressed vowel [ɪ], [-əʊ], [-ə(r)] or a syllabic [l̩]. (For the purposes of this rule the diphthong [-əʊ] counts as light – a fact that is not surprising since many speakers weaken this vowel and pronounce it as [ə] when it is unstressed at the end of a word, e.g., *narrow* is often rendered as [nærə].) Disyllabic adjectives with a heavy second syllable containing a tense vowel, a diphthong (except [-əʊ]) or a vowel followed by a consonant take *more* (regardless of whether the heavy second syllable is stressed or not). Longer adjectives, with three or more syllables, also take *more*. (Note in passing that the use of the *-er* suffix with disyllabic adjectives ending in [-ə(r)] is in decline. While *cleverer* is acceptable to all speakers, most people find *slenderer*, *securer*, *maturer* and *obscurer* odd.)

Table 6.4 Comparative degree of English adjectives

a.	*A + er*	*Monosyllabic*
bigger	deeper	tougher

b.	*A + er*	*Disyllabic with light second syllable*
busier	prettier	dirtier
narrower	mellower	shallower
gentler	simpler	nobler
purer	obscurer	maturer
cleverer	slenderer	tenderer

c.	*More A*	*Disyllabic with heavy second syllable*
more timid	more wooden	more handsome

d.	*More A*	*Adjective with three or more syllables*
more similar	more competent	more ferocious

Templatic morphology

Prime justification for the prosodic morphology model has come from Semitic languages such as Arabic which have *nonconcatenative morphology*. In languages of this type, word-building typically involves some sort of modification of the segments that form the root of a word rather than the straightforward chaining together of affixes and roots. The Arabic verb root typically consists of three consonants which represent the word's identity. Thus, as the examples in Table 6.5 show, verbs with the meaning 'write' have the root consonants *ktb* while those with the meaning 'kill' have the root consonants *qtl*.

Table 6.5 Arabic verbs

a.	kataba	'he wrote'	b.	qatala	'he killed'
	kattaba	'he caused to write'		qattala	'he caused to kill'
	kutiba	'it was written'		qutila	'it was killed'

A three-tiered autosegmental representation accounts simply for the observed patterns. A template (or mould) with CV skeletal positions can be set up to represent the canonical form of the **binyan** (verbal class). For instance, the CVCVCV template represents 'past tense/completed action', the CVCCVC template represents 'causative', etc. Information about the actual segments that occur in a particular word is represented separately on the vocalic and consonantal tiers. The consonantal tier represents the root, and this contains the word's meaning (e.g., *ktb* 'write', *qtl* 'kill', etc.), while the vocalic tier represents verbal categories such as 'causative' and 'aspect' (indicating whether an action is in progress or completed).

Vocalic and consonantal tiers are referred to as **melodies**. Melodies are mapped onto the appropriate C and V positions of the **CV-tier** (also called the **phonological skeleton**) that are capable of bearing those units, going from left to right. So, consonants are mapped onto C positions and vowels onto V positions. If there are more skeletal positions than there are segments, spreading may take place. One segment may be multiply linked with several skeletal positions so that ultimately every segment ends up being associated with a skeletal position, and every skeletal position also ends up being linked to at least one segment. But spreading is not automatic. Where spreading entails multiple linking of a vowel or consonant to several skeletal positions, it has to be expressly sanctioned by the grammar of the language.

Finally, as already mentioned in Chapter 3, section 7.2, association lines are not allowed to cross. This is a formal way of indicating the fact that one entire segment cannot be inserted inside another distinct segment. For instance, a sequence like *tkt* must be represented as having two instances of the consonant *t*, as shown in Figure 6.9*a*, and not as having just a single, discontinuous *t* as in Figure 6.9*b*. (We omit the vocalic tier since it is not relevant here.) Figure 6.9*a* shows that the speaker produces the first *t,* then produces a *k* before going on to pronounce the second *t*.

```
Consonantal tier     a.  t  k  t          b. *t  k  t
                         |  |  |               └──┘│
CV-tier                  C  C  C               C  C
```

Figure 6.9   Association lines do not cross.

Using these principles in Figure 6.10, we can represent *qattala* 'he caused to kill' and *qutila* 'it was killed' in this way:

qattala   qutila

'he caused to kill'   'it was killed'

Figure 6.10   Arabic verb templates.

Thus, the CV positions of the phonological skeleton can be used to deal with the interaction of sound structure with word-building elements.

Reduplication and prosodic morphology

It has been shown by linguists working in the framework of prosodic morphology that genuine units of prosody such as the **mora**, a rhythmic unit corresponding to a short syllable nucleus (cf. Chapter 3, section 4.5), the syllable and the foot often play a key role in conditioning or determining the application of morphological rules. We have already observed this in the discussion of English comparative degree adjectives above: the -*er* comparative degree ending only goes with adjective bases that do not exceed two syllables.

Even stronger evidence of prosodic units conditioning morphological processes is provided by a number of languages that employ **partial reduplication**. This phenomenon typically involves manufacturing a reduplicative affix by making a copy of a portion of the base. The copy has a pre-specified canonical prosodic shape stipulated by the morphological template. But it has a great variety of vowel and consonant segments – with its exact shape always depending on the segments available in the base. For instance, in Ilokano (spoken in the Philippines) the morpheme meaning 'covered/filled with' is *si* followed by a templatic target which is a syllable containing just one mora (σ_μ) while the plural morpheme has for its templatic target a bimoraic prefix ($\sigma_{\mu\mu}$). (By convention the mora is symbolised by $_\mu$.) In both cases the template is satisfied by factoring out and copying appropriate segments, starting from the left edge of the base, until the template is satisfied. (In the examples in Table 6.6, the dot indicates syllable boundaries.)

Table 6.6   Ilokano prefixal reduplication

$si + \sigma_\mu$ – 'covered/filled with'				
bu .neŋ	'buneng'	→	si-<u>bu</u>.–bu .neŋ	'carrying a buneng'
dʒja .ket	'jacket'	→	si-<u>dʒja</u>-dʒja.ket	'wearing a jacket'
pan .di.liŋ	'skirt'	→	si-<u>pa</u>-pan.di.liŋ	'wearing a skirt'
$\sigma_{\mu\mu}$ – 'plural'				
pu.sa	'cat'	→	<u>pus</u>-pu .sa	'cats'
dʒja.nitor	'janitor'	→	<u>dʒjan</u>-dʒja.nitor	'janitors'
kal.diŋ	'goat'	→	<u>kal</u>-kal.diŋ	'goats'

2

PHONOLOGY AND SYNTAX

We saw in the first section of this chapter that some phonological rules include reference to subclasses of words and thus interact with the morphological component of a grammar. There are also rules that depend on certain kinds of syntactic information. Some stress patterns of English, for example, are determined by the syntactic category of the form to which the rules apply.

2.1

English stress

In English, there are pairs, such as those in Table 6.7, which show differing stress placement.

Table 6.7 Contrasting stress patterns in English

A		B	
gréenhòuse	'a place to grow flowers'	grèen hóuse	'a house that's green'
blúebòttle	'a large fly that defecates on food'	blùe bóttle	'a bottle that's blue'
féatherbèdding	'overemployment'	fèather bédding	'bedding with feathers'
bláckbird	'the blackbird' *Agelaius phoniceus*	blàck bírd	'any bird that's black'

In Chapter 4, section 3.1, it was shown that when words are grouped together to form compounds or phrases, one of the primary word stresses is usually more prominent than the others. We will now see how the stress patterning of compounds and phrases is represented on metrical levels respectively called the **compound level** and the **phrase level**.

The column A forms in Table 6.7 are all compounds. The rule for stress placement in English noun compounds places the primary stress over the leftmost word. Stated in terms of feet, the rule is as follows.[2]

1)

In English noun compounds, build a left-headed unbounded foot over the leftmost stress on the compound level.

The column B forms in Table 6.7 are all syntactic phrases. Unlike the compounds, they have been constructed by syntactic rules rather than rules of word formation. The rule for stress placement in English places the primary stress over the rightmost word. Stated in terms of feet, the rule is as follows.

2)

In English phrases, build a right-headed unbounded foot over the rightmost stress on the phrase level.

Presented step by step, the assignment of stress to compounds is shown in Figure 6.11 (overleaf). Foot-level stress is present for completeness in the examples.

This stressing procedure results in a primary stress on *green* and a secondary stress on *house*: gréenhòuse.

Foot- and word-level stress

(x)	(x)	Word level
(x)	(x)	Foot level
[green] _{Adj}	[house] _N	

Compound stress

(x	)	Compound level
(x)	(x)	Word level
(x)	(x)	Foot level
[[green] _{Adj}	[house] _N] _N	

(also: Blúebòttle, féatherbèdding, and other compounds)

Figure 6.11 Stress assignment in compounds.

Stress assignment in phrases undergoes the steps shown in Figure 6.12.

Foot- and word-level stress

(x)	(x)	Word level
(x)	(x)	Foot level
[green] _{Adj}	[house] _N	

Phrase-level stress

(	x)	Phrase level
(x)	(x)	Word level
(x)	(x)	Foot level
[[green] _{Adj}	[house] _N] _{NP}	

(also: Blùe nóse, fèather bédding, and other phrases)

Figure 6.12 Stress assignment in phrases.

Here, the stressing procedure provides a primary stress on *house* and a secondary stress on *green*: *grèen hóuse*.

2.2
Embedded compound stress

When a compound is embedded in a larger compound, the rule that stresses the leftmost word applies again. For example, if the compound *bláckbird* is joined with *nést*, the new compound still shows primary stress on the leftmost element: *bláckbird nèst*. This stress assignment takes place in stages as each part of the compound has stress assigned to it. Another metrical level at which compound stress applies is added to the representation. Since the same rule of stressing applies at more than one level, each application is called a **cycle**.

Note that each time a new x is added to a compound at one level, a matching stress must be added to the word(s) outside the parentheses as well (as it is to *nest* here). This procedure assures that the secondary stresses will be correctly placed. (The italic x in Figure 6.13 indicates the matching stress that must be added to the other word(s) outside the parentheses.)

Foot- and word-level stress

(x)	(x)	(x)	Word level
(x)	(x)	(x)	Foot level
[black] $_N$	[bird] $_N$	[nest] $_N$	

Compound stress

(first cycle)

(x	)	x	Compound level (first cycle)
(x)	(x)	(x)	Word level
(x)	(x)	(x)	Foot level
[[black] $_N$	[bird] $_N$] $_N$	[nest] $_N$	

Compound stress

(second cycle)

(x	)	Compound level (second cycle)
(x	) x	Compound level (first cycle)
(x)	(x)	(x)	Word level
(x)	(x)	(x)	Foot level
[[[black] $_N$	[bird] $_N$] $_N$	[nest] $_N$] $_N$	

Figure 6.13 Stress assignment in an embedded compound.

Since *bird* did not receive an x at the compound level, its stress, after all metrical levels have been assigned, is less than that of *nest*.

2.3

Stress clash (advanced)

The interface beween metrics and syntax can lead to some subtle changes in speech rhythm. An example of this phenomenon can be heard clearly in the case of personal names in English.

The stressing of personal names in English patterns like phrases, in that the first and last names are stressed as words, and the rightmost element of the full name normally receives primary stress: *Frèd Smíth*, *Màry Devíne*, *Fiòna McCáwley*, and so on. Each word in the name *Fred Smith* is composed of one stressed foot; word-level stress applies to the (single) stressed foot, as shown earlier in Figure 3.40, and phrase-level stress applies as shown in Figure 6.14.

(	x)	Phrase level
(x)	(x)	Word level
(x)	(x)	Foot level
[[Fred] $_N$	[Smith] $_N$] $_{NP}$	

Figure 6.14 Phrasal stress applied to an English proper name.

In everyday speech, however, certain first names such as *Jo-ann*, *John-Paul*, *Mary-Lou*, and so on, may optionally show an altered stress pattern when combined with a last name. In Table 6.8, note how the stress pattern of the first names in column A changes when the last name is added, while the stress placement in the first names in column B does not change.

Table 6.8 Proper names undergoing/not undergoing stress clash resolution in English

A			B		
Jò-ánn	→	Jò-ann Wátson	Yvónne	→	Yvònne Wátson
Jòhn-Pául		Jòhn-Paul Cámpbell	Akím		Akìm Cámpbell
Màry-Lóu		Màry-Lou Hénner	Annétte		Annètte Hénner

Represented on a grid, a name such as *Jo-ann Watson* takes the form shown in Figure 6.15 before any adjustment to the stress pattern takes place. Stressing of the first name and full name takes place cyclically. (The italic *x* indicates the matching stress that must be added to the other words in the group; see section 2.2.)

Note that in Figure 6.15, two stresses (x's) stand immediately next to each other on the phrase level (first cycle) and also have corresponding x's on the (word) level below. Such a configuration of stresses is known as **stress clash**. (To see a different configuration that does not show stress clash, compare the two x's in Figure 6.15 with the x's over *black* and *nest* in Figure 6.13, where there is a gap between the two x's at the compound level.)

The shift from what is represented in Figure 6.15, *Jo-ànn Wátson*, to the

(			x)	Phrase level (second cycle)
(		x)	*x*	Phrase level (first cycle)
(x)		(x)	(x)	Word level
(x)		(x)	(x .)	Foot level
[[[Jo] N		[ann] N] NP	[Watson] N] NP	

Figure 6.15 Phrasal stress with a compound proper name.

commonly heard pronunciation *Jò-ann Wátson* can be described in metrical terms as (optionally) occurring in order to resolve stress clash. As long as there is a stress on a lower level for the clashing stress to shift back to, it may. This adjustment is shown in Figure 6.16, where the 0 stands for a syllable with no x on the given level. The phrase level (first name) is boldfaced to emphasize that the metrical adjustment takes place there. Remember that this adjustment can only take place because there is an x over the name *Jo* on the level below that where the clash occurs. The abbreviations *1c* and *2c* stand for *first cycle* and *second cycle*, respectively.

(		x)		(		x)	Phrase level 2c
(	x)	x	→	(x	0)	x	**Phrase level 1c**
(x)	(x)	(x)		(x)	x)	(x)	Word level
(x)	(x)	(x .)		(x)	x)	(x .)	Foot level
[[Jo] N [ann] N] NP		[Watson]] N] NP	[[[Jo] N [ann] N] NP		[Watson]] N] NP	

Figure 6.16 Stress clash resolution.

We must now ask ourselves two questions. First, why is there no stress clash resolution on names like *Frèd Smíth*? The answer to this question is easy: there is no other syllable in the name *Fred* for a stress to fall back onto. The second question is more interesting. Why do names like *Yvonne* and *Akim* in column B of Table 6.8 not undergo stress clash resolution?

The answer to the second question lies in the formulation of stress-clash resolution presented above. Stress is shifted one syllable to the left *where possible*. All of the examples in column A above resolve stress clash by shifting a stress back to a syllable which is already stressed on the foot level since the names consist of two stressed feet. In the first names *Yvonne*, *Akim*, and *Annette* however, the first syllable is not stressed, and so does not constitute a proper landing site for a retracted stress. Figure 6.17 shows this on a metrical grid.

(x)		(x)		Phrase level
(x)	(x) →	**resolution not possible**		**Word level**
(. x)	(x .)	(. x)	(x .)	Foot level
[[Yvonne] N	[Watson] N] NP	[[Yvonne] N	[Watson] N] NP	

Figure 6.17 Stress clash resolution does not apply.

Subtle details like these govern many aspects of stress and rhythm in everyday speech and provide convincing evidence for an interface between phonology and syntax.

3

MORPHOLOGY AND SYNTAX

Many linguistic phenomena reflect the interaction of the morphological and syntactic components of the grammar. An important example of this interaction involves case, which indicates an NP's position in syntactic structure. Case is usually marked by inflecting the head of the NP (which will always be a noun or a pronoun).

We noted earlier (see sections 1.4 and 6.3 of Chapter 4) that the English noun has only one case ending – the element written as -'s which marks an NP that occupies the specifier position within a larger NP, as depicted in Figure 6.18. (We extend the system of phrase structure presented in Chapter 5 by allowing an NP to serve as specifier of an N.)

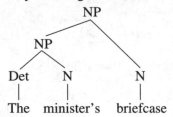

Figure 6.18 The genitive case marks on NP that function as specifier of an NP.

As also noted in Chapter 4 and shown in Table 6.9, a somewhat richer system of contrasts is found in English pronouns, whose forms reflect a three-way case distinction.

Table 6.9 Case for the 3rd person singular masculine pronoun in English

Form	Name	Function	Example
he	nominative	subject	He left.
his	genitive	specifier of N	his book
him	accusative	complement of V or P	Mary saw him. Mary sat near him.

Figure 6.19 shows that Japanese also makes a three-way case distinction, with the nominative suffix *-ga* used for a subject, the genitive suffix *-no* for a specifier of N, and the accusative suffix *-o* for a complement of V. (Complements of P do not take a case suffix in Japanese.)

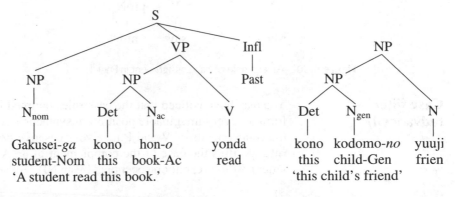

a The nominative and accusative   *b The genitive*

Figure 6.19   Case contrasts in Japanese.

The case rules of English

In order to account for the case contrasts found in English nouns and pronouns, the grammar must include a set of rules that associate case with specific syntactic positions. The following rules capture the generalizations about English case noted above.

3)

The case rules for English NPs:

a.   The complement of V receives accusative case.

b.   The complement of P receives accusative case.

c.   The specifier of N receives genitive case.

d.   The subject receives nominative case.

Let us assume that the lexicon of English includes a list of the various case forms that each word can have. So, the entry for the third person singular masculine pronoun, for example, will include the following information.

4)

Case forms: *he* (nominative)
            him (accusative)
            his (genitive)

According to the rules in *3)*, Figure 6.20 shows that a sentence such as *Mary saw him* is well-formed since the pronoun in the complement NP is accusative, as required by rule *3a)*.

In contrast, a sentence such as **Mary saw he* is ungrammatical since the pronoun in the complement NP has the nominative form, in violation of rule *3a)*.

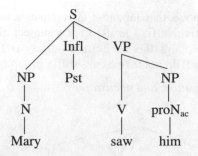

Figure 6.20 An example of case assignment in English.

Case filter (advanced)

You may have noticed that the case rules outlined in *3)* do not specify a case form for every imaginable position in syntactic structure. For instance, while the complements of V and P receive accusative case (rules *3a)* and *3b))*, no rule specifies the case of the complement of an A or N. Interestingly, these latter positions cannot be occupied by an NP.

5)

V with NP complement:	P with NP complement:
criticize [NP the girl]	near [NP the girl]
N with NP complement:	A with NP complement:
*criticism [NP the girl]	*critical [NP the girl]

We account for this by requiring that every NP receive case, regardless of whether the case is overtly expressed through inflection. This requirement is known as the **Case Filter**.

6)

The Case Filter:
Each NP in a grammatical sentence must be in a position to which case is assigned.

Phrases such as *criticize the girl* and *near the girl* satisfy the Case Filter since the NP *the girl* is in a position to receive accusative case (Figure 6.21). (Although nouns have no visible case inflection for the accusative case, a pronoun that occurred in this position would have the form *her* rather than *she*, so we know that the accusative case is assigned here.)

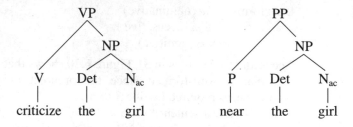

Figure 6.21 Case assignment for the complement of V and P.

In contrast (see Figure 6.22), the ill-formed phrases *criticism the girl* and *critical the girl* in *5)* above violate the Case Filter since the NP *the girl* is not in a position to which case is assigned. (Recall that no rule assigns case to the complement of N or A.)

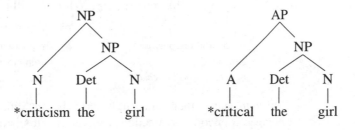

Figure 6.22 The absence of case on the complement of N and A.

In order for these phrases to be grammatical, the complement must be realized as a PP, as shown in Figure 6.23.

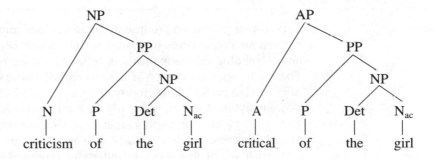

Figure 6.23 Case assignment when the complement of N and A is realized as a PP.

As you can see, this structural pattern avoids the problem found in Figure 6.22 since the complement of P receives accusative case according to the rules in *3)*.

Sometimes, an NP's case is determined by its position in deep structure rather than surface structure. A good example of this involves *wh* questions, in which the *wh* word appears in a position (the specifier of C) to which no case is assigned. In such circumstances, the NP's deep structure position determines its case. Direct evidence for this comes from conservative varieties of English, in which *who* is associated with the subject position and the special accusative form *whom* with the direct object position.

7)

In summary, then, although case is an inflectional (morphological) category, it encodes syntactic information. This is captured by means of the rules outlined in *3)*, which associate each of the various case forms of English with a different position in syntactic structure (subject, specifier of N, complement of V, and so on). Taking this idea and extending it one step further, the Case Filter then ensures that NPs can only occur in positions to which case is assigned. This explains why an NP may serve as complement of a V or P (Figure 6.20), but not of an N or A (Figure 6.21).

Summing up	This chapter provides a glimpse of the sometimes complex interaction among the various components of grammar. Interaction between the phonological and morphological components is reflected by the presence of allomorphs. The use of underlying representations and derivation by **morphophonemic** rules accounts for these morphophonemic alternations. In some cases, allomorphy is determined by the fact that only certain classes of forms undergo a given morphophonemic rule. Dealing with allomorphy leads to underlying representations, which in many cases are **abstract**. The use of a certain amount of abstraction in underlying representations allows allomorphs with distinct phonetic forms to be derived from single underlying forms. A further aspect of the phonology–morphology interface dealt with involves the ways in which **prosodic phonology** characterized in terms of the skeleton may affect or determine the application of morphological rules. This chapter also shows how morphological and syntactic structure play a role in determining stress assignment in compounds and phrases in English. Finally, it demonstrates that **case** marking reflects an interaction between the form of words (**morphology**) and the positions they occupy in syntactic structures (**syntax**).

Notes	1 In many varieties of British English, the phoneme /ɪ/ at the end of a word (e.g., *electricity*, *witty* and *pity*) is realized by the allophone [i] rather than [ɪ].
	2 The account of stress in compounds presented here has been somewhat simplified. We have omitted the less common right-headed noun compounds such as *woman dóctor*, *apple-píe*, and *kitchen táble* which are stressed on the second element. (See the article by Cinque cited below for a treatment of these.)

Sources	The problem of an underlying form for the plural suffix and of morphophonemic variation in general is discussed in Arnold Zwicky's article 'Settling on an underlying form: the English inflectional endings', in *Testing Linguistic Hypotheses*, edited by D. Cohen and J. Wirth (New York: John Wiley & Sons, 1975). The account of templatic morphology is based on J. McCarthy, *Formal problems in Semitic phonology and morphology*, MIT PhD thesis, distributed by Indiana University Linguistic Club, 1979. The discussion of Ilokano and prosodic morphology is based on John McCarthy and Alan Prince, 'Prosodic morphology' (cited below). For a more detailed discussion of the Case Filter, see *A Course in GB Syntax* by H. Lasnik and J. Uriagerecka (Cambridge, Mass.: MIT Press, 1988).

Recommended reading	Cinque, G. 1993. 'A null theory of phrase and compound stress.' *Linguistic Inquiry* 24: 239-398.
	Dressler, W.U. 1985. *Morphonology: The Dynamics of Derivation.* Ann Arbor: Karoma Publishers.
	Gleason, Jr, H.A. 1961. *An Introduction to Descriptive Linguistics.* New York: Holt, Rinehart & Winston.
	Inkelas, S. and Zec, D. eds. 1990. *The Phonology–Syntax Connection.* Chicago: The University of Chicago Press.
	Katamba, F. 1995. 'Skeleta and the prosodic circumscription of morphological domains.' In J. Durand, and F. Katamba (eds). *Frontiers of Phonology.* London: Longman.
	Kenstowicz, M. 1994. *Phonology in Generative Grammar.* Oxford: Blackwell.
	Kenstowicz, M. and Kisseberth, C. 1979. *Generative Phonology.* New York: Academic Press.
	McCarthy, J. and Prince, A. 1995. 'Prosodic morphology.' In John Goldsmith (ed.) *The Handbook of Phonological Theory.* Oxford: Blackwell.
	Pullum, G. and Zwicky, A. 1988. 'The syntax–phonology interface.' In *Linguistics: The Cambridge Survey.* Vol. 1. Edited by F. Newmeyer, pp. 255–80. Cambridge: Cambridge University Press.

Questions	**1.** The following data provide the possible forms of the regular past tense morpheme of English.

a)	walked	/wɔːkt/	l)	heaved	/hiːvd/
b)	cracked	/krækt/	m)	wheezed	/wiːzd/
c)	flipped	/flɪpt/	n)	fined	/faɪnd/
d)	hissed	/hɪst/	o)	flitted	/flɪtɪd/
e)	huffed	/hʌft/	p)	butted	/bʌtɪd/
f)	hushed	/hʌʃt/	q)	padded	/pædɪd/
g)	munched	/mʌntʃt/	r)	loaded	/ləʊdɪd/
h)	drubbed	/drʌbd/	s)	collided	/kəlaɪdɪd/
i)	dragged	/drægd/	t)	allowed	/əlaʊd/
j)	jogged	/dʒɒgd/	u)	sowed	/səʊd/
k)	fudged	/fʌdʒd/			

i) List the alternate forms of the past tense morpheme.

ii) Which alternate makes the best underlying form? Why?

iii) State in words the conditioning factors that account for the presence of the alternate forms of the past tense morpheme.

2. Vowel harmony is a process that results in all vowels of a word sharing a certain feature or features. Morphophonemic rules of vowel harmony are found in many languages, among them Turkish.
(Note:ö = ø; ü = y)

		Singular	*Plural*
a)	'eye'	göz	gözler
b)	'candle'	mum	mumlar
c)	'gun'	top	toplar
d)	'horse'	at	atlar
e)	'sheath'	kuun	kunlar
f)	'thread'	ip	ipler
g)	'rose'	gül	güller
h)	'hand'	el	eller

i) List the allomorphs of the plural morpheme in the preceding data.

ii) What phonological feature is shared by the vowels of both allomorphs of the plural?

iii) What phonological feature distinguishes the vowels of the allomorphs?

iv) Is it possible in this case to pick one allomorph as the best underlying form?

v) Choose one allomorph as underlying, and provide a representation using the feature hierarchy that derives the other one from it. Provide derivations for the words for 'eye' and 'gun'.

3. Provide derivations for the following English compounds and phrases using the model presented in Figures 6.11 and 6.12. Be careful! Some phrases may contain compounds.

Compounds		*Phrases*	
a)	basketball net	e)	drive-in movie
b)	night club act	f)	electric pencil sharpener
c)	wetsuit designer	g)	second language learning
d)	Mississippi mudpie	h)	Princes Street Gardens

4. Account for stress clash resolution in the following examples. Be sure your answer accounts for the following questions. Why does the stress retract across a syllable? Why is there no reversal of stress in forms d) and e)?

a)	Jàpanése	Jàpanese cár
b)	Mìrimachí	Mìrimachi Ríver
c)	Tènnessée	Tènnessee Wáltz
d)	Amánda	Amànda Kíng
e)	Missóuri	Missòuri Wáltz

5. The following Russian sentences contain several different forms for the pronoun 'I' – *ya*, *menya*, *mnoy*, and *mne*.
    (Note: y = j, š = ʃ, and č = ʒ)

    Nominative
    a) ya ponimayu urok
        I understand lesson
        'I understand the lesson.'
    b) ya vižu yožika
        I see hedgehog
        'I see the hedgehog.'

    Accusative
    c) on uvidel menya
        he saw me
        'He saw me.'
    d) oni vstretili menya
        they met me
        'They met me.'

    Instrumental
    e) vi pošli sa mnoy
        you went with me
        'You went with me.'
    f) oni pogovorili sa mnoy
        they spoke with me
        'They were speaking with me.'

    Dative
    g) oni pošli k mne
        they arrived to me
        'They came to my place.'
    h) on podošol k mne
        he approached to me
        'He approached me.'

    i) Draw the tree structure for each of these sentences, and make a statement about the context in which each case form for the first person pronoun occurs.
    ii) Does the complement of a preposition receive the same case as the complement of a verb in Russian?
    iii) Is the case assigned to the complement of a preposition the same for the two prepositions used in the data?

7

Semantics: the analysis of meaning

William O'Grady

... in every object there is inexhaustible meaning

❧ Thomas Carlyle

Up to now, this book has focused on the form of utterances – their sound pattern, morphological structure, and syntactic organization. But there is more to language than just form. In order for language to fulfil its communicative function, utterances must also convey a message; they must have content. Speaking very generally, we can call this message or content the utterance's **meaning**.

This chapter is concerned with **semantics**, the study of meaning in human language. Because some work in this complicated area of linguistic analysis presupposes considerable knowledge of other disciplines (particularly logic, mathematics, and philosophy), not all aspects of contemporary semantics are suitable for presentation in an introductory linguistics textbook. We will restrict our attention here to four major topics in semantics: (1) the nature of meaning, (2) some properties of the conceptual system underlying meaning, (3) the contribution of syntactic structure to the interpretation of sentences, and (4) the role of non-grammatical factors in the understanding of utterances.

1

THE NATURE OF MEANING

Long before linguistics existed as a discipline, thinkers were speculating about the nature of meaning. For thousands of years, this question has been considered central to philosophy. More recently, it has come to be important in psychology as well. Contributions to semantics have come from a diverse group of scholars, ranging from Plato and Aristotle in ancient Greece to Bertrand Russell in the twentieth century. Our goal in this section will be to consider in a very general way what this research has revealed about meaning in human language. We will begin by considering some of the basic analytic notions used in evaluating the meanings of words and sentences.

1.1

Semantic relations among words

By virtue of their meaning, words and phrases are able to enter into a variety of semantic relations with other words and phrases in the language. Because these relationships help identify those aspects of meaning relevant to linguistic analysis, they constitute a good starting point for this chapter.

Synonymy

Synonyms are words or expressions that have the same meanings in some or all contexts. The pairs of words in Table 7.1 provide plausible examples of synonymy in English.

Table 7.1   Some synonyms in English

youth	adolescent
begin	start
remember	recall
purchase	buy
vacation	holidays
big	large

Although it is easy to think of contexts in which both words in each pair have essentially the same meaning (*I spent my holidays/vacation in the Swiss Alps*), there are also contexts in which their meanings diverge at least slightly. For example, Christmas and Spring Bank Holiday are holidays, but they are not necessarily part of one's vacation. Similarly, although *youth* and *adolescent* both refer to people of about the same age, only the latter word has the meaning of 'immature' in a phrase such as *He's such an adolescent!* Many linguists believe that it would be inefficient for a language to have two words or phrases whose meanings are absolutely identical in all contexts, and that complete synonymy is therefore rare or non-existent.

Antonymy

Antonyms are words or phrases that are opposites with respect to some component of their meaning. The pairs of words in Table 7.2 provide examples of antonymy.

Table 7.2   Some antonyms in English

dark	light
boy	girl
hot	cold
up	down
in	out
come	go

In each of these pairs, the two words contrast with respect to at least one component of their meaning. Thus, the meanings of *boy* and *girl* are opposites with respect to gender, although they are alike with respect to species (both are human). Similarly, *come* and *go* are opposites with respect to direction, although both involve the concept of movement.

Polysemy and homophony

Polysemy occurs where a word has two or more related meanings. Table 7.3 contains some examples of polysemous words in English.

Table 7.3 Some polysemy in English

Word	Meaning A	Meaning B
bright	'shining'	'intelligent'
to glare	'to shine intensely'	'to stare angrily'
a deposit	'minerals in the earth'	'money in the bank'

If you consult a reasonably comprehensive dictionary for any language, you will find numerous examples of polysemy. The ease with which words acquire additional related meanings allows language to accommodate the new concepts and perspectives that accompany technological and cultural change. For instance, with the advent of the internet, surfers are nowadays found not only on the ocean wave but also on the Web in cyberspace.

Homophony exists where a single form has two or more entirely distinct meanings (Table 7.4). In such cases, it is assumed that there are two (or more) separate words with the same pronunciation rather than a single word with different meanings.

Table 7.4 Some homophones in English

Word	Meaning A	Meaning B
bat	'a flying, mouse-like nocturnal mammal'	'a piece of equipment used in cricket or baseball'
bank	'a financial institution'	'a small cliff at the edge of a river'
club	'a social organization'	'a blunt weapon'
plot	'a plan of a literary work'	'a small piece of ground'
pen	'a writing instrument'	'a small cage'

Polysemy and homophony create **lexical ambiguity** in that a single form has two or more meanings. Thus, a sentence such as *1)* could mean either that Liz purchased an instrument to write with or that she bought a small cage.

1)

Liz bought a pen.

Of course, in actual speech the surrounding words and sentences usually make the intended meaning clear. The lexical ambiguity in sentences such as the following therefore normally goes unnoticed.

2)

He got a loan from the *bank*.

3)

Because Liz needed a place to keep her guinea pig, she went to the pet shop and bought a *pen* for £10.

1.2

Semantic relations involving sentences

Like words, sentences have meanings that can be analysed in terms of their relation to other meanings. We consider three such relations here – paraphrase, entailment, and contradiction.

Paraphrase

Two sentences that can have the same meaning are said to be **paraphrases** of each other. The following pairs of sentences provide examples of paraphrases.

4)

a.   The police chased the burglar.

b.   The burglar was chased by the police.

5)

a.   I gave the summons to Chris.

b.   I gave Chris the summons.

6)

a.   It is unfortunate that the team lost.

b.   Unfortunately, the team lost.

7)

a.   Paul bought a car from Sue.

b.   Sue sold a car to Paul.

8)

a.   The game will begin at 3.00 p.m.

b.   At 3.00 p.m., the game will begin.

The *a)* and *b)* sentences in each of the above pairs are obviously very similar in meaning. Indeed, it would be impossible for one sentence in any pair to be true without the other also being true. Thus, if it is true that the police chased the burglar, it must also be true that the burglar was chased by the police. Similarly, if it is false that the police chased the burglar, then it must also be false that the burglar was chased by the police. (Sentences whose meanings are related to each other in this way are said to have the same **truth conditions**.)

For some linguists, this is enough to justify saying that the two sentences have the same meaning. However, you may notice that there are subtle differences in emphasis between the *a)* and *b)* sentences in *4)* to *8)*. For instance, it is natural to interpret *4a)* as a statement about what the police did and *4b)* as a statement about what happened to the burglar. Similarly, *8b)* seems to place more emphasis on the starting time of the game than *8a)* does. As is the case with synonymy, many linguists feel that languages do not permit two or more structures to have absolutely identical meanings and that paraphrases are therefore never perfect.

Entailment

A relation in which the truth of one sentence necessarily implies the truth of another, as happens in examples *4)* to *8)* above, is called **entailment**. In the cases we have been considering, the entailment relation between the *a)* and *b)* sentences is mutual since the truth of either sentence guarantees the truth of the other. In some cases, however, entailment is asymmetrical. The following examples illustrate this.

9)
a.   The park wardens killed the tiger.
b.   The tiger is dead.

10)
a.   Robin is a man.
b.   Robin is human.

The *a)* sentences in *9)* and *10)* entail the *b)* sentences. If it is true that the park wardens killed the tiger, then it must also be true that the tiger is dead. However, the reverse does not follow since the tiger could be dead without the park wardens having killed it. Similarly, if it is true that Robin is a man, then it is also true that Robin is human. Once again though, the reverse does not hold: even if we know that Robin is a human, we cannot conclude that Robin is a man rather than a woman or a child.

Contradiction

Sometimes, it turns out that if one sentence is true, then another sentence must be false. This is the case with the examples in *11)*.

11)
a.   Charles is a bachelor.
b.   Charles is married.

If it is true that Charles is a bachelor, then it cannot be true that he is married. When two sentences cannot both be true, we say that there is a **contradiction**.

1.3

What is meaning?

Although it is relatively easy to determine whether two words or sentences have identical or different meanings, it is much more difficult to determine precisely what meaning is in the first place. In fact, despite many centuries of study, we still know very little about the nature of meaning or how it is represented in the human mind. Nonetheless, it is worth while to review briefly some of the better known proposals and the problems that they encounter.

Connotation

One notion that is closely linked with the concept of meaning is **connotation**, the set of associations that a word's use can evoke. For most Scots, Scandinavians, and Canadians, for example, the word *winter* evokes thoughts of snow, bitter cold, short evenings, frozen fingertips and the like. These associations make up the word's connotation, but they cannot be its meaning (or at least not its entire meaning). This is because *winter* could still be used for the season stretching from December to March even if none of these other things was present (perhaps because it is a mild year, perhaps because one spends the period in Florida or Crete). We must therefore look beyond connotation for our understanding of what meaning is.

Denotation

One well-known approach to semantics attempts to equate the meaning of a word or phrase with the entities to which it refers – its **denotation** or **referents**. The denotation of the word *winter*, for example, corresponds to the season between autumn and spring (regardless of whether it is cold and unpleasant). Similarly, the denotation of the word *dog* corresponds to the set of canines, and so on.

Although a word's denotation is clearly connected to its meaning in some way, they cannot be one and the same thing. This is because there are words such as *unicorn* and phrases such as *the present king of France*, which have no referents in the real world even though they are far from meaningless.

A problem of a different sort arises with expressions such as *the Prime Minister of the United Kingdom* and *the leader of the Conservative Party*, both of which refer (in 1995, at least) to John Major. Although these two expressions may have the same referent, it seems wrong to say that they mean the same thing. Thus, we would not say that the phrase *Prime Minister of the United Kingdom* is defined as 'the leader of the Conservative Party' or that the definition of the phrase *leader of the Conservative Party* is 'Prime Minister of the United Kingdom'.

Extension and intension

The impossibility of equating an element's meaning with its referents has led to a distinction between **extension** and **intension** (Table 7.5). Whereas an expression's extension corresponds to the set of entities that it picks out in the world (its referents), its intension corresponds to its inherent sense, the concepts that it evokes. Thus, the extension of *woman* is a set of real world

Table 7.5 Extension versus intension

Phrase	Extension	Intension
Prime Minister of the UK	John Major	leader of the governing party
The Rugby World Champions (1995)	The Springboks	South Africa's Rugby team, winners of the 1995 Rugby World Cup Tournament
Capital of New Zealand	Wellington	city containing the seat of government

entities (women) while its intension involves notions like 'female' and 'human'. Similarly, the phrase *Prime Minister of the United Kingdom* has as its extension an individual (John Major), but its intension involves the concept 'leader of the governing party'.

The distinction between intension and extension does not allow us to resolve the question of what meaning is. It simply permits us to pose it in a new way: What are intensions?

One suggestion is that intensions correspond to mental images. This is an obvious improvement over the referential theory since it is possible to have a mental image of a unicorn or even the king of France although there are no such entities in the real world. However, problems arise with the meanings of words such as *dog*, which can be used to refer to animals of many different sizes, shapes, and colours. If the meaning of this word corresponds to a mental image, that image would have to be general enough to include Chihuahuas and St Bernards, yet still exclude foxes and wolves. If you try to draw a picture that satisfies these requirements, you will see just how hard it is to construct an image for word meanings of this sort.

Componential analysis

Still another approach to meaning tries to represent a word's intension by breaking it down into smaller semantic components. Sometimes known as **componential analysis** or **semantic decomposition**, this approach has long been used to analyse the meaning of certain types of nouns in terms of semantic features. The analysis in Figure 7.1 for the words *man*, *woman*, *boy*, and *girl* illustrates this. (Nothing depends on the choice of feature names here; the analysis would work just as well with the feature ±FEMALE as ±MALE.)

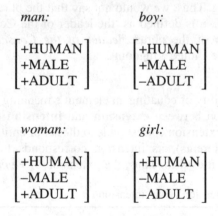

man:

$$\begin{bmatrix} +\text{HUMAN} \\ +\text{MALE} \\ +\text{ADULT} \end{bmatrix}$$

boy:

$$\begin{bmatrix} +\text{HUMAN} \\ +\text{MALE} \\ -\text{ADULT} \end{bmatrix}$$

woman:

$$\begin{bmatrix} +\text{HUMAN} \\ -\text{MALE} \\ +\text{ADULT} \end{bmatrix}$$

girl:

$$\begin{bmatrix} +\text{HUMAN} \\ -\text{MALE} \\ -\text{ADULT} \end{bmatrix}$$

Figure 7.1 Semantic feature composition for *man, woman, boy, girl.*

An obvious advantage of this approach is that it allows us to group entities into natural classes (much as we do in phonology). Hence, *man* and *boy* could be grouped together as [+HUMAN, +MALE] while *man* and *woman* could be put in a class defined by the features [+HUMAN, +ADULT].

Componential analysis can also be used to analyse verb meaning, although here the semantic components tend not be written as binary features. A semantic component that is especially useful for the analysis of verb meaning is GO, which is used to represent change of various sorts. As the following examples help show, the notion of change associated with GO can be manifested in different ways.

12)

Manifestations of the concept GO

a. Positional
Patel went from Delhi to Sydney.

b. Possessional
The inheritance went to Mary.

c. Identificational
Max went from being a rational gentleman to being a stark raving maniac.

This concept is manifested in many verbs other than just *go*. For example, positional GO is present in the meaning of *fly* ('go through the air'), *walk* ('go on foot'), *crawl* ('go on hands and knees'), and so forth. Possessional GO is manifested in the meaning of *give*, *buy*, and *inherit*, all of which involve a change of possession, while identificational GO shows up in *become* and *turn into* (as in *The caterpillar turned into a butterfly*).

Componential analysis is most useful for uncovering and representing similarities among semantically related words. As illustrated above, a few simple features allow us to capture the similarities and differences among subclasses of people – men, women, boys, and girls. Similarly, componential analysis reveals a surprising similarity in the meaning of (for instance) *travel*, *give*, and *become*, all of which incorporate the GO concept (positional in the first case, possessional in the second, and identificational in the third).

However, there are limits on the insights into word meaning offered by componential analysis. What value, for example, is there in characterizing the meaning of *dog* as [+ANIMAL, +CANINE] so long as there is no further analysis of these features? Similarly, do we say that the meaning of *blue* consists of the feature [+COLOUR] and something else? If so, what is that other thing? Isn't it blueness? If so, then we still have not broken the meaning of *blue* into smaller components, and we are back where we started.

Meaning and concepts

What, then, can we say about meaning? From the preceding survey, it seems that meaning must be something that exists in the mind rather than the world and that it must be more abstract than pictures and that there is more to it than just features. The seventeenth century philosopher John Locke suggested that words are 'marks of ideas in the mind'. This proposal is typical of a wide range of traditional and modern approaches to semantics, all of which try to relate meaning to mental concepts of some sort. Since concepts don't have to correspond to objects in the world and need not be images or sets of features, these approaches can avoid the problems outlined above. However, they face a serious problem of their own. Unless it is possible to determine what a concept is, it does little good to equate the meaning of linguistic forms with concepts in the mind. In the next section of this chapter, we will consider the human conceptual system from the point of view of linguistic meaning and try to determine some of its basic properties.

2

THE CONCEPTUAL SYSTEM

Underlying the use of words and sentences to express meaning in human language is a conceptual system capable of organizing and classifying every imaginable aspect of our experience, from inner feelings and perceptions, to cultural and social phenomena, to the physical world that surrounds us. This section focuses on what the study of this conceptual system reveals about how meaning is expressed through language. We will begin by considering some examples that illustrate the way in which these concepts are structured, extended, and interrelated.

2.1

Fuzzy concepts

We tend to think that the concepts expressed by the words and phrases of our language have precise definitions with clear-cut boundaries that distinguish them from other concepts. Some concepts may indeed be like this. For example, the concept expressed by the phrase *Member of Parliament* seems to be clear cut enough: one is a Member of Parliament if and only if one is duly elected to a particular legislative body; no other person can be truthfully called a Member of Parliament.

But are all concepts so straightforward? Consider the concept associated with the word *rich*. How much does one have to be worth to be called rich? Five hundred thousand pounds? Eight hundred thousand? A million? Is there any figure that we can give that would be so precise that a person who is short by just five pence would not be called rich? It seems not. While one could miss out on being a Member of Parliament by five votes, it does not seem possible to miss out on being rich by just five pence. Moreover, whereas some people clearly qualify as rich and others do not, an indefinitely large number of people fall into the unclear area at the borderline of the concept and it is just not possible to say definitively whether or not they count as rich. This is because the notion of 'richness' does not have clear-cut boundaries; it is what we call a **fuzzy concept**.

Many linguists believe that this type of fuzziness pervades the human conceptual system. Certainly, it is not hard to think of everyday concepts whose boundaries are fuzzy in the same way as the preceding example – *shrub*, *tree*, *tall*, *old*, *clever*, *strong*, *grey-haired*, *fast*, *clean*, *genius*, *bargain*, and so on.

Graded membership

A second important fact about concepts is that their members can be graded in terms of their typicality. Consider first a fuzzy concept such as 'film star'. Even within the set of people who we can agree are film stars, some provide better examples of this concept than others. At the time of writing, for instance, Tom Hanks, Arnold Schwarzenegger, and Julia Roberts are better examples of a film star than Ben Kingsley, Anthony Hopkins, or Meryl Streep. Although movie fans agree that all these actors are stars, in recent years the former have received more media attention, enjoyed more fan adulation, achieved greater box office success – and hence have demanded and received more colossal financial rewards, and so on. This makes Tom Hanks, Arnold Schwarzenegger, and Julia Roberts better examples of a star than Ben Kingsley, Anthony Hopkins, or Meryl Streep.

Even concepts whose boundaries can be scientifically defined exhibit this type of graded membership. A good example of this involves the concept 'bird' (Figure 7.2). Even assuming that English speakers all think of birds as 'warm-blooded, egg-laying, feathered vertebrates with forelimbs modified to form wings' (the dictionary definition), they still feel that some of these creatures are more bird-like than others. Thus, robins and magpies, for example, are intuitively better examples of birds than are hummingbirds, ostriches, or penguins.

Examples like these suggest that concepts have an internal structure, with the best or **prototypical** exemplars (for instance Arnold Schwarzenegger in the case of 'film stars', robins in the case of 'birds') close to the core and less typical members arranged in successively more peripheral regions.

The existence of fuzzy concepts and of graded membership in concepts provides important insights into the nature of the human conceptual system. In particular, it seems that many (perhaps even most) concepts expressed in

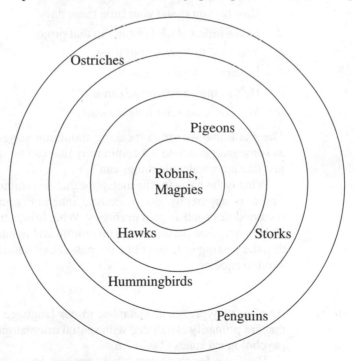

Figure 7.2 Possible internal structure of the concept 'bird'.

language are not rigid all-or-nothing notions with precise and clear-cut boundaries. Rather, they are characterized by an internal structure that recognizes degrees of typicality as well as by fuzzy boundaries that make categorization uncertain in some cases.

2.2

Metaphor

The concepts expressed through language are not isolated from each other. Rather, they make up a giant network, with many interconnections and associations among the various subparts. A good example of these interconnections involves **metaphor**, the understanding of one concept in terms of another.

We have a tendency to think of metaphor as a literary device reserved for the use of authors and poets. In fact, however, there is reason to think that it has a prominent place in the conceptual system shared by all human beings. The effects of this prominence are seen in the way in which we use language to talk about various abstract notions.

A simple example of this involves the concept of time, which we analyse metaphorically by treating it as if it were a concrete commodity. Consider in this regard the following sentences, which illustrate how we talk about time.

13)

a.   You're *wasting* my time.

b.   This gadget will *save* you hours.

c.   How do you *spend* your time these days?

d.   I have *invested* a lot of time in that project.

e.   You need to *budget* your time.

f.   Is that *worth* your while?

g.   He's living on *borrowed* time.

h.   You don't use your time *profitably*.

The words that we use in speaking about time suggest that it is conceptualized as something concrete – a commodity that can be saved, wasted, and invested just like other valuable things can.

What is the basis for the metaphor that determines how we talk about time? There is apparently no objective, inherent similarity between time and commodities such as gold or money. What brings these two concepts together is the *perception*, based in part on culture and in part on the subjective feeling that the passing of time is like the passage of valuable commodities from one hand to another.

A spatial metaphor

Another very prevalent metaphor in our language involves the use of words that are primarily associated with spatial orientation to talk about physical and psychological states (Table 7.6).

The basis for these metaphors appears to lie in our physical experience. Unhappiness and ill health tend to be associated with lethargy and inactivity,

Table 7.6 Metaphorical use of spatial terms

EMOTIONS: HAPPY IS UP, SAD IS DOWN	
I'm feeling *up*.	I'm feeling *down*.
That *boosted* my spirits.	He *fell* into a depression.
My spirits *rose*.	Her spirits *sank*.
You're in *high* spirits.	He's feeling *low*.
The *height* of ecstasy	The *depths* of misery.
That gave me a *lift*.	That *depressed* me.

PHYSICAL HEALTH: UP IS HEALTH AND LIFE, DOWN IS SICKNESS AND DEATH	
He's at the *peak* of health	He's *sinking* fast.
Lazarus *rose* from the dead.	He *fell* ill.
She's in *top* shape.	She came *down* with the flu.
	Her health is *declining*.
	She's feeling *under* the weather.

which often involve being on one's back (physically down). In contrast, happiness and good health are often correlated with energy and movement, which involve being on one's feet (physically up).

These few examples illustrate a more general point about language and meaning. The innumerably many concepts that we express through language do not all exist independent of each other. Rather, many concepts are structured and understood metaphorically in terms of notions more basic to our physical and cultural experience. Thus, time is understood in terms of a commodity metaphor, health and happiness in terms of a spatial metaphor, and so on. By studying how concepts are represented in language, we can gain valuable insights into the role of experience and metaphor in the human conceptual system.

2.3

The lexicalization of concepts

Do all human beings share the same conceptual system? Do all languages express concepts in the same way? These are questions that have fascinated and puzzled researchers for many decades. At the present time, there is no reason to believe that human beings in different linguistic communities have different conceptual systems. But there is ample evidence that languages can differ from each other in terms of how they express concepts.

Lexicalization

The classic and frequently distorted example of how languages can differ from each other in the expression of concepts involves the words for 'snow' in Eskimo (Inuktitut). Sometimes estimated in the hundreds by unknowledgeable commentators, the set of simple words for 'snow' in Eskimo is in fact much smaller. For example, one well-known dictionary gives only four items shown in Table 7.7 (although other dictionaries give several more for at least some varieties of Eskimo).

Table 7.7   Words for 'snow' in Eskimo

aput	'snow on the ground'
qana	'falling snow'
piqsirpoq	'drifting snow'
qimuqsuq	'snow drift'

As you can see, there is nothing particularly startling about this list of words. In fact, even in English there is more than just one word to describe snow in its various forms – *snow, slush, blizzard,* and *sleet* come to mind, for example.

The types of differences we are considering involve **lexicalization**, the process whereby concepts are encoded in the words of a language. Thus, Eskimo lexicalizes the concepts 'falling' and 'snow' in a single word (*qana*) while English uses two separate words. While some lexicalization differences may correlate with cultural factors (the relative importance of types of snow in traditional Eskimo culture), this is not always so. For example, Table 7.8 shows that English has an unusually rich set of vocabulary items pertaining to the perception of light.

Table 7.8   Some verbs pertaining to 'light' in English

glimmer	glisten
gleam	glow
glitter	flicker
shimmer	shine
flare	glare
flash	sparkle

Although most English speakers know and use the words in this list, it is hard to see how the variety found in this particular area of vocabulary can be correlated with any identifiable feature of English-speaking culture or society.

Contrary to popular belief, the lexicalization differences just illustrated are generally not considered by linguists to have any special importance. As we have tried to emphasize throughout this book, the focus of linguistic analysis is on the *system* of knowledge that makes it possible to speak and understand a language. The fact that a particular language has more words pertaining to snow or light does not in and of itself provide any insight into the nature of the human linguistic system, and therefore does not merit special attention. However, as we will see in the next subsection, there are lexicalization differences whose properties can shed light on how linguistic systems express meaning.

Motion verbs

All languages have words that can describe motion through space (in English, *come, go,* and *move,* among many others). However, recent work suggests that there may be systematic differences in terms of how languages express motion and the concepts related to it. In English, for example (Table 7.9), there are many verbs that simultaneously express both the concept of motion and the manner in which the motion occurs.

Table 7.9   Some verbs expressing motion and manner in English

The rock *rolled* down the hill.
The skate *slid* across the ice.
She *limped* through the house.
The smoke *swirled* through the opening.

Notice how each of these verbs expresses both the fact that something moved and the manner in which it moved (by rolling, sliding, limping, and so on).

Interestingly, Romance languages (descendants of Latin) cannot express motion events in this way. Thus, while Spanish has a verb *rodar* with the meaning 'to roll', it does not use this verb to express both manner and motion as English does.

14)

*La botella rodó en la cueva.
'The bottle rolled into the cave.'

Instead, the motion and its manner have to be expressed separately.

15)

La botella entró en la cueva, rodando.
'The bottle entered the cave, rolling.'

However, Spanish *does* have a series of verbs (Table 7.10) that jointly express the concept of motion and the path along which it occurs.

Table 7.10   Some verbs expressing motion and path in Spanish

El globo   *bajó*   por la chimenea.
'The balloon moved-down through the chimney.'

El globo   *subió*   por la chimenea.
'The balloon moved-up through the chimney.'

La botella   *volvió*   a la orilla.
'The bottle moved back to the bank.'

La botella   *cruzó*   el canal.
'The bottle moved-across the canal.'

La botella   *salió*   de la cueva.
'The bottle moved-out from the cave.'

As the English translations show, Spanish verbs of motion express both the concept of movement and the direction of its path – down, up, back, across, out, and so forth. (English, too, has verbs that can express both motion and path – *descend*, *ascend*, *return*, and so on – but these words are not part of its native vocabulary. Rather they were borrowed into English from latinate sources, usually through French.)

Another lexicalization option is found in the Amerindian language Atsugewi (Table 7.11), in which verbs can express both motion and the type of thing that moves.

Table 7.11   Some verb roots expressing motion and the thing moving in Atsugewi

lup	for movement of a small, shiny spherical object (a hailstone)
t	for movement of a smallish, flat object that can be attached to another (a stamp, a clothing patch, a shingle)
caq	for movement of a slimy, lumpish object (a toad, a cow dropping)
swal	for movement of a limp linear object, suspended by one end (a shirt on a clothesline, a hanging dead rabbit)
qput	for movement of loose, dry dirt
staq	for movement of runny, unpleasant material (manure, guts, chewed gum, rotten tomatoes)

We learn two things from these facts. First, the concept of motion is associated with a number of other concepts, including 'path', 'manner of movement', and 'moving thing'. Second, the way in which these concepts are grouped together for purposes of lexicalization can differ systematically from language to language. Languages such as English have verbs that simultaneously lexicalize motion and manner while other languages have verbs that simultaneously lexicalize motion and path (Spanish) or motion and the type of thing that moves (Atsugewi).

The general picture that is emerging from this type of work is that within particular semantic domains, there may be a small universal set of concepts (motion, manner, path, thing that moves, and so on) and a small set of options for how these concepts can be combined for purposes of lexicalization. Unlike the lexicalization differences involving snow and light discussed earlier, these differences appear to be highly systematic and to reveal some general tendencies about the way in which meaning can be expressed in human language. Further work of this type should provide additional insights into the organization of the human conceptual system as well as the ways in which its component notions can be lexicalized in human language.

2.4

The grammaticization of concepts

Of the indefinitely large set of concepts expressible in human language, a relatively small subset enjoys a special status. These are the concepts that are expressed by affixes and non-lexical (functional) categories in one language or another. Some of the concepts that are treated this way in English are listed in Table 7.12.

Concepts that are expressed as affixes or non-lexical categories are said to have been **grammaticized**.

Some concepts tend to be highly grammaticizable in that most, if not all, languages lexicalize them as affixes or special non-lexical categories. Negation and conjunction are possible examples of concepts that are grammaticized in all languages. Contrasts involving singular versus plural and past versus non-past are encoded by special affixes in many languages, but not all. (Recall the discussion of Nancowry in section 6.1 of Chapter 4.) Still other concepts are grammaticized in a smaller number of languages, as the following example from the Siouan language Hidatsa illustrates.

Table 7.12   Some concepts associated with affixes and non-lexical categories in English

Concept	Affix
Past	-ed
More than one	-s
Again	re-
Negation	in-, un-

Concept	Non-lexical category
Obligation	must
Possibility	may
Definite, specific	the
Indefinite, non-specific	a
Disjunction	or
Negation	not
Conjunction	and

Hidatsa assertion morphemes

In Hidatsa, each statement is accompanied by a morpheme to indicate which of the five categories in Table 7.13 (overleaf) it exemplifies. (Still other markers are used for questions, commands, and wishes.)

Choice of the appropriate assertion morpheme is extremely important in Hidatsa. A speaker who makes an utterance containing the morpheme -ski, which turns out to be false, is considered to be a liar. Had he used the morpheme -c, on the other hand, it would be assumed that he simply made a mistake.

While English has ways of indicating these contrasts (by using expressions such as *perhaps*, *I heard that*, and *I guess* (American)), it does not have a grammatical system of morphemes that obligatorily encodes this information in every sentence. By investigating the grammaticization options found in different languages, it may eventually be possible to identify the factors that determine which concepts are singled out for association with affixes and non-lexical categories.

Table 7.13 Assertion morphemes in Hidatsa

ski	*The speaker is certain of the statement's truth*
	Waceo iikipi kure heo -<u>ski</u>
	'The man (definitely) carried the pipe.'
c	*The speaker believes the statement to be true*
	Waceo iikipi kure heo -<u>c</u>.
	'The man (supposedly) carried the pipe.'
wareac	*The speaker regards the statement to be common knowledge*
	Waceo iikipi kure heo -<u>wareac</u>.
	'The man carried the pipe (they say).'
rahe	*The statement is based on an unverified report from someone else*
	Waceo wiira rackci heo -<u>rahe</u>.
	'The man roasted the goose (it is rumoured).'
toak	*The truth of the statement is unknown to both speaker and listener*
	Waceo cihpa rakci heo -<u>toak</u>.
	The man roasted the prairie dog (perhaps).'

3

SYNTAX AND SENTENCE INTERPRETATION

The two preceding sections have focused on the meaning conveyed by the individual words and phrases that make up a sentence. In this section, we turn to the problem of sentence interpretation, with an emphasis on how the positioning of words and phrases in syntactic structure helps determine the meaning of the entire sentence, consistent with the following principle.

16)

The Principle of Compositionality:
The meaning of a sentence is determined by the meaning of its component parts and the manner in which they are arranged in syntactic structure.

There are many different ideas about precisely how the meaning of a sentence's component words and their arrangement in syntactic structure determine sentence meaning. For purposes of illustration, we will consider the relevance of syntactic structure to three aspects of sentence interpretation – the representation of structural ambiguity, the assignment of thematic roles, and the interpretation of pronouns.

3.1

Structural ambiguity

Some sentences are **structurally ambiguous** in that the meanings of their component words can be combined in more than one way. A simple example of this is found in the phrase *wealthy men and women*, where 'wealthy' can be seen as a property of both the men and the women or of just the men alone. These two interpretations or **readings** are depicted in Figure 7.3 (Con = conjunction).

Figure 7.3*a* corresponds to the reading in which *wealthy* modifies both *men* and *women*. This is shown by having the adjective combine with a category that includes both nouns. In Figure 7.3*b*, on the other hand, the

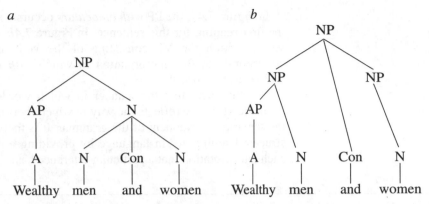

Figure 7.3   An ambiguous phrase. The structure on the left indicates that both the men and women are wealthy; in the structure on the right, only the men are said to be wealthy.

adjective combines only with the N *men*. This structure corresponds to the reading in which 'wealthy' applies only to the men.

Another case of structural ambiguity is found in sentences such as *17)*.

17)

Nicole can see the people with binoculars.

In one interpretation of *17)*, the people had binoculars when Nicole noticed them (the phrase *with binoculars* modifies the noun *people*) while in the other interpretation Nicole saw the people by using the binoculars (the PP modifies the verb). Figure 7.4 shows how these two readings can be represented.

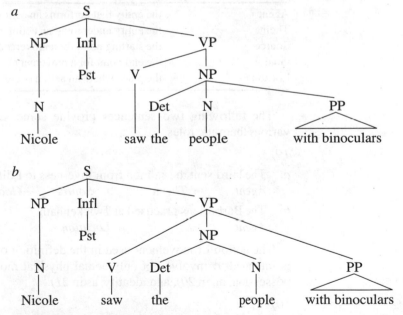

Figure 7.4   An ambiguous sentence. In the first structure, the people have the binoculars; in the second structure, Nicole uses the binoculars to see the people.

In Figure 7.4*a*, the PP *with binoculars* occurs with the N *people*, reflecting the first reading for this sentence. In Figure 7.4*b*, on the other hand, the PP occurs within the VP consisting of the verb and its complement. This corresponds to the interpretation in which *with binoculars* describes how Nicole saw the people.

We see, then, that the manner in which words are grouped together in syntactic structure reflects the way in which their meanings are combined by the semantic component of the grammar. It is therefore possible to represent structural ambiguity in language by providing a different tree structure for each interpretation that a particular utterance has.

3.2

Thematic roles

Another aspect of semantic interpretation involves determining the roles that the referents of NPs play in the situations described by sentences. Consider in this regard the sentence in *18*).

18)

The laird sent the salmon from Inverness to Edinburgh.

It would be impossible to understand this sentence if we could not identify the laird as the person who is responsible for sending something, the salmon as the thing that is sent, and so on. The term **thematic role** is used to describe the part played by a particular entity in an event. In most linguistic analyses, at least the thematic roles in Table 7.14 are recognized.

Table 7.14 Thematic roles

Agent	the entity that performs an action
Theme	the entity undergoing an action or a movement
Source	the starting point for a movement
Goal	the end point for a movement
Location	the place where an action occurs

The following two sentences provide some simple examples of these various thematic roles.

19)

a. The laird sent the salmon from Inverness to Edinburgh.
    Agent   *Theme*   *Source*   *Goal*

b. The Barbarians practised at Twickenham.
    Agent   *Location*

The notion of movement used in the definition of theme, source, and goal is intended to involve not only actual physical motion, but also changes in possession, as in *20)*, and identity, as in *21)*.[1]

20)

Terry gave the keys to Mary.
Agent   *Theme*   *Goal*

21)

The magician changed the ball into a rabbit.
Agent   *Theme*   *Goal*

Thematic role assignment

Where do thematic roles come from, and how does the grammar ensure that the appropriate thematic role is associated with each NP in a sentence? Thematic roles originate in word meaning (Table 7.15). Thus, if the sentence *Harry hit the ball* contains an agent and a theme, it is because the verb *hit* has the type of meaning that implies an entity that does the hitting (an agent) and an entity that gets hit (a theme). Similarly, if we understand *Inverness* as a source and *Edinburgh* as a goal in sentence *19a)*, it is because of the difference in the meaning of the prepositions *from* and *to* that occur with these NPs.

Table 7.15   Some words and the thematic roles implied by their meanings

hit	‹agent, theme›
walk	‹agent›
to	‹goal›
from	‹source›
near	‹location›

These roles are then assigned to NPs based on their position in syntactic structure, with each NP receiving one and only one role.

As a first example of this, let us consider the complement of a preposition. In such cases, the process of thematic role assignment can be summarized as follows.

22)

A P assigns a thematic role to its complement NP.

The operation of this convention is illustrated in Figure 7.5.

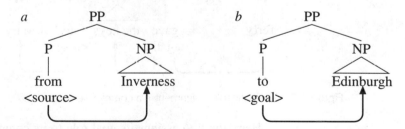

Figure 7.5   Thematic role assignment by prepositions.

Matters are slightly more complicated in the case of Vs. Here we must distinguish between the theme role, which is assigned to the V's complement, and the agent role, which is assigned to its subject (the NP immediately under S).

23)

A V assigns a theme role (if it has one) to its complement NP.
A V assigns an agent role (if it has one) to its subject NP.

This is exemplified in Figure 7.6.

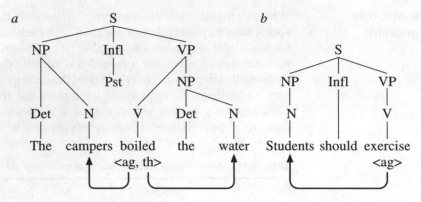

Figure 7.6 Thematic role assignment by verbs.

In accordance with 23), the theme role (where present) is assigned to the V's NP complement while the agent role is assigned to the subject. The NP assigned the theme role – which is typically the first NP that follows the verb – is normally referred to as the **direct object**.

The structure in Figure 7.7 illustrates the assignment of thematic roles in a sentence that contains a P in addition to a V.

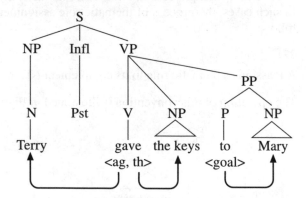

Figure 7.7 Thematic role assignment in a complex sentence.

Here, the P *to* assigns its goal role to its complement NP *Mary* while the verb *give* assigns its theme role to the complement *the keys* and its agent role to the subject *Terry*.

Deep structure and thematic roles

In the examples considered to this point, it is unclear whether an NP receives its thematic role on the basis of its position in deep structure or surface structure. This is because our example sentences are all formed without the help of movement transformations, so that each NP occupies the same position in both deep structure and surface structure. But now consider a sentence such as 24), which is formed with the help of *Wh* Movement.

24)

What should the man bring?

This sentence has the deep structure depicted in Figure 7.8.

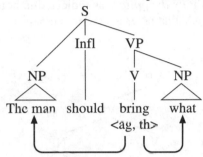

Figure 7.8   Thematic role assignment in a *wh* question.

Since the theme role is assigned to the complement of V (see *23)* and Figure 7.7 above), it follows that the NP *what* in the above example receives this role by virtue of its position in deep structure, not surface structure (where it occurs at the beginning of the sentence). This allows us to draw the following conclusion.

25)

An NP's deep structure position determines its thematic role.

The relevance of deep structure to the assignment of thematic roles is important for two reasons. First, it shows that syntactic structure not only represents the way in which words are organized into phrases, but also is relevant to semantic interpretation. Second, the fact that an NP's position in deep structure determines its thematic role provides additional support for the existence of this underlying level of syntactic structure. This, in turn, lends support to the claim that there must be at least two types of syntactic rules: phrase structure rules, which form the deep structure, and transformations, which convert it into surface structure.

Passives (advanced)

Now let us reconsider the passive structures first discussed in section 6 of Chapter 5.

26)

The thief was arrested (by the police).
Theme   *Agent*

From the point of view of thematic role assignment, this sentence is strange in two respects. First, the NP that occurs in subject position in this sentence (*the thief*) bears the theme role since it refers to the person who is placed in custody. Yet, as we saw earlier, the theme role should be assigned to the complement functioning as the direct object of the verb, not to its subject. Second, instead of being assigned to the subject position, the agent role (corresponding to the person doing the arresting) is assigned to an NP that occurs in an optional PP headed by the P *by*. How are we to account for these facts?

The first of these facts follows straightforwardly from the type of deep structure assigned to passive sentences (see Figure 7.9). (For the time being, we ignore the PP *by the police*; as indicated in note 2 of Chapter 5, auxiliary *be* is treated as a V that takes a VP complement.)

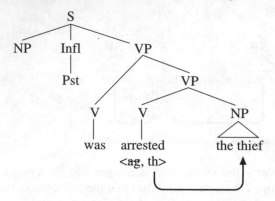

Figure 7.9   Deep structure for *The thief was arrested*; the line through the 'ag' symbol beneath the verb indicates that the agent role is suppressed.

Since the NP *the thief* appears as complement (direct object) of the verb *arrest* in deep structure and since an NP's deep structure position determines its thematic role, it follows that it will be assigned the theme role, as desired.

But what of the agent role? The crucial assumption is that the passive form of a verb loses the ability to assign an agent role – which is why the 'ag' symbol beneath the verb in Figure 7.9 has a line through it. This is why passive sentences are perfectly acceptable even when there is no agent NP (for example, *The thief was arrested*). When an NP bearing the agent role does appear, it occurs not in the subject position but rather as complement of the preposition *by*. Because the verb is unable to assign an agent role, some other element must take responsibility for the assignment of this role. *By* is that element, being unique among prepositions in having the type of meaning that assigns an agent role. Thus, the sentence *The thief was arrested by the police* has the deep structure depicted in Figure 7.10. (This *by* should not be confused with the *by* in *He stood by the tree*, which assigns a locative role.) In this structure, the passive verb *(was) arrested* assigns its theme role to its complement (the NP *the thief*) while the special preposition *by* assigns its agent role to its complement (the NP *the police*). This ensures that the sentence has the correct interpretation, with the police doing the arresting and the thief getting arrested.

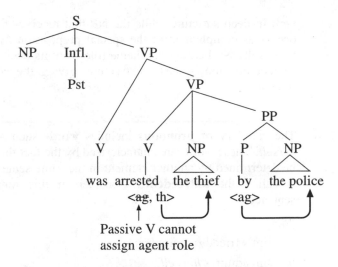

Figure 7.10 Deep structure for *The thief was arrested by the police.*

In order to form the correct surface structure for passive sentences, we need a transformation that will move the NP bearing the theme role from the direct object position to the subject position when the latter is empty.[2]

27)

NP Movement
Move NP into the subject position.

This transformation applies to the deep structure in Figure 7.10 to give the surface structure depicted in Figure 7.11.

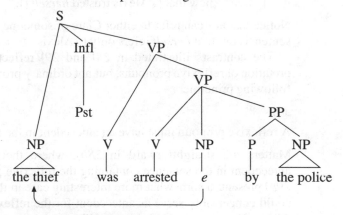

Figure 7.11 Surface structure resulting from NP movement. (In this figure *e* stands for *trace* which was introduced in section 3.4 of Chapter 5.)

In sum, then, the transformational analysis of passives makes use of both deep structure and surface structure. In order to account for thematic role assignment, the NP that receives the theme role occurs as complement of the verb in deep structure while the NP that receives the agent role, if present, occurs as complement of the special preposition *by*. A transformation then moves the NP bearing the theme role from its deep structure position to the subject position in surface structure, giving the correct final form of the sentence.

The interpretation of pronouns (advanced)

The category of **pronouns** includes words such as *he*, *she*, *himself*, and *herself*. These words are characterized by the fact that their interpretation can be determined by another element in the same sentence. (This other element is called the **antecedent**.) Consider in this regard the following two sentences.

28)

a.   Jim's friends admire *him*.

b.   Jim admires *himself*.

In the first of these sentences, the pronoun *him* can have the same referent as the NP *Jim* or can be taken to refer to someone not mentioned in the sentence (say, Jim's father). In the second sentence, in contrast, the pronoun *himself* must have the same referent as *Jim*; no other interpretation is possible. The former type of pronoun is called a **pronominal** and the latter type a **reflexive pronoun**.

The interpretation of pronominals and reflexive pronouns also differs in the following sentences.

29)

a.   [$_S$ Clare knew that [$_S$ Alexis trusted *her*]].

b.   [$_S$ Clare knew that [$_S$ Alexis trusted *herself*]].

Notice that *her* can refer to either Clare or someone else not mentioned in the sentence, but that *herself* refers only to Alexis.

The contrasts illustrated in *28)* and *29)* reflect the fact that the interpretation of reflexive pronouns, but not ordinary pronominals, is subject to the following principle.

30)

A reflexive pronoun must have an antecedent in the smallest S containing it.

Matters are straightforward in *28b)*, where there is only one potential antecedent in the sentence containing the reflexive pronoun. The sentence in *29b)* presents a somewhat more interesting case in that there are two NPs that could conceivably serve as antecedent for the reflexive pronoun – *Clare* and *Alexis*. However, only the latter NP can serve as antecedent since only it occurs in the smallest S containing the reflexive pronoun.

Principle A

A somewhat more abstract feature of syntactic structure enters into the interpretation of the reflexive pronouns in sentences such as *31)*, which has the tree structure in Figure 7.12. (Pronouns are treated as N-type categories that head NPs; to save space, some word-level category labels are omitted. As noted in the previous chapter, possessor NPs occur in the specifier position within larger NPs.)

31)

The boy's uncle admired himself.

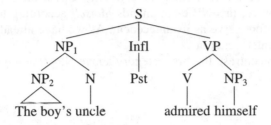

Figure 7.12 Structure containing a reflexive pronoun.

Although there are two NPs in the same S as *himself* (namely, *the boy* and *the boy's uncle*), only one (*the boy's uncle*) can serve as antecedent for the reflexive pronoun. Thus, the person who was admired in *31)* must have been the boy's uncle, not the boy.

The principle needed to ensure this interpretation makes use of the notion **c-command**, which is defined as follows.

32)

NP_a c-commands NP_b if the first category above NP_a contains NP_b.

Although c-command might appear to be a rather technical notion, the underlying idea is very simple. Figure 7.13 illustrates the type of configuration in which c-command occurs.

Figure 7.13 The c-command configuration.

When trying to determine c-command relations, you can either use the definition in *32)* or apply the template in Figure 7.13 to the tree structure being analysed.

We can now formulate the constraint on the interpretation of reflexives, called **Principle A**, as follows. In order to keep the discussion at an introductory level, we consider only the version of this principle required for simple, one-clause sentences.

33)

Principle A:

A reflexive pronoun must have an antecedent that c-commands it.

When using Principle A, the key step involves determining whether a potential antecedent c-commands the reflexive pronoun. Compare in this regard the status of the NPs *the boy* and *the boy's uncle* in Figure 7.12.

Since the first category above *the boy's uncle* (namely, S) contains the reflexive, this NP c-commands *himself* according to our definition and can therefore serve as its antecedent. As we have already seen, the sentence has this interpretation.

In contrast, the first category above NP₂ (*the boy*) is NP₁, as illustrated in Figure 7.14.

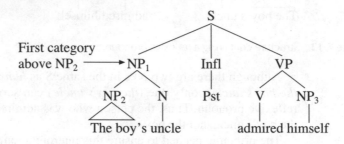

Figure 7.14 Structure illustrating the absence of a c-command relation between NP₂ and NP₃.

Since NP₁ does not contain the reflexive, there is no c-command relationship between NP₂ and *himself* according to our definition. It is therefore not possible for *the boy* to serve as antecedent for *himself*.

Principle B

Now let us consider the interpretation of pronominals. As the following example shows, the interpretation of the pronominal *him* contrasts sharply with that of the reflexive *himself* in the structure that we have been considering. Thus, *him* can refer to the boy, but not to the boy's uncle – the opposite of what we observed for *himself*.

34)

The boy's uncle admired him.

How are we to account for these facts? The relevant constraint, called **Principle B**, is stated in *35)*. (As with Principle A, we present only the version of this principle relevant to simple one-clause sentences.)

35)

Principle B:

A pronominal must not have an antecedent that c-commands it.

To see how this principle works, consider the structure shown in Figure 7.15, in which, NP₁ (*the boy's uncle*) c-commands *him* since the first category above it (namely, S) also contains *him*. Principle B therefore prevents NP_1 from serving as antecedent for *him*. In contrast, NP_2 (*the boy*) does not c-command *him* since the first category above it (namely, NP_1) does not contain the pronoun. Thus, nothing prevents the interpretation in which *him* and *the boy* refer to the same person.

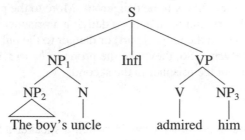

Figure 7.15 Structure containing a pronominal.

There is much more that can and should be said about the interpretation of pronouns. A more detailed examination of this very complex phenomenon would reveal the need for even more abstract principles referring to additional properties of syntactic structure. However, the examples we have already considered suffice to illustrate the crucial point in all of this, which is that syntactic structure plays an important role in the interpretation of both pronominals and reflexive pronouns.

4

OTHER FACTORS IN SENTENCE INTERPRETATION

Syntactic structure provides only part of the information needed to determine the meaning of a sentence. Other necessary information comes from **pragmatics**, which includes the speaker's and addressee's background attitudes and beliefs, their understanding of the context in which a sentence is uttered, and their knowledge of how language can be used to inform, to persuade, to mislead, and so forth. This section focuses on the role of pragmatics in the interpretation of utterances.

4.1

The role of beliefs and attitudes

As we saw in the preceding section, the grammar includes a structural principle (Principle B) that regulates the interpretation of pronominals such as *he* and *they*. However, as the following sentences show, non-linguistic knowledge and beliefs can also play an important role in selecting the antecedent for a pronominal.

36)

a. The judge denied the prisoner's request because he was cautious.

b. The judge denied the prisoner's request because he was dangerous.

These two sentences have identical syntactic structures, differing only in the choice of the adjective in the second clause (*cautious* in the first sentence versus *dangerous* in the second). Yet, most people feel that *he* refers to the judge in *36a)* but to the prisoner in *36b)*.

These preferences have nothing to do with structural principles. Rather, the crucial factor involves our shared beliefs about different groups within society. Most people believe that a judge is more likely to be cautious and a prisoner more likely to be dangerous. More to the point, they also believe that a plausible reason for a judge's denying a prisoner's request is more likely to be caution (on the judge's part) or danger to the public (on the prisoner's part) than vice versa. So, they take the pronoun *he* to refer to the judge in the first sentence but the prisoner in the second.

Presupposition

There are many other ways in which a speaker's beliefs can be reflected in language use. Compare in this regard the following two sentences.

37)

a. Have you stopped exercising regularly?

b. Have you tried exercising regularly?

Use of the verb *stop* implies a belief on the part of the speaker that the listener has been exercising regularly. No such assumption is associated with the verb *try*.

The assumption or belief implied by the use of a particular word or structure is called a **presupposition**. The following two sentences provide another example of this.

38)

a. Nick admitted that the team had lost.

b. Nick said that the team had lost.

Choice of the verb *admit* indicates that the speaker who utters *38a)* is presupposing the truth of the claim that the team lost. No such presupposition is associated with choice of the verb *say* in *38b)*. The speaker is simply reporting Nick's statement without taking a position on its accuracy.

Still another type of presupposition is illustrated in *39)*.

39)

a. D'Arcy McGee was assassinated in 1868.

b. D'Arcy McGee was murdered in 1868.

Notice that use of the verb *assassinate* in *39a)* involves the assumption that D'Arcy McGee was a prominent political figure, but that no such presupposition is associated with the verb *murder*. (For the same reason it is all right to say *'John Kennedy was assassinated'* if the John Kennedy referred to is the late American president and not a Dublin docker.)

4.2

Setting

As noted at the beginning of this section, the pragmatic factors relevant to sentence interpretation can include knowledge of the context in which a sentence is uttered. Two types of contextual information are involved here, the first having to do with the physical environment in which a sentence is uttered (the **setting**) and the second having to do with the other utterances in the speech event (the **discourse**). In this subsection we will consider an example of how information about the setting enters into language use; the role of discourse will be examined in the next subsection. Both these issues are examined from a slightly different perspective in chapter 14.

Deictics

All languages have forms whose use and interpretation depend on the location of the speaker and/or addressee within a particular setting. Called spatial **deictics**, these forms are exemplified in English by words such as *this* and *here* (proximity to the speaker) versus *that* and *there* (proximity to the addressee and/or distance from the speaker). Thus, if Steve and Brian are sitting across from each other at a table, each would refer to a plate directly in front of him as *this plate* and to a plate in front of the other person or a plate distant from both as *that plate*. Without an understanding of how the setting in which a sentence is uttered can influence the choice of words such as *this* and *that*, it would be impossible for speakers of English to use or interpret these forms correctly.

As the preceding examples show, English makes a two-way distinction in its expression of deictic contrasts. However, many languages use a third set of forms in this part of their grammar, as shown in Table 7.16.

Table 7.16 A three-way deictic distinction

Language	'this'	'that'	'that over there'
Spanish	este	ese	aquel
Korean	i	ku	ce
Japanese	kono	sono	ano
Palauan	tia	tilęcha	se
Turkish	bu	ʃ	o

An even more complex system is found in the Amerindian language Tlingit, which makes a four-way distinction: *yáa* 'this one right here', *héi* 'this one nearby', *wée* 'that one over there', and *yóo* 'that one far off'.

Determiners are not the only type of element whose use and interpretation require reference to features of the setting. In English, for example, deictic contrasts are also crucial to the understanding of such commonly used verbs as *come* and *go*. Notice in this regard the striking difference in perspective found in the following two sentences.

40)

a. The bear is coming into the tent!

b. The bear is going into the tent!

Whereas *come* with a third person subject implies movement towards the speaker (hence we know that the person who utters *39a)* must be in the tent), *go* with the same type of subject suggests movement away from the speaker. Use of *come* with a first person subject (*I*) is different again. Hence the sentence *I'm coming over* implies that the speaker is about to go to where the *addressee* is. As was the case with deictic determiners, we could not fully understand these sentences without reference to the physical setting in which they are uttered.

4.3

Discourse

Properties of other utterances in the same speech event (the discourse) are also crucial to understanding a sentence. A very simple example of this involves the interpretation of elements such as *he*, *it*, and *there*, whose referent is often determined by a word or phrase in a preceding utterance. Consider in this regard the following passage.

41)

A child went for a walk in the park. While *there*, *he* saw a rabbit. Since *it* was injured, *he* took *it* home.

Each of the italicized words in this passage relies for its interpretation on information encoded in a preceding sentence. Thus, we interpret *there* with reference to *in the park*, *he* with reference to *a child*, and *it* with reference to *a rabbit*.

Old and new information

One of the most important contrasts in the study of discourse is the distinction between new and old information. **Old** (or **given**) **information** consists of the knowledge that the speaker assumes is available to the addressee at the time of the utterance, either because it is shared by both or because it has already been introduced into the discourse. In contrast, **new information** involves knowledge that is introduced into the discourse for the first time. Consider the contrast between the following two sentences.

42)

a. The woman is at the front door.

b. A woman is at the front door.

Choice of *the* as the determiner for *woman* in *42a)* suggests that the referent of the phrase is someone who has been mentioned in the previous discourse and is therefore already known to the addressee (old information). In contrast, choice of the determiner *a* in *42b)* implies that the referent is being introduced into the discourse for the first time (new information).

Notice that both sentences in *42)* use *the* as the determiner for *front door*. This is because the setting for the conversation presumably includes only one front door, whose identity and location is known to both speaker and addressee. As noted, old information can consist of shared knowledge such as this and need not always be explicitly stated in the previous discourse.

Topics

Another important notion for the study of discourse is that of **topic**, which corresponds to what a sentence or group of sentences is about. Consider the following passage.

43)

Once upon a time there was a merchant with two daughters. The older daughter wanted to be a scholar. She spent her time reading and studying. As for the younger daughter, she preferred to travel and see the world.

The first sentence in this passage introduces a merchant and his two daughters as new information. A topic (the older daughter) is selected in the second sentence and maintained in the third, in which *she* refers back to *the older daughter*. The final sentence then switches to a new topic (the younger daughter), providing some information about her. This switch is facilitated by the expression *as for*, which can be used in English as a marker of new topics.

In English, the subject of the sentence tends also to be the topic. This is why (as mentioned in section 1.2 above) it is natural to interpret the active sentence in *44a)* as being about the police and the passive sentence in *b)* as being about the burglar (see also section 6.2 of Chapter 5).

44)

a.   The police chased the burglar.

b.   The burglar was chased by the police.

In some languages, a special affix is used to identify the topic. The following sentences from Japanese illustrate this phenomenon. (Nom = nominative, the subject marker; Top = topic marker; Q = question marker)

45)

Speaker A: Dare-ga kimasita-ka?
               Who-Nom came-Q?

Speaker B: Akira-ga kimasita.
               Akira-Nom came.

Speaker A: Akira-wa dare-to kimasita-ka?
               Akira-Top who-with came-Q?
               'Who did Akira come with?'

The topic marker in Japanese (the suffix *-wa*) is distinguished from the subject marker (*-ga*) by its use to mark old or background information. This is why speaker B responds to A's first question by using the subject marker on the NP *Akira*. Because this NP provides new information here (an answer to A's question), the topic marker would be inappropriate. However, once it has been established that Akira is the person who came, the corresponding NP can then bear the topic marker. This is precisely what happens in Speaker A's final utterance, wherein the NP *Akira* (which is now associated with previously established information) is marked by the topic suffix *-wa*.

Conversational strategies

In addition to background beliefs, the setting, and the discourse context, there is at least one other major type of information that enters into the interpretation of utterances. This information has to do with the 'rules for conversation', our understanding of how language is used in particular situations to convey a message. If, for example, I ask someone, *'Would you like to go to the cinema tonight?'* and I receive as a response *'I have to study for an exam'*, I know that the other person is declining my invitation even though there is nothing in the literal meaning of the sentence that says so. Moreover, even though the response does not contain an explicit answer to my invitation, I recognize it as a perfectly appropriate way to respond. (Notice that the same could not be said of a response like *'I have to comb my hair'* or *'I enjoy reading books'*.)

As speakers of a language, we are able to draw inferences about what is meant but not actually said. Information that is conveyed in this way is called a **conversational implicature**. The ease with which we recognize and interpret implicatures stems from our knowledge of how people in our linguistic community use language to communicate with each other.

The general overarching guideline for conversational interactions is often called the **Co-operative Principle**.

46)

The Co-operative Principle:
Make your contribution appropriate to the conversation.

More specific **maxims** or guidelines ensure that conversational interactions actually satisfy the Co-operative Principle.

Table 7.17   Some conversational maxims

The Maxim of Relation:
Be relevant.
The Maxim of Quality:
Try to make your contribution one that is true. (Do not say things that are false or for which you lack adequate evidence.)
The Maxim of Quantity:
Do not make your contribution more or less informative than required.
The Maxim of Manner:
Avoid ambiguity and obscurity; be brief and orderly.

The maxims in Table 7.17 are responsible for regulating normal conversation but, as we will see directly, each can be suspended in certain circumstances to create particular effects.

Relation

The Maxim of Relation is crucial to evaluating the appropriateness of responses to the question *'Would you like to go to the cinema tonight?'* (the example given at the beginning of this section). Because we assume that the conversational contributions of others are relevant to the topic at hand, we are able to infer from the response *'I have to study for an exam'* that the speaker is unable or unwilling to go to the movie. Similarly, because it is hard to see a connection between combing one's hair and being able to go to a movie, we judge the response *'I have to comb my hair'* to be irrelevant and hence inappropriate.

Of course, the Maxim of Relation can sometimes be suspended by a speaker who wants to create a particular impression. For example, if someone asks you *'Have you finished that essay yet?'*, and you respond *'It's been raining a lot lately, hasn't it?'*, you violate the Maxim of Relation by not responding in a relevant way. On the other hand, by giving this response you signal to the other person that you want to move away from the topic of conversation that has been raised.

Quality

The Maxim of Quality requires that the statements used in conversations have some factual basis. If, for example, I ask *'What's the weather like?'* and someone responds *'It's snowing'*, I will normally assume that this statement provides reliable information about the current weather.

In order to achieve irony or sarcasm, however, it is sometimes possible to abandon the Maxim of Quality and say something that one knows to be false. Thus, if two people live in the middle of a sweltering desert and one person insists on asking every morning *'What's the weather like?'*, it might be appropriate for the other person to respond sarcastically *'Oh, today it's snowing, as usual'*, perhaps with a particular facial expression or intonation to indicate that the statement was not intended as a true report of the facts.

Quantity

The Maxim of Quantity introduces some very subtle guidelines into a conversation. If, for example, someone asks me where a famous English author lives, then the nature of my response will depend in large part on how much information I believe to be appropriate for that point in the conversation. If I know that the other person is simply curious about which part of the country the author lives in, it might suffice to respond *'in Birmingham'*. On the other hand, if I know that the person wants to visit the author, then much more specific information (perhaps even an address) is appropriate.

The Maxim of Quantity can be suspended in order to mislead a conversational partner. For example, if Mary's estranged partner asks me where Mary is and I know that Mary does not want to see this person, I might respond by saying *'I think she moved to the south of England or something'* even though I know her precise address in London. In responding in this vague manner, I am not being untruthful since I have said nothing false, but by giving less information than is appropriate, I am violating the Maxim of Quantity and hence being misleading.

Manner

The Maxim of Manner imposes several constraints on language use, two of which will be exemplified here. First, imagine that I refer to a particular person as *the man whom Mary lives with*. A listener would be justified in concluding that the man in question is not Mary's husband. This is because, by the Maxim of Manner, a briefer and less obscure description, *Mary's husband*, would have been used if it could have correctly described Mary's companion.

Second, imagine that I am writing a letter of recommendation to an employer and, choosing my words carefully, I say about a former student of mine, *'You will be fortunate indeed if you can get Henry to work for you'*. By deliberately using a sentence that can be interpreted in two dramatically different ways ('You will be glad to have Henry on your staff' versus 'It is not easy to get Henry to do any work'), I violate the Maxim of Manner by using an ambiguous structure. Since the maxims are violated only for specific purposes (as when the Maxim of Quality is suspended to yield sarcasm), the person to whom the letter is written would be justified in concluding that my choice of language constitutes a veiled warning about Henry. (See also the discussion in Chapter 17, section 5.)

The maxims in other societies

The preceding maxims represent constraints on conversation that may well be an integral part of language use in all cultures. This is not to say that the maxims are employed in exactly the same way in all linguistic communities, however. In fact, we know that the circumstances under which it is appropriate to suspend a maxim can differ. A good example of this involves the Maxim of Quantity as it is used in rural areas of the Malagasy Republic (formerly called Madagascar), the large island off the east coast of Africa.

Because rural villages in the Malagasy Republic form small, tightly integrated societies, new information is rare and considerable prestige accrues to its holder. Speakers are therefore often reluctant to impart it to just anyone. When asked about a particular event, then, they may reply evasively, avoiding mention of the information being sought by their conversational partner. Thus, a visit to the market might be described by saying simply *'there were many people there'* rather than giving any specific details. This suggests not only that the Maxim of Quantity can be overridden, but that the conditions under which this happens may be intertwined with the cultural practices of a particular society.

Relevance (advanced)

How do we interpret utterances in context? As we saw at the beginning of the previous section, conversation that appears superficially disjointed may be quite well-ordered. *'I have to study for an exam'* can be an appropriate reply to *'Would you like to go to the cinema tonight?'*. Why and how does the hearer draw from the addressee's response the inference that the invitation is being declined?

It is this problem of drawing inferences that **Relevance Theory** is designed to address. The essence of Relevance Theory is that when interpreting utterances, we focus on information that is **relevant**, as seen from the addressee's stance. In this theory the term 'relevance' has a specialized technical meaning. It refers to information that produces a '**contextual effect**'. And information is said to produce a contextual effect if it interacts with the linguistic and extra-linguistic context by having implications that yield new information that confirms, contradicts or otherwise modifies the hearer's previously held assumptions and beliefs with regard to some proposition. An important aspect of Relevance Theory is the claim that the context in which utterances are interpreted is not prefabricated in advance, but rather is continuously created and modified using linguistic and extra-linguistic clues present in the unfolding situation. To illustrate this, let us consider the exchange in *47)*.

47)

Barbara: Did you enjoy the meal?
Janet: The soup was lumpy, the steak was gristly, the vegetables were overcooked and the desert was musty.

The information contained in Janet's list produces for Barbara the contextual effect from which she draws the implicature *'No, I did not enjoy the meal'*.

We are assuming, of course, that though she is not answering directly, nonetheless Janet is being co-operative and providing relevant information. Since we know that lumpy soup, gristly steak and overcooked vegetables, followed by a musty pudding is not anyone's idea of a lovely meal, the inference that Janet did not enjoy the meal is justified.

How do we assess the degree of relevance that a particular piece of information has? The degree of relevance of an utterance depends on a **cost–benefit analysis**. Ideally, an interpretation which maximizes contextual effects and minimizes the processing cost is preferred. A simple example will make this clear. Suppose you at a cheese-and-wine party which is part of a university student recruitment fair, and you notice a bearded, bald person who is wearing a kilt. From his appearance and attire you infer *48)*.

48)

The bald, bearded person in a kilt is a Scotsman.

The cost of arriving at this inference is minimal as the clues are obvious and require very little processing.

Moments later, you are introduced to this man and you are told his name is Mr Hamish MacTavish. From his name you confirm the inference in *48)*. As soon as you exchange greetings and hear his very strong Glasgow accent you get further confirmation of *48)*, and you also draw a further inference:

49)

Mr Hamish MacTavish is a Scotsman from Glasgow.

Now, let us suppose that you are a football fan and adore the Glasgow Rangers. Suppose you also have other interests. You are interested in ballet and you know that Glasgow is the headquarters of Scottish Ballet; you are a history of technology enthusiast and last night you saw a documentary which mentioned that John Logie Baird, the inventor of low definition television and James (Paraffin) Young, who founded the oil industry in Scotland and Pennsylvania, were both graduates of Glasgow's Royal College of Science and Technology. You have read somewhere that this college merged with the Scottish College of Commerce and became Strathclyde University in 1964. Furthermore, you remember from your school geography lessons that Glasgow is on the river Clyde and used to be a leading shipbuilding centre – the *Queen Elizabeth II* was built there. You also happen to have seen recent newspaper reports about pirated videos and computer programmes sold by criminal syndicates in *the Barras* (you are aware that *the Barras* is slang for 'the Barrows', Glasgow's famous open-air market). Theoretically, it would be possible to combine all these pieces of information and derive *50)*.

50)

Mr Hamish MacTavish is a Scot from Glasgow, home of the Rangers, a city on the Clyde, which used to be a major shipbuilding centre – where the *Queen Elizabeth II* was built; it is the headquarters of Scottish Ballet and home of Strathclyde University (which was created by merging the Royal College of Science and Technology (whose alumni include John Logie Baird who invented low definition television and James (Paraffin) Young, who founded the oil industry in Scotland and Pennsylvania) with the Scottish College of Commerce; unfortunately, it is also a city where pirated videos and computer programmes are sold by criminal syndicates in the Barras.

In principle there are a million and one other pieces of information one could process about Glasgow. But one wouldn't. The sensible thing would be to determine a suitable cutoff point because processing information costs time and effort. (In real life conversation we do not have all day to process information before saying something to our interlocutors.) The bigger the context taken into account gets, the greater the number and complexity of possible inferences becomes. Therefore it is necessary to determine whether the benefits obtained in the processing of various strands of information outweigh the cost involved. The hearer selects for processing the context that yields the greatest contextual effect for the least amount of processing cost. In our example, the cost of processing *50)*, which is so complex and unwieldy, would far exceed any likely benefits in terms of yielding a contextual effect.

Supposing you are at this cheese-and-wine-party because you are thinking about choosing a university at which to study, the most relevant information will probably be that Strathclyde University which boasts of some famous alumni (and which is presumably a reputable institution) is in Glasgow. If the person introducing you then says,

51)

Mr MacTavish is the Director of Admissions at Strathclyde . . .

Strathclyde University produces the greatest contextual effect in this situation. So, it would be more natural if the next contribution to the conversation had something to do with Strathclyde University rather than kilts, Mr MacTavish's bald head, Scottish Ballet or the Barras.

If as a conversation opener, Mr MacTavish asks you an apparently vague question like:

52)

Where do you want to go next year?

His question will not be vague. Cost–benefit analysis will suggest that since this is a student recruitment fair and Mr MacTavish's job is to recruit students, he wants to find out where you want to go to university next year rather than where you plan to go for your summer holidays.

To sum up, relevance is a cognitive principle that lies behind information processing. From the multitude of available pieces of information and potential inferences the hearer selects the optimally relevant ones.

Relevance Theory is not without its critics. While not discounting its merits, some pragmaticists have criticized Relevance Theory for being too one-sided. Communication is a two-way street. Being oriented towards the listener at the expense of the speaker/writer's point of view, Relevance Theory does not seem to deal adequately with the ways in which speakers go about the task of encoding their communicative intentions, which is a major part of communication.

Summing up

Semantics and pragmatics are concerned with complementary and overlapping aspects of study of meaning. The boundary between the two cannot be clearly drawn. As a rule of thumb, **semantics** deals with a broad range of phenomena including the nature of **meaning** and the role of syntactic structure in the interpretation of sentences. **Pragmatics**, on the other hand, investigates how the meaning that the speaker intends to communicate by using a particular utterance in a particular context is understood by the addressee. Although serious problems and obstacles remain in all these areas, work in recent years has at least begun to identify the type of relations and principles involved in the understanding of language. These include the notions of **extension** and **intension** in the case of word meaning, **thematic role** assignment in the case of sentence interpretation, and **c-command** in the case of pronoun interpretation. Other factors known to be involved in an utterance's interpretation include the speaker's and addressee's background beliefs (as manifested, for example, in **presuppositions**), the context provided by the **setting** and the **discourse**, and the **maxims** associated with the **Co-operative Principle**. Finally, **relevance** plays a key role in understanding utterances.

Notes

1 A similar set of contrasts in the manifestation of the GO concept was noted in section 1.3. This is no coincidence: many linguists believe that thematic roles should be defined in terms of the atomic concepts (such as GO) out of which word meanings are constructed. Hence, we might say that the theme corresponds to the

entity undergoing the change associated with GO.

2 The movement may be triggered by considerations relating to the Case Filter, which requires that each NP in a grammatical sentence receive case (Chapter 6, section 3). On the assumption that passive verbs lose the ability to assign case to their complement, the postverbal NP in Figure 7.10 must move to a case position elsewhere in the sentence if the Case Filter is to be satisfied. The subject slot is the only such open position.

Sources

Surveys of the nature of word meaning and semantic relations can be found in many sources, including the book by Allan cited below. The discussion of fuzzy categories and graded membership in section 2 draws from Part 1 of *Women, Fire, and Dangerous Things* by G. Lakoff (Chicago: University of Chicago Press, 1987) and the references cited there. The discussion of metaphor takes as its starting point the book *Metaphors We Live By*, cited below. The four Eskimo words for snow in Table 7.7 are from *The Handbook of American Indian Languages* by F. Boas (Washington: Smithsonian Institute, 1911) and are also cited on p. 123 of the book by Allen referenced below; for a longer list of words for snow, see *Dictionnaire français-eskimau du parler de l'Ungava* (Québec: Presses de l'Université Laval, 1970); see also 'The Great Eskimo Vocabulary Hoax' by G. Pullum in *Natural Language and Linguistic Theory* 7: 275–81 (1989). The discussion of verbs of motion is based on the paper 'Lexicalization patterns: semantic structure in lexical form' by L. Talmy in *Language Typology and Syntactic Description*, Vol. 3, edited by T. Shopen, pp. 57–149 (Cambridge, Cambridge University Press, 1985). The definition of grammaticization used in section 2.4 is based on D. Slobin's 'Crosslinguistic evidence for the language-making capacity', in *The Crosslinguistic Study of Language Acquisition*, Vol. 2, edited by D. Slobin, pp. 1172–73 (Hillsdale, NJ: Erlbaum, 1985). The data on Hidatsa assertion morphemes in the same section is from *Hidatsa Syntax* by G.H. Matthews (The Hague: Mouton, 1965).

The treatment of structural ambiguity, thematic role assignment, and pronoun interpretation in this chapter presents slightly simplified versions of views widely held within generative grammar in the early 1990s. For a simple summary of the last two issues, see *Lectures on Contemporary Syntactic Theories* by P. Sells (Stanford, Calif.: Center for the Study of Language and Information, 1985).

The data used in the discussion of deixis come from 'Deixis' by S. Anderson and E. Keenan in *Language Typology and Syntactic Description*, Vol. 3, edited by T. Shopen, pp. 259–308 (Cambridge: Cambridge University Press, 1985). The discussion of topicalization draws on the 'Major functions of the noun phrase' by A. Andrews in *Language Typology and Syntactic Description*, Vol. 1, edited by T. Shopen, pp. 62–154 (Cambridge: Cambridge University Press, 1985). The discussion of the Co-operative Principle and the maxims of conversation is based primarily on 'Logic and conversation' by Paul Grice in *Syntax and Semantics*, Vol. 3, edited by P. Cole and J. Morgan, pp. 41–58 (New York: Academic Press, 1975) and the paper by L. Horn cited below. The discussion of Malagasy conversation is based on 'The universality of conversational postulates' by E. Ochs in *Language in Society* 5: 67–80 (1976). The treatment of Relevance Theory draws on Diane Blakemore, *Understanding Utterances: An Introduction to Pragmatics* (Oxford: Blackwell, 1992, especially Chapter 2), which in turn is based on Sperber and Wilson 1986 (cited below). The data in question 18 are from the chapter entitled 'Disorder in court' in Richard Lederer's *Anguished English* (London: Robson Books, 1989).

The exercises for this chapter were prepared by Joyce Hildebrand.

Recommended reading   Allan, Keith. 1986. *Linguistic Meaning*. Vols 1 and 2. London: Routledge & Kegan Paul.

Horn, Laurence. 1988. 'Pragmatic theory.' In *Linguistics: The Cambridge Survey*. Vol. 1. Edited by F. Newmeyer, pp. 113–45. Cambridge: Cambridge University Press.

Hurford, James, and Brendan Heasley. 1983. *Semantics: A Coursebook*. Cambridge: Cambridge University Press.

Ladusaw, William. 1988. 'Semantic theory.' In *Linguistics: The Cambridge Survey*. Vol. 1. Edited by F. Newmeyer, pp. 89–112. Cambridge: Cambridge University Press.

Lakoff, George, and Mark Johnson. 1982. *Metaphors We Live By*. Chicago: University of Chicago Press.

Levinson, Stephen. 1983. *Pragmatics*. Cambridge: Cambridge University Press.

McCawley, James. 1993. *Everything That Linguists Have Always Wanted to Know About Logic*. 2nd edn. Chicago: University of Chicago Press.

Mey, Jacob. 1993. *Pragmatics: An Introduction*. Oxford: Blackwell.

Prince, Ellen. 1988. 'Discourse analysis: a part of the study of linguistic competence.' In *Linguistics: The Cambridge Survey*. Vol. 2. Edited by F. Newmeyer, pp. 164–82. Cambridge: Cambridge University Press.

Sperber, Dan and Deidre Wilson. 1986. *Relevance: Communication and Cognition*. Oxford: Blackwell.

Questions

1. Two relations involving word meanings are antonymy and synonymy. Which relation is illustrated in each of the pairs of words below?
   a) flourish–thrive
   b) intelligent–stupid
   c) casual–informal
   d) young–old
   e) uncle–aunt
   f) intelligent–able
   g) flog–whip
   h) drunk–sober

2. It was noted in this chapter that a single form can have two or more meanings. Depending on whether these meanings are related to each other, this phenomenon involves polysemy or homophony. Which of these two relations is exemplified by the forms below?
   a) grass   herbage used for grazing animals; marijuana
   b) leech   a bloodsucking worm; a hanger-on who seeks advantage
   c) range   a cooking stove; a series of mountains
   d) key   an instrument used to open a lock; an answer sheet for a test or assignment
   e) reel   a spool for photographic film; round device at the butt end of a fishing rod for the line
   f) race   the act of running competitively; people belonging to the same genetic grouping
   g) /flaʊə/   a blossom; finely ground wheat

3. Three semantic relations among sentences were covered in this chapter: paraphrase, entailment, and contradiction. Which of these relations is exemplified in each of the following pairs of sentences?

a) I saw Terry at the anniversary party.
    It was Terry that I saw at the anniversary party.
b) Jim is Mary's husband.
    Mary is married.
c) My pet cobra likes the taste of chocolate fudge.
    My pet cobra finds chocolate fudge tasty.
d) Vera is an only child.
    Olga is Vera's sister.
e) It is fifty kilometres to the nearest service station.
    The nearest service station is fifty kilometres away.
f) My cousin Bryan teaches at the Adult College for a living.
    My cousin Bryan is a teacher.

4. In discussing the nature of meaning, we noted that it is necessary to distinguish between intension and extension. Describe the intensions and the extensions of each of these phrases.
a) the President of the United States
b) the Queen of England
c) the capital of Germany
d) women who have walked on the moon
e) the Prince of Wales
f) Princess Diana's husband
g) Henry VIII's wife
h) Father Christmas

5. In our discussion of semantic decomposition, we noted that at least some words have meanings that can be represented in terms of smaller semantic features. Four such words are *dog*, *puppy*, *cat*, and *kitten*.
a) Attempt to provide the semantic features associated with each of these words.
b) How are the pairs *dog–puppy* and *cat–kitten* different from *man–boy* and *woman–girl*?
c) Try to provide semantic features for the words *circle*, *triangle*, and *quadrangle* What problems do you encounter?

6. Each of the following words is associated with a concept.
a) island   e) food
b) soft   f) husband
c) white   g) cricket bat
d) wristwatch   h) mountain

i) Determine which of these examples are fuzzy concepts.
ii) Choose one of the fuzzy concepts above. Name one prototypical member of that concept and one member that is closer to the concept boundary.
iii) Draw a diagram for the concept 'dwelling' similar to that of Figure 7.2 in this chapter. Do the same for the concept 'vehicle'.

7. Examine the following sets of sentences, each of which include words or phrases used metaphorically.

a)   She gave him an icy stare.
   He gave her the cold shoulder.
   He exudes a lot of warmth towards people.
   They got into a heated argument.

b)   He drops a lot of hints.
   The committee picked up on the issue.
   She dumps all her problems on her friends.
   Although he disagreed, he let it go.

c)   the eye of a needle
   the foot of the bed
   the hands of the clock
   the arm of a chair
   the table legs

d)   I'm looking forward to it.
   She can foretell the future.
   I can remember back to when I was two years old.
   He drags up old conflicts.
   You must plan ahead for retirement.

e)   This lecture is easy to digest.
   He just eats up the lecturer's words.
   Chew on this thought for a while.
   Listen to this juicy piece of gossip.

For each set of sentences:

i)   Identify the words or phrases that are used metaphorically in each
   sentence.

ii)   Determine the basis for each of these metaphor sets.
   Use the pattern: 'The metaphors in (x) describe _____ in terms
   of _____.'
   Example: The metaphors in (a) describe human relationships in
   terms of temperature.

8. The section on lexicalization of concepts discussed how some languages
   simultaneously express motion and path, motion and movement, and/or
   motion and thing moving in motion verbs. Can you change the sentence
   He moved the goods by cart to the warehouse so that both movement and
   vehicle used to move are lexicalized in one verb? What other verbs
   express a similar combination of concepts?

9. Grammaticized concepts are expressed with the use of affixes or non-
   lexical categories. Consider the following Fijian pronouns.

   a)   au   1st person singular 'me'
   b)   iko   2nd person singular 'you'
   c)   koya   3rd person singular 'him/her/it'
   d)   kedaru   1st person dual 'you and me'
   e)   keirau   1st person dual 'one other (not you) and me'
   f)   kemudrau   2nd person dual 'you two'
   g)   rau   3rd person dual 'them two'
   h)   kedatou   1st person trial 'two others (including you) and me'

i) keitou   1st person trial 'two others (excluding you) and me'
j) kemudou   2nd person trial 'you three'
k) iratou   3rd person trial 'those three'
l) keda   1st person plural 'us (more than three, including you)'
m) keimami   1st person plural 'us (more than three, excluding you)'
n) kemuni: 2nd person plural 'you (more than three)'
o) ira   3rd person plural 'them (more than three)'

i) Some concepts are grammaticized in the Fijian pronoun system which are not grammaticized in the English pronoun system. Can you identify them?

ii) Which concept is grammaticized in the English pronoun system but not in the Fijian system?

10. Each NP in the following sentences has a thematic role that represents the part that its referent plays in the situation described by the sentence.
a) The man chased the intruder.
b) The cat jumped from the chair onto the table.
c) Aaron wrote a letter to Marilyn.
d) The premier entertained the guests in the lounge.
e) Henry posted the manuscript from Inverness.
Using the terms described in this chapter, label the thematic role of each NP in these sentences and identify the assigner for each thematic role.

Example: *Bill* wrote *a novel* in *the park*.

11. Each of the following sentences has undergone a movement transformation.
a) What has Larry given to the bride?
b) Who will Chris kiss?
c) Which house will the group leave from?
d) What has Tim forgotten on the bus?
e) The necklace was stolen by the burglar.
f) The ball was thrown to Jo by Louise.
Write out the deep structure string for each of these sentences and mark all thematic roles and thematic role assigners.

Example: a) *Larry* has given *what* to *the bride*.

12. One of the relations involved in the interpretation of pronouns is that of c-command. Examine the following tree structure for the sentence *Jack's brother gave himself a haircut*.
a) Who does *himself* refer to in this sentence?
b) Does NP$_2$ c-command NP$_3$?
c) How does your answer to b) relate to your answer to a)?
d) Does the antecedent change if you change *himself* to *him*? Why?

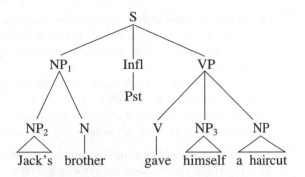

13. In the following sentence, the pronoun *she* can refer to either *the architect* or *the secretary*.

The architect gave the secretary a rise after she typed the report.

a) Which interpretation for *she* comes to mind first?
b) Why?
c) What happens to the pronoun's interpretation if you change the word *secretary* to *janitor*?

14. In the following pairs of sentences, one of the two sentences contains a presupposition relating to the truth of the complement clause.
a) John regrets that Maria went to the graduation ceremony.
   John believes that Maria went to the graduation ceremony.
b) The captain thought that the ship was in danger.
   The captain realized that the ship was in danger.
c) It is significant that the criminal was sentenced.
   It is likely that the criminal was sentenced.

For each pair:
i) Identify the sentence that contains this presupposition.
ii) Locate the word that is responsible for the presupposition.

15. In Malagasy, the use of the deictics *ety* 'here' and *aty* 'there' depend on whether the object in question is visible to the speaker. How does this differ from the English use of *here/there*?
a) Ety ny tranony. 'Here is his house (visible to the speaker).'
b) Aty ny tranony. 'There is his house (not visible to the speaker).'

16. The syntactic construction *It was* _____ *that* _____ is called a cleft construction and is used in certain discourse contexts. Consider the following conversations involving cleft constructions.
a) *A*: Did Sally claim that she saw a flying saucer last night?
   B: No, it was a meteorite that Sally claimed she saw last night.
b) *A*: Did Sally claim that she saw a flying saucer last night?
   B: No, it was Sally that claimed she saw a meteorite last night.
c) *A*: Did Sally claim that she saw a flying saucer last night?
   B: No, it was last week that Sally claimed she saw a flying saucer.

i) Is B's response equally acceptable in all three interactions?

ii) Choose one of the discourses in which B's response is appropriate. How do the underlined parts correspond to new and old information?

iii) For the discourse in which B's response is unacceptable, can you now explain why it is unacceptable?

iv) In addition to the cleft construction, identify the way in which new information is marked phonetically in B's responses.

17. Each of the following examples contains a conversational implicature.

a) *A*: Have you washed the floor and done the dishes?
    B: I've washed the floor.

b) *A*: Did you get hold of Carl yet?
    B: I tried to call him yesterday.

c) *A*: What did you think of the film?
    B: Well, the supporting actor was great.

d) *A*: Do you have any pets?
    B: Yes, I have two cats.

i) What is the implicature for each example?

ii) For each example, which maxim of the Co-operative Principle is relevant to the implicature?

18. Using the various dimensions of pragmatics, including Relevance Theory, explain the peculiarity of the following extracts from Richard Lederer's *Anguished English* which are all taken from records of snippets of exchanges from American courtrooms. (*Q* = Question; *A* = Answer)

a) *Q* What is your brother-in-law's name?
    A Borofkin.
    Q What is his first name?
    A I can't remember.
    Q He's your brother-in-law for 45 years, and you can't remember his first name?
    A No. I tell you I'm too excited. (Rising from the witness chair and pointing to Mr Borofkin) Nathan, for god's sake, tell them your first name!

b) *Q* Please state the location of your right foot immediately prior to impact.
    A Immediately before impact, my right foot was located at the end of my right leg.

c) *Q* What is your name?
    A Ernestine McDowell.
    Q And what is your marital status?
    A Fair.

Historical linguistics: the study of language change

Robert W. Murray

Many men sayn that in sweveninges
Ther nys but fables and lesynges;
But men may some swevenes sene
Whiche hardely that false ne bene,
But afterwarde ben apparaunt.

➤ Chaucer, *The Romance of the Rose* (c. 1370)

Language change is both obvious and rather mysterious. The English of the late fourteenth century, for example, is so different from Modern English that without special training it is difficult to understand the opening lines to *The Romance of the Rose* cited above. Not only would these sentences have a foreign sound, but words and structures such as *sweveninges*, *lesynges*, and *false ne bene* are unfamiliar.[1] The existence of such differences between early and later variants of the same language raises questions as to how and why languages change over time.

Historical linguistics is concerned with both the description and explanation of language change. In this chapter we examine the nature and causes of language change and survey in some detail phonological, morphological, syntactic, lexical, and semantic change. We also explore techniques used to reconstruct linguistic pre-history and briefly discuss interrelated research into language acquisition and linguistic universals.

1

THE NATURE OF LANGUAGE CHANGE

All languages undergo change over time. English has undergone continuous and dramatic change throughout its three major periods Old English (roughly from 450 to 1100), Middle English (from 1100 to 1500), and Modern English (from 1500 to the present). While Chaucer's Middle English is at least partially comprehensible today, Old English looks like a completely foreign language. The following is an extract from an eighth-century Old English document, a translation of Bede's *Latin History of England*. (The letter þ called 'thorn', represented the phoneme /θ/ in Old English; here and elsewhere in this chapter ⁻ marks a long vowel in the orthography.)

1)

and Seaxan þā sige geslōgan.
and Saxons the victory won
'And the Saxons won the victory.'

þā sendan hī hām ǣrenddracan.
then sent they home messenger
'Then they sent home a messenger.'

These Old English sentences differ from their Modern English counterparts in many respects. In terms of pronunciation, for instance, the Old English word *hām* [ha:m] 'home' in the second sentence became [hɔ:m] in Middle English, and then [howm] (and eventually [həʊm]) in Modern English. In its morphology, Old English differed significantly from Modern English. The suffix *-an* on the Old English word for 'sent' indicates both past tense and plurality of the subject (*hī* 'they'). Differences in word order are also readily apparent, with the verb following both the subject and the object in the first sentence and preceding both the subject and the object in the second. Neither of these word orders would be acceptable in the Modern English forms of these sentences.

In addition, some Old English words have disappeared from use, as the unfamiliar *ǣrenddracan* 'messenger' and *sige* 'victory' indicate. Still other words have been maintained, but with a change in meaning. For example, the Old English word *geslōgan* (which we translated as 'won') is the past tense of the verb *slēan* the Old English predecessor of our word *slay*. Although the Modern English meaning of this word in normal usage is restricted to the act of killing, the Old English verb could also mean 'to strike, beat, coin (money), and forge (weapons)'. As these examples imply, all components of the grammar from meaning (semantics) to individual sounds (phonology) are subject to change.

1.1

Systematicity of language change

A striking fact about language change in general is its regularity and systematicity. For example, the development of a fixed subject–verb–direct object (SVO) basic word order in English did not affect just a few verbs; all verbs in Modern English appear before rather than after the direct object. Similarly, the changes affecting the vowel in the word *hām* did not occur in that word only; they represent the regular development of the Old English vowel *ā* ([a:]) (see Table 8.1).

Table 8.1 Changes affecting Old English [a:]

Old English	Middle English	Modern English		
[ba:t]	[bɔ:t]	([boʊt]>	[bəʊt]	'boat'
[a:θ]	[ɔ:θ]	([oʊθ]>	[əʊθ]	'oath'
[sta:n]	[stɔ:n]	([stoʊn]>	[stəʊn]	'stone'

1.2

Causes of language change

The inevitability of language change is guaranteed by the way in which language is 'handed down' from one generation to the next. Children do not begin with an intact grammar of the language being acquired but rather must construct a grammar on the basis of the available data (see Chapter 12). In such a situation it is hardly surprising that differences will arise, even if only subtle ones, from one generation to the next. Moreover, since all children use the same physiological and cognitive endowment in learning language, it is to be expected that the same patterns of change will be consistently and repeatedly manifested in all languages. Following is a brief overview of the principal causes of language change.

Articulatory simplification

As might be expected, most sound changes have a physiological basis. Since such sound changes typically result in articulatory simplification, they have traditionally been related to the idea of 'ease of articulation'. Although this notion is difficult to define precisely, we can readily identify cases of articulatory simplification in our everyday speech (Table 8.2) such as the deletion of a consonant in a complex cluster or, in some dialects, the insertion of a vowel to break up a complex cluster.

Table 8.2 Simplification of complex clusters

Deletion of a consonant		
[fɪfθs]	→	[fɪfs] *'fifths'*
Insertion of a vowel		
[æθliːt]	→	[æθəliːt] *'athlete'*

Spelling pronunciation

Not all changes in pronunciation have a physiological motivation. A minor, but nevertheless important, source of change in English and other languages is **spelling pronunciation**. Since the written form of a word can differ significantly from the way it is pronounced, a new pronunciation can arise which seems to reflect more closely the spelling of the word. A case in point is the word *often*. Although this word was pronounced with a [t] in earlier English, the voiceless stop was subsequently lost resulting in the pronunciation [ɒfən] (compare *soften*). However, since the letter *t* was retained in the spelling, [t] has been reintroduced into many speakers' pronunciation of this word.

Another case in point is the pronunciation of [s] in words such as *assume* and *consume*. Although in earlier English such words were pronounced with [s], sound change resulted in a pronunciation with [ʃ] (as in *assure*). Similar to the case of *often*, a pronunciation with [t] has been reintroduced into many dialects on the basis of the spelling (which remained unchanged even after the sound change took place). Since spelling tends to remain stable even though sound changes have occurred (English spelling began stabilizing more than three hundred years ago), spelling pronunciation can reintroduce a pronunciation that was earlier altered through sound change.

Note also that changes induced by spelling pronunciation tend to reduce the notorious arbitrariness of the relationship between spelling and pronunciation which is a feature of many names. For example, the Scottish surname *Menzies* which used to be always pronounced [mɪŋɪs] or [meŋɪs] is nowadays normally pronounced [menzɪz]. The same applies to place names. Thus, *Frithsden* (near Berkhamsted in Hertfordshire) is often pronounced [frɪθsdən] rather than [frɪzdən], and *Cambuslang* in Glasgow, which was originally [kəmzlæŋ], today tends to be pronounced [kəmbəslæŋ] – especially by those who are not from that district of the city.

Spelling pronunciation may sometimes be triggered by social factors. This is obviously what lies behind the change that has affected words of French origin such as *human*, *herb*, *humble*, *humour* and *hotel*. These words used to start with a vowel sound, and had an initial 'silent *h*', as they still do in French. But most of us now pronounce the initial orthographic *h* because 'dropping one's aitches' (as in [aʊs] for 'house') is generally negatively evaluated.

Analogy and reanalysis

Cognitive factors also play a role in change in all components of the grammar. Two sources of change having a cognitive basis are **analogy** and **reanalysis**. Analogy reflects the preference of speakers for regular patterns over irregular ones. It typically involves the extension or generalization of a regularity on the basis of the inference that if elements are alike in some respects, they should be alike in others as well. Both phonological and semantic characteristics can serve as a basis for analogy. For example, on the basis of its phonological similarity with such verbs as *sting/stung* and *swing/swung*, in some dialects *bring* has developed a form *brung*, as in *I('ve) brung it into the house*. Children create forms such as *goed* by analogy with regular past tense forms like *played*. As we will see, analogy plays a very important role in morphological change.

Reanalysis is particularly common in morphological change. Morphological reanalysis often involves an attempt to attribute a compound or root + affix structure to a word that formerly was not broken down into component morphemes. A classic example in English is the word *hamburger*, which originally referred to a type of meat patty deriving its name from the city of Hamburg in Germany. This word has been reanalysed as consisting of two components, *ham + burger*. The latter morpheme has since appeared in many new forms including *fishburger*, *chickenburger*, *veggieburger* and even as a free morpheme *burger*. Note that the resulting reanalysis must not necessarily be correct. (There is usually no ham in a burger!)

Language contact

Another cause of linguistic change is **language contact**, which occurs when speakers of one language frequently interact with the speakers of another language or dialect. As a consequence, extensive **borrowing** can occur, particularly where there are significant numbers of bilinguals or multilinguals. Although borrowing can affect all components of the grammar, the lexicon is typically most affected. English, for example, has borrowed many French words such as *parent, cousin, animal, soup, colour, major, cuisine, gateau,* and *blasé.* In North America, many Amerindian words including *Canada, moccasin, totem, tomahawk, chinook, moose,* and *skunk* have also been added to the English lexicon.

Among the effects that borrowing can have on the sound system are the introduction of new phonemes or allophones and changes in their distribution. For example, some English speakers pronounce the name of the classical composer, *Bach,* with the final velar fricative [x] found in the German pronunciation. If there is a significant number of borrowings from another language, the borrowed foreign segment can eventually become a new phoneme. In the early Middle English period, the London dialect had [f] but not [v] in word-initial position. The [v] was later introduced as a result of contact with other English dialects and with French, in which it did occur word-initially. As a result of this contact, a contrast developed between /f/ and /v/ word-initially, as found in Modern English pairs such as *file* and *vile.*

Language (as well as dialect) contact also results in another minor but nevertheless important source of language change, **hypercorrection**. Hypercorrection occurs when a speaker who is attempting to speak another (perhaps more prestigious) dialect or language overgeneralizes particular rules. For example, many speakers from the north of England have the vowel [ʊ] in words like *cut, grumpy,* and *stump* where RP and other dialects have [ʌ]. But there are also a few words such as *put, sugar, butcher,* and *Buddha* in which both RP and Northern English have the vowel [ʊ]. (This is because Northern English is conservative and did not take on board a historical change that occurred elsewhere which resulted in the split of the short /ʊ/ of Middle English into the phonemes /ʊ/ and /ʌ/ in certain words.) The problem is that in present-day English there is no way of distinguishing between words that belong to the *cut* (/kʌt/) class, which underwent the change of /ʊ/ to /ʌ/, from words in the *put* (/pʊt/) class that evaded the change. So, sometimes speakers of Northern English wishing to adopt an RP accent, overgeneralize the rule that makes their [ʊ] correspond to RP [ʌ]. The result is the hypercorrect pronunciation of a word like *butcher* as [bʌtʃə], although this word is an exception to the historical change of [ʊ] to [ʌ]. They may also pronounce *rubella* ([rʊbelə]) as [rʌbelə], not realizing that when this word was borrowed from Latin (cf. *rubellus* 'reddish') in the late nineteenth century, the Latin pronunciation of *u* as [ʊ] was retained.

Another example of hypercorrection is the use of *I* in constructions such as *He saw John and I.* This usage is an overgeneralization of the rule that only *I* should be used in subject position, never *me.* According to this rule, *John and I are going* is correct but *John and me/me and John are going* is incorrect. For some speakers, hypercorrection has resulted in the inference that all coordinate phrases containing *me* (such as *John and me*) are incorrect even when they serve as the direct object (complement) of the verb. Note that the person who says *He saw John and I* would not say *He saw I.*

2

SOUND CHANGE

Although all components of the grammar are susceptible to change over time, some types of change yield more obvious results than others. Variation and change are particularly noticeable in the phonology of a language. Several common types of sound change can be distinguished.

Most sound changes begin as subtle alterations in the sound pattern of a language in particular phonetic environments. The linguistic processes underlying such **phonetically conditioned** change are identical to the ones found in the phonology of currently spoken languages (see Chapter 2, section 9). The application of such processes usually brings about an articulatory simplification and over time significant changes in the phonology of a language can result.

Although all aspects of phonology (for example, tone, stress, and syllable structure) are subject to change over time, we will restrict our attention here to change involving segments. Since most sound changes involve sequences of segments, the main focus will be on **sequential change**. However, we will

Table 8.3 Catalogue of sound changes

Assimilation
    Place and/or manner of articulation
    Palatalization/affrication
    Nasalization
    Umlaut
Dissimilation
Epenthesis (segment addition)
Metathesis (segment movement)
Weakening and deletion
    Vowels
        Vowel reduction
        Syncope
        Apocope
    Consonants
        Degemination
        Voicing
        Frication
        Rhotacism
        Deletion
Consonant strengthening
    Glide strengthening

Segmental change
Deaffrication

Auditorily-based change
Substitution

also discuss one common type of **segmental** change, involving the simplification of an affricate. In addition, in order to indicate that more than just articulatory factors play a role in sound change, we will discuss a case of sound change based on auditory factors. All important sound changes discussed in this section and referred to in this chapter are found in the catalogue of sound changes, presented in Table 8.3.

2.1

Sequential change

Assimilation

The most common type of sequential change is **assimilation**, which has the effect of increasing the efficiency of articulation through a simplification of articulatory movements. We will focus here on the four main types indicated in the catalogue.

Partial assimilation involving **place** or **manner of articulation** is a very common change which, over time, can result in total assimilation. In the Spanish and Latin examples in Table 8.4, the place of articulation of the nasal assimilated to the following consonant.

Table 8.4 Assimilation (place of articulation) in Spanish and Latin[2]

| Old Spanish | semda | Modern Spanish | senda | 'path' |
| Early Latin | inpossibilis | Later Latin | impossibilis | 'impossible' |

The first of the Old English examples in Table 8.5 shows voicing assimilation and the second shows the assimilation of nasality.

Table 8.5 Assimilation in voice and manner of articulation in Old English

Early Old English	*Later Old English*	
slæpde	slæpte	'slept'
stefn	stemn	'stem (of a tree)'

In the Italian examples in Table 8.6, a stop assimilates totally to a following stop.

Table 8.6 Total assimilation in Italian

Latin	*Italian*	
octo (*c* = [k])	otto	'eight'
septem	sette	'seven'
damnum	danno	'damage'

Another type of assimilation is **palatalization** – the effect that front vowels and the palatal glide [j] typically have on velar, alveolar, and dental stops, making their place of articulation more palatal. If you compare your pronunciation of *keep* as opposed to *cot*, you will notice that the pronunciation of [k] in the former is much more palatal than in the latter due to the influence of [i]. Palatalization is often the first step in **affrication** (Table 8.7), a change in which palatalized stops become affricates, either [tˢ] or [tʃ] if the original stop was voiceless or [dᶻ] or [d³] if the original stop was voiced.

Table 8.7 Palatalization/affrication induced by front vowels and [j]

Examples from the Romance languages

Latin	centum [k]	Old French	cent	[tˢ]	'one hundred'
Latin	centum [k]	Italian	ciento	[tʃ]	'one hundred'
Latin	medius [d]	Italian	mezzo	[dᶻ]	'half'
Latin	gentem [g]	Old French	gent	[d³]	'people'

Nasalization refers to the nasalizing effect that a nasal consonant can have on an adjacent vowel (Table 8.8). This change occurred in both French and Portuguese, with the subsequent loss of the nasal consonant. (The pronunciation of the vowels in our examples underwent additional changes in height and tenseness in French.)

Table 8.8 Nasalization in Portuguese and French

Latin	Portuguese		French		
bon-	bon	[bõ]	bon	[bɔ̃]	'good'
un-	um	[ũ]	un	[œ̃]	'one'

Although assimilation is probably most common in the case of adjacent segments, it can also apply at a distance. A case in point is **umlaut**, the effect a vowel or sometimes a glide in one syllable can have on the vowel of another syllable, usually a preceding one. Umlaut (resulting in front rounded vowels [y] and [ø]) played an important role in Old English, as it still does in modern German, and is the source of irregular plurals such as *goose/geese* and *mouse/ mice* in Modern English. For example, the plural of the pre-Old English words *gōs* 'goose' and *mūs* 'mouse' was formed by adding a suffix -[i]. As a result, umlaut of the vowel in the preceding syllable occurred in the plural forms (see pre-Old English stages 1 and 2 in Table 8.9) but not in the singular forms. By early Old English, the suffix -[i] had been lost in a separate change, leaving the umlauted vowel as the marker of the plural form. (Subsequent changes included the derounding of the umlauted vowels [y] and [ø] yielding [ī] and [ē] respectively by Middle English, and the Great Vowel Shift as described in section 2.4.)

Table 8.9 Umlaut in English

Pre-OE 1		Pre-OE 2		Early OE		Subsequent changes	
[gōs]	>	[gōs]	>	[gōs]	>	[gu:s]	'goose'
[gōsi]	>	[gøsi]	>	[gøs]	>	[gi:s]	'geese'
[mūs]	>	[mūs]	>	[mūs]	>	[maʊs]	'mouse'
[mūsi]	>	[mȳsi]	>	[mȳs]	>	[maɪs]	'mice'

Dissimilation

Dissimilation, the process whereby one segment is made less like another segment in its environment, is much less frequent than assimilation. This type of change typically occurs when it would be difficult to articulate or perceive two similar sounds in close proximity. The word *anma* 'soul' in Late Latin, for example, was modified to *alma* in Spanish, thereby avoiding two consecutive nasal consonants. Like assimilation, dissimilation can also operate at a distance to affect non-adjacent segments. For instance, the Latin word *arbor* 'tree' became *arbol* in Spanish and *alboro* in Italian, thereby avoiding two instances of [r] in neighbouring syllables. (By contrast, dissimilation did not occur in French where *arbre* has retained both instances of [r].)

Epenthesis

Another common sound change, **epenthesis**, involves the insertion of a consonant or vowel into a particular environment (Table 8.10). In some cases, epenthesis results from the anticipation of an upcoming sound.

Table 8.10 Epenthesis in Old English

Earlier form	Change		Later form		
ganra	VnrV	>	VndrV	gandra	'gander'
simle	VmlV	>	VmblV	simble	'always'
æmtig	Vmtv	>	VmptV	æmptig	'empty'

In these examples, the epenthetic [b], [d], or [p] has the place of articulation of the preceding nasal but agrees with the following segment in terms of voice and nasality. The epenthetic segment therefore serves as a bridge for the transition between the segments on either side (Table 8.11).

Table 8.11 The nature of epenthesis

[m]	[b]	[r]	[m]	[p]	[t]
labial	labial	non-labial	labial	labial	non-labial
nasal	non-nasal	non-nasal	nasal	non-nasal	non-nasal
voiced	voiced	voiced	voiced	voiceless	voiceless

In other cases, vowel epenthesis serves to break up a sequence of sounds which would otherwise be difficult to pronounce or even inconsistent with the phonotactic patterns of the language (Table 8.12). As mentioned, some English speakers avoid [θl] clusters by inserting an epenthetic [ə] in their pronunciation of words such as *athlete* as *ath*[ə]*lete*. In the history of Spanish, word-initial [sk] clusters were avoided by inserting a vowel.

Table 8.12   Examples of epenthesis

Latin	schola	[sk]	Spanish	escuela	[esk]	'school'
Latin	scribere	[sk]	Spanish	escribir	[esk]	'write'

Metathesis

Metathesis involves a change in the relative positioning of segments. This change, like assimilation and dissimilation, is shown in Table 8.13 and can affect adjacent segments or segments at a distance.

Table 8.13   Metathesis of adjacent segments in Old English

Earlier form	*Later form*	
wæps	wæsp	'wasp'
þridda	þirdda	'third'

As shown in Figure 8.1, metathesis at a distance is found in the change from Latin *mīrāculum* 'miracle' to Spanish *milagro*, in which [r] and [l] have changed places although they were not adjacent.

Figure 8.1   Metathesis of non-adjacent segments in Spanish.

Weakening and deletion

Both vowels and consonants are also susceptible to outright **deletion** as well as to various **weakening** processes. We will first treat the effects of these processes on vowels and then turn to their effects on consonants.

Vowel deletion (Table 8.14) may involve a word-final vowel (**apocope**) or a word-internal vowel (**syncope**). A vowel in an unstressed syllable is particularly susceptible to deletion, especially when a nearby neighbouring syllable is stressed.

The effects of syncope are also apparent in the loss of the medial vowel in Modern English words such as *vegetable*, *interest*, and *family*, which are frequently pronounced as [védʒtəbl̩], [íntrest], and [fæmlɪ].

Vowel deletion is commonly preceded by **vowel reduction** (Figure 8.2) in which a full vowel is reduced to a short central vowel [ə]. Vowel reduction typically affects short vowels in unstressed syllables and may affect all or only a subset of the full vowels.

Table 8.14   Vowel deletion in French

Apocope: Latin	French	
cū́r*a*	cure [kyʁ]	'cure'
ōrnā́r*e*	orner	'decorate'

Syncope: Latin	French	
pér*d*e*re*	perdre	'lose'
ví*ve*re	vivre	'live'

Figure 8.2   Vowel reduction.

Vowel reduction with subsequent deletion (syncope and apocope) occurred in Middle English and Early Modern English, as shown in Table 8.15.

Table 8.15   Vowel reduction and deletion in English

Old English		Middle English (vowel reduction)		Early Modern English (vowel deletion)	
Syncope					
stan*as*	[a]	ston*es*	[ə]	ston*es*	Ø
stan*es*	[e]	ston*es*	[ə]	stone's	Ø

Old English		Middle English (vowel reduction)		Early Modern English (vowel deletion)	
Apocope					
nam*a*	[a]	nam*e*	[ə]	nam*e*	Ø
tal*u*	[u]	tal*e*	[ə]	tal*e*	Ø

Consonant deletion is also a very common sound change. For example, the word-initial cluster [kn] was found in Old and Middle English, as the spelling of such words as *knight, knit, knot,* and *knee* implies, but the [k] was subsequently lost giving us our modern pronunciation. The loss of word-final consonants has played a major role in the evolution of Modern French. The final letters in the written forms of the words listed in Table 8.16 reflect consonants which were actually pronounced at an earlier stage of the language.

Table 8.16 Consonant loss in French

French spelling (masculine form)	Current pronunciation	
gros	[gro]	'large'
chaud	[ʃo]	'warm'
vert	[vɛʁ]	'green'

Just as vowel reduction can be identified as a weakening process since it represents an intermediate step on the pathway from a full vowel to deletion of the vowel, so too can pathways of **consonant weakening** be identified. The scale of **consonantal strength** shown in Figure 8.3 can be helpful in identifying cases of weakening.

Consonantal strength

stronger ↑ voiceless stops
voiceless fricatives, voiced stops
voiced fricatives
nasals
liquids
weaker ↓ glides

(*Note*: Geminate consonants are stronger than their non-geminate counterparts.)

Figure 8.3 Scale of consonantal strength.

Accordingly, geminates weaken to non-geminates (**degemination**), stops weaken to fricatives (**frication**), and voiceless stops or voiceless fricatives weaken to voiced stops or voiced fricatives respectively (**voicing**).[3] Weakening can ultimately result in the deletion of the consonant. Figure 8.4 is a typical pathway of weakening.

Figure 8.4 Typical pathway of consonant weakening.

Consonants are particularly subject to weakening in an intervocalic environment. Parts of the pathway of consonantal weakening are exemplified with developments from the Romance languages shown in Table 8.17.

Rhotacism is a relatively common type of weakening that typically involves the change of [z] to [r]. Often rhotacism is preceded by a stage involving the voicing of [s] to [z]. Within the Germanic family of languages

Table 8.17   Consonantal weakening in Romance

Degemination (tt > t)	Latin	mit̲tere	Spanish	met̲er	'to put'
Voicing (t > d)	Latin	māt̲ūrus	Old Spanish	mad̲uro	'ripe'
Frication (d > ð)	Old Spanish	mad̲uro	Spanish	mad̲uro [ð]	'ripe'
Deletion (ð > Ø)	Old French	[mað̲yr]	French	mûr	'ripe'

for instance, [s] first became [z] in a particular intervocalic environment. This [z] remained in Gothic, an early Germanic language, but became [r] in other Germanic languages such as English, German, and Swedish. The effects of the latter part of this change can be seen in the standard spellings of the words presented in Table 8.18.

Table 8.18   Rhotacism in English, German, and Swedish

Gothic	English	German	Swedish
maiza	more	mehr	mera
diuzam	deer	Tier	djur
huzd	hoard	Hort	—

In Modern English, rhotacism is the source of the alternation between [z] and [r] in *was* and *were*. The [r] resulted from earlier [z] which was originally intervocalic.

Consonantal strengthening

Just as consonants weaken, they can also strengthen. **Glide strengthening** (the strengthening of a glide to an affricate) is particularly common, especially in word-initial position. In the Italian examples given in Table 8.19, the glide [j] (spelt *i*) has been strengthened to [d³].

Table 8.19   Glide strengthening in Italian

Latin	iūdicium	[j]	Italian	giudizio	[d³]	'justice'
Latin	iuvenis	[j]	Italian	giovane	[d³]	'young'

2.2

Segmental change

Segments such as affricates are considered phonologically complex because they represent the fusing of a stop plus a fricative into a single segment, for example, [d³] or [tˢ]. Such complex segments are commonly subject to simplification. A very common type of segmental simplification is **de-affrication** (Table 8.20, overleaf), which has the effect of turning affricates into fricatives by eliminating the stop portion of the affricate.

Since deaffrication of [tʃ] (as well as [d³]) has not occurred in English, early borrowings from French (Table 8.21) maintain the affricate, while later borrowings have a fricative.

Table 8.20   Deaffrication in French

| Old French | cent | [tˢ] | French | cent | [s] | 'one hundred' |
| Old French | gent | [dȝ] | French | ggent | [ȝ] | 'people, tribe' |

Table 8.21   Borrowings from French

Early borrowings (before deaffrication occurred in French)

Old French [tˢ]	*English* [tˢ]
chaiere	chair
chaine	chain
(Compare *Modern French* [ʃ] in chaire 'throne, seat' and chaîne 'chain'.)	

Later borrowings (after deaffrication occurred in French

Modern French [ʃ]	*English* [ʃ]
chandelier	chandelier
chauffeur	chauffeur

2.3

Auditory-based change

Although articulatory factors (particularly relating to 'ease of articulation') are of central importance in sound change as indicated in the preceding discussion, auditory factors also play a role. **Substitution** is a type of auditorily-based change involving the replacement of one segment with another similar sounding segment (Table 8.22). A common type of substitution involves [f] replacing either [x] or [θ]. Earlier in the history of English, [f] replaced [x] in some words; today [f] replaces [θ] in the speech of some Londoners who speak the Cockney dialect.

Table 8.22   Auditorily-based substitution

| [x] > [f] | Middle English | laugh | [x] | English | laugh [f] |
| [θ] > [f] | English | thin | [θ] | Cockney | [fɪn] |

So far we have treated sound changes without consideration of their effect on the sound pattern of the particular language as a whole. But, in reality, since languages are integrated systems, a phonetic or phonological change in one part of the system may have implications for the rest of the sound system. Thus, all of the foregoing sound changes can lead both to new types of allophonic variation, and to the addition or loss of phonemic contrasts. Examples of such cases are presented in the next section.

2.4

Phonetic versus phonological change

The sound changes outlined in the previous sections can affect the overall sound pattern (phonology) of a language in different ways. Commonly, the first stage of a sound change results in the creation of a new allophone of an already existing phoneme. The term **phonetic sound change** can be used to refer to this stage.

A good example of phonetic sound change involves the laxing of short high vowels that has developed in Canadian French (Table 8.23). This change can be seen in closed word-final syllables, among other environments.

Table 8.23   Vowel laxing in Canadian French

European French	Canadian French	
Closed syllable		
[vit]	[vɪt]	'quick'
[libʁ]	[lɪbʁ]	'free'
[ekut]	[ekʊt]	'listen'
[pus]	[pʊs]	'thumb'
Open syllable		
[vi]	[vi]	'life'
[li]	[li]	'bed'
[vu]	[vu]	'you'
[lu]	[lu]	'wolf'

Whereas Canadian French has the lax vowels [ɪ] and [ʊ] in closed final syllables, European French has kept the tense vowels [i] and [u]. Both dialects retain [i] and [u] in open syllables. This suggests that Canadian French has developed the following rule.

$$\begin{bmatrix} V \\ +high \\ -long \end{bmatrix} \longrightarrow [-tense] \ / \ \_\_\_ \ C \ (C)\#$$

Figure 8.5   Vowel laxing rule in Canadian French.

While this rule did introduce an allophone not present in European French, it did not create any new phonemes since there is no contrast between lax vowels and their tense counterparts in Canadian French.

Splits

Sometimes sound change can lead to changes in a language's phonological system by adding, eliminating, or rearranging phonemes. Such **phonological change** can involve **splits**, **mergers**, or **shifts**.

In a phonological split, allophones of the same phoneme come to contrast with each other due to the loss of the conditioning environment, with the result that one or more new phonemes are created. The English phoneme /ŋ/ was the result of a phonological split. Originally, [ŋ] was simply the allophone of /n/ that appeared before a velar consonant. During Middle English, consonant deletion resulted in the loss of [g] in word-final position after a nasal consonant, leaving [ŋ] as the final sound in words such as *sing* (Table 8.24). (Note that this change did not take place in the area of the midlands and the north of England stretching from Coventry and Birmingham in the south to Liverpool and Manchester in the north. There, even today postnasal [g] in word-final position is still pronounced by many speakers in words like *sing* [sɪŋg], *bring* [brɪŋg], *wing* [wɪŋg] etc.)

Table 8.24   Phonological split resulting in /ŋ/

Original phonemic form	/sɪng/
Original phonetic form	[sɪng]
Deletion of [g]	[sɪng] > [sɪn]
New phonemic form	/sɪŋ/

The loss of the final [g] in words created minimal pairs such as *sin* (/sɪn/) and *sing* (/sɪŋ/), in which there is a contrast between /n/ and /ŋ/. Figure 8.6 represents a typical phonological split. When the conditioning environment of an allophonic variant of a phoneme is lost through sound change, the allophone is no longer predictable and thus itself becomes phonemic. The original phoneme (in our example /n/) splits into two phonemes (/n/ and /ŋ/).

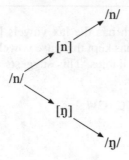

Figure 8.6   A phonological split.

Mergers

In a phonological merger (Figure 8.7), two or more phonemes collapse into a single one, thereby reducing the number of phonemes in the language. The case of auditorily-based substitution discussed above has this effect in Cockney English, where all instances of the interdental fricative /θ/ have become /f/. Consequently, the phonemes /θ/ and /f/ have merged into one (/f/) and words such as *thin* and *fin* have the same phonological form (/fɪn/). Similarly, /v/ and /ð/ have merged (for example, /smuːv/ for *smooth*).

Figure 8.7   A phonological merger.

Shifts

A phonological shift is a change in which a series of phonemes is systematically modified so that their organization with respect to each other is altered. A well-known example of such a change is called the Great English Vowel Shift (Table 8.25). Beginning in the Middle English period and continuing into the eighteenth century, the language underwent a series of modifications to the long vowels.

Table 8.25 The Great English Vowel Shift

Middle English	Great Vowel Shift (and later diphthongization)	Modern English	
[ti:d]	[i:] > [aɪ]	[taɪd]	'tide'
[lu:d]	[u:] > [aʊ]	[laʊd]	'loud'
[ge:s]	[e:] > [i:]	[gi:s]	'geese'
[sɛ:]	[ɛ:] > [i:]	[si:]	'sea'
[go:s]	[o:] > [u:]	[gu:s]	'goose'
[brɔ:kən]	[ɔ:] > [o:] > [ow]	[broʊkən] > [brəʊkən]	'broken'
[na:mə]	[a:] > [e:] > [eɪ]	[neɪm]	'name'

Figure 8.8 illustrates the effect of these changes on English long vowels.

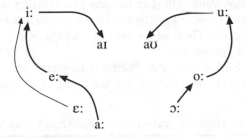

Figure 8.8 Changes brought about by the Great English Vowel Shift.

2.5

Explaining phonological shift

The causes and even the details of the Great English Vowel Shift still remain unclear. In fact, the causes of phonological shift in general are not well understood. A possible motivation in some cases appears to involve the notion of phonological space within phonemic systems. As in the case of 'ease of articulation', phonological space is difficult to define precisely. For our purposes, and focusing on vowels only, we can consider the vowel 'trapezium' (a schematicization of the oral cavity) as the phonological space that vowels must occupy. Although the vowel systems of languages can be arranged in various ways (see Chapter 9), there is a tendency for languages *a* Typical distribution of vowels in phonological space

b Atypical distribution of vowels in phonological space

Figure 8.9 Vowel distribution.

to maximize the use of space in the trapezium. Accordingly, if a language has only three vowel phonemes, they will likely be /i/, /a/, and /o/ or /u/, not (for example) /i/, /e/, /ɛ/. Similarly, if a language has five vowels, they will be distributed throughout the phonological space, typically as /i/, /e/, /a/, /o/, /u/ rather than /u/, /ʊ/, /a/, /o/, and /ɔ/, for example.

Languages with seven (or more) vowels (the case in English at the starting point of the Great English Vowel Shift in Figure 8.8) often undergo **diphthongization**. This can be seen as a reaction to the overcrowding of the phonological space. Its effect is to reduce the seven-vowel system to a five-vowel system. (Think of the two diphthongs as not infringing on the space of the simple vowels.)

Table 8.26 shows that overcrowding appears to have resulted in diphthongization in many languages, including Old High German and Spanish.

Table 8.26 Diphthongization in Old High German and Spanish

Old High German dipthongization	*Spanish diphthongization*

i: u: i   u
    ia   ua   e   ie   we   o
e: ↗   ↖ o: ɛ ↗   ↖ ɔ
ɛ: ɔ: a
          a:

Old High German			*Latin*	*Spanish*	
Earlier	*Later*				
hēr	hiar	'here'	petra	piedra	'stone'
flōt	fluat	'flood'	mortem	muerte	'death'

The diphthongization in these two languages differs from that of the Great English Vowel Shift in two ways. The mid vowels and not the high vowels are affected, and different sets of diphthongs result. Nevertheless, in terms of phonological space all these cases of diphthongization achieve the same result: namely, the reduction of an overcrowded seven-vowel system to a five-vowel system. (Of course, the Great English Vowel Shift is further complicated by other developments.)

2.6

Sound change and rule ordering (advanced)

In describing language change, it is often crucial to identify the relative chronology, or times at which different changes have occurred. Three important changes in the history of English can be given as the (somewhat simplified) rules presented in Figure 8.10.

1) Voicing
   $$C \longrightarrow [+\text{voice}] \, / \, [+\text{voice}] \, \underline{\quad} \, [+\text{voice}]$$

2) Syncope
   $$V \longrightarrow \emptyset \, / \, \underline{\quad} \, C \, \#$$
   $$[-\text{stress}]$$

3) Assimilation
   $$C \longrightarrow [+\text{voice}] \, / \quad C \quad \underline{\quad}$$
   $$[+\text{voice}]$$

Figure 8.10 Three rules in the history of English.

These changes have played an important role in the evolution of English plural forms such as *hooves* (versus *hoof*) and *wolves* (versus *wolf*). Of the possible orderings of these three rules, only one will derive the contemporary pronunciation from the earlier (Old English) phonemic form. Two of the possible orderings are shown in Table 8.27.

Table 8.27 Rule ordering in the history of English

Hypothesis A	
Original phonemic form	wulfas
Voicing	wulvas
Syncope	wulvs
Assimilation	wulvz
Hypothesis B	
Original phonemic form	wulfas
Voicing	wulvas
Assimilation	(cannot apply)
Syncope	wulvs (incorrect)

If we assume hypothesis A with the ordering voicing, syncope, and assimilation, we can account for the [vz] in the modern pronunciation of a word such as *wolves*. By contrast, the ordering proposed in hypothesis B would not account for the present pronunciation.

3

MORPHOLOGICAL CHANGE

3.1

In this section we discuss morphological changes resulting from analogy and reanalysis as well as changes involving the addition or loss of affixes.

Addition of affixes

Borrowing has been a very important source of new affixes in English. For instance, during the Middle English period, many French words containing the suffix *-ment* (as in *accomplishment*, *commencement*) made their way into the language. Eventually, *-ment* established itself as a productive suffix in English and was used with bases that were not of French origin (for example, *acknowledgement*, *merriment*). The ending *-able*, which converts a verb into an adjective (for example, *readable*, *lovable*, etc.), followed a similar pattern. Although words with this ending (for example, *favourable*, *conceivable*) were initially borrowed into English as whole units, eventually the suffix became productive and was used with new bases.

Not all new affixes are the result of borrowing. Lexical forms can become grammatical forms over time through a process called **grammaticalization** or **grammaticization** (see section 2.4 of Chapter 7). In the case where two words are frequently adjacent, over time they can become fused together to form a single unit consisting of a base and an affix. **Fusion** (Table 8.28) refers to this specific type of grammaticalization where words develop into affixes (either prefixes or suffixes).

Table 8.28 Fusion

word word	>	base + affix (suffixation)
word word	>	affix + base (prefixation)

Table 8.29 shows that a number of Modern English suffixes are derived from earlier words by means of fusion.

Table 8.29 English suffixes resulting from fusion

Suffix		Old English word
-hood (childhood)	hād	'state, condition, rank'
-dom (freedom)	dōm	'condition, power'
-ly (fatherly)	(ge-)līc	'similar, equal, like'

Another case of fusion is the development of the future tense affixes in Italian which are derived from various forms of the Latin word *habere* 'to have' (Table 8.30).

Table 8.30 Fusion resulting in a future tense affix in Italian

Latin	Italian	
amāre + habēo	amerò	'I will love'
amāre + habēmus	ameremo	'we will love'

3.2

Loss of affixes

Just as affixes can be added to the grammar, they can also be lost. Sometimes affixes simply fall into disuse for no apparent reason. For example, a number of Old English derivational affixes, including -*bǽre* and -*bora*, are no longer used.

Table 8.31 Affixes no longer found in English

N + bǽre	→	A	lustbǽre	'pleasant, agreeable' from *lust* 'pleasure'
N + bora	→	N	*mundbora*	'protector' from *mund* 'protection'

It is also very common for affixes to be lost through sound change. For example, Old English had a complex system of affixes marking case and gender. Nouns were divided into three gender classes – masculine, neuter, and feminine. Assignment to a class was not based on sex (natural gender) but on grammatical gender; for example, the word for *stone* (Old English *stān*) and even a word for *woman* (*wīfmann*) were masculine, the word for *sun* (*sunne*) was feminine, and another word for *woman* (*wīf*) was neuter. Each gender class was associated with a different set of case endings (see Table 8.32).

Table 8.32 Old English case affixes

	Masculine		Neuter		Feminine	
Singular						
	hund	'dog'	dēor	'animal'	gief	'gift'
Nominative	hund		dēor		gief-u	
Accusative	hund		dēor		gief-e	
Genitive	hund-es		dēor-es		gief-e	
Dative	hund-e		dēor-e		gief-e	
Plural						
	hund	'dog'	dēor	'animal'	gief	'gift'
Nominative	hund-as		dēor		gief-a	
Accusative	hund-as		dēor		gief-a	
Genitive	hund-a		dēor-a		gief-a	
Dative	hund-um		dēor-um		gief-um	

The following Old English sentence contains all four case categories.

2)

Se cniht	geaf	gief-e	þæs hierd-es	sun-e
the youth-Nom	gave	gift-Acc	the shepherd-Gen	son-Dat

'The youth gave a gift to the shepherd's son.'

By the fifteenth century, English case endings had changed radically. Consonant deletion resulted in the loss of the earlier [m] of the dative plural suffix and through vowel reduction all the unstressed vowels of the case endings were reduced to the central vowel [ə] (which was later lost through vowel deletion). Consequently, many of the earlier case and gender distinctions were obliterated. (The examples in Table 8.33 also include changes to the base-internal vowels as the result of various processes, including the Great English Vowel Shift.)

Table 8.33   The loss of case affixes through sound change (in English *hound*)

Singular			
Nominative	hund	hund	hound
Accusative	hund	hund	hound
Genitive	hund-es	hund-(e)s	hound's
Dative	hund-e	hund-(e)	hound
Plural			
Nominative	hund-as	hund-(e)s	hounds
Accusative	hund-as	hund-(e)s	hounds
Genitive	hund-a	hund-(e)	hounds'
Dative	hund-um	hund-(e)	hounds

Whereas Old English had five distinct affixes for cases, Middle English had only two suffixes, *-e* and *-es* which, with the loss of schwa, were ultimately reduced to a single suffix *-s*, still used in Modern English for the plural and the possessive. This represents a typical example of how sound change can result in modification to the morphological component of the grammar.

3.3

From synthetic to analytic to synthetic

Since languages vary greatly in the complexity of their morphology, linguists often make a distinction between analytic and synthetic languages (see Chapter 9). Whereas analytic languages have very few affixes (for example, Modern English), synthetic languages have many (for example, Latin, Old English).

Even in the absence of borrowing, sound change and fusion ensure that there is a constant flux in the morphology of a language over time. As we have seen, due to the loss of case endings through sound change English has developed from a synthetic language with many inflectional affixes to an analytic one with very few, as the above discussion of nouns such as *hound* indicates.

By contrast, fusion ensures the rise of new synthetic forms. Fusion can be observed in some Modern English dialects in forms such as *coulda* (for example, *I coulda won*) which represents the fusion of *could* and *have*. For many speakers, the -*a* is treated as a suffix that is no longer related to *have*, as evident in spellings such as *could of* which result from confusion over how to represent the pronunciation of *coulda* in written English. Through fusion, a language with an analytic morphology can become much more synthetic over time.

3.4

Analogy

The drastic effects that sound change can have on the morphology of a language are often alleviated through analogy. For example, the plural of Old English *hand* 'hand' was *handa* (Table 8.34). Vowel reduction and apocope applying to *handa* would have yielded a Modern English plural form identical to the singular form, namely *hand*.

Table 8.34 Sound changes applied to Old English *handa* 'hands'

handa	
handə	vowel reduction
hand	apocope

Obviously, then, the Modern English plural *hands* cannot be the direct consequence of sound change. Rather, it is the result of earlier analogy with words such as Middle English *hund* 'hound' (see Table 8.33) which did form the plural with the suffix -*s*. This suffix, whose earlier form -*as* was predominant even in Old English, was extended by analogy to all English nouns with a few exceptions (*oxen, men, geese*, etc.). Other plural forms besides *hands* that were created on the basis of analogy include *eyes* (*eyen* in Middle English) and *shoes* (formerly *shooen*).

Continuing analogy along these lines is responsible for the development of the plural form *youse* (from *you*) in some English dialects. Each generation of English-speaking children temporarily extends the analogy still further by producing forms such as *sheeps, gooses*, and *mouses*. To date, however, these particular innovations have not been accepted by adult speakers of Standard English and are eventually abandoned by young language learners.

3.5

Reanalysis

As mentioned in section 1.2, reanalysis can result in a new morphological structure for a word. It can affect both borrowed words and, particularly in cases where the morphological structure of the word is no longer transparent, native words. Reanalysis can result in new productive patterns, as in the case of (-)*burger*, (see page 316 above) or it can remain quite isolated affecting perhaps only one word. Since the type of reanalysis exemplified by *hamburger* is not based on a correct analysis of a word (at least from a historical perspective) and does not usually involve a conscious or detailed study of the word on the part of the speaker, it is often called **folk etymology**.

Although in the case of *hamburger*, the only evidence of folk etymology is the productive uses of (-)*burger* (for example, as an independent word and in compounds of the type *fishburger*), folk etymology commonly involves changes in pronunciation reflecting the new morphological analysis. For example, our word *earwig* derives from Old English *ēarwicga* [ǣərwidʒa], a compound consisting of 'ear' and 'insect'. Taking into consideration sound change alone, the expected Modern English pronunciation of this word would be *earwidge* [ɜːwɪdʒ]. However, the second part of the compound was lost as an independent word by Middle English, so speakers could no longer associate it with the meaning of 'insect'. Subsequently, reanalysis related the second part of the compound to the verb 'wiggle' resulting in Middle English *arwygyll* (literally 'ear + wiggle'). The end result is Modern English *-wig* and not *-widge*. Another example of folk etymology is *belfry*, meaning 'bell tower' which comes from Middle English *berfry* 'defensive tower'. *Berfry* originally had nothing to do with bells. It was borrowed from Old French *berfrei* 'movable siege tower'. The reanalysis resulting in the meaning of 'bell tower' came later, partly as a result of dissimilation which turned *ber* into *bel*, yielding *bel̲f̲r̲y̲* from *berf̲r̲y̲*. This no doubt encouraged the semantic association of *bel* with 'bell'. More examples of folk etymology are found in Table 8.35.

Table 8.35 Folk etymology in English (native words and borrowings)

bridegroom	Middle English *bridegroom* (unrelated to *groom*) (compare Old English *brȳd'* 'bride' and *guma* 'man')
muskrat	Algonquian *musquash* (unrelated to either *musk* or *rat*)
woodchuck	Algonquian *otchek* (unrelated to either *wood* or *chuck*)

Although reanalysis of individual words is common, affixes can also be affected, sometimes with new productive morphological rules developing as a result. This is the case of the Modern English adverbial suffix *-ly* (developing from Old English *-lic(e)*). In Old English, adjectives could be derived from nouns by adding the suffix *-lic*. Adverbs, in turn, could be derived by adding the suffix *-e* to adjectives (including those derived with *-lic*), as can be seen in Table 8.36.

Table 8.36 The derivation of Old English adjectives and adverbs

Formation of an adjective from a noun
[dæg]$_N$ + lic   →   [dæglic]$_A$ *'daily' (as in 'daily schedule')*

Formation of an adverb from an adjective
[dēop]$_A$ + e   →   [dēope]$_A$ *'deeply'*

Formation of an adverb from a derived adjective with -lic
[dæg+lic]$_A$ + e   →   [dæglice]$_{Adv}$ *'daily' (as in 'she ran daily')*

At some point, the entire complex suffix *-lic+e* was reanalysed as an adverbial suffix (rather than as an adjectival suffix *-lic* plus an adverbial suffix *-e*). It was then used by analogy to derive adverbs from adjectives in forms where it was not used before, resulting in Modern English *deeply* and other such words.

4

SYNTACTIC CHANGE

Like other components of the grammar, syntax is also subject to change over time. Syntactic changes can involve modifications to phrase structure rules or transformations, as the following examples illustrate.

4.1

Word order

All languages make a distinction between the subject and direct object. This contrast is typically represented through case marking or word order. Since Old English had an extensive system of case marking, it is not surprising that its word order was somewhat more variable than that of Modern English. The most common word order in unembedded clauses was subject–verb–object (SVO).

3)

S	V	O
Hē	geseah	þone mann.

'He saw the man.'

However, when the clause began with an element such as þa 'then' or ne 'not', the verb occurred in second position and preceded the subject.

4)

	V	S	O
þa	sende	sē cyning	þone disc
then	sent	the king	the dish

'Then the king sent the dish.'

Although this word order is still found in Modern English, its use is very limited and subject to special restrictions, unlike the situation in Old English.

5)

	V	S		O
Rarely	has	he	ever deceived	me.

When the direct object was a pronoun, the subject–object–verb order was typical.

6)

S	O	V
Hēo	hine	lærde.
She	him	advised

'She advised him.'

The subject-object-verb order also prevailed in embedded clauses, even when the direct object was not a pronoun.

7)

	S	O	V	
þa	hē	þone cyning	sōhte,	hē bēotode.
when	he	the king	visited,	he boasted

'When he visited the king, he boasted.'

Since case markings were lost during the Middle English period through sound change, fixed subject–verb–object order became the means of marking grammatical relations. As Table 8.37 shows, a major change in word order took place between 1300 and 1400, with the verb–object order becoming dominant.

Table 8.37   Word order patterns in Middle English

	Year (AD)				
	1000	*1200*	*1300*	*1400*	*1500*
Direct object before the verb (%)	53	53	40	14	2
Direct object after the verb (%)	47	47	60	86	98

From SOV to SVO

Just as languages can be classified in terms of their morphology, they can also be grouped on the basis of the relative order of subject (S), object (O), and verb (V) in basic sentences. Almost all languages of the world fall into one of three types: SOV, SVO, or VSO, with the majority being one of the first two types. Just as languages change through time from one morphological type to another, they can also change from one syntactic type to another. A case in point is found in the history of English, which shows the development from SOV to SVO syntax.

Evidence indicates that the earliest form of Germanic (from which English descended), was an SOV language. One of the earliest recorded Germanic sentences, for example, has this word order. The sentence in 8) was inscribed on a golden horn (now called the Golden Horn of Gallehus) about sixteen hundred years ago.

8)

Horn of Gallehus
S			O	V
ek	HlewagastiR	HoltijaR	horna	tawido
I	Hlewagastir	of Holt	horn	made

'I, Hlewagastir of Holt, made the horn.'

Another type of evidence for an earlier SOV order is found in compounding. Since compounding depends on frequently occurring syntactic patterns, it can sometimes serve as an indicator of earlier syntax. The OV compound, very common in Old English (as well as in Modern English), very probably reflects an earlier stage of OV word order.

Table 8.38   Old English compounds with OV structure

manslæht	'man' + 'strike'	'manslaughter, murder'
æppelbǣre	'apple' + 'bear'	'apple-bearing'

If the earliest Germanic was SOV and Modern English is firmly SVO, then Old English represents a transitional syntactic type. In developing from SOV to SVO syntax, languages seem to follow similar pathways. For example, Modern German, which developed from the same Germanic SOV source as English, shares two of Old English's distinguishing characteristics. First, the verb is typically placed in the second position of the sentence in main clauses, preceded by the subject or some other element (such as an adverb). Second, the SOV order is employed for embedded clauses.

9)

Modern German word order

a. Verb in second position in unembedded clauses:
(Compare the Old English sentence in 4).)

	V	S	O
Gestern	hatte	ich	keine Zeit.
yesterday	had	I	no time

'I had no time yesterday'

b. SOV in embedded clauses:
(Compare the Old English sentence in 7).)

S	O	V
Als er	den Mann	sah ...
when he	the man	saw

'When he saw the man ...'

The change from SOV to SVO is not restricted to English and other Germanic languages. The same change is evident, for example, in completely unrelated languages such as those of the Bantu family of Africa. Since linguists are still not sure why languages change from one syntactic type to another, the causes of such change will undoubtedly remain an important area of investigation, especially since the relative order of verb and object (OV versus VO) has been closely linked with other word order patterns (see Chapter 9).

4.2

Inversion in the history of English

In Old and Middle English the Inversion transformation (see Chapter 5) involved in the formation of *yes–no* questions could apply to all verbs, not just auxiliaries, yielding forms like those in 10) from Shakespeare that would be unacceptable in Modern English.

10)

a. And what make you from Wittenberg, Horatio? (*Hamlet*, Act 1: i)

b. Spake you with him? (*Lear*, Act 1: ii)

During the sixteenth and seventeenth centuries, the Inversion rule was changed to apply solely to auxiliary verbs.

11)

Inversion (old form):
The (first) V moves to the left of the subject.
They speak → Speak they?
They can speak →Can they speak?

Inversion (new form):
The Aux moves to the left of subject.
They speak → *Speak they?
They can speak → Can they speak?

With this change, structures such as *Speak they the truth?* were no longer possible. The corresponding question came to be formed with the auxiliary *do* as in *Do they speak the truth?*[4]

5

LEXICAL AND SEMANTIC CHANGE

Another obvious type of language change involves modifications to the lexicon. Since we have already dealt with some changes relating to derivational and inflectional morphology in section 3, the main focus here will be on lexical change involving entire words. Simply stated, there are two possible types of lexical change: addition and loss. The addition or loss of words often reflects cultural and technological changes that introduce novel objects and notions and eliminate outmoded ones.

5.1

Addition of lexical items

Addition is frequently the result of technological innovations or contact with other cultures. Such developments result in **lexical gaps** which can be filled by adding new words to the lexicon. New words are added either through the word formation processes available to the language or through borrowing.

Word formation

The most important word formation processes are compounding and derivation, although other types, including conversion, blending, backformation, clipping, and acronyms (see Chapter 4) can play a significant role.

Compounding and derivation have always been available to English speakers for the creation of new words. In fact, much of the compounding and derivation in Old English (see Table 8.39) seems very familiar.

Just as speakers of Modern English can use compounding and derivation to create new words (for example, the N + N compound *airport*), so could Old English speakers create new words such as the poetic N + N compound *hwælweg*, literally 'whale' + 'path' to mean 'sea'.

Note, however, that even though many Old English compounding and derivational rules have been maintained in Modern English, words which were acceptable in Old English are not necessarily still in use in Modern English (Table 8.40), even though many of them are quite understandable.

However, not all word formation processes available to Modern English speakers were also found in Old English. For example, conversion (as in

Table 8.39   Compounding and derivation in Old English

Noun compounds

N + N	sunbēam	'sunbeam'
A + N	middelniht	'midnight'

Adjective compounds

N + A	blōdrēad	'bloodred'
A + A	dēadboren	'stillborn'

Derived nouns

[bæc]$_V$ + ere	→	bæcere	'baker'
[frēond]$_N$ + scipe	→	frēondscipe	'friendship'

Derived adjectives

[wundor]$_N$ + full	→	wundorfull	'wonderful'
[cild]$_N$ + isc	→	cildisc	'childish'

Table 8.40   Old English compound and derived forms no longer used

Noun compounds

N + N	bōccræft ('book' + 'craft')	'literature' (compare *witchcraft*)
A + N	dimhūs ('dim' + 'house')	'prison'

Adjective compounds

N + A	ælfscīene ('elf' + 'beautiful')	'beautiful as a fairy'
A + A	eallgōd ('all' + 'good')	'perfectly good'

Derived nouns

[sēam]$_V$ + ere	→	sēamere	'tailor' (compare *seamster, seamstress*)
[man]$_N$ + scipe	→	manscipe	'humanity' (compare *friendship*)

Derived adjectives

[word]$_N$ + full	→	wordfull	'wordy' (compare *wonderful*)
[heofon]$_N$ + isc	→	heofonisc	'heavenly' (compare *childish*)

Modern English [summer]$_N$ → [summer]$_V$) was not possible in Old English. In fact, conversion is typically not available to (synthetic) inflectional languages such as Old English since change in a word category in such languages is usually indicated morphologically and conversion, by definition, does not involve the use of affixes.

Borrowing

As discussed in section 1.2, language contact over time can result in an important source of new words, borrowing. Depending on the cultural relationship holding between languages, three types of influence of one language on the other are traditionally identified: **substratum**, **adstratum**, and **superstratum**.

Substratum influence is the effect of a politically or culturally non-dominant language on a dominant language in the area. Both Canadian and

American English and Canadian French, for instance, have borrowed vocabulary items from Amerindian languages (see examples in section 1.2). From a much earlier period in the history of English, the influence of a Celtic substratum is also evident, particularly in place names such as *Thames*, *London*, and *Dover*. Substratum influence does not usually have a major impact on the lexicon of the borrowing language. Borrowed words are usually restricted to place names and unfamiliar items or concepts. This situation reflects the fact that it is usually the speakers of the substratum language who inhabited the area first.

Superstratum influence is the effect of a politically or culturally dominant language on another language or languages in the area. For example, Swahili (spoken in East African countries which were colonized by the British) has borrowed a number of governmental terms from English, including *meya* 'mayor', *polisi* 'police', *jaji* 'judge', *inspekta* 'inspector', *afisa* 'officer, official', *korti* 'court', *koloni* 'colony' and *gavana* 'governor'. This pattern is replicated in other colonial situations around the world.

In the case of English, Norman-French had a superstratum influence. The major impact of French on the vocabulary of English is related to a historical event – the conquest of England by French-speaking Normans in 1066. As the conquerors and their descendants gradually learned English over the next decades, they retained French terms for political, judicial, and cultural notions. These words were in turn borrowed by native English speakers who, in trying to gain a place in the upper echelons of society, were eager to imitate the speech of their social superiors (Table 8.41). Not surprisingly, borrowing was especially heavy in the vocabulary areas pertaining to officialdom: government, the judiciary, and religion. Other areas of heavy borrowing include science, culture, and warfare.

Table 8.41 Some French loanwords in English

Government	tax, revenue, government, royal, state, parliament, authority, prince, duke, slave, peasant
Religion	prayer, sermon, religion, chapel, chaplain, friar
Judiciary	judge, defendant, jury, evidence, jail, verdict, crime
Science	medicine, physician
Culture	art, sculpture, fashion, satin, fur, ruby
Warfare	army, navy, battle, soldier, enemy, captain

In some cases, French loanwords were used in conjunction with native English words to convey distinctions of various sorts. For a minor crime, for example, the English word *theft* was employed, but for a more serious breach of the law the French word *larceny* was used. The English also kept their own words for domesticated animals, but adopted the French words for the meat from those creatures (Table 8.42).

Table 8.42   French loanwords used in conjunction with native English words

English origin	French origin
cow	beef
calf	veal
sheep	mutton
pig	pork

Adstratum influence refers to the situation where two languages are in contact and neither one is clearly politically or culturally dominant. In a city such as Montreal with its large number of bilingual speakers, Table 8.43 shows that English and French inevitably influence each other.

Table 8.43   French influence on Montreal English

Montreal English	
subvention	'subsidy'
metro	'subway'
autoroute	'highway (+ motorway)'

Earlier in the history of English, when the Scandinavians settled part of England beginning in 800 AD, there was substantial contact between the speakers of English and Scandinavian resulting in an adstratum relationship. As evident in the examples in Tables 8.43 and 8.44, adstratum contact usually results in the borrowing of everyday words. In fact, without consulting a dictionary, most English speakers could not distinguish between borrowings from Scandinavian and native English words.

Table 8.44   Some loanwords from Scandinavia

anger, cake, call, egg, fellow, gear, get, hit, husband, low, lump, raise, root, score, seat, skill, skin, take, their, they, thrust, ugly, window, wing

Borrowed words from many other languages attest to various types of cultural contact and serve often to fill the lexical gaps such contact inevitably brings (Table 8.45).

Table 8.45   Some lexical borrowings into English

Italian	motto, artichoke, balcony, casino, mafia, malaria
Spanish	comrade, tornado, cannibal, mosquito, banana, guitar, vigilante, marijuana
German	poodle, noodle, kindergarten, seminar, pretzel
Dutch	sloop, cole slaw, smuggle, gin, cookie, boom
Slavic languages	czar, tundra, polka, intelligentsia, robot
Australian languages	boomerang, dingo, koala, billabong
Indian languages	nirvana, cot, curry, paddy, tattoo, juggernaut, thug
Amerindian languages	toboggan, oppossum, parka, wigwam, chipmunk

Although borrowing has been a very rich source of new words in English, it is noteworthy that the most frequently used vocabulary items have been the least susceptible to replacement by loanwords. This reflects a general tendency for highly frequent words to be relatively resistant to loss or substitution, as shown by Table 8.46.

Table 8.46   Origin of the 5000 most frequent words in English

	(Source language %)			
Degree of frequency	English	French	Latin	Other
First 1000	83	11	2	4
Second 1000	34	46	11	9
Third 1000	29	46	14	11
Fourth 1000	27	45	17	11
Fifth 1000	27	47	17	9

5.2

Loss of lexical items

Just as words can be added to the lexicon, they can also be lost (Table 8.47). Loss of a word frequently occurs as a result of changes in society, particularly in the case where the object or notion a word refers to has become obsolete.

Table 8.47   Some Old English words lost through cultural change

dolgbōt	'compensation for wounding'
þeox	'hunting spear'
eafor	'tenant obligation to the king to convey goods'
flȳtme	'a blood letting instrument'

5.3

Semantic change

Although changes in word meaning take place continually in all languages, words rarely jump from one meaning to an unrelated one. Typically, the changes are step by step and involve one of the following phenomena.

Semantic broadening (Table 8.48) is the process in which the meaning of a word becomes more general or more inclusive than its historically earlier form.

Table 8.48   Semantic broadening

Word	Old meaning	New meaning
bird	'small fowl'	'any feathered vertebrate with a beak'
barn	'place to store barley'	'any agricultural building'
aunt	'father's sister'	'father or mother's sister'

Semantic narrowing (Table 8.49) is the process in which the meaning of a word becomes less general or less inclusive than its historically earlier meaning.

Table 8.49   Semantic narrowing

Word	Old meaning	New meaning
hound	'any dog'	'a hunting breed'
meat	'any type of food'	'flesh of an animal'
fowl	'any bird'	'a domesticated bird'
disease	'any unfavourable state'	'an illness'

In **amelioration** (Table 8.50) the meaning of a word becomes more positive or favourable.

Table 8.50   Amelioration

Word	Old meaning	New meaning
pretty	'tricky, sly, cunning'	'attractive'
knight	'boy'	'a man of honourable military rank'

The opposite change, **pejoration** (Table 8.51), also occurs.

Table 8.51   Pejoration

Word	Old meaning	New meaning
silly	'happy, prosperous'	'foolish'
wench	'girl'	'wanton woman, prostitute'

Given the propensity of human beings to exaggerate, it is not surprising that the **weakening** of meaning frequently occurs. For example, our word *soon* used to mean 'immediately' but now simply means 'in the near future'. Other examples are shown in Table 8.52.

Table 8.52   Weakening

Word	Old meaning	New meaning
wreak	'avenge, punish'	'to cause, inflict'
crucify	'kill by nailing to a cross'	'to cause pain'
quell	'kill, murder'	'to put down, pacify'

Semantic shift (Table 8.53) is a process in which a word loses some aspect of its former meaning, taking on a partially new, but related, meaning.

Table 8.53   Semantic shift

Word	Old meaning	New meaning
immoral	'not customary'	'unethical'
bead	'prayer'	'prayer bead, bead'

Sometimes a series of semantic shifts occurs over an extended period of time, resulting in a meaning which is completely unrelated to the original sense of a word. The word *hearse*, for example, originally referred to a triangular harrow. Later, it denoted a triangular frame for church candles and later still was used to refer to the device which held candles over a coffin. In a subsequent shift it came to refer to the framework on which curtains were hung over a coffin or tomb. Still later, *hearse* was used to refer to the coffin itself before finally taking on its current sense of the vehicle used to transport a coffin.

One of the most striking types of semantic change is triggered by **metaphor** (Table 8.54), a figure of speech based on a perceived similarity between distinct objects or actions. (See Chapter 7, section 2.2 for a discussion of metaphor.) Metaphorical change usually involves a word with a concrete meaning taking on a more abstract sense, although the word's original meaning is not lost. The meanings of many English words have been extended through metaphor.

Table 8.54   Some examples of metaphor in English

Word	Metaphorical meaning	Word	Metaphorical meaning
grasp	'understand'	down	'depressed'
yarn	'story'	sharp	'clever, smart'
high	'on drugs'	dull	'stupid'

6

THE SPREAD OF CHANGE

Up to this point, we have been concerned with the causes and description of linguistic change. Still to be dealt with is the question of how linguistic innovations spread. This section focuses on two types of spread, one involving the way in which an innovation is extended through the vocabulary of a language and the other the way in which it spreads through the population.

6.1

Diffusion through the language

Sometimes linguistic change first manifests itself in a few words and then gradually spreads through the vocabulary of the language. This type of change is called **lexical diffusion**. A well-attested example in English involves an ongoing change in the stress pattern of disyllabic words such as *convert*, which can be used as either a noun or a verb. Although the stress originally fell on the second syllable regardless of lexical category, in the latter half of the sixteenth century three such words, *rebel*, *outlaw*, and *record*, came to be pronounced with the stress on the first syllable when used as nouns. As the Figure 8.11 illustrates, this stress shift was extended to an increasing number of words over the next decades.

This change has still not diffused through the entire vocabulary of English. There are about a thousand nouns of the relevant sort which still place the

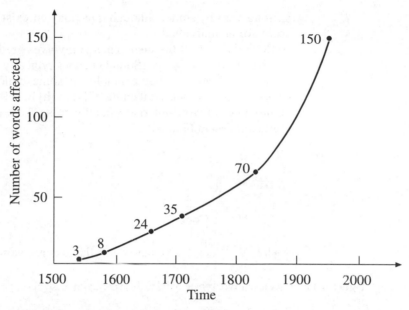

Figure 8.11 Diffusion of stress shift in English.

stress on the second syllable (for example, *report*, *mistake*, and *support*). Table 8.55 illustrates the spread of this change to date.

Table 8.55 Stress shift in English (nouns)

Before the 16th century	During the 16th century	During the 18th century	Today
rebél	rébel	rébel	rébel
affíx	affíx	áffix	áffix
recéss	recéss	recéss	récess
mistáke	mistáke	mistáke	mistáke

This ongoing change can be observed in progress today. The noun *dispute*, for example, is pronounced by many people with stress on the first syllable as [díspju:t], although the older pronunciation [dɪspjú:t] is still heard. Some speakers alternate between the two. This change may continue to work its way through the language until all nouns in the class we have been considering are stressed on the first syllable.

The changes discussed in the section on analogy also spread word by word. For example, the transition of strong (irregular) verbs (the *sing/sang/sung* type) to the weak verb class (regular verbs with past tense *-ed*) is an ongoing change. Both strong and weak past tense forms of original strong verbs such as *shine* and *dive* are heard in current English. In many dialects, the past tense of *shine* may be *shined* or *shone*, depending on the speaker. In Britain the change of the past tense of *dive* from *dove* to *dived* is complete and only *dived* is heard in the past tense, but in North America *dive* may still be treated as a strong verb by some, although *dove* may co-exist with *dived*, – even in the speech of an individual.

However, not all linguistic change involves gradual diffusion through the vocabulary of a language. Sound changes typically affect all instances of the segment(s) involved. For example, in some dialects of Spanish (such as Cuban) the consonant weakening of [s] to [h] in syllable-final position affects all instances of word-internal *s* in all words. The relevant rule is stated in the representation in Figure 8.12.

Figure 8.12   Consonant weakening of [s] to [h] in certain Spanish dialects.

This rule has resulted in changes such as those exemplified in Table 8.56.

Table 8.56   The effects of the [s] to [h] change in some Spanish dialects

Standard pronunciation	New pronunciation	
[felismente]	[felihmente]	'happily'
[estilo]	[ehtilo]	'type'
[espaɲa]	[ehpaɲa]	'Spain'

This change is entirely regular, affecting all instances of a word-internal syllable-final [s] in the speech of individuals who adopt it.

Accordingly, two types of language change can be identified. One, exemplified by the stress shifts in bisyllabic English nouns of the type we have discussed, affects individual words one at a time and gradually spreads through the vocabulary of the language. The other, exemplified by the consonant weakening of syllable-final [s] to [h] in some dialects of Spanish, involves an across-the-board change that applies without exception to all words.

6.2

Spread through the population

For a language change to take place, the particular innovation must be accepted by a sizeable section of the linguistic community. For example, although as mentioned, children acquiring English typically form the past tense of *go* as *goed* instead of *went*, *goed* has never received widespread acceptance. Doubtless the verb form in *he throve on fame* would be equally unacceptable to most speakers today. In earlier English, however, *throve* was the past tense form of *thrive* (compare *drive/drove*). At some point in the past, then, the novel form *thrived* did receive general acceptance.

Just as change sometimes begins with a small number of words, effects of a change often appear first in the speech of a small number of people. Social pressures play an important role in determining whether a particular innovation will spread through the entire linguistic community. Since speakers can consciously or unconsciously alter the way they speak to approximate to what they perceive to be a more prestigious or socially acceptable variety of speech, once a change has taken hold in the speech of a high prestige group it may gradually spread to other speakers and ultimately affect the entire linguistic community.

There have been numerous examples of this in the history of English, notably the loss of postvocalic [r] in a syllable coda in most parts of England and along the east coast of the United States. This change, which resulted in an 'r-less' pronunciation of words such as *far* as [fɑ:], originated in the southeast of England in the seventeenth and eighteenth centuries. At that time, postvocalic [r] was still pronounced throughout English-speaking settlements in North America. Two factors accounted for its loss in parts of that continent. First, the children of the New England gentry picked up the new pronunciation in British schools and subsequently brought it back to the colony. Second, the speech of newly arrived immigrants, including colonial administrators and church officials who enjoyed high social status in the colony, typically lacked the postvocalic [r]. As a result, the innovation was widely imitated and ultimately spread along much of the east coast and into the south. Dialects where postvocalic r is retained are referred to as *rhotic*, and those where it was lost as *non rhotic*.

Social pressures were also involved in limiting the spread of this innovation. It did not penetrate Pennsylvania or the other Midland states since the most prestigious group of settlers there were Quakers from northern England, an area which at that time retained the postvocalic [r]. Similarly, in Canada, the influence of Scottish and Irish settlers, whose dialects did not undergo the change in question, helped ensure the survival of postvocalic [r] in all but a few areas where contact with New England was strongest, most notably in the Canadian regions of Lunenberg County in Nova Scotia and Grand Manan Island in New Brunswick. More recently (probably in part because of the decline of British prestige) the 'r-less' pronunciation has become stigmatized in North America, even in areas where it was previously firmly entrenched, and we now see a trend to restoration of [r] in environments where it had been deleted. However, in England no such reversal in the fortunes of 'r-less' pronunciation has occurred.

7

LANGUAGE RECONSTRUCTION

When we compare the vocabulary items of various languages, we cannot help but notice the strong resemblance certain words bear to each other. By systematically comparing languages, we can establish whether two or more languages descended from a common parent and are therefore genetically related (see Chapter 9). The **comparative method** refers to the procedure used to reconstruct earlier forms on the basis of a comparison of later forms. In this way, we can reconstruct properties of the parent language with a great degree of certainty.

7.1

Comparative reconstruction

The most reliable sign of family relationships is the existence of **systematic phonetic correspondences** in the vocabulary items of different languages. Many such correspondences can be found, and Table 8.57 shows a sample of vocabulary items from English, Dutch, German, Danish, and Swedish, all of which are members of the Germanic family of languages.

Table 8.57   Some Germanic cognates

English	Dutch	German	Danish	Swedish
man	man	Mann	mand	man
hand	hand	Hand	hånd	hand
foot	voet	Fuß (ß = [s])	fod	fot
bring	brengen	bringen	bringe	bringa
summer	zomer	Sommer	sommer	sommar

Since the relationship between the phonological form and meaning of a word is mostly arbitrary, the existence of systematic phonetic correspondences in the forms of two or more languages must point towards a common source. Conversely, where languages are not related, their vocabulary items fail to show systematic similarities. This can be seen by comparing words from Turkish (Table 8.58), which is not related to the Germanic languages, with their counterparts in the languages cited in Table 8.57.

Table 8.58   Some words in Turkish, a non-Germanic language

adam	'man'
el	'hand'
ajak	'foot'
getir	'bring'
jaz	'summer'

Words that have descended from a common source (as shown by systematic phonetic correspondences and, usually, semantic similarities) are called **cognates**. Cognates are not always as obvious as the Germanic examples in Table 8.57. Where languages from the same family are only distantly related, the systematic correspondences may be considerably less striking. This is exemplified in Table 8.59, showing data from English, Russian, and Hindi, all of which are distantly related to each other. Forms from the unrelated Turkish are included to emphasize the similarities among the first three languages.

Table 8.59   Some distinctly related cognates compared to non-related Turkish

English	Russian	Hindi	Turkish
two	dva	dō	iki
three	tri	tīn	ytʃ
brother	brat	bhāī	kardeʃ
nose	nos	nahī̃	burun

Once the existence of a relationship between two or more languages has been established, an attempt can be made to reconstruct the common source. This reconstructed language, or **proto-language**, is made up of **proto-forms**, which are written with a preceding * (for example, *hand*) to indicate their hypothetical character as reconstructions of earlier forms that have not been recorded or are not directly observable.

7.2

Techniques of reconstruction

Reconstruction can be undertaken with some confidence because (as discussed in the previous sections) the processes underlying language change are systematic. Once the processes are uncovered by linguists, they can be reversed allowing us to infer earlier forms of the language. Although it is possible to reconstruct all components of a proto-language (its phonology, morphology, syntax, lexicon, and semantics), we will focus in the following on phonological reconstruction, the area in which linguists have made the most progress.

Reconstruction strategies

Reconstruction of a proto-form makes use of two general strategies. The most important one is the **phonetic plausibility strategy**, which requires that any changes posited to account for differences between the proto-forms and later forms must be phonetically plausible. Secondarily, the **majority rules strategy** stipulates that if no phonetically plausible change can account for the observed differences, then the segment found in the majority of cognates should be assumed. It is important to note that the first strategy always takes precedence over the second; the second strategy is a last resort.

Consider the following cognates (somewhat simplified) from members of the Romance family.

Table 8.60   Romance cognates

French	Italian	Rumanian	Spanish	
si	si	ʃi	si	'yes'

The data exemplify a correspondence between [s] and [ʃ] before the vowel [i]. To account for this, we could assume either that Rumanian underwent a change that converted [s] to [ʃ] before [i] or that the other three languages underwent a change converting [ʃ] to [s] before [i].

Both reconstruction strategies in Figure 8.13 favour hypothesis A. Most importantly, the phonetic change needed to account for the Rumanian pronunciation involves palatalization before [i]. Since palatalization in this context is a very common phenomenon in human language, it is reasonable to assume that it occurred in Rumanian. It would be much more difficult to argue that the proto-language contained [ʃ] before [i] and that three languages underwent the change posited by Hypothesis B since depalatalization before [i] would be an unusual phonetic process. (The reconstructed *s posited in Hypothesis A is also compatible with the majority rules strategy since three of the four languages in the data have [s] before [i].)

Hypothesis A

Proto-form for:	*si
Sound change (Rumanian only):	*s > ʃ / ___ i

Hypothesis B

Proto-form:	*ʃi
Sound change (French, Italian and Spanish):	*ʃ > s / ___ i

Figure 8.13   Romance cognates.

Reconstruction and the catalogue of sound changes

Although there are factors that can confound our attempt to determine the relative plausibility of various sound changes, the changes listed in the catalogue in Table 8.3 can generally be considered highly plausible. Table 8.61 lists some plausible versus less plausible or even implausible changes based on that catalogue.

Table 8.61   Different rules in terms of their plausibility based on catalogue of sound changes

Rule	Name of sound change in catalogue
t > tˢ / __i	palatalization/affrication
n > m / __b	assimilation (place of articulation)
t > d / V__V	voicing
k > Ø / V__st	consonant deletion
Low probability	
tˢ > t / __i	(does not correspond to any listed change)
m > n / __b	(does not correspond to any listed change)
d > t / V__V	(does not correspond to any listed change)
Ø > k / V__st	(does not correspond to any listed change)

Reconstructing Proto-Romance

Consider now a slightly more complex example involving data from several languages of the Romance family.

Table 8.62 Some Romance cognates

Spanish		Sardinian	French		Portuguese	Rumanian	Original meaning
riba	[ß]	ripa	rive	[ʁiv]	riba	rîpă	'embankment'
amiga	[ɣ]	amica	amie	[ami]	amiga	—	'female friend'
copa		cuppa	coupe	[kup]	copa	cupă	'cup, goblet'
gota		gutta	goutte	[gut]	gota	gută	'drop'

(*Note:* Orthographic c represents [k] in all the above examples and Rumanian ă represents [ə]. [ß] is a bilabial voiced fricative and [ɣ] a velar voiced fricative. Some details of vowel quality have been ignored.)

Our goal here is to reconstruct the proto-forms for these words in Proto-Romance, the parent language of the Modern Romance languages, which stands very close to Latin.

Let us first consider the reconstruction of the Proto-Romance form for 'embankment' in Table 8.62. Since the first two segments are the same in all the cognate languages, we can reconstruct Proto-Romance *r and *i on the basis of the majority rules strategy. In the case of the second consonant (Table 8.63), however, there are differences between the cognates.

Table 8.63 Systematic correspondences in the second consonant of the cognates for 'embankment'

Spanish	Sardinian	French	Portuguese	Rumanian
-ß-	-p-	-v-	-b-	-p-

It is most important that we first think in terms of phonetic plausibility. In the absence of evidence to the contrary, we will assume that one of the segments found in the cognates ([p], [b], [v], or [ß]) should be reconstructed for Proto-Romance. Logically possible changes ranked with respect to their phonetic plausibility are found in Table 8.64.

Table 8.64 Changes based on phonetic plausibility

Change in V__V	Name of change based on catalogue	Phonetic plausibility
p > b	voicing	high
p > v	voicing (p > b) and frication (b > v)	high
p > ß	voicing (p > b) and frication (b > ß)	high
b > p	—	low
ß > p	—	low
v > p	—	low

In terms of plausibility, the only possible reconstruction for Proto-Romance is *p. Proto-Romance *p undergoes no change in Sardinian and

Rumanian, but in Portuguese it underwent intervocalic voicing and in Spanish it underwent both voicing and frication (that is, weakening). (We assume that voicing preceded frication since Portuguese shows voicing but no frication.) If we assume that the final vowel of the proto-form was still present in French when the consonant changes took place, we can conclude that voicing and frication occurred in this language as well – see Table 8.65. (In its written form, *rive* retains a sign of the earlier reduced vowel [ə].) These changes are phonetically plausible and thus expected.

Table 8.65 Summary of the changes affecting Proto-Romance *p

*p > p /V__V	no change in Sardinian or Rumanian
*p > b /V__V	voicing in Portuguese
*p > b > ß /V__V	voicing and frication in Spanish
*p > b > v /V__V	frication in French

Turning now to the final vowel, we note that three languages have full vowels, Rumanian has [ə], and French has no vowel. Since vowel reduction and apocope are identified as phonetically plausible changes in the catalogue, it is appropriate to posit a full vowel for the proto-language. Furthermore, since the three languages with a full vowel all have [a], we can posit this vowel on the basis of the majority rules strategy. Accordingly, the reconstructed proto-form is *ripa*.

Table 8.66 Summary of the changes affecting Proto-Romance *a

Language	Change (word-final)	Name of change(s)
Rumanian	*a > ə	vowel reduction
French	*a > ə > Ø	vowel reduction and deletion

We can now outline in Table 8.67 the development of the word in French, which has the most complicated development of the five languages.

Table 8.67 Evolution of French *rive* from *ripa

Change	*ripa	Name of change
p > b /V__V	riba	voicing
b > v /V__V	riva	frication
a > ə /__#	rivə	vowel reduction
ə > Ø /__#	riv	apocope

In the case of the cognates for 'female friend' (the second row of Table 8.62), the first three segments are the same in all the languages in the data. According to the majority rules strategy, we can reconstruct the first three segments as *ami-*. In the reconstruction of the second consonant, however, we must appeal to our strategy of phonetic plausibility.

Table 8.68 Systematic correspondences in the second consonant of the cognates for 'female friend'

Spanish	Sardinian	French	Portuguese	Rumanian
ɣ-	-k-	-ø	-g-	—

Once again, since intervocalic voicing, frication, and deletion are phonetically plausible changes, it is most appropriate to posit *k for the proto-form (see Table 8.69).

Table 8.69 Summary of the changes affecting Proto-Romance *k

Language	Change (in V__V)	Name of change(s)
Portuguese	*k > g	voicing
Spanish	*k > g > ɣ	voicing and frication
French	*k > g > ɣ > Ø	voicing, frication, and deletion

In the case of the final vowel, we have the same situation we had in the previous form. The full vowel is found in Spanish, Sardinian, and Portuguese, but there is no vowel in French. We can therefore assume the full vowel *a for the proto-form, with subsequent vowel reduction and apocope in French. Consequently, we arrive at the proto-form *amika.

Finally, applying the same procedure to the cognates in the final two rows of Table 8.62 yields the proto-forms *kuppa 'cup' and *gutta 'drop'. All the languages in the data retain the initial consonant of both proto-forms. The vowel *u is reconstructed on the basis of the majority rules strategy, since we have no phonetic grounds for choosing either [u] or [o] as the older vowel. The systematic correspondences involving the intervocalic consonants are given in Table 8.70.

Table 8.70 Systematic correspondences of the medial consonants of *kuppa and *gutta

Spanish	Sardinian	French	Portuguese	Rumanian
-p-	-pp-	-p	-p-	-p-
-t-	-tt-	-t	-t-	-t-

Regardless of whether we are dealing with original *pp or *tt, the same pattern is evident in the case of both geminate types. There is a geminate stop consonant in Sardinian and a single consonant in Spanish, French, Portuguese, and Rumanian. Since degemination is an expected sound change (see the catalogue), we assume that the proto-forms contained geminate consonants which underwent degemination except in Sardinian. This is an example of a case where the phonetic plausibility strategy overrules the majority rules strategy (since four of the five languages have [p]/[t] whereas only one language has [pp]/[tt]). As far as the final vowels are concerned, the same pattern found in the previous examples is once again evident. Proto-Romance *a* was retained in Spanish, Sardinian, and Portuguese, reduced to [ə] in Rumanian, and deleted in French (see Table 8.66).

Of the languages exemplified here, Sardinian is considered the most **conservative** since its forms stand closest to those of the proto-language. (In fact, the Sardinian words in the examples happen to be identical with the proto-forms, but this degree of resemblance would not be maintained in a broader range of data.) In the case of the other Romance languages and changes we have discussed, the most to least conservative are: Portuguese (degemination, voicing) and Rumanian (degemination, vowel reduction); Spanish (degemination, voicing, frication); French (degemination, voicing, frication, consonant deletion, vowel reduction, apocope).

Although there is no reason to expect Proto-Romance to be identical with Classical Latin, close similarity is expected (Table 8.71).[5] Accordingly, the fact that our reconstructions are so close to the Latin words gives us confidence in our methods of reconstruction.

Table 8.71 Comparison of Latin and Proto-Romance forms

Latin	Proto-Romance form
rīpa	*ripa
amīca (c = [k])	*amika
cuppa	*kuppa
gutta	*gutta

Notice that it is sometimes not possible to reconstruct all characteristics of the proto-language. For example, on the basis of our data we were not able to reconstruct vowel length (Latin had a distinction between long and short vowels) since there was no evidence of this characteristic in the cognate forms.

It is also worth noting that we are not always so fortunate as to have written records of a language we expect to be very close to our reconstructed language. In the case of the Germanic languages, for example, there is no ancient written language equivalent to Latin. We must rely completely on our reconstruction of Proto-Germanic to determine the properties of the language from which the modern-day Germanic languages descended. Furthermore, for many languages of the world (for example, the majority of African and South American languages) we have no written historical records at all and for other languages, such as the Amerindian languages of North America, it is only very recently that we have written records.

In summary, when the forms of two or more languages appear to be related, we can, through a consideration of systematic phonetic correspondences of cognates, reconstruct the common form from which all the forms can be derived by means of phonetically plausible sound changes. Genetically related lexical forms of different languages are called **cognates**, the reconstructed forms, **proto-forms**, and a reconstructed language, a **proto-language**.

7.3

Internal reconstruction

Sometimes it is possible to reconstruct the earlier form of a language even without reference to comparative data. This technique, known as **internal reconstruction**, relies on the analysis of morphophonemic variation within a single language. The key point is that the sound changes that create allomorphic and allophonic variation can be identified and then used to infer an earlier form of the morpheme. The data in Table 8.72 are from French; because of borrowing, English exhibits a parallel set of contrasts involving [k] and [ʃ].

Table 8.72   [k]–[s] correspondence in French

maʒik	'magic'	maʒis-jɛ̃	'magician'
loʒik	'logic'	loʒis-jɛ̃	'logician'
myzik	'music'	myzis-jyɛ̃	'musician'

The root morpheme in each row exhibits two forms, one ending in [k], the other ending in [s]. The same methods and principles used in comparative reconstruction can be applied here to reconstruct the historically earlier form of the root morpheme. If a root ending in *$*s$ is posited, no phonetically plausible change can account for the [k] in the left-hand column. By contrast, if a root-final *$*k$ is posited, the [s] can be accounted for by assuming that the *$*k$ was fronted under the influence of the high front vowel of the suffix (palatalization) and became an affricate [tˢ] (affrication), which was later simplified to a fricative [s] (deaffrication). All of these changes are phonetically plausible and listed in the catalogue in Table 8.3. Accordingly, internal reconstruction indicates that at an earlier point in the development of French, the root morphemes in Table 8.72 ended in the consonant *$*k$.

7.4

The discovery of Indo-European

The late eighteenth-century discovery that Sanskrit (the ancient language of India) was related to Latin, Greek, Germanic, and Celtic revolutionized European linguistic studies. Sir William Jones, a British judge and scholar working in India, summed up the nature and implications of the findings in his 1786 address to the Royal Asiatic Society in Calcutta, a part of which follows:

The Sanskrit language, whatever be its antiquity, is of a wonderful structure; more perfect than the Greek, more copious [having more cases] than the Latin, and more exquisitely refined than either, yet bearing to both of them a stronger affinity, both in the roots of the verbs and in the forms of the grammar, than could possibly have been produced by accident; so strong indeed, that no philologer could examine them all three, without believing them to have sprung from some common source, which, perhaps, no longer exists; there is a similar reason ... for supposing that both the Gothic and the Celtic ... had the same origin with the Sanskrit; and the old Persian might be added to the same family.

This discovery led to several decades of intensive historical-comparative work and to important advances in historical linguistics during the nineteenth century. By studying phonetic correspondences from an ever-increasing number of languages, linguists eventually ascertained that most of the languages of Europe, Persia (Iran), and the northern part of India belong to a single family, now called Indo-European. By applying the techniques of the comparative method, they began reconstructing the grammar of the proto-language from which these languages evolved, **Proto-Indo-European (PIE)**.

A number of individuals advanced this research. In 1814, the Danish linguist Rasmus Rask carefully documented the relationships among cognates in a number of Indo-European languages, and at the same time established the methods that would govern the emerging science of historical-comparative linguistics. He wrote:

When agreement is found in [the most essential] words in two languages, and so frequently that rules may be drawn up for the shift in letters [sounds] from one to the other, then there is a fundamental relationship between the two languages; especially when similarities in the inflectional system and in the general make-up of the languages correspond with them.

Rask worked without access to Sanskrit. The first comparative linguistic analysis of Sanskrit, Greek, Persian, and the Germanic languages was done by the German scholar Franz Bopp in 1816. In 1822, another German, Jakob Grimm, extended Rask's observations and became the first person to explain the relationships among the cognates noted by Rask in terms of a **sound shift**, the systematic modification of a series of phonemes. Some of the correspondences on which he based his work are given in Table 8.73.

Table 8.73 Some Indo-European phonetic correspondences

Greek	Latin	English
pat<u>é</u>r	<u>p</u>ater	<u>f</u>ather
<u>t</u>reîs	<u>t</u>rēs	<u>th</u>ree
he<u>k</u>atón	<u>c</u>entum	<u>h</u>undred

The crucial observation is that where English has [f], [θ], and [h] (here, in word-initial position), Greek and Latin have [p], [t], and [k]. Grimm tabulated a series of consonant shifts for Proto-Germanic which differentiated it from other Indo-European languages. **Grimm's Law** (Table 8.74) is the name given to the consonant shifts which took place between Proto-Indo-European and Proto-Germanic.

Table 8.74 The sound shifts underlying Grimm's Law

Proto-Indo-European	p	t	k	b	d	g	bh	dh	gh
Germanic	f	θ	x	p	t	k	b	d	g

Some additional examples of the relationships captured by these shifts are given in Table 8.75. The Proto-Indo-European consonants were either maintained in Sanskrit, Greek, and Latin or in some cases underwent changes different from those found in Germanic.

Table 8.75 Some examples of the consonant shifts underlying Grimm's Law

Shift in Germanic	Sanskrit	Greek	Latin	English
p > f	pād-	pod-	ped-	foot
t > θ	tanu-	tanaós	tenuis	thin
k > x	çatam	hekatón	centum	hundred
b > p	—	—	lūbricus	slippery
d > t	daça	déka	decem	ten
g > k	ajras	agrós	ager	acre
bh > b	bhrātā	phrátēr	fräter	brother
dh > d	vidhavā	éítheos	vidua	widow
gh > g	hansas	khén	(h)änser	goose

Although there appeared to be exceptions to Grimm's Law (Table 8.76), they turned out to be systematic and could be traced to specific environments. For example, voiceless stops were not subject to Grimm's Law when they were immediately preceded by *s*.

Table 8.76 A systematic exception to Grimm's Law

Original s + voiceless stop				
Latin	spu ō	English	spit	[sp] (not [sf])
Latin	stāre	English	stand	[st] (not [sθ])
Latin	piscis	Gothic	fisks	[sk] (not [sx])

A particularly important discovery was made by Karl Verner, who traced a group of exceptions to Grimm's Law to the original accentual pattern of Proto-Indo-European. In a generalization that came to be known as Verner's Law, he proposed that a word-internal voiceless fricative resulting from Grimm's Law underwent voicing if the original Proto-Indo-European accent did not immediately precede it. Since stress came to be fixed on the root syllable in Germanic subsequent to the changes covered by Verner's Law, the original environment was obscured. However, Sanskrit provides direct evidence for Verner's claim since Sanskrit was very conservative in its maintenance of the original Proto-Indo-European accent. Although the English forms are complicated by other developments, the effects of Verner's Law are apparent in the Gothic examples shown in Table 8.77 (overleaf). In the Gothic word for *brother*, PIE **t* becomes [θ] according to Grimm's Law, whereas in the word for *father* it becomes [ð] in accordance with both Grimm's and Verner's Laws.

Table 8.77   Verner's Law

PIE	Sanskrit	Grimm's Law	Verner's Law	Gothic	
*t	bhrátā	*t > θ	—	[bro:θar]	'brother'
*t	pitā́	*t > θ	θ > ð	[faðar]	'father'

It should also be noted here that borrowing is an important factor which must be taken into consideration when comparative reconstruction is being carried out. For example, Table 8.78 shows that English has many words that do not show the effects of Grimm's Law.

Table 8.78   English words not showing the effects of Grimm's Law

Expected by Grimm's Law	Latin	English
p > f	ped-	pedestrian
t > θ	tenuis	tenuous
k > h	canalis	canal

The apparent failure of Grimm's Law here stems from the fact that the English words were borrowed directly from Latin or French many centuries after the sound shifts described by Grimm's Law had taken place. The task of reconstruction can often be complicated by such borrowings.

Subsequent developments

By the middle of the nineteenth century, the study of language had made great strides, especially in the field of phonetics, which opened the way for the detailed comparison of linguistic forms. One influential hypothesis at that time was that sound laws operated without exception. A group of linguists known as the **Neogrammarians** adopted this idea and made many important contributions to the fledgling science of linguistics by applying it to new and more complicated data. Although such factors as lexical diffusion and social pressures were more or less ignored by the Neogrammarians, their hypothesis represented an important and daring advance in the scientific study of language.

The nineteenth century also saw major advances in the classification of languages. A German scholar, August Schleicher, developed a classification for the Indo-European languages in the form of a genealogical tree. Genetic classification is discussed in much more detail in the chapter on language typology that follows.

Work in comparative reconstruction is far from finished. In particular, linguists are now considering the possibility of superfamilies. One such proposed family is Nostratic, which includes Indo-European, Afro-Asiatic (for example, Arabic, Hebrew), Altaic (for example, Japanese, Korean, Turkish), and Uralic (for example, Finnish, Hungarian). Comparative reconstruction is also playing an important role in determining the genetic relationships of the hundreds of North American indigenous languages, a topic which still remains highly controversial.

7.5

Reconstruction and typology

Since the 1800s, when the reconstruction of Proto-Indo-European was carried out, linguists have accumulated vast amounts of information on thousands of languages. This is in part due to the explosion of studies in the field of linguistic typology, which is concerned with the investigation of structural similarities among languages regardless of whether they are genetically related. Even languages that do not belong to the same family can have striking similarities. For example, in addition to shared word order patterns (see section 2.3 in Chapter 9), SOV languages commonly exhibit a strong tendency towards agglutinating morphology (a type of complex affixation; see Chapter 9) and the phonological process known as vowel harmony, where all the vowels in a word are selected from one of two sets that are incompatible with each other (such as front vs back vowels, rounded vs unrounded vowels, etc.). Typological studies play an important role in the linguist's search for universals of language – statements which are true for all languages.

The extensive information on the languages of the world available to modern linguists was, of course, not available at the time the original reconstruction of Proto-Indo-European was undertaken. Modern linguists involved in comparative reconstruction now take a keen interest in typological studies and the role of **typological plausibility** in reconstruction has become an important topic. For example, a linguist would be very reluctant to propose a reconstruction that violated a universal property of language or that had no parallel in any known language.

Some linguists have argued that the traditional reconstruction of the PIE obstruent system (given in Table 8.79) should be rejected on the basis of typological plausibility.

Table 8.79   The traditional reconstruction of the Proto-Indo-European obstruents

p	t	ḱ	k	kʷ	(voiceless stops)
(b)	d	ǵ	g	gʷ	(voiced stops)
bh	dh	ǵh	gh	gʷh	(voiced aspirated stops)
	s				

This reconstruction is typologically questionable in at least two respects. First, reconstructed forms with PIE *b are extremely rare, almost as if there were a gap in the labial system. Such a gap is very uncommon in the languages of the world. Typically, if there is a missing labial stop, it is the voiceless stop that is missing, not the voiced stop. Second, the traditional reconstruction posits a series of voiced aspirated stops but no corresponding series of voiceless aspirated stops, even though some typologists have argued that all languages which have a voiced series also have the voiceless one.

Such facts have led some linguists to propose what they believe is a more typologically plausible reconstruction of Proto-Indo-European (Table 8.80) involving a voiceless stop series, an ejective series,[6] and a voiced stop series (as well as *s as in the traditional reconstruction).

Table 8.80   A recent reconstruction of the Proto-Indo-European obstruents

p	t	ḱ	k	kʷ	(voiceless stops)
(p′)	t′	ḱ′	k′	k′ʷ	(ejectives)
b	d	ǵ	g	gʷ	(voiced stops)
	s				

Not only does this reconstruction avoid the problem with the aspirated stops, it is also common for languages with an ejective series to lack the labial. From this perspective, this reconstruction seems much more plausible than the traditional one.

Both reconstructions have their supporters. In fact, however, it is difficult to come to a definitive decision on the basis of typological considerations since it is common for a proposed universal to have exceptions. For example, a few languages have been found with the characteristics attributed to Proto-Indo-European by the traditional reconstruction. These languages have labial gaps in the voiced series (for example, Amerindian languages of the Athapaskan and Caddoan families) and a voiced aspirate series but no voiceless counterpart (Madurese, an Indonesian language). Accordingly, as long as the traditional reconstruction is linguistically possible, it would not seem right to reject it simply because the phonological system proposed would be a rare one.

Typological plausibility will likely continue to play a secondary role in reconstruction until linguists can draw a clear line between what is linguistically possible and what is not possible. Nevertheless, as our knowledge and understanding of language universals continues to improve, it is certain that linguists involved in the reconstruction of proto-languages will maintain an interest in typological plausibility.

8

LANGUAGE CHANGE AND NATURALNESS

A striking fact about language change is that the same patterns of change occur repeatedly, not only within the same language at different periods in its history but also across languages. Both the similarity of changes across languages as well as the directionality of language change suggest that some changes are more natural than others. This notion of **naturalness** is implicit in the phonetic plausibility strategy introduced in the section on comparative reconstruction.

If naturalness is a factor in language change, its manifestations should also be found in the language acquisition process and in language universals. This does seem to be the case. As a specific example, let us consider the frequently made claim that the CV syllable is the most natural of all syllable types. At least three different kinds of evidence can be brought forth in support of this claim.

First, in terms of universals, all languages of the world have CV syllables in their syllable type inventory. Second, a variety of sound changes have the effect of reducing less natural syllable types to the more natural CV type (Table 8.81).

Table 8.81   Sound changes yielding CV syllables

Deletion

CCV	>	CV		Old English	cnēow	English	knee	/ni:/
CVC	>	CV		Old Spanish	non	Spanish	no	

Vowel epenthesis

CCVCV	>	CVCVCV	Italian	croce	Sicilian	kiruci	'cross'

By contrast, note that such changes rarely if ever apply to a CV syllable to yield a different syllable type. Deletion of the C in a word-initial CV syllable is extremely rare, as is vowel epenthesis in a CV syllable or a sequence of CVCV syllables.

Third, in terms of language acquisition, the CV syllable type is one of the first syllable types to be acquired and many phonetic processes found in child language have the effect of yielding CV syllables, just like the sound changes listed above (see Chapter 11 on language acquisition).

Table 8.82   Phonetic processes in language acquisition yielding CV syllables

CCV	→	CV	tree	→	[ti:]	(simplification of consonant clusters)
CVC	→	CV	dog	→	[dɑ]	(deletion of final consonants)

It is clear, however, that it is inappropriate to take a simplistic view of linguistic naturalness. For example, some sound changes produce less natural syllables. Thus, syncope has the effect of reducing a sequence of CVCVCV syllables to the less natural CVCCV. Usually in such cases, a different motivation can be identified, such as the preference for shorter phonological forms over longer forms. But given the complexity of human language, not to mention human behaviour in general, it should not be surprising that there are many different parameters of linguistic naturalness and that these can, in turn, lead to apparently conflicting changes in language over time. It remains an important task of the linguist to identify, rank, and ultimately explain relations of linguistic naturalness. The study of language change will continue to make an important contribution to this area.

Summing up

Historical linguistics studies the nature and causes of language change. The causes of language change find their roots in the physiological and cognitive makeup of human beings. Sound changes usually involve articulatory simplification as in the case of the most common type, **assimilation**. **Analogy** and **reanalysis** are particularly important factors in morphological change. **Language contact** resulting in **borrowing** is another important source of language change. All components of the grammar, from phonology to semantics, are subject to change over time. A change can simultaneously affect all instances of a particular sound or form, or it can spread through the language word by word by means of **lexical diffusion**. Sociological factors can play an important role in determining whether or not a linguistic innovation is ultimately adopted by the linguistic community at large. Since language change is systematic, it is possible, by identifying the changes that a particular language or dialect has undergone, to reconstruct linguistic history and thereby posit the earlier forms from which later forms have evolved. Using sets of **cognates**, **comparative reconstruction** allows us to reconstruct the properties of the parent or **proto-language** on the basis of **systematic phonetic correspondences**.

Studies in historical linguistics can provide valuable insights into relationships among languages and shed light on prehistoric developments. Furthermore, historical studies of language are of great importance to our understanding of human linguistic competence. In fact, it has often been stated that language change provides one of the most direct windows into the workings of the human mind. Furthermore, the study of language change contributes to our understanding of how social, cultural, and psychological factors interact to shape language. Finally, the integration of studies on language change, language acquisition, and language universals remains one of the most important challenges facing linguists today.

Notes

1   The translation for these lines is as follows:
     Many men say that in dreams
     There is nothing but talk and lies
     But men may see some dreams
     Which are scarcely false
     But afterward come true.

2   In these and other examples throughout this chapter, orthographic forms are given where these clearly reflect the sound change(s) in question. If required, partial or full phonetic transcriptions are provided .

3   Since voicing commonly occurs between voiced segments, it can also be considered a type of assimilation. It is treated here as a weakening since it is often part of a larger pattern of change involving various weakening processes.

4   We have simplified here in two respects. First, we ignore the fact that the verbs *be* and *have* can undergo Inversion even when they do not function as auxiliaries.
     Are they here?
     Have you no sense?
     Second, we have not traced the emergence of the auxiliary verb *do* in the formation of questions.

5   Classical Latin was the literary language of ancient Rome whereas Proto-Romance represents an attempt to reconstruct the spoken language of the Romans which spread throughout much of Europe and which was the source of the various Romance languages.

6   Ejectives are produced by a closing of the glottis and raising of the larynx. (See Chapter 2, section 10.)

Sources

This chapter is based on a chapter in the original edition by James M. Anderson – the advanced textbooks by Anttila, Hock, and McMahon (cited below) provide much more detailed discussions of most of the major topics in this chapter. They are also excellent sources for references relating to particular topics. Hock is particularly important for providing detailed discussions of syntactic change and the role of typology in reconstruction.

Overviews of historical linguistics as it applies to the development of English are presented in the books by Williams, Pyles and Algeo, Baugh and Cable, and Millward and Strang cited below.

The catalogue of sound changes is adapted from catalogues proposed by Theo Vennemann in the article 'Linguistic typologies in historical linguistics', *Società di linguistica italiana* 23: 87–91 (1985) and a book entitled *Preference Laws for Syllable Structure and the Explanation of Sound Change* (Amsterdam: Mouton de Gruyter, 1988). Section 2 has also benefited from unpublished material (particularly the manuscript 'Linguistic change') kindly made available by Theo Vennemann (University of Munich) to the author (Robert Murray) during his stay in Munich from 1980 to 1985.

The data on vowel laxing in Canadian French are from Douglas C. Walker's book *The Pronunciation of Canadian French* (Ottawa: University of Ottawa Press, 1984). The discussion of borrowing and semantic change in English as well as the material on word order in Old and Middle English come from the book by Joseph Williams *Origins of the English Language* (New York: The Free Press, 1975). The data in Table 8.46 on the origin of the 5000 most common words in English also come from p. 67 of the same book.

Figure 8.11 depicting lexical diffusion of the stress change in English nouns derived from verbs is taken from the book by Jean Aitchison cited below. Aitchison's remarks are based on the article by M. Chen and W. Wang, 'Sound change: actuation and implementation', *Language* 51: 255–81 (1975). The data on the realization of [s] as [h] in Spanish were provided by Herbert Izzo of the University of Calgary.

The Germanic cognates used to illustrate family relationships are based on Leonard Bloomfield's classic work *Language* (New York: Holt, Rinehart & Winston, 1933). The data on sound change in Muskogean come from Mary Haas's book *The Prehistory of Languages* (Amsterdam: Mouton, 1969). The quote from Jones is taken from *A Reader in Nineteenth-Century Historical Indo-European Linguistics*, edited and translated by Winfred P. Lehmann (Bloomington: Indiana University Press, 1967) and the quote from Rask is taken from Holger Pedersen's book *The Discovery of Language: Linguistic Science in the Nineteenth Century* (Bloomington: Indiana University Press, 1959).

Question 2 is based on data provided by Dr George Patterson, whose generosity we hereby acknowledge. The data for questions 3 and 4 are from F. Columbus's *Introductory Workbook in Historical Phonology* (Cambridge, Mass.: Slavica Publishers, 1974). Question 10 is based on data provided by David Bellusci. The data for question 18 are drawn from *Source Book for Linguistics* by W. Cowan and J. Rakušan (Philadelphia: John Benjamins, 1987).

Recommended reading   Aitchison, Jean. 1981. *Language Change: Progress or Decay?* London: Fontana.

Anttila, Raimo. 1989. *Historical and Comparative Linguistics*. Amsterdam and New York: John Benjamins.

Arlotto, Anthony. 1972. *Introduction to Historical Linguistics*. Lanham, New York and London: University Press of America.

Baldi, P. 1983 *An Introduction to the Indo-European Languages*. Carbondale and Edwardsville: Southern Illinois University Press.

Baugh, Albert C., and Cable, Thomas. 1993. *A History of the English Language*. 4th edn. London: Routledge.

Hock, Hans Henrich. 1986. *Principles of Historical Linguistics.* Berlin, New York, and Amsterdam: Mouton de Gruyter.

Jeffers, Robert J., and Lehiste, Ilse. 1979. *Principles and Methods for Historical Linguistics.* Cambridge, Mass.: MIT Press.

Leith, Dick. 1983. *A Social History of English.* London: Routledge & Kegan Paul.

McMahon, A.M.S. 1994 *Understanding Language Change.* Cambridge: Cambridge University Press.

Millward, C.M. 1989. *A Biography of the English Language.* New York: Holt, Rinehart & Winston.

Pyles, Thomas, and Algeo, John. 1992. *The Origins and Development of the English Language.* 4th edn. New York: Harcourt Brace Jovanovich.

Strang, B. 1970. *A History of English.* London: Methuen.

Williams, Joseph. 1975. *Origins of the English Language: A Social and Linguistic History.* New York: The Free Press.

Questions

1. Identify the following sound changes with reference to the catalogue of sound changes provided in Table 8.3. In each pair of examples, focus on the segment(s) in bold only. The form on the left indicates the original segment(s) before the change and the form on the right indicates the segment(s) after the change.

   a) Sanskrit **sn**eha — Pali **sin**eha — 'friendship'
   b) Old English **hl**āf — English **l**oaf
   c) Latin **i**uvenis [j] — Italian **gi**ovane[dʒ] — 'young'
   d) English triath**l**on — dialect triath[ə]lon
   e) Latin vi**du**a [dw] — Spanish viu**d**a [wd] — 'widow'
   f) Sanskrit sa**pt**a — Pali sa**tt**a — 'seven'
   g) Latin turtu**r** — English turt**le**
   h) *ven**r**é — Spanish *ven**dr**é — 'I will come'
   i) Italian mu**nd**o — Sicilian mu**nn**u — 'world'
   j) Old French **ci**re [tˢ] — French **ci**re [s] — 'wax'
   k) Latin p**ān**- — French p**ain** [ɛ̃] — 'bread'
   l) Latin **mul**gēre — Italian **mun**gere — 'to milk'
   m) Latin pa**c**āre [k] — Italian pa**g**are — 'to pay'
   n) Latin pe**cc**ātum [kk] — Spanish pe**c**ado [k] — 'sin'
   o) *hon**ōs**is — Latin *hon**ōr**is — 'honor (gen sg)'
   p) English ra**ge** — French ra**ge** [ʒ] — 'rage'
   q) English co**ff**ee — Chipewyan [ka**θ**i]
   r) Latin ma**re** — Portuguese ma**r** — 'sea'
   s) Latin **vī**cīnitās — Spanish **ve**cindad — 'neighbourhood'
   t) Gothic **þ**liuhan [θ] — English **f**lee
   u) Old English (ic) sin**ge** — English (I) sin**g**
   v) Latin su**mm**a — Spanish su**m**a — 'sum, gist'
   w) Latin ōrn**ā**mentum — Old French orn**e**ment [ə] — 'ornament'
   x) *l**ū**si — Old English l**ȳ**s [y:] — 'lice'

2. a) Describe the difference between the two French dialects in the following data given in phonetic transcription.

b) What sound change would you posit here? Why?

c) State the sound change in the form of a rule.

	Standard French	Acadian French	
i)	okyn	otʃyn	'none'
ii)	kør	tʃør	'heart'
iii)	ke	tʃe	'wharf'
iv)	kẽːz	tʃẽ̃ːz	'fifteen'
v)	akyze	atʃyze	'accuse'
vi)	ki	tʃi	'who'
vii)	kav	kav	'cave'
viii)	kɔr	kɔr	'body'
ix)	kurir	kurir	'run'
x)	ãkɔːr	ãkɔːr	'again'

3. a) What sound changes differentiate Guaraní from its parent language, Proto-Tupí-Guaraní, in the following data?

b) State these changes in rule form.

	Proto-Tupí-Guaraní	Guaraní	
i)	jukɨr	jukɨ	'salt'
ii)	moajan	moajã	'push'
iii)	puʔam	puʔã	'wet'
iv)	meʔeŋ	meʔẽ	'give'
v)	tiŋ	tʃĩ	'white'
vi)	potiʔa	potʃiʔa	'chest'
vii)	tatatiŋ	tatatʃĩ	'smoke'
viii)	kɨb	kɨ	'louse'
ix)	men	mẽ	'husband'

4. a) Describe the three changes that took place between Proto-Slavic and Bulgarian in the following data. (The symbol ˘ over a vowel indicates that it is short.)

b) State these changes as rules and indicate, as far as possible, the order in which they must have applied.

c) Apply these rules to the Proto-Slavic word for 'adroit' to show how the Bulgarian form evolved.

	Proto-Slavic	Bulgarian	
i)	gladŭka	glatkə	'smooth'
ii)	kratŭka	kratkə	'short'
iii)	blizŭka	bliskə	'near'
iv)	ʒeʒĭka	ʒeʃkə	'scorching'
v)	lovŭka	lofkə	'adroit'
vi)	gorĭka	gorkə	'bitter'

5. Determine all the sound changes required to derive the later form from the proto-form. Where possible, give the chronology of the sound changes.

a)	*feminam	Old French	femme (final e = [ə])	'woman'
b)	*lumine	Spanish	lumbre	'fire'
c)	*tremulare	Spanish	temblar	'tremble'
d)	*stuppam	Spanish	estopa	'tow'
e)	*populu	Rumanian	plop	'poplar'

6. Taking into consideration the Great Vowel Shift, give all the changes necessary to derive the Modern English forms from the Old English forms. (*Note*: Assume, simplifying somewhat, that the Old English forms were pronounced as they are written.)

	Old English	*Modern English*
a)	brōde (sg acc)	brood
b)	cnotta (c=[k])	knot
c)	wīse	wise
d)	hlǣfdige (g=[j])	lady

7. Place names are often subject to spelling pronunciation. Transcribe your pronunciation of the following words and then compare your pronunciation with that recommended by a good dictionary. Do you think any of your pronunciations qualify as spelling pronunciations?
   a) Worcestershire
   b) Thames
   c) Plymouth
   d) Dyfed
   e) Grosvenor
   f) Newfoundland
   g) Hawick
   h) Birmingham
   i) Morecambe
   j) Reading
   k) Derby

8. Compare the Old English singular and plural forms:

   Singular *Plural*
   bōc   bēc   'book(s)'
   āc   ǣc   'oak(s)'

   Although the Old English words have an umlaut plural (as in Old English gōs/gēs 'goose/geese'), the Modern English forms do not. Explain how the change in plural formation could have come about.

9. As evident in the following sentence, Shona, a modern Bantu language spoken in Zimbabwe, has SVO word order. (*Note*: The morpheme *ano-* marks present tense.)

   mwana   anotengesa   miriwo
   child   sells   vegetables
   'The child sells vegetables'

   By contrast, Shona's morphology reflects a different pattern as evident in the following examples.

mwana   ano**mu**ona
child   **him**+*see*
'The child sees him'

mukadzi   ano**va**batsira
woman   **them**+*help*
'The woman helps them'

What do these examples indicate about earlier Shona or possibly Proto-Bantu word order?

10. All of the following English words at one time had meanings that are quite different from their current ones. (In the case of borrowed words, the semantic change may have occurred before the word came into English.) Identify each of these semantic changes as an instance of narrowing, broadening, amelioration, pejoration, weakening, or shift.

	Word	*Earlier meaning*
a)	moody	'brave'
b)	uncouth	'unknown'
c)	aunt	'father's sister'
d)	butcher	'one who slaughters goats'
e)	witch	'male or female sorcerer'
f)	sly	'skilful'
g)	accident	'an event'
h)	argue	'make clear'
i)	carry	'transport by cart'
j)	grumble	'murmur, make low sounds'
k)	shrewd	'depraved, wicked'
l)	praise	'set a value on'
m)	ordeal	'trial by torture'
n)	picture	'a painted likeness'
o)	seduce	'persuade someone to desert his or her duty'
p)	box	'a small container made of boxwood'
q)	baggage	'a worthless person'
r)	virtue	'qualities expected of a man'
s)	myth	'story'
t)	undertaker	'one who undertakes a task'
u)	hussy	'housewife'
v)	astonish	'strike by thunder'
w)	write	'scratch'
x)	quell	'kill'

11. Look up the following words in a good dictionary. Discuss any semantic changes that have affected the underscored portions since Old English. Do you think speakers of Modern English have reanalysed any of these forms in terms of folk etymology?

a) wed<u>lock</u>
b) witch<u>craft</u>
c) stead<u>fast</u>
d) after<u>ward</u>

12. The following line is from *Troilus and Criseyde V* by Geoffrey Chaucer.
    His lighte goost ful blisfully is went.
    [hɪs liçtə gɔːst fʊl blɪsfʊlli ɪs wɛnt] ([ç] is a voiceless palatal fricative.)
    'His light spirit has gone very blissfully.'
    a) How has the meaning of the word *ghost* changed since Chaucer's time?
    b) Describe the changes that have taken place in the pronunciation of *light* and *ghost*.

13. Consider the following lyrics from the Middle English song 'Sumer Is I-cumen In'. Compare the Middle English lyrics with the Modern English translation and answer the questions that follow.

Original text	*Transcription*
Sumer is i-cumen in;	[sʊmər ɪs ɪkʊmən ɪn
Lhude sing, cuccu!	luːdə sɪŋg kʊkkʊ
Grōweþ sēd, and blōweþ mēd,	grɔːwəθ seːd and blɔːwəθ meːd
And springþ þe wude nū.	and sprɪŋgθ ðə wʊdə nuː]

    Translation
    'Summer has come in;
    Loudly sing, cuckoo!
    Seed grows and meadow blooms
    And the wood grows now.'

    a) What affix converted the adjective *loud* into an adverb in Middle English?
    b) What accounts for the difference between the Middle English and Modern English pronunciation of the vowel in *loud*?
    c) What other words in this poem reflect this general shift?
    d) How has the relative ordering of the subject and verb changed since this was written?
    e) How has the third person singular present tense suffix changed since Middle English?

14. The following Cree words were borrowed from French as the result of contact between the two groups on the Canadian prairies. (Notice that the French determiner was not treated as a separate morpheme and was carried along with the borrowed word.) What types of considerations could one plausibly assume played a role in the borrowing of these words into Cree?

	Cree	*French*	
a)	labutōn	le bouton	'button'
b)	lībot	les bottes	'boots'
c)	lamilās	la mélasse	'molasses'
d)	lapwīl	la poêle	'frying pan'
e)	litī	le thé	'tea'

15. The following Latin roots are found in words that have been borrowed into English. Since these words were borrowed after Grimm's Law had

applied, they do not show its effects. All of these roots, however, do have Germanic cognates that did undergo Grimm's Law. On the basis of your knowledge of this law and the meaning of the borrowing, try to determine the Modern English (Germanic) cognate for each root. Consult a good dictionary if you need help. (*Note*: Focus on the portion of the Latin word in bold only; vowel changes must also be taken into consideration.)

	Latin root	Related borrowing	English cognate
a)	**ped**is	pedestrian	*foot*
b)	**nep**os	nepotism	
c)	**pisc**is	piscine	
d)	**ten**uis	tenuous	
e)	**corn**u	cornucopia	
f)	**duo**	dual	
g)	**ed**ere	edible	
h)	**gen**us	genocide	
i)	**ager**	agriculture	

16. Attempt to reconstruct the Proto-Germanic form for each pair of cognates. Focusing on the vowels, describe the changes which affected the Old English forms. (*Note*: y = [y], œ = [ø] and j = [j].)

	Gothic	Old English	
a)	kuni	cyn	'kin'
b)	badi	bed	'bed'
c)	dōmjan	dœman	'to judge'
d)	sōkjan	sœcan	'to seek'
e)	bugjan	bycgan	'to buy'
f)	nati	net	'net'

17. Reconstruct the Proto-Romance form for each set of cognates. Give all the changes necessary to derive each of the modern forms from the proto-forms.

	Spanish	Sardinian	Rumanian	
a)	vida	bita	vită (ă = [ə])	'life'
b)	sí	si	şi (ş = [ʃ])	'yes'
c)	riso	rizu	rīs	'laugh'
d)	miel	mele	miere	'honey'
e)	hierro	ferru	fier	'iron'
f)	piedra	pedra	piatră (ă = [ə])	'stone'
g)	hierba	erva	iarbă (ă = [ə])	'grass'
h)	oso	ursu	urs	'bear'
i)	roto	ruttu	rupt	'broken'
j)	lecho	lettu	–	'bed'

(*Note*: The Spanish and Rumanian spelling 'ie' represents the sequence /je/, and the Rumanian spelling 'ia' represents the sequence /ja/.)

9

The classification of languages

Aleksandra Steinbergs

Everything it is possible for us to analyse depends on a clear method which distinguishes the similar from the not similar.

✦ Linnæus, *Genera Plantarum* (1754)

In the world today there are thousands of different languages, each with its own sound patterns, grammar and vocabulary, However, regardless of how different these languages are, they have important similarities that allow linguists to group them into a relatively small number of families and types. This chapter describes the methods of classification linguists use, and some of the findings which have resulted from this type of research.

1

SOME PRELIMINARIES

We will begin by considering two topics – the problem of distinguishing between a language and a dialect, and the chief methods of language classification used in linguistics today.

1.1

Dialect and language

It is often difficult to determine whether two linguistic communities speak different languages or merely different dialects of the same language. One test that linguists use to decide this involves the criterion of **mutual intelligibility**. Mutually intelligible varieties of a language can be understood by speakers of each variety. According to this criterion, the English of London, the English of Edinburgh, the English of Cape Town, the English of Sydney, the English of Toronto and the English of Miami qualify as dialects of the same language. On the other hand, if two speakers cannot understand one another, then linguists normally conclude that they are speaking different languages. The Italian of Florence and the French of Paris are examples of varieties of speech that are not mutually intelligible.

Political, cultural, social, historical, and religious factors often intervene in the determination of linguistic boundaries. For example, Serbs and Croatians often maintain that they speak different languages. However, even though their history, religion, and spelling systems differ, standard Serbian and standard Croatian are mutually intelligible dialects of the same language, which linguists call Serbo-Croatian. In contrast, we often speak of Chinese as if it were a single language, even though, according to the mutual intelligibility test, it is actually a number of separate languages (Cantonese, Mandarin, Hakka, and so on), each with a multitude of dialects of its own.

In addition to the problems presented by these non-linguistic considerations, complications also arise when we try to divide a continuum of mutually intelligible dialects whose two end points are not intelligible. Dutch and German, for example, are mutually intelligible around the border area between Germany and Holland; however, the Dutch of Amsterdam and the German of Munich are not. Similarly, Palestinian Arabic and Syrian Arabic are mutually intelligible, but Moroccan Arabic and Saudi Arabian Arabic are not.

Taking these considerations into account, how many distinct languages are there in the world today? The best available estimate places the current figure at about six thousand. However, many of these languages have only a few hundred speakers and many others are in grave danger of demise as indigenous peoples throughout the world lose their traditional culture and homelands. Indeed, according to one estimate, only around three hundred of the world's languages have a secure future.

1.2

Types of classification

Within the field of linguistics, three different approaches to language classification are used.

Genetic classification categorizes languages according to their descent. Languages that developed historically from the same ancestor language are grouped together and are said to be **genetically related**. This ancestor may be attested (that is, texts written in this language have been discovered or preserved, as in the case of Latin), or it may be a reconstructed hypothetical proto-language for which no original texts exist (as is the case for Proto-Indo-European). Genetic classification is discussed further in section 3.

Although genetically related languages often share structural characteristics, they do not necessarily bear a close structural resemblance. For example, Latvian and English are genetically related (both are descended from Indo-European), but their morphological structure is quite different. An English sentence like *It has to be figured out/ascertained* can be expressed in Latvian by a single word.

1)

jāizgudro
(one) must out figure (it)
'It has to be figured out.'

Of course, Latvian and English are very distantly related, and languages that are more closely related will typically share a larger number of similarities. On the other hand, it is also necessary to recognize that even languages that are totally unrelated may share some structural properties. Thus, English and Swahili, which are unrelated, both employ subject–verb–object word order in simple declarative sentences.

2)

Maria anapenda Ali
'Maria likes Ali.'

For these reasons, a second approach to language classification is required. Known as **linguistic typology**, it classifies languages according to their structural characteristics without regard for genetic relationships. Thus, typologists might group together languages with similar sound patterns or, alternatively, ones with similar word order. Typological studies also seek to identify **linguistic universals**, structural characteristics which occur across the languages of the world. We return to this type of classification in section 2.

Finally, **areal classification** identifies characteristics shared by languages which are in geographical contact. Languages in close contact often borrow words, sounds, morphemes, and even syntactic patterns from each other. As a result, neighbouring languages can come to resemble each other even though they may not be genetically related. Due to space considerations, this chapter will not deal with areal classification specifically; however, a description of borrowing can be found in sections 1.2 and 5.1 of Chapter 8.

2

TYPOLOGICAL CLASSIFICATION

As already noted, the classification of languages according to their structural characteristics is known as linguistic typology. Typological research groups together languages on the basis of similarities in their word order patterns, morphological structures, or phonological systems. An important area of research within the study of linguistic typology involves the search for linguistic universals – structural patterns and traits that occur in all or most human languages. Patterns or traits that occur in all languages are called **absolute universals**, whereas those that occur in most languages are known as **universal tendencies**.

Many typological generalizations involve **implicational universals**, which specify that the presence of one trait implies the presence of another (but not vice versa). For instance, languages with fricative phonemes (such as /f/ and /s/) will also have stop phonemes (such as /p/ and /t/), although the reverse is not necessarily true.

Another way to analyse linguistic universals is through **markedness theory**. Within this theory, **marked** traits are considered to be either more complex and/or universally rarer than **unmarked** characteristics. In addition, a marked trait is typically found in a particular language only if its unmarked counterpart also occurs. Thus, markedness theory is closely related to the study of implicational universals.

An example can help to clarify these terms. Nasalized vowels are said to be marked, while non-nasalized (oral) ones are said to be unmarked. Phonologically, oral vowels can be considered less complex: oral vowels allow the airstream to exit only through the mouth, while nasal vowels allow air to escape from both the mouth and the nose. Cross-linguistically, we find that all languages have oral vowel phonemes, while only some languages have nasal vowel phonemes. Moreover, even in the languages which have both, there are usually fewer nasal vowels than oral ones. Thus, nasal vowels (which are considered to be marked) are both rarer and phonologically more complex than oral vowels (which are unmarked).

The following sections present some of the typological classifications and universals that have been proposed in the areas of phonology, morphology, and syntax.

2.1

Phonology

In this section, we represent all vowel and consonant systems phonemically. This simplifies the presentation; note, however, that the exact phonetic realization of these systems may vary in the individual languages.

Vowel systems

Languages are often classified according to the size and pattern of their vowel systems. The most common vowel system has five phonemes – two high vowels, two mid vowels, and one low vowel (Figure 9.1). The front vowels are unrounded, as is the low vowel, and the back vowels are rounded.

i u

e o

a

Figure 9.1   The most common vowel system.

About half the world's languages, including Basque, Hawaiian, Japanese, Spanish, and Swahili, have such a system.

The majority of the world's other languages have three, four, six, seven, eight or nine different vowel phonemes (disregarding contrasts based on length or nasalization, which can double or triple the number of phonemic vowels). Languages with fewer than three, or more than nine distinctive vowels are rare. Some typical vowel systems are presented in Figure 9.2.

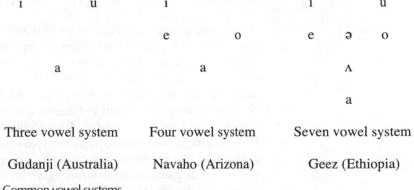

Three vowel system Four vowel system Seven vowel system

Gudanji (Australia) Navaho (Arizona) Geez (Ethiopia)

Figure 9.2   Common vowel systems.

Analysis of many languages has led to the discovery of a number of universal tendencies with respect to vowel systems. Some of these tendencies are listed here, along with a description of the most commonly occurring vowels.

- The most commonly occurring vowel phoneme is /a/, which is found in almost all of the languages of the world. The vowels /i/ and /u/ are almost as common as /a/.
- Front vowel phonemes (/i, e, ɛ, æ/) are generally unrounded, while non-low back vowel phonemes (/ɔ, o, u/) are generally rounded.
- Low vowels (/æ, a, ɑ/) are generally unrounded.

Although English has an above-average number of vowels, these phonemes all comply with the above tendencies. Thus, RP English has only front unrounded vowels, all the low vowel phonemes are unrounded, and all of the back, non-low vowels are rounded. The only asymmetry found is that there is no front unrounded vowel corresponding to /ɒ/. The English vowel system (excluding length, diphthongs and schwa) can be presented as shown in Figure 9.3. (Here the vowel in *set* is represented as /ɛ/ rather than /e/ in order to highlight the symmetry; see the discussion on pages 37 and 38.)

i		u
ɪ		ʊ
ɛ	ʌ	ɔ
—		ɒ
æ		ɑ

Figure 9.3   The English vowel system.

The relationship among contrasting vowel types (such as oral vs nasal and long vs short) can also be expressed in terms of implicational universals, since the presence of one vowel phoneme type implies the presence of another (but not vice versa).

- If a language has contrastive nasal vowels, then it will also have contrastive oral vowels. For example, French contrasts different nasal vowels (/lɔ̃/ 'long' and /lã/ 'slow'), and contrasts oral vowels with nasal vowels (/la/ 'weary' and /lã/ 'slow'). Predictably, French also contrasts different oral vowels, as in /klo/ 'shut' and /klu/ 'nail'. English shows contrasts among oral vowels but does not contrast nasal vowels with oral vowels. There are no contrasts in English like /bɑt/ and /bãt/.
- If a language has contrasting long vowels, then it will also have contrasting short vowels. For example, Finnish shows contrasting long vowels, and, predictably, contrasting short vowels. The reverse is not necessarily the case. Swahili shows contrasting short vowels (/i e a o u/)

but does not contrast long vowels with short ones, although the second-to-last syllable of a word, which is stressed, is lengthened allophonically.

Table 9.1 Finnish vowel contrasts

Long versus long	/vi:li/	'junket'	/va:li/	'election'
Short versus short	/suka/	'bristle'	/suku/	'family'
Short versus long	/tuli/	'fire'	/tu:li/	'wind'

Consonant systems

It is not particularly useful to classify languages according to the number of consonants that they contain, since languages may have as few as eight consonant phonemes (as in Hawaiian), or more than ninety. (!Kung, a language spoken in Namibia, has ninety-six consonant phonemes.) Nevertheless, typological analysis of consonant systems has produced a number of well-substantiated universals.

- All languages have stops.
- The most common stop phonemes are /p, t, k/. Very few languages lack any one of these, and there are no languages that lack all three. If any one of these three stops is missing, it will probably be /p/; for example, Aleut, Nubian, and Witchita have no /p/ phoneme. The most commonly occurring phoneme of the three is /t/.
- The most commonly occurring fricative phoneme is /s/; few languages lack it. If a language has only one fricative, it is most likely to be /s/. This is the only fricative found in Nandi (a language of Kenya) and Weri (a language of New Guinea). The next most common fricative is /f/.
- Almost every known language has at least one nasal phoneme; in cases where a language has only one nasal phoneme, that phoneme is usually /n/ (as in Arapaho, spoken in Wyoming). If there are two contrasting nasals, they are normally /m/ and /n/.
- The majority of languages have at least one phonemic liquid. However, a small number of languages have none at all (Dakota, Blackfoot, which is spoken in Alberta, Saskatchewan and Montana , Efik, which is spoken in Nigeria, and Siona, which is spoken in Ecuador). English, of course, has two: /l/ and /r/.

Consonant phonemes are also subject to various implicational universals.

- If a language has voiced obstruent phonemes (stops, fricatives, or affricates), then it will also have voiceless obstruent phonemes. The reverse is not necessarily true; for example, Ainu (a language of northern Japan) has only voiceless obstruent phonemes: /p, t, k, tʃ, s/.
- Sonorant consonants (nasals, liquids, and glides) are generally voiced. Very few languages have voiceless sonorants and those that do always have voiced sonorants as well. For example, Burmese contrasts voiced and voiceless nasals and laterals.
- If a language has fricative phonemes, then it will also have stop

phonemes. There are no languages that lack stops; however, there are some languages that lack fricatives. For example, Gilbertese (Gilbert Islands), Kitabal (eastern Australia), and Nuer (south-eastern Sudan) have no fricative phonemes.

- Languages which have affricates will also have fricatives and stops. This is not surprising, since an affricate is, in essence, a sequence of a stop followed by a fricative. However, many languages lack affricates altogether. French, for example, has fricatives and stops, but no affricates. By contrast, English has all three.

Suprasegmental systems

Languages can also be classified according to their prosodic, or suprasegmental, type. Languages in which pitch distinctions are phonemic are called *tone languages*. (The phonetics and phonology of tone were introduced in Chapters 2 and 3.)

A great many of the world's languages are tone languages. Mandarin Chinese, for instance, has four contrastive tones as shown in Table 9.2.

Table 9.2   Tone contrasts in Mandarin Chinese

High level	dā	'build'
High rising	dá	'achieve'
Low falling rising	dǎ	'hit'
High falling	dà	'big'

The other Chinese languages as well as many languages of Southeast Asia, Africa, and the Americas also use tone contrastively. A few tone languages are also found in Europe; for example, in one of the dialects of Latvian, a three-way tonal distinction is made.

Table 9.3   Tone contrasts in Latvian

Falling	loks	[lùoks]	'arch, bow'
Level (high)	loks	[lūoks]	'green onion'
Rising-falling (broken)	loks	[lûoks]	'window'

As noted in the chapter on phonetics, tones are of two types, *level* tones and *contour* tones. Tone languages most often contrast only two tone levels (usually high and low); however, contrasts involving three tone levels (such as high, low, and mid) are also relatively common. Five or more levels of tonal contrast are almost unknown.

Tone systems, too, exhibit various universal tendencies.

- If a language has contour tones (such as rising or falling tone), then it will also have level tones (such as high, mid, or low tone). Burmese, Crow, Latvian, and Mandarin are examples of languages that fit this pattern. In contrast, languages with contour tones but no level tones (for example, Dafla, spoken in northern India) are very rare.

- If a language has complex contour tones (such as rising–falling or falling–rising), then it will also have simple contour tones (like rising or falling). Both the Mandarin and Latvian examples fit this pattern.

Differences in stress, discussed in Chapter 2, are also useful in classifying languages. **Fixed stress** languages are those in which the position of stress on a word is predictable. For example, in French and Mayan, stress always falls on the last syllable of a word; in Polish, Swahili, and Samoan, stress falls on the penultimate (second-to-last) syllable of words, while in Czech, Finnish, and Hungarian, it always occurs on the first syllable of a word. In **free stress** languages, the position of stress is not predictable and must be learned on a word-by-word basis. Free stress is also called phonemic stress because of its role in distinguishing between words. Russian is an example of a language with free stress.

Table 9.4 Stress contrasts in Russian

múka	'torture'	muká	'flour'
zámok	'castle'	zamók	'lock'
rúki	'hands'	rukí	'hand' (gen sg)

Syllable structure

All languages permit V and CV syllable structures (where V stands for a syllabic element and C for a non-syllabic element). These structures are assumed to be unmarked, since they appear in all languages. However, the universality of the CV structure is not merely due to its structural simplicity; the syllable structure VC appears to be equally 'simple', but it is not found universally. The presence of an onset (as in a CV syllable) is apparently more valued than the presence of a coda (as in a VC syllable), perhaps because an onset may help to signal the beginning of a new syllable.

In any given language, the structure of onsets may be different from that of codas. For example, in English, a nasal + stop sequence is permitted in a coda (in a word like *hand*), but not in an onset (there are no English words that begin with the sequence *nd*). However, Swahili has precisely the opposite restrictions: the *nd* sequence is permitted in onset position (in words like *ndizi* 'banana'), but not in coda position since Swahili syllables are coda-less – they can only end in vowels.

Differing syllable structure constraints can have interesting consequences when languages come in contact. For example, in Hawaiian only V and CV syllables are permitted. So, when a word is borrowed from a language like English, which allows more complicated syllable structures, vowels are inserted to produce the only allowed syllable structures. For example, when *Merry Christmas* was borrowed into Hawaiian, it was rendered as *mele kalikimaka*. (Of course, some consonant changes were made as well, since Hawaiian lacks /r/ and /s/ phonemes.)

Two implicational universals referring to syllable structure are presented below. Both deal with the relative complexity of permitted onsets and codas.

- If a language permits sequences of consonants in a syllable onset, then it will also permit single consonants or zero consonants in an onset.
- If a language permits sequences of consonants in a syllable coda, then it will also permit single consonants or zero consonants in a coda.

2.2

Morphology

Words and the morpheme are both cross-linguistically legitimate categories. However, there are clear differences in the ways in which individual languages combine morphemes to form words. Four types of systems are usually distinguished.

The isolating type

A language which is purely **isolating** or **analytic** would contain only words that consist of a single (root) morpheme. In such a language there would be no affixes, and categories such as number and tense would therefore have to be expressed by a separate word. For instance, in Mandarin Chinese, which is primarily an isolating language, the morpheme *le* is often used to indicate that an action was done in the, or is completed. Although this morpheme is thus semantically similar to a past tense morpheme in English, it acts just like an independent word since its position in a sentence may vary – it can be separated from the verb with which it is semantically associated.

3)

a. Ta chi *le* fan.
he eat past meal
'He ate the meal.'

b Ta chi fan *le*.
he eat meal past
'He ate the meal.'

Other languages that are primarily isolating include Cantonese, Vietnamese, Laotian, and Cambodian.

The polysynthetic type

In a **polysynthetic** language, single words can consist of long strings of roots and affixes that often express meanings associated with entire sentences in other languages. The following word from Inuktitut illustrates this.

4)

Qasuiirsarvigssarsingitluinarnarpuq.
Qasu -iir -sar   -vig -ssar -si -ngit -luinar   -nar   -puq
tired not cause-to-be place-for suitable find not   completely someone 3/sg
'Someone did not find a completely suitable resting place.'

Polysynthetic structures are found in many native languages of North America, including Inuktitut, Cree, and Sarcee.

The terms *isolating* and *polysynthetic* refer to two extremes: words consisting only of single morphemes versus words which can be complete sentences. Few if any languages are either purely isolating or purely polysynthetic. Rather, the vast majority of languages are **synthetic**, in that they admit words containing several morphemes. Two types can be distinguished.

The agglutinating type

An **agglutinating** language has words which can contain several morphemes, but the words are easily divided into their component parts (normally a root and affixes). In such languages, each affix is clearly identifiable and typically represents a single grammatical category or meaning.

Turkish words can have a complex morphological structure, but each morpheme has a single clearly identifiable function. In the words in Table 9.5, for instance, *-ler* marks plurality, and *-in* marks the genitive (which is used to indicate the possessor).

Table 9.5 Affixes in Turkish

køj	'village'	
køj-ler	'villages'	(plural)
køj-ler-in	'of the villages'	(plural, genitive)

The fusional type

Words in a **fusional** language can also consist of several morphemes. However, in contrast to agglutinating systems, the affixes in fusional languages often mark several grammatical categories simultaneously. In Russian, for example, a single inflectional affix simultaneously marks the noun's gender class (masculine, feminine, or neuter), its number (singular or plural), and its grammatical role (subject, direct object, and so on). The suffix *-u*, for instance, can be used to indicate that a noun belongs to the feminine gender class, is singular, and functions as direct object.

5)
mi vid^jim ruk-u.
we see hand-fem/sg/Ac
'We see a/the hand.'

This situation is typical of the entire Russian case system.

The distinction between agglutinating and fusional is sensitive to the number of 'bits' of information normally packed into an affix; in an agglutinating language, each affix normally contains only one element of grammatical or lexical meaning, while in a fusional language, affixes normally have several simultaneous functions.

Mixed types

Many languages, including English, do not belong exclusively to any of these four categories. English employs isolating patterns in many verbal constructions, where each notion is expressed by a separate word. Futurity, for instance, is indicated by the free morpheme *will* (rather than an affix) in structures such as *I will leave*. In contrast, English exhibits considerable agglutination in derived words, such as *re-en-act-ment*, which consist of a series of clearly identifiable morphemes, each with its own unique meaning and function. The English pronoun system, on the other hand, is largely fusional since a single form can be used to indicate person, number, gender, and case. The word *him*, for instance, is used to express a third person, singular, masculine direct object.

Implicational universals: morphology

A variety of generalizations can be made about word structure in human language.

- If a language has inflectional affixes, it will also have derivational affixes. For example, English not only has inflectional affixes such as the past tense *-ed* and plural *-s,* but it also contains derivational affixes like *un-* (*unhappy*, *unwanted*) and *-ly* (*quickly*, *slowly*).
- If a word has both a derivational and an inflectional affix (Table 9.6), the derivational affix is closer to the root. (DA = derivational affix; IA = inflectional affix.)

Table 9.6   The ordering of derivational and inflectional affixes

English					
friend-ship-s			*friend-s-ship		
Root DA IA			Root IA DA		
Turkish					
iʃ	-tʃi	-ler	*iʃ	-ler	-tʃi
work	-er	-pl	work	-pl	-er
Root	*DA*	*IA*	*Root*	*IA*	*DA*

- If a language has only suffixes, it will also have only postpositions. (As noted in Chapter 5, postpositions are the equivalent of prepositions in languages that place the head at the end of the phrase.) Turkish, for example, has only suffixes; as expected, it also has postpositions rather than prepositions. This is illustrated in the following sentence.

6)

ahmet ajʃe itʃin kitab-ɯ al-dɯ
Ahmet Ayshe for   book-Ac buy-Pst
'Ahmet bought the book for Ayshe.'

2.3

Syntax

Because we lack detailed descriptions for most of the world's languages, much of the work on syntactic universals has been restricted to the study of word order in simple declarative sentences such as *The women built the house*. Patterns are classified in terms of the order of the subject (S), direct object (O), and verb (V). The three most common word orders (in descending order of frequency) are SOV, SVO, and VSO. Over 95 per cent of the world's languages use one of these patterns as their basic word order.

7)

SOV (Turkish):
Hasan öküz-ü al-dɯ
Hasan ox-Ac buy-Pst
'Hasan bought the ox.'

8)

SVO (English):
The athlete broke the record.

9)

VSO (Welsh):
Lladdodd y ddraig y dyn.
killed the dragon the man
'The dragon killed the man.'

SOV, SVO, and VSO patterns have one property in common: in all three cases, the subject occurs before the direct object. The prevalence of this type of pattern may stem from the fact that the subject usually corresponds to the topic (what the sentence is about – Chapter 7, section 4.3), and therefore is more useful at an early point in the utterance.

Although an overwhelming majority of the world's languages place the subject before the direct object in their basic word order, this practice is not universal. There is a small number of VOS languages, the best-known example of which is Malagasy.

10)

VOS (Malagasy):
Nahita ny mpianatra ny vehivavy.
saw the student the woman
'The woman saw the student.'

As well, there are a very few OVS and OSV languages, all of which seem to be spoken in the Amazon basin of South America.

11)

OVS (Hixkaryana):
Kana yanɨmno bɨryekomo
fish caught boy
'The boy caught a fish.'

12)

OSV (Apurinã):
Anana nota apa
pineapple I fetch
'I fetch a pineapple.'

Word order universals

Sometimes, the order of elements within one kind of structure has implications for the order of elements in other structures. Many of these implications concern the relationship between the verb and its (direct) object.

- If a language has VO word order, then it will have prepositions rather than postpositions. Languages of this type include Berber (spoken in Morocco), Tagalog (the Philippines), Maori (New Zealand), Maasai (Kenya), Welsh, and Irish Gaelic.

  13) Irish Gaelic

  a. VSO pattern:
  Chonaic mé mo mháthair
  saw   I   my mother
  'I saw my mother.'

  b Preposition pattern:
  sa teach
  in house
  'in the house'

- If a language has OV word order, then it will probably have postpositions rather than prepositions. Languages with this structural pattern include Basque, Burmese, Hindi, Japanese, Korean, Quechua, Turkish, and Guugu Yimidhirr, an aboriginal language of Australia.

  14) Guugu Yimidhirr
  a. S–OV pattern:
  Gudaa-ngun yarrga dyinday.
  dog-Erg   boy   bit (Erg= Ergative, see Chapter 4, section 6.3)
  'The dog bit the boy'

  b. Postposition pattern:
  yuwaal nganh
  beach from
  'from the beach'

- PPs almost always precede the verb in OV languages, and usually follow the verb in VO languages.

  15) Japanese
  a. S–OV pattern:
  Gakusei-ga hon-o   yonda
  student-Nom book-Acc read
  'The student read a book'

  b. PP precedes verb:
  Taroo-ga   [PP nitiyoobi ni] tsuita
  Taroo-Nom   Sunday   on   arrived
  'Taroo arrived on Sunday.'

16) English

a. S–VO pattern:
   Hamish likes haggis.

b. PP follows verb:
   Georgina left [$_{PP}$ on Sunday].

- Manner adverbs overwhelmingly precede the verb in OV languages and generally follow the verb in VO languages.

17) Japanese (S–OV pattern, as seen in *15a)*):
   Manner adverb precedes verb:
   hayaku hasiru
   fast   run

18) English (S–VO pattern, as seen in *16a)*):

   Manner adverb follows verb:
   Sally runs fast.

- With respect to possessive structures, there is an overwhelming preference for Genitive + N order in OV languages, and a (somewhat weaker) preference for N + Genitive order in VO languages.

19) Japanese (S–OV pattern, as seen in *15a)*):
   Genitive structure precedes head N:
   Taroo-no   hon
   Taroo-Gen book
   'Taroo's book'

20) French

a. S–VO pattern
   Pierre aime Marie
   'Pierre likes Marie.'

b. Genitive structure follows head N:
   la maison de   Marie
   the house of (Gen) Marie
   'Marie's house'

English, although an SVO language, exhibits both Gen + N and N + Gen patterns:

21)

a. Gen + N pattern:
   Mary's friend

b. N + Gen pattern
   a friend of Mary

Examples like *21)* do not invalidate the universals we have presented, since these universals are intended to capture tendencies only.

Grammatical hierarchies

Implicational universals are often stated in terms of hierarchies of categories or relations. One of the most important hierarchies of this type refers to the grammatical relations of subject and direct object (see Chapter 5).

Hierarchies represent degrees of markedness, with the least marked option at the top and the most marked at the bottom. According to the hierarchy in Figure 9.4, then, a process that applies only to subjects is less marked than a process that applies to direct objects, and so on. Given the definition of markedness outlined at the beginning of section 2, this entails that if a particular phenomenon applies to direct objects, it should also apply to subjects. The converse, however, need not be true: it would not be surprising to find a process that applies to subjects but not to direct objects.

Least marked

> Subject
> Direct object
> Other

Most marked ↓

Figure 9.4 Hierarchy of grammatical relations.

Among the many typological phenomena that comply with this hierarchy is verb agreement, first mentioned in Chapter 4 (section 6.4). As the following examples show, there are languages in which the verb agrees with just the subject and there are languages in which it agrees with both the subject and the direct object. (3 = 3rd person, sg = singular, pl = plural, pst= past)

22)
Agreement with subject only (Spanish):

Subject
Juan parti-ó.
Juan leave-3/sg/Pst
'Juan left.'

23)
Agreement with subject and direct object (Swahili):

Subject   *Direct object*
Juma a- li- wa- piga watoto
Juma 3/sg Pst 3/pl hit children
'Juma hit the children.'

However, as predicted by the hierarchy, however, there are no languages in which the verb agrees with just the direct object.

2.4

Explaining universals

Linguists are still uncertain about how to explain the existence of many linguistic universals. Nonetheless, a number of interesting proposals have been made, and it is worthwhile to consider some of them here.

Phonology

Perceptual factors play a role in shaping phonological universals. For example, the fact that /s/ is the most commonly occurring fricative may have to do with its acoustic prominence: varieties of [s] are inherently louder than other kinds of fricatives.

Vowel systems (discussed in section 2.1) develop so as to keep vowel phonemes as different from each other as possible. A three-vowel system such as that shown in Figure 9.5 allows for plenty of 'space' around each vowel, which may make each phoneme easier to distinguish from the others.

i u

a

Figure 9.5 A three-vowel system.

The same holds true of stop phonemes. It may be that /p/, /t/, and /k/ are the three most common stops because they occur at three maximally distant places of articulation within the supralaryngeal vocal tract. These stops are perceptually much easier to distinguish from each other than a sequence of dental, alveolar and palatal stops, for example, all of which are produced in the central region of the oral cavity. (See Figures 2.1 and 2.4 in Chapter 2.)

It has been recently suggested that consonant systems in general respond to the articulatory pressures that give rise to unmarked sounds and systems. Thus, for example, articulatorily basic obstruents such as [p], [t], and [k] are found much more widely than more complex articulations such as [tɬ] and [qʷ]. Table 9.7 shows the set of obstruents that is exploited first cross-linguistically.

Table 9.7 Obstruents found cross-linguistically

p	t	k	ʔ
b	d	g	
f	s		h
	tʃ		

Languages tend to have consonant systems that consist of about 70 per cent obstruents and 30 per cent sonorants, no matter what the total size of their consonant inventories may be. These figures appear to reflect the kind of space that is available for consonant contrasts: more distinctions can be made among obstruents than among sonorants. There are, for example, no nasal fricative sonorants, because the air pressure needed to force air through the narrow articulatory opening characteristic of fricatives cannot be built up when so much air is flowing through the nasal passage at the same time. For reasons such as this, the number of obstruent consonants in any language is potentially larger than the number of sonorant consonants. This is just one example of how considerations involving articulatory complexity can play a role in the shaping of consonant systems.

Morphology

Other types of explanations may be appropriate for morphological universals. For example, the fact that languages with suffixes but no prefixes always have postpositions (section 2.2) may have a historical explanation. In these languages, some postpositions may have gradually become attached to a preceding word and thus eventually became suffixes. Because suffixes in such languages have evolved from postpositions, the link between the two elements can be traced to their common origin.

The requirement that derivational affixes occur closer to the root than inflectional affixes has another type of explanation. As noted in Chapter 4, derivation typically changes the category of the base to which it applies whereas inflection simply marks the subclass (for example, plural for Ns, past tense for Vs) to which a word belongs. Given that a word's category must be known before its subclass can be determined, it follows that derivational processes should precede inflection. This is reflected in word structure, where derivational affixes appear closer to the root than inflectional markers. In Figure 9.6, for example, the verbal root *treat* is converted into a noun by the affix *-ment* before the plural inflectional marker is added.

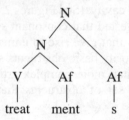

Figure 9.6 The structure of a word containing a derivational affix and an inflectional affix.

Syntax

At least some syntactic universals may be explained in terms of the way that the human brain processes sentence structure. Consider the summary of word order patterns in Table 9.8, which is based on the implicational universals discussed in section 2.3.

Table 9.8 Word order patterns

Constituents	Order in VO language	Order in OV language
P & NP	preposition–NP	NP–postposition
V & PP	verb–PP	PP–verb
V & manner Adv	verb–manner Adv	Manner Adv–verb
Gen & N	noun–genitive	genitive–noun

One recent explanation as to why the word order properties in the second and third columns cluster together involves contrast between right-branching and left-branching languages. In right-branching languages the more elaborate part of a phrase's structure occurs on its right branch; in left-branching languages, it occurs on the left. Thus, in Figure 9.7, a verb–object pattern is right-branching since a phrasal constituent (an XP) appears on its right branch, but an object–verb pattern is left-branching.

a) Right-branching (VO)   *b)* Left-branching (OV)

Figure 9.7 Right-branching and left-branching patterns.

As you can easily determine for yourself, the P–NP, V–PP, V–Adv and N–Gen patterns commonly associated with VO languages are also all right-branching (both genitives and adverbials are a type of phrase). In contrast, the NP–P, PP–V, Adv–V and Gen–N patterns typically found in OV languages are all left-branching. In other words, it seems that languages are fairly consistent in using one or the other type of branching structure. This sort of uniformity may make it easier for speakers and hearers to process syntactic structure. Thus, just as some human beings are right-handed and others left-handed, it appears that some languages prefer to use consistently right-branching systems, while others prefer left-branching systems.

The study of linguistic typology and language universals is a relatively new field within linguistics. There is obviously much still to be learned about linguistic universals, and it must be admitted that some of the current work is speculative and incomplete. No doubt many interesting new facts will eventually come to light.

3

GENETIC CLASSIFICATION

The world's languages can be grouped into a relatively small number of language families. However, genetic classification is sometimes difficult for a number of reasons.

Perhaps the biggest problem is simply the amount of data that must be collected before linguists can be confident about the status of a group of languages. It is only in the last three or four decades, for example, that enough information has been accumulated to propose a detailed classification of the languages of Africa. Many of the languages of South America, New Guinea, and Australia are still relatively unknown.

In many cases, linguists face the problem of establishing the tests or criteria to be used in proposing genetic relationships. There is some disagreement over the degree of similarity that should exist among languages before a genetic relationship can be proposed. This issue arises because unrelated languages are often typologically similar (that is, share structural characteristics). This is particularly likely if languages have been in contact long enough to have borrowed a large number of words, sounds, morphemes, or syntactic structures from one another.

Additional difficulties stem from the fact that genetically related languages need *not* be typologically similar. This is especially true if the relationship is a distant one, as is the case with English and Russian. Russian has numerous inflectional affixes, an extensive case system, and free word order, while English has relatively few inflectional affixes, virtually no case marking, and fixed word order. Yet, both belong to the Indo-European family.

To complicate matters even further, linguists also disagree as to the number of cognates that must be uncovered before a genetic relationship between languages can be established. The more distant the genetic relationship between languages, the less likely it is that a large number of obvious cognates will be found. Sound changes, for example, can obscure similarities between cognate words. English and Latin are related (though distantly), but the similarity between cognates like Latin *unda*, meaning 'wave', and English *water* is certainly not striking.

Matters are not helped either by semantic change which may mask the relatedness of erstwhile cognates. For instance, in Bantu we find the form *galo*, meaning 'arm' in Zulu and Xhosa, but 'finger' in Ganda, while in Swati, the apparently corresponding form -*kalo* means 'nail'. Whether 'arm', 'finger,' and 'nail' are sufficiently similar in meaning to warrant their treatment as cognates is open to some debate.

Assuming that cognates can be identified, the standard method of establishing genetic relationships is comparative reconstruction (also called the comparative method) which was introduced in section 7 of Chapter 8. Using this method, linguists can show that languages are genetically related if systematic sound-meaning correspondences can be established. Unfortunately, this task becomes increasingly difficult as the time depth increases. Reliable, systematic sound correspondences are barely establishable at a time depth of around 5000 years. If we go back 10,000 or 20,000 years or more, research is greatly hampered by the fact that words which may be excellent indicators of a genetic relationship can drop out of the lexicon. In fact, the problem of lexical loss obliterating the evidence may arise even at a shallower time depth. For example, Old English had a word *leax* ('salmon') which was cognate with German *Lachs* and Yiddish *lox*, but this lexical item has since been lost from native English vocabulary (although *lox* has, of course, been borrowed back into some varieties of English as the name for a popular delicatessen food). Since word loss is a common historical fact, linguists prefer to use the oldest available form of a language for their research; thus, our knowledge of Proto-Indo-European (see Chapter 8, section 7.4) is heavily based on Old English, Sanskrit, and Latin rather than their modern descendants: English, Hindi-Urdu, French, and so on.

Some language families contain many hundreds of languages; in other cases, only one language may remain to represent a family; in still other cases, families have become extinct. The following sections present some information about the makeup and membership of a few of the language families represented in the world today.

3.1

The Indo-European family

With only about a hundred languages, Indo-European is not a large family in terms of total number of languages. However, it is the largest language family in the world in terms of the total number of speakers: there are about 1.7 billion native speakers of an Indo-European language. Living Indo-European languages can be assigned to one of the nine branches illustrated in Table 9.9.[1]

Table 9.9 Main branches of the Indo-European family

Germanic	Hellenic	Baltic
Celtic	Albanian	Slavic
Italic	Armenian	Indo-Iranian

Germanic

The Germanic branch of Indo-European can be divided into three sub-branches. The East Germanic branch included Gothic, the oldest Germanic language for which written texts exist (dating from the fourth century AD). Gothic and any other languages belonging to this branch of Germanic have long been extinct. The North Germanic (or Scandinavian) branch originally included Old Norse (including Old Icelandic), a dialect of which was spoken by the Vikings. From it descended Icelandic, Norwegian, and Faroese (spoken on the Faroe islands, north of Scotland); the other North Germanic languages are Swedish and Danish.

The West Germanic branch includes German, Flemish (spoken in Belgium), Dutch, Afrikaans, Frisian, and English. Afrikaans is descended from the Dutch spoken by seventeenth-century settlers in South Africa (the Boers). Frisian is spoken on the north coast of Holland and on the Frisian islands just off the coast, as well as on the northwestern coast of Germany. English descended from the speech of the Angles, Saxons, and Jutes, Germanic tribes who lived in northern Germany and southern Denmark (in an area just east of the Frisians) before invading England in the fifth century and settling here.

Table 9.10 The Germanic family

(East Germanic)	North Germanic	West Germanic
(Gothic)	Icelandic	German
	Faroese	Dutch
	Norwegian	Frisian
	Danish	English
	Swedish	Afrikaans
		Yiddish

The organization of the Germanic family of languages is illustrated in Table 9.10. (In this and other tables, parentheses are used to indicate languages that no longer have any native speakers. The tables are intended to illustrate the organization and membership of language families; they do not necessarily provide a complete list of the languages in each family.)

Celtic

The Celtic branch of Indo-European (see Table 9.11) has two main sub-branches – Insular and Continental (now extinct). Gaulish, a member of the Continental branch, was once spoken in France but has long been extinct. The Insular sub-branch can be subdivided into two groups of languages: Brythonic and Goidelic. Brythonic languages include Welsh and Breton (which is spoken in northwestern France) as well as Cornish, which was formerly spoken in southwest England but is now extinct. The Goidelic branch contains Irish (or Irish Gaelic), which is still spoken natively in the western parts of Ireland, and Scots Gaelic, which is native to some of the northwestern parts of Scotland (especially the Hebrides Islands) and, to a lesser extent, Cape Breton Island in Nova Scotia in Canada.

Table 9.11   The Celtic family

Insular		Continental
Brythonic	*Goidelic*	
Welsh	Irish [= Irish Gaelic]	(Gaulish)
Breton	Scots Gaelic	
(Cornish)	(Manx)	

Italic

The Italic family originally consisted of a variety of languages spoken in the area corresponding roughly to modern-day Italy. The surviving members of the Italic family are all descended from Latin, the language of the Roman Empire, and are therefore called Romance languages. They can be divided into a Southern group (consisting of Sardinian and Corsican), an Eastern group (consisting of Italian and Rumanian) and a Western group, consisting of all the other Romance languages. The Western group is further divided into Ibero-Romance (Spanish, Portuguese, and Catalan) and Gallo-Romance, which includes the Romance languages spoken in France and Switzerland. These divisions are illustrated in Table 9.12.

Table 9.12   The Romance family

Eastern	*Western*		*Southern*
	Ibero-Romance	*Gallo-Romance*	
Italian	Spanish	French	Sardinian
Rumanian	Portuguese	Occitan	Corsican
Catalan	Romansch		

Hellenic

The Hellenic branch of Indo-European has only one living member, Greek. All modern Greek dialects are descended from the classical dialect known as Attic Greek, which was the speech of Athens during the Golden Age of Greek culture (500 to 300 BC). Hellenic Greek, which was used in subsequent centuries, was the language of commerce throughout the Middle East. (Hellenic Greek was also Cleopatra's native language; Egyptian was long extinct by her time.)

Albanian

The Albanian branch of Indo-European has only one member, Albanian, which is spoken not only in Albania, but also in parts of Yugoslavia, Greece, and Italy.

Armenian

The Armenian branch also has only one member, Armenian. This language is concentrated in Armenia (formerly part of the USSR, and located between the Black Sea and the Caspian Sea, in the area known as the Caucasus) and in northeastern Turkey.

Baltic

The Baltic branch contains only two surviving languages, Latvian (or Lettish) and Lithuanian. They are spoken in Latvia and Lithuania (located just west of Russia and northeast of Poland). Lithuanian has an elaborate case system, which resembles the one proposed for Proto-Indo-European.

Slavic

The Slavic branch of Indo-European can be divided into three sub-branches: East, South, and West. The East Slavic branch is made up of Russian (also called Great Russian), Ukrainian, and Byelorussian (or White Russian); the latter is spoken in Byelorussia, which is just east of northern Poland. The West Slavic branch includes Czech, Slovak, Polish and Lusatian (the last two both spoken in Poland). The South Slavic branch includes Bulgarian, Macedonian, Serbo-Croatian, and Slovene (or Slovenian). The latter three languages are all spoken in the former Yugoslavia. Note that although Alexander the Great was king of Macedonia, he spoke Hellenic Greek, not (Slavic) Macedonian; Slavic-speaking tribes did not move into the area until several centuries later. The organization of the Slavic group of languages is represented in Table 9.13.

Table 9.13   The Slavic family

East Slavic	South Slavic	West Slavic
Russian	Slovene	Czech
Ukrainian	Serbo-Croatian	Slovak
Byelorussian	Macedonian	Polish
	Bulgarian	Lusatian

Indo-Iranian

The Indo-Iranian branch of Indo-European is divided into Iranian and Indic sub-branches. The Iranian sub-branch contains about two dozen different languages, including Modern Persian (also called Parsi or Farsi, spoken in Iran), Pashto (the principal language of Afghanistan), and Kurdish (found in Iran, Iraq, Turkey, and Syria). Other Iranian languages are spoken in Pakistan, southern parts of the former USSR, and China.

Table 9.14 The Indo-Iranian family

Iranian	Indic
Persian [= Farsi]	Hindi-Urdu
Pushtu	Bengali
Kurdish	Panjabi
	Marathi
	Gujerati
	Romany [= Gypsy]

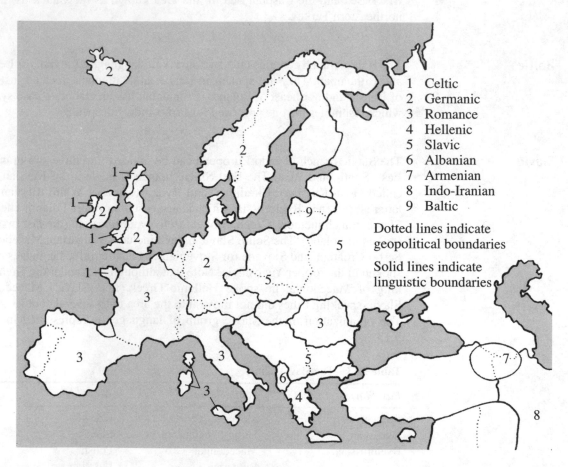

1 Celtic
2 Germanic
3 Romance
4 Hellenic
5 Slavic
6 Albanian
7 Armenian
8 Indo-Iranian
9 Baltic

Dotted lines indicate geopolitical boundaries

Solid lines indicate linguistic boundaries

Figure 9.8 Location of Indo-European languages.

There are about thirty-five different Indic languages. Most of the languages spoken in northern India, Pakistan, and Bangladesh belong to this branch of Indo-European. Some of the most widespread (in terms of number of speakers) are Hindi-Urdu, Bengali, Punjabi, Marathi, and Gujarati. Although Hindi and Urdu are two dialects of the same language, they have totally different writing systems and are associated with different cultures; Urdu is spoken principally in Pakistan by Muslims whereas Hindi is spoken primarily in India by Hindus.

Less well known as an Indic language is Romany, or Gypsy. It is believed that the Gypsies were an entertainment caste in India who were invited to perform in the Middle East some time in the Middle Ages. They never returned to India, but travelled instead to Turkey and, eventually, Europe. Romany contains many borrowed words – particularly from Greek, which was spoken in Turkey at the time of their stay. Table 9.14 depicts the organization of Indo-Iranian.

Figure 9.8 illustrates the geographic location of the Indo-European families identified in this chapter.

3.2

Some other families

Although no introductory text could hope to present a complete survey of all of the world's language families, some further discussion of this topic is warranted in order to illustrate the extraordinary diversity of human language (see Figure 9.9 on p. 402).

Uralic

The Uralic family (see Table 9.15) contains about twenty languages and has approximately twenty-two million speakers. Uralic languages are spoken in a band across the northern part of Europe, all the way from northern Norway to Siberia. Uralic has two major branches: Samoyedic and Finno-Ugric. The Samoyed branch contains a handful of languages spoken in the Arctic region of Russia, particularly in areas around the Ural mountains, and also in Siberia.

Table 9.15 The Uralic family

Finno-Ugric		Samoyed
Finnic	*Ugric*	
Finnish	Hungarian	Nganasan
Estonian	Ostyak	Selkup
Saame (Lapp)	Vogul	Nenets
Karelian		Enets
Livonian		
Vepsian		
Mordvin/Mordva		
Mari (Cheremis)		
Votyak		
Komi		

The most widely spoken Finno-Ugric language is Hungarian. Other Finno-Ugric languages are Finnish, Saame (also known as Lapp, spoken in northern Scandinavia and northwestern Russia), Estonian (Estonia), Livonian (Latvia), Karelian (eastern Finland and northwestern Russia), and Mordvin (or Mordva, spoken in the Mordva republic of the former USSR and other parts of Russia).

Uralic languages are primarily agglutinating and most have postpositions with SOV or SVO word order. The nouns often have many cases (Finnish has fifteen), which appear to have developed historically from postpositions that became attached to nouns as suffixes.

Altaic

Languages belonging to the Altaic family form a continuum from Turkey to Siberia, China, and possibly Korea and Japan. The membership of the Altaic family (see Table 9.16) is still very much in dispute, but it probably includes at least three branches: Turkic, Mongolian, and Tungusic. Recent scholarship has collected substantial evidence that Korean and Japanese are also members of the Altaic family. However, dissenting scholars argue that the similarities among Japanese, Korean, and the other languages in this proposed family are primarily typological, and that there are few reliable cognates encompassing the complete spectrum of the proposed Altaic family.

Table 9.16   The Altaic family

Turkic	Mongolian	Tungusic		
Turkish	Khalkha	Evenki	Korean	Japanese
Uzbek	Buriat	Chakar		
Azerbaijani				
Tatar [= Tartar]				
Uighur				
Kazakh				
Saxa (Yakut)				
Chuvash				

The best known Turkic language is Turkish, which is spoken by over forty million people. Turkish accounts for about 40 per cent of the speakers of Turkic languages. Other languages of this family (most of which are spoken in the former USSR) include Uzbek (Uzbekistan), Azerbaijani (Azerbaijan Republic and Iran), Tatar (Tatarstan and Kazakhstan), Uighur (China and Kazakhstan), Kazakh (Kazakhstan, China, and Mongolia), and Yakut (northern Siberia).

The Mongolian languages are spoken by around ten million people, primarily in Mongolia and China, while the Tungusic languages are found in central Siberia and Mongolia. The number of speakers of Tungusic languages probably does not exceed one million people.

Altaic languages are usually agglutinating, often with several suffixes in the same word. They normally employ SOV word order and typically use postpositions rather than prepositions. Many Altaic languages have vowel harmony, a phonological phenomenon in which all vowels of a word share certain features, such as [round] or [back].

Caucasian

The languages that are normally grouped together as Caucasian have not yet been assigned to families in a definitive way. These languages are primarily spoken in northeastern Turkey and in the southeast of the former USSR (between the Black Sea and the Caspian Sea, in and around the Caucasus Mountains). The best evidence so far points to three distinct language families – Northwest Caucasian, Northeast Caucasian, and South Caucasian (see Table 9.17). South Caucasian (sometimes called Kartvelian) consists of Georgian, Svan, and Laz-Mingrelian. Northwest Caucasian contains Circassian (or Kabardian) and Abkhaz, while Northeast Caucasian consists of about two dozen languages; of these, Chechen, Lezghian, and Avar have the largest number of speakers. Altogether there are about thirty-five languages in the three separate families, with a total of approximately five million speakers.

Although no genetic relationship has been proven to exist among these three families, they do seem to share a number of areal features (probably brought about through mutual borrowing): many Caucasian languages have glottalized consonants, complex consonant clusters, a large consonantal inventory, and very few vowel phonemes.

Table 9.17 The Caucasian languages

The South Caucasian (Kartvelian) family
Georgian
Svan
Laz-Mingrelian

The Northwest Caucasian family
Kabardian [= Circassian]
Abkhaz

The Northeast Caucasian family
Chechen
Lezghian
Avar

Dravidian

There are twenty-five Dravidian languages, which are primarily found in the southern half of India, but also in Sri Lanka, Pakistan, and Nepal. About a hundred and seventy-five million people are native speakers of a Dravidian language. The most widely spoken languages in this family are Telugu, Tamil, Kannada, and Malayalam (Table 9.18). Dravidian languages are normally SOV. They are agglutinating and non-tonal, and usually have initial stress.

Table 9.18 The Dravidian family

North	Central	South-central	South
Kurux	Kolami	Telugu	Tamil
Malto	Naiki	Savara	Malayalam
Brahui	Parji	Konda	Kannada
	Ollari	Manda	Kota
	Gadaba	Gondi	Toda
			Tulu
			Kodagu

Austroasiatic

The Austro-Asiatic family of languages (see Table 9.19) consists of about a hundred and fifty languages with approximately fifty million speakers. The Munda branch of Austro-Asiatic includes languages spoken in central and northeastern India, such as Santali and Mundari. Mon-Khmer is the largest branch of Austro-Asiatic and contains languages such as Cambodian (also called Khmer) and many other languages of Cambodia, Vietnam, Burma, and southern China. Other Austro-Asiatic languages are spoken in Malaysia and on the Nicobar Islands (northwest of Sumatra). Some Austro-Asiatic languages are tonal (for example, Vietnamese) and some are characterized by large and complex vowel systems. Word order is generally SVO or SOV.

Table 9.19 The Austro-Asiatic family

Munda	Mon-Khmer	Nicobarese
Santali	Vietnamese	Car
Mundari	Cambodian [= Khmer]	Nancowry
Ho	Mon	
	Khasi	
	Bahnar	

Sino-Tibetan

In terms of numbers of speakers, the Sino-Tibetan family (see Table 9.20) is the largest language family after Indo-European. There are about three hundred Sino-Tibetan languages, with a total of approximately seven hundred million speakers. There are two major branches: the Tibeto-Burman branch and the Sinitic branch. To the first branch belong the Tibetan languages, Burmese, and many other languages spoken in northeastern India, Nepal, Burma, and Tibet.

The Sinitic branch contains the languages that we call 'Chinese'. From a purely linguistic point of view, Chinese consists of several distinct, mutually

Table 9.20 The Sino-Tibetan family

Tibeto-Burman			Sinitic		
	Mandarin	*Wu*	*Min*	*Yue*	*Hakka*
Burmese	Mandarin	Wu	Taiwanese	Cantonese	Hakka
Tibetan			Amoy		
Sharpa			Hokian		
Newari			Fukian		

unintelligible languages. Yet, the speakers themselves, as well as linguists, normally call them 'dialects' for historical and cultural reasons – in particular because the same writing system is used across China and can be understood by speakers of different Chinese languages (see Chapter 15, section 4.1). However, the Sinitic branch contains several different languages (each of which may have a multitude of different dialects). For instance, Mandarin Chinese has dialects spoken in Peking (Beijing), Szechuan, and Nanking. The other major Sinic languages are Wu (with dialects in Shanghai and Suchow), Min (which includes Taiwanese, Amoy, Hokian, and Fukian), Cantonese (spoken in Hong Kong), and Hakka.

The Sino-Tibetan languages typically have SVO or SOV word order. The Sinitic languages are all tonal (as are many of the Tibeto-Burman languages) and are predominantly isolating. Morphemes generally consist of a single CV(C) syllable.

Austronesian

The Austronesian family contains over nine hundred (and according to some estimates over twelve hundred) languages which are spoken from the island of Madagascar, off the southeast coast of Africa, halfway across the world to Southeast Asia, Hawaii, Easter Island and New Zealand. Some of the languages of Taiwan also belong to this family; however, Taiwanese, which is spoken by most of the island's residents, is a Sinitic language (see above).

The largest branch within the Austronesian family consists of the Malayo-Polynesian languages. These include Malagasy (spoken in Madagascar), Malay (which is essentially identical to Indonesian), Tagalog (the basis for Philipino, the official language of the Philippines), Javanese, and hundreds of other languages spoken in Malaysia, Vietnam, Cambodia, and the islands of Indonesia. The Polynesians were intrepid ocean travellers and colonized Hawaii, Easter Island, and New Zealand, some time between 200 and 1000 AD. Well-known Malayo-Polynesian languages in the Pacific include Fijian, Tongan, Samoan, Tahitian, Maori, and Hawaiian (which now has fewer than one thousand native speakers).

Some recent research has confirmed earlier attempts to link the Austronesian family with the Austro-Asiatic family of India and Southeast Asia, and this relationship is now widely accepted.

One feature characteristic of Austronesian languages is the use of reduplication. Many of these languages also use infixes, a phenomenon which is extremely rare in other language families. Word order is usually SVO, although VSO is more prevalent in Taiwan, the Philippines and Polynesia.

Table 9.21 The Austronesian family

Formosan	Malayo-Polynesian		
	Western	*Central*	*Eastern*
Amis	Tagalog	Soboyo	Samoan
Bunun	Malay	Manggarai	Tongan
Paiwan	Javanese	Ngadha	Fijian
Puyuma	Malagasy	Tetum	Tahitian
Rukai	Sundanese		Hawaiian
Seediq	Balinese		Maori
Atayal	Cebuano		Gilbertese
Tsou	Chamorro		

Indo-Pacific

Indo-Pacific (or Papuan) languages are all spoken on the island of New Guinea, on nearby islands such as New Britain or Bougainville, or on the Andaman Islands (just southwest of Burma). Little is known about many of these languages, but they appear to be about seven hundred in number, with just under three million speakers. Two languages with relatively large speaker populations are Enga (a hundred and sixty-five thousand speakers, spoken in the western highlands of New Guinea) and Bunak (fifty thousand speakers, spoken on the island of Timor, west of New Guinea).

Indo-Pacific languages are normally tone languages. Nouns are often marked for case, but not always for number. Word order is usually SOV.

Australian

Recent studies have established that all of the aboriginal languages of Australia belong to the same family. There are about one hundred and seventy such languages, but many have very few speakers. There are currently only about thirty thousand speakers of aboriginal Australian languages.

The majority of Australian languages are spoken in Arnhem Land (north central Australia) and the northern part of Western Australia. The languages with the largest number of speakers are Mabuiag (seven thousand speakers on the Torres Straits Islands, north of Australia) and the Western Desert Language (five thousand speakers in Western Australia).

Australian languages are characterized by simple vowel systems. Nouns are normally marked for case, sometimes in unusual and intricate ways, and word order can be very free.

Afro-Asiatic

Afro-Asiatic languages (see Table 9.22) are spoken primarily in a band across the northern half of Africa and in the Middle East. There are about two hundred and fifty Afro-Asiatic languages and a hundred and seventy-five million speakers of these languages. Afro-Asiatic has five main branches of which one, the Egyptian branch, no longer contains any living languages. Although Old Egyptian was spoken from around 3000 BC onwards (including during the life of Ramses II, who was Pharaoh at the time of Moses), it was already a dead language by the time of Cleopatra.[2] Its descendant, Coptic, is now used only as the liturgical language of the Coptic church.

Table 9.22 The Afro-Asiatic family

(Egyptian)	*Cushitic*	*Berber*	*Chadic*	*Semitic*
(Coptic)	Somali	Tuareg	Hausa	Arabic
	Oromo	Tamazight		Modern Hebrew
		Shilha		Amharic
		Kabyle		(Babylonian)
		Zenaga		(Old Canaanite)
				(Aramaic)

A second branch of Afro-Asiatic is Cushitic, whose member languages are spoken in the Sudan, Ethiopia, Somalia, and Kenya. A third branch, Berber, includes several languages of Algeria, Morocco, and Niger, such as Tuareg and Tamazight. Still another branch of Afro-Asiatic, Chadic, contains many of the languages of Chad and Nigeria, such as Hausa. Unlike other Afro-Asiatic languages, Chadic languages are tonal.

The fifth and largest branch of Afro-Asiatic (in terms of number of speakers) is the Semitic branch. Many (now extinct) languages mentioned in the Bible were of Semitic origin, such as Babylonian (also known as Assyrian or Akkadian), (Old) Canaanite, Moabite, Classical Hebrew, and Biblical Aramaic. Biblical (or Palestinian) Aramaic was the language spoken in Palestine at the time of Jesus, and was probably his native language.

Classical Hebrew has not been spoken as a native language for two millennia, although it has been maintained as a written language by Hebrew scholars. Modern Hebrew (or Israeli) is not directly descended from Classical Hebrew; rather, it was created (or re-created) at the beginning of this century by regularizing some aspects of Classical Hebrew and adding new vocabulary. Modern Hebrew has only had a community of native speakers for the past few decades.

Still another Semitic language, Arabic, has various dialects, not all of which are mutually intelligible. Varieties of Arabic are spoken all across North Africa and throughout the Middle East. All of these are descended from Classical Arabic, which was the language of the Prophet Mohammed, the founder of Islam, and is the language of the Koran, the holy book of Islam.

The Semitic languages are characterized by a system of consonantal roots. Most roots consist of three (sometimes two) consonants, with vowels being inserted to indicate various inflectional and derivational categories (see Chapter 3, section 9.1 and Chapter 4, section 1.3). For example, Arabic has the root *k–t–b* (denoting the concept of writing) from which a variety of words

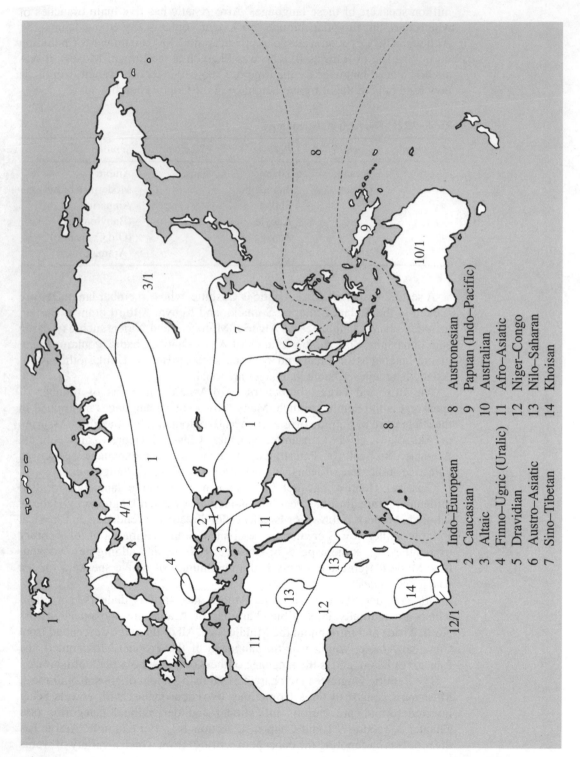

Figure 9.9   Location of some non-Indo-European language families.

1	Indo–European
2	Caucasian
3	Altaic
4	Finno–Ugric (Uralic)
5	Dravidian
6	Austro–Asiatic
7	Sino–Tibetan
8	Austronesian
9	Papuan (Indo–Pacific)
10	Australian
11	Afro–Asiatic
12	Niger–Congo
13	Nilo–Saharan
14	Khoisan

can be formed, including *kitaabun* 'book', *kaatibun* 'writer', *kataba* 'he had written', and *yaktubu* 'he will write'. The Semitic languages frequently have complex consonant clusters and pharyngeal or pharyngealized consonants.

Niger-Congo

Most of the languages spoken in sub-Saharan Africa belong to the Niger-Congo family of languages (see Table 9.23). In all, this family contains over 900 languages, with a total of approximately a hundred and eighty million speakers. It can be divided into nine major subfamilies: Mande, Kordofanian, Atlantic, Ijoid, Kru, Gur, Adamawa-Ubangi, Kwa and Benue-Congo.

Table 9.23 The Niger-Congo family

Kordofanian	Atlantic	Ijoid	Mande	Gur	Kwa	Adamawa-Ubangi	Benue-Congo	Kru
Koalib	Fula	Ijo	Bambara	Mooré	Twi	Banda	Yoruba	Grebo
Katla	Wolof	Defaka	Mende	Dagaari	Fante	Ngbandi	Igbo	Guéré
	Temne		Maninka		Ewe	Ngbaka	Efik	Bassa
	Drola					Zande	Bemba	Klao
	Manjanku						Kongo	
							Ganda	
							Swahili	
							Shona	
							Xhosa	
							Zulu	

The Atlantic branch of Niger-Congo contains west coast languages such as Wolof (Senegal) and Fula (Guinea). The Mande branch also contains many West African languages, such as Mende, Bambara, and Maninka. The Benue-Congo subfamily constitutes the largest branch within Niger-Congo. It includes the Bantu group of languages, which number over 200 and have more than 60 million speakers. Some of the principal Bantu languages are Swahili (Tanzania and Kenya), Zulu (South Africa), Ganda (Uganda), Shona (Zimbabwe), and Kongo (Republic of the Congo and Zaïre).

Niger-Congo languages are typically SVO and usually have tone systems (with the notable exception of Swahili). The Bantu languages are usually agglutinating with verb–subject and verb–direct object agreement. Languages in the Bantu group also exhibit a complex system of noun classes, each of which is marked by a distinctive set of prefixes.

Nilo-Saharan

The Nilo-Saharan family is found primarily in eastern and central Africa and includes approximately one hundred and twenty languages, with about thirty million speakers. Some of the languages in this family are Maasai, Luo (both spoken in Kenya), Nubian (Sudan), Kanuri (Nigeria), and Songhai (Niger and Mali). Nilo-Saharan languages generally have tonal systems, and nouns are usually marked for case.

Khoisan

The Khoisan family is quite small, containing only about thirty languages, spoken by a hundred and twenty thousand speakers. The majority of Khoisan languages are spoken in the southern and southwestern areas of Africa. Some Khoisan languages are Hottentot [= Nama], !Kung, and Sandawe (one of only two Khoisan languages spoken in eastern Africa). Khoisan languages have click sounds in their consonantal systems, which is unusual. These clicks have been borrowed by a few neighbouring Bantu languages, such as Zulu and Xhosa.

3.3

North, Central, and South America

Contrary to popular belief, not all native American Indian (also called **Amerindian**) languages belong to the same family. Although many of the relationships are still unclear, it appears that there are several different families in the Americas.

The major language families found in North (and Central) America are exemplified in Table 9.24.

Table 9.24   North, Central and South American families

Language family	Some member languages
Eskimo-Aleut	Inuktitut
Athapaskan	Navajo, Apache, Chipewayan, Dogrib
Algonquian	Cheyenne, Shawnee, Cree, Ojibwa, (Mohican)
Siouan	Crow, Winnebago, Omaha
Iroquoian	Seneca, Mohawk, Oneida, Cherokee
Caddoan	Caddo, Witchita, Pawnee
Wakashan	Makah, Nootka, Nitinat
Salish	Flathead, Spokan, Kalispel, Coeur d'Alene
Klamath-Sahaptin	Nez Perce, Sahaptin, Klamath
Penutian	Patwin, Wintu, Nomlaki
Muskogean	Choctaw, Koasati, Mikasuki
Hokan	Diegueño, Yuma, Mohave
Coahuiltecan	Comecrudo, Cotoname, Pakawa, Carrizo
Uto-Aztecan	Northern Paiute, Snake, Comanche
Otomian-Pame	Otomi, Pame, Pirinda, Mazahua
Mayan	Huastecan, Cholan, Maya, Tzeltal, Tojolabal
Andean-Equatorial	Quechua, Aymara, Arawak, Guaraní
Ge-Pano-Carib	Carib, Bororo, Witoto, Mataco
Macro-Chibchan	Cuna, Cayapa, Epera, Warao, Talamanca

The map in Figure 9.10 shows the geographic distribution of the widely accepted Amerindian language families and **isolates** of North America, an isolate being a language that cannot be shown to share a common descent with any other living language (see the end of this section). Of course, the political border between Canada and the United States is not a linguistic boundary. As

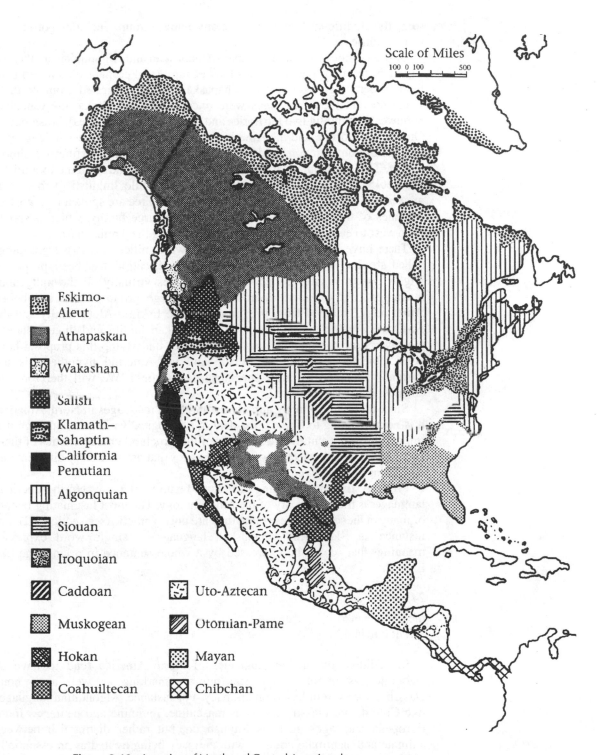

Figure 9.10   Location of North and Central American language groups.

seen, the traditional homeland of many native groups includes portions of both countries.

Of the families shown on the map, Athapaskan and Algonquian are the two largest in terms of the land mass they occupy (and perhaps also in terms of the number of speakers). The Athapaskan people migrated from north to south, so that their languages were once spoken in Alaska, the Canadian northwest (including two territories and four western provinces), Washington, Oregon, California, and the American southwest. The Athapaskan languages in Washington, Oregon, and California are now either extinct or almost extinct. The Algonquian languages of Canada are spread from the foothills of the Rocky Mountains to the Atlantic coast. While linguistic variation is greatest around the five Great Lakes, dialects of Cree are spoken in almost all localities of the Algonquian territory. Another large family, which is spread from west to east, is Eskimo-Aleut, spoken along the Arctic coast.

There have been attempts to place known families into larger groupings called **stocks**. Recently, a very daring classification has been proposed. Highly controversial, this classification places virtually all the indigenous languages of the Americas into a single large group, which is labelled **Amerind**. (Excluded from this group are the Eskimo-Aleut family and the Na-Dene, a stock consisting of the Athapaskan family and three isolates.) However, both the methodology and the data underlying this proposal have been subjected to severe criticism, and the Amerind hypothesis is not currently accepted by most specialists in the field. We will therefore not consider it any further here.

Since there are so many apparently unrelated languages in North America, it is not surprising to find a great deal of typological variation. Although it is impossible to present even a synopsis of the structural characteristics of these languages, a small selection of characteristics that are strikingly different and interesting will be given.

Probably the most striking structural features of many North American languages is the compexity of their morphology. The most fascinating feature of many of these languages is that they are polysynthetic (see section 2.2). For instance, in Slave (an Athapaskan language) a single word expresses meanings that would be expressed by a whole sentence in a language like English:

24)

mewõhníendiʔõ
'I lent it to him.'

In addition, the native languages of North America tend to have an elaborate system of person and number marking as well as a noun classification system based on animacy. For instance, Algonquian languages like Cree do not classify nouns as masculine, feminine and neuter as Indo-European languages such as English do, but rather distinguish between animate and inanimate nouns – with animacy being treated as an essentially grammatical concept so that men, pipes and ducks all count as animate.

Another type of classification is found in the verb system of Athapaskan. Every Athapaskan language has up to twelve classificatory verbs, the selection of which is governed by factors such as the shape, texture, and animacy of the referent of the subject or direct object. This set of contrasts may be viewed as a sort of noun classification system within the verb.

South America is home to at least six hundred different Amerindian languages, with a total of eleven million speakers. However, our knowledge of these languages is often minimal and some linguists estimate that there may actually be over a thousand South American Amerindian languages. Most of these languages belong to one of three families: Andean-Equatorial, Ge-Pano-Carib, and Macro-Chibchan.

The Andean-Equatorial family contains languages that are found throughout South America and may have as many as ten million speakers all together. The principal language in this family is Quechua, which has over six million speakers. Dialects of Quechua are spoken in Peru, Ecuador, and Bolivia. This was the language of the Inca empire, which reached its height in the sixteenth century AD, before being destroyed by the Spanish conquistadors. Other languages belonging to this family are Aymara (Peru), Arawak (Surinam), and Guaraní (the major native language of Paraguay). One of the interesting typological features of Andean-Equatorial languages is that some of them have no lateral consonants whatsoever.

The Ge-Pano-Carib family is also spread over much of South America. Some of the languages belonging to this family are Carib (Surinam), Bororo (Brazil), Witoto (Peru), and Mataco (Argentina). Languages of the Ge-Pano-Carib family also often lack lateral phonemes; the dominant word order in these languages is usually SOV.

Languages of the Macro-Chibchan family are found in Central America and the northwestern part of South America. Some languages belonging to this family are Cuna (Panama), Cayapa (Ecuador), Epera (Colombia), and Warao (Venezuela). Macro-Chibchan languages generally have SOV word order.

Language isolates

Although linguists have succeeded in placing thousands of the world's languages into families, there are still many other languages that cannot be so classified. A language that is not known to be related to any other living language is called an **isolate**. Basque, which is spoken in northern Spain and south-western France, is such a language. Examples of other language isolates throughout the world include Ainu (northern Japan), Burushaski (Pakistan), Kutenai (British Columbia), Gilyak (Siberia), Taraskan (California), and Yukagir (Siberia).

However, in recent years some linguists have claimed that all languages are ultimately related. Advocates of this position have attempted to set up a few, large macrofamilies to which all the languages of the world belong. Should this claim turn out to be valid, the idea of language isolates will have to be abandoned (see the next section).

3.4

Language phyla

In recent years attempts have been made to group many of the language families presented in sections 3.1, 3.2, and 3.3 into even larger groupings called **phyla** (singular **phylum**) or **macrofamilies**. These attempts are, as yet, extremely controversial, as they challenge established modes of thought within linguistics. However, they also afford a number of intriguing possibilities. In this section we will attempt to provide a balanced view of these ventures into long-range comparison.

One of the best known of the proposed phyla is Nostratic (also called Eurasiatic by some). It includes Indo-European, Uralic, Altaic and (depending on the linguist) various other languages and language families. A number of reconstructed forms have been proposed for this phylum; two of the most convincing are the reconstructed first and second person singular pronouns:

Table 9.25   Twelve phyla of the world's languages

1. Khoisan
2. Niger-Kordofanian
3. Nilo-Saharan
4. Australian
5. Indo-Pacific
6. Austric:
    a)   Austro-Asiatic
    b)   Miao-Yao
    c)   Daic
    d)   Austronesian
7. Dene-Caucasian:
    a)   Basque
    b)   North-Caucasian
    c)   Burushaski
    d)   Nahali
    e)   Sino-Tibetan
    f)   Yeniseian
    g)   Na-Dene
8. Afroasiatic
9. Kartvelian (South Caucasian)
10. Dravidian
11. Nostratic/Eurasiatic:
    a)   Indo-European
    b)   Uralic
    c)   Altaic
    d)   Korean-Japanese-Ainu
    e)   Gilyak
    f)   Chuckchi-Kamchatkan
    (g)   Eskimo-Aleut
12. Amerind

*m- 'I' and *t- 'you (sg)'. These forms are particularly persuasive, since pronoun systems are normally extremely stable, and thus are among the most likely forms to have remained constant for the extended period of time (about 20,000 years) since the existence of Proto-Nostratic .

Another proposed phylum is Dene-Caucasian. It includes Sino-Tibetan, Na-Dene, North Caucasian, and a number of other individual languages. A third proposal for a phylum is Austric, which would include Austro-Asiatic, Austronesian, Daic (the family to which Thai belongs), and the Miao-Yao group of languages.

If all of these phyla were to be accepted by linguists, the total number of linguistic groupings would be reduced to a mere twelve (as opposed to the fifty or more which have at times been proposed). Table 9.25 contains a list of the proposed phyla.

To take this approach still further, some linguists have gone so far as to reconstruct a single, common ancestor for all human languages, which has been called Proto-World or Proto-Sapiens. This putative ancestor language would have been spoken approximately 60,000 to 70,000 years ago. For the sake of interest, we provide a (simplified) example of one of the more than two dozen Proto-World etymologies which have been reconstructed to date. (It must be acknowledged that the semantic correspondences among the proposed cognates are rather loose.)

- Proto-World *mena 'to think (about)'. Proposed cognates: Latin men(s) 'mind', Basque munak (pl.) 'brains', Hungarian mon(-d) 'say', Telugu manavi 'prayer, humble request', Shawnee menw 'prefer, like', Bambara me 'know', Tumale aiman 'think', Songhai ma 'understand', Masa min 'wish'.

It is certainly possible that all human languages descended from a single ancestor language. It is generally agreed that all human beings are closely biologically related; indeed, recent genetic studies have proposed that all living human beings are descended from a particular woman of the species *Homo sapiens sapiens* who lived in Africa some 200,000 years ago.

Most linguists would probably agree that all human languages must have descended from a small number of languages, if not a single mother language. However, many argue that the tools used for reconstruction (the historical-comparative method) are not able to provide any linguistic evidence for long-range comparisons that go back more than about 8000 or 10,000 years. There are a number of reasons for this.

First, it is argued, the pronunciation and meaning of words can change radically over even a much shorter period of time, rendering cognates completely unrecognizable. Thus, Latin aqua [akwa] 'water' developed into French eau [o] 'water' in less than 2000 years, Proto-Indo-European (PIE) *dwo 'two' developed into Armenian erku 'two' in 5000 to 8000 years, and Old English hūswīf 'housewife' radically changed its meaning, to become hussy 'a strumpet, or trollop' in less than 1500 years. Of course, as noted in section 3 above, languages also lose words altogether, which can make it all the more difficult to uncover the cognates needed to establish a genetic relationship.

Another argument against long-range comparison has to do with the complications introduced by borrowings. For instance, for many years Thai was thought to be a Sino-Tibetan language, because it contained so many Chinese loanwords. However, painstaking research has finally made it clear that Thai is not Sinitic, but that it belongs to the Daic family.

A further difficulty arises when words that appear to be cognates may have evolved independently as instances of onomatopoeia. Since onomatopoeic words (e.g., *cuckoo*, *vroom*) are intended to sound like real world noises, it would not be surprising to find that such words would be similar even in unrelated languages.

Another argument against long-range comparison is that certain cross-linguistic similarities among sounds may stem from the fact that all human beings have the same vocal tract configuration. Thus, the presence of universally common sounds like / p t k s i a u / in suspected cognates may be due not to a shared ancestor, but rather to the fact that these sounds have articulatory and acoustic properties that favour their frequent use.

In defence of their endeavour, supporters of long-range comparison claim that loanwords and onomatopoeic words are easily identifiable by the experienced researcher, and can thus be easily discounted. Furthermore, they note, language change need not affect all of the words of a language; some words retain a similar meaning and pronunciation for thousands of years. Thus, Old English *fisc* [fɪʃ] apparently had the same pronunciation and the same meaning as modern English *fish* [fɪʃ], despite a lapse of 1500 years; Latin *aqua* [akwa] 'water' did not change its meaning or pronunciation in Italian: *acqua* [akwa] (2000 years), PIE **dwo* changed very little in pronunciation in Latin *duo* (about 6000 years), and PIE **nepōt* 'nephew, grandson' had a meaning and pronunciation almost identical to those of its descendant *nepot* 'nephew, grandson' in modern Rumanian (about 8000 years).

Supporters of long-range comparison claim that both anthropological and biological evidence show the relationship of all human beings and that it is therefore plausible to believe that all human languages must be related as well. It only remains, they claim, for linguists to determine the degree of relationship between individual families.

This controversy is far from being resolved, and it is fair to say that most linguists remain very sceptical about the evidence and conclusions associated with comparative research involving a time depth greater than eight or ten thousand years. Nonetheless, the debate has presented new and intriguing possibilities in the study of linguistic classification.

Summing up

The focus of this chapter is on the criteria that linguists use to classify languages, and on the enormous variety of languages found throughout the world. Linguists sometimes attempt to classify languages solely in terms of their structural similarities and differences (that is, in terms of their **linguistic typology**). Analysis of cross-linguistic data has identified a number of linguistic **universals**, indicating the most common characteristics of human language. The other major type of classificatory work in linguistics is concerned with genetic **relationships** – establishing language families whose members are descended from a common ancestor. While research in this area is hampered both by the large number of languages involved and the scarcity of the available data, a sizeable portion of the world's several thousand languages have been placed in families. Finally, we present the controversial work recently done on linguistic phyla or **macrofamilies**. Research in these areas can shed light on the nature of language change, as well as the movement of peoples throughout the world.

Notes	1 Hyphenated names for language families may refer to two major linguistic branches (for example, Sino-Tibetan) or to the two branches found at the end points of the family's geographical territory (for example, Indo-European). Single names often refer to a prominent geographical phenomenon (for example, Uralic – the Ural mountains and Altaic – the Altai mountains). 2 A descendent of one of Alexander the Great's generals, Cleopatra had Hellenic Greek as her native language.

Sources

The estimate that approximately six thousand languages are spoken in the world today comes from *Ethnologue: Languages of the World*, 11th edn, edited by B. Grimes (Dallas: Summer Institute of Linguistics, 1988). The suggestion that only three hundred of these languages have a secure future is due to K. Hale, professor of linguistics at MIT, cited in *Time* magazine (23 September 1991, p. 48). For further discussion, see 'Endangered languages' by K. Hale *et al.* (*Language* 68: 1–42, 1992).

The section on linguistic typology draws on data from the books by B. Comrie and J. Greenberg cited below as recommended reading. Other material for this section comes from *Tone: A Linguistic Survey*, edited by V. Fromkin (New York: Academic Press, 1978); J. Hawkins's article 'On implicational and distributional universals of word order', *Journal of Linguistics* 16: 193–235 (1980); M. Dryer's article 'The Greenbergian word order correlations', *Language* 68: 81–138 (1992); *Patterns of Sounds* by I. Maddieson (Cambridge: Cambridge University Press, 1984); M. Ruhlen's book *A Guide to the Languages of the World* (Language Universals Project: Stanford University, 1976); *The World's Major Languages*, edited by B. Comrie (Oxford: Oxford University Press, 1990), and the four volume series *Universals of Human Language*, edited by J. Greenberg (Stanford, California: Stanford University Press, 1978).

The discussion of morphological typology draws on information presented in B. Comrie's book recommended below; examples 7) to 10) are from this same source (p. 87). The estimate of the relative frequency of languages in which the subject precedes the direct object is based on information in the book by W. Croft recommended below. The data on OVS and OSV languages is from 'Object-initial Languages' by D. Derbyshire and G. Pullum, *International Journal of American Linguistics* 47: 192–214 (1981). The discussion of consonant systems in section 2.4 is based on 'Phonetic universals in consonant systems' by B. Lindblom and I. Maddieson in *Language, Speech and Mind: Studies in Honor of Victoria Fromkin*, edited by L. Hyman and C. Li, pp. 62–78 (New York: Routledge & Kegan Paul, 1988).

The section on language families is based on B. Comrie's book *The Languages of the Soviet Union* (London: Cambridge University Press, 1981); J. Greenberg's *The Languages of Africa* (Bloomington: Indiana University Press, 1966); C.F. Voegelin, and F.M. Voegelin, 'Classification of American Indian languages', Languages of the World, Native America fascicle 2, section 1.6, *Anthropological Linguistics* 7: 121–50 (1965); the book by M. Ruhlen cited previously, another book by Ruhlen entitled A *Guide to the World's Languages. Volume 1: Classification* (Stanford: Stanford University Press, 1987), and C.F. and F.M. Voegelin's *Classification and Index of the World's Languages* (cited below). The maps used to illustrate the geographic location of language families are adapted from those found in *The Origins and Development of the English Language* by T. Pyles and J. Algeo (New York: Harcourt Brace Jovanovich, 4th edn, 1992).

The Amerind hypothesis is presented by J. Greenberg in his book *Language in the Americas* (Stanford, Calif.: Stanford University Press, 1987). For some sample criticism see 'On Megalocomparison' by J. Matisoff, *Language* 66: 106–20 (1990).

The section on language phyla is based on the book by M. Ruhlen cited below as recommended reading, and on *Sprung from Some Common Source*, ed. by S. Lamb and E. Mitchell (Stanford: Stanford University Press, 1991).

The data for questions 1 to 3 are found in A *Guide to the Languages of the World* by M. Ruhlen, cited above.

Recommended reading   Comrie, Bernard. 1989. *Language Universals and Linguistic Typology.* 2nd edn. Oxford: Blackwell.

Croft, William. 1990. *Typology and Universals.* Cambridge: Cambridge University Press.

Greenberg, Joseph, ed. 1966. *Universals of Language.* 2nd edn. Cambridge, Mass.: MIT Press.

Hawkins, Peter. 1984. *Introducing Phonology.* London: Hutchinson.

Ruhlen, Merritt. 1994. *On the Origin of Languages.* Stanford: Stanford University Press.

Voegelin, C.F., and Voegelin, F.M. 1977. *Classification and Index of the World's Languages.* New York: Elsevier.

Questions

1. Which tendencies and universals are manifested in the following two vowel systems?

   a) *Afrikaans* (South Africa)

i	y		u
	ø	ə	o
ɛ			ɔ
		a	

b) *Squamish* (Washington State)

```
i        u
    ə
    a
```

2. As noted in section 2.1, the presence of long and nasal vowel phonemes is governed by implicational universals. Do the vowel systems below comply with the implicational universals that make reference to length and nasality?

a) *Maltese Arabic*

```
i        u        i:        u:
e        o        e:        o:
    a             a:
```

b) *Awji* (North New Guinea)

```
i        u        ĩ         ū
e    ə   o        ẽ    ə̃    õ
    a             ã
```

3. Consider the following consonant systems. To what extent do they comply with the implicational universals mentioned in this chapter?

a) *Tuhitian* (Tahiti)

```
p    t    ?
f         h
v    r
m    n
```

b) *Palauan* (Palau Islands)

```
     t    k    ?
b
     ð
     s
m         ŋ
     l, r
```

c) *Nengone* (Loyalty Islands, South Pacific) – Stop system only

```
pʰ  tʰ  tʰ     kʰ  ?
b   d   ḍ      g
m   n      ɲ   ŋ
m̥  n̥         ŋ̥
```

(*Note*: [ṭ] and [ḍ] are retroflex consonants; [̥] marks a voiceless nasal; [ɲ] represents a palatal nasal.)

d) *Mixe* (South Mexico)

p	t	k	?
	d	g	
ts	tʃ		
s		x	h
v		ɣ	
m	n		

4. Describe the morphological characteristics of each of the following languages in terms of the four-way system of classification outlined in section 2.2. (indic = indicative or statement)

a) *Swahili*
tu- li- som- a
we pst read indic
'we read'

b) *Latvian*

las-u	las-ām	rakst-u	rakst-ām
read-1sg/Prs	read-1pl/Prs	write-1sg/Prs	write 1pl/Prs
'I read'	'we read'	'I write'	'we write'

c) *Japanese*
gakusei-wa   homer-are-na-i.
student-Top   praise-Pass-Neg-Prs
'The student is not praised.'

5. Do a morphological analysis of the following data from Latvian. After you have segmented and identified the morphemes, describe how the data reflect the implicational universals in section 2.2. (j=[j])
   a) lidotājs   'pilot (nominative)'
   b) lidotāju   'pilot (accusative)'
   c) lidotājam   'to the pilot (dative)'
   d) lidot   'to fly'
   e) rakstītājs   'writer (nominative)'
   f) rakstītāja   'writer's (genitive)'
   g) rakstīt   'to write'

6. Note the following data from Malagasy, an Austronesian language spoken on the island of Madagascar. Does Malagasy comply with all the word order tendencies mentioned earlier in section 2.3?
   a) Avy any Amerika izy.
      comes from America he
      'He comes from America.'

   b) entin' ny labiera ny mpiasa.
      brings the beer   the waiter
      'The waiter brings the beer.'

c)   tanana-nay
      country our
      'our country'

7.   To which families do the following languages belong?

a)   Gujarati
b)   Hakka
c)   Lapp
d)   Uzbek
e)   Sandawe
f)   Huastecan
g)   Faroese
h)   Twi
i)   Santali
j)   Yuma
k)   Korean
l)   Kabardian
m) Koasati
n)   Aramaic
o)   Flathead
p)   Telugu
q)   Javanese
r)   Navajo

8.   Make a list of up to fifteen languages spoken by friends and acquaintances and identify the language family to which each belongs.

10

Brain and language

Gary Libben

The goal of neurology is to understand humanity

ை Wilder Penfield

In this chapter we will be concerned with the understanding of how language is represented and processed in the brain. This field of study is called **neurolinguistics**. Although the study of the relationship between brain and language is still in its infancy, much has already been learned about which parts of the brain are involved in various aspects of language production and comprehension. The field of neurolinguistics has also done much to deepen the way we think about the nature of linguistic competence.

The chapter provides a brief survey of brain structure and the methods that are currently available to study the brain. This is followed by a discussion of the different types of language disturbance that result from brain damage and by a discussion of how phonology, morphology, syntax, and semantics may be represented in the brain. The chapter concludes by reviewing the current answers to the important neurolinguistic question: Where is language?

1

THE HUMAN BRAIN

Contained within your skull is about 1400 grams of pinkish-white matter. It may be the most complex 1400 grams in the galaxy. For most of human history, however, the role of the brain as the centre of mental life remained completely unknown. Even the Greek philosopher Aristotle believed that its primary function was to cool the blood.

We now know much more about the structure and functioning of the brain. But in many ways we are still quite like Aristotle, finding it hard to believe that this wrinkled mass of nerve cells could be the stuff that dreams, fears, and knowledge are made of. Nevertheless it is, and the task of brain science (or **neuroscience**) is to understand how the breadth and depth of human experience is coded in brain matter.

The brain is composed of nerve cells or **neurons** that are the basic information processing units of the nervous system. The human brain contains about ten billion neurons that are organized into networks of almost unimaginable complexity. This complexity results from the fact that each neuron can be directly linked with up to ten thousand other neurons. But the brain is not simply a mass of interconnected neurons. It is composed of structures which seem to play specific roles in the integrated functioning of the brain. The following sections provide a brief overview of these structures.

1.1

The cerebral cortex

The brain encompasses all the neurological structures above the spinal cord and appears to have evolved from the bottom up. The lower brain structures are shared by almost all animals. These structures are responsible for the maintenance of functions such as respiration, heart rate, and muscle co-ordination that are essential to the survival of all animals. As we move farther away from the spinal cord, however, we begin to find structures that have developed differently in different species. At the highest level of the brain, the **cerebral cortex**, the differences are most pronounced. Reptiles and amphibians have no cortex at all, and the progression from lower to higher mammals is marked by dramatic increases in the proportion of cortex to total amount of brain tissue. The human brain has the greatest proportion of cortex to brain mass of all animals.

In humans, the cortex is a grey wrinkled mass that sits like a cap over the rest of the brain. The wrinkled appearance results from the cortex being folded in upon itself. This folding allows a great amount of cortical matter to be compressed into the limited space provided by the human skull (in much the same way as the folding of a handkerchief allows it to fit into a jacket pocket). It has been estimated that up to 65 per cent of the cortex is hidden within its folds.

It is the human cortex that accounts for our distinctness in the animal world and it is within the human cortex that the secrets of language representation and processing are to be found. The remainder of our discussion of brain structure, therefore, will focus on the features of the cerebral cortex.

1.2

The cerebral hemispheres

The most important orientation points in mapping the cortex are the folds on its surface. The folds of the cortex have two parts: **sulci** (pronounced /sʌlsaɪ/; singular: **sulcus**), which are areas where the cortex is folded in, and **gyri** (singular: **gyrus**), which are areas where the cortex is folded out towards the surface.

Figure 10.1 shows a human brain as seen from above, illustrating the many sulci and gyri of the cortex. A very prominent feature is the deep sulcus (in this case called a **fissure** because its size) which extends from the front of the brain to the back. This fissure is known as the **longitudinal fissure**. It separates the left and right **cerebral hemispheres**. In many ways, the cerebral hemispheres can be considered to be separate brains and indeed are often referred to as the left brain and the right brain. There are two main reasons for this: the first reason is that the hemispheres are almost completely anatomically separate. The main connection between them is a bundle of nerve fibres known as the **corpus callosum**, whose primary function is to allow the two hemispheres to communicate with one another.

Central sulcus
(Rolandic fissure)

Postcentral
gyrus

Precentral gyrus

Angular gyrus

Longitudinal
fissure

Front of
the head

Back of
the head

Frontal
lobe

Parietal
lobe

Occipital
lobe

Figure 10.1 The cerebral hemispheres seen from above the head. Note the many fissures and gyri of the cortex and the prominence of the longitudinal fissure, which separates the left and right hemispheres.

The other reason for considering the hemispheres to be separate brains is that they show considerable functional distinctness. In terms of muscle movement and sensation, each hemisphere is responsible for half the body – oddly enough, the opposite half. Thus the left hemisphere controls the right side of the body and the right hemisphere controls the left side of the body. These **contralateral** (contra = opposite, lateral = side) responsibilities of the cerebral hemispheres account for the fact that people who suffer damage to one hemisphere of the brain (as a result of a stroke or accident) will exhibit paralysis on the opposite side of the body.

The hemispheres also show functional distinctness with respect to higher cognitive functions. In general, the left hemisphere seems to excel in analytic tasks such as arithmetic, whereas the right hemisphere excels in tasks which require an overall appreciation of complex patterns such as the recognition of familiar faces and melodies.

Despite the fact that the hemispheres show such specialization, we should be cautioned against sweeping generalizations about left brain versus right brain abilities or strategies. In all probability, complex mental activities involve the coordinated functioning of both hemispheres. The representation of language in the brain provides a useful example of this.

Most right-handed individuals have language represented in the left cerebral hemisphere (Figure 10.2) and are therefore said to be left **lateralized** for language. But not every aspect of language is represented in the left hemisphere of right-handers. Adults who have had their left cerebral hemispheres surgically removed lose most, but not all, of their linguistic competence. They typically lose the ability to speak and process complex syntactic patterns but retain some language comprehension ability. Clearly, it must be the right hemisphere that is responsible for whatever language processing ability remains.

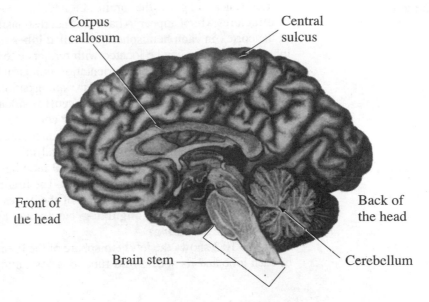

Corpus callosum

Central sulcus

Front of the head

Back of the head

Brain stem

Cerebellum

Figure 10.2   The left hemisphere seen from the inside. In this picture the corpus callosum has been cut so that one hemisphere may be separated from the other. Note how the grey cortex caps the lower structures (the brain stem and cerebellum) which are whitish in colour.

It has also been reported that right-handed patients who suffer damage to the right cerebral hemisphere exhibit difficulty in understanding jokes and metaphors in everyday conversation. These patients are able to provide only a literal or concrete interpretation of figurative sentences such as *He was wearing a loud tie*. They also frequently misunderstand people because they cannot use loudness and intonation as cues to whether a speaker is angry, excited, or merely joking. Thus the right hemisphere has a distinct role to play in normal language use.

Finally, a consideration of language representation in the brains of left-handers makes matters even more complex. Contrary to what might be expected, few left-handers have a mirror image representation for language (that is, language localization in the right hemisphere). Rather, they tend to show significant language representation in both hemispheres. Thus left-handers are generally less lateralized for language.

To sum up, although the left and right hemispheres have different abilities and different responsibilities, complex skills such as language do not always fall neatly into one hemisphere or the other. Research into why this is the case constitutes an important part of neuroscience. This research promises to reveal much about the cerebral hemispheres and about the individual representations and processes that comprise language.

1.3

The lobes of the cortex

We have seen that the cerebral hemispheres make distinct contributions to the overall functioning of the brain. In addition, each hemisphere contains substructures which appear to have distinct responsibilities. The substructures of the cortex in each hemisphere are called **lobes**. Like the hemispheres, the lobes of the cortex can be located with reference to prominent fissures, sulci, and gyri, which are useful as orientation points in much the same way that rivers and mountain ranges are useful in finding particular locations on a map.

As can be seen in Figure 10.3, the **central sulcus** (also called the fissure of Rolando) extends from the top of the cortex to another groove known as the **lateral fissure** (also called the Sylvian fissure). These two features are important in the delineation of the cerebral lobes. The **frontal lobe** lies in front of the central sulcus and the **parietal lobe** lies behind it. The **temporal lobe** is the area beneath the lateral fissure. The fourth lobe, the **occipital lobe**, is not clearly marked by an infolding of the cortex, but can be identified as the area to the rear of the **angular gyrus** (which has been found to play an important role in reading).

Figure 10.3 shows the left hemisphere of the brain. It indicates the location of each lobe and its specialized functions. Assuming that this is the brain of

Frontal lobe
Planning
Prediction
Speech
Discrete movements
of the body

Central
sulcus

Parietal lobe
Reading ability
Sensation of
–pain
–temperature
–touch
–pressure
–taste

Angular
gyrus

Lateral
fissure

Temporal lobe
Audition
Memory processing
Sensory integration

Occipital lobe
Visual processing

Figure 10.3   The left hemisphere seen from the outside.

a right-hander, it is also possible to identify those areas of the cortex that have a particular role to play in language processing, as we will see.

2

INVESTIGATING THE BRAIN

Imagine that you could open the top of a living human being's skull and observe the brain while the individual is engaged in activities such as reading, writing, watching a football match, or having a heated argument. What would you see? The answer is – nothing! To the outside observer, the working brain shows no evidence of its activity. This is clearly a problem for the field of neurolinguistics, which requires the use of special investigative techniques to uncover the secrets of where and how language is processed in the brain. In addition, these special techniques must meet the stringent ethical requirements of research with human subjects. While other neuroscientists are able to do much of their research using animal subjects (which raise ethical questions in a somewhat less acute manner) this option is not available to neurolinguists.

Imposing as they may be, the problems of investigating the processing of language in the brain are not insurmountable. Recent decades have seen a number of technological advances which have greatly facilitated the investigation of the question: What is going on in the brain when people are engaged in language behaviour? In the following sections, we discuss some of the techniques of neurolinguistic investigation.

2.1

Autopsy studies

Until recently the only way to study the brain was through **autopsy** (or **post-mortem**) **studies**. This technique was most often carried out with patients who were admitted to hospital displaying a neurological disorder. Careful observations were made of a patient's behaviour, and subsequent to his or her death, the brain was examined to determine which areas were damaged. By comparing the area of brain damage and the type of disorder the patient displayed while alive, neurologists could develop theories about the role of the damaged brain parts in normal brain functioning.

A famous example of this type of analysis comes from the work of Paul Broca, a nineteenth-century French neurologist. In 1860, Broca observed a patient who had been hospitalized for over twenty years in Paris. For most of his hospitalization, the patient was almost completely unable to speak, but appeared to understand everything that was said to him. Towards the end of his life (he died at age 57) the patient also developed a paralysis of the right arm and leg. Immediately after his death (as a result of an unrelated infection) Broca examined the brain. It showed severe damage (called a **lesion**) in the lower rear area of the left frontal lobe.

Broca concluded that because the patient was unable to speak, this part of the frontal lobe must normally be responsible for speech production. Since that time, many other autopsy studies have supported Broca's conclusions. This lower rear portion of the left frontal lobe is now called **Broca's area** (see Figure 10.4 overleaf which shows this and other language-processing areas of the left hemisphere). As will be discussed in section 3.1, the impairment of the ability to speak as a result of brain damage is called **Broca's aphasia**.

Precentral gyrus   Central sulcus   Postcentral gyrus

Angular gyrus
Reading

Broca's area
Speech
production

Wernicke's area
Language
comprehension

Figure 10.4   Language processes in the left hemisphere. Damage to Broca's area is usually associated with non-fluent speech and difficulty in processing complex syntactic patterns. Damage to Wernicke's area is usually associated with comprehension disturbances. Damage to the area around the angular gyrus results in reading impairment.

2.2

Images of the living brain

Autopsy analysis has been and continues to be an important tool in the understanding of the brain. But an autopsy can only be carried out after the patient's death. Therefore, whatever information it reveals about the nature and extent of the patient's brain damage comes too late to be of any use in treating the patient.

Computerized Axial Tomography (also called **CT scanning**) is a relatively new technique which uses a narrow beam of X-rays to create brain images that take the form of a series of brain slices. CT scans have offered neuroscientists their first opportunity to look inside a living brain. However, like autopsy, CT scanning provides a static image of the brain. It is most useful in identifying brain lesions and tumours.

Recently a number of new techniques have emerged that also make it possible to study the brain in action. One such technique is **Positron Emission Tomography** (**PET**). PET capitalizes on one of the brain's many interesting properties – it is extremely hungry for oxygen. Although the brain accounts for only about 2 per cent of total body weight, it consumes about 20 per cent of the oxygen the body uses while at rest. This oxygen is, of course, carried to the brain by the blood. What is important for this technique is the fact that the areas of the brain that are most active during any particular activity require more oxygen to be transported to them.

In a PET experiment, a subject inhales a minute quantity of some radioactive gas, or is injected with a safe dose of radioactive fluid (glucose or water) – which soon renders the blood radioactive. The subject then places his or her head in a device fitted with gamma-ray detectors. Since the blood is (momentarily) radioactive, the detectors are able to register the intensity of radiation in various parts of the brain, which directly reflects the amount of blood going to those areas. Cerebral metabolic activity can then be modelled by a computer program which displays a picture, with bright colours – reds and yellows – indicating the areas of intense activity, and dull indigos representing areas that are less active. By comparing the computer-generated pictures of the brain when the subject is listening to non-linguistic sounds like bird song or taking in non-linguistic visual information (say by watching a film of city traffic) with pictures obtained when the subject engages in linguistic behaviour such as reading, listening to speech or talking, neurologists can see which areas of the brain play a role in language comprehension, processing and production.

Cerebral blood flow studies have greatly increased our knowledge of where language processing takes place in the brain. It has been found, for example, that when subjects speak, much blood flows to the left hemisphere of the cortex and to Broca's area in particular. When subjects read, much blood flows to the occipital lobe (because it is responsible for visual processing), to the angular gyrus (which has a special role to play in reading), and to other areas of the left hemisphere. These observations support the view that the left hemisphere is primarily responsible for language and that there are specific language areas within the left hemisphere.

2.3

Learning from hemispheric connections and disconnections

In the techniques that have been described, information about language representation in the brain is gained through an investigation of the brain itself. In this section, we review an alternate approach – one which examines behaviour that can be associated with a particular brain hemisphere.

Dichotic listening studies

Dichotic listening studies have been extremely important in the accumulation of the knowledge we possess about the specialization of the cerebral hemispheres. The technique capitalizes on the property of the brain which we have discussed in section 1.2, namely, that each hemisphere is primarily wired to the opposite side of the body (including the head). So, most of the input to your right ear goes to the left hemisphere of your brain. Now, if the left cerebral hemisphere is indeed specialized for language processing in right-handers, these individuals should process language better through the right ear.

If you are right-handed, you will most probably be able to verify this by observing the difference between holding a telephone receiver to your right ear and holding it to your left ear during a conversation. When the receiver is held to the right ear, it will appear that the speech is louder and clearer. This phenomenon is known as the **right ear advantage (REA)**. In the laboratory technique, stereo earphones are used and different types of stimuli are presented to each ear. In general, the right ear shows an advantage for words, numbers, and Morse code, whereas the left ear shows an advantage for the perception of melodies and environmental sounds such as bird songs.

Split brain studies

If the left hemisphere is wired to the right ear, why is it possible to understand speech presented to the left ear? There are two reasons for this. The first is that the auditory pathways to the brain are not completely crossed – there are also secondary links between each hemisphere and the ear on the same side of the body. The second is that after the right hemisphere receives information from the left ear, that information can be transferred to the left hemisphere via the corpus callosum – the bundle of fibres that connects the two hemispheres.

Evidence concerning the crucial role that the corpus callosum plays in normal brain functioning comes from the study of patients who have had this pathway surgically severed.[1] Studies that have investigated the effects of this surgery on cognition are referred to as **split brain experiments**. They have provided dramatic illustrations of what happens when the hemispheres cannot communicate with one another.

It appears from the behaviour of split brain patients that although the right hemisphere does show some language understanding, it is mute. In one of the many split brain experiments, a patient is blindfolded and an object (for example, a key) is placed in one hand. When the key is held in the right hand, the patient can easily name it, because the right hand is directly connected to the left hemisphere, which can compute speech output. However, when the key is placed in the left hand, the patient cannot say what it is. The right hemisphere, which receives information from the left hand, knows what is there, but it can neither put this into words nor transfer the information across the severed corpus callosum to the left brain.

Split brain experiments have presented new and important knowledge about the functioning of the brain. In terms of overall investigative methodology, however, they are not quite as exotic as they seem. In fact, the logic of split brain experiments is identical to the logic employed by Broca in 1860. In both cases the researcher endeavours to learn how the normal brain works by examining which functions are lost as a result of the brain damage. In the case of split brain studies, the damage is surgically induced. In the case of Broca's patient, disease caused an experiment in nature. In the following section, we return to these experiments in nature and examine what they reveal about language representation in the brain.

3

APHASIA

Occasionally, humans suffer damage to particular parts of their brains. The most common cause of such brain damage is a **stroke** (also called a **cerebrovascular accident**). A language deficit caused by damage to the brain is called **aphasia**. The study of aphasia is by far the most important tool in the investigation of language in the brain. By observing and documenting the varieties of aphasic symptoms, neurolinguists have the best chance of identifying the major components of language in the brain.

In general, the amount and type of aphasic disturbance that a patient will exhibit depends on how much the brain is damaged and where it is damaged. There are many varieties of aphasia. In the following sections, we will describe some of the more important types.

C.S. Moss was a psychologist who became aphasic subsequent to a stroke. He later wrote a book about the experience entitled *Recovering with Aphasia*. The following is an excerpt from that book:

I recollect trying to read the headlines of the *Chicago Tribune* but they didn't make any sense to me at all. I didn't have difficulty focusing; it was simply that the words, individually or in combination, didn't have meaning, and even more amazing, I was only a trifle bothered by that fact. . . .

The second week I ran into a colleague who happened to mention that it must be very frustrating for me to be aphasic since prior to that I had been so verbally facile. [I] later found myself wondering why it was not. I think part of the explanation was relatively simple. If I had lost the ability to converse with others, I had also lost the ability to engage in self-talk. In other words, I did not have the ability to think about the future – to worry, to anticipate or perceive it – at least not with words.

It took a great deal of effort to keep an abstraction in mind. For example, in talking with the speech therapist I would begin to give a definition of an abstract concern, but as I held it in mind it would sort of fade, and chances were that I would end up giving a simplified version rather than the one at the original level of conception. It was as though giving an abstraction required so much of my added intelligence that halfway through the definition I would run out of energy available to me and regress to a more concrete answer.

A consideration of Moss's recollections leads to some provocative questions about the relationship between language and thought. Is it possible that the ability to think about the future is dependent on language? Does language support abstract thought?

The type of aphasia that Moss reports involves a mixture of deficits – speaking, listening, reading, and writing. Some other forms of aphasia, however, are much more specific. In these more specific forms, particular skills are lost, and others remain intact. The study of the specific aphasias can tell us much about the building blocks of language in the brain. Sections 3.1 and 3.2 discuss the two most important specific aphasias.

3.1

Non-fluent aphasia

Non-fluent aphasia (also called **motor aphasia**) results from damage to parts of the brain in front of the central sulcus. Recall that an important part of the frontal lobe is concerned with motor activity and that the bottom rear portion of the frontal lobe (Broca's area) is responsible for the articulation of speech (see Figure 10.4). Not surprisingly, therefore, non-fluent patients show slow effortful speech production (hence the term *non-fluent*). The most severe form of non-fluent aphasia is **global aphasia**. In this type of aphasia, the patient is completely mute. Of the less severe forms, **Broca's aphasia** is the most important.

The speech of Broca's aphasics is very halting. Patients have great difficulty in accurately producing the needed phonemes to say a word. For example, an Edinburgh patient who wishes to produce the sentence in *1a)* would be likely to produce the utterance in *1b)*.

1)

a. 'It's hard to eat with a spoon.'

b. [. . . har i:t . . . wɪt . . . pun]

The ellipsis dots (. . .) between the words in *1b)* indicate hesitation – periods of silence in the production of the utterance. Utterances produced at this slow rate tend to also lack normal sentence intonation. This is a common characteristic of the speech of Broca's aphasics and is called **dysprosody**. Note how the patient, who speaks Scottish English (which is a rhotic dialect, see page 349) and would normally have pronounced *hard* as [hard], simplifies the consonant cluster at the end of this word by dropping the [d]. Similarly, in the word *spoon* the word-initial cluster is simplified by deleting the [s]. In addition, the patient also changes the /θ/ to /t/ in the word *with*. The speech errors which result from these sorts of phonemic errors are called **phonemic paraphasias**.

It is tempting to think that the impairment of speech production in Broca's aphasia is caused by the fact that Broca's area is adjacent to the motor strip that controls movement of the facial muscles. The problem with this hypothesis is that damage to Broca's area usually only produces mild weakness of the muscles on the opposite side of the face and no permanent damage. Yet, for some reason, even people who can still control the muscles used in speech cannot use language properly after damage to Broca's area. This suggests that Broca's area has a language specific responsibility.

Broca's aphasia as a syntactic disorder

Returning to the utterance in *1b)*, note that the patient also omits a number of words that would normally be used in this utterance. The words that are omitted are: *it*, *is*, *to*, *a* – the sorts of words that we too would be likely to omit if we were writing a telegram (for example, *I will meet you in the airport lounge* → *Meet you in airport lounge*). These 'little words' are often called **function words** and their omission in the speech of Broca's aphasics has been referred to as **telegraphic speech**. (We will return to the problem of determining which items belong to the set of function words in section 5.)

One possible account of the speech of Broca's aphasics is that it results from an economy of effort. Speech production is very effortful for these patients so they use as few words as possible because, like telegram writers, they are 'paying' by the word. But there are other characteristics of their linguistic abilities that point to a deeper cause – the disturbance of syntactic competence.

In addition to omitting function words, Broca's aphasics tend to omit inflectional affixes such as *-ing*, *-ed*, and *-en* in words such as *running*, *chased*, and *broken*. They also show difficulty judging the grammaticality of sentences. For example, given sentences such as the ones in *2)*, Broca's aphasics will not always be able to determine which ones are grammatical and which ones are not.

2)

a. The boy ate it up.

b. * The boy ate up it.

c. * Boy ate it up.

d. The boy ate up the cake.

Finally, a close examination of the comprehension of Broca's aphasics offers further support to the view that there is a syntactic component to the disorder. The nature of the problem will become clear when we consider the following sentences:

3)

a. The mouse was chased by the cat.

b. The dog was chased by the ostrich.

c. The cat was chased by the mouse.

Broca's aphasics tend to interpret sentences such as *3a)* correctly. In a sentence such as this, knowledge about the typical behaviour of cats and mice helps the patient to guess correctly at the meaning of the sentence. For sentences such as *3b)*, however, in which knowledge of the world is not a reliable guide to comprehension, patients are unsure about the meaning. Finally, Broca's aphasics tend to interpret a sentence such as *3c)* as though it had the same meaning as *3a)*. When we read a sentence like *3c)*, we recognize it as describing an unlikely event, but our interpretation is driven by the syntax of the sentence, not by our knowledge of the world. Many Broca's aphasics appear not to have this ability.

These sorts of observations have led many neurolinguists to reconsider the traditional view that Broca's aphasia is simply a production deficit. The possibility that Broca's aphasia also involves some central disturbance of syntactic competence is intriguing and may lead to a deeper understanding of how syntactic knowledge is represented in the brain. We will return to this question in section 5.

A final point about Broca's aphasia is of a less technical nature but is of great importance to the understanding of the syndrome as a whole. Unlike patients such as C.S. Moss, Broca's aphasics are acutely aware of their language deficit and are typically very frustrated by it. It is as though they have complete understanding of what they should say, but to their constant dismay, find themselves unable to say it. This plight of Broca's aphasics is consistent with our understanding of the role of the frontal lobe, which is usually the site of lesion in the syndrome. Broca's area of the frontal lobe plays an extremely important role in language; however, it does not seem to be involved in the semantic relationships between words and the relationship between units of language and units of thought. The neurological basis of these meaning relationships remains almost entirely unknown. From the analysis of non-fluent aphasia in general and Broca's aphasia in particular, however, we suspect that these semantic relationships are the responsibility of areas of the brain that lie behind the central sulcus–in the temporal and parietal lobes of the brain (see Figure 10.3). This suspicion is supported by the type of language deficits associated with damage to the temporal–parietal lobes.

3.2

Fluent aphasia

The type of aphasia which results from damage to parts of the left cortex behind the central sulcus is referred to as **fluent aphasia** (or **sensory aphasia**). This type of aphasia stands in sharp contrast to non-fluent aphasia. Fluent aphasics have no difficulty producing language, but have a great deal of difficulty selecting, organizing, and monitoring their language production.

The most important type of fluent aphasia is called **Wernicke's aphasia**. The syndrome is named after the German physiologist, Carl Wernicke, who in 1874 published a now famous report of a kind of aphasia that was almost the complete opposite of Broca's aphasia. It was determined from autopsy data that this type of aphasia was associated with a lesion in the temporal lobe just below the most posterior (rear) portion of the lateral fissure. In severe cases, the lesion could also extend upwards into the lower portion of the parietal lobe. This area of the brain is now known as Wernicke's area (see Figure 10.4).

In contrast to Broca's aphasics, Wernicke's aphasics are generally unaware of their deficit. Their speech typically sounds very good: there are no long pauses; sentence intonation is normal; function words are used appropriately; word order is usually syntactically correct. The problem is that the patient rarely makes any sense. The following is a conversation between an examiner (*E*) and a Wernicke's patient (*P*).

4)

E: How are you today, Mrs A?

P: Yes.

E: Have I ever tested you before?

P: No. I mean I haven't.

E: Can you tell me what your name is?

P: No, I don't I . . . right I'm right now here.

E: What is your address?

P: I cud /kʌd/ if I can help these this like you know . . . to make it.
       We are seeing for him. That is my father.

The patient in this conversation produces a number of errors. But note that most of these errors are different in kind from the errors of Broca's aphasia. While the patient is able to produce some well-formed structures (for example, *No, I don't*), these structures appear intermittently amidst various unrelated fragments. Not only are these constructions unrelated to each other, they are also totally irrelevant to the examiner's questions. It appears that the patient has no understanding of the questions being asked.

This patient displays a significant but not severe form of Wernicke's aphasia. Her speech appears to result from a semi-random selection of words and short phrases. In very severe cases of this syndrome, phonemes are also randomly selected and the result is speech that has the intonational characteristics of English but actually contains very few real words of the language. This is termed **jargonaphasia**.

The type of deficit found in Wernicke's aphasia leads us to a greater understanding of the role of the temporal–parietal area of the brain known as Wernicke's area and to a deeper consideration of the nature of language comprehension. Wernicke's aphasia is primarily a comprehension deficit. But as we have seen, when comprehension breaks down, most of what we call language ability breaks down with it. Patients cannot express themselves because they cannot understand what they have just said and use that understanding in the planning of what to say next. In a very real sense, these patients have lost contact with themselves (and therefore with the rest of the world). Wernicke's patients cannot have coherent trains of thought – the brain damage does not allow the elements of the train to be connected.[2]

In summary, our discussion of fluent and non-fluent aphasia has demonstrated how normal language use is a marriage of content and form. In the case of non-fluent aphasia, form is compromised but the content of language remains relatively intact. In contrast, fluent aphasia is characterized by a rapid flow of form with little content.

4

ACQUIRED DYSLEXIA AND DYSGRAPHIA

Reading and writing involve a complex array of perceptual and motor skills. In this section we will consider impairments of reading and writing which are caused by damage to the brain. The impairment of reading ability is called **acquired dyslexia** (or **acquired alexia**). The impairment of writing ability is called **acquired dysgraphia** (or **acquired agraphia**). In both cases the term *acquired* indicates that the patient possessed normal reading and/or writing ability prior to brain damage and distinguishes the syndromes from developmental dyslexia and developmental dysgraphia, which deal with disturbances of reading and writing development in children.

4.1

Reading and writing disturbances in aphasia

Acquired dyslexia and dysgraphia typically accompany the aphasic syndromes which we considered in section 3. Most Broca's aphasics show writing disturbances that are comparable to their speaking deficits. In other words, a patient who cannot pronounce the word *spoon* will also not be able to write it correctly. The resulting error in writing (for example, *poon*) is called a **paragraphia**. In spontaneous writing, Broca's aphasics also tend to omit function words and inflectional affixes. Finally, while the silent reading of Broca's aphasics is very good, their reading aloud shows the same telegraphic style as their spontaneous speech. These observations reinforce the view that the deficit in Broca's aphasia is much more than a speech articulation deficit. It is a production deficit at a very deep level of language planning.

Wernicke's aphasics also show reading and writing deficits that match their deficits in speaking and listening. The writing of Wernicke's aphasics is formally very good. They typically retain good spelling and handwriting. Their written production, however, like their speaking, makes little sense. Reading comprehension is also severely impaired in Wernicke's aphasia. Like C.S. Moss, patients can see the letters and words, but cannot make any sense of them. Again the conclusion to be drawn is that Wernicke's aphasia, like Broca's aphasia, is a central disturbance of language competence – the knowledge that underlies language functioning. In such cases of central language disturbance, whatever impairment the patient has in listening and speaking will be matched in reading and writing.

4.2

Acquired dyslexia as the dominant language deficit

In addition to the reading and writing deficits that accompany aphasia, there are many cases in which the disruption of reading and writing ability is the dominant symptom. This typically follows damage in and around the angular gyrus of the parietal lobe. An analysis of these types of disabilities has led to some very interesting theories about the nature of reading (at least in English).

Before we proceed to discuss two contrasting types of acquired dyslexia, it might be worth while to reflect on the abilities involved in the reading of words. Up to this point in the chapter you have read over five thousand words. Some of these words (such as the function words) are very familiar to you and you probably recognized them as wholes. But others, such as *angular gyrus* are words that you probably read for the first time. How then could you know how to pronounce them? Many theorists believe that readers maintain a set of spelling-to-sound rules that enables them to read new words aloud. These rules are important in the development of reading ability and in the addition of new words to our reading vocabulary.

Phonological dyslexia is a type of acquired dyslexia in which the patient seems to have lost the ability to use spelling-to-sound rules. Phonological dyslexics can only read words that they have seen before. Asked to read a word such as *blug* aloud, they either say nothing or produce a known word that is visually similar to the target (for example, *blue* or *bug*).

Surface dyslexia is the opposite of phonological dyslexia. Surface dyslexics seem unable to recognize words as wholes. Instead they must process all words through a set of spelling-to-sound rules. This is shown by the kinds of errors they make. Surface dyslexics do not have difficulty reading words such as *bat* that are regularly spelled. They read irregularly spelled words such as *yacht* however, by applying regular rules and thus producing the incorrect form /jɒtʃt/. The most interesting aspect of surface dyslexics' reading ability is that they understand what they produce, not what they see. So, if they read out a word incorrectly, they assign it a meaning that is appropriate to their incorrect pronunciation. For example, if the patient read the word *sweat* as /swiːt/ (and not /swet/), when asked what the word means, they would answer: the opposite of bitter.

Data from acquired dyslexia allow researchers to build models which specify the components of normal reading ability and their relationship to each other. Clearly, this type of analysis plays a very important role in the development of our understanding of language, the mind, and the brain.

5

LINGUISTIC THEORY AND APHASIA

Looking at aphasia in terms of linguistic theory gives us a new perspective on language in the brain. Linguistic theory has been traditionally concerned with the structure of language, not with how it is used in the processes of listening, speaking, reading, and writing. In contrast, the traditional way of looking at aphasia has been in terms of what the patient can and cannot do. The involvement of theoretical linguists in the study of aphasia has caused a minor revolution in the field. Aphasia researchers have begun to think about the deficit in terms of the loss of knowledge representations such as semantic features, phonological rules, and perhaps syntactic tree structures. Theoretical linguists have also found that the study of aphasia offers an important area for testing theoretical distinctions such as the one between derivational suffixes and inflectional suffixes. In this section, we will look at some of the areas in which the marriage of theoretical linguistics and neurolinguistics has been most fruitful. This fruitfulness has usually meant an increase in the sophistication of the questions which are asked about aphasia. It has also meant the discovery of new and often bizarre aphasic phenomena.

5.1

Features, rules, and underlying forms

In the area of phonology, we have found that the phonemic paraphasias of Broca's aphasics usually differ from the target phoneme by only one distinctive feature (recall section 3.1, sentence *1*): 'with' → ['wɪt'] and can therefore be easily described by phonological rules. Observations such as these lead us to believe that phonological features and rules might be good tools to characterize how language is represented and produced.

In the area of morphology, the study of aphasia has offered empirical support for the theoretical distinction between inflection and derivation. As we have discussed, Broca's aphasics show a sensitivity to this distinction in their omission of affixes in speech. Inflectional affixes are commonly dropped, but derivational affixes are usually retained. Perhaps most interesting is the tendency of some aphasics to produce underlying forms of morphemes in reading and repetition. Asked to repeat the word *illegal*, for example, some aphasics will produce *inlegal*, using the underlying form of the negative prefix rather than the allomorph that should occur before a base beginning with /l/. Again, errors such as these point to the possibility that phonological processes such as nasal assimilation and the notion of underlying form are not only an elegant way to represent linguistic competence but are also relevant to the processing of language in the brain.

The study of aphasia also stands to shed light on the nature of semantic representations. Most of the work in this area has concentrated on the many subvarieties of acquired dyslexia. In a syndrome known as **deep dyslexia**, patients produce reading errors which are systematically related to the word which they are asked to read (in the sense that they share some semantic features but not others). Given the word *mother*, for example, a deep dyslexic is likely to read *father*.

The detailed study of semantic deficits associated with brain damage has also led to some very surprising discoveries. Most aphasics and dyslexics find abstract words much more difficult to process than concrete words. But there have been reports of concrete word dyslexia in which the patient shows exactly the opposite problem (having difficulty with concrete words such as *table*). There has even been a report of a patient who shows a selective inability to read words that refer to fruits and vegetables.

5.2

Agrammatism

In section 3.1, we observed that many theorists now believe that Broca's aphasia involves a central syntactic deficit. The syndrome which is characterized by telegraphic speech has been given the name **agrammatism** – to indicate that grammatical ability has been lost. Agrammatism is the aphasic disturbance which has been most studied by linguists. As was discussed in section 3.1, it is characterized by the omission of function words such as *it*, *is*, *to*, and *a*, the omission of inflectional affixes, and by comprehension deficits in cases where the correct interpretation of a sentence is dependent on syntax alone.

In recent years, many linguists have become involved in the problems of characterizing the agrammatic deficit. These problems have raised both specific questions such as: What exactly is a function word? and general questions such as: Is it possible to lose syntax? The involvement of linguists has also generated cross-linguistic studies of agrammatism that provide interesting insights into the interaction between characteristics of the syndrome and characteristics of particular languages.

5.3

Function words

Intuitively, function words are grammatical words that can be distinguished from content words such as nouns, verbs, and adjectives. In terms of formal syntax, however, they are quite heterogeneous. They include pronouns, auxiliaries, determiners, and prepositions – items that do not fall into any single syntactic category. Much of the recent work in this area by linguists has concentrated on working out what exactly the so-called function words have in common. Some researchers have suggested that they form a phonological group – they are all words that do not normally take stress. Others have pointed to the fact that function words do not normally take affixes and therefore form a morphological group. Still others have suggested that syntactic theory should be modified so that all the words that are lost in agrammatism fall under the heading *functional category* (this would involve changing the status of prepositions, which are currently treated as lexical categories – see Chapter 5).

Whatever the outcome of this debate, it is clear that neurolinguistic evidence has presented a new set of challenges to the field of formal linguistics. One of these challenges is to build bridges between normal and pathological linguistic competence by finding units of analysis that are appropriate to both.

The loss of syntactic competence

Another, much more general, challenge is to define what it means to possess syntactic competence such that we can speak of its loss. This challenge has forced researchers to address the question: What is the essence of syntactic knowledge? Is it the hierarchical arrangement of elements? Is it the representation of abstract entities such as traces? (See section 3.4 of Chapter 5.)

Some researchers have suggested that agrammatism involves the loss of the ability to form hierarchical representations. They claim that agrammatics interpret sentences as strings of content words and assign thematic roles to nouns (as opposed to NPs) according to a default strategy such as: The first noun is the agent. This strategy works reasonably well for simple sentences in which the first noun can be assigned the thematic role of agent and the second noun can be assigned the role of theme as in sentence 5a). It results in miscomprehension, however, for sentences such as 5b) and 5c), where the first NP does not have the role of agent.

5)

a. The girl kissed the boy.

b. The girl was kissed.

c. It was the girl that the boy kissed.

Other researchers have argued that agrammatism does not involve the loss of syntactic competence, but rather an alteration of that competence. They have claimed that agrammatics show hierarchical arrangements of elements but can no longer represent the traces that indicate an NP's position in deep structure. As a result, they are unable to recognize that the subject NP bears the theme role since they do not realize that it is the complement of the verb in deep structure (see section 3 of Chapter 7).

Agrammatism in other languages

Data from other languages have suggested that the original characterization of agrammatism as a syndrome in which function words and inflectional affixes are lost may not reflect the true nature of this deficit, but rather reflects the fact that such deletions are possible in English.

In English, affixes are typically attached to a base that is itself a free form. The past form of the verb *watch*, for example, is created by the addition of *-ed*; the third person singular is created by the addition of *-s*. However, not all languages work this way. In Semitic languages, such as Arabic and Hebrew, the base is typically a string of three consonants, which is unpronounceable in its uninflected form. Inflections are produced by inserting vowels into this triconsonantal 'skeleton' (cf. the discussion of prosodic morphology and the treatment of the phonological skeleton in section 1.6 of Chapter 6). For example, the Hebrew root for the verb to write is /ktv/. The masculine third person present form of the verb is /kɔtɛv/ and the masculine third person past form is /katav/. If Hebrew agrammatics simply 'lose' inflectional affixes the way they do in English, they should not be able to produce any verbs. As it turns out, Hebrew agrammatics do produce verbs, but instead of dropping inflectional forms, they choose randomly among them. This sort of evidence has provided a convincing argument against the view that agrammatic language results from a simple economy of effort. Rather, it seems that it is a linguistic deficit that involves the mis-selection of linguistic forms. It is only in languages such as English, where the base is also a legal free form, that the agrammatism is characterized by affix omission.

6

WHERE IS LANGUAGE?

In this chapter we have outlined some important findings that have greatly increased our understanding of the types of language disturbances which result from damage to the brain, as well as our understanding of the association between specific areas of the brain and particular language functions. We have seen that Broca's area plays a crucial role in the articulation of speech and in the ability to create syntactic representations. Wernicke's area plays a key role in language comprehension, and the area surrounding the angular gyrus plays a special role in reading.

On the other hand, we have seen that, in an important sense, normal language use involves the integrated functioning of the entire cortex. Even right-handers who are strongly left lateralized for language show some language deficit in cases of damage to the right hemisphere. Finally, virtually all forms of aphasia are accompanied by word-finding difficulties. This observation suggests that the storage and retrieval of word forms may be diffusely represented in the brain.

There is, therefore, no simple answer to the question: Where is language? Even if there were, the task of neurolinguistics would be far from done, for the truly important question concerning language in the brain is not: Where is it? but: What is it? Indeed, the answer to the first question may have little to do with the answer to the second question. Consider, by analogy, the goal of understanding the British parliamentary system: To what extent does the knowledge that Parliament is to be found in London advance the understanding of how Parliament works?

Ultimately, the goal of neurolinguistics is to understand, in neurological terms, what language is. The field of neurolinguistics is still a long way from being able to specify how syntax is coded in brain matter, or even how a word is represented. Nevertheless, as our discussion of agrammatism has revealed, recent work by neurolinguists has resulted in important new perspectives on the nature of language competence.

Summing up

This chapter is concerned with how language is represented and processed in the human brain. **Dichotic listening** studies and **split brain** studies have shown that the **left hemisphere** of the brain carries most of the responsibility for language processing in right-handed individuals. **Neuroscientists** have also used **autopsy** studies, **computerized axial tomography**, and **cerebral blood flow** studies to determine the relationship between particular areas of the left hemisphere and specific language functions. It has been found that **Broca's area** is primarily responsible for speech production, **Wernicke's area** is primarily responsible for language comprehension, and the area surrounding the **angular gyrus** plays an important role in reading. Most of our knowledge concerning language representation in the brain comes from the study of **aphasia** – language disturbance resulting from damage to the brain. **Neurolinguists**, trained in both linguistics and neuroscience, carefully examine the manner in which linguistic competence is affected by brain damage. Their goal is to increase our understanding of how linguistic knowledge is coded in brain matter and how this knowledge is used in the processes of language comprehension and production.

Notes

1   Callosumectomy is a rare surgical procedure used to treat severe forms of epilepsy. It prevents epileptic seizures from spreading to both hemispheres.
2   It is interesting to note that Wernicke patients have difficulty planning and executing many types of sequenced behaviour such as purchasing groceries, getting home by bus, or doing a wash.

Sources

David Caplan's 1987 book *Neurolinguistics and Linguistic Aphasiology: An Introduction* is an excellent introduction to neurolinguistics. A more practical approach to aphasia and its treatment is to be found in the Rosenbek *et. al.* book *Aphasia: A Clinical Approach*. The discussion of the PET technique draws on Steven Pinker's 1994 book *The Language Instinct* (page 301) which is cited below.

The discussion of agrammatism was drawn from the rich literature that includes M.-L. Kean's edited volume *Agrammatism* (New York: Academic Press, 1985) and Yosef Grodzinsky's challenging proposals in *Theoretical Perspectives on Language Deficits* (Cambridge, Mass.: MIT Press, 1990). An alternative approach to Grodzinsky's is well represented in David Caplan and Nancy Hildebrandt's book *Disorders of Syntactic Comprehension* (Cambridge, Mass.: MIT Press, 1988).

C.S. Moss's autobiographical account of his aphasic experience is to be found in *Recovery with Aphasia* (Urbana, Ill.: University of Illinois Press, 1972). Another book that offers an experiential perspective on aphasic disturbance is Howard Gardner's *The Shattered Mind* (New York: Knopf, 1975).

The material on acquired dyslexia is drawn from the volumes *Deep Dyslexia* and *Surface Dyslexia* (see Recommended reading), as well as Y. Zotterman's book *Dyslexia: Neuronal, Cognitive and Linguistic Aspects* (Oxford: Pergamon Press, 1982).

Recommended reading

Caplan, D. 1987. *Neurolinguistics and Linguistic Aphasiology*. Cambridge: Cambridge University Press.

Caplan, D. 1988. 'The biological basis for language.' In *Linguistics: The Cambridge Survey*. Vol. 3. Edited by F. Newmeyer, pp. 237–55. Cambridge: Cambridge University Press.

Coltheart, M., Patterson, J., and Marshall, J.C. eds. 1980. *Deep Dyslexia*. London: Routledge & Kegan Paul.

Jackendoff, R. 1993. *Patterns in the Mind*. Hemel Hempstead, Hertfordshire: Harvester Wheatsheaf.

Patterson, K.E., Marshall, J.C., and Coltheart, M. eds. 1986. *Surface Dyslexia*. Hillsdale, NJ: Erlbaum.

Pinker, S. 1994. *The Language Instinct*. London: Allen Lane (The Penguin Press).

Rosenbek, J.C., Lapointe, L.L., and Wertz, R.T. 1989. *Aphasia: A Clinical Approach*. Boston: College-Hill Press.

Segalowitz, S. 1983. *Two Sides of the Brain*. Englewood Cliffs, NJ: Prentice Hall.

Questions

1. What distinguishes the human brain from a non-human brain?

2. In what ways can the cerebral hemispheres be considered to be two separate brains?

3. What are the relative advantages and disadvantages of the various techniques used to investigate the brain? Consider ethics, cost, intrusiveness, and type of information yielded.

4. Following is an unlabelled diagram of the left hemisphere. Choose four contrasting colours and colour each lobe of the cortex. Use arrows to point to the central sulcus, the lateral fissure, and the angular gyrus. Finally, use a pencil to indicate areas of lesion that would result in Broca's aphasia, Wernicke's aphasia, and acquired dyslexia. Label these lesions.

Front

Back

5. What do dichotic listening tests tell us about the specialization of the cerebral hemispheres? Can you think of types of stimuli that would be interesting to present dichotically?

6. Do you think it is possible to learn how the normal brain functions by studying brain-damaged patients? What can the study of aphasia tell us about normal language competence?

7. Contrast the differences in behaviour between fluent and non-fluent aphasics. What could explain these differences?

8. Describe the differences between phonological and surface dyslexia.

9. Re-read the introduction to section 3. What do you think Moss's account tells us about the relationship between language and thought?

10. Many researchers have claimed that agrammatism involves a loss of syntactic knowledge. Imagine a type of aphasia that involves a loss of phonological knowledge. How would patients with this type of aphasia behave?

11

Psycholinguistics: the study of language processing

Gary Libben

Leaving one still with the intolerable wrestle
With words and meanings

❧ T.S. Eliot

We engage in language processing almost every day of our lives. This processing takes place when we watch television, listen to the radio, read a passing signboard while driving, write a letter or have a conversation. Usually these language activities are carried out with great ease and in a completely subconscious manner. We might sometimes be aware that we are searching for a word, composing a sentence, or straining to understand someone else, but we are never aware of the actual mechanisms and operations involved in producing and understanding language.

Psycholinguistics is the study of these language-processing mechanisms. Psycholinguists study how word, sentence, and discourse meaning are represented and computed in the mind. They study how complex words and sentences are composed in speech and how they are broken down into their constituent parts during listening and reading. In short, psycholinguists seek to understand *how language is done*.

This chapter introduces the field of psycholinguistics by first discussing some methods used by psycholinguists to probe language representation and processing in the mind. This is followed by a summary of recent research on language processing in the domains of phonetics, phonology, morphology, and syntax. Finally, we will discuss how these various aspects of linguistic processing work together to make the everyday acts of speaking, listening, and reading appear so simple and effortless.

1

METHODS OF PSYCHOLINGUISTIC RESEARCH

As was noted, language users are not able to introspect on the details of language processing. Just paying attention to what they are doing will not provide reliable insights into how they access words or build sentences. Perhaps the reason for this is that, in normal use, language processing must occur very quickly. By shielding mental linguistic operations from the conscious mind, it is possible that the language-processing system is maximizing its ability to operate with speed and efficiency.

In order to get a sense for the extent to which language processing is subconscious, you might try the following exercise: Give a friend a page of text to read silently and sit opposite him or her. Carefully observe your friend's eyes as they move across the text. You will notice that the eyes do not move smoothly from left to right but rather proceed in a series of jerks called **saccades**. Like most of us, your friend probably has the subjective impression that his or her eyes are moving very evenly across the page. But that subjective impression is incorrect. As humans, it seems that we are simply not constructed to be able to monitor many of our automatic activities, including language processing.

A substantial additional challenge for the psycholinguistic researcher is presented by the fact that most language-processing does not involve observable physical events such as eye-movement, but rather involves mental events that cannot be observed directly. Research therefore requires that language processing events in the mind be inferred from observable behaviour. Consequently, a large part of psycholinguistic research is concerned with the development of new (and often very clever) techniques to uncover how language processing is accomplished. Some of these techniques are presented in the following sections.

1.1

Slips of the tongue

Some of the earliest and most influential studies of language processing examined the spontaneous slips of the tongue produced during speech. **Spoonerisms** are slips of the tongue named after the Reverend William A. Spooner who was warden of New College, Oxford, between 1903 and 1924. The Reverend Spooner was famous for producing a great many, often humorous, speech errors. Some of his more well-known mistakes are provided below.

1)
What he intended: '*You have missed all my history lectures*'.
What he said: '*You have hissed all my mystery lectures*'.

2)
What he intended: '*Noble sons of toil*'.
What he said: '*Noble tons of soil*'.

3)
What he intended: '*You have wasted the whole term*'.
What he said: '*You have tasted the whole worm*'.

4)
What he intended: '*The dear old Queen*'.
What he said: '*The queer old dean*'.

Beginning in the 1960s, Victoria Fromkin began to study these and other naturally occurring slips of the tongue and noted that they can be very revealing of the manner in which sentences are created in speech. For example, as can be seen in the preceding examples, the characteristic pattern in Reverend Spooner's errors is a tendency to exchange the initial consonants of words in the utterance. When this creates new words (as opposed to non-words as in 'fire and brimstone → bire and frimstone'), the result is often humorous. But here's the important psycholinguistic point: In order for these exchanges to occur, there must be considerable pre-planning before an utterance is actually produced. Otherwise, how would it be possible in example *1)* for the first segment of the sixth word '<u>h</u>istory' to be transported backwards so that it becomes the first segment of the third word (<u>m</u>issed → hissed)?

Another important observation that Fromkin made was that speech errors also often involve 'mixing and matching' morphemes within words. Consider the following slips of the tongue:

5)
Intended: *'rules of word formation'*.
Produced: *'words of rule formation'*.

6)
Intended: *'I'd forgotten about that'*.
Produced: *'I'd forgot aboutten that'*.

7)
Intended: *'easily enough'*.
Produced: *'easy enoughly'*.

All these errors involve morphemes being exchanged within a sentence. As is the case for sound exchange errors, these slips of the tongue provide evidence that a sentence must be planned out before speech begins. They also provide evidence that the morpheme, rather than the word, is the fundamental building block of English sentence production. Note how in example *5)*, although the nouns *rule* and *word* are exchanged in the sentence, the inflectional suffix *-s* remains in its original position. In examples *6)* and *7)*, it is the suffixes that move while the stems remain in their original positions. These examples all suggest that morphological components of words can function independently during sentence production (and of course also in sentence *mis-production*).

As can be seen from these examples, slips of the tongue can offer fascinating insights into the mechanisms involved in language production and the role that linguistic units such as phonemes and morphemes play in that production. But because slips of the tongue are naturally occurring events, the researcher has no control over when and where they will happen and must simply wait for them. In this way, the analysis of slips of the tongue is a **field technique** and differs from the **experimental paradigms** discussed in the following sections. In these experimental paradigms the researcher takes an active role in controlling the circumstances in which language is processed, the stimuli to which the experimental subjects are exposed, and the ways in which subjects may respond to these stimuli.

1.2

Experimental methods: words in the mind

One of the most intense areas of psycholinguistic research has been the investigation of how words are organized in the mind. We are all in possession of a vocabulary that forms the backbone of our ability to communicate in a language. In many ways, this vocabulary must be used just as a normal dictionary is used. It is consulted to determine what words mean, how they are spelled, and what they sound like. But the dictionary in our minds – our mental lexicon – must also be substantially different from a desktop dictionary. It must be much more flexible, accommodating with ease the new words that we learn. It must be organized so that words can be looked up extremely quickly – word recognition takes less than one-third of a second and the average adult reads at a rate of about 250 words per minute. It must allow access to entries in terms of a wide variety of characteristics. The 'tip-of-the-tongue' phenomenon, in which we are temporarily unable to access a word, is particularly revealing of how flexible access to the mental lexicon can be. We have all experienced episodes in which we eventually retrieve words on the basis of their meaning, sound, spelling, first letter, or even what they rhyme with.

Many psycholinguists conceive of the mental lexicon as a collection of individual units as in Figure 11.1. In this figure, the lexicon is shown as a space in which entries of different types are stored and linked together. The main questions that are asked about the mental lexicon are: (1) How are entries linked? (2) How are entries accessed? (3) What information is contained in an entry?

Although these questions are simple and straightforward, there is no way to answer them directly because the human mental lexicon cannot be observed. So, the psycholinguist must use experimental methods that are indirect to understand how words are organized, accessed, and represented in

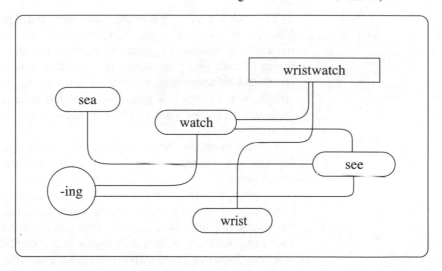

Figure 11.1 Units in the mental lexicon.

the mind. We will briefly discuss the two most common of these methods – **lexical decision** and **priming**.

Lexical decision

In the lexical decision paradigm, the experimental subject (in this example, a native speaker of English) is seated in front of a computer screen. A word appears in the middle of the screen and the subject must judge as quickly as possible whether or not the word is a real English word by pressing a button labelled 'yes' or a button labelled 'no' (see Figure 11.2).

Figure 11.2   A lexical decision experiment.

This task is very easy for subjects to carry out. They typically see and judge hundreds of words in a single fifteen-minute lexical decision experiment. In most lexical decision experiments there are two **dependent variables**, that is, things that are being measured: the time that it takes for a subject to respond (**response latency**) and whether or not the subject's judgement is correct (**response accuracy**). A response is judged as correct if a subject responds 'yes' to a real word such as *glove* or *sadness* and 'no' to a non-word such as *blove* or *sadding*.

Lexical decision experiments usually involve comparing subjects' performance on one set of stimuli (e.g., nouns) to their performance on another set of stimuli (e.g., verbs). The key to the importance of the experimental paradigm is that in order for a subject to respond 'no' to a stimulus such as *blove* or 'yes' to a real word such as *glove*, the subject's mental lexicon must be accessed. The lexical decision task can therefore be used to measure the speed and accuracy with which words in the mental lexicon are accessed. It has been found in many experiments, for example, that subjects take about half a second (500 milliseconds) to press the 'yes' button for frequently used words such as *free* but almost three-quarters of a second to press the 'yes' button for less common words such as *fret*. This finding has been called the **frequency effect**. Assuming that longer response times reflect processing that is more difficult or complex, this finding suggests that our mental dictionaries are organized so that words we typically need more often (the frequent words) are more easily and quickly available to us.

Another way in which the lexical decision task can be used to explore language representation and processing is to investigate the speed and accuracy with which subjects press the 'no' button for different types of stimuli. It has been found, for example, that pronounceable non-words, such as *plib*, show slower 'no' response times than unpronounceable non-words such as *nlib*. Thus subjects' lexical decisions seem to take into account the phonotactic constraints of the language. It has also been found that non-words that sound like real words (e.g., *blud*, *phocks*) take longer to reject than stimuli that are non-words both visually and phonologically. Again this tells us that aspects of phonology are automatically activated during word reading (although in the lexical decision task, the subject never has to pronounce the word).

The priming paradigm	The **priming paradigm** very often involves the lexical decision task and can be considered an extension of it. Recall that in lexical decision tasks different categories of stimuli (e.g., concrete versus abstract words) are compared in terms of subjects' response latency and accuracy. Priming experiments typically involve the same procedure as the lexical decision task except that the word to be judged (now called the **target**) is preceded by another stimulus (called the **prime**) What is measured is the extent to which the prime influences the subject's lexical decision performance on the target stimulus.

The priming paradigm is an excellent technique for probing how words are related in the mind. One of the first experiments using this paradigm showed that response time is faster when a target is preceded by a semantically related prime (e.g., *cat–dog*) as compared to when it is preceded by an unrelated prime (e.g., *cat–pen*). Results of this sort lead us to the view that words are related in the mind in terms of networks. On the basis of evidence from these priming experiments, psycholinguists reason that when a word such as *cat* is seen, its image is activated in the mind and that activation spreads to other words in the lexical network that are semantically related (e.g., *dog*). Now, because the mental representation for *dog* has already been activated through the prime, it is in a sense 'warmed up' so that when the subject later sees it on the screen as the target, response time is faster than it otherwise would have been. This is called the **priming effect**.

In recent years, the priming paradigm has been used to explore many aspects of the representation of words in the mind, and researchers have explored many types of priming in addition to the semantic priming above. For example, priming effects have been found for orthographically related words (e.g., *couch*, *touch*), and phonologically related words (e.g., *light, bite*); they are also found between word roots and complex forms (e.g., *legal*, *illegality*). This last finding suggests that words are represented in the mind in terms of their constituent morphemes. This will be discussed further in section 2.2 below in this chapter. (See also the discussion of the computational lexicon in Chapter 17, section 4).

1.3

Experimental methods: sentence processing

The lexical decision and priming paradigms offer interesting insights into how words are processed, but are of limited use in exploring the processing of sentences. The main reason for this is that the types of questions asked about sentence processing tend to be different from those asked about the mental lexicon. The majority of the sentences that we hear are unique events. Therefore, sentence processing must be fundamentally a process that relies on a particular type of computation (as opposed to a particular type of storage in the case of words in the mind). It is presumed that in sentence processing (i.e., in reading or listening) a sentence is understood through the analysis of the meanings of its words and through the analysis of its syntactic structure. Psycholinguists refer to this type of subconscious automatic analysis as **parsing**. Much of the research on sentence processing is concerned with the principles and steps involved in sentence parsing, the speed of parsing, and the manner and conditions under which parsing can break down. (See also Chapter 17, section 3 for a discussion of parsers and grammars in computational linguistics.)

In this section, we review two groups of experimental paradigms that have been used extensively to study sentence processing. These are timed-reading experiments and eye-movement experiments.

Timed-reading experiments

Timed-reading experiments begin with the assumption that the more difficult sentence processing is, the longer it should take. Therefore, by timing how long it takes subjects to read particular sentence types or parts of sentences, we can study the determinants of sentence-processing difficulty.

One of the more common and revealing timed-reading experimental paradigms is the *bar-pressing paradigm* in which subjects are seated in front of a computer screen and read a sentence one word at a time. The subject begins by seeing the first word of the sentence in the middle of the screen. When the subject presses a bar on the keyboard, the first word disappears and the second word of the sentence appears in its place. This process continues until the subject has read all the words in the sentence. The dependent variable in these experiments is the amount of time it takes subjects to press the bar after seeing a particular word (i.e., the amount of time they need to process that word in the sentence).

Bar-pressing experiments can be very revealing of the manner in which sentence processing occurs. Subjects do not show equal bar-pressing times across a sentence, but rather a pattern that reflects the syntactic structure of the sentence. An example of such a pattern is shown in Figure 11.3, which displays bar-pressing times for the sentence *The Chinese, who used to produce kites, used them in order to carry ropes across the rivers*.

As can be seen in Figure 11.3, subjects show longer bar-pressing times for

Figure 11.3 Bar-pressing times in sentence reading (adapted from Stine 1990).

processing most nouns and verbs and relatively less time for function words such as determiners, conjunctions, and prepositions. What is particularly interesting is how subjects pause at the end of clause boundaries. This increased processing time is interpreted as reflecting the extra amount of time required to integrate preceding information into a complete clause structure. Thus the greatest bar-pressing time is required for *rivers*, the final noun in the sentence, and the second greatest for *kites*, which is the last word in the embedded relative clause that modifies Chinese.

8)

[CP The Chinese [CP who used to produce *kites*] used them in order to carry ropes across the *rivers*]

Eye movements

We have already noted that sentence reading involves a series of jerky eye movements called saccades. A number of events occur during these jerky movements. When the eyes are at rest they take a 'snapshot' of two or three words. These snapshots usually last from 200 to 250 milliseconds. While the snapshot is being taken, the language-processing system calculates where to jump to next. During a jump to the next fixation location (usually about eight letters to the right), the subject is essentially blind.

The details of eye movements in sentence reading are studied with sophisticated laboratory procedures in which a subject is seated in front of a computer screen on which text is displayed. A low-intensity infra-red beam of light is bounced off the subject's eyeball and registered on a video camera. The image from the video camera is fed to a computer which is also controlling the display of text on the screen. The computer calculates where on the screen the subject is currently fixating.

This technique has revealed that fixation times are typically longer for less frequent words, and the points of fixation are typically centred on content words such as nouns and verbs rather than on function words such as determiners and conjunctions. Difficult sentence structures create longer fixation times as well as many more regressive (backward) saccades. **Regressive saccades** are backward jumps in a sentence and are usually associated with mis-parsing or miscomprehension. On average, backward saccades make up 10 to 15 per cent of the saccades in sentence reading, but syntactically complex sentences and semantically anomalous sentences (e.g., *The pizza was too hot to drink*) create many more regressive saccades. It has also been found that poor readers jump back and forth through sentences much more often than good readers do.

1.4

Brain activity: event-related potentials

Perhaps the most exciting new technique to be used in psycholinguistic research is the study of **event-related potentials** (**ERPs**) produced by the brain during language processing. As a research technique, the ERP paradigm has the same basic advantage as eye-movement studies. The subject simply sits in front of a computer screen and reads. This is a relatively natural language-processing activity that, unlike lexical decision or bar-pressing, is similar to what subjects do in normal language-processing situations.

ERP experiments measure electrical activity in the brain. Electrodes are placed on a subject's scalp and recordings are made of voltage fluctuations resulting from the brain's electrical activity. The difference between ERP recordings and the more familiar EEG recordings is that, in the EEG, all the electrical activity of the brain is recorded. This electrical activity results from a very large number of background brain activities that are always going on. The advantage of the ERP approach is that it uses a computer to calculate what part of the electrical brain activity is related to a stimulus event (in our case, words or sentences on a screen). This is done by a process of averaging. The computer records the instant at which a stimulus is presented and compares the voltage fluctuation immediately following the stimulus presentation to the random background 'noise' of the ongoing EEG. By repeating this process many times with stimuli of a particular type, random voltage fluctuations are averaged out and the electrical potentials related to that stimulus type can be extracted. The resulting wave forms are called the event-related potentials.

The ERP pattern is typically illustrated in terms of a line graph in which time is shown from left to right and voltage is shown on the vertical axis with negative values on top and positive values on the bottom. An example of an ERP graph is provided in Figure 11.4.

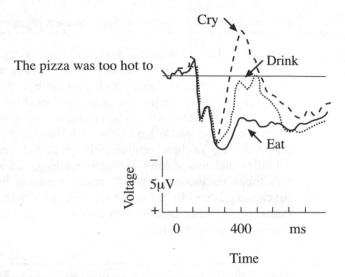

Figure 11.4   ERPs elicited by sentence-final words that are congruent, incongruent, and very incongruent with the sentence context.

Figure 11.4 also displays one of the most interesting psycholinguistic findings using ERPs. It turns out that in the processing of sentences, the brain displays a characteristic ERP sign of surprise. Consider the following sentences:

9)

a.   The pizza was too hot to eat.

b.   The pizza was too hot to drink.

c.   The pizza was too hot to cry.

The sentences in *9)* are arranged in order of semantic plausibility. In the first case, the last word fits in perfectly well with the sentence and would typically be expected by the reader. As can be seen in Figure 11.4, the ERP for this sentence shows a positive voltage associated with the last word. In the case of *9b)*, however, in which the last word does not make sense (people do not drink pizza), the ERP is much more negative. As is shown in the horizontal axis, this negative spike occurs 400 milliseconds after the onset of the word. For this reason this signal of semantic anomaly is called the N400 (negative spike at 400 milliseconds after stimulus presentation). Note how the N400 is even stronger in the case of sentence *9c)*, which is less congruent with the sentence context (*drink* is at least associated with food).

The N400 effect can be obtained not only at the ends of sentences but also in any sentence position. This fact suggests that sentence processing is immediate and online. When reading a sentence we do not wait until the entire string is complete, but are rather constantly building interpretations of the sentence as it unfolds. Whenever what we see or hear contradicts our expectations based on our ongoing interpretative processes, an N400 ERP spike is observed.

2

LANGUAGE PROCESSING AND LINGUISTICS

In the preceding sections we discussed some of the methods that psycholinguists use to investigate the manner in which language is processed. One of the most important results of such psycholinguistic investigations has been that many of the concepts and principles used by linguists to describe and understand the structure of language in terms of phonetics, phonology, morphology, and syntax have been found also to play an important role in the understanding of how language is produced and comprehended during activities such as speaking, listening, reading, and writing. In this section we will focus on these points of contact between theoretical linguistics and psycholinguistics. In doing so we will also highlight the correspondence between the study of language processing and the concepts discussed in Chapters 1 to 6 of this book.

2.1

Phonetics and phonology

The study of phonetics and phonology reveals that the sound structure of language is richly structured into many different levels of representation. Thus, as is discussed in Chapters 2 and 3, individual segments can be characterized in terms of place and manner of articulation or with respect to a hierarchy of phonological features. Sequences of sounds can be grouped into syllabic structures, and allophonic variation can be described in terms of underlying phonemes and surface allophones. How much of this structure plays a role in language processing?

The simple answer to this question is: 'All of it!' The more complex answer and, of course, also the more accurate answer is that language processing shows evidence that features, phonemes, and syllable structure all capture some aspects of the way in which we process language, but that speech production and perception is a complex activity that involves much more than these phonetic and phonological representations.

To see why this is the case, consider what might occur when you hear the sentence: *The dog bit the cat*. Because the utterance unfolds in time, you will first hear the segment /ð/ and then the segment /ə/. (In fact, you do not hear these segments separately but rather you create them out of a continuous sound stream.) As soon as these segments are identified you have already accessed the representation for the word *the* in your mental lexicon. When the next segment comes up in the sound stream, you already know that it is the beginning of a new word and you also know that this word is likely to be a noun. The phonetic analysis that follows identifies the segments *d-o-g* and the corresponding lexical entry. Now come the first segments of the word *bit*. In principle, the first two phonemes /bɪ/ could be the first two segments of the word *built*, but you are not likely to consider this possibility because your developing interpretation of the sentence is biasing you towards the word *bit*, which is associated in your mind with *dog*.

As can be appreciated from this example, language processing involves the interplay of information that develops simultaneously at many different levels of analysis. The person hearing the sentence *The dog bit the cat* is performing phonetic analysis to isolate phonemes and word boundaries, and to relate these to representations in the mental lexicon. This inductive analysis is referred to as **bottom-up processing**. But we do not wait until we have analysed all the phonemes in a sentence before we begin to try to understand it. Rather, we begin interpretation of a sentence spontaneously and automatically on the basis of whatever information is available to us. For this reason, by the time we get to the word *bit* in the sentence, we are not only recognizing it using bottom-up processing but we are also employing a set of expectations to guide phonetic processing and word recognition. This is called **top-down processing**. In normal language use we are always engaged in both bottom-up and top-down activities. We never process just features, or phonemes, or syllables. We process language for the purposes of understanding each other.

In section 3 of this chapter, we will discuss how phonetic and phonological analysis fits into other processes involved in speaking and listening. For now, however, we will concentrate on three levels of linguistic structure that seem fundamental to phonetic and phonological representation: features, phonemes, and syllables.

Features

In both linguistics and psycholinguistics, the term *feature* is used to refer to the most basic level of representation. It is therefore always associated with bottom-up processing in language. In the processing of sound, it refers to characteristics of individual phonemes (e.g., [± voice] [± continuant], etc.). The most straightforward evidence concerning the role of such features comes from the analysis of slips of the tongue. Some examples of these slips are presented in Table 11.1.

Table 11.1   The role of features in speech errors

	Intended	Actually produced
a)	big and fat	pig and vat
b)	Is Pat a girl?	Is bat a curl?
c)	Cedars of Lebanon	Cedars of Lemmanon

The errors in Table 11.1 follow a pattern, but that pattern can only be understood with reference to a system of phonological features. In all three examples, the errors involve a *phonological feature*. In example (a) the feature [voice] has been exchanged between the words *big* and *fat* to create the new words *pig* and *vat* (the phoneme pairs /b–p/ and /f–v/ only differ in the feature [voice]). This same pattern of the exchange of the feature voice can be seen in example (b) where *Pat* becomes *bat* and *girl* becomes *curl*. Finally, the error in (c) is particularly intriguing because we normally think of /b/ and /m/ as completely different phonemes. In fact, however, they are both voiced bilabial stops that only differ in terms of the feature [± nasal]. Changing the /b/ in *Lebanon* from [−nasal] to [+nasal] creates the error *Lemmanon*.

These examples offer evidence that language production makes use of the individual feature components of phonemes and that the phonemes that we produce in speech may actually be put together 'on the fly' out of bundles of such features.

Phonemes

We have seen in section 1.1 that Spoonerisms show evidence of entire phonemes being misplaced during sentence planning. The phonemic unit of representation also plays a central role in psycholinguistic models of speech processing, such as the **cohort model**. This model states that, in word comprehension, words are analysed by hearers from beginning to end. So, for example, when we hear the word *glass*, we initially consider all the words that begin with the sound [g]. When the next sound [l] is recognized, the number of possible words (the cohort) is reduced to those words that begin with [gl]. This process continues until the cohort of possible words is reduced to one – the word that is being recognized. Evidence in favour of the cohort model comes from a number of experiments in which it has been found that the beginnings of words play a more important role in word recognition than the middle or end portions. The cohort model has also been supported by experiments that found that the beginning-to-end analysis of spoken words proceeds one phoneme at a time, rather than one cluster or one syllable at a time.

Syllables

Although in the cohort model, the phoneme rather than the syllable seems to be the fundamental unit of auditory word recognition, there is other evidence that the syllable plays an important role in speech perception. In one study, subjects were presented with disyllabic words (e.g., *bullet*) and disyllabic non-words (e.g., *sullet*) and were asked to press a button if a particular target unit was in the stimulus. The target units were either syllables (e.g., *let*) or segments (e.g., *t*). It was found both for words and non-words that subjects were significantly faster at identifying syllable targets than at identifying single segment targets. It was concluded that syllable identification was faster because, in normal auditory analysis, subjects first break down stimuli into syllables and then into individual segments as the situation demands.

Another source of evidence on the role of the syllable in language processing comes from observing subjects' performance on word games. For example: You are given two words such as *bug* and *cat*. In this game, you are required to blend the words together to make a new word. Now, what sounds better: (*bug* + *cat* = *bat*) or (*bug* + *cat* = *but*)? The difference between these two possibilities is that the first one takes the onset of the first syllable and combines it with the rhyme of the second syllable (Figure 11.5). The other possibility does not split the words at a natural point of English syllable structure. As you might expect, subjects are much better at creating word blends that correspond to the syllable structure of their language and prefer such blends when presented with a choice. The fact that English speakers find such onset–rhyme divisions easier and more natural suggests that the sound of words is represented in speakers' minds in terms of their syllables and syllable constituents (e.g., Onset and Rhyme).

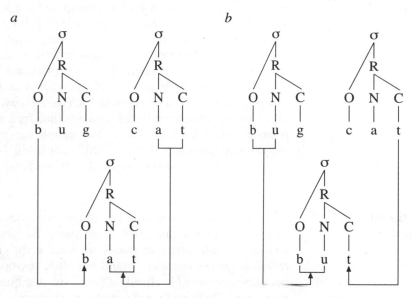

Figure 11.5 Speakers of English find the word blend in *a* easier and more natural than the word blend in *b* because the former involves breaking the words at natural syllable-structure boundaries.

2.2

Morphological processing

The linguistic study of morphology is the study of word structure. It seeks to characterize the system of categories and rules involved in word formation and interpretation. The psycholinguistic study of morphological processing seeks to understand how this word structure plays a role in language processing. In the following sections, we will summarize some psycholinguistic research that reveals how morphological structures and principles play a substantial role in the representation of words in the mind and in word recognition.

Morpheme activation

Words such as *blackboard*, *happiness*, and *watched* are made up of two morphemes. In the case of the compound *blackboard*, both these morphemes are roots. In the case of *happiness*, one morpheme is a root and the other is a derivational suffix. Finally in the case of *watched*, one morpheme is a root and the other is an inflectional affix. The first question we will address is whether the individual morphological components of words play a role in processing.

The answer to this question seems to be a straightforward yes. For most multimorphemic words, individual morphemes are automatically activated during word recognition. One source of evidence for this conclusion comes from priming experiments in which it is found that words like *happiness* will prime their constituents and vice versa in a lexical decision experiment (cf. section 1.2 above). When a subject is exposed to a multimorphemic word such as *happiness*, the activation of that word in the mind automatically activates the lexical entry for its root *happy*, which results in its showing a faster response time as the target in a lexical decision task.

Another source of evidence for this view comes from semantic priming in lexical decision experiments involving compounds. For example, it was found that presentation of a compound such as *crowbar* will produce a priming effect for the subsequent lexical decision time for a word such as *bird*. For this priming effect to take place, the morpheme *crow* would have to be individually activated during word recognition because, as a whole, the compound *crowbar* has nothing to do with birds.

Selectional restrictions

As is discussed in Chapter 4, one of the properties of English morphology is that not all affixes can attach to all stems. So, for example, the suffix *-ize* attaches to adjectives or nouns to form verbs. For this reason, English morphological constraints would not allow a word such as **understandize* because *understand* is already a verb. Now the question for psycholinguistic research is: Do these formal restrictions play a role in the way in which native speakers of English process new words? In a recent experiment in morphological processing, subjects were presented with nonsense roots (e.g., *birm*) that had prefixes and suffixes attached to them. Because they contained nonsense roots, none of these words made much sense (e.g., *re-birm-able*, *re-birm-ize*, *re-birm-ity*). Notice that as is shown in Figure 11.6, however, *re-birm-able* and *re-birm-ize* are morphologically legal whereas *re-birm-ity* violates a morphological constraint – the prefix *re-* must attach to a verb and the suffix *-ity* must attach to a noun. The construction is illegal because the nonsense root *birm* cannot be both a noun and a verb at the same time. In experiments with these sorts of stimuli, it was found that response times were significantly longer for the illegal nonsense words than for the morphologically legal words. These results suggest that knowledge of the selectional restrictions of affixes does indeed form part of the word-processing system.

Figure 11.6 Morphologically legal and illegal affixed nonsense roots.

Hierarchical structure

In Figure 11.6, trimorphemic words are represented in terms of a tree diagram in which constituent morphemes are arranged in a hierarchy. The last question we will consider in our discussion of morphological processing is whether there is evidence that the representation of multimorphemic words in the mind includes a representation of hierarchical structure.

This question has been investigated in priming experiments that use lexical decision response times as the dependent variable. In these experiments, stimuli such as *refillable*, which have a left-branching structure, are compared to stimuli such as *unbearable*, which have a right branching structure (see Figure 11.7). This means that for the word *refillable*, the substring *fillable* is not a morphological component of the tree structure (even though it is a real word of English). However, because the word *unbearable* is right-branching, its final two morphemes *bear* and *-able* make up a component of the morphological tree.

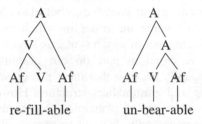

Figure 11.7   Left-branching and right-branching trimorphemic words.

In the priming experiments, subjects were first shown the right substrings such as *fillable*, and then the full trimorphemic word, such as *re-fill-able*. Priming effects were measured in terms of the lexical decision response times for the full word. It was found that those substrings that were real morphological constituents produced a significantly larger priming effect than those that were not.

Note that if hierarchical structure were not part of the representation of multimorphemic words in the mind, that is, if these words were simply strings of morphemes (e.g., *re + fill + able*), then there should be no difference between the priming effects for right-branching versus left-branching stimuli. The fact that such priming effects were observed is evidence that our representation of complex words is organized in terms of hierarchical morphological structure.

2.3

Syntax

Syntax is the system of rules and categories that underlies sentence formation in human language. Sentences are unique events – virtually all of the sentences you read in this chapter are sentences that you have never encountered before. They are typically made up of familiar words, but the arrangement of those words into a syntactic structure is normally unique to each sentence. The question that we will consider in this section is: How are these syntactic structures created during sentence processing?

The syntax module

One very simple possibility for how sentences are processed is that production and comprehension employ the system of rules that are used by linguists to describe sentence structure. This possibility suggests that speakers would begin with deep structure representations and employ a series of transformations to derive the surface structure characteristics of a sentence. Many psycholinguistic experiments examined this possibility by testing, for example, whether sentences with many transformations take longer to process than sentences with fewer transformations. It turned out that the number of transformations in a sentence did not predict processing time. Researchers concluded that there is at least some difference between the rules that native speakers use to generate and comprehend sentences and the rules that linguists use to characterize the linguistic knowledge of native speakers.

As a result, it was necessary to postulate a special module for sentence processing and another for grammatical knowledge. The processing module is called the **syntactic parser**. This parser is understood to be the system that makes use of grammatical knowledge but also contains special procedures and principles that guide the order in which elements of a sentence are processed and the manner in which syntactic structure is built up. Because our parsing ability is based in part on our grammatical knowledge of our language, it is usually the case that there is a close correspondence between sentence parsing and grammatical structure. However, because the parsing module has its own set of principles, sentences that are grammatically complex are not necessarily difficult to parse and sentences with relatively simple syntactic structure can be. (See also the discussion of parsers in computational syntax in Chapter 17, section 3.)

It should be noted that in discussing how processing takes place, the term **module** has a special meaning. It refers to a unit of processing that is relatively autonomous from other processing units. The idea of processing modules has been very important and controversial in many domains of human information processing. To get a sense of how processing may involve the co-ordination of separate modules, consider what occurs when you watch a film. The film director, in order to obtain a variety of effects, tries to manipulate how the audience will respond by relying on processing modularity. The director knows that when an aeroplane on the screen goes into a dive or when a canoe goes over the falls you, the viewer, will experience a physical sensation of falling. The director knows that you cannot stop this from happening even though you are aware that you are sitting in a chair that is not moving. Similarly, you will be frightened by the sudden appearance of a monster, even though you know that you are really in no danger. All these effects result from processing modularity. The bottom-up information that comes from processing modules cannot be turned off by the top-down information that you are seated in a stationary and safe cinema environment.

Psycholinguistic studies have investigated whether this same sort of modularity is present in syntactic processing – in other words, whether syntactic parsing operates in an automatic and obligatory manner that is relatively independent of the activity of other processing systems. Two sources of evidence have been very important in the exploration of the principles of modularity of sentence processing. These are **garden path sentences** and **sentence ambiguity**. (Both of these dimensions of language processing are treated also in Chapter 17 from a computational perspective.)

Garden path sentences

Some sentences are extraordinarily difficult to understand even though they are not very complex syntactically. These sentences are called garden path sentences because they lead the syntactic parser down the garden path to the wrong analysis. Perhaps the most famous garden path sentence is the one given in *10)*:

10)

The horse raced past the barn fell.

This sentence is perfectly grammatical, but almost impossible to understand. The reason for this is that, as we read the sentence, we build up a syntactic structure in which *The horse* is the subject of the sentence and *raced past the barn* is the main VP of the sentence. When we get to the word *fell*, we are surprised because the sentence we have built has no room for an extra VP. In the correct interpretation for the sentence, *fell* is the head of the main VP and *raced past the barn* is a clause that attaches to the NP *the barn* (see Figure 11.8; for expository convenience, *Infl* is not represented here).

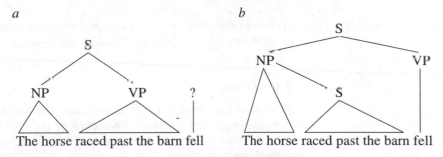

Figure 11.8   A garden path sentence. The garden path effect is shown in *a*. The correct interpretation is represented in *b*.

The ways in which native speakers misunderstand garden path sentences reveals how the parser might work. It seems that we construct syntactic representations from the beginning of the sentences to the end and that our sentence parsers are organized so that we make a number of assumptions about how a sentence will proceed. This can be seen by considering the garden path sentence in *11)*:

11)

Since Keith always walks a mile seems like a short distance to him.

This sentence is not as difficult to process as the one in *10)*, but you probably noticed yourself having to backtrack after an initial mis-analysis. Your parser is inclined to build a single VP out of the string *walks a mile*, when in fact *walks* and *a mile* belong to different clauses. This tendency has been extensively studied by psycholinguists. The backtracking that you might have noticed in your own reading shows up significantly in eye-movement studies in which it is found that subjects show more regressive saccades for these sentences as well as longer fixation times.

It has been claimed that the garden path effect results from two principles of parsing. These are **minimal attachment** and **late closure**. The principle of minimal attachment states that we do not postulate new syntactic nodes (like the extra imbedded S in Figure 11.8 *b*), unless it is clear that we absolutely have to. The principle of late closure states that we prefer to attach new words to the clause currently being processed as we proceed through a sentence from beginning to end. The result of late closure is shown in Figure 11.8*a* where we are inclined to continuously add words to the VP until we arrive at the last word *fell*, which cannot be integrated into the syntactic structure that is being created.

Now, there is one last point to be made concerning what garden path sentences can tell us about how people process sentences. Try reading the sentence in *11)* again. You should find that although you now know the correct analysis for the sentence, you misread it the second time just as you did the first time. This suggests that the parsing system is in fact a module that operates automatically and independently of top-down knowledge.

Sentence ambiguity

Another important clue to how syntactic processing is accomplished comes from the study of ambiguity. Consider the sentence in *12)*.

12)

They all rose.

In fact the last word in *12)* is ambiguous. The word *rose* can either be related to *stand* or related to *flower*. The sentence context, however, leads us clearly to favour the *stand* version of the word. Does the sentence context therefore inhibit activation of the other meaning of *rose*? This question was investigated in a lexical decision experiment in which the sentence in *12)* served as the prime. After seeing the sentence, subjects were presented with either the word *flower* or *stand*. The researchers found that the sentence facilitated lexical decision response times to both words; that is, both meanings for the word *rose* in the sentence were activated, even though the sentence clearly presented a bias in favour of one reading over the other.

This experimental finding is one of many that reveal a fundamental property of human language processing. We create all representations possible and then discard the ones that are either incorrect or unnecessary. This last characteristic was found in a follow-up priming experiment which was identical to the one just described except that there was a pause of several hundred milliseconds between the prime and the target. When the pause was present, the priming effect disappeared for the meaning that was unrelated to the sentence context (i.e., *flower*). This suggests that, in fact, sentence processing proceeds in two stages. In the first stage, all possible representations and structures are computed. In the second stage, one of these structures is selected and all others are abandoned. Of course, all this happens very quickly and subconsciously so that, as native speakers of a language, we are never aware that for a sentence such as *13)*, we compute two possible interpretations.

13)

The tuna can hit the boat.

In reading this sentence, you ended up imagining either:

a)   tuna meat that is packed in a small round can; or
b)   a large fish swimming towards a boat.

The point of the psycholinguistic experiments just described is this: no matter which interpretation you arrived at, a) or b), you probably considered both of them, chose one, discarded the other, and forgot about the whole thing in less than a second.

3

PUTTING IT ALL TOGETHER: PSYCHOLINGUISTIC MODELLING

Up to this point, our discussion of psycholinguistic research has examined characteristics of phonetic, phonological, morphological, and syntactic processing as well as the relation between the concepts used in theoretical linguistics and in psycholinguistics. It is important to note, however, that research in language processing seeks not only to discover which types of representations play a role in language processing, but also how these representations and processes fit together to make activities such as speaking, listening, reading, and writing possible.

Psycholinguistic researchers present their ideas of how *language is done* in terms of models. These models very often take the form of flow charts made up of boxes and arrows. A psycholinguistic model incorporates the results of experiments into a proposal of how processing takes place. In other words, it is a statement of *what happens when*.

Suppose, for example, we wished to present the finding discussed in section 2.3 that a sentence such as *They all rose* will prime both the words *flower* and *stand*. The model might look like Figure 11.9.

For our present purposes, it is not important whether this model is actually correct. The purpose of the model is simply to illustrate how psycholinguistic statements can be represented as flow chart models. The model in Figure 11.9 says that we first perform phonological processing. So, at this stage the input is processed into a representation such as /ðeɪ ɔːl rəʊz/. At the lexical access stage, units of the mental lexicon corresponding to *rose* (1), *rose* (2), *they*, and *all* are activated. Information from lexical access 'feeds' the syntactic parsing module which might produce a representation such as [S[NPThey all][VP rose]]. The model also claims that information from both the lexical access module and the syntactic parsing module are fed to the representation pruning

Figure 11.9 A simplified psycholinguistic model.

module (the module that discards extra/unneeded representations). So, this module is the one that would determine that rose is related to *standing* and not related to *flower*. Finally, the model states that interpretation only becomes conscious in the final stage of analysis and that information flows to conscious interpretation along a 'one-way street' (the conscious mind cannot 'peek' at how things are going).

You will note that in creating this model we have taken two kinds of shortcuts: first, we have created a novel name (e.g., representation pruning) to describe an operation that has been deduced from the results of psycholinguistic experimentation. Second, our model uses the box notation as a shorthand for a constellation of processes. Thus, it is understood that as the model becomes more elaborate, each one of the boxes in Figure 11.9 would be expanded into a flow chart of its own.

As you inspect the model in Figure 11.9 you should find that it is really very inadequate. It is missing much important detail, it seems to characterize only one aspect of sentence processing, and it avoids any mention of how meaning is accessed or how sentence interpretation actually takes place. To be a model of any real value, it would have to be much more elaborate.

Indeed, the types of psycholinguistic models that have been proposed in recent years are very elaborate. This is a good thing. We want models to be as detailed and comprehensive as possible, to take a great deal of experimentation into account and, perhaps most importantly, to show how linguistic and non-linguistic operations work together in the processing of language.

In Figure 11.10, a real psycholinguistic model is presented. This model is a proposal about how speech is produced, and is fairly complex. In principle, however, it is no different from the 'pretend' model in Figure 11.9. It contains boxes that stand for constellations of activities. These boxes are given creative names (e.g., Formulator) to give an indication of the action they perform. The boxes are connected by arrows that indicate what takes place first, second, and so on. Finally, the boxes are arranged in space so as to show what activities may take place simultaneously.

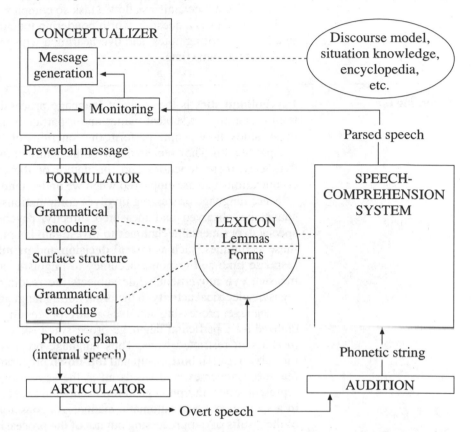

Figure 11.10 Levelt's model of speech production.

The model presented in Figure 11.10 is currently the most influential model of speech production and is based on a wide array of psycholinguistic results. It states that speech production begins in the Conceptualizer (in which a message is formed). The message is then given linguistic form in the Formulator. This Formulator contains grammatical and phonological processes and draws upon the lexicon (represented in the centre of the model). From the Formulator, information is passed to the Articulator, which actually produces the utterance.

Note that in Levelt's model, information does not flow in one direction only. Rather there is feedback so that while producing language, a speaker monitors through the comprehension system whether the utterance makes sense. This is represented as an arrow that feeds back to the Conceptualizer.

Although Levelt's model might look quite complex, it is clear that the model, as presented in Figure 11.10, is a great simplification of what might actually occur in the mind during language processing. The more we think about the details of language processing, the more we realize that the study of *how people do language* is still in its infancy. The fundamental mystery remains: What mechanisms allow a task so complex to be accomplished with such ease? This is a question worth pondering the next time you are listening to a lecture, writing notes, and overhearing a whispered conversation next to you all at the same time.

Summing up

Psycholinguistics is the study of language processing. The field is defined both by an area of subject matter and a particular methodology. Psycholinguists study how people perform the functions of language comprehension and production. They seek to discover the nature of the mental representations that serve these functions and the nature of the cognitive operations and computations that are employed when we understand and produce language.

Since language processing involves computations and representations that cannot be observed and measured directly, psycholinguists have devised special experimental techniques to investigate language processing. Some of these techniques, such as **lexical decision** and **priming**, measure a subject's response time and response accuracy to linguistic stimuli. Other techniques measure **eye movement** while subjects are reading silently and yet others measure electrical activity in the brain during language processing.

Language processing involves many processing **modules** that are specialized for a particular language-processing task and that interact with other modules in restricted ways. Thus language processing involves a constant interplay between **bottom-up** and **top-down** processing. We process phonetic features, phonemes, and words all at the same time. We construct syllable representations, morphological representations, and syntactic representations in a spontaneous and automatic manner. As conscious beings, we are aware of the results of our processing but not of the processing itself.

In general, psycholinguistic studies have revealed that many of the concepts employed in the analysis of sound structure, word structure, and sentence structure also play a role in language processing. An account of language processing, however, also requires that we postulate additional processing units such as a **parser**, as well as the non-linguistic components of models of language processing. These language-processing models are often presented in flow chart form and seek to provide explicit accounts of how particular language tasks are accomplished.

Sources

In recent years, many new books on psycholinguistics have appeared. These include *Psycholinguistics* by Joseph Kess (Philadelphia: John Benjamins, 1992), *Psycholinguistics* by Jean Berko-Gleason and Nan Bernstein Ratner (Philadelphia: Harcourt Brace, 1993) and Michael Garman, *Psycholinguistics* (Cambridge: Cambridge

University Press, 1990). Another excellent source is the 1994 *Handbook of Psycholinguisics* edited by Morton Ann Gernsbacher (New York: Academic Press, 1994).

Some of the 'slip of the tongue' material in section 1.1 is drawn from Victoria Fromkin's chapter on speech production (pp. 272–300) in the Berko-Gleason and Ratner volume cited above.

The experiment in which bar-pressing times were found to correspond to clause boundaries was originally reported by E.A. Stine (1990) in an article titled 'On-line processing of written text by younger and older adults' (*Psychology and Ageing*, 5: 68–78) and is discussed in Arthur Wingfield's chapter 'Sentence processing' in the Berko-Gleason and Ratner text.

The discussion of eye-movement data in psycholinguistics was based on the article by K. Rayner and S. Sereno, 'Eye-movements in reading', in *Handbook of Psycholinguistics* edited by M.A. Gernsbacher as well as in the book by K. Rayner and A. Pollatsek, *The Psychology of Reading* (Englewood Cliffs, NJ: Prentice Hall, 1989).

The material on event-related potentials is discussed in an article by Marta Kutas and Cyma Van Petten (pp. 83–133) in *Handbook of Psycholinguistics*. The syllable-processing experiment cited in the syllable section was reported in an article by J. Segui, U. Frauenfelder, and J. Mehler, 'Phoneme monitoring, syllable monitoring, and lexical access', in *British Journal of Psychology*, 72: 471–7 and is discussed in R.E. Remes's article 'On the perception of speech', in *Handbook of Psycholinguistics*.

The word-blending studies are reported in a series of studies conducted by Rebecca Treima, e.g., 'The structure of spoken syllables: Evidence from novel word games', *Cognition* 15: 49–74 (1983). A cross-linguistic study using a forced-choice version of these word games is reported in G.E. Wiebe and B.L. Derwing, 'A forced-choice blending task for testing intra-syllabic break points in English, Korean, and Taiwanese', in *Twenty-First LACUS Forum* (Chapel Hill, North Carolina: LACUS, 1994).

The morphological priming experiments are summarized in an article by William Marslen-Wilson, Lorraine Komisarjevsky Tyler, Rachelle Waksler, and Lianne Older, 'Morphology and meaning in the English mental lexicon', *Psychological Review*, 101(1): 3–33 (1994). The experiments on selectional restrictions are reported in G. Libben's 'Are morphological structures computed during word recognition?', *Journal of Psycholinguistic Research*, 22 (5): 535–544.

The section on the processing of garden path sentences is taken from Lynn Frazier's article 'Sentence processing: a tutorial review', in *Attention and Performance, vol. 12. The Psychology of Reading*, edited by M. Coltheart (London: Lawrence Erlbaum, 1987, pp. 559–96). These sentence types are also discussed in David Caplan's book *Language: Structure, Processing and Disorders* (Cambridge, Mass.: MIT Press, 1994).

The study of sentence ambiguity is reported in M.K. Tannenhaus, G.N. Carlson and M.S. Seidenberg, 'Do listeners compute linguistic representations?' in *Natural Language Parsing*, edited by D.R. Dowty, L. Karttunen, and A.M. Zwicky (Cambridge: Cambridge University Press, 1985).

Recommended reading   Berko-Gleason, J. and Ratner, Nan Bernstein. 1993. *Psycholinguistics*. Philadelphia: Harcourt Brace.

Garman, Michael. 1990. *Psycholinguistics*. Cambridge: Cambridge University Press.

Gernsbacher, M.A. 1994. *Handbook of Psycholinguistics*. New York: Academic Press.

Kess, J. 1992. *Psycholinguistics*. Philadelphia: John Benjamins.

Questions

1. How do psycholinguistic investigations of language differ from theoretical linguistic investigations?

2. Consider the following slips of the tongue. What does each reveal about the process of language production?
   a) They *laked* across the *swim*.
   b) The spy was *gound* and *bagged*
   c) I will *zee* you in the *bark*.

3. Imagine that you read that a psycholinguist has reported an experiment in which a priming effect was found for morphological roots on suffixed past tense forms in a lexical decision task.
   a) State the dependent variable in the experiment.
   b) Give an example of a prime stimulus.
   c) Give an example of a target stimulus.

4. Imagine that ERP researchers find that a positive spike is consistently observed half a second after the presentation of a particular sentence type. What do you think this new ERP spike would be called?

5. Complete the following sentences by filling in the blanks. In each case, what type of top-down processing and bottom-up processing guided your decision?
   a) The children __ running in the park.
   b) All __ movies I like have happy endings.
   c) He tends to see everything as __ and white.

6. Recall that according to the cohort model, a word is recognized from beginning to end, one phoneme at a time. According to the cohort model, how many phonemes of each of the following words would have to be processed before a hearer would be sure which word had been spoken?
   a) giraffe
   b) splat
   c) computerize

7. Write the garden path sentences in examples *10)* and *11)* of this chapter on index cards. Take a few other cards and write a normal sentence on each of them. Now, have some friends try to read the sentences on the cards aloud. Do they show evidence that garden path sentences are more difficult to process?

8. What is a processing module? Try to describe the process of reading single words in terms of a processing model that contains specific modules.

9. In this chapter, parsing has been discussed in the context of sentence

processing. The notion of parsing, however, can also be used to describe how morphologically complex words are analysed. Describe, in terms of parsing, how you think the following multimorphemic words would be processed.
a) bookmark
b) unredoable
c) overbearing

10. Imagine yourself as a psycholinguist trying to devise experiments to investigate how people do language. What experiments would you make up to address the following questions? Be as specific as possible about how you would interpret the question and what you would do to try to find an answer through a psycholinguistic experiment.
a) Are semantically abstract words easier to process than semantically concrete ones?
b) Are simple clauses more difficult to understand than conjoined clauses?
c) Do people read words from beginning to end?
d) Do people with different degrees of education process language in fundamentally different ways?
e) Does the way you parse a sentence depend on what language you speak?

12

Language acquisition: the emergence of a grammar

Sook Whan Cho and William O'Grady

Human brains are so constructed that one brain responds in much the same way to a given trigger as does another brain, all things being equal. This is why a baby can learn any language; it responds to triggers in the same way as any other baby.

❧ D. Hofstadter

One of the most intriguing phenomena studied by linguists is children's acquisition of language. So rapid and commonplace is it that it is taken for granted by most people. In fact, language acquisition is a major intellectual achievement. In recent decades, an increasingly large amount of linguistic research has focused on the question of how children the world over are able to master the complexities of human language in the space of a few short years.

This chapter deals with some of the major findings of research into the nature of the language acquisition process. We will begin by considering the research strategies used by linguists and psychologists in the study of linguistic development. We will then describe some of the major findings concerning children's acquisition of the phonological, morphological, syntactic, and semantic systems of their language. The chapter concludes with a brief examination of the contribution of the linguistic environment to language acquisition, the relationship between the emergence of language and cognitive development, and the possible existence of inborn linguistic knowledge.

1

THE STUDY OF LANGUAGE ACQUISITION

Although we commonly refer to the phenomenon of linguistic development as 'language acquisition', the end result of this process is actually a *grammar* – the mental system that allows people to speak and understand a language. There are at least two reasons for believing that the development of linguistic skills must involve the acquisition of a grammar.

First, as noted in Chapter 1, mature language users are able to produce and understand an unlimited number of novel sentences. This can only happen if, as children, they have acquired a system of productive grammatical rules that are applicable to novel cases. Simple memorization of a fixed inventory of words and sentences would not equip the language learner to deal with previously unheard utterances – a basic requisite of normal language use.

A second indication that children acquire grammatical rules is found in their own utterances. For example, rather than simply memorizing all the regular and exceptional past tense forms for English verbs, children formulate a general rule that adds *-ed* to the verb stem. This rule sometimes produces forms such as *doed, *leaved, and *goed in addition to *washed, walked,* and so forth. Such errors provide clear signs of children's attempts to construct grammatical rules.

Because language acquisition involves the emergence of a grammar, its study is closely tied to the type of linguistic analysis with which we have been concerned in preceding chapters. Indeed, linguists and psychologists studying language acquisition must often look to the study of phonology, syntax, and other components of the grammar for help in identifying and describing the rules and categories that children acquire during the first years of life.

1.1

Methods

A good deal of research on the acquisition of language focuses on children's early utterances, the order in which they emerge, and the kinds of errors they contain. The study of these phenomena not only contributes to a description of the language acquisition process, but also provides valuable clues about the nature of the mental mechanisms involved in linguistic development.

Investigators concerned with these problems draw on two basic methods – naturalistic observation and experimentation. Although both methods provide valuable information about the nature of the language acquisition process, they do so in different ways.

The naturalistic approach

In the **naturalistic** approach, investigators observe and record children's spontaneous verbal behaviour. One type of naturalistic investigation is the so-called **diary** study, in which a researcher (often a parent) keeps daily notes on a child's linguistic progress. Alternatively, a researcher may visit individual children on a regular basis and record (or videotape) a sample of utterances (perhaps one hour every second week over a period of five months). In both cases, attention is paid to the context in which children's speech occurs, the toys they are playing with, the pictures they are looking at, and the like.

The experimental approach

In **experimental** studies, researchers typically make use of specially designed tasks to elicit linguistic activity relevant to the phenomenon that they wish to study. The child's performance is then used to formulate hypotheses about the type of grammatical system acquired at that point in time.

Experimental research is typically **cross-sectional** in that it investigates and compares the linguistic knowledge of different children (or groups of children) at a particular point in development. A typical cross-sectional study might involve conducting a single experiment with a group of two year olds, a group of four year olds, and a group of six year olds – taking each of these groups to be representative of a particular stage or 'cross-section' of the developmental process. In contrast, naturalistic studies tend to be **longitudinal** in that they examine language development in a particular child or group over an extended period of time (sometimes as long as several years). As the name suggests, longitudinal studies take a long time to conduct, but unlike cross-sectional studies they have the advantage of permitting researchers to observe development as an ongoing process in individual children.

Experimental studies usually employ tasks that test children's comprehension, production, and imitation skills. One widely used method for testing children's comprehension makes use of a picture selection format. For example, in order to test the interpretation of reflexive pronouns, an experimenter might show children a picture of Big Bird scratching himself as the Cookie Monster looks on and a picture of Big Bird scratching the Cookie Monster, and then ask which picture goes with the sentence *Big Bird is scratching himself*. A second method involves supplying children with an appropriate set of toys and then asking them to act out the meaning of a sentence – perhaps a passive structure such as *The truck was bumped by the car*. Children's responses can provide valuable clues about the type of grammatical rules being used to interpret sentences at particular stages of development.

In a typical production task, the child is shown a picture and asked to describe it. Although production tasks can be useful for assessing certain types of linguistic knowledge, there are many structures (such as passives) which are hard to elicit even from adults since they are used only in special contexts. Moreover, because children's ability to comprehend language is often more advanced than their ability to produce sentences of their own, production tasks can provide an overly conservative view of linguistic development unless they are accompanied by other types of tests.

Both comprehension and production tests are often used in conjunction with imitation tasks. Although one might think that imitation would be excessively easy, it has been found that children's ability to repeat structures reflects the state of their current grammatical knowledge and that a form that has not been mastered will probably not be correctly repeated. Thus, a child who has not yet acquired auxiliary verbs will repeat the sentence *Mummy is talking* as *Mummy talking*.

By using naturalistic observation together with experimental techniques, linguists and psychologists have made significant progress in the study of the language acquisition process. Much of this chapter is devoted to a survey of this progress, beginning with the development of speech sounds.

2

PHONOLOGICAL DEVELOPMENT

From birth, children are exposed to a variety of noises in their environment. Before they can begin to acquire language, they must first separate non-speech noises from speech sounds. The rudiments of this ability seem to be present at birth, since newborns respond differently to human voices than to other sounds and can recognize their mother's voice within a matter of weeks.

From around one month of age, children exhibit the ability to distinguish among certain speech sounds. In one experiment, infants were presented with a series of identical [ba] syllables. These were followed by an occurrence of the syllable [pa]. A change in the children's sucking rate (the normal reaction to a new stimulus) indicated that they perceived the difference between the two syllables, and were therefore able to distinguish between [p] and [b].

Despite this early sensitivity to contrasts among speech sounds, children initially cannot distinguish between meaningful words. The emergence of this ability has been examined in a task in which children are presented with two toy animals named *bok* and *pok* and are asked to respond to sentences such as *Show me pok*. To respond correctly, children must not only hear the difference between [p] and [b] but also recognize that this difference is linguistically significant – that it is used to distinguish between words in their language. Children under eighteen months have little success in this type of task.

2.1

Babbling

Even before children master the phonemic contrasts of their language, they begin to develop the articulatory movements needed to produce these distinctions in speech. Although there is considerable variation in the pattern of phonological development, a number of general trends can be identified.

The emergence of articulatory skills begins around six months of age, with the onset of babbling. It is likely that babbling provides children with the opportunity to experiment with and begin to gain control over their vocal apparatus – an important prerequisite for later speech. Children who are unable to babble for medical reasons[1] can subsequently acquire normal pronunciation, but their speech development is significantly delayed.

Despite obvious differences among the languages to which they are exposed, children from different linguistic communities exhibit significant similarities in their babbling. The tendencies in Table 12.1 are based on data from fifteen different languages, including English, Thai, Japanese, Arabic, Hindi, and Mayan. (We focus here on consonant sounds, for which the data are somewhat more reliable than for vowels.)

Table 12.1 Cross-linguistic similarities in babbling

Frequently found consonants			Infrequently found consonants			
p	b	m	f	v	θ	ð
t	d	n	ʃ	ʒ	tʃ	dʒ
k	g		l	r	ŋ	
s	h	w	j			

Such cross-linguistic similarities suggest that early babbling is at least partly independent of the particular language to which children are exposed. In fact, even deaf children babble, although their articulatory activity is somewhat less varied than that of hearing children.

2.2

The developmental order

Babbling increases in frequency until the age of about twelve months, at which time children start to produce their first understandable words. Babbling may overlap with the production of real words for several weeks before dying out. By the time children have acquired fifty words or so, they begin to adopt fairly regular patterns of pronunciation.

Language acquisition researchers have expended a good deal of effort trying to determine the order in which speech sounds are mastered in production and perception. Although this work has been hindered by difficulties in determining precisely when a contrast has been acquired, as well as by a shortage of reliable data from a sufficiently broad range of languages, some general trends seem to exist.

- As a group, vowels are acquired before consonants (by age three).
- Stops tend to be acquired before other consonants.
- In terms of place of articulation, labials are acquired first, followed, with some variation, by velars, alveolars, and palato-alveolars. Dentals (such as [θ] and [ð]) are acquired last.
- New phonemic contrasts manifest themselves first in word-initial position. Thus, the /p/–/b/ contrast, for instance, will be manifested in pairs such as *pat–bat* before *mop–mob*.
- All other things being equal, a sound (like [s] in English) that occurs in many different words will be acquired before a sound (like [ʒ]) that occurs in relatively few words.

By age two, the average English-speaking child can produce the inventory of consonant phonemes listed in Table 12.2.

Table 12.2 Consonant inventory at age two

Stops			Fricatives	Other
p	b	m	f	w
t	d	n	s	
k	g			

By age four, this inventory is considerably larger and includes the sounds listed in Table 12.3. Still to be acquired at this age are the interdental fricatives [θ] and [ð] and the voiced palato-alveolar fricative [ʒ].

In general, the relative order in which sounds are acquired during the language acquisition process reflects their distribution in languages of the world. The sounds that are acquired early are generally the ones that are most widely found in the world's languages while the sounds that are acquired late tend to be the ones that are less common across languages.

Table 12.3   Consonant inventory at age four

Stops			Fricatives		Affricates		Other	
p	b	m	f	v	tʃ	dʒ	w	j
t	d	n	s	z			l	r
k	g	ŋ	ʃ					

Early phonetic processes

The sound patterns found in child language are quite different from those used by adults in terms of both the segments they contain and the phonotactic combinations they allow. These differences are the product of a small number of universal phonetic processes that replace certain sounds with others that children find easier to produce and/or perceive. In discussing examples of these processes, we will assume that children's mental representation of a word's pronunciation is close to that of an adult even though its spoken form may be quite different.

Syllable simplification

One frequent process in children's speech involves the systematic deletion of certain sounds in order to simplify syllable structure. In the data shown in Table 12.4 – typical of the speech of two- and three-year-old children – consonant clusters are reduced by deleting one or more segments.

Table 12.4   Reduction of consonant clusters

[s] + stop (strategy: delete [s])
stop → [tɒp]
small → [mɒ]
desk → [dek]

stop + liquid (strategy: delete liquid)
try → [taɪ]
crumb → [gʌm]
bring → [bɪŋ]

fricative + liquid (strategy: delete liquid)
from → [fʌm]
sleep → [si:p]

nasal + voiceless stop (strategy: delete nasal)
bump → [bʌp]
tent → [det]

Another common deletion process in early child language involves the elimination of final consonants. Initial consonants, in contrast, are typically retained if they precede a vowel.

1)

dog → [dɒ]
bus → [bʌ]
boot → [bu:]

Both the reduction of consonant clusters and the deletion of final consonants have the effect of simplifying syllable structure, bringing it closer to the CV pattern that is universally favoured by children and that is the most widely found pattern in human language in general.

Substitution

One of the most widespread phonetic processes in early language involves substitution – the systematic replacement of one sound by an alternative that the child apparently finds easier to articulate. Common substitution processes include **stopping**, the replacement of a fricative by a corresponding stop; **fronting**, the moving forward of a sound's place of articulation; **gliding**, the replacement of a liquid by a glide; and **denasalization**, the replacement of a nasal stop by a non-nasal counterpart. These processes are illustrated with the help of English examples in Table 12.5.

Table 12.5　Substitution in early speech

Process	Example	Change
Stopping (continuant → stop)	sing → [tɪŋ]	s → t
	sea → [ti:]	s → t
	zebra → [di:brə]	z → d
	thing → [tɪŋ]	θ → t
	this → [dɪt]	ð → d, s → t
	shoes → [tu:d]	ʃ → t, z → d
Fronting	ship → [sɪp]	ʃ → s
	jump → [dzʌmp]	dʒ → dz
	chalk → [tsɔ:k]	tʃ → ts
	go → [dou]	g → d
Gliding	lion → [jaɪn]	l → j
	laughing → [jæfɪŋ]	l → j
	look → [wʊk]	l → w
	rock → [wɒk]	r → w
	story → [stowi:]	r → w
Denasalization	spoon → [bu:d]	n → d
	jam → [dæb]	m → b
	room → [wu:b]	m → b

Assimilation

Still another widespread phonetic process in child language is assimilation – the modification of one or more features of a segment under the influence of neighbouring sounds. In the following examples, initial consonants have been voiced in anticipation of the following vowel.

2)

tell	[del]
pig	[bɪg]
push	[bʌs]
soup	[zu:p]

Assimilation is also observed in children's tendency to maintain the same place of articulation for all of the consonants or vowels in a word. This can lead to the pronounciation of *doggy* as [gɒgi:] (with two velar stops) or as [dɒdi:] (with two alveolar stops). Other examples of this include [felf] for *self* (with identical consonants) and [bibi] for *baby* (with identical vowels in both syllables).

2.4

Production versus perception

As noted at the beginning of section 2, children are initially unable to use phonemic contrasts to distinguish between words in their language. Do children develop the ability to perceive the phonemic contrasts of their language at the same time as they learn how to produce them, or do perceptual skills emerge first? According to one study, a child who could not produce a distinction in his own speech between *mouse* and *mouth*, *cart* and *card*, or *jug* and *duck* was nonetheless able to point to pictures of the correct objects in a comprehension task. Evidently, this child's ability to perceive the phonemic contrasts in question exceeded his ability to produce them.

Another indication that children's perceptual abilities are more advanced than their articulatory skills comes from their reaction to adult speech that fails to respect the normal phonemic contrasts. The following report describes one such incident.

One of us, for instance, spoke to a child who called his inflated plastic fish a *fis*. In imitation of the child's pronunciation, the observer said: 'This is your *fis*?' 'No,' said the child, 'my *fis*.' He continued to reject the adult's imitation until he was told, 'That is your fish.' 'Yes,' he said, 'my fis.'

The child's reaction to the adult's initial pronunciation of *fish* shows that he could perceive the difference between [s] and [ʃ] even though he could not yet produce it himself.

3

MORPHOLOGICAL DEVELOPMENT

As is the case with the sound pattern of language, the details of morphological structure emerge over a period of several years. Initially, the words of English-speaking children seem to lack any internal morphological structure. Affixes are entirely absent and most words consist of a single root morpheme. Gradually, inflectional and derivational morphemes appear, marking an increased capacity for word formation.

In a language such as English, which has many examples of irregular inflection (*men* as the plural of *man*, *ran* as the past of *run*), children often begin by simply memorizing forms on a case-by-case basis without regard for general patterns or rules. Thus, they may initially produce the correct plural form for *man* and the correct past tense for *run*. When they subsequently observe the generality of *-s* as a plural marker and *-ed* as a past tense marker around age 2;6 (two years, six months), they sometimes incorrectly use these suffixes for the irregular forms – producing words such as **mans* and **runned*. (Errors that result from the overly broad application of a rule are called **overgeneralizations** or **overregularizations**.) Even occasional mixed forms such as *felled*, a blend of *fell* and *falled*, may be used.

Table 12.6   The development of affixes

Stage 1:	case-by-case learning
Stage 2:	overuse of general rule
Stage 3:	mastery of exceptions to the general rule

Recent work has shown that inflectional overgeneralization, which can last into the school years, is much less frequent than traditionally thought: pre-school children seem to overregularize irregular verbs less than 25 per cent of the time at any point in development. This suggests that the over-generalization errors observed in early speech reflect lapses in accessing the appropriate irregular form from the lexicon rather than the failure to learn irregular forms *per se*.

3.1

A developmental sequence

An important result of child language research during the 1970s was the discovery that the development of bound morphemes and functional categories (such as determiners and auxiliaries) takes place in an orderly sequence with relatively little variation from child to child. In a pioneering study of three children between the ages of twenty months and thirty-six months, the developmental sequence shown in Table 12.7 for English morphemes was found to be typical.

Table 12.7   Typical developmental sequence for non-lexical morphemes

1. *-ing*
2. plural *-s*
3. possessive *-'s*
4. *the, a*
5. past tense *-ed*
6. third person singular *-s*
7. auxiliary *be*

An interesting feature of this developmental sequence is that it seems to be largely unrelated to the frequency of the different morphemes in the speech heard by children. For example, as Table 12.8 shows, the determiners *the* and *a* are the most frequent non-lexical morphemes in the children's environments even though they are acquired relatively late.

Table 12.8   Typical relative frequency of morphemes in parental speech

1.   *the, a*
2.   *-ing*
3.   plural *-s*
4.   auxiliary *be*
5.   possessive *-'s*
6.   third person singular *-s*
7.   past tense *-ed*

This shows that frequency by itself cannot explain the relative developmental order for non-lexical morphemes, although it may have some role to play in conjunction with other factors.

Determining factors   What, then, determines the order of acquisition of non-lexical categories and bound morphemes? Research on a variety of languages suggests that several factors are involved.

1. Frequent occurrence in utterance-final position   Children show a greater tendency to notice and remember elements that occur at the end of the utterance than those found in any other position.

2. Syllabicity   Children seem to take greater notice of morphemes such as *-ing*, which can constitute syllables on their own, than the plural or possessive suffix *-'s*, whose principal allomorphs (/s/ and /z/) are single consonants.

3. A straightforward relation between form and meaning   Whereas the word *the* functions only as a determiner in English, the verbal suffix *s* simultaneously represents three linguistic categories: person (third), number (singular), and tense (non-past). This latter type of morpheme is more difficult for children to acquire.

4. Few or no exceptions in the way it is used   Whereas all singular nouns form the possessive with *-'s*, not all verbs use *-ed* to mark the past tense (cf. *saw, read, drove*). Such exceptions hinder the language acquisition process.

5. Allomorphic invariance   Whereas the affix *-ing* has the same form for all verbs, the past tense ending *-ed* has three major allomorphs – /t/ for verbs such as *chase*, /d/ for forms such as *crave* and /ɪd/ for verbs such as *recite*. This type of allomorphic variation, which also occurs with the plural, possessive, and third person singular affixes in English, slows morphological development.

6. Clearly discernible semantic function   Whereas morphemes such as plural *-s* express easily identifiable meanings, some morphemes (such as the third person singular *-s*) make no obvious contribution to the meaning of the sentence. Acquisition of this latter type of morpheme is relatively slow.

The status of the English morphemes whose developmental order we have been considering is indicated in Table 12.9; as before, morphemes are listed in order of emergence. (The ± symbol in the second column indicates that the morphemes in question have both syllabic and non-syllabic allomorphs. The plural suffix, for example, is realized as /s/ in some contexts but as /ɪz/ in others.)

Table 12.9 Factors affecting development

Morphemes	Factors					
	1	2	3	4	5	6
-*ing*	+	+	+	+	+	+
plural -*s*	+	±	+	+	−	+
possessive -'*s*	−	±	+	+	−	+
the, a	−	+	+	+	−	−
past tense -*ed*	+	±	+	−	−	+
third person singular -*s*	−	±	−	+	−	−
auxiliary *be*	−	±	−	+	−	−

As Table 12.9 helps show, the morphemes that are acquired first generally exhibit more of the properties just outlined than those that emerge at a later point.

3.2

Allomorphic rules

As children's productive and perceptual abilities improve, they start to follow the rules regulating the sort of allomorphic variation associated with the English plural (/s/ in *hats*, /z/ in *pens*, /ɪz/ in *judges*) and the past tense (/t/ in *taped*, /d/ in *played*, /ɪd/ in *hunted*). Initially, even allomorphic variation as straightforward as the *a/an* alternation in English can cause difficulty for language learners, and it is not unusual to hear children aged two to three produce utterances such as *a apple*.

A well-known technique for studying the development of morphophonemic rules involves presenting children with nonsense words and asking them to form plurals or past tense forms. If the children have mastered productive rules for allomorphic variation, they ought to be able to add appropriate endings even to words they have never heard before. In a classic experiment, children were shown a picture of a strange creature and told, 'This is a wug.' A second picture was then presented and the children were given the following type of question.

3)

Now, there's another wug. There are two of them.
Now, there are two . . . ?

Children who knew the plural formation rule were able to respond with the form /wʌgz/. Table 12.10 indicates the average scores attained by preschoolers (aged four to five) and first graders (aged five and a half to seven) on specific nonsense words in this experiment.

Table 12.10   Percentage of correct responses on wug test

Allomorph	Nonsense word	Pre-schoolers (%)	First graders (%)
/s/	heafs	79	80
/z/	wugs	76	97
	luns	68	92
	tors	73	90
	cras	58	86
/ɪz/	tasses	28	39
	gutches	28	38
	kashes	25	36
	nizzes	14	33

These results suggest that the various allomorphs of the plural are acquired at different times. Particularly problematic is the /ɪz/ allomorph, which is needed in the last four items in Table 12.10. Even first grade children fail to produce the correct form of the plural here in well over half the cases studied, perhaps because /ɪz/ is the least frequent of the plural allomorphs and occurs in the most restrictive context (after a strident; see Chapter 6, section 1.2).

3.3

Word formation rules

Like inflectional morphemes, derivational affixes and compounding appear to be acquired in a more or less fixed order. In one experiment, children were given sentence frames that required the formation of a new word from a real or made-up root. For the agentive -*er*, for example, a typical frame would be *A person who niches is called a* __. As Table 12.11 shows, not all word formation processes were equally easy for the children.

Table 12.11   Percentage correct for made-up roots

Construction	Pre-school (%)	Early School (%)	Middle School (%)
Agentive -*er*	7	63	80
Compound	47	50	65
Adjectival -*y*	0	30	55
Instrumental -*er*	7	35	45
Adverbial -*ly*	0	13	20

The crucial factor in determining the order of emergence of these word formation processes seems to be productivity. The two processes that apply most freely in English (the formation of a noun by the addition of the agentive affix -*er* to a verb and compounding) were the first to emerge. On the other hand, morphemes that can apply to only a restricted set of roots (e.g., -*ly*, which can combine with *quick* but not *fast*) seem to be mastered at a much later age. This supports the earlier suggestion that the relative lack of exceptions facilitates morphological development (factor 4 in the list given in section 3.1).

Even the subtlest properties of word formation seem to be acquired in the pre-school years. One such property, first discussed in section 3.1 of Chapter 4, involves the fact that an inflectional suffix such as the plural cannot occur inside compounds (compare *dogs catcher* with *dog catcher*). In one study, children as young as three years of age produced compounds that obeyed this constraint. Thus, when asked a question such as 'What do you call someone who eats cookies?', they responded by saying *cookie eater* rather than *cookies eater*.

Of course, the acquisition of word formation processes is not entirely error-free. Three- and four-year-old children, for example, have been observed to make word order errors in compounds, producing forms such as *breaker bottle* (for *bottle breaker*) and *builder wall* (for *wall builder*). However, such errors typically disappear by age five.

4

SYNTACTIC DEVELOPMENT

Like phonological and morphological development, the emergence of syntactic rules takes place in an orderly sequence. Beginning with the production of one-word utterances near the end of the first year of life, children gradually master the rules for sentence formation in their language. Some of the milestones in this developmental process are considered here.

4.1

The one-word stage

As noted earlier, children begin to produce one-word utterances between the ages of twelve months and eighteen months. A basic property of these one-word utterances is that they can be used to express the type of meaning that would be associated with an entire sentence in adult speech. Thus, a child might use the word *dada* to assert 'I see Daddy', *more* to mean 'Give me more juice', and *up* to mean 'I want up'. Such utterances are called **holophrases** (literally 'whole sentences').

In forming holophrastic utterances, children seem to choose the most informative word that applies to the situation at hand. A child who wanted a drink, for example, would say *juice* rather than *want* since the former word is more informative in this situation. Similarly, a child who notices a new doll

Table 12.12   Semantic relations in children's one-word utterances

Semantic relation	Utterance	Situation
Agent of an action	*dada*	as father enters the room
Action or state	*down*	as child sits down
Theme	*door*	as father closes the door
Location	*here*	as child points
Recipient	*mama*	as child gives mother something
Recurrence	*again*	as child watches lighting of a match

would be more likely to say *doll* than *see*, thereby referring to the most novel feature of the situation he or she is trying to describe.

Table 12.12 lists some of the semantic relations that children commonly try to express during the one-word stage.

4.2

The two-word stage

Within a few months of their first one-word utterances, children begin to produce two-word 'mini-sentences'. Table 12.13 provides a sampling of these utterances and the types of meaning they are commonly used to express. (Although these examples are from English, similar patterns are found in the early development of all languages.)

Table 12.13   Some patterns in children's two-word speech

Utterance	Intended meaning	Semantic relation
Baby chair	'The baby is sitting on the chair.'	agent-location
Doggie bark	'The dog is barking.'	agent-action
Ken water	'Ken is drinking water.'	agent-theme
Hit doggie	'I hit the doggie.'	action-theme
Daddy hat	'Daddy's hat.'	possessor-possessed

As these examples help illustrate, the vast majority of two-word utterances employ an appropriate word order, suggesting a very early sensitivity to this feature of sentence structure. It is somewhat less clear whether children have acquired syntactic categories such as noun, verb, and adjective at this point in their development. This is because the inflectional affixes that help distinguish among syntactic categories in adult English (such as the plural and the past tense) are absent during this period. To complicate matters still further, the relative shortness of the utterances produced during the two-word stage means that the positional differences associated with category distinctions in adult speech are often not manifested. Thus, words such as *busy* (an adjective in adult speech) and *push* (a verb) may appear in identical patterns.

4)

Mummy busy.
Mummy push.

While this does not show that children lack syntactic categories, it makes it very difficult to demonstrate that they possess them. For this reason, linguists and psychologists are split over whether to describe children's utterances in terms of the semantic relations that they express (as in Table 12.13) or the syntactic categories of adult speech.

4.3

The telegraphic stage

After a period of several months, during which their speech is limited to one- and two-word utterances, children begin to produce longer and more complex grammatical structures. Some representative utterances from the first part of this period follow.

5)

Chair broken.
Daddy like book.
What her name?
Man ride bus today.
Car make noise.
Me wanna show Mommy.[2]
I good boy.

At first, these utterances lack bound morphemes and most non-lexical categories. Because of their resemblance to the style of language found in

Table 12.14   Sample utterances from a child's speech over a twelve-month period

Age	Sample utterances
28 months	Play checkers.
	Big drum.
	I got horn.
	A bunny-rabbit walk.
30 months	Write a piece of paper.
	What that egg doing?
	I lost a shoe.
	No, I don't want to sit seat.
32 months	Let me get down with the boots on.
	Don't be afraid a horses.
	How tiger be so healthy and fly like kite?
	Joshua throw like penguin.
34 months	Look at that train Ursula brought.
	I simply don't want put in chair.
	Don't have paper.
	Do you want little bit, Cromer?
	I can't wear it tomorrow.
36 months	I going come in fourteen minutes.
	I going wear that to wedding.
	I see what happens.
	I have to save them now.
	Those are not strong mens.
	They are going sleep in wintertime.
	You dress me up like a baby elephant.
38 months	So it can't be cleaned?
	I broke my racing car.
	Do you know the lights went off?
	What happened to the bridge?
	Can I put my head in the mailbox so the mailman can know where I are and put me in the mailbox?
	Can I keep the screwdriver just like a carpenter keep the screwdriver?

telegrams, this acquisitional stage is often dubbed telegraphic. Over a period of several months, affixes, determiners, and auxiliary verbs emerge in accordance with the developmental sequence discussed in section 3.

A noteworthy feature of the telegraphic stage is that despite the emergence of complex new syntactic structures, children make virtually no word order errors. As the previous examples illustrate, adult word order patterns are employed even though individual words may not have the appropriate endings. In languages with variable word order (such as Korean and Russian), children use the various word order patterns with roughly the same relative frequency as adults do.

Language development from age two onward is rapid. As the examples in Table 12.14 help illustrate, children move from relatively primitive two- and three-word utterances at the beginning of the telegraphic stage to a broad range of syntactically intricate sentence types in the space of just a few months.

Because of the diversity and sophistication of the utterances produced during the telegraphic stage, there is general agreement that this period is characterized by the emergence of powerful grammatical devices. Foremost among these are the phrase structure rules, which regulate the order and composition of syntactic units. If you reconsider the examples in 5) above, you will see evidence for the rule that forms phrases consisting of a head (especially a V) and a complement (*like book*, *ride bus*, *show Mummy*). Modifiers, including adjectives like *good* and adverbs like *today*, also exist during this period. (The place of modifiers in phrase structure is discussed in section 5.2 of Chapter 5.)

As already noted, determiners and other non-lexical categories are conspicuously absent from the telegraphic stage. Since these are the types of words that generally serve as specifiers, children's speech sometimes gives the impression that XP categories are acquired in steps, with lexical heads and complements emerging before specifiers. Table 12.15 summarizes the development of phrase structure.

Table 12.15   The development of phrase structure

Stage	Approx. age	Developments
Holophrastic	1–1.5 years	single word utterances; no structure
Two-word	1.5–2 years	early work combinations; presence of syntactic categories unclear
Telegraphic	2–2.5 years	emergence of phrase structure, especially head-complement and subject-VP patterns
Later	2.5 years up	emergence of non-lexical categories (Det, Aux) including those used as specifiers

4.4

Later development

In the years following the telegraphic stage, children continue to acquire the complex grammar that underlies adult linguistic competence, including the system of transformational rules outlined in Chapter 5. Some highlights of this period of development are reviewed in this section.

Inversion

In the very early stages of language acquisition, children signal *yes–no* questions by means of rising intonation alone. (Recall that auxiliary verbs are a relatively late development.)

6)
See hole?
I ride train?
Ball go?
Sit chair?

Even after individual auxiliary verbs appear in child language, there is often a delay of a few months before they undergo Inversion and appear at the beginning of the sentence in *yes–no* questions. In one study, for example, a young boy began using the auxiliary verb *can* at age two years, five months, but did not invert it in questions until six months later.

An interesting error in children's early use of Inversion in both *yes–no* and *wh* questions is exemplified in 7).

7)
Can he *can* look?
What *shall* we *shall* have?
Did you *did* came home?

In these sentences, the auxiliary verb occurs twice – once to the left of the subject (in the position that it occupies after Inversion) and once to the right (in the position it occupies in deep structure). It has been suggested that this pattern reflects an error in the application of the Inversion transformation in that a copy of the moved auxiliary is left behind in its original position.

Experimental work has shown that this type of error is more likely in a sentence such as 8), which has a complex subject NP.

8)
[The girl who is crying] should leave →
*Should [the girl who is crying] should leave?

This presumably happens because the subject NP stands directly between the auxiliary's deep structure position and the position to which it is moved in surface structure. As such, its complexity can interfere with the Inversion operation.

Wh questions

Wh questions emerge gradually between the ages of two and four. For many children, the following three stages are involved.

Stage 1 Children produce both *yes–no* questions and *wh* questions, but Inversion is not possible since auxiliary verbs are not yet acquired. The first *wh* words to be acquired are typically *what* and *where*, followed by *who, how,* and *why*; *when*, *which*, and *whose* are relatively late acquisitions.

9)

Where that?
What me think?
Why you smiling?
Why not me drink it?

Stage 2   Auxiliary verbs make their appearance and undergo Inversion, but more frequently in *yes–no* questions than in *wh* questions.

10)

Yes–no questions (with Inversion):
Did Mummy pinch her finger?
Can't you fix it?
Do I have it?
Will you help me?
Is Mummy talking to Robin's grandmother?

11)

Wh questions (no Inversion):
What I did yesterday?
Why Kitty can't stand up?
Where I should put it?
Where I should sleep?
Why you are smiling?

Stage 3   Inversion is common in *wh* questions as well as *yes–no* questions.

12)

Where did my mitten go?
Where should I sleep?
Why are you smiling?

For some children, Inversion in *wh* questions develops in two substages, appearing later in negated sentences. In these cases, children who are able to produce the constructions in *12)* still use ill-formed negated sentences such as the following:

13)

Why you can't sit down?
Why Kitty can't stand up?

5

SEMANTIC DEVELOPMENT

By age eighteen months or so, the average child has a vocabulary of fifty words or more. Common items include the words listed in Table 12.16.

As Table 12.16 shows, noun-like words make up the single largest class in the child's early vocabulary, with verb- and adjective-like words being the

Table 12.16 Common items in the first fifty words

Entities

Names for people: *daddy, mummy,* etc.

Words referring to

humans:	*baby*
food/drink:	*juice, milk, water, toast, apple, cake*
animals:	*dog, cat, duck, horse*
clothes:	*shoes, hat*
toys:	*ball, doll, blocks*
vehicles:	*car, boat, truck*
other:	*bottle, key, book*

Properties

hot, allgone, more, dirty, cold, here, there

Actions

up, sit, see, eat, go, down

Personal-social

hello, bye, no, yes, please, thank-you

next most frequent category types. Among the most frequent individual words are expressions for displeasure or rejection (such as *no*) and various types of social interaction (such as *please* and *bye*). Over the next months this vocabulary grows rapidly, sometimes by as much as ten or twelve words a day. By age six, most children have mastered about thirteen thousand words.

Children seem to differ somewhat in the types of words that they focus on, especially in the early stages of language acquisition. One of these differences is reflected in the number of nouns in early vocabulary. Whereas some children have a relatively high proportion of such words (75 per cent or more) by age two, other learners exhibit a much lower percentage of nouns (50 per cent or less). Making up for the smaller number of nouns is a larger vocabulary in the area of socially useful expressions such as *bye, go-away, stop-it, thank-you, I-want-it,* and so on. (Hyphens are used here to indicate that these expressions are not yet segmented into their component words.)

5.1

The acquisition of word meaning

A major factor in lexical development is the child's ability to make use of contextual clues to draw inferences about the category and meaning of new words. For instance, from early in the language acquisition process, children can use the presence or absence of determiners to distinguish between names and ordinary nouns. Two-year-old children who are told that a new doll is *a dax* will apply this label to similar-looking dolls as well. However, if they are told that the new doll is *Dax,* they will restrict use of the new word to the doll they have actually been shown. Like adults, these children treat *dax* as an ordinary noun when it is preceded by *a,* but as a name when there is no determiner.

Children are also able to use the meaning of other words in the sentence and their understanding of the non-linguistic context to form hypotheses about new words. In one experiment, for example, three- and four-year-old children were asked to act out the meaning of sentences such as 'Make it so there is *tiv* to drink in this glass (of water)'. The only clues to the interpretation of the nonsense word *tiv* come from the meaning of the rest of the sentence and from the child's understanding of the types of changes that can be made to a glass of water. Not only did more than half the children respond by either adding or removing water, some even remembered what *tiv* 'meant' two weeks later!

The meanings that children associate with their early words sometimes correspond closely to the meanings employed by adults. In many cases, however, the match is less than perfect. The two most typical semantic errors involve overextension and underextension.

Overextension

In cases of **overextension**, the meaning of the child's word is more general or inclusive than that of the corresponding adult form. The word *dog*, for example, is frequently overextended to include horses, cows, and other four-legged animals. Similarly, *ball* is sometimes used for any round object, including a balloon, an Easter egg, a small stone, and so on. Table 12.17 gives some additional examples of overextension.

Table 12.17   Examples of overextension

Word	First referent(s)	Subsequent extensions
tick tock	watch	clocks, gas meter, fire hose on a spool, scale with round dial
fly	fly	specks of dirt, dust, small insects, child's toes, crumbs of bread
quack	duck	all birds and insects, flies, coins (with an eagle on the face)
candy	candy	cherries, anything sweet
apple	apples	balls, tomatoes, cherries, onions, biscuits
turtle	turtles	fish, seals
cookie	cookies	crackers, any dessert
kitty	cats	rabbits, any small furry animal
box	boxes	lifts (elevators)
belt	belts	watchstrap

The basis for overextension

An important issue in the study of language acquisition has to do with whether children's overextensions are the result of similarities in the appearance (shape, size, texture) or the function of the objects to which the overextended word refers. The evidence collected to date suggests that perceptual properties form the critical factor in children's first hypotheses about word meanings. As a result, children often overextend a word to include a set of perceptually similar objects that they know to have diverse functions. For example, one child used the word *moon* for the moon, grapefruit halves, and a crescent-shaped car light. Another child used the word *money* for a set of objects ranging from pennies to buttons and beads. If you reconsider the examples of overextension given in Table 12.17, you will see that they too are more plausibly explained in terms of perceptual similarities than a shared function.

Children seem to overextend more in their production than in their comprehension. A child who overextends the word *dog* in his or her own speech, for example, may well point only to the appropriate animal when asked by an adult to find a dog in a picture. This suggests that children sometimes deliberately overextend words in production to compensate for their limited vocabulary.

Underextension

While overextensions are the most frequent type of word-meaning error in early language (about one-third of children's words are overextended at the fifty-word stage of vocabulary development), children also frequently employ **underextension** by using lexical items in an overly restrictive fashion. Thus, *kitty* might be used to refer to the family pet, but not to any other cats. Or the word *dog* might be used for collies, spaniels, and beagles, but not for Chihuahuas.

Underextension errors often reflect children's propensity to focus on prototypical or core members of a category. As noted in section 1.3 of Chapter 7, the potential referents of many words differ in terms of how well they exemplify the properties associated with a particular concept. Thus, among the potential referents of the word *dog*, collies and spaniels have more of the properties associated with the concept 'dog' (long hair, relative size, type of bark, and so on) than do Chihuahuas. While the preference for a prototype can be overruled by factors such as the presence of a non-typical category member in the child's everyday experience (e.g., a Chihuahua as a family pet), it is clear that the internal structure of concepts can have an important influence on semantic development.

5.2

Spatial and dimensional terms

English has many words that are used to express spatial relations (such as *in*, *on*, and *behind*). Although syntactically similar (most are prepositions), these words differ from each other in terms of their semantic complexity. Notice, for example, that the relation expressed by *on* and *in* does not depend on the speaker's viewpoint: if two marbles are on a box, then they are on it no matter where the speaker is standing. However, matters are more complicated in the case of the relations expressed by *behind* and *in front of* since we would say that the marbles are behind the box only if the box is between us and the marbles. If we stand on the opposite side of the box, the marbles would then appear to be in front of the box. Matters are slightly simpler when the object with respect to which the marbles are situated has an inherent front and back (such as a television). In this case, we can ignore our own position and focus on the marbles' location with respect to the front part of the television.

These considerations seem to be directly reflected in the order in which words expressing spatial relations are acquired.

Table 12.18   Order of acquisition for words expressing spatial relations

Step	Words	Description
1	*in, on, under, beside*	independent of speaker's perspective
2	*behind, in front of*	used with objects with inherent fronts and backs
3	*behind, in front of*	used with objects without inherent fronts or backs

Interestingly, the developmental order shown in Table 12.18 has been observed in a number of languages (Italian, Turkish, and Serbo-Croatian) other than English. This suggests that the considerations that determine the semantic complexity of spatial words are universal and therefore are manifested in the acquisition of all languages.

Dimensional terms

Like words referring to spatial relations, terms describing size and dimensions are also acquired in a relatively fixed order, depending on their generality. The first dimensional adjectives to be acquired, *big* and *small*, are the most general in that they can be used for talking about any aspect of size (height, area, volume, and so on). In contrast, the second group of adjectives to emerge – *tall*, *long*, *short*, *high*, and *low* – can only be used for a single dimension (height–length). The remaining modifiers (*thick–thin*, *wide–narrow*, and *deep–shallow*) are still more restricted in their use since they describe the secondary or less extended dimension of an object (Table 12.19). For instance, the dimension of a stick that we describe in terms of width or thickness is almost always less extended than the dimension that we describe in terms of height or length, which tends also to be perceptually more salient.

Table 12.19   Order of acquisition for dimensional adjectives

Step	Words	What they describe
1	*big–small*	any aspect of size
2	*tall–short*, *long–short*, *high–low*	a single dimension
3	*thick–thin*, *wide–narrow*, *deep–shallow*	a secondary dimension

The importance of the salient dimension in the development of adjectives is underlined by a peculiar error that has been observed in children's early use of the modifier *big*. When asked to choose which of the two figures is the 'big one', children between the ages of three and five tend to choose Figure 12.1*b* over 12.1*a* (p. 486).

Although figure *a* is larger in overall area, figure *b* is greater on the vertical dimension. The fact that children take *b* to be bigger suggests that height is more salient to them than is overall area.

Figure 12.1   The importance of salience in the development of adjectives.

5.3

The interpretation of sentence structure (advanced)

As noted in Chapter 7, the interpretation of sentences draws heavily on information about how words are hierarchically organized to form phrase structure. In this section we will briefly consider some aspects of the acquisition of two interpretive phenomena that rely on information about syntactic structure.

Thematic roles

In Chapter 7, we saw that thematic roles are assigned to particular (deep structure) positions in accordance with the following generalizations.

14)

A preposition (P) assigns its role (location, source or goal) to an NP complement.

A verb (V) assigns its theme role to an NP complement (traditionally called the object).

A verb (V) assigns its agent role to the subject.

Children learning English are able to associate thematic roles with particular structural positions at a very early point in the acquisition process. By the time their average utterance length is two words, they are able to respond correctly about 75 per cent of the time to comprehension tests involving simple active sentences such as *15)*, in which the truck is the agent and the car is the theme.

15)

The truck bumped the car.

However, children find it much harder to interpret passive sentences correctly. This is especially true for passive sentences such as the one in *16)*, which contains no semantic clues about which NP is agent and which one is theme. (Note that it makes just as much sense for the car to bump the truck as it does for the truck to bump the car. Such sentences are said to be 'reversible'.)

16)

The car was bumped by the truck.

Although children produce passive sentences in their own speech from around age three, Table 12.20 shows that they have continuing difficulty responding appropriately to passive constructions in comprehension tests.

Table 12.20 Comprehension of reversible passive constructions

Group	Percentage correct
Nursery school (around age 3–4)	20
Kindergarten (around age 4-5)	35
Grade 1 (around age 5-6)	48
Grade 2 (around age 6–7)	63
Grade 3 (around age 7–8)	88

Why should this be so? Thematic role assignment in passive structures is complicated by the fact that the NP bearing the theme role occurs in the subject position while the agent (marked by the preposition *by*) appears after the verb.

17)

Passive sentence: The car was bumped by the truck
                   Theme   *Agent*
Active sentence: The truck bumped the car.
                   Agent   *Theme*

Thus, passive sentences are almost mirror images of their active counterparts in that the agent occurs after the verb and the theme before it rather than vice versa. Significantly, the most common error made by children is to assume that the first NP in passive sentences is the agent and the second NP the theme. This suggests that they tend to overgeneralize the thematic role pattern found in active sentences, thereby systematically erring on passive patterns.

As the data in Table 12.20 show, children begin to apply this strategy randomly around six, suggesting that they are starting to realize that it is not always appropriate. A year or so later, their scores start to rise dramatically, indicating that they recognize the special properties associated with thematic role assignment in the passive construction.

Pronominals and reflexives

In Chapter 7, we saw that a reflexive pronoun (*himself, herself*, and so on) must have a 'higher' (i.e., c-commanding) antecedent in the minimal clause containing it. Thus, *himself* must refer to Gary in the following sentence.

18)

Sam said that [$_S$ Gary slapped *himself* on the wrist].

In contrast, a pronominal (*him, her*) in this position can refer only to Sam or to someone not mentioned in the sentence.

19)

Sam said that [$_S$ Gary slapped *him* on the wrist].

In terms of language acquisition, there is some reason to believe that children are able to interpret reflexives correctly before pronominals. Thus, children between the ages of three and five correctly interpret *himself* as Gary.

However, they often misinterpret *him* as if it were a reflexive, allowing it to refer to Gary in *19)*. It is not until age seven or so that language learners are able to uniformly give the correct interpretation for pronouns in this type of structure.

6

DETERMINANTS OF LANGUAGE ACQUISITION

In the preceding sections, we have seen that children acquire the grammar of their language over a period of several years. While it is relatively easy to describe the order in which children acquire various phonemic contrasts, morphemes, and syntactic rules, it is much more difficult to explain *how* they do this. The sections that follow outline some of the factors that may help children discover the categories and rules that make up the grammar of their language.

6.1

The role of imitation and correction

At one time, it was widely believed that children learn language by simply imitating the speech of those around them. We now know that this cannot be true, since many utterance types produced by children do not closely resemble structures found in adult speech. Plural forms such as *foots* and question structures such as *Why the sun shining?* are obvious examples of patterns that are unique to child language. As noted earlier, such utterances reflect children's attempts to formulate grammatical rules, not the imitation of adult speech.

The importance of imitation to language acquisition is placed in further doubt by the fact that children are typically unable to imitate structures that they have not yet learned. For instance, a child who has not yet acquired the Inversion rule for *wh* questions will imitate sentence *20a)* by producing *20b)*.

20)

a. What can you see? (*model*)
b. What you can see? (*child's imitation*)

Findings like these suggest that children rely on their current grammatical rules to process the speech they hear and that they are therefore not able to imitate sentences exactly as they are produced by adults.

This is not to say that imitation plays no role in language learning. While many children rarely attempt to repeat utterances, some language learners do seem to make selective use of imitation. They imitate new words in constructions they have already learned and repeat novel constructions that contain words already familiar to them. Thus, they might imitate the new word *computer* in a familiar subject–verb–object pattern (such as *Daddy bought a computer*). Similarly, they might imitate a new structure such as the passive if it contained familiar words (*Daddy was called by Mummy*). But they would not imitate a sentence whose structure and vocabulary were both new to them. Such selective imitation suggests that children do not blindly mimic adult speech, but rather exploit it in very restricted ways to improve their linguistic skills.

Correction

Another classic attempt to explain language development is based on the assumption that parents provide children with direct linguistic training by correcting ill-formed utterances. However, such an assumption has not been supported by studies of actual interactions between parents and children. Instead, it has been found that parents evaluate the truth of children's utterances rather than their grammaticality. In one case, a parent even reacted to the utterance *Mama isn't boy, he's a girl* by responding *That's right*.

Even when adults do attempt to correct children's grammatical errors, their efforts seem to have little effect. The following exchange between a child and his mother is typical in this regard.

21)

Child:	Nobody don't like me.
Mother:	No, say 'Nobody likes me.'
Child:	Nobody don't like me.

[*Exchange is repeated eight times.*]

Mother:	No, now listen carefully; say 'Nobody likes me.'
Child:	Oh! Nobody don't LIKES me.

A more subtle form of correction occurs when adults repeat a child's utterance, making adjustments to its form and/or content.

22)

Child:	Daddy here.
Mother:	Yes, Daddy is here.
Child:	Boy chasing dog.
Mother:	Yes, the boy is chasing the dog.
Child:	Him go.
Mother:	Yes, he is going.
Child:	The dog is barking.
Mother:	Yes, he is barking at the kitty.

A study of upper-middle-class families in the United States suggests that mothers of two-year-old children exhibit a slightly greater tendency to revise ungrammatical utterances than grammatical utterances (26 per cent vs 14 per cent). (No such tendency was found in response to the speech of older children.) However, no mothers revised all ungrammatical utterances produced by their children and even grammatical utterances were often revised (the fourth example in 22)). The mothers' responses therefore apparently do not provide language learners with reliable information about whether their utterances are well formed.

6.2

The role of adult speech

Linguistic development obviously depends in crucial ways on the child's linguistic experience. Children who are exposed to English learn to speak English, those exposed to Zulu learn Zulu, and so on. Moreover, children who are not exposed to language do not develop linguistic skills beyond the babbling stage.

A good deal of recent work has been devoted to the search for a possible relationship between language acquisition and the type of speech that is typically addressed to young language learners. Such speech is often called **motherese** or **caregiver speech**. A valuable product of this research has been the discovery that speech addressed to young children has special properties that could well heighten its comprehensibility. Phonologically, for example, motherese is known to consist of clearly articulated utterances with pauses between phrases and exaggerated intonation contours to signal questions, imperatives, and statements. Maternal speech also tends to concentrate on the here and now, consisting primarily of statements relating to the child's current surroundings, activities, and needs. The examples in Table 12.21 help to illustrate this.

Table 12.21 Some examples of caregiver speech

Mother's utterance	Context
That's right, pick up the blocks.	the child is picking up a box of building blocks
That's a puppy.	the child is looking at a young dog
The puppy's in the basket.	the child is examining a puppy in a basket

It seems reasonable to suppose that exposure to this type of language makes it easier for children to match forms (morphemes, words, and phrases) with meanings, and thereby to acquire the vocabulary and structure of their language. Table 12.22 lists some features commonly found in the speech of middle-class English-speaking mothers to their children.

Although potentially helpful, it is not clear that these phenomena are actually crucial to the language acquisition process. In some cultures, for instance, children are not considered to be potential conversational partners until they are fluent speakers. Little speech is addressed directly to them, although they do spend a lot of time with their mothers and are exposed to a good deal of conversation among adults. The fact that these children seem to learn language in a normal fashion indicates that exposure to the speech style typical of middle-class mothers in North American society is not necessary for language acquisition. Indeed, working-class American mothers have been observed to talk considerably less to their babies than their middle-class counterparts. But, of course, this does not prevent babies brought up in working-class families from acquiring language with apparent ease.

We also know that maternal speech has highly selective effects on child

Table 12.22   Some features of English caregiver speech

Phonetic
Slower speech
Higher pitch
Exaggerated intonation and stress
Longer pauses

Lexical and semantic
More restricted vocabulary
Concrete reference to here and now

Syntactic
Fewer incomplete sentences
Short sentences
More commands and questions

Conversational
More repetitions
Fewer utterances per conversational turn

language. In one widely cited study, the speech of fifteen mothers to their daughters (aged one to two years and three months) was analysed. It was found that there were correlations between only some aspects of motherese and child speech. For instance, the number of *yes–no* questions in maternal speech was correlated with the rate at which auxiliary verbs developed. This was presumably because auxiliaries occur in the salient sentence-initial position in *yes–no* questions (*Can Jennifer go?*). However, many other features of maternal speech seem not to influence child language. As we saw earlier (section 3.1), for example, the relative frequency of bound morphemes and non-lexical categories in maternal speech apparently does not determine their order of acquisition.

In and of itself, maternal speech cannot explain how language acquisition occurs. However, research into motherese may contribute to this goal in less direct ways by helping to determine the types of linguistic experience that are most valuable to children. This in turn should help identify the types of mechanisms and strategies involved in language acquisition.

6.3

The role of cognitive development

Cognitive development is the name given to the emergence of the various mental abilities and skills that make up the human intellect. Because there are dramatic changes in both linguistic and non-linguistic abilities during the first years of life, it is tempting to think that the two are somehow linked. Indeed, prominent psychologists have suggested both that general cognitive development shapes language acquisition (a view put forward by the late Swiss psychologist Jean Piaget) and that language acquisition is crucial to other aspects of cognitive development (a position associated with the late Russian psychologist Lev Vygotsky).

There are many suggestive similarities between language acquisition and cognitive development. During the first two years of life, for example, several cognitive advances that could facilitate language acquisition take place. One of these involves the development of object permanence, the ability to recognize that objects have an existence independent of one's interaction with them. Prior to the development of this ability, children seem to assume that an object ceases to exist when it moves out of sight, and is a different entity when it reappears. They therefore do not know where to look for an object that they observe being hidden; from their perspective, it has apparently simply ceased to exist. Object permanence emerges around age eighteen months, just prior to a period of rapid growth in the child's vocabulary. The relative timing of these two events suggests a possible connection: children's ability to learn the names for objects increases dramatically once they understand that those objects have an independent existence.

During the first twenty-four months of their lives, children also acquire the ability to classify objects and actions. They seem to understand that certain things are eaten, others can be sat upon, still others serve as toys, and so on. It is conceivable that these classification skills also play a role in dividing words into linguistic categories such as noun and verb on the basis of their semantic, morphological, and syntactic properties. It has also been suggested that a general ability to arrange and order elements with respect to each other is manifested in children's attempts to organize words into sentences.

Still another link between cognitive development and language acquisition involves seriation, the ability to arrange elements (such as sticks) in order of increasing or decreasing size. Children who are unable to perform this type of task typically describe the objects on which they are working simply as *long* or *short*. In contrast, children who are capable of seriation (age five and older) use comparative terms such as *longer* and *shorter*. Here again, there is an apparent connection between an aspect of language (the *-er* suffix for adjectives) and a more general cognitive skill (seriation).

Just as cognitive development may influence language acquisition, so may the emergence of linguistic skills have an effect on cognition. At the very least, language seems to provide its users with an enhanced capacity for complex reasoning. It is also conceivable that language may help draw children's attention to certain conceptual distinctions that would otherwise develop more slowly. For instance, in the course of learning words such as *father*, *mother*, *brother*, and so on, children may make discoveries about family relationships that would otherwise develop more slowly.

Special cases

Considerations such as these notwithstanding, there is reason to think that language acquisition and other types of cognitive development are to a very significant degree independent of each other. A rich source of evidence for this conclusion comes from the study of children with particular types of mental deficits, including those whose general cognitive development is quite good but whose language is deficient in some respect.

One important study of this type focused on Rick, a severely retarded fifteen year old whose performance on a variety of non-linguistic tasks suggests that his general cognitive level is that of a pre-school child. Yet, as the following examples illustrate, Rick's speech shows signs of syntactic and morphological sophistication – with appropriate use of affixes, non-lexical categories, and word order.

23)

She must've got me up and thrown me out of bed.
She keeps both of the ribbons on her hair.
If they get in trouble, they'd have a pillow fight.
She's the one that walks back and forth to school.
I wanna hear one more just for a change.

Case studies such as this suggest that certain aspects of language (in particular, morphology and syntax) are independent of non-linguistic types of cognitive development. This in turn implies that the mental mechanisms responsible for the acquisition of those parts of the grammar are relatively autonomous and that their operation neither follows from nor guarantees general cognitive development.

6.4

The role of inborn knowledge

Although both cognitive development and exposure to the speech of others are clearly crucial to language acquisition, other factors must be involved. Apes have many of the cognitive skills of two-year-old children, but they do not acquire language even when they are exposed to speech (see Chapter 16). This suggests that there is something about the human mind that equips it to acquire language.

A very influential view among linguists is that children are born with prior knowledge of the type of categories and rules that are found in the grammar of any human language. They therefore know, for example, that the words in the language they are acquiring will belong to a small set of syntactic categories (N, V, and so on) and that there will be rules of a certain sort to create larger phrases (NP, VP, S). The set of inborn categories and principles common to all human languages makes up Universal Grammar (UG), first mentioned in Chapter 5.

Of course, not every feature of a language's grammar can be inborn. In the case of phrase structure, for example, UG stipulates that an XP constituent can include a head X and its complements, but it does not specify the relative order of these elements. This differs from language to language, so that a child acquiring English must learn that Vs and Ps precede their complements while a child acquiring Japanese must learn that heads follow their complements. As noted in section 4 of Chapter 5, Universal Grammar includes a parameter (set of options) for word order. As illustrated in Table 12.23 overleaf, these options include head-initial order versus head-final order. (We ignore the positioning of specifiers for the purposes of this illustration.)

The view that certain grammatical knowledge is inborn is known as **nativism**. Although nativism has roots in philosophy that date back thousands

Table 12.23   The word order parameter

Stipulated by UG	Resulting options
XP → X, Complement	XP → X Complement (head-initial)
	XP → Complement X (head-final)

of years, its popularity in linguistics is due largely to the theories of Noam Chomsky, a linguist at the Massachusetts Institute of Technology. Chomsky's basic claim is that the grammars for human language are too complex and abstract to be learned on the basis of the type of experience to which children have access. Therefore, he argues, significant components of the grammar must be inborn. To illustrate this, we must consider a relatively complex example involving the notion of c-command introduced in Chapter 7 (section 3.3).

Principle A (advanced)

As you may recall, c-command is defined as follows.

24)

NP_a c-commands NP_b if the first category above NP_a contains NP_b.

The c-command relation plays a crucial role in the statement of Principle A, which restricts the interpretation of reflexive pronouns (in English, pronouns ending in *self* or *selves*).

25)

Principle A:
A reflexive pronoun must have an antecedent that c-commands it.

Principle A is responsible for the fact that *himself* in Figure 12.2 takes *the boy's father* as its antecedent, but not *the boy*. That is, the sentence must be taken to mean that the father of the boy is the person who was hurt. (As mentioned in Chapter 7, a possessor NP can occur in the specifier position within a larger NP.)

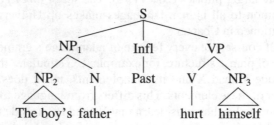

Figure 12.2   The reflexive pronoun takes the c-commanding NP_1 as its antecedent.

In Figure 12.2, there is only one category above the NP *the boy's father* – namely S. Since this category contains the reflexive pronoun, NP1 c-commands *himself* according to our definition and can therefore serve as its antecedent in accordance with Principle A. The same is not true of *the boy*

(NP$_2$) since the first category above it is NP$_1$, which does not contain the reflexive. This means that NP$_2$ does not c-command the reflexive and cannot serve as its antecedent.

There are two major reasons for believing that Principle A must be inborn. First, the notion of c-command is quite abstract. It is not the type of concept that we would expect young children to discover simply by listening to sentences. Since we also know that no one teaches them about c-command, it makes sense to think that this notion is inborn and therefore does not have to be discovered or taught.

Second, the c-command component of Principle A seems to be universal. Thus, there appear to be no languages in which the equivalent of English *himself* can refer to the boy rather than the boy's father in structures such as the one in Figure 12.2. The universality of this restriction would be explained if it were innate and hence part of the inborn linguistic knowledge of all human beings.

The claim that children are born with abstract linguistic principles is controversial, and research on alternatives continues. However, the hypothesis that the grammar is genetically structured is an exciting and intriguing development in linguistics. It is one of the many areas in the field of language acquisition where important breakthroughs remain to be made.

6.5

Is there a critical period?

One of the most intriguing issues in the study of language acquisition has to do with the possibility that normal linguistic development is possible only if children are exposed to language during a particular time frame or **critical period**. Evidence for the existence of such a period comes from the study of individuals who do not experience language during the early part of their lives.

One such individual is the much discussed Genie, who was kept in a small room with virtually no opportunity to hear human speech from around age two to age thirteen. After many years of therapy and care, Genie's non-linguistic cognitive functioning was described as 'relatively normal' and her lexical and semantic abilities as 'good'. In terms of syntax and morphology, however, many problems remained, as evidenced in the following sample utterances presented in Table 12.24.

Table 12.24   Some of Genie's utterances

Utterance	Meaning
Applesauce buy store	'Buy applesauce at the store.'
Man motorcycle have	'The man has a motorcycle.'
Want go ride Miss F. car	'I want to go ride in Miss F.'s car.'
Genie have full stomach	'I have a full stomach.'
Mama have baby grow up	'Mama has a baby who grew up.'

As these examples show, Genie makes word order errors (the second example above) and her speech does not contain non-lexical categories or affixes.

Another revealing case study involved Chelsea, a deaf child who was misdiagnosed as retarded and emotionally disturbed. Chelsea grew up without language and was not exposed to speech until the age of thirty-one, when she was finally fitted with hearing aids. After intensive therapy, she is able to hold a job and to live independently. However, her vocabulary consists of only 2000 words and her sentences are badly ill formed, as the following examples help to show.

26)

The woman is bus the going.
Combing hair the boy.
Orange Tim car in.
The girl is cone the ice cream shopping buying the man.

It is now widely believed that the ability to acquire a first language in an effortless and ultimately successful way begins to decline from age six and is severely compromised by the onset of puberty.

If at first blush this claim appears odd, one may be persuaded of its essential correctness when one realizes that elsewhere in the animal kingdom the idea of critical periods for the acquisition of certain kinds of behaviour has received unambiguous support from a number of experiments.

The best known of these experiments was conducted by Konrad Lorenz. It involved the study of 'imprinting' in goslings – the ability to follow mother goose, wherever she leads. Lorenz showed that in early infancy, goslings can be fooled into being imprinted by anything that looks more or less like a goose, moves more or less like a goose and makes sort of goose-like noises. This he did by pretending to be a goose – by waddling and quacking – in the presence of recently hatched goslings. The goslings proceeded to follow him as they would the real thing. Lorenz was also able to show that this ability disappears after a few days. A gosling unexposed to geese in the days following hatching does not get imprinted if later on it is presented with the appropriate stimulus.

Imprinting is by no means unique in this regard. As we will see in Chapter 16, the acquisition of birdsong is another aspect of avian behaviour which (at least in some species) is subject to a critical period.

Summing up

This chapter has been concerned with the problem of how children acquire the **grammar** of their first language. Research in this area deals with two major issues: the nature of the **developmental sequence** leading to the emergence of mature linguistic competence and the factors that make it possible for children to acquire complex grammatical rules. We have seen that over a period of several years children gradually acquire different subsystems of the grammar (**phonology**, **morphology**, **syntax**, and **semantics**). In many cases, acquisition of a rule will involve a number of intermediate stages, each of which marks a successively closer approximation to the adult grammar. A number of factors may contribute to the child's acquisition of language, including the properties of maternal speech (**motherese**), the effects of general cognitive development, and **inborn** linguistic knowledge. We look to future research for deeper insights into the precise role of these and other factors.

Notes

1 In the case of certain breathing disorders, physicians must insert a tube into the child's trachea. The tube, which must sometimes be left in place for a period of months, interferes with the production of speech sounds.

2 Obviously, this child is acquiring North American English.

Sources

Pioneering work on infant perception is reported in 'Developmental studies of speech perception' by P. Eimas, in *Infant Perception*, edited by L. Cohen and P. Salapatek (New York: Academic Press, 1975); the ability to use phonetic contrasts to distinguish between words is examined in 'Perception and production in child phonology: the testing of four hypotheses' by M. Edwards, *Journal of Child Language* 1: 205–19 (1974). The cross-linguistic data on babbling are summarized and discussed on pp. 9–11 of *Phonological Acquisition and Change* by J. Locke (cited below); see also 'Adaptation to language: evidence from babbling and first words in four languages' by B. de Boysson-Bardies and M. Vihman, *Language* 67: 297–319. For a recent discussion of the relevance of babbling to the development of control over the vocal tract, see S. Pinker's *The Language Instinct* (New York: Morrow, 1994, p. 266). Differences between children's production and perception of speech sounds are found in *The Acquisition of Phonology: A Case Study* by N. Smith (Cambridge: Cambridge University Press, 1973); the '*fis* phenomenon' is reported in 'Psycholinguistic Research Methods' by J. Berko and R. Brown, *Handbook of Research Methods in Child Development*, edited by P. Mussen (New York: John Wiley & Sons, 1960). David Ingram's *Phonological Disability in Children* (London: Edward Arnold, 1976) contains many useful examples of early phonetic processes. The data on developmental order for speech sounds comes from Chapter 8 of *First Language Acquisition* by D. Ingram, cited below.

The remarks on inflectional overgeneralization are based in part on *Over-regularization in Language Acquisition* by G. Marcus, S. Pinker, M. Ullman, M. Hollander, T. Rosen and F. Xu (Monographs of the Society for Research in Child Development, Serial No. 228, Vol. 57, No. 4, 1992). The pioneering work on the developmental order for English bound morphemes and lexical categories was done by R. Brown and reported in his book *A First Language: The Early Stages* (Cambridge, Mass.: Harvard University Press, 1973). The cross-linguistic data on the factors determining morphological development come from 'Universal and particular in the acquisition of language' by D. Slobin, in *Language Acquisition: The State of the Art*, edited by E. Wanner and L. Gleitman (Cambridge: Cambridge University Press, 1982). The original '*wug* test' was done by J. Berko and is reported in her article 'The child's learning of English morphology', *Word* 14: 150-77 (1958). The work on the development of derivational affixes and compounding in English is from 'Recent research on the acquisition of English morphology' by B. Derwing and W. Baker, in *Language Acquisition*, edited by P. Fletcher and M. Garman (Cambridge: Cambridge University Press, 1979).

The data on the acquisition of the prohibition against inflection within compounds is from 'Level-ordering in lexical development' by P. Gordon, *Cognition* 21: 73–93

(1985). Word order errors within compounds are reported in 'Coining complex compounds in English: affixes and word order in acquisition' by E. Clark, B. Hecht and R. Mulford, *Linguistics* 24: 7–29 (1986).

The data in Table 12.14 in section 4.3 are taken from S. Pinker, *The Language Instinct* (London: Allen Lane (The Penguin Press), 1994, pp. 269–71). The data on the development of question structures are based on the classic article by E. Klima and U. Bellugi, 'Syntactic regularities in the speech of children', in *Psycholinguistic Papers*, edited by J. Lyons and R. Wales (Edinburgh: Edinburgh University Press, 1966). The auxiliary copying error in question structures is the subject of an experiment reported by M. Nakayama, 'Performance factors in subject-auxiliary inversion', *Journal of Child Language* 14: 113–26 (1987). The developmental order for *Wh* words is documented by L. Bloom, S. Merkin and J. Wootten, '*Wh* questions: Linguistic factors that contribute to the sequence of acquisition', *Child Development* 53: 1084–92 (1982). Other descriptions confirming the main points of this account can be found in Chapter 9 of the book by Ingram cited below.

The sample fifty-word vocabulary in section 5 is from p. 149 of the book by Ingram, cited below. The estimate that children know thirteen thousand words by age six is from the book by Pinker cited above. The differences in the type of words in children's early vocabulary were first noted by K. Nelson, 'Structure and strategy in learning to talk', *Monographs of the Society for Research in Child Development* 38, no. 149, 1973. The '*dax* experiment' on proper and common nouns is reported by N. Katz, E. Baker, and J. Macnamara in their article 'What's in a name? a study of how children learn common and proper nouns', *Child Development* 45: 469–73 (1974); the '*tiv* experiment' is from 'The child as word learner' by S. Carey, in *Linguistic Theory and Psychological Reality*, edited by M. Halle, J. Bresnan, and G. Miller (Cambridge, Mass.: MIT Press, 1978). The contrast between overextension in production and comprehension is described on pp. 152–3 of the book by Ingram cited below; see also 'Overextensions in production and comprehension revisited' by L. Naigles and S. Gelman, *Journal of Child Language* 22: 19–46 (1995). The literature on spatial and dimensional terms is reviewed both in the book by Ingram and in 'Cognitive prerequisites: the evidence from children learning English' by J. Johnston, in *The Crosslinguistic Study of Language Acquisition*, Vol. 2, edited by D. Slobin (Hillsdale, NJ: Erlbaum, 1985), pp. 961–1004.

The data on the acquisition of passive structures come from a study by E. Turner and R. Rommetveit, reported in their article 'The acquisition of sentence voice and reversibility', *Child Development* 38: 650–60 (1967).

The role of correction in language development is examined in 'Derivational complexity and the order of acquisition in child speech' by R. Brown and C. Hanlon, in *Cognition and the Development of Language*, edited by J. Hayes (New York: John Wiley & Sons, 1970). The data on mothers' reactions to children's ungrammatical and grammatical utterances come from 'Brown and Hanlon revisited: mothers' sensitivity to ungrammatical forms' by K. Hirsh-Pasek, R. Treiman, and M. Schneiderman, *Journal of Child Language* 11: 81–8 (1984). The relationship between *yes–no* questions in maternal speech and the development of auxiliaries is discussed by E. Newport, H. Gleitman, and L. Gleitman in their article, 'Mother, I'd rather do it myself: some effects and noneffects of maternal speech style', in *Talking to Children*, edited by C. Snow and C. Ferguson (Cambridge: Cambridge University Press, 1977). General reviews of the role of the cognitive development in language acquisition can be found in the article by J. Johnston (cited above) and the book by D. Ingram (below). The description of Genie and of Rick is based on 'Abnormal language acquisition and the modularity of language' by S. Curtiss, in *Linguistics: The Cambridge Survey*, Vol.

2, edited by F. Newmeyer (Cambridge: Cambridge University Press, 1988), pp. 96–116. Chelsea's case is discussed by S. Curtiss in 'The independence and task-specificity of language', in *Interaction in Human Development*, edited by A. Bornstein and J. Bruner (Hillsdale, NJ: Erlbaum, 1989).

The discussion of the critical period and imprinting in geese is based on Konrad Lorenz's book *King Solomon's Ring* (New York: Thomas Y. Crowell, 1952).

Questions for this chapter were prepared by Joyce Hildebrand.

Recommended reading

Bloom, Paul, ed. 1993. *Language Acquisition: Core Readings*. New York: Harvester Wheatsheaf.

De Villiers, Jill, and de Villiers, Peter. 1985. 'The acquisition of English.' In *The Crosslinguistic Study of Language Acquisition*. Vol. 1. Edited by D. Slobin. Hillsdale, NJ: Erlbaum.

Fletcher, Paul. 1985. *A Child's Learning of English*. Oxford: Blackwell.

Goodluck, Helen. 1991. *Language Acquisition*. Oxford: Blackwell.

Ingram, David. 1989. *First Language Acquisition: Method, Description and Explanation*. Cambridge: Cambridge University Press.

Locke, John. 1983. *Phonological Acquisition and Change*. New York: Academic Press.

O'Grady, William. 1997. *Syntactic Development*. Chicago: University of Chicago Press.

Piattelli-Palmarini, Massimo, ed. 1980. *Language and Learning: The Debate between Jean Piaget and Noam Chomsky*. Cambridge, Mass.: Harvard University Press.

Questions

1. One piece of evidence that children acquire a grammar is their production of forms like *doed*, *leaved*, and *goed*. From recollections of your experience with children, what are some other forms (not related to the past tense rule) that children produce that indicate they are acquiring and overgeneralizing grammatical rules?

2. In one naturalistic study, a search for passive structures in a sample of 18,000 utterances from sixty children yielded only nineteen examples produced by twelve of the children.
   a) Does this mean that the other forty-eight children had not yet mastered the passive structure?
   b) How are the disadvantages of the naturalistic method exemplified here?

3. The following transcriptions represent the pronunciation of a two-year-old child. Indicate which phonetic processes have applied in each case.

a)	skin	[kɪd]	h)	tent	[det]
b)	spoon	[bu:n]	i)	teddy	[dedi:]
c)	zoo	[du:]	j)	brush	[bʌt]
d)	John	[dɒn]	k)	bump	[bʌp]
e)	bath	[bæt]	l)	play	[pweɪ]
f)	other	[ʌdə]	m)	breakfast	[brekpəst]
g)	Smith	[mɪt]	n)	cheese	[tʃi:s]

4. Drawing on the phonetic processes posited for the preceding exercise, predict one or more plausible immature pronunciations for each of the following words. Justify your predictions.

a) show   e) juice
b) please   f) thumb
c) spit   g) zebra
d) under   h) ring

5. Based on the discussion in section 3.1 of the developmental sequence for morpheme acquisition, consider the acquisition in other languages of the morphemes corresponding to those listed in Table 12.7. Would you predict that these morphemes would be acquired in exactly the same order as their English equivalents? Why or why not?

6. Considering children's tendency to overgeneralize morphological rules, what might we expect a young child to use in the place of the following adult words? Justify your choice in each case.

a) fish (plural)   f) geese
b) went   g) brought
c) mice   h) hit (past tense)
d) ate   i) himself
e) has   j) women

7. Each of the following utterances is from the speech of a child in the two-word stage. Identify the semantic relation expressed by each of these utterances.

	Intended meaning	*Child's utterance*
a)	Jimmy is swimming.	Jimmy swim
b)	Ken's book	Ken book
c)	Daddy is at his office.	Daddy office
d)	You push the baby.	push baby
e)	Mummy is reading.	Mummy read

8. Consider the following data from Jordie, a two-and-a-half-year-old child, in the light of the list of morphemes in Table 12.7.

	Intended meaning	*Jordie's utterance*
a)	Where's my blanket?	Where my blanket?
b)	Does it go right here, Mummy?	Go right here, Mummy?
c)	It's running over.	Running over.
d)	Here, it goes here.	Here, go here.
e)	No, that's mine.	No, that mine.
f)	Dinosaurs say gronk.	Dinosaur say gronk.
g)	There's more.	There's more.

i) Which of the morphemes in Table 12.7 are missing in Jordie's sentences but present in the equivalent adult utterance?

ii) List the morphemes that are present in both the adult interpretations and in Jordie's speech.

9. Now consider the following utterances from a child named Krista.

	Intended meaning	*Krista's utterance*
a)	My name is Krista.	Mine name Krista.
b)	My last name is Pegit.	Last name Pegit.
c)	The tape is right there.	Tape right there.
d)	Daddy's book	Daddy book.
e)	I've got a book.	I'm got a book
f)	Read me a story.	Read me story.
g)	I'll do it.	I'm do it.
h)	He went outside.	He went outside.
i)	Open the gate, please.	Open a gate, please.
j)	Gramma's house.	Gramma's house.
k)	Smell the flowers.	Smell flowers.
l)	Shoes on.	Shoes on.
m)	The wee boy fell down.	Wee boy fell down.
n)	That's my ball.	That's mines ball.

i) Which morphemes are missing in Krista's speech, but present in the adult interpretations? Does this comply with Table 12.7?

ii) Krista uses the past tense twice in the above utterances. Do you think this is evidence that she has acquired the past tense morpheme? Justify your answer.

iii) Comment on Krista's difficulty with possessive pronouns.

iv) Do you think she has acquired possessive -'s? Justify your answer.

10. The allomorphic variation associated with the 3rd person singular verbal ending -*s* is identical to that found with plural -*s*.
   a) Make up a test parallel to the one discussed in section 3.2.
   b) If possible, give your test to children between the ages of three and seven. Are your results similar to the ones discussed in the chapter?

11. The following utterances were produced spontaneously by Holly, aged three years.
   a) I learned about loving mums.
   b) Put him in the bathtub.
   c) We eated gummy snakes.
   d) Thank you for giving these books us.
   e) I don't know.
   f) He bited my finger. (When corrected, she said: He bitted my finger.)
   g) I runned in the water.
   h) I rided on a elephant.

   i) Has Holly acquired the past tense morpheme? How do you know?
   ii) What is the evidence in Holly's speech that she has learned the XP rule? the S rule?
   iii) What is the evidence that she has acquired the category noun? the category verb?

12. The following sentences were uttered by a child aged two and a half.
   a) What's this is called?
   b) Mum, what these is called?

c) Did you don't go to school today?

d) You gonna don't go to school?

Considering these four sentences, describe in detail the child's current knowledge of the Inversion transformation.

13. Consider the following speech sample from a child.

a) What Evan will read?

b) Where Evan will read?

c) Why you see seal?

d) Why she want to?

i) Determine the stage of development of this child in terms of his acquisition of question structures.

ii) What do we expect to happen next?

14. Consider the following examples of overextensions, all of which have actually been observed in children's speech. What is the basis for each of these overextensions?

Word	First referent	Overextensions
a) sch	sound of a train	music, noise of wheels, sound of rain
b) bow-wow	dog	sheep, rabbit fur, puppet
c) baby	baby	people in pictures
d) sizo	scissors	nail file, knife, screwdriver, spoon
e) policeman	policeman	postman, sailor, doctor
f) strawberry	strawberry	grapes, raspberry
g) fireworks	fireworks	matches, light, cigarette
h) Batman	Batman logo on a T-shirt	any logo on a T-shirt

15. Since children have a tendency to focus on the prototypical members of categories in the acquisition of word meanings, how might you expect children to underextend the following words? What members of the category might you expect children not to include?

a) car   d) flower

b) tree   e) fruit

c) ball   f) shoe

16. As mentioned in this chapter, children acquire certain spatial terms like *behind* and *in front of* relatively late. They also acquire words like *those*, *this*, *here*, and *there* relatively late and they find the meaning of the words *left* and *right* difficult to master. What do all of these words have in common that delays their acquisition?

17. Reports of hearing children growing up in homes with non-speaking deaf parents show that children cannot learn language from radio or even television (S. Pinker *The Language Instinct*. London: Allen Lane (The Penguin Press), 1994, p. 278.)

a) Can you think of any reasons for this?

b) What are the implications of these findings for our understanding of the type of experience that is required for language acquisition?

13

Second language acquisition

John Archibald

When we talk about acquisition in SLA research, we are not talking about acquisition in the sense that one acquires polo ponies, Lladró figurines, or CBS, but rather in the sense that one acquires vicious habits, a taste for Brie, or a potbelly.

❧ Kevin R. Gregg

The field of **second language acquisition** (SLA) research investigates how people attain proficiency in a language which is not their mother tongue. So, whether we are looking at someone learning to read Greek in university, or someone becoming fluent in a fifth language in their forties, or a child acquiring a new language after moving to a new country, we refer to it as second language acquisition. The interesting phenomenon of children simultaneously acquiring two languages is generally investigated in the field known as **bilingualism** (which may be thought of as a subdiscipline of SLA research). In this chapter, we will primarily be concerned with second language acquisition in adults.

Over the years, the study of second language acquisition has been undertaken from a variety of different perspectives. In the 1950s and 1960s the primary objective was pedagogic. Researchers were interested in trying to improve the way in which second languages were taught. Hence, they were interested in discovering how those languages were learned. From the 1970s on, the focus shifted from the teacher to the learner.

The reason for this has something to do with what was going on in linguistics, psychology, and first language acquisition research. All three of these areas shifted focus from the external to the internal in the 1960s. Linguistics became concerned with the mental grammar of the speaker, not just the description of the linguistic structures of a given language. Psychology shifted from behaviourism (which denied the importance of mental representations) to cognitive psychology. And research on first language acquisition focused on children's internal grammars. These source fields are also crucial to the study of SLA. Linguistics gives us a sophisticated and accurate description of what learners are trying to learn (the second language), and what they already know (the first language). Psychology can provide us with a learning theory to account for how people acquire knowledge. And the field of first language acquisition (which has been around longer than the field of second language acquisition) offers various findings that can be productively applied to SLA. For example, we know that children who are acquiring their first language (L1) have grammars that are systematic and that their utterances are not just bad imitations of the adult target. As we will see, second language learners too are developing a grammar that is systematic even if it is not nativelike.

1

THE STUDY OF SECOND LANGUAGE ACQUISITION

In the case of first language acquisition, we may ascribe the difference between child and adult grammars to either cognitive or biological immaturity in the child. In the case of second language learning by adults, however, we cannot say that the learners are either cognitively or biologically immature. Rather, they are subject to an influence that is absent from the child's situation: the first language itself. Let us diagram the situation as follows:

L1 $\longrightarrow$ Interlanguage Grammar $\longleftarrow$ L2

Figure 13.1 Influences on an Interlanguage Grammar.

This diagram illustrates the fact that second language learners have a systematic **interlanguage** (IL) grammar – so-called because it is influenced by both the first and the second language and has features of each.

1.1

The role of the first language

One of the most easily recognizable traits of a second language learner's speech is that it bears a certain resemblance to the first language. Thus, someone whose first language is French is likely to sound different from someone whose first language is German when they both speak English. Consider in this regard the following typical pronunciation of the English word *have* by speakers of French and German.

English target	*French speaker*	*German speaker*
have [hæv]	[æv]	[hæf]

Figure 13.2 Phonological transfer.

The form produced by the French speakers reflects the fact that French lacks the phoneme /h/ while the pronunciation associated with German speakers can be traced to the fact that German includes a rule of Syllable Final Obstruent Devoicing (which changes the /v/ to a [f]). The term **transfer** is used to describe the process whereby a feature or rule from a learner's first language is carried over to the IL grammar. Other examples can be seen in Table 13.1.

Table 13.1   More phonological transfers

L1	L2	Example	Comment
Spanish	English	I espeak Espanish.	Spanish does not allow s + consonant sequences word–initially.
English	French	[ty] (you) → [tu]	English does not have the front, rounded vowel [y]. The English speaker substitutes the [u] sound.
Quebec French	English	Over dere.	The [ð] sound is replaced by [d].
European French	English	Over zere.	The [ð] sound is replaced by [z].
English	Spanish	[paɾa] 'for' → [para]	As English does not have the tapped [ɾ] as an allophone of /r/, [r] is substituted.

1.2

The role of the L2

The first language is not the only influence on the interlanguage grammar, since some properties of the IL can be traced to aspects of the L2. In the case of a German speaker who is learning English, for example, the IL grammar will contain some features of both German and English. Consider in Figure 13.3 how a German speaker learning Canadian English might pronounce the word *eyes*.

Target form	Result of Final Obstruent Devoicing	Result of Canadian Vowel Raising
/aɪz/	[aɪs]	[ʌɪs]

Figure 13.3   One possible pronunciation of the English word *eyes* by a German-speaking learner.

Here, the learner first applies the rule of Syllable Final Obstruent Devoicing (transferred from German), changing /aɪz/ to [aɪs]. But the learner also has acquired some knowledge of the target language – in this case, the rule of Canadian Vowel Raising, which states that [aɪ] becomes [ʌɪ] before a voiceless consonant in the same syllable. Thanks to application of the Syllable Final Obstruent Devoicing Rule, the input form now ends in a voiceless consonant ([s]) which triggers Canadian Raising. This example serves to show us something about the nature of an interlanguage: it contains features of both the L1 and the L2.

1.3

The nature of an interlanguage

The dual nature of IL grammars is captured in the **Ontogeny Model** of second language acquisition. According to this model, there are two types of error in an IL grammar: **transfer errors** and **developmental errors**. As we have seen, the former type of error reflects transfer from the L1. In contrast, developmental errors involve the same sort of mistakes that children make in acquiring their L1. For example, as we saw in Chapter 12, children learning English as a first language sometimes produce forms like *goed* and *breaked*, apparently overgeneralizing the regular rule for past tense formation. A similar developmental error is observed in second language learners, who also overgeneralize rules as they acquire a grammar.

It is possible that the processes of transfer and overgeneralization in L2 learning are the result of a single cognitive strategy that could be informally stated as 'use what you know' or 'go with what you have'. This predicts that the kind of errors made by second language learners will be dependent on their level of proficiency. Beginning learners may have nothing to draw on but their L1. However, more advanced learners have acquired a certain amount of knowledge about the L2 and this knowledge becomes a potential source of errors. This is illustrated in Table 13.2.

Table 13.2   Error patterns in L2 acquisition

Level of proficiency	Transfer errors	Developmental errors
Beginner	High	Low
Intermediate	Medium	High
Advanced	Low	Low

Graphically, the predictions of the Ontogeny Model are illustrated in Figure 13.4. The number of transfer errors should decrease over time while the number of developmental errors should initially be small, but then should increase before finally decreasing.

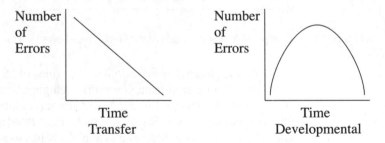

Figure 13.4   Error patterns predicted by the Ontogeny Model.

The IL grammar, then, is influenced by both the L1 and the L2, though the proportion of influence is dependent on the learner's level of overall proficiency. Note that advanced learners have low numbers of both transfer and developmental errors. Not all learners, however, reach this advanced stage. It is common in second language acquisition for learners to reach a plateau in their development. For example, even after many years of exposure to English, a second language learner may still produce sentences like *I don't know what should I do* (meaning 'I don't know what I should do') in spite of hearing the grammatical version from native speakers and perhaps being corrected. When the interlanguage grammar stops changing, it is said to have **fossilized**.

Second language learners can exhibit non-nativelike characteristics in any linguistic domain, as can be seen in Table 13.3.

Table 13.3 Types of errors found in the acquisition of English

L1	Example	Error type	Comment
Spanish	My wife is embarrassed. (Meaning 'pregnant')	Lexical	Spanish *embarasada* = 'pregnant'
Various	I live in a two bedroom department. (Meaning 'apartment')	Lexical	Sometimes the wrong word can be chosen.
Various	I didn't took the car.	Morphological	English doesn't mark the past tense on both auxiliary and main verbs.
Various	She get ups late.	Morphological	The speaker adds the agreement marker to the particle not the verb.
French	He drinks frequently beer.	Syntactic	French places the main verb before the adverb.
Various E.g., Turkish, Arabic	There's the man that I saw him.	Syntactic	Some languages allow pronouns in this position in a relative clause.

1.4

The final state

So far we have been talking about the characteristics of the intermediate grammar. But a discussion of what an IL grammar looks like must consider the **target**, i.e., what is to be acquired. The field of SLA, then, must address the issue of actual proficiency or **communicative competence**. While knowledge of a language's grammar allows us to distinguish between grammatical and ungrammatical sentences, successful communication requires much more than this. The learner must also be able to use the language in a way that is appropriate to the situation or context. As Figure 13.5 helps to illustrate, both grammatical accuracy and communicative ability are part of communicative competence.

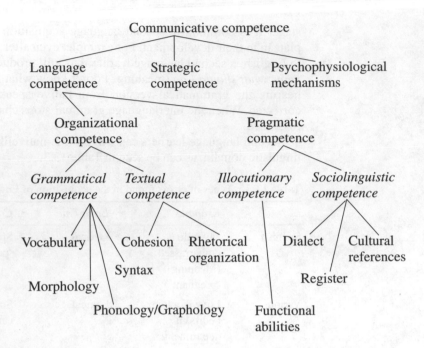

Figure 13.5 A model of communicative competence.

Let us now briefly consider each of the major subparts of the model.

Grammatical competence

Grammatical competence has to do with knowledge of the core components of the grammar: phonetics, phonology, morphology, syntax, and semantics. We will address these areas in detail in section 2.

Textual competence

Textual competence involves knowledge of well-formedness above the sentence level, including the rules that string sentences together to make a well-formed text in the spoken or written language. As the following examples help show, a **text** is not just a sequence of grammatical utterances.

1)

MGs can be very temperamental. MGs won't start if they are wet. When they work, MGs are fun to drive. They do not work often.

2)

Like most sports cars, MGs can be very temperamental. For example, they won't start if they are wet. However, on the rare days when they work, they are fun to drive.

The difference between the two texts does not involve the grammaticality of individual sentences, but rather relates to differences in the use of inter-sentential links such as *like*, *for example*, and *however*. To be proficient, second language learners have to acquire the ability to organize and link sentences in this way.

Sociolinguistic competence

As we will see in Chapter 14, language use can vary according to the context. For example, we use a different style of language in informal situations than we do in formal ones. This can affect phonology, syntax, and lexical choice, as can be seen in the following two utterances.

3)

I assume we will be working late again this evening? What a shame!

4)

Workin' late again! Dammit!

In order to be communicatively competent, second language learners need to be able to produce and comprehend a variety of social dialects.

Illocutionary competence

The meaning of an utterance is not always directly reflected in its surface structure. For example, when uttering the sentence *Have you ever considered professional help?*, a speaker could have in mind a variety of intended meanings. He might mean 'I can't help you, but maybe somebody else could' or 'I think you are a truly disturbed individual; get help'. The speaker's intent in producing an utterance is referred to as **illocutionary force**. Illocutionary competence, then, refers to the ability to comprehend a speaker's intent, and to produce a variety of syntactic structures to convey a particular intent in various circumstances (e.g., *Are you cold?*, *Could I close the window?*, *Why on earth is the window open?*). This, too, is something that second language learners need to acquire. (See also the earlier discussion in Chapter 7, section 4.)

In sum, communicative competence is a model of proficiency that allows us to measure second language knowledge and ability, to construct second language proficiency tests, and to design balanced second language courses.

1.5

Variation in performance

An important goal of L2 research is to integrate the study of competence (linguistic knowledge) and performance (actual language use in particular situations). One of the characteristics of the output of second language learners is that it is quite variable. For example, a learner might well produce the following sentence:

5)

I <u>didn't</u> like <u>th</u>at movie so I told her I <u>no</u> want to go <u>d</u>ere.

In the preceding (hypothetical) example, the learner is inconsistent, getting one of the two negatives right and correctly pronouncing one of the interdental fricatives. The question that intrigues researchers has to do with what causes this sort of variation. We usually think of knowledge as fairly stable within an individual. So, for example, if you make a mistake while speaking in your native language, you tend not to question your competence in that language, but rather to assume that you made some kind of performance error. So how do we account for learners who behave as if they know how to negate a verb or pronounce [ð] on some occasions, but not others? Do they have the knowledge or don't they?

It is difficult to answer this question, in part because of considerations involving error frequency. If a second language learner gets something wrong 10 per cent of the time, is it the same (in terms of competence) as getting it wrong 60 per cent of the time? We would probably say that a non-native speaker who gets the English past tense correct 10 per cent of the time doesn't know it, and that someone who gets it right 90 per cent of the time does. But what of someone who gets it right somewhere between those two scores? This is a complex research question. The (admittedly simplistic) view adopted in this chapter is that variation falls into the realm of linguistic performance.

Linguistic performance clearly involves the interaction of a number of cognitive systems and has much in common with other skills. A crucial notion for the study of how skills develop involves the distinction between controlled and automatic processing. When acquiring a new skill (e.g., playing golf) we begin by having to devote a lot of conscious or controlled processing to the activity. Feet apart, head down, elbow straight, white shoes, etc. Once we become proficient, we 'just' hit the ball; the activity has become automatic.

We need to shift processing from controlled to automatic because, as humans, we have a fixed processing capacity. We cannot consciously process everything at once. Shifting some material into automatic processing frees up space for more controlled processing. Consider an example from reading. When we first learn how to read, we devote much of our cognitive processing to determining what the written symbols stand for. When we are focusing on decoding the letters, we do not have the processing capacity to deal with things like reading for prejudice or bias. After a time, though, letter recognition happens automatically in our first language and learners can devote more of their cognitive capacity to higher level skills.

That native speakers do this kind of thing automatically can be seen by the difficulty we have in proofreading. It is hard to suppress the information we're getting from the context since the mind tries to make sense of what it's reading. Conversely, when we are forced by exceptional circumstances to devote a lot of energy to decoding the print (e.g., a bad photocopy or fax), our higher-level processing slows down; we can't focus as much on the message when we are focusing on the form.

All this is relevant to second language acquisition in that it can help explain the variable performance of L2 learners. When learners are focusing on the form of the L2 utterance, they may be able to produce it accurately. However, when there are extra demands, such as trying to communicate a complex thought or carry on a conversation in a noisy room, errors may occur. This suggests that the learner has a mental representation of the form in question (say a negated verb or a [ð]) but can have difficulty implementing or accessing it under certain conditions.

2

INTERLANGUAGE
GRAMMARS

Let us turn now to a discussion of the specifics of what is acquired when learning the phonology, morphology, and syntax of a second language. The general question we are trying to answer here is: 'What is the structure of an interlanguage?' Second language learners are acquiring grammars, and those grammars involve mental representations. Therefore we can investigate the nature of those representations within the various subdomains of linguistic theory. We begin with phonology.

2.1

L2 phonology

Let us consider what is to be acquired in the domain of phonology. Broadly speaking, we can distinguish between segmental and prosodic phonology. Segmental phonology has to do with the characteristics of phonological segments, like consonants (C) and vowels (V). Prosodic phonology, on the other hand, has to do with phonological phenomena that affect more than a single segment (e.g., syllables and stress).

Segmental phonology

As we saw in Chapter 3, languages vary in their segmental inventory in that they choose a subset of the sounds found in human languages. There is thus a good chance that a second language learner will have to learn to produce and perceive some new sounds when acquiring a second language.

One of the most obvious characteristics of adult second language speech is that it is 'accented' as the result of phonological and phonetic transfer from the native language. This is why native speakers of English can usually distinguish French-accented English from German-accented English. Consider the examples in Figure 13.6.

English target	Quebec French speaker	German speaker
[ðə] 'the'	[də]	[zə]

Figure 13.6 French- and German-accented English.

As both French and German lack the interdental fricative [ð], native speakers of those languages substitute a sound from their L1 where English has that sound. Generally, the learners substitute a sound that shares some features with the target sound. In the above example, the French speaker substituted a voiced alveolar (coronal) stop, while the German speaker substituted a voiced alveolar (coronal) fricative for the English voiced, interdental (coronal) fricative. Particularly at a beginning level of proficiency, L2 learners pronounce words using their L1 phonological system.

A similar phenomenon can be seen in the phonology of loan words. When a language borrows a word from another language, it makes the word fit into its own phonological system. For example, as we saw in Chapter 3, when English borrowed the word _pterodactyl_ from Greek, it reduced the onset cluster [pt], which is well-formed in Greek but not English. However, no such change was made in the word *helicopter* (also from Greek) since it already complied with the phonological pattern of English.

Markedness

One question that has received a lot of attention in SLA research is whether some sounds are harder to acquire in a second language than others. Perhaps some sounds are simpler than others. Or perhaps some sound systems are easier for speakers of a certain language to acquire. Would it be easier for a Japanese speaker to acquire English or Vietnamese? As might be expected, these are not simple issues. We cannot talk about the ease or difficulty of entire languages, but we may have something to say about individual sounds.

When linguists try to deal with the notions of ease or simplicity, they make use of the notion *markedness*. Structures that are simple and/or especially common in human language are said to be **unmarked**, while structures that are complex or less common are said to be **marked**. So, we might say that a sound that is found in relatively few of the world's languages (e.g., [θ] is marked while a sound that occurs in many of the world's languages (e.g., [t]) is unmarked.

Markedness is commonly approached from the perspective of language typology, which is concerned with the comparative study of similarities and differences among languages. As noted in Chapter 9, researchers have discovered certain implicational universals of the form 'if a language has *x*, it will also have *y*'. For example, if a language has nasal vowels (e.g., [ã]), then it will also have oral vowels (e.g., [a]). Crucial to the understanding of implicational universals is the fact that the implication is unidirectional. Thus a language that has oral vowels does not necessarily have nasal vowels. This allows us to identify [a] as less marked than [ã], in accordance with the following generalization.

6)

x is more marked than *y* if the presence of *x* implies the presence of *y*, *but not vice versa*.

It is interesting to ask whether IL grammars obey such implicational universals and whether this can tell us something about the question of ease and difficulty of learning.

The **Markedness Differential Hypothesis** investigates second language acquisition by comparing the relative markedness of structures in the L1 and the L2. Remember the earlier example of Syllable Final Obstruent Devoicing in German, which explains why a word like *hund* 'dog' is pronounced with a [t] at the end. German speakers learning English typically transfer Syllable Final Obstruent Devoicing into their IL (producing [hæt] for [hæd] 'had') and must learn to make the contrast between [t] and [d] at the ends of words. We might be tempted to think that the principle underlying this phenomenon is something like 'it's hard to learn to make contrasts that your L1 doesn't make'. But when we look at another set of data we see that this is not the case.

French makes a contrast between [ʃ] and [ʒ] in places where English does not, as Figure 13.7 indicates.

	English [ʃ]/ [ʒ]	*French* [ʃ]/ *[ʒ]
Initial	<u>s</u>ure [ʃ]/ *[ʒ]¹	<u>ch</u>ant ([ʃ]) / <u>g</u>ens ([ʒ]) 'song' 'people'
Medial	a<u>ss</u>ure ([ʃ]) / a<u>z</u>ure ([ʒ])	bou<u>ch</u>er ([ʃ]) / bou<u>g</u>er ([ʒ]) 'to fill up' 'to budge'
Final	lea<u>sh</u> ([ʃ]) / lie<u>ge</u> ([ʒ])	ha<u>ch</u>e ([ʃ]) / a<u>ge</u> ([ʒ]) 'axe' 'age'

Figure 13.7   The [ʃ]/[ʒ] contrast in English and French.

If it were invariably difficult for second language learners to make contrasts that are not found in their L1, we would expect English speakers to have difficulty learning to produce [ʒ] at the beginning of words. But they don't. English speakers seem able to learn to pronounce French words like *jaune* 'yellow' and *jeudi* 'Thursday' without trouble.

The notion of markedness can be used to explain why German speakers have difficulty making a new contrast in English, while English speakers don't have difficulty making a new contrast in French. The typological situation is as follows:

- There are languages that have a voicing contrast initially, medially, and finally (e.g., English).
- There are languages that have a voicing contrast initially and medially, but not finally (e.g., German).
- There are languages that have a voicing contrast initially, but not medially or finally (e.g., Sardinian).

These generalizations allow us to formulate the following implicational universal.

7)

The presence of a voicing contrast in final position implies the presence of a voicing contrast in medial position, which in turn implies the presence of a voicing contrast in initial position.

We can represent this universal graphically as follows:

8)

initial < medial < final
C   B   A

The presence of A implies the presence of B (but not vice versa), and the presence of B implies the presence of C (but not vice versa). Therefore A is the most marked and C is the least marked. This markedness differential explains the differing degrees of difficulty exhibited by the German and

English L2 learners. The German speakers learning English are attempting to acquire a contrast in a universally more marked position (final) whereas the English speakers learning French are attempting to acquire a contrast in a universally unmarked position (initial).[2]

In addition to the segmental inventory, second language learners also have to acquire the prosodic phonology of the target language. For example, they have to acquire the principles of syllabification and stress assignment. We will now look at each in turn.

L2 syllabification

We saw in Chapter 3 that syllables have the hierarchical structure shown in Figure 13.8.

Figure 13.8   The internal structure of the syllable.

The languages of the world vary according to such things as whether syllabic nodes can branch. Some languages (e.g., Japanese) do not allow branching onsets or codas. Ignoring some complexities, let us assume that all syllables must be CV or CVC. More complex syllables such as CCVCC are not allowed. A common phenomenon in second language learning involves modifying an L2 word so that it fits the L1 syllable structure. Consider the following words spoken by someone whose L1 is Arabic:

9)

English target	Non-native speaker's version
plant	pilanti
Fred	Fired
translate	tiransilet

Arabic does not allow branching onsets or codas, so an English word like *plant* cannot be mapped onto a single Arabic syllable. A characteristic of Arabic is that illicit consonant clusters are broken up by an epenthetic [i].[3]

With this in mind, let us look at the steps that an Arabic speaker would go through in syllabifying 'plant'.

Step 1   Initial syllabification: Assign vowels to a nucleus (N) and the nucleus to a rhyme (R), and the rhyme to a syllable (σ).

Step 2 Assign allowable onset (O) consonants (in Arabic, one)

Step 3 Assign allowable coda (C) consonants (in Arabic, one).

Step 4 Insert an epenthetic [i] to the right of an unsyllabified consonant.

Step 5 Assign vowels to a nucleus, the nucleus to a rhyme, and the rhyme to a syllable (σ).

Step 6 Assign allowable onset consonants (in Arabic, one).

As this example helps to show, we can explain why Arabic speakers pronounce English words in the way that they do by investigating the principles of syllabification in the L1. Especially at the beginning levels of proficiency, the structure of the IL is influenced by the structure of the L1.

Stress assignment

L2 learners also have to acquire the stress patterns of the language they are trying to learn. Consider an example from Polish. Polish is a language in which word-level stress is assigned to the penultimate syllable (regardless of syllable weight). These metrical principles transfer and result in one of the characteristics of a Polish accent in English: the tendency to place stress on the penultimate syllable regardless of syllable weight. Remember from Chapter 3 that in English heavy syllables tend to attract stress (e.g., aróma, agénda). The following examples illustrate a non-native stress pattern in which the second to last syllable is always stressed.

10)

English target	Non-Native form
astónish	astónish
maintáin	máintain
cábinet	cabínet

2.2

L2 syntax

L2 learners also have to acquire the syntax of their new language. In this section, we will look at two facets of syntactic structure: the null subject parameter and verb movement.

Null subjects

As we saw in Chapter 5, Universal Grammar includes universal principles (that account for what all natural languages have in common) as well as parameters (that account for cross-linguistic variation). Parameters are like linguistic switches (often binary) that can be set to a particular value as a result of the linguistic input. One of the first parameters to be discussed in the generative literature was the null subject (or pronoun-drop) parameter. Essentially, this parameter is designed to account for the contrast between languages like French and English, which require overt grammatical subjects (e.g., *He speaks French/*Speaks French*), and languages like Spanish and Italian, which allow subjects to be omitted (e.g., Spanish *Él habla español/ Habla español* '[S/he] speaks Spanish').

11)

The Null Subject Parameter:
The subject of a finite clause 'may/may not' be null.

Languages that allow null subjects tend to have other grammatical traits associated with them. For one, they tend to allow declarative sentences with the word order Verb + Subject as well as Subject + Verb, as in the following examples from Spanish.

12)

a. Juan llegó.
John arrived.

b. Llegó Juan
arrived John.

Second, they tend to allow sentences like the following, in which a complementizer (here *que* 'that') is immediately followed by the trace (represented as t) of a moved *Wh* word.

13)

Quién dijo usted que t̲ llegó?
who said you that arrived?
'Who did you say that arrived?'

As the following example shows, such sentences are unacceptable in English.

14)

*Who did you say [CP that [S t̲ arrived]?
(deep structure *you did say that who arrived*)

In other words, languages like English ([–null subject]) do not allow *that*-trace sequences, whereas languages like Spanish ([+null subject]) do.

Studies on L2 learners of English show that Spanish speakers are more likely to judge subjectless English sentences to be grammatical than are French speakers. This is consistent with the assumption that L1 parameter settings are transferred into the IL grammar, at least in the early stages. Learning a second language can be seen as involving the resetting of parameters that have different values in the L1 and the L2.

Moreover, when Spanish subjects are given a task that requires them to change a declarative sentence into a question, they are more likely to produce a sentence that contains a *that*-trace sequence than are French subjects. For example, if Spanish subjects are given a sentence like *Joshua believed that his father would be late* and have to form a question asking about the underlined element, they are more likely than French subjects to produce a sentence like *Who did Joshua believe that t̲ would be late?* This points towards the possibility that the admissibility of null subjects and the acceptability of *that*-trace sequences are somehow both related to the null subject parameter (i.e., speakers of null subject languages are more likely to permit *that*-trace sequences).

However, there are complications. Remember that the study just described had the Spanish and French speakers form new sentences. Another study had both French and Spanish subjects judge the grammaticality of English sentences with a *that*-trace violation. Both groups were quite able to reject those sentences as ungrammatical. For some reason, there is a stronger L1 influence when learners have to form new sentences themselves.

Verb movement

A difference between French and English involves the setting of the Verb Movement Parameter (see Figure 13.9).

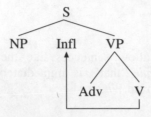

Figure 13.9 Verb movement.

15)

The Verb Movement Parameter
V 'raises/does not raise' to Infl.

We saw in Chapter 5 that the transformation of verb movement takes a verb from within the VP and moves it up in Infl. Simplifying slightly, let us say that English does not allow verb movement but French does. Thus, in French the verb raises to Infl past a preverbal adverb, but in English it does not. This difference can be seen in the following sentences, in which movement of the verb over the adverb separating it from the Infl position gives a bad result in English but a good result in French.

16)

a. *Marie watches often television.

b. Marie regarde souvent la télévision.

Studies have shown that French speakers learning English initially assume that English allows verb raising. In order to learn English they have to reset the value of their verb-raising parameter.

Markedness and the subset principle

Another interesting facet of a parameter-setting approach to SLA has to do with whether adult L2 learners can reset their parameters, and whether the notion of directionality of difficulty captured by the Markedness Differential Hypothesis (see above, section 2.1) can be captured in a parameter-setting model. The Null Subject Parameter can be used to address these questions. To understand how, we must first consider how a parameter-setting model instantiates the notion of markedness.

If we consider the two settings of the Null Subject Parameter (+/−), we can see that the different values generate different grammars, as shown in the following sentences from English and Spanish.

17)

[− null subject]:   I speak Spanish.
[+ null subject]:   Yo hablo español.
                     Hablo español.

As you can see, the [+ null subject] setting generates more grammatical utterances than the [– null subject] setting does. Therefore the [–] setting is said to be a subset of the [+] setting. Graphically, this can be represented in Figure 13.10.

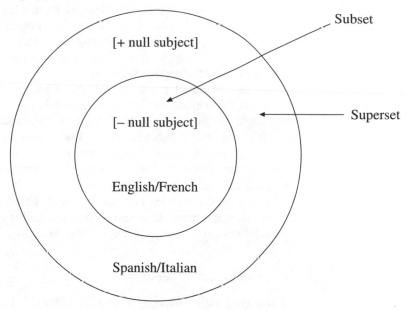

Figure 13.10 Subset/superset relation for the Null Subject Parameter.

The **Subset Principle** stipulates that the initial or default setting of a parameter will correspond to the most restrictive option (i.e., the option that permits the fewest patterns). Hence, for first language learners, the initial or default setting will be the subset value (i.e., [– null subject] in the case of the Null Subject Parameter).[4]

Second language learners may have to reset their parameters. When attempting to reset from subset to superset or from superset to subset, there are different types of evidence available to the learner. Imagine a learner of English (who has the [–] setting) trying to learn Spanish. The learner's initial assumption will be the L1 parameter setting, which leads to the expectation that all sentences will have overt subjects. When faced with Spanish input, the learner will be exposed to grammatical utterances in the L2 which do not have overt subjects (e.g., *Hablo español* '[I] speak Spanish'), which indicates that the L1 setting is incorrect and needs to be reset. Data like these, which involve grammatical utterances to which one is actually exposed, are referred to as **positive evidence**.

Now imagine a learner whose L1 is Spanish ([+]) who is trying to learn English ([–]). The learner's initial assumption will be that English should be [+null subject], like the L1. The learner's IL grammar will allow sentences with overt subjects and sentences without. Crucially, there will be no positive evidence in the English input directed at this learner to show that the L1 parameter setting is wrong. The learner will hear sentences with overt subjects, which are sanctioned by the current IL grammar, but there will be no direct indication that sentences with null subjects are not allowed. There is no pressure to reset the parameter. In this case, the learner will have to rely on **negative evidence** (i.e., observations about what is missing or ungrammatical in the data) to reset the parameter. In particular, the learner would either have to be explicitly told what is ungrammatical (**direct** negative evidence), or infer that it is ungrammatical on the basis of the fact that no one else ever says it (**indirect** negative evidence).

Given that direct positive evidence is available in one case (English → Spanish), and negative evidence is required in the other (Spanish → English), we might predict that it is harder for Spanish speakers to learn the English value of the Null Subject Parameter than vice versa. In fact, the prediction is borne out. Studies have shown that it is easier for English speakers to reset to the Spanish value of the Null Subject Parameter, than it is for Spanish subjects to reset to the English setting.

Let us now consider how an approach based on typological universals would treat the same phenomenon. The possibility of null subjects implies the possibility of overt subjects, but not vice versa.

18)

overt subjects > null subjects

Therefore, null subjects would be thought of as more marked, and, consequently, more difficult to acquire. The Markedness Differential Hypothesis predicts that structures that are more marked typologically will cause difficulty in SLA because they are more marked. The Subset Principle, on the other hand, predicts that structures that are more marked will not cause difficulty because there will be clear evidence that the L1 setting is wrong. Although only the Subset Principle seems to make the correct prediction in the case of the null subjects, further research is necessary in order to see which approach is better able to handle a wider range of data.

2.3

L2 morphology

The study of second language morphology has a slightly different flavour than the study of either L2 phonology or syntax. L2 phonology has been studied for a long time, though the analyses have changed to reflect changes in linguistic theory. L2 syntax is a much younger field, and much of it has been informed by current linguistic theory. By contrast, L2 morphology has been studied more or less in a theoretical vacuum. In the 1970s, a number of studies collected data on the accuracy of second language learners on a variety of morphemes. This research drew on previous studies in the field of first language acquisition that had attempted to determine the order of acquisition of morphemes in L1 development. The developmental sequence in Table 13.4 was found:

Table 13.4   Developmental order for first language acquisition

1.	*-ing* The present participle affix	(e.g., she is work*ing*)
2.	Plural *-s*	(e.g., bottle*s*)
3.	Irregular past	(e.g., she *taught* French)
4.	Possessive *-s*	(e.g., a child*'s* toy)
5.	Copula *be*	(e.g., I *am* happy)
6.	Articles	(e.g., *a*, *the*)
7.	Regular past	(e.g., she walk*ed* quickly)
8.	3rd person *-s*	(e.g., she walk*s* quickly)
9.	Auxiliary *be*	(e.g., she *is* working)

Research on second language acquisition focused on whether the developmental sequence in L2 learning was the same as for L1 learning. The order in Table 13.5 was found.

Table 13.5   Developmental order for second language acquisition

1.	*-ing*
2.	Copula *be*
3.	Articles
4.	Auxiliary *be*
5.	Plural *-s*
6.	Irregular past
7.	Regular past
8.	3rd person *-s*
9.	Possessive *-s*

There are many similarities but there are also some differences. For example, note that auxiliary and copula *be* are acquired at a relatively earlier point in L2 than in L1, and that the possessive morpheme -*'s* is acquired later in L2 than in L1. To attempt to explain these patterns, we need to look a little more closely at the structures that implement inflectional morphology.

In the syntax section we saw that, in English, main verbs do not raise to Infl. However, Figure 13.11 on the next page shows that the verb *be* does raise to Infl if no modal is present (see section 4.3 in Chapter 5).

19)

a.   No modal is present: the auxiliary verb moves from inside the VP to Infl.
He is [VP probably t eating].

b.   A modal is present: the auxiliary verb does not raise.
He should [VP probably be eating].

c.   Main verbs do not raise.
He [VP probably likes eating] vs *He likes [VP probably t eating].

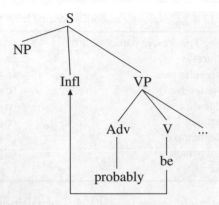

Figure 13.11   Raising *be* to Infl.

Children acquire *be* as a main verb before they acquire *be* as an auxiliary verb. So, children start by producing sentences that are simpler in that they have only a copula (linking) verb (e.g., *He is hungry*) before they produce sentences that include an auxiliary plus a main verb (e.g., *He was working*) as shown in Figure 13.12.

Figure 13.12   *a.* Sentence with copula verb *be*.   *b.* Sentence with auxiliary verb *be* plus main verb.

Structure 13.12*b* has an extra level of complexity in that it has a complex verb phrase (one VP within another). Adults, on the other hand, appear to be able to use both the simple copula and auxiliary verbs quite early on. Whether this difference is because of the adult's greater ability to handle complexity in general cognitive terms or because children's linguistic systems are maturing remains a controversial and unresolved issue.

In addition, note that children acquire the three -*s* morphemes in the order plural, possessive, third person in their first language. Phonetically, these morphemes have the same realization, so we can't say that the order reflects phonological complexity. The order might be explained by noting that plural is a word-level phenomenon (e.g., *dogs*), possessive (as we saw in Chapter 4, section 1.3) is a phrase-level phenomenon (e.g., [*the king of England*]'*s horse*, not *[*the king*]'*s of England horse*), and third person marking involves a relation between the verb and a phrase (the subject) elsewhere in the sentence (e.g., *[That man] usually thinks too much*). Like the pattern noted for the development of copula and auxiliary *be*, children seem to be acquiring structures in order of complexity, as shown in Figure 13.13.

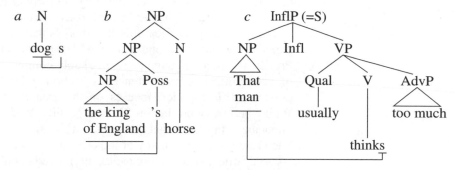

Figure 13.13   The effect of complexity on the order of the morphological acquisition by children.

In contrast, adults acquire the plural quite early, but then seem to get both the possessive and the third person marking quite late – perhaps for reasons involving processing. (When concentrating on getting the words right, we do not always have the processing capacity to produce well-formed higher-level structures.) Interestingly, the adults do not seem to find interphrasal morphology (like Figure 13.13*c*) more difficult than phrasal morphology (like Figure 13.13*b*). This may be because the adults have already acquired the grammar for their first language and that grammar most likely has both phrase-level and interphrasal morphological phenomena. In contrast, children have to set up hierarchical structure of a grammar for the first time, and could conceivably be building the structure from the bottom up (words → phrases → sentences).

In summary, we note that the order of acquisition data are intriguing in both first and second language acquisition, even though we await a conclusive explanation of the facts.

3

FACTORS AFFECTING SLA

So far, we've looked at some of the characteristics of an IL grammar. Now let's turn to a variety of factors that can influence second language acquisition. It is clear that there is much more variation in the grammars of people learning second languages than in the grammars of people learning first languages. This brings us to the question of what factors might help to account for that variation.

3.1

Age

One of the obvious ways that language learners vary is in their age. People start learning second languages at different points in their lives. Could the age of onset of L2 learning cause different levels of final proficiency?

This is a question usually considered under what is known as the *Critical Period Hypothesis* (see Chapter 12, section 6.5). We know that biologically based critical periods exist in other species. For example, some birds can learn the song of their species only if exposed to it during a particular window of opportunity. If they only hear the song too early or too late, then learning will not take place. (See Chapter 16 for further discussion.)

Is second language learning like this? Is there an optimal time (or critical period) to acquire a second language? The answer appears to be 'yes and no'. Proficiency in a language is a remarkably complex thing (see the discussion of communicative competence in section 1.4). Usually discussion of a possible critical period focuses on the area of phonological competence. While people who begin SLA as adults tend to retain non-nativelike phonology in the target language, it is much more difficult to predict knowledge or ability in any of the other areas of communicative competence (syntax, cohesion, sociolinguistics, etc.) based upon age of acquisition.

In fact, even L2 phonology is not as straightforward as it might first appear to be. We can predict with fair certainty that people who start learning their L2 before the age of seven will have nativelike L2 speech and that people who start learning after fourteen or fifteen will probably have non-nativelike speech. But the results of people who start learning between the ages of seven and fourteen are much more varied. Some end up with accents, and some do not.

There is no current evidence of anything biological that prevents adults from acquiring proficiency in a second language. Factors that have been considered in the past (like brain **lateralization**; see Chapter 11) are now thought to be of little predictive value in determining L2 ability. The question of 'ultimate attainment' in L2 acquisition is still hotly debated, and the literature has cited cases of adult L2 learners who apparently perform virtually identically to native speakers in a variety of domains (including phonology).

Currently, the critical period debate in SLA research is usually couched in terms of the question, 'Do adults have access to Universal Grammar?' Rather than looking for changes in the brain that coincide with ageing, researchers now look to see whether IL grammars are governed by the same constraints as primary languages (e.g., Swahili, Yoruba). If adults are engaged in the same kind of development process as children, then we would expect their IL grammars to be describable in terms of the same principles and parameters of UG that we use to describe primary languages. Conversely, if adults are acquiring their second languages using qualitatively different learning mechanisms than are used to acquire an L1 (e.g., if they use general problem-solving abilities), then we might expect them to adopt hypotheses that are not sanctioned by Universal Grammar. Something like this may in fact happen in the acquisition of gender in French. Children learning French as a first language seem to have very little trouble learning gender as they learn the words themselves (e.g., *le livre*, 'the book' is masculine; *la table*, 'the table' is feminine) and so on. On the other hand, adults whose first language does not have gender often have great difficulty learning French gender. They seem to set up complex (but incorrect) rules for predicting the gender of a given noun. (For example, they may assume that words naming colours (or some other semantic category) are of one gender, or that words that end with a certain sound sequence are of another.) Rules like this sometimes allow non-native speakers to guess the gender correctly, but they still perform significantly differently from native speakers. This is an example, of how adults' greater capacity to formulate general rules can sometimes lead them down the wrong path.

3.2

Individual differences

Learners vary in ways other than age. Broadly speaking, the research asks the question, 'If learners have a particular quality x, does this make them better at second language acquisition?' For example, we might look at the effect of inhibition, left-handedness, or some other individual trait on L2 ability. As intuitively appealing as this avenue is, it is one that must be taken carefully. In particular, there are three points on which we must be explicit:

- how we define and measure x
- what it means to be *better*
- what aspect of communicative competence we are referring to.

Consider in this regard a trait like empathy. It has been argued that people who are empathetic are better language learners. This is an intuitively appealing notion. People who are empathetic can imagine what it feels like to be in someone else's shoes and they can look at things from another perspective. And second language learning certainly involves looking at things from a different perspective. But in SLA research, we need to find a more precise way to evaluate this hypothesis.

There are tests that claim to measure a person's empathy, but is this notion really a well-defined construct? Is one simply empathetic or not, or are there degrees of empathy? If there are degrees, do we see a correlation between degree of empathy and degree of success? And what does it mean for empathetic learners to be better language learners than people who aren't empathetic? Do they make fewer errors? Less serious errors? Should we expect people with greater empathy to be better at everything in the L2? Or maybe just at phonology and sociolinguistic competence? On what basis could we make a prediction? These are not simple issues. We raise them not to argue that research in individual variation is misguided, but to show some of the complex areas that need to be addressed before we can hope to establish a causal connection between a particular personality trait and success at second language learning.

We can distinguish between two kinds of factors in terms of which individuals can vary: affective factors and cognitive factors. First we will look at the role of affect.

Affective factors

Affective factors have to do with the emotional side of learning a second language. Clearly there is a great deal at stake emotionally when learning a second language, and it is possible that emotions affect how successful a second language learner is. Affective factors that have been studied include empathy, anxiety, inhibition, and risk-taking. In this section we will look at one such factor: **motivation**.

Learners can vary with respect to the amount or type of motivation they have to learn a second language. If someone is highly motivated to learn, will that person do better at learning? In order to answer this question, we need to say a bit more about what it means to be motivated.

Traditionally, two types of motivation have been proposed: **instrumental** and **integrative**. Instrumental motivation involves wanting to learn the L2 for a specific goal or reason. For example, someone might need to pass a language requirement in order to get a graduate degree, or a job with a government agency. Integrative motivation, on the other hand, involves wanting to learn the L2 in order to learn more about a particular culture or fit into it better. For instance, someone might want to learn Japanese in order to learn more about a fascinating culture.

Studies have shown that the degree of integrative motivation correlates with the degree of success in language learning. That is to say, subjects who score highly on tests of integrative motivation do better on certain language tests than comparable subjects who score poorly on the same tests. However, subjects with instrumental rather than integrative motivation can also do well if their level of motivation is high. One study found that subjects who were offered a cash reward if they obtained a certain score on a language test performed much the same as subjects with high integrative motivation. All this seems to suggest that degree of motivation is a better predictor of future learning success than is type of motivation.

Cognitive factors

While affective factors have something to do with the emotional side of learning, cognitive factors involve the mechanics of how an individual learns something. Different people seem to learn via different cognitive styles and different learning strategies. We will first address **cognitive style**.

As individuals, we tend to tackle mental tasks using a particular 'cognitive style'. In contrast with an affective factor like motivation, which may vary from domain to domain (e.g., someone might be more motivated to learn French cooking that to learn the French language), cognitive style is a stable trait across domains.

The study of cognitive style often focuses on a contrast between field dependence and field independence. Learners who are **field independent** are not distracted by irrelevant background information when trying to learn something. These are people who can see the trees without being distracted by the forest. On the other hand, learners who are **field dependent** tend to see the forest but may miss the characteristics of individual trees. Of course, this is not to say that, overall, one trait is good and the other is bad. Field-dependent learners probably are able to synthesize the overall picture better than field-independent learners, but field-independent learners are probably better able to pick out relevant facts.

In terms of second language acquisition, it seems that field-independent learners do better on language tests that focus on analytic tasks such as providing the correct grammatical form in a given sentence:

20)

Yesterday, we __ the kids to the zoo. (take)

In contrast, field-dependent learners tend to do better on tasks that involve synthesizing their knowledge. For example, they may demonstrate broader communicative competence in that they are more concerned with getting the message across than with the grammatical accuracy of the sentences they use to form their message.

Ultimately, the proficient L2 learner needs to be concerned with both **accuracy** and **fluency**. Broadly speaking, accuracy has to do with whether the learner has the correct representation of a particular linguistic structure (i.e., it involves *knowledge*). Fluency, on the other hand, has to do with the rapid retrieval or processing of those representations (i.e., it involves *skills*). Someone who is not fluent may well have accurate representations, but take considerable time and energy to retrieve them. Different learners, though, are probably going to have a natural affinity to emphasize either accuracy or fluency, depending perhaps on their individual cognitive style. Performance issues of this type are discussed in greater depth in Chapter 12.

While cognitive styles appear to be relatively stable traits in an individual, there are elements of learning that we have some control over. Each of us has certain **learning strategies** that we can employ to try to fill gaps in our linguistic knowledge. These strategies can be contrasted with **communication strategies**, which are designed to keep communication happening in spite of gaps in knowledge – as when someone uses paraphrase to describe an object for which he or she has no vocabulary item (e.g., *Could you pass me the thing you use for hitting nails?*).

In contrast, a learning strategy is used to discover something new about the L2. Many different learning strategies have been proposed. For example, using the strategy of directed attention, learners may decide in advance to focus on particular aspects of a task and to ignore others. So, when reading a text or listening to a lecture, they might decide to focus only on the main points. Another strategy involves repetition: to retain a lexical item or to improve the pronunciation of a sequence of sounds, the learner may repeat a word or phrase over and over. A third strategy makes use of clarification requests (to the teacher, a peer, or the others in a conversation) about something that is not understood (e.g., How come *stood* doesn't rhyme with *food*? What's a *liege*?). Under this view, learners have a variety of strategies at their disposal and have to discover which ones work best for them.

3.3

The good language learner

The question of individual variation in second language learning has received quite a bit of attention under the heading 'the good language learner'.

What makes a good language learner? One researcher has presented the characteristics listed in Table 13.6. For the most part, this list is concerned with the learning strategies that people invoke in an attempt to acquire an L2.

Table 13.6 Characteristics of the 'good language learner'

1.	Has an [effective] personal learning style or positive learning strategies.
2.	Has an active approach to the learning task.
3.	Has a tolerant and outgoing approach to the target language and empathy with its speakers.
4.	Has technical know-how about how to tackle a language.
5.	Has strategies of experimentation and planning with the object of developing the new language into an ordered system and revising this system progressively.
6.	Is consistently searching for meaning.
7.	Is willing to practise.
8.	Is willing to use the language in real communication.
9.	Has self-monitoring ability and critical sensitivity to language use.
10.	Is able to develop the target language more and more as a separate reference system and is able to learn to think in it.

By focusing on such characteristics, the learning strategy approach seeks to account for differences in L2 proficiency by referring to the way in which individuals try to acquire new knowledge. Some people have gone so far as to suggest that this type of research will make it possible to teach not-so-good language learners the learning strategies necessary to be good language learners.

This brings us to the interesting question of second language learning in classrooms and the effect that instruction has on L2 learning. Is it really possible to teach someone a second language? Or can teachers simply create an environment in which second language learning can take place? We turn now to the research that has looked specifically at L2 classrooms.

4

THE L2 CLASSROOM

It has been flippantly said that people have been successfully acquiring second languages for thousands of years, but when teachers get involved, the success rate plummets. This comment is probably more a reflection of people's unfortunate experience in certain types of language classrooms (that may have been dull or even physically threatening, depending on the century) than it is a statement about general pedagogic utility. However, the fact remains that language classrooms can be sheltered environments where students can be given the opportunity to learn and practise without being subject to the penalties for failure that can be imposed outside the classroom.

We should acknowledge at this point that there is really no such thing as the typical second language classroom. In reality, all classrooms are different because they have different people in them. Nevertheless, there are certain statements that can be made. There are three relevant characteristics of a second language classroom that we wish to explore:

- modified input
- modified interaction
- focus on form.

4.1

Modified input

In Chapter 12, it was noted that adults do not talk to children in the same way that they talk to other adults. Just as the input directed to children has certain simplifying characteristics, so speech directed at non-native speakers tends to be simplified compared to the speech directed at native speakers. In all communicative situations – whether dealing with a child or an adult, a non-native speaker or a native speaker – we seem to make a rapid assessment of the level of proficiency or background knowledge of the listener, and adjust the input accordingly.

The input aimed at non-native speakers is referred to as **foreigner talk**. The subset of this speech that takes place in classrooms is known as **teacher talk**. Teacher talk tends not to be as evenly matched to the proficiency of the listener as foreigner talk is, for the simple reason that teachers are usually addressing a class rather than an individual. As a result, some learners may find the modified speech too hard or too easy.

The pedagogic goal of teacher talk is crystal clear: make sure the students know what is being talked about by providing **comprehensible input**. Perhaps surprisingly, this idea has generated an extraordinary amount of conflict in the field of SLA research. Although it seems to be useful to provide learners with comprehensible input, teachers must guard against simplifying too much, which might give the appearance of patronizing the learners or talking to them as if they were stupid rather than on the way to becoming bilingual.

4.2

Modified interaction

Second language classrooms also differ from the outside world in terms of the kind of interactions that go on there. However, the difference appears to be mainly one of degree, not quality. Inside a classroom, the teacher may engage in the following kinds of strategies:

- More comprehension checks; e.g., *Do you understand? OK?*
- More prompting; e.g., *Who knows where the Tower of London is?*
- More expansions; e.g., Student: *Me red sweater.*
  Teacher: *Yes, you're wearing a red sweater, aren't you?*

This modified interaction appears to be one of the characteristics that differentiates classrooms from other communicative settings. While all these devices (e.g., comprehension checks) occur in non-classroom discourse as well, they appear to occur more frequently in second language classrooms. Assuming that the teacher realizes that the purpose of the classroom is to prepare the student to understand input and interaction outside the classroom as well, modified interaction is beneficial.

4.3

Focus on form

The final characteristic of the second language classroom to be discussed here involves focus on form. The term 'focus on form' encompasses two distinct practices that tend to occur in most L2 classrooms: instruction about the language and explicit correction.

Most second language classes present the students with some sort of information about the language – noting, for example, that 'English has voiced and voiceless dental fricatives' or that 'French has nasal vowels'. Instruction of this type is designed to improve the form (or **accuracy**) of the student's L2. In all likelihood, other activities that happen in the class will focus on giving the student a chance to improve fluency or particular sociolinguistic skills.

Error correction is also designed to improve the form of the student's L2. Regardless of the methodology used in most classes today, there is some focus on form and some error correction. The interesting research question is whether either of these practices can be shown to have a positive effect on the learner. Do students who get corrected do better than students who don't?

The question may not be as straightforward as it appears. Remember that it has frequently been argued in first language acquisition research that attempts at error correction are relatively infrequent and don't really affect children's grammars. Could it be different for adult second language learners? The learning environment is different in that adult learners (unlike children) are usually exposed to a fair amount of error correction. But does that make a difference? Not surprisingly, this question is difficult to answer. Some studies have argued that second language learners who receive correction develop at about the same pace as those who do not. Other studies have shown certain increases in accuracy as the result of correction.

These results may not be as contradictory as they seem, though. The areas where correction seems to be most useful involve the lexicon. When someone tries to learn the relevant properties of a lexical item, they benefit from feedback. However, feedback concerning certain structural phenomena may not be as effective. For example, the previously mentioned study of French speakers learning about the lack of verb movement in English (see section 2.2) found that while there were short-term improvements in the subjects who were explicitly taught the relevant facts, there were no significant long-term effects. When the subjects were tested a year later, they were found to have reverted to their pre-instructional performance.

This doesn't necessarily mean either that students should not be corrected or that there should be no focus on form in the second language classroom. If a balance is struck between classroom activities that focus on form and those that focus on meaningful communication, then there is certainly no evidence that feedback causes any trouble. Indeed, to the contrary, there is evidence that students in classes that focus primarily on communication but also include some instruction on form are significantly more accurate than students who are exposed only to instruction that focuses on communication.

In sum, adult students usually expect error correction, and teachers are accustomed to providing it. Assuming that the class is not devoted entirely to instruction that focuses on form (with no opportunity for meaningful practice), error correction doesn't seem to cause any harm. And in a class with activities that focus on both form and fluency, the students tend to emerge with greater accuracy.

4.4

Bilingual education

We will conclude this chapter with a discussion of two types of bilingual education programme: minority language maintenance programmes and **immersion** programmes. Both are designed to produce bilingual children, but there are important differences. French immersion programmes in Canada – and similar Spanish immersion programmes in the United States – involve children from a majority language (English) being immersed in a minority language (French or Spanish). As English-speaking children in North America, they are in no danger of losing their first language since it is so dominant in the culture. Their situation is clearly different from that of children who speak a minority language (e.g., Cree, Greek, or Korean) and who are submersed in the majority language (English). Not only are these children in some danger of losing their first language, the sink-or-swim approach can have strongly negative consequences on their future schooling. For these reasons, it should be emphasized that even if we argue for the benefits of immersing English-speaking children in French classrooms, it does not follow that we should submerse speakers of other languages in English classrooms.

Let us look in more detail at some of the issues surrounding bilingual education. We begin with minority language maintenance programmes.

Minority language maintenance programmes

Minority language maintenance programmes, which are also known as 'heritage language programmes' or 'L1 maintenance programmes', have been introduced around the world to try to address the fact that minority language children often have difficulty in majority language schools. Even with separate classes of instruction, they tend to have more than their share of problems later in school (including a higher than expected drop-out rate). One reason for this becomes evident when one thinks of what these children face. Up to the age of five, they are exposed to a language at home (say, Bengali or Greek). Then at age five, they are put into an English-speaking school in a class of primarily native English speakers. Typically, they do not understand everything that the teacher is saying, and do not have the opportunity to develop the basic cognitive skills necessary for functioning in school. These children may thus suffer a setback from which they will never recover.

This poor beginning can lead to minority language students underachieving and being placed in classes which are not designed for students intending to pursue post-secondary education, which in turn can lead to an early exit from the educational system. To try to change this recurring pattern, a number of bilingual education programmes have been set up in places like Britain, Canada, Finland and the United States. In all of these programmes, the children of minority language background receive their initial instruction in the minority language. Over the years of their elementary education, instruction in the majority language is gradually introduced so that by the third to sixth year of primary school, the children receive about half of their instruction in the majority language as well.

The question raised in evaluating these programmes (and indeed the question that led policy-makers to adopt the competing sink-or-swim approach to minority language education) is, 'What is the effect on the children's English?' Obviously, knowledge of English in places like Britain, Australia, Canada and the United States is essential. But is submersion in English the only way to acquire proficiency in English? It would seem that the answer is no, since children can become bilingual with relative ease. In virtually all of the bilingual education programmes studied, the subjects ended up performing as well as their monolingual L1 and L2 peers by the end of primary school. So, for example, a child in London who received all instruction in Bengali for the first couple of years of schooling and was getting 50 per cent English and 50 per cent Bengali instruction by the end of the sixth year in primary school would be performing in Bengali like a monolingual Bengali speaker and in English just like a monolingual English speaker.

Thus, receiving instruction in the L1 does not have negative consequences on the L2. On the contrary, it seems to have significant positive effects on success in school, on linguistic proficiency, and even on the family situation of the students. The students can understand the teacher (which helps them at school), and they can understand their parents and grandparents (which helps them at home).

Immersion

Another very popular kind of bilingual education programme involves immersing a majority language student in a minority language class.

Over the last decade, **immersion programmes** have become increasingly popular as a way of teaching children a second language, especially for Spanish in the United States and French in Canada. In this context, immersion means that pupils are taught most of their subjects in the second language and school activities are also conducted in that language. Schooling is usually begun in the second language and eventually incorporates the native language.

The main objective of any immersion programme is that all pupils acquire a high level of proficiency in oral, listening, and literacy skills. Attempts to achieve literacy in the second language prior to achieving literacy in the native language have been successful. Moreover, immersion has also exerted a positive influence on the L2 learner's attitude towards the L2 culture.

Fundamental to an immersion programme is the belief that normal children have the inherent capacity to learn a second language without jeopardizing their native language expertise. The success rate of immersion programmes to date has convinced parents and educationists that such a belief is valid.

Let us now focus on the French immersion programmes in Canada as they are the best known, large-scale programmes of this type. French immersion differs from traditional French instruction (also known as Core French) and from submersion programmes. It is different from a Core French course in that French is the medium of communication, not the subject of the course. It is teaching *in* French, not teaching *of* French. In a Core French course, French is just another subject (say forty minutes a day). In French immersion, all of the instruction is in French, even when the content is geography or music.

French immersion is different from submersion programmes in that no one in the class is a native speaker of the medium of instruction. Native speakers of French do not enrol in French immersion classes, so all the students are starting from approximately the same place. Contrast this with a native Cree or Cantonese speaker who is thrown into an English-only class with a large number of native speakers of English.

Probably the two biggest questions that get asked about immersion programmes are (1) what effect does such a programme have on the students' English? and (2) how good is their French? The answer to the first question is remarkably similar to the answer provided by the heritage language programmes. Children can become bilingual, and instruction in one language does not necessarily mean a diminished capacity for the other language. Often, though, children in French immersion programmes exhibit a delay in productive skills (talking and writing) in English in the early years. However, by grade six, on average they are outperforming their monolingual English peers. Boldly stated, children in French immersion learn English.

So how good is their French? Concerns are often expressed that the children who come out of French immersion programmes end up speaking a kind of mixed language (that has been called *Frenglish*, or *Franglais*). It is true that immersion students tend to make mistakes in things like French gender, the *tu/vous* distinction (where *vous* is used as an honorific second person singular pronoun), and polite conditionals such as *Je voudrais un crayon* 'I would like a pencil' versus the somewhat less polite simple present form *Je veux un crayon* 'I want a pencil'. Overall, however, their receptive skills (reading and listening) end up virtually native-like and their productive skills, while not native-like, are at an advanced level.

In sum, the positive features of French immersion programmes can be stated as follows. Children who emerge from French immersion suffer no negative effects on their English, do well in school, outperform their monolingual counterparts in a number of ways, and know a heck of a lot of French.

A different version of the immersion idea is provided by the European Schools model. Since 1958, West European governments have financed a network of nine elitist European Schools (Bergen, Brussels 1, Brussels 2, Culham, Karlsruhe, Luxembourg, Mol, Munich and Varese), whose mission is to provide education for about 14,500 children of Eurocrats (other children may also be admitted, if there is spare capacity). The schools take pupils from kindergarten to the end of secondary education at age eighteen.

The philosophy of the schools is to foster the pupils' first language and national identity while at the same time promoting a European, supranational identity. All the European Schools are multilingual, and instruction is given in at least two languages. Each school is split into different linguistic subsections in which the same curriculum is taught, regardless of the language of instruction. The Brussels 1 school, which is the largest and most polyglot of them all, has three thousand students and contains eight subsections in which education is provided in English, Danish, Dutch, French, German, Italian, Greek, and Spanish.

Are the European Schools a success? At one level they clearly are. They prepare extremely well the able students for the very demanding academic standards of the European Baccalaureate. And, for the most part, they turn out bilingual young people upon whom is inculcated a strong European identity. But they have been criticized for not serving the needs of the less academically inclined students adequately. Also, socially, the European Schools form an enclave of privilege: most of their pupils come from a very restricted and privileged background and they are insulated from their peer group in neighbouring schools. At a practical level, there has been concern expressed about the cost of educating a pupil at these schools. For instance, in 1990, each European School pupil cost on average approximately US$7469, compared with US$4029 for a pupil at a Belgian state school.

On a less ambitious scale, there are a number of national initiatives which, to varying degrees, provide pupils with a near immersion experience. For instance, in France there are many secondary schools in which English is the main foreign language offered where, as well as having English lessons taught in English, English is also used as the medium of instruction for several other subjects such as geography, history, and computer science.

Summing up

This chapter has dealt with a number of issues in the field of second language acquisition. We investigated the notion of an **interlanguage grammar** and the influence of both the source and target languages on this grammar in terms of **transfer** and **developmental errors**. Proficiency in a second language requires both knowledge and ability, something captured in a model of **communicative competence**. One must acquire knowledge in all linguistic domains (phonetics, phonology, morphology, syntax, and semantics) as well as the ability to use that knowledge in a variety of social contexts.

What is easy or difficult to acquire in a second language has been investigated from a variety of perspectives. We focused on **Universal Grammar** (the **subset principle**) and **typological universals** (the **markedness differential hypothesis**). However, it is not just universals that influence second language learning; the specific characteristics of an individual can also affect the process. **Affective** factors and **cognitive** factors both influence second language learning. So too do factors such as **modified input**, **modified interaction**, **focus on form** and **bilingual education**.

The field of second language acquisition is remarkably diverse, in part because of what is involved in L2 learning. Someone who is attempting to learn an additional language must develop new mental representations, and develop facility at accessing those representations in a variety of circumstances. The field of SLA research must therefore draw on philosophy (theories of mind), psychology (theories of learning, theories of performance), linguistics (theories of linguistic structure), and pedagogy (theories of instruction). This is probably the main reason why we have not established anything like a comprehensive theory of how second languages are learned. But bit by bit, piece by piece, we're starting to put together some pieces of the puzzle.

Notes	1 The asterisk indicates that this sound is not allowed in initial position (except in a few words that have been borrowed from French – e.g., *genre*, *gendarmes*, and so forth)

1   The asterisk indicates that this sound is not allowed in initial position (except in a few words that have been borrowed from French – e.g., *genre*, *gendarmes*, and so forth)

2   Note that English phonology in general respects the implicational universal given in *7)*, as can be seen in pairs such as *sip/zip*. The lack of contrast of [ʃ]/[ʒ] in initial position is an accidental gap. Even with this gap, however, it seems that English speakers respect the universal when learning the phonology of a second language. The voicing contrast is easier to acquire in the universally unmarked position.

3   This might happen in Arabic if two morphemes are put together and, as a result, two consonants occur adjacent to each other.

4   As we will see, linguists infer the initial setting of a parameter on the basis of the kind of input or evidence available to the language learner. It is a separate question to empirically validate whether children's early grammars actually have the [+] or [–] setting of the Null Subject Parameter. For example, children's early sentences in English often lack overt subjects, which might lead us to believe that the grammars have the [+] setting. However, the early sentences of English-speaking children do not contain the other structures associated with the [+ null subject] parameter setting: *that*-trace effects and VS order in declaratives. Given the complexity of this issue, we will assume the relationship shown in Figure 13.8 when discussing second language learners.

Sources	The Ontogeny Model was proposed by R. Major in 'Foreign accent: recent research and theory', *International Review of Applied Linguistics* 15: 185–202 (1987).

The Ontogeny Model was proposed by R. Major in 'Foreign accent: recent research and theory', *International Review of Applied Linguistics* 15: 185–202 (1987). The model of communicative competence is an adaptation of L. Bachman's *Fundamental Considerations in Language Testing* (Oxford: Oxford University Press, 1990). The Markedness Differential Hypothesis was developed by F. Eckman in 'Markedness and the contrastive analysis hypothesis', *Language Learning* 27: 315–30 (1977). The data from Arabic syllabification come from E. Broselow, 'Prosodic phonology and the acquisition of a second language', in S. Flynn and W. O'Neil, eds, *Linguistic Theory in Second Language Acquisition* (Dordrecht: Kluwer, 1988). The stress data were reported in J. Archibald, *Language Learnability and L2 Phonology* (Dordrecht: Kluwer, 1993). The Null Subject analysis is drawn from L. White, *Universal Grammar and Second Language Acquisition* (Amsterdam: John Benjamins, 1989). The Verb Movement study can be found in L. White, 'Adverb placement in second language acquisition: some effects of positive and negative evidence in the classroom', *Second Language Research* 7: 133–61 (1991). The L2 morphology data can be found in H. Zobl and J. Liceras, 'Functional categories and acquisition order',

Language Learning 44(1): 159–80 (1994). The French gender information is discussed in S. Carroll, 'Second-language acquisition and the computational paradigm', *Language Learning* 39(4): 535–94. (1989). The instrumental/integrative distinction comes from R. Gardner, J.B. Day, and P.D. MacIntyre, 'Integrative motivation, induced anxiety and language learning in a controlled environment', *Studies in Second Language Acquisition* 14(2): 197–214 (1992). The Good Language Learner profile of Table 13.5 can be found in H.H. Stern, 'What can we learn from the good language learner?', *The Canadian Modern Language Review* 34: 304–18 (1975), but see also J. Rubin, 'What the "good language learner" can teach us', *TESOL Quarterly* 9(1): 41–51 (1975), and R. Ellis, *Understanding Second Language Acquisition* (Oxford: Oxford University Press, 1986). The L2 classroom discussion owes much to R. Allwright and K. Bailey, *Focus on the Language Classroom: An Introduction to Classroom Research for Language Teachers* (Cambridge: Cambridge University Press, 1991). The evidence from focus on form was presented by P. Lightbown and N. Spada, 'Focus-on-form and corrective feedback in communicative language teaching: effects on second language learning', *Studies in Second Language Acquisition* 12(4): 429–48 (1990). Bilingual education and French Immersion programmes are discussed in J. Cummins and M. Swain, *Bilingual Education* (London: Longman, 1986). The discussion of European Schools draws on H.B. Beardsmore, 'The European School experience in multilingual education', in T. Skutnabb-Kangas, *Multilingualism for All* (Lisse, the Netherlands: Swets & Zeitlinger B.V., 1995)

Recommended reading

Archibald, J. and Libben, G. 1995. *Research Perspectives on Second Language Acquisition.* Toronto: Copp Clark.

Cook, V. 1993. *Linguistics and Second Language Acquisition.* London: Macmillan.

Cummins, J. and Swain, M. 1986. *Bilingual Education.* London: Longman.

Long, M. and Larsen-Freeman, D. 1991. *Second Language Acquisition Research.* London: Longman.

Selinker, L. 1992. *Rediscovering Interlanguage.* London: Longman.

Sharwood Smith, M. 1994. *Second Language Learning: Theoretical Foundations.* London: Longman.

White, L. 1989. *Universal Grammar and Second Language Acquisition.* Amsterdam: John Benjamins.

Appendix:
L2 pedagogy

It has probably become clear that this chapter (and the field of second language acquisition research) is not directly concerned with second language *teaching*. Anyone interested in a catalogue of approaches to language teaching could consult *Fundamental Concepts of Language Teaching* by H.H. Stern (Oxford: Oxford University Press, 1983) and *Approaches and Methods in Language Teaching* by J.C. Richards and T.S. Rodgers (Cambridge: Cambridge University Press, 1986).

Historically, there have been a number of specific methods proposed as the best way to teach a language. There have been methods that emphasize physical activity (**total physical response**), and methods that emphasize relaxed learning (**Suggestopedia**). Some methods encourage translation (**grammar-translation**) while others discourage it (**direct method**). There are approaches that encourage repetitive drilling (**audiolingualism**) and other that discourage it (**communicative language teaching**).

Recent trends in second language pedagogy have tended to downplay the idea that a single method of instruction will work for all people. As second language acquisition research identified the large number of ways in which second language learners can vary, it became evident that not everybody learns in the same way. Therefore, not everybody can be taught in the same way.

Currently, teachers tend to adopt an eclectic approach to second language instruction. What this means is that a variety of methods and approaches are utilized. A class may include some time for drilling and some time for physical activity (just to name two possibilities). The metaphor of multiple bridges may help to explain the rationale of this eclectic approach. If teachers want to get as many students as possible to a particular destination (call it proficiency) then they have a better chance if there are multiple bridges (i.e., techniques) than if there is only one bridge (i.e., a single methodology).

The activities that make up a class will be determined by the needs and preferences of the learners, as well as by the experience and preferences of the teacher. Together they attempt to negotiate a programme of instruction that is best-suited for those concerned.

Questions

1. Some dialects of Arabic break up clusters by inserting an epenthetic vowel to the <u>left</u> of an unsyllabified consonant (unlike the dialect discussed in this chapter). How would a speaker of this dialect pronounce the words *plant*, *transport*, and *translate*? Draw trees depicting the necessary syllable structures.

2. The following is a sample of non-native writing. The assignment was to write about whether you prefer to live in the city or the country. Look through the sample and 'correct' the errors. Do you have any idea what the student's first language might be? Compare your corrected copy with that of someone else in the class and see if you agree on the corrections. If you disagree, justify to each other the corrections that you made.

Are you among the number of people who have to choose their place to live? Whenever they have to move from another country, they even change the profession, they want to have a house outside the big city, or they can't find a place in Downtown.

Its possible to move as well as you are supported by some essential condition of life I've mention in the following lines.

Most of people are living in the Big city to have many of the opportunities that offer the Downtown lifestyle, jobs, studies, activities or whatever but nowadays for instance in London its really difficult to find a place to live because the percentage of vacancy is slightly under 0% so many people are constrained to move on the suburb, by this way some of these get along this phenomene because they want to avoid the noise, the smog of the city and even they try to find their own place to live with garden and everything, actually to invest money to owe their house which is better than to rent a flat in the city, therefore they have to consider the transportation problem to reach the city even to have a car or use the public transportation.

To have your own house outside the city required a great initial capital that you have to draft from any bank or you dispose in your account but afterwhat the house become your possession with the years and couple of more will increase the house value, although it is expensive furthermore it should be a great benefit for the owner even though he decided to rent the unoccupied room into the house.

Moreless the frienship beetween the person in the subrub is closer they are ore contact with each other and maybe can meet themselves doing gardenwork or other kind of activities belong to the suburb lifestyle.

But in another (illegible) it should be difficult for the people who haven't ever lived in the suburb to move from th big city because they have to adapt their habits but they can fin amonst a great number of things that they use to have in the city. Otherwise during the last 15 years the business activites has developing around the city quickly in the Europe also the supermarket company, manufacture and so on offered the job opportunity to the people outside the big aglomeration in that way it was created some apartments vacaint in the city.

For me I don't even care where I have to live but I will observe which part could be the less expensive as well as transportation to reach my job but I will be sure that I'd like to live outside the downtown.

3. Given what you know about implicational universals, do you think it would be easier for an English speaker to acquire French nasal vowels (e.g., *gant* [gã], 'glove') or for French speakers to acquire English oral vowels?

4. What explanation would you give for a native speaker of French who produced the English sentence *I drink frequently coffee*. How could you explain the fact that when the same speaker produces the sentence *He is frequently late*, it is grammatical? Do any other English verbs behave like this?

5. Which of the following sentences would you classify as positive evidence and which as negative evidence for the learner?
   a) Non-native speaker (NNS):   He study a lot.
      Native speaker (NS):   He *studies* a lot.
   b) NS: What kind of books do you like to read?
      NNS: Mysteries.
   c) NNS: I was born in Saltillo.
      NS: Pardon me?
   d) NNS: I goed to Manchester on the weekend.
      NS: Remember that *go* has an irregular past.

6. Discuss why second language learners, regardless of their first language, might produce forms such as *goed*, *sheeps,* and *coulds* given that they never hear these forms in input from native speakers of English. Give some other forms analogous to the above that might be generated.

7. What factors can you think of that might influence fossilization? In other

words, do you think that some people are more likely to fossilize than others? Do you think it can be reversed? How?

8. Acquiring a second language involves both knowing something about the language, and being able to do something with the language. Do you think that knowledge and skills are related? Can you see any trade-off between accuracy and fluency?

9. Why do you think that non-native speakers of English would be more at risk of leaving the education system than native speakers?

10. Respond to the following statement:

It's the school system's job to make sure that non-native speakers of English learn English. They need English in order to be able to suceed in this country. We want them to succeed. If we encourage them to speak their own language, then ghettoes will form and they'll never learn English. And if we want them to learn English, then obviously they need to be exposed to more English. What good is it knowing how to speak another language in England? What they need is English, English and more English.

14

Language in social contexts

Ronald H. Southerland and Francis Katamba

… il est évident que les causes dont dépendent les faits linguistiques doivent être de nature sociale …

❧ Antoine Meillet

This chapter treats a variety of social contexts in which one can examine both the use of language and the impact of extra-linguistic factors on language. The topics range from regional variation in language through social variation in language to studies of language use in interaction. The uses of language examined reflect the real world. Utterances are given in their natural form and are not edited or censored with respect to content or choice of vocabulary. A reading of this chapter should create an awareness that the reality of language in social contexts is not one of proper speech versus all other speech but of a set of complementary speech varieties that are used by members of the **speech community**. In promoting this awareness, the chapter also discusses analytical techniques and theoretical assumptions that underlie the topics examined.

1

FUNDAMENTAL CONCEPTS

The subdiscipline of linguistics that treats the social aspects of language is called **sociolinguistics**. In this chapter, this label will be used to refer to all research about language in social contexts. Such research ranges from the very limited and localized context of a single conversation to studies of language use by whole populations. Given these quite diverse areas of research interest, it might be assumed that many sociolinguists do not share the same fundamental concepts or goals. This is to some extent true.

Despite the fact that there are a number of ways of approaching the study of language in social context, there are nevertheless certain terms and concepts that are common to most of them. The locus of all sociolinguistic investigation is the speech community. A speech community can be as small as a town, village, or even a club or as large as a nation or a group of nations. The important characteristics of a speech community are that its members share a particular language (or variety of a language) as well as the norms (or rules) for the appropriate use of their language in social context, and that these speakers be distinguished from other comparable groups by similar socio-linguistic criteria.

The term **speech variety** is the label given to that language (or form of language) used by any group of speakers. It is an ambiguous term, which can refer to the basic lexicon, phonology, syntax, and morphology shared by members of the group or to the speech used by members of the group in particular situations. Speech varieties are of four types: the **standard** language, social speech varieties (also called social dialects or **sociolects**), regional speech varieties (or **regional dialects**), and functional speech varieties (or **registers**).

In modern, developed societies there is one variety, the **standard**, that ranks above the others. This superposed variety is employed by the government and communications media, used and taught in educational institutions, and is the main or only written language. It is more fixed (allowing less variation in pronunciation, spelling and grammar) and more resistant to change than any other variety in the community and is something of a yardstick against which other varieties are measured. It is to the written standard that prescriptivists, those who seek to regulate how others use language, usually appeal when they condemn some usage as incorrect, improper, or even barbarous.

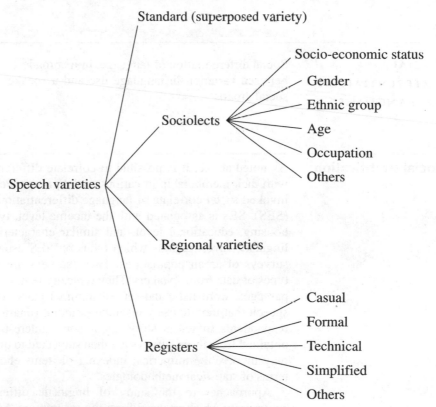

Figure 14.1 Types of speech varieties in the speech community.

Sociolects are subdivisible into several smaller categories, largely as a function of the type of social group that shares the particular speech variety. Most often, one thinks of sociolects in terms of the socio-economic status of the speakers. Other sociolects, however, may be associated with ethnic, gender, occupational, or age groups.

While sociolects are often seen as arranged along a vertical dimension corresponding to social status, regional dialects are usually thought of as distributed across a horizontal dimension. Their domains can be easily represented on a map. Regional dialects differ from each other systematically in terms of lexical or phonological criteria; they are not usually defined in terms of morphological or syntactic properties.

Functional speech varieties, more commonly called registers, are bits of talk (or pieces of writing) that are appropriate to particular speech situations. This concept, along with other basic concepts and terms associated with interactional sociolinguistics, is somewhat different from the concepts used by sociolinguists concerned with regional and social variation. Interactional sociolinguists are primarily interested in language use in speech situations, and their research thus centres on the dynamics of ongoing speech between people. The notions relevant to this type of study are treated in section 5.

2

SOCIAL DIFFERENTIATION OF LANGUAGE

Social differentiation of language, in its broadest sense, refers to correlations between variation in language use and a speaker's membership in various social groups.

2.1

Social stratification

As noted above, it is possible to correlate differences in how people speak with their membership in various social groups. Perhaps the most frequently invoked social correlate of language differentiation is socio-economic status (SES). SES is associated with the income level, type of occupation, type of housing, educational level, and similar characteristics of speakers. Socio-linguistic investigations which focus on SES usually involve large random surveys of urban populations. These surveys are designed to elicit several types of data from speakers. They typically require respondents to read aloud passages, word lists, and sets of minimal pairs. They also attempt to elicit speech that more closely resembles natural (unaffected) language by asking respondents to tell a story about some interesting experience. The data obtained from these surveys are then subjected to quantitative analysis, which may involve the numerical indexing of items elicited and treating them in terms of statistical methodologies.

Approaches to the study of linguistic differentiation in the speech community which proceed from the assumption that SES is an important (or the most important) correlate of differences in language usage generally arrive at (or proceed from) a view of vertical variation which is referred to as the **social stratification** of language. It is probably fair to say that most sociolinguistic studies over the past two decades or so have been concerned with this vertical variation of language and that most have viewed it as a function of the speaker's membership in a particular socio-economic class.

Stratification of language, while widespread in the world, is probably not universal. It is, on the other hand, reasonable to claim that social differentiation of one sort or another is universal. Underlying this claim is the belief that there are always differences in speech communities and that these differences correlate with the existence of social groups within the community. These social groups may be functions of the socio-economic status, gender, age, ethnic, or other characteristics of their members.

Until recently most conventional sociolinguistic investigations have relied on random sampling in a speech community. Generally this research has also reflected the researcher's preconceptions about the most important social correlates of linguistic behaviour in the community and, as well, has assumed that individuals sampled were representative of such social categories as those listed in the previous paragraph. There is some concern, however, that, while linguistic variation clearly does correlate with social variation, the results of particular studies may be based on invalid (or incomplete) assumptions made by the investigator who has failed to consider a full range of possible correlates.

In other words, if one undertakes a study of social differentiation, assuming that the primary social correlate of observed differences in speech will be the socio-economic status of speakers (however that may be defined), one may overlook other factors which could offer an equal or better explanation of the differentiation. Indeed, some recent studies (and attempts to re-evaluate older studies in terms of newer methodologies) have suggested that assumptions about the primacy of SES as an explanation for linguistic variation have obscured the role of gender in that regard. Some research supports the conclusion that gender may, in fact, be a more powerful underlying cause for the social differentiation of language than socio-economic status.

2.2

Other ways of studying social variation

Two alternative approaches which are challenging the traditional methodology are **social network analysis** and **principal components analysis**.

Social network analysis

A sociolinguist using the social network approach does not rely on large random samplings of a population but, rather, examines first-hand from the perspective of a participant-observer the language use of a pre-existing social group. Just as more traditional sociolinguists may assume that social stratification exists and that this has significance for the interpretation of data, researchers using the social network approach also make certain assumptions. These researchers attach importance to the nature of the relationships (and resulting interactions) of a speaker and interpret linguistic variation in terms of the kinds and densities of relationships the individual enjoys in various groups.

The density of a network is related to the potential for communication among members of the network and can be either closeknit or looseknit. A person's social network will consist of everyone in every group in which the person plays some role. Closeknit networks, which typically characterize speakers of the highest and lowest SES groups, exert a great deal of peer pressure on speakers. They are thus associated with language maintenance since speakers in such a network – owing to the fact that they interact with the same relatively limited set of people in a number of different kinds of relationships – reinforce each other's speech habits. Closeknit networks among the high SES groups reinforce either a standard speech variety or one with high status. Closeknit networks among low SES groups are loci for non-standard speech varieties.

Social networks have been likened to a Chinese fan (as in Figure 14.2), in which each group is both separate but at the same time exhibits overlap with other groups and all groups converge on the person at its centre. Thus the nature and frequency of interactions in the family group will differ from those among fellow workers, members of the same sports team, neighbours, and the like. In a sense, such studies can lend weight to the notion that we 'talk like those we talk to', more especially where those interactants are in a closeknit network.

Figure 14.2   Social networks.

Figure 14.3 shows a portion of a closeknit network investigated by Lesley Milroy in the working-class Clonard area of Belfast. This network had a 100 per cent density index; that is to say, everybody in the network of the researcher's original contact (John R.) knew everybody else and talked to them frequently. John R. himself lived in a neighbouring block of flats but his family lived in the Clonard. He introduced Lesley Milroy to his friend Martin Convery whose immediate and extended family and friends also lived in the Clonard and met up with each other often.

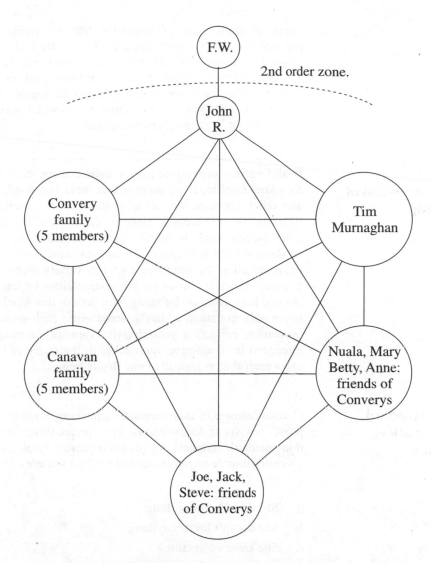

Figure 14.3 A portion of the Clonard network, showing density of 100 per cent.

Principal components analysis

The newest technique to challenge the traditional approach is Principal Components Analysis (PCA). This approach has been used in studies of the Sydney, Australia, and St John's, Newfoundland, speech communities. PCA is highly quantitative. It uses statistical techniques which allow the investigator to examine a large number of linguistic variants, to compare speakers with similar linguistic characteristics (displayed on graphs in clusters) and, only as a last step, to determine what social similarities are shared by these linguistically categorized groups of speakers. A particular 'Principal Component' is a set of variables (such as the phonological ones in Table 14.1 on p. 548) which can be shown statistically to give the best account of the data. Groups of people who share particular linguistic features are categorized in terms of those sets of linguistic features rather than with respect to preconceived sociological features. Given the lack of *a priori* assumptions about the relevance of particular social categories, the results of PCA studies are seen by the investigators as more reliable pictures of social differentiation than was possible using traditional methodologies. In the section below on non-standard phonological features we consider some of the results of the PCA study of St John's, Newfoundland.

2.3

Social differentiation of English

In all English-speaking countries, there is a speech variety that can be termed *Standard English*. If we assume that there is a single standard and there are also other varieties, we can label these other varieties non-standard. Sociolinguists use this term in place of the more commonly used non-technical label *substandard*. It might seem reasonable to call a particular usage substandard if it is in fact other than standard, since we have already defined the standard as the superposed speech variety. *Substandard* is, however, not a neutral label. It carries with it connotations of inferiority and even social stigma. It is assumed by many who do use this label that substandard usage is not only not standard but in some sense perhaps wrong or illogical. This, of course, reflects a prescriptivist view of language. Since linguists are interested in descriptive approaches to the study of language, they prefer to use a neutral term instead of one that is biased.

Non-standard grammatical features

Certain features of non-standard varieties of English are often singled out by prescriptivists as demonstrating the inherent illogic or lack of systematicity of non-standard varieties. An oft-cited grammatical feature of this sort is the so-called double negative, seen in the first sentence in *1)*.

1)

a. She don't know nothing.

b. She doesn't know anything.

c. She knows something.

A prescriptivist asserts that the two negations in the first sentence (*-n't* and *no-*) cancel each other out. Thus the speaker in *1a)* has supposedly uttered an affirmative sentence with the meaning of *1c)*. Anyone who hears the sentence in *1a)*, however, knows that its meaning is the same for the non-standard speaker as the meaning of *1b)* is for the speaker of the standard. The non-standard and standard negative sentences differ from the affirmative sentence in the same two ways: both verbs are marked as negative and both indefinite pronouns are marked differently from the pronoun in the affirmative sentence. When the verb is negated in Standard English, an indefinite pronoun in the verb phrase is also negated, by changing *some-* to *any-*. In the non-standard variety, negating the verb causes the pronoun to be negated by changing *some-* to *no-*. Both varieties mark negation twice and thus are equally logical – or illogical.

There is another non-standard feature in *1a)* – the verb *do* – which co-occurs with the subject pronoun *she*. This sort of usage and the similar one seen in non-standard *She know* are also condemned by prescriptivists. These two sentences violate the Standard English subject–verb agreement rule, which requires present tense English verbs with third person subjects to have a special ending (*-s*). An examination of the morphology of Standard English verbs and a look at the historical development of these forms, however, show that over time all but the third person singular ending *-s* has been lost in the present tense. A non-prescriptivist view of those non-standard varieties that lack a special ending in this form would hold that they have simply carried this particular linguistic change to its logical conclusion by eliminating the last remaining inflectional ending in the present tense.

Non-standard phonological features

The phonological entities of interest to sociolinguists are called socio-linguistic variables. These variables are speech sounds (either single segments or syllables) that do not occur uniformly across a speech community or, occasionally, even in the speech of an individual. For instance, a particular variable may be realized one way in one speech variety and a different way in another speech variety. Similarly, a variable might be rendered one way by speakers when they are speaking carefully and another way in a more casual speaking style. Traditional sociolinguistic studies have concentrated on small numbers of phonological variables, most of them binary (exhibiting only two realizations) in nature.

Perhaps the most widespread variable in English is (ing). We use parentheses to set off sociolinguistic variables, thus distinguishing them formally from phonemes and phones. Since (ing) is a variable, it is not always realized the same way in speech. Its two realizations are [ɪn] and [ɪŋ]. The same word might be pronounced with one or the other realization by the same speaker or by different speakers: *swimming* might thus be realized as [swɪmɪn] or as [swɪmɪŋ].

These realizations do not occur randomly in speech. There are well-established correlations between the two realizations of (ing) and such extra-linguistic factors as the socio-economic status and gender of the speaker, the relative formality (or informality) of the speech situation, its physical location, and the nature of the particular lexical item. The variable tends to be realized as [ɪŋ] by speakers of higher socio-economic status, by females, and in formal situations. Words such as *analysing* (in general, formal vocabulary) are pronounced more frequently with [ɪŋ] than with [ɪn], while words such as *chucking* are more often heard with the [ɪn] than with [ɪŋ]. Words such as *everything* may be heard with either realization (depending often on the regional origin of the speaker), but we do not expect to hear any native speaker of English pronounce *sing* [sɪn], nor *sin* [sɪŋ]. One study showed that in school situations, with respect to student speakers, more [ɪŋ]s were heard in the classroom and more [ɪn]s were heard on the playground.

The St John's study mentioned above isolated some five consonantal and eight vocalic variables in the speech of its 120-person sample. Various statistically based groupings of these variables constituted particular Principal

Components. Any one variable might appear in more than one Principal Component (PC) (along with other variables) but each PC was a set of variables linked to (and defining) some group of speakers. Principal Component 1 [PC1] was expressed in terms of the non-standard realizations of each of the six variables given in Table 14.1. (The standard being contrasted with Newfoundland English is Standard Canadian English.)

Table 14.1   Phonological variables in Newfoundland English PC1

Variable	Word	Phonetic realization	
(e)	bay	a)	standard diphthongal [eɪ]
		b)	non-standard monophthongal [e:]
(o)	boat	a)	standard diphthongal [ou]
		b)	non-standard monophthongal [o:]
(θ)	three	a)	standard interdental fricative [θ]
		b)	non-standard alveolar stop [t]
(l)	mole	a)	standard dark [ɫ]
(post-vocalic)		b)	Irish-like clear [l]
		c)	vocalic [ɤ] (mid-back unrounded)
(or)	bore	a)	standard [ɔr]
		b)	non-standard [ar]-like pronunciation
(ð)	them	a)	standard interdental fricative [ð]
		b)	non-standard alveolar stop [d] or flap [ɾ]

Speakers evidencing high values (i.e., high percentages of occurrence) of the *non-standard* realizations of the variables in Table 14.1 turned out almost exclusively to be older males. There were no correlations with socio-economic status or religion.

Principal Component 2 [PC2], on the other hand (Table 14.2), consisted of another grouping of variables.

Table 14.2   Phonological variables in Newfoundland English PC2

Variable	Word	Phonetic realization	
(ing)	fishing	a)	standard [ɪŋ]
		b)	non-standard or casual [ɪn]
(ð)	them	a)	standard interdental fricative [ð]
		b)	non-standard alveolar stop [d] or flap [ɾ]
(θ)	three	a)	standard interdental fricative [θ]
		b)	non-standard alveolar stop [t]

Speakers with high values of the *standard* realizations of the variables in Table 14.2 clustered together and showed a greater proportion of women than men and also a higher proportion of the uppermost SES groups than did other clusters of speakers. This is consistent with other findings which tend to show standard features occurring more in the speech of women and persons of higher socio-economic status and less in the speech of men and persons of lesser socio-economic status.

The Newfoundland examples also exhibit evidence of the sort needed to understand socially motivated linguistic change. Newfoundland English owes many of its characteristics to Irish English because many settlers in this province were of Irish stock. But Newfoundland exists in the wider English-speaking North American community and for more than forty years has been a province of Canada. These phonological variables show something of the conflict between older linguistic norms and newer ones. Here the older men in the first group are adhering to older norms, while the women and higher status persons of the second group are reflecting incoming (general Canadian) norms.

2.4

Language and gender

Using the words *language* and *gender* in the same context can lead to confusion. Linguists use the word *gender* as the label for certain ways languages may subcategorize their lexicons (see Chapter 4, section 6.2). The word does not ultimately refer to sex. In popular usage, however, and in other social sciences *gender* refers to social distinctions drawn between men and women. In the following section, *gender* used by itself will have this sociological sense and the term *grammatical gender* will be used when referring to internal language categories. Any discussion of language and sex would imply that observed differences between the speech of men and women are biological rather than social. It is far from clear at the present stage of research what correlations can be made between the (biological) sex of an individual and his or her speech.

There is a considerable literature on the general topic of language and gender, which may be taken as including all of the following:

- differences in language use associated with the gender (or sexual orientation) of the speaker or addressee (person spoken to)
- differences in language use associated with the gender (or sexual orientation) of the referent (person spoken about)
- efforts to alter the language with respect to ways gender is or is not encoded.

Two different, but not necessarily contradictory, views have been advanced as to the relationship between language and gender. One view, which has characterized much sociolinguistic research in this area, holds that gender differences in language are simply a reflection of the way society works. Another view, one often associated with some feminists, claims that, far from merely reflecting the nature of society, language serves as a primary means of encoding ideas used in constructing and maintaining that society. The continued use in English, for instance, of male forms (such as *chairman*) in a generic sense (as we will see below) excludes women and is seen as perpetuating a social order in which women are invisible. Thus attitudes as to how people should talk and, indeed, how they are to regard their own status within society are formed by language and continue to be reinforced unless language changes (or is altered).

There is certainly truth in both of these views insofar as they recognize the ideological role of language. Clearly, language does mirror society's ideas, underlying assumptions as well as practices with respect to what is seen as important and even normal. On the other hand, if groups (whether gender, ethnic, or other) are marginalized by the ways they are categorized or labelled by language, then this issue must be addressed and certain aspects of the language may need to be changed in order to include rather than exclude particular groups. In the following sections we will explore some specific types of gender differentiation in language and will examine some efforts to remove sexist language from English. The correlation between sexual orientation of speaker and language use is treated below in section 2.7.

Gender-exclusive differentiation

Gender-exclusive differentiation refers to the radically different speech varieties used by men and women in particular societies. In these societies, a woman or a man may, except in special circumstances, not be allowed to speak the variety of the other gender. It is in this sense that the varieties are gender-exclusive. A society in which this is the norm is typically one in which the roles assigned to the genders are rigid, and in which there is little social change.

This phenomenon has been observed in some Amerindian societies but is no longer as widespread as it may have been in the remote past. A study of Koasati (a Muskogean language spoken in Louisiana) showed that members of this speech community possessed different verb forms based on the gender of the speaker. Some of these differences are illustrated in Table 14.3. The men's speech can be most efficiently described as being derived from the women's speech by rules. Where the women's form had falling pitch-stress (marked ^) on its final syllable and ended in a short vowel followed by [l], the men's form showed high pitch-stress (marked ´) and [s] for the [l]. If the women's form ended in a short or long vowel followed by one or two consonants, the men's form added [s] ([t] + [s] → [tʃ]). If the women's form ended in [tʃ], the men's form was the same. (W in Table 14.3 stands for female speaker and M for male speaker.)

Table 14.3 Gender-exclusive verb forms in Koasati

W	M	
lakawwîl	lakawwís	'I am lifting it'
lakáwtʃ	lakáwtʃ	'you are lifting it'
lakáw	lakáws	'he is lifting it'
lakáwwilit	lakáwwilitʃ	'I lifted it'

In traditional Koasati society, women and men normally used the forms appropriate to their gender, but they were not forbidden the use of forms associated with the other gender. In quoting a member of the other gender as in relating a story, a Koasati used the form appropriate to the person being quoted.

Gender-exclusive differentiation has assumed an even more radical form in some societies. In the most extreme form, which was decidedly rare, the gender of the speaker and that of the addressee were both encoded in an utterance. In Biloxi (an extinct language of the Siouan family), all of the forms shown in Table 14.4 (each meaning 'carry it!') were found.

Table 14.4   Gender-exclusive differentiation in Biloxi

	One addressee	*More than one addressee*
M to M	kikankó	kítakankó
M or W to W	kitkí	kítatkí
W to M	kitaté	kítatuté

Furthermore, in addition to morphological differences of the kind discussed above, gender-exclusive differences may also be found to a limited extent in the lexicon. In Japanese, for example, there are a few vocabulary items that vary according to the gender of the speaker. Some examples are listed in Table 14.5.

Table 14.5   Gender-exclusive lexical differentiation in Japanese

Women's form	*Men's form*	
ohiya	mizu	'water'
onaka	hara	'stomach'
oisii	umai	'delicious'
taberu	kuu	'eat'

Gender-variable differentiation

Gender-variable differentiation is much more common in the languages of the world than is gender-exclusivity. This phenomenon is reflected in the relative frequency with which men and women use the same lexical items or other linguistic features. If, as is often asserted, female English speakers use words such as *lovely* and *nice* more often than do male speakers, we can claim that in this respect English speakers exhibit gender-variable differentiation.

Women have been shown to possess a greater variety of specific colour terms than men in English-speaking speech communities. If this is true, it is probably due to the tasks traditionally performed by women. There is no evidence to show that women have more acute colour perception than do men. Indeed, one study showed that younger men had larger vocabularies of colour terms than did older men but still less extensive ones than women. Thus there is evidence that gender-variability in this area is undergoing change.

Men are reputed to possess larger lexicons in areas associated with traditional male activities (such as occupations like bricklaying and deep sea fishing) and male-dominated sports (like football, boxing, and rugby). These examples may appear stereotypical, but they do reflect the sometimes subtle, sometimes blatant, differences between the activities and thus the language of members of the two genders.

Other differences between men's and women's language in English-speaking speech communities are seen in women's more frequent use of **politeness formulas**. There are a number of ways in which requests (or commands) can be mitigated in English. Instead of simply saying to someone *'Open the window!'* we might say *'Please open the window!'*, *'Would you please open the window?'*, *'Could you open the window?'*, *'Would you mind opening the window?'*, *'Do you find it stuffy in here?'*, and so on. These are all less direct ways of making the request than the straightforward imperative and, it is claimed, would more likely be employed by women.

Similarly, some studies suggest that women use more **verbal hedges** than do men. These are words such as *perhaps* or *maybe* (as in *We could perhaps go to Greece next summer for our holidays*) which are less assertive in conversations than utterances without hedges (e.g., *We should go to Greece next summer for our holidays*). (See also section 5.3.)

Finally, it has been noted that men tend to use more vernacular as opposed to standard forms. Men tend to attach positive value to non-standard forms. Their use is seen as having in-group **covert prestige** (as opposed to the overt prestige of standard forms). Indeed, in a study in Norwich, it was found that men often claimed to use more non-standard forms than they actually did use. Normally men also use 'bad language' considerably more than women who belong to the same social class. Indeed, among some men it is considered *macho* – rather than plain vulgar – to spice one's utterances richly with maximally taboo four letter words like *shit*, *fuck*, and *cunt*.

What do the three phenomena that we have considered have in common? Why does women's usage differ from that of men? The answer seems to have to do with saving **face** (i.e., showing respect and consideration for others). Men's less frequent use of politeness formulas, reluctance to use hedges and the predilection for the vernacular (and in particular 'bad language') has been attributed to the fact that in the social construction of masculinity, being 'tough' – and hence inconsiderate of the face-protection needs of the addressee – is often considered a virtue. By contrast, in the construction of femininity the opposite is the case. So, in the linguistic behaviour of women, behaviour that is considerate and protects the face of the addressee is preferred.

Since we are discussing gender-variable usage here, we must emphasize that all of the above ways of phrasing a request are available to all speakers but are not equally selected by male and female speakers. An important factor that affects the use of politeness formulas, hedges, and non-standard vernacular forms is the degree of formality of the situation. The more formal the situation the more likely are speakers of either gender to use standard forms, hedges, and politeness formulas.

Talking about women and men

The most obvious way in which gender differences with respect to a referent are manifested in English is grammatical gender. The use of English pronouns is instructive in this regard. We do not employ *he*, for instance, to refer only to males. In Standard English, it is prescribed as a generic third person singular pronoun when the gender of the referent is unknown or irrelevant.

Thus, we might encounter sentences such as '*Did everyone hand in his assignment today?*' even if the entire group of referents is composed of women. However, nowadays in naturally occurring speech we more often hear utterances such as the following: '*No one can with impunity take the law into* their *own hands*' (asserted by former Mayor Koch of New York City) and '*Why don't we go to our first caller and see what* their *concerns are?*' (from a television talk-show host). In these sentences, we have instances of singular (gender-indefinite) *they*, which is widespread in non-conservative, non-prescriptivist English and which denotes an indefinite number of individuals of unspecified (or possibly mixed) gender. For speakers who utter sentences of this sort, the pronouns *she* and *he* are reserved for reference to individuals of a single gender whose gender is known.

English nouns, though not overtly marked for grammatical gender like those in Latin, Russian, or many other languages, do distinguish between women and men. Generally in English, nouns referring to certain occupations are at once both masculine and generic, thus the traditional terms *postman* or *fireman*, until comparatively recently, were used both for men and women in those professions. There occasionally are female forms for the names of occupations (*manageress, sculptress, actress, poetess, usherette*) but these have evolved to connote more than just the gender of the practitioner of the occupation. Many observers feel that these and similar forms trivialize women so labelled. A woman who acts in films pointedly identified herself as an *actor* in an interview, not as an *actress*. She said that *actor* connoted for her someone who was serious about the craft, while *actress* did not.

The form -*man* has been under considerable scrutiny in the recent past with respect to its reference. The pervasiveness of male-referential forms used generically (as in *chairman, postman*, and *Museum of Man*) has disturbed many observers, who have felt that such language not only reflects sexist values but also perpetuates and reinforces them. This concern has resulted in moves to eliminate generic masculine forms from the language. In many instances, the suffix -*man* has been changed to gender-neutral -*person*. Other morphological processes have resulted in the creation of new forms (a *postman* becomes a *letter carrier*, a *fireman* becomes a *fire fighter*, and a *chairman* becomes a *chairperson* or *chair*). The *Museum of Man* became the *Museum of Civilization*.

Changes have also come about in the use of pronouns. In many cases, regulations, laws, and the like have been rewritten to eliminate discriminatory masculine forms, replacing them with forms such as *he/she* or the gender-neutral singular *they*.

Replacement of sexist nouns with gender-neutral ones and a few adjustments in the use of third-person pronouns contribute, of course, to the creation of a less biased language. Advocates of the view (discussed earlier) that language does not merely mirror society but rather moulds it would point to further and more wide-ranging examples of sexism which should be reformed. Deferential uses of language by women (the use of politeness formulas or hedges, for example) would be supplanted by more assertive behaviour. Unequal treatment of men and women in various areas of the language would be levelled out. For, in this view, as long as these inequalities exist, they reinforce the status quo and leave women as a marginalized group. (For further examples of the unequal treatment of women and men – in the context of university slang – see section 2.6 below.)

Of course, important though it is for the reasons outlined above, language reform in itself is not sufficient to guarantee equality. It is instructive to note that there are many languages that appear reasonably non-sexist – e.g., the Bantu languages of sub-Saharan Africa which make no grammatical gender distinctions on the basis of sex and which have relatively few gender-biased lexical items – but which, nonetheless, are used in societies which harbour many deeply ingrained sexist attitudes. Feminists recognize the fact that eliminating sexist language is only a part of a wider programme of political and social reform leading to a more just distribution of power and opportunities.

2.5

Euphemism

Euphemism is the avoidance of words which may be seen as offensive, obscene, or somehow disturbing to listeners or readers. Items which are euphemized are said to be tabooed. The word **taboo** was borrowed from the Tongan language and, in its most general sense, refers to a prohibition on the use of, mention of, or association with particular objects, actions, or persons. As originally used in Polynesia, *taboo* had religious connotations, but in sociolinguistics it now denotes any prohibition on the use of particular lexical items. Taboo and euphemism are thus two faces of the same coin.

In the English-language speech community, the most obvious taboos are not religious but have to do with bodily functions, body parts, and death. In addition, there is a noticeable tendency for governments to resort to euphemism to mask otherwise unpleasant concepts or to conceal aspects of their policy. Table 14.6 contains a variety of types of euphemisms which have been employed in the past or are currently in use.

Table 14.6   Some common euphemisms in English

Euphemism	Tabooed word or expression
private parts	'penis, cock, vagina, cunt, etc.'
make love	'fuck'
perspire	'sweat'
cold feet	'cowardice'
budget	'cheap'
pee	'piss'
sit-down job	'defecation'
pink slip	'dismissal notice'
pass away	'die'
neutralize	'kill'
collateral losses	'civilian casualties'

The existence of taboo and euphemism represent the exercise of power by dominant groups over their subordinates. Controlling what one can say is an aspect of controlling one's overall behaviour. Taboos in English on language related to sex are, after all, not uniform across the speech community. As we saw above, in section 2.4, men have historically been allowed much greater freedom to use such terms in public than have women. Taboos serve to support the status quo, the existing power structure. They may help to maintain the dominance of one gender over another, a political or religious elite over the general population or the like. Since no words are inherently 'dirty' or 'offensive', it is unclear what salutary effect taboos and euphemisms have. Below in sections 2.6 and 2.7 there are examples of some terms which, although not seen as offensive by the speakers who use them, may cause offence (and thus may be tabooed) in the wider speech community.

2.6

Slang

Slang is a label that is frequently used to denote certain informal or faddish usages of nearly anyone in the speech community. The term was first attested in English in the mid-eighteenth century, used in reference to 'special vocabulary used by any set of persons of a low or disreputable character; language of a low and vulgar type' (according to the *Oxford English Dictionary*). Nowadays, it is often applied to aspects of the language of adolescents or others who are perceived as speaking non-standard varieties of the language.

Slang exists alongside jargon and argot (treated below in section 2.7) as members of a class of speech varieties of limited usage in the speech community. Each of these last two mentioned varieties, whether characteristic of an occupational or social group, is confined to a comparatively small number of speakers and is obscure to outsiders. Slang, while it may be fleeting and subject to rapid change, is more widespread and more familiar to large numbers of speakers. Particular 'slangs', however, are very much associated with membership of groups and, when used in the presence of another member of the same group, serve as an affirmation of solidarity with other members.

Studies have shown that slang usage is abundant, creative, and socially important. We will focus on a study of a Glasgow working-class boys' gang in the 1960s. This study contains many interesting examples of Glasgow underworld slang (Table 14.7 overleaf), some of which is used in the wider working-class community.

The use of slang plays a major role in the maintenance of the gang's group identity. It separates the in-group, who use the slang, from the rest of society who do not and are not part of the gang.

A study of slang at a major American university (UCLA) produced a dictionary which included details of syntax and word formation as well as some indications of the origins of many of the slang expressions (Table 14.8).

The students were also found to use particular word formation processes in producing slang (Table 14.9).

Table 14.7   Glasgow slang

gemmie	a hard man who never runs away from a fight
crap-bag	coward
punters	fellow gang members
square-going	unarmed combat
malky	weapon
chib (noun)	weapon
chib (verb)	strike with a weapon
haas	bastard
gallous gear	very flashy suits
snide gear	unfashionable clothes
sleekit	cunning
peter	police or prison cell

Table 14.8   Origins of UCLA slang

Slang expression	*Meaning*	*Origin*
homeboy	'very close male friend'	Black English
mazeh	'gorgeous guy'	Hebrew
happa	'half-Asian person'	Japanese
have missile lock	'concentrate on'	popular film

Table 14.9   Processes of word formation in UCLA slang

Slang	*Meaning*	*Source*	*Process*
sucky	'awful'	suck	derivation [V → A]
mazehette	'gorgeous girl'	mazeh	derivation [N → N]
gork	'nerd'	geek + dork	blending
cas [kæʒ]	'all right'	casual	clipping
TFA	'great!'	**T**otally **F**ucking **A**wesome	acronymy
fake-bake	'tanning salon'	fake + bake	compounding

In addition to these morphological techniques of word formation there was substantial use of the semantic technique of metaphor, in which an existing lexical item is replaced by another which suggests an image similar to that associated with the item replaced. Often the new coinage can be seen as more dramatic than the original. A typical instance of this process is seen in the phrase *blow chunks* 'vomit'. This replaces the older phrase *throw up* with a new phrase which has greater impact. Although speakers of this slang can also be expected to exhibit phonological variability with respect to (ing) (discussed in section 2.1) in their usual speech, they consistently realize (ing) as [ɪn] in the slang word *bitchin'* 'good, excellent' so that there is no **bitching* alternating with it.

Interestingly, the slang items gathered in this study had a relatively limited semantic range. That is, the overwhelming majority of forms referred to comparatively few concepts. Many concerned the appearance of males (most were flattering, such as *hoss* 'stud; muscular male'; only a few were not: *eddie* 'ugly guy'). A large proportion of the terms referring to women were denigrating (as, *wilma* 'ugly girl', or *turbobitch* 'crabby female'). Some descriptive labels were gender-neutral (e.g., *studmuffin* both 'strong, muscular person' and 'cute person; achiever' and *gagger* 'disgusting person or thing'). Other frequently attested semantic domains in the UCLA slang included every aspect of university life, sexual relations, and bodily functions.

As seen, the UCLA slang is rich in vocabulary denigrating women. In this it stands in a long and regrettable tradition which is firmly entrenched in traditional dialects. Dialect studies have revealed a rich vocabulary of insults directed at women for their looks (see examples in Table 14.10*a*), allegedly loose morals (see Table 14.10*b*) or apparent lack of femininity (see Table 14.10*c*).

Table 14.10   Traditional dialectal insults for women

	Word	Meaning
a.	bamsey	fat, red-faced woman
	bussock	fat, heavy woman
	cloffy	slattern, tawdrily dressed woman
	driggle-draggle	slovenly, untidy woman
	sess	great, fat woman
b.	rompstall	rude, romping girl
	fiz-gig	frivolous woman
	vuddicks	coarse, fat woman
c.	shammel	masculine woman
	twanker	virago
	fuz	fat, idle woman

It is no accident that there is no comparable wealth of insults for men: the fact that men do but women do not fashion language in this way both reflects and helps to maintain unequal power relations in society.

2.7

Jargon and argot

The terms **jargon** and **argot** are often used almost interchangeably to refer to 'obscure or secret language' or 'language of a particular occupational group'. Since the term *argot* arose in the seventeenth century as the label for a speech variety used by French beggars and street merchants and later was applied to the secret language of criminals, we will use it to denote 'secret language'. It is a label for speech varieties associated with social groups whose members wish to or must conceal themselves or some aspects of their communication from non-members. We will use jargon as the label for 'vocabulary peculiar to some field; occupational sociolect'.

Cockney rhyming slang

A famous example of an English argot is Cockney rhyming slang which is exemplified in Table 14.11. It arose among navvies in London's East End in the nineteenth century and was soon appropriated by the criminal elements who found it an effective way of concealing what they were up to from the authorities. Rhyming slang eventually diffused into the speech of the general working-class population of the East End. It is still thriving today.

Table 14.11   Cockney rhyming slang

Slang	Meaning
bird lime	time
bees and honey	money
merry-go-round	pound sterling
Hampstead Heath	teeth
Daily Mail	tail
Russian-Turk	(casual) work

Some of this rhyming slang has passed on into the slang used by the wider speech community. For instance, even those of us who are unfamiliar with Cockney rhyming slang know that '*telling porkies*' (shortened from '*telling pork pies*') is slang for 'telling lies' and that '*to take the Micky*' is to 'to faze or humiliate' (which is a variant of 'to take the piss' – it is derived from *Mike Bliss*, the rhyming slang for 'piss' (urinate)).

Interestingly, rhyming slang is not restricted to Cockney. In many urban working-class English speech communities there exists some form of rhyming slang. For example, in Glasgow, *House of Fraser* (the name of a department store chain) is rhyming slang for 'razor' and *pineapple* can mean '(catholic) chapel'. In Australia an 'idiot' (i.e., mug) may be called a *milk jug* (*jug* for short). In American rhyming slang 'cocaine' (shortened to 'coke') is called *big bloke*, 'jail' is called *ginger ale*, and so on.

Gay lingo

Language used by members of the male homosexual community is, in historical perspective at least, another example of an argot (Table 14.12). It was either used covertly or its use in public was not meant to be understood by non-gays. The lexicon of this argot covers a variety of concepts but is particularly rich in terms denoting sexual practices, categories of homosexuals, physical appearance, and matters of taste, among others.

Table 14.12   Some words from 'gay lingo' which have attained wider usage in the speech community

butch	'(of a woman) very "masculine"; (of a man) macho'
camp	'a playful appreciation of the ridiculous or kitsch'
come out	'disclosing one's homosexuality'
(in the) closet	'relating to the concealing of one's homosexuality (or other trait) from public knowledge'

Only *butch* preserves most of the original notion in non-gay casual speech. The other three terms in Table 14.12, though clearly arising in the gay subculture, have gained wider usage. Thus one can now refer not only to a 'closet homosexual' but, in an age which increasingly frowns on the use of tobacco, to a 'closet smoker'. While a homosexual can 'come out' so can anyone else who wishes to acknowledge some aspect of his or her identity which has previously been masked. The notion of camp has become so well-known that a philosopher wrote an essay on it and it frequently appears in discussions of art and entertainment. These words are excellent examples of the fact that argots, jargons, and, especially, slang are productive sources of lexical items which later become part of the linguistic resources of the wider speech community.

Hacker jargon

Practitioners of many professions are often accused by others of having obscure jargons which deny communicative access to non-members of the group. Although jargons may offer effective and efficient ways of communication within the group, they are confusing to outsiders. One contemporary jargon which is notably unclear to the non-initiate but nevertheless important and increasingly influential in the language is hacker jargon. Hackers are perhaps best defined as 'particularly enthusiastic and resourceful computer users and programmers'. Their jargon is characterized by a substantial vocabulary associated with computers but also evidences unusual rules both in its syntax and word formation. The word *hardware* 'the computer or its attachments', for instance, provided, via reanalysis of -*ware*, the neologism *software* 'instructions, applications which are distinct from the computer and require use of the computer in order to function'. Over time the use of -*ware* has been further extended so that hackers have coined terms such as those in Table 14.13 (overleaf).

Hackers, of course, very often use computers for communication. In so doing they have adapted some features of face-to-face interaction to this electronic medium. Thus an e-mail (electronic mail) message may be filled with typed utterances such as <*groan*> or <*chortle*>. These usages may then be transferred into the hackers' verbal interaction so that they actually say 'groan' in the course of speaking. There are also numerous 'emoticons' – use of standard keyboard characters to convey the emotions or attitudes of the communicator, such as ;-) 'a smile and a wink' or :-('a frown or anger'. LISP, a programming language, uses a *p* suffix to denote functions resembling questions. A LISP programmer may then appropriate this (normally written) usage in his or her speech and utter '*Foodp?*' which means perhaps 'Do you want to eat?' All of the examples in this paragraph are instances of usage from one register (see section 5.1) being adapted for use in another. Hackers offer in microcosm an example of a very resourceful use of the devices available to speakers of the language and an indication of ways in which language changes.

Table 14.13   Some instances of -*ware* in hacker jargon

freeware	'software provided without fee by its developer'
shareware	'software for which the developer requires a voluntary payment of a small fee by the user'
guiltware	'shareware which contains a message detailing how much effort the developer has put into it and implying that the user should immediately pay the fee'
crippleware	'shareware which has some important functionality removed, so as to entice the user to remit the fee in order to receive a fully functional version'
crudware	'large quantities of low-quality freeware available from users' groups'
postcardware	'freeware for which the developer's only requested payment is a postcard from the user's hometown'
happiware	'freeware which contains a message stating the developer hopes it will make the user happy'
vapourware	'products (software or hardware) announced far in advance of their appearance, which may never take place'
wetware	'the human brain; human beings such as programmers'

Cyberspace jargon

Recent growth in the importance and popularity of the *Internet* has been matched by an explosion in the growth of *cyberspace* related jargon, some of which is percolating into everyday, non-technical language. Not only do many of us who do not consider ourselves to be computer buffs use *e-mail* to contact our local radio station or to write a letter to our newspaper, we also go *netsurfing* using *browsers* like *Mosaic* or *Netscape* to see what news, entertainment, shopping or educational offerings are available at various *sites* on the *World Wide Web*. Table 14.14, on the next page, lists some of the cyberspace jargon that has entered the language.

2.8

Ethnicity and language

The link between one's language and one's membership of a particular ethnic group is complex. As we will see below, not all ethnic groups exhibit the same degree of maintenance of their language from generation to generation. Ethnic sociolects, those speech varieties associated with specific ethnic groups, exist in a spectrum including varieties as diverse as Black English (a kind of English) on the one hand, and Xhosa in South Africa or Maori in New Zealand (indigenous languages, unrelated to English) on the other. In a complex speech community these varieties are in competition with whatever standard or official languages may be present. Often these ethnic varieties succumb to the overriding influence of the dominant language.

Table 14.14   Some Internet-related jargon

archive site	A machine that provides access to a collection of files across the internet.
bounce	The return of a piece of mail because of an error in its delivery.
bridge	A device that forwards traffic between network segments based on datalink layer information. These segments would have a common network layer address.
client	A computer system or process that requests a service of another computer system or process. A workstation requesting the contents of a file from a file server is a client of the file server.
cyberspace	A term coined by William Gibson in his fantasy novel *Neuromancer* to describe a 'world' of computers, and the society that gathers around them.
e-mail	Electronic mail.
Internet (net)	A global network of computer networks.
mailing list	A list of e-mail addresses, used by a mail exploder, to forward messages to groups of people. Generally, a mailing list is used to discuss certain set topics. And different mailing lists discuss different topics.
moderator	A person, or small group of people, who manage moderated mailing lists. Moderators are responsible for determining which e-mail submissions are passed onto the list.
netiquette	A pun on 'etiquette' referring to proper behaviour on a network.
network	A computer network is a data communications system which interconnects computer systems at various sites.
World Wide Web (WWW or W3)	A hypertext-based, distributed information system created by researchers at CERN. Users may create, edit or browse hypertext documents. The clients and servers are freely available.

Language maintenance, language shift, and language death

Broadly speaking, when languages come in contact one of three things may happen: there may occur *language maintenance*, *language shift*, or *language death*. In cases of language maintenance, the languages co-exist in a fairly stable relationship, with speakers of the less influential language managing to hold on to it and to pass it on to their children. This is most likely to happen if the speakers wish to assert their separate identity – for instance, if they strongly value maintaining their language for cultural or religious reasons. The chances of language maintenance are enhanced if the speakers form a substantial speech community and belong to closeknit social networks. It is also an advantage if the economic imperatives – the desire to 'get on' – can be satisfied without abandoning their language. That is most likely to be the case if the less influential language has media, economic, educational, and political institutions that are capable of counter-balancing the power of the dominant language. These conditions are met, for example, in Switzerland where French holds its own despite the dominance of the German-speaking majority.

If, however, increasing numbers of speakers of the less influential language succumb to the pressure of the dominant language, their language which would have been used previously in their homes and communities is supplanted from these vital domains by the dominant language. In that event, language shift is inevitable. Increasing numbers of younger speakers fail to acquire their parents' language and instead grow up as monolingual speakers of the dominant language. That has been the fate of Breton in France and Gaelic in Scotland.

If the process of squeezing the range of domains in which the weaker language is used goes much further, and if at the same time the decline in the number of people who speak that language continues unchecked, the final result is language death. When the last speaker of the language dies, the language becomes extinct. That is what happened to Cornish towards the end of the eighteenth century. It was elbowed out by English. The same fate is suffered every year by dozens of languages spoken by small minority groups round the world today.

English multilingualism

Like most other countries in the world today, England is multilingual. This was shown in a report documenting the extent of multilingualism in schools entitled *Linguistic Minorities in England* which was commissioned by the Department of Education and was published in 1983. The report demonstrated that in many major cities there are significant minority communities using more than one language in their everyday lives. Normally, in such communities, while English is used in formal education settings and in dealings with the state's bureaucratic machine, home life, shopping, recreational and cultural activities are carried out in community languages such as Greek, Gujerati, Cantonese, Turkish or Jamaican Creole.

Table 14.15, which shows the main languages reported in five Local Education Authorities (LEAs), gives a good indication of the extent of multilingualism in England. It also shows that the distribution of minority languages is very uneven. In any one area a handful of important minority languages may account for over 85 per cent of the total number of minority language speakers. The distribution of the different languages reflects patterns of settlement by immigrants, most of whom came to the UK after World War II. Typically, immigrants tended to settle in areas where significant numbers of other members of their ethnic group were already living. This is to be expected since earlier immigrants could offer new arrivals assistance with housing and provide them with elaborate support networks.

Table 14.15   Main languages reported in five LEAs

		Bradford	Coventry	London Borough of Harringey	Peter-borough	London Borough of Waltham Forest
(1)	Total no. of pupils recorded as using a language other than English at home	14,201	7189	7407	2408	5521
(2)	Total no. of identifiably distinct languages reported	64	50	87	42	65
(3)	The most frequently reported spoken languages or language groupings as a % of (1) to the nearest whole number	Panjabi 53 Urdu 19 Gujerati 9 Bengali 3 Pushtu 3 Italian 3 Polish 1 Hindi 1 Chinese 1 Creoles* 1 Ukranian 1	Panjabi 59 Gujerati 16 Urdu 7 Hindi 3 Italian 2 Bengali 2 Polish 2 Chinese 1 Creoles* 1	Greek 34 Turkish 15 Creoles* 9 Gujerati 6 Italian 6 French-based Creoles 4 Bengali 3 Urdu 2 Panjabi 2 Spanish 2 Chinese 2 French 1	Panjabi 24 Italian 24 Urdu 18 Gujerati 12 Chinese 4 Polish 2 German 2 Hindi 2 Creoles* 1 French 1	Panjabi 31 Urdu 21 Gujerati 8 Greek 8 Creoles* 7 Turkish 4 French-based Creoles 3 Bengali 3 Chinese 2 Italian 2 Hindi 1 French 1
(4)	Total of (3) as cumulative % of (1)	95%	93%	86%	90%	91%

*'Creoles' here means English-based and other non-French-based Creole languages.

Dialectology is the study of linguistic variation in terms of the geographical distribution of speakers. Dialectology arose in Europe about a century ago as a result of the interest of some historical linguists in observing the spread of sound changes across particular regions, especially rural areas. Later dialectological studies came to include lexical variation.

Methods

Dialectologists gather data from speakers in a variety of ways. Originally, aspects of speech were recorded by hand on worksheets in interviews and then subjected to analysis. Today dialectologists use sophisticated interviews and record speakers' utterances on tape, thus lending greater accuracy to their work. Many dialectologists use computers for quantitative analysis or visualization of their data.

The work of dialectologists may be published in the form of articles, but may take the form of a dialect atlas. A dialect atlas contains numerous maps that exhibit regional variation in a language. These maps may plot features which characterize a particular group of speakers or they may, for instance, be used to show features which separate one group of speakers from another. The computer-generated map in Figure 14.4 is designed to show similarities in shared vocabulary between francophone fishing villages in Atlantic Canada and France, thus demonstrating the probable geographical origins of the settlers of the Maritime villages.

Figure 14.4 Words for 'fishhook' [Standard French *hameçon*] in French dialects of Atlantic Canada and western France (Peronnet and Arsenault, 1990).

Sometimes it is possible to discern clear boundaries between speakers of one dialect and speakers of another. These boundaries are represented on maps by means of lines called **isoglosses**. The latter may be drawn with respect to one feature (generally phonological or lexical) but the more significant boundaries occur in the form of bundles of isoglosses. These lines are meant to indicate that with respect to the feature or features in question, people on one side share one variant while those on the other share a different one.

Dialect continua

In many parts of the world dialects do not have clear boundaries which can be definitively marked by isoglosses. Rather, what one observes is a **dialect continuum**. The differentiation of dialects increases cumulatively as one travels in one direction away from the starting point. Some of the differences may be minute and others quite big, but there is no evidence of a single place on the map which can be marked as the endpoint of one dialect and the start of another. If the distance travelled is long enough, the places at the extreme ends of the journey may be distinct languages.

The situation we have just described is found in many parts of Europe. In the Romance family, there is a West Romance continuum. Though standard varieties of French, Catalan, Spanish, Portuguese, and Italian are separate languages, speakers of any two of these languages in border areas have no difficulty in understanding each other's local dialect. Similarly, we can recognize a West Germanic continuum. As one travels from one village or town to the next in Austria, through Germany and into Holland, fairly small differences that do not impede mutual intelligibility are observed in neighbouring places along the route. But by the time one gets from, say, Innsbruck in Austria to Rotterdam in the Netherlands, the cumulative differences are quite considerable: Dutch and Austrian German are definitely separate languages. Moving north in Europe, we find another continuum – the Scandinavian language continuum. Some of the forms below are Swedish and others are Norwegian. But comparison of the versions of the sentence does not enable us to tell which is which. The first two are classified as 'Swedish' and the last two as 'Norwegian'. The classification is linguistically arbitrary: it is motivated by political and cultural considerations.

2)

a. /hem:ɑ hɑʀ ja intə sɔ meːd   sɔm et gam:ɑlt gɑusabɑin/
b. /hem:a har ja intə sɔ myk:ət sɔm et gam:ɑlt gɔːsbeːn/
c. /jem:ə har jæ ik:ə sɔ myːə   sɔm et gam:əlt gɔːsəbeːn/
d. /heimə har eg içːə sɔ myçːə sɔm et gam:ɑlt gɔːsəbein/
     At home have I not so much as an old goose-leg

Dialect and accent

In the study of language variation, it is necessary to distinguish between **accent** and **dialect**. The term dialect is used to refer to varieties of a particular language that differ in vocabulary, grammar, and pronunciation. In Britain virtually every county has its own distinctive traditional dialect(s) (e.g., Lancashire, Yorkshire, Somerset, etc.). Major cities too have their own popular dialects (e.g., Cockney in London, Scouse in Liverpool, Geordie in Newcastle, Glaswegian in Glasgow, etc.) which are normally used by people who do not belong to the higher social groups.

The term accent is used for less drastic differences which are restricted to variation in the pronunciation. Thus, British speakers of Standard English (for example doctors or lawyers) may have different accents and hence sound different depending on whether they are from, say, Inverness, Cardiff or London. But any lexical or grammatical differences that they exhibit would be negligible.

Questionnaires

The most important tool used in conducting surveys of dialects and accents is the questionnaire. This method has two advantages. First, it is easy to use; and, second, the results obtained from different speakers are easy to compare. (This contrasts, for instance, with naturalistic observation and recording of conversation, which usually yields more interesting but less readily comparable results.) The very earliest questionnaires devised in the nineteenth century by the German and French pioneers of dialectology used **direct questions**. Informants were asked in Standard German or French a question like 'What do you call a pig?' and they would be expected to supply their dialect word. It was not long before scholars realized that direct questions have the disadvantage of not encouraging informants to give natural dialectal responses. More authentic results are likely to be obtained if the information is elicited using **indirect questions**. Respondents might be asked to circle the form they ordinarily use, or to respond verbally to questions like those in Table 14.16 which are adapted from the questionnaire used by Eugen Dieth and Harold Orton in their *Survey of English Dialects*. These questions illustrate the rural bias of much of traditional British dialectology.

Table 14.16   Typical questions from an English dialect survey

Definitions for the terms sought	Possible responses
What do you call the place where you keep cows?	barn, beef-house, (cow-)byre, cow-hole/house/hull/shade/shed, lathe, mistall, shippon
What do you call the animal that makes a noise like *hee-haw*?	donkey, cuddy, fussock, pronkus, nirrup, mokus, moke, neddy

Linguistic maps and lexical variation

The data obtained from questionnaires are processed and the results are displayed in maps that show the geographical area where a particular linguistic feature occurs. For instance, dialectologists focusing on lexical differences have produced maps like that in Figure 14.5.

Lexical items unique to a particular dialect may be **archaisms** – survivors of forms previously more widely used, such as *shippon* in Table 14.16 or *fell*, an Old English word for 'hill' which today only survives in the north of England – or may be innovations, or **neologisms**, such as American *homeboy* (see Table 14.8) or *sad* (meaning 'massively uncool') in current British slang. A dialect may also evidence unique senses of lexical items that have different meanings in other dialects. For instance, in Northern Ireland *wither* means 'hesitate' and in Scotland *stay* means 'reside'.

A similar situation is found when we compare certain words that have the same form but different meanings in British and American English (Table 14.17).

Figure 14.5 Map showing the distribution of words for *Cow-house*.

Table 14.17 Same word but different meanings in British and American English

Word	British English	American English
homely	'down to earth'	'ugly (of people)'
nervy	'nervous'	'bold, full of nerve, cheeky'
pants	'underpants'	'trousers'
pavement	'footpath, sidewalk (US)'	'road surface'
to tick off	'to scold'	'to make angry'

Morphological variation

In addition to exhibiting lexical differences, dialects may also show morphological differences. We will first illustrate this with some verb forms. Compare the forms of the verb *be* in Table 14.18 overleaf.

Table 14.18   The present tense of the verb *be* in Standard English and in the East Somerset dialect

Standard English		East Somerset dialect	
I am	we are	I be	we be
you are	you are	thou art	you be
she/he is	they are	she/he be	they be

As seen, whereas in Standard English the verb *be* has the three forms *am*, *are*, and *is*, in east Somerset it only has two, namely *be* and *art*. Moreover, the subject–verb agreement patterns are also different. In Standard English *am* and *is* occur with the first and third person singular respectively, and *are* with the rest while in east Somerset *art* is used with the second person singular and *be* occurs elsewhere.

A more widespread pattern of morphological variation involves irregular verbs (Table 14.19). In some non-standard dialects, many irregular verbs which have distinct past tense and past participle forms in Standard English have undergone regularization. The result is that the same form realizes both the past tense and the past participle. This morphological simplification has brought those irregular verbs in line with regular verbs like *jump, jumped, jumped*, which use the *-ed* for both the past tense and the past participle.

Table 14.19   Dialectal morphological variation in irregular verbs

Standard English			Non-Standard English		
Present	*Past*	*Past participle*	*Present*	*Past*	*Past participle*
see	saw	seen	see	saw	seed
do	did	done	do	done	done
go	went	gone	go	went	went
take	took	taken	take	took	took
write	wrote	written	write	writ	writ

For our last example of morphological variation we will consider the formation of reflexive pronouns. In Standard English reflexive pronouns fall into two sets. One set is formed by suffixing *-self* in the singular and *-selves* in the plural to the corresponding possessive pronoun, as in Table 14.20*a*, while the other set is formed by adding *-self/-selves* to the corresponding

Table 14.20   Reflexive pronouns in Standard English

a. Possessive pronoun as base	b. Object pronoun as base
myself	himself
yourself	itself
herself	herself
ourselves	themselves

object pronoun, as in Table 14.20*b*. (*Herself* appears in both columns because it is impossible to say whether *her* is a possessive or objective form.)

Many non-standard dialects have simplified the system so that all reflexive pronouns use the possessive as the base, as shown in Table 14.21.

Table 14.21 Regularized reflexive pronouns in non-Standard English

Possessive pronoun as base	Possessive pronoun as base
myself	hisself
yourself	herself
herself	itsself
ourselves	theirselves

Syntactic variation

We briefly highlighted syntactic variation earlier (in section 2.3) when we showed that negation is one of the areas in which non-standard varieties differ from Standard English. Our next example of syntactic dialectal variation involves the behaviour of modal verbs. The data are taken from the dialect of Hawick in the Scottish Borders region which shows patterns that are found in several other regional, non-standard dialects in Scotland.

Whereas in Standard English only one modal verb is allowed under the INFL node in a sentence, various combinations of modals are allowed in this position in the Hawick dialect. The sentences in *3)* contain examples of '*double modal auxiliary constructions*' with *can* or *could* following another modal auxiliary.

3)

You <u>should can</u> do it.
(= 'You ought to be able to do it')
Rose <u>would could</u> visit Archie if she went to Melrose.
(= Rose would be able to visit Archie if she went to Melrose.)

There are also '*embedded modal auxiliary constructions*' (as shown in *4)*), in which *can* or *could* appears after the complementizer *to* in embedded constructions. This type of syntactic structure is outlawed in Standard English.

4)

You'll <u>have to can see</u> her whether you like it or not.
(= 'you'll have to be able to see her whether you like it or not')
I would <u>like to could speak</u> Gaelic.
(= 'I would like to be able to speak Gaelic.')

Phonological variation

Let us now turn to pronunciation. Where there are dialectal differences in vocabulary and grammar, they are normally accompanied by phonological differences. For example, speakers of traditional southwest of England dialects (who say *I be, we be, thou art, they be,* etc.) have voiced word-initial fricatives corresponding to voiceless initial fricatives in other dialects in Table 14.22.

Table 14.22   Initial fricative voicing in south west England

Southwest	Standard	
[v]ace	[f]ace	'face'
[v]armer	[f]armer	'farmer'
[v]eed	[f]eed	'feed'
[ð]ing	[θ]ing	'thing'
[ð]atch	[θ]atch	'thatch'
[ð]umb	[θ]umb	'thumb'
[ʒ]ugar	[ʃ]ugar	'sugar'
[ʒ]illing	[ʃ]illing	'shilling'

Differences among accents

Most of the variation among geographical varieties of British English can be characterized in terms of accent: the differences are normally at the level of phonology rather than grammar or vocabulary. (The case of the west country dialect outlined in the last paragraph is untypical.)

The phonological differences fall into a number of major categories. The most straightforward variation is at the level of the realization of allophones of the same phoneme in different areas. For example, the vowels in words like *may* and *know* are realized by the diphthongs [eɪ] and [əʊ] in RP but by the monophthongs [e] and [o:] in Scottish English. Likewise, the vowel of *mat*, is realized as [æ] in the kind of mainstream RP one hears on the BBC newscasts, but in old-fashioned RP spoken, for example, by upper-class older ex-public schoolboys it is somewhat higher, and is very close to [ɛ] . (It may also be diphthongized and be realized as [ɛ°].) The raised [ɛ] vowel is also used in Australia, New Zealand, and South Africa. By contrast, in northern England, the same phoneme is realized by [a], a lower front vowel.

Allophonic realizational differences may involve consonants as well. A good example of this is provided by /l/. Usually in British English 'dark l' (in which the body of the tongue has a fairly high back position) occurs before a consonant (as in [sɪɫk]) *silk* or in word-final position (as in [beɫ] *bell* , and 'clear l' (in which the body of the tongue has a rather high front position) is found elsewhere. By contrast, 'dark l' is absent from Irish English and so there 'clear l' is heard in all environments.

Furthermore, in some cases accents/dialects may have different phonological inventories. One dialect may possess a phoneme that is not found in some other dialect. For example, Scottish (and possibly Irish) English has the velar fricative phoneme /x/, as in /lɒx/ *loch*, which contrasts with /k/, as in /lɒk/ *lock*. This phoneme is not found elsewhere.

Similarly, the phoneme /ʌ/ is absent from the speech of most people in the Midlands and the north of England (Table 14.23). For such speakers, the vowel /ʊ / corresponds to RP /ʌ/.

Table 14.23   Variation in vowel inventories

Midland and North				RP			
[kʊt]	[bʊs]	[ʃʊt]	[skrʊm]	[kʌt]	[bʌs]	[ʃʌt]	[skrʌm]
cut	bus	shut	scrum	cut	bus	shut	scrum

Additionally, variation may be due to differences in the deployment of the same phonemes in different words. This is evidenced by the distribution of the phonemes /æ/ and /ɑ:/ in northern English and RP. Both varieties have the vowels /æ/ and /ɑ:/ – they both contrast /hæd/ *had* with /hɑ:d/ *hard*, /pæk/ *pack* with /pɑ:k/ *park*, etc. But they differ in the choice of phoneme they use in certain words. This is particularly true if the next sound in the word is a fricative. Normally, RP has /ɑ:/ before a fricative while northern English uses /æ/ in that environment (Table 14.24).

Table 14.24   The vowels /æ/ and /ɑ:/ before a fricative

Northern English		RP
/pæθ/	'path'	/pɑ:θ/
/pæst/	'past'	/pɑ:st/
/dɪzæstə/	'disaster'	/dɪzɑ:stə/
/læf/	'laugh'	/lɑ:f/

Finally, variation may be due to different phonotactic constraints. The distribution of what is traditionally called 'post-vocalic r' – but is more accurately described as 'coda /r/' since it follows a vowel that belongs to the same syllable – provides a good example of this. In the accents of English spoken in Scotland, Ireland, southwest England, parts of Lancashire and North America (except in parts of the eastern states), coda /r/ is pronounced in words like *hard* and *herd*, where it is followed by a consonant, and in words like *fir* and *fur* where it is at the end of a word. Such accents are described as **rhotic**. By contrast, in non-rhotic accents such as accents found in the rest of England and in Australia, New Zealand, South Africa, and Trinidad, 'coda r' is dropped. (See also the discussion of 'post-vocalic r' in Chapter 8, section 6.2 .)

4

MIXED LANGUAGES

No natural language is in any sense 'pure' or free from all influence from other languages and cultures. Some languages in the world are, however, mixtures composed of elements from many sources. This very quality of being 'mixed' rather than the product of one clear historical evolution lends a unique character to these languages.

4.1

Pidgins

The term **pidgin** is used by linguists as the label for speech varieties that develop when speakers of two or more different languages come into contact with each other and do not know each other's language. A pidgin is not the native language of any group. Where pidgins still exist their use may be confined to the marketplace or similar domain. There are numerous theories as to why and how pidgins have come about. Some pidgins have been called 'trade languages' or 'trade jargons' and have clearly arisen as the result of contact situations between people, without a language in common, who were seeking to do business with each other. Sailors have been ascribed a particular role in the genesis of certain pidgins. Some scholars have claimed that jargons called 'nautical English' or 'maritime French' served as the basis for later pidgins in various parts of the world. Clearly sailors did at least play an important role in spreading major colonial languages (English, French, Spanish, Portuguese, and Dutch) throughout the world but it is unclear that their jargons formed the basis for resulting pidgins.

There is some evidence to support the claim that pidgins may have arisen as a result of the apparently quite normal tendency for speakers in language contact situations to 'simplify' their speech both syntactically and lexically. Linguists use the term *foreigner talk* for such simplified registers (see Chapter 13, section 4.1). This term is used to describe the way an adult native speaker of English attempts to communicate with a non-English speaker, relying on simple concepts and avoiding more complicated syntactic devices such as embedded clauses or passives. Foreigner talk is similar to *baby talk*, which is the label for the simplified register adults use to talk with babies (see section 5.1 below in this chapter and section 6.2 of Chapter 12).

However they may have arisen, pidgins typically present a syntactic structure that is comparatively simple and they exhibit certain characteristic relationships to their source languages. They normally reflect the influence of the higher status (or dominant) language in their lexicon and that of the lower status language in their phonology (and occasionally syntax). For example, the following sentence from the Hawaii Pidgin English spoken by Philippine labourers in Hawaii prior to 1930 consists of English words but has the verb in initial position (where it occurs in Philippine languages):

5)

wok had dis   pipl
work hard these people
'These people work hard.'

Pidgins are an important subset of a larger group of languages termed **lingua francas**. A lingua franca may be a pidgin or it may be the native language of a people (as is modern English). These are 'third' languages that are used for communication among speakers of different languages. The name derives from a medieval trade language (called Lingua Franca) used in the Mediterranean region and based largely on Romance languages (Italian, French, and Spanish) but also containing elements of Greek, Arabic, and

Turkish. In the modern world, it is fair to say that English is the most important lingua franca, since it is used as a means of communication for purposes of business among large numbers of people who do not otherwise share a common language.

<table>
<tr><td>4.2</td></tr>
</table>

Creoles

A **creole** is a language which, having originated as a pidgin, has become established as a first language in some speech community. In most instances, creoles that have become established as first languages in particular countries continue to exist alongside the standard (higher status) language that was originally pidginized. The standard language usually serves as the language of education and administration. The creole, not having the stabilizing base of a written tradition and being prone to the influence of the standard, tends to change more rapidly over time.

Typically, different varieties of the creole emerge, some resembling the standard more than the others. The standard may serve as a source for new lexical items in the creole. In such situations, the creole may develop varieties that to greater or lesser extents resemble the standard. Those varieties that show the greatest lexical influence from the standard and are otherwise most similar to the standard are labelled **acrolects**. Those which evidence the least influence from the standard are called **basilects**. Varieties between these two extremes are called **mesolects**.

Along with most pidgins, most creoles have existed in a relatively narrow belt between the Tropics of Cancer and Capricorn (see Figure 14.6 on pp. 574–5). There are a number of them in the West Indies, the East Indies, and West Africa. Two important and opposing views on the origin and development of these creoles are the notions of **relexification** and the **language bioprogram** hypothesis. Both of these theories are based on the fact that creoles the world over show remarkable similarities in their grammars, such as SVO word order.

In brief, the relexification hypothesis holds that creoles either (1) all go back to a single historical source (such as the sixteenth-century West African slaver's jargon Pidgin Portuguese or the original Lingua Franca) and have essentially retained the grammar (syntax) of that pidgin but have undergone changes in their vocabulary (relexification) in different subsequent linguistic and cultural contexts, or (2) may have more than one historical source but still are largely re-formed over time through the replacement of lexical items while the comparatively simple grammars remain relatively unchanged.

The language bioprogram hypothesis holds that similarities among creoles are not the result of historical transmission from an original 'proto-pidgin' grammar but reflect linguistic universals both in terms of first language acquisition and with respect to processes and structures which are putatively innate in the human brain. A pattern of similar innovations in the development of the first generation of creoles has been observed which, it is claimed, can only be explained in terms of a theory of linguistic universals. These innovations include, for example, the use of various preverbal particles to indicate notions such as completeness, ongoing action, and the like. In the following sentence from Hawaiian Creole, for example, the particle *stei* (from

Figure 14.6   Some English- and French-based pidgins and creoles of the world.

English 'stay') is used to indicate an action currently taking place:

6)

ai no kea hu   stei hant insai dea
I   no care who stay hunt inside there
'I don't care who's hunting in there.'

Pidgins are seen as structurally deficient in many respects and inadequate as input to children acquiring their first language. Children are thus said to be thrown back on their innate language bioprogram to provide a basic structure for the creole. This produces a generation of speakers of a language which can serve as the basis for further generations of learners and can, for instance, undergo the sorts of lexical changes mentioned above in which it may come to resemble the original higher status language more.

Cape York Creole

Among the English-based creoles of the world is Cape York Creole (CYC), spoken in the northern tip of Australia opposite Papua-New Guinea. The data from this creole in Tables 14.25 to 14.27 will help to illustrate the fact that creoles are not simply deformed or bastardized languages but, in fact, have interesting characteristics of their own that are not shared with the standard.

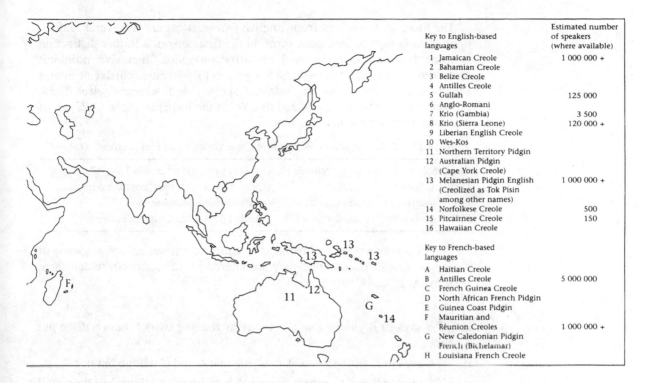

Key to English-based languages	Estimated number of speakers (where available)
1 Jamaican Creole	1 000 000 +
2 Bahamian Creole	
3 Belize Creole	
4 Antilles Creole	
5 Gullah	125 000
6 Anglo-Romani	
7 Krio (Gambia)	3 500
8 Krio (Sierra Leone)	120 000 +
9 Liberian English Creole	
10 Wes-Kos	
11 Northern Territory Pidgin	
12 Australian Pidgin (Cape York Creole)	
13 Melanesian Pidgin English (Creolized as Tok Pisin among other names)	1 000 000 +
14 Norfolkese Creole	500
15 Pitcairnese Creole	150
16 Hawaiian Creole	

Key to French-based languages	
A Haitian Creole	
B Antilles Creole	5 000 000
C French Guinea Creole	
D North African French Pidgin	
E Guinea Coast Pidgin	
F Mauritian and Réunion Creoles	1 000 000 +
G New Caledonian Pidgin French (Bichelamar)	
H Louisiana French Creole	

Table 14.25 Singular pronouns in Cape York Creole

1st person	ai, mi
2nd person	yu
3rd person	i, im

Differences from Standard English include the fact that in the third person there is no three-way gender distinction and that all of these pronouns can serve as a subject. Only *mi*, *yu*, and *im*, however, can serve as objects. This is reminiscent of the Standard English pronouns *me* and *him*, which only serve as non-subjects (as object of a verb or following a preposition). The main difference between the CYC pronominal system and that of Standard English lies in the non-singular forms. CYC exhibits two non-singular categories: dual and plural. The forms for second and third person are shown in Table 14.26.

Table 14.26 Dual and plural pronouns in Cape York Creole (2nd and 3rd person)

Dual, 2nd person	yutu(pela)
Dual, 3rd person	tupela
Plural, 2nd person	yu(pela)
Plural, 3rd person	ol, dempela

The form -*pela* derives from English *fellow*. It occurs in several realizations, -*fela* being the acrolectal form. In the first person, a further distinction is made between *inclusive* and *exclusive* pronouns. Inclusive pronouns *include* the speaker and the addressee ('you and I'), while exclusive pronouns *exclude* the addressee but include the speaker and someone else. These pronominal categories are realized in CYC in the forms in Table 14.27, all of which are first person, non-singular.

Table 14.27   Dual and plural pronouns in Cape York Creole (1st person)

Dual, inclusive	yumi, yumtu	(speaker plus one addressee)
Dual, exclusive	mitu	(speaker plus one other, not the addressee)
Plural, inclusive	mipela, wi	(speaker plus addressees)
Plural, exclusive	mitupela, wi	(speaker plus others, not addressee)

The following example illustrates the semantic differences among some of these categories. Assume that they are uttered in a situation in which three persons (A, B, and C) are present.

7)

a.   If A says to B *yumi go nau*, A is saying that the two of them will go but not C.

b.   If A says to B *mitu go nau*, A is saying that A and C will go but not B.

c.   If A says to B and C *mipela go nau*, A is saying that all three of them will go.

It should be apparent from these few examples that creoles, far from being less than a standard, are capable of distinctions not found in the standard. The existence of a dual category of number alongside those of plural and singular, for example, affords CYC speakers a precision not available to speakers of Standard English. The dual is often seen in languages spoken in small-scale, mainly agricultural societies in which it is useful to be able to designate items as occurring in pairs. The distinction between inclusive and exclusive pronouns is widespread in languages of the world, being present in many Amerindian languages, for example. Note how, in the foregoing translations, English can only somewhat clumsily paraphrase the ideas expressed by these CYC pronouns. These distinctions are, however, important to CYC speakers – and probably to speakers of neighbouring indigenous languages – and thus are incorporated into the pronominal system. Like other English-based creoles, CYC shares a number of features with Standard English but has its own linguistic system and its own history.

5

**SPEECH
SITUATIONS**

…the social situation is the most powerful determinant of verbal behavior…

❧ William Labov

Speech situations are those social situations in which there is appropriate use of language. They are the main locus for research by interactional sociolinguists. **Interactional sociolinguistics** may be said either to include or to exhibit considerable overlap with the subdisciplines of ethnography of communication, discourse analysis, and pragmatics. The methods of description and analysis of language used in speech situations differ markedly from the techniques we have previously examined in this chapter, yet we have already referred to several concepts which can only be adequately discussed using this approach.

A speech situation consists of a number of components. In analysing a speech situation, the sociolinguist (or an ethnographer of communication) seeks to specify how each of these components is realized. Once this has been done, an understanding of the how, what, and why of the interaction is achieved. In Table 14.28, the components of the speech situation have been mnemonically arranged to form the acronym SPEAKING.

Table 14.28 Components of the speech situation arranged mnemonically

S	–	the setting and scene of a speech situation, distinguishing between the physical locale and the type of activity
P	–	the participants, often characterized by terms such as addresser, addressee, speaker, performer, audience, questioner, answerer, caller, interviewer, interviewee, and so on
E	–	the ends, including both functions and outcomes; functions may be broadly classified as those circumstances in which the content of talk is important (transactional function) and those which serve to reinforce or establish social or interpersonal relations (interactional function); outcomes have to do with what effect the speech has on the addressee or other aspect of the situation
A	–	the act sequence, including the content and form of speech
K	–	the key, tone, mood or manner, distinguishing among serious, facetious, formal, sarcastic, and so on
I	–	the instrumentalities, including the 'channel' (verbal, non-verbal, face-to-face, written, electronic mail, and so on) and 'code' (the language and/or variety used)
N	–	the norms of interaction and interpretation (the basic rules that seem to underlie the interaction)
G	–	the genre, any of a class of named speech acts (greeting, leave-taking, sermon, lecture, joke, and so on)

These notions become more concrete in the context of a specific example. Consider the following situations, which might occur in a university.

- **Setting, Scene** A classroom could be the setting and might accommodate a number of scenes, among them a lecture, tutorial, club meeting, or conversation.
- **Participants** The different scenes provide for a number of possible

relationships between interactants: teacher–student, leader–member, addresser–addressee, among others.

- **Ends** Among the numerous possible functions might be the instructional (in a lecture), the consultative (in a tutorial), and the interactional (in a friendly conversation). The outcomes could include whatever has been learned in the lecture or tutorial, the plans for a party in the club meeting, or the sharing of gossip in a conversation.
- **Act sequence** The content and form might vary from the structured lecture material, to the question-and-answer or problem-solving of the tutorial, to the agenda of the meeting, to the small talk of the conversation.
- **Key** The mood would range from the comparative formality of the lecture to the relative informality (even jocularity) of the conversation.
- **Instrumentalities** All the situations would be face-to-face, mostly verbal (aside from appropriate non-verbal aspects such as the raising of a hand for recognition and the performance of written tasks). The variety of English would likely be Standard English in the lecture but might contain significantly more non-standard features in the conversation. Recalling the sociolinguistic variable (ing) from section 2.3, we might expect to hear it realized as [ɪŋ] in the lecture but as [ɪn] more often in the conversation.
- **Norms** The norms would vary considerably from situation to situation. The rights (or status) of participants would differ markedly. In the lecture, tutorial, and, perhaps to a lesser extent, the club meeting, the teacher (or leader) would probably control the situation. He or she might do most of the talking and generally determine the course of the interaction. Other participants would normally be required to secure the permission of the leader in order to speak. In the conversation, there would be greater equality between participants.
- **Genre** A lecture can be termed a genre in itself. It is recognizable by its form, limited number of topics, speaker–audience format, and relative formality. A tutorial would include questions and answers, among other acts. A conversation consists of a number of possible speech acts (or genres). Among these might be an initial greeting ('*Hi!*'), a concluding leave-taking ('*Bye!*'), and intervening narratives (including perhaps a joke). Thus, it can be seen that genre is a component that can be understood on more than one level. A lecture can be a genre but so can a greeting or a joke, which is included in the lecture.

As we can see from these examples, speaking in social contexts involves more than simply being able to form grammatical sentences. Sociolinguists claim that speakers possess **communicative competence**, or underlying knowledge of the linguistic system combined with knowledge of the rules (or norms) for the appropriate use of language in speech situations. (See Chapter 13, section 1.4.) In interactional sociolinguistics, the concern is not so much with the grammaticality of utterances but rather with their appropriateness. The next section treats this matching of language with situation in its discussion of the concept of functional speech variety, or register.

5.1

Register

The form that talk takes in any given context is called a **register**. Different registers may be characterized in phonological, syntactic, or lexical terms. A register is also a function of all the other components of a speech situation discussed in the previous section. A formal setting may condition a formal register, characterized by particular lexical items, greater adherence to the rules of Standard English, absence of stigmatized sociolinguistic variables, and so on. An informal setting may be reflected in a casual register that exhibits less formal vocabulary, more non-standard features, greater instances of stigmatized variables, and so on. Registers can also be categorized in terms of their relative explicitness.

Two good friends discussing a matter well known to both do not need to make every detail of their conversation explicit. Each may correctly assume that the other knows basically what the conversation is about. Such an assumption can result in the appropriate use of pronouns and elliptical sentences, both of which are less explicit (more implicit) than nouns or full sentences. The speakers' shared background knowledge will fill in the blanks. Similarly, shared knowledge in an ongoing situation, such as experienced by spectators at a football match, means that one fan can say *'Oh heck! He blew it!'* and be understood by another (as they both watch their hero kick the ball wide after beating the defence). A university lecture (or a textbook), on the other hand, requires both a formal and an explicit register and perhaps a technical one as well, since new and unfamiliar concepts are being introduced and explained.

The following examples of some registers of spoken and written language are mainly differentiated from each other in terms of relative formality and explicitness.

8)

'OK. I'm . . . I'll come over this afternoon and look at the other one.'

This utterance, which was part of a telephone conversation, is entirely context-bound (and maximally implicit) in its meaning. It contains the deictic expressions *I, this afternoon*, and *come* which are only properly interpretable because the hearer knows the setting in which they appear. Also, the expression *the other one*, which seems to be very vague, is in fact sufficiently specific in this situation given the shared knowledge of the interlocutors of what has been said before. (The speaker who was calling from out of town had just been told by the estate agent that one of the houses that she wanted to view had just been withdrawn from the market.) Furthermore, note that false starts, syntactically incomplete sentences, and restarts like that found at the beginning of the utterance in *8)* are common in impromptu spoken language.

9)

*'*That's what I ought to look like is like that.'

This sentence is again entirely context-bound (and maximally implicit) in its meaning. It was appropriate, however, when uttered. Its speaker and addressee both understood what *that* referred to. Its convoluted syntax that remains uncorrected is also consistent with its informality.

10)

'In that jacket you really look like a zhlub.'

Again, the interpretation of the precise reference is limited to the context in which the sentence was uttered. Also, the use of an ethnic slang term *zhlub* (meaning 'gauche or coarse person' in Yiddish) signals an informal register.

11)

'Wilt thou have this man to thy wedded husband . . .'

Lexical, morphological, and syntactic archaisms signal this formal and ritualized register. (Syntactically it may be an open yes–no question, but only a 'yes' answer is expected.)

12)

'Pellagra is characterized by cutaneous, mucous membrane, CNS, and gastrointestinal symptoms.'

This quotation from a medical handbook illustrates features of a formal register (in the written channel) by its fully formed sentence, high degree of explicitness, use of the passive, and the presence of medical jargon. It is an example of a technical register.

13)

'Mangled by the nightmare-made-flesh from Mangere.'

This appeared as a sports page headline in *The Guardian* newspaper the day after the semi-final match in Cape Town between England and New Zealand's *All Blacks* in the 1995 Rugby World Cup. This headline is elliptical in form, as is customary in the style of newspaper headlines. But it is appropriate to the written channel of communication and illustrates the importance of shared knowledge in the interpreting of elliptical utterances. A rugby fan would know that the caption refers to the defeat of England (45–29) which was in a large measure due to the *All Blacks'* phenomenal player, Jonah Lomu, born in Mangere (a suburb of Auckland).[1]

14)

'Time to go bye-bye.'

The minimal syntax and choice of lexical items characterize this utterance as one which might be directed by a parent to a child. It is an example of a simplified register called *baby talk* (termed *motherese* in Chapter 12). Baby talk is widespread, perhaps even universal, in speech communities in the world. In English it is specifically characterized by its limited lexicon, simple syntax, and relatively wide pitch. In these respects it is most similar to the registers we use to speak to a pet or a lover and is thus both non-threatening and nurturing. With respect to its simplified grammar and lexicon, baby talk resembles the foreigner talk register mentioned in the discussion of the genesis of pidgins (see section 4.1).

The preceding quotations are a small sample of the variety of registers available to English speakers. All competent speakers of the language are able to produce at least a few registers, thereby making their speech appropriate for particular speech situations.

5.2

Forms of address

One aspect of speech that has been productively analysed by interactional sociolinguists is that of **address term** usage. This phenomenon has been observed in a variety of languages and cultures. It seems clear that all languages have address forms and specific rules that determine their appropriate use. Every time one calls someone, or refers to him or her, by name, one indicates something of one's social relationship to or personal feeling about that individual. One might be on first-name terms with a friend but not with an uncle or a mother. A grandparent might be addressed by a pet name coined in one's childhood, but an employer might be called Ms Smith and might address an employee by using the latter's first name. There is nothing unusual about these examples. Not everyone functions with precisely this assortment of address forms, but they are probably quite representative of general usage in our society.

Compared to most of the world's languages, English has a relatively simple system of address terms, such as those shown in Table 14.29.

Table 14.29 Types of address terms in English

Term	Example
First name (FN)	Chris!
Title + last name (TLN)	Mr Thickpenny!
Title alone (T)	Nurse!
Last name (LN)	Smith!
Kin terms (KT*)	Granny!

*alone or with FN or LN, as appropriate.

Address terms can be used reciprocally or non-reciprocally. In the first case, speakers address each other with the same type of term (FN or TLN). This is a sign of symmetrical social relationship in which both parties have the same status (friends, colleagues, and so on). In the case of non-reciprocal usage, there is an asymmetrical relationship, one in which the difference in power and status between participants is marked. Thus, one person might use FN, and the other TLN. This is typical of a doctor–patient or teacher–student relationship.

In English, and other languages as well, it is also possible to avoid address terms altogether when participants are unsure which term to use. This practice is called **no-naming**. In the case of English speakers, it results in participants using *you* while scrupulously avoiding terms such as FN or TLN. A familiar example of this occurs in the university setting when students no-name a tutor if unsure whether to call her or him by a more specific address term.

Changes in power relations in society in this century have resulted in a strong tendency to move away from the more formal terms of address. For instance, in the university setting of the early 1900s it would have been most unusual for junior colleagues, let alone undergraduates, to address a professor by her or his first name, rather than by T or TLN, but nowadays in many British university departments symmetrical use of first names is the norm.

Other European languages have one complication that has been largely missing from English since the seventeenth century: the choice of two pronouns in the second person. On one level in the grammars of these languages, choosing between these two pronouns (*tu* and *vous* in French) is a function of the number of people being addressed – singular versus plural. These pronouns, however, also encode the sociolinguistic dimensions mentioned above. Thus, the form *tu* is like our FN in connoting friendship or intimacy when used mutually and in connoting lower status of the addressee when used non-reciprocally. The form *vous* used with a singular addressee is similar to our TLN in these respects. The details of these usages vary from language to language, but these broad outlines are indicative of the general tendencies.

Outside Europe and other areas where European languages dominate, these overall patterns still hold, but often in complex systems with vast numbers of address forms. In many instances, we also have to take into account not only the second person pronouns, but first and third person pronouns as well. In many languages (especially those in highly traditional, stratified societies), there are a number of first person singular pronouns. In Thai, for example, there are seventeen different forms that translate English *I*. Their appropriate use is based on the status of the addresser, that of the addressee, and the relationship between the two. In the same language, there are a further seventeen second person forms and eleven third person forms. In addition, there are numerous categories of nouns that can be used in direct address. The rules for deciding which form is appropriate are complex and require that participants have some knowledge about each other's status (Table 14.30). Given these complications and the possibility that selecting an inappropriate form might be rude or insulting, there is also a provision for no-naming.

Table 14.30   Some Thai address forms

Speaker	Addressee	Term
friend/kin/spouse	friend/kin/spouse	/nii/
adult/superior	child/inferior	/nuu/
Buddhist monk	superior monk	/pradeedprakhun/
inferior/non-monk	superior/monk	/than/

These forms, all equivalent to English *you*, are but a small sample of the set of address terms available in the Bangkok speech community.

5.3

Discourse and text

Language used in naturally occurring situations takes many forms. Any bit of talk produced by a speaker, which is distinct from other bits of talk from the same speaker and from other speakers in a speech situation, is an **utterance**. An utterance may realize a complete sentence ('*I have to leave now*'), an elliptical sentence ('*Time to go*'), a sequence of sentences (as in a long response to a question), or a single word ('*Yes*'). Any utterance will also be analysable in terms of the components of SPEAKING (discussed earlier in section 5) and thus will have, in addition to a particular form, an appropriate speaker and hearer, function, and so forth. The set of utterances produced by a speaker can be referred to as that speaker's **discourse**. The written (or transcribed) version of any utterance or body of discourse is called a **text**. The field that deals with the organization of texts, ways in which parts of texts are connected, and the devices used for achieving textual structure is **discourse analysis**.

Discourse analysis is very much a multidisciplinary field. Its practitioners are drawn from linguistics, anthropology, sociology, philosophy, psychology, computer science, and other disciplines. Linguists working in this area tend to focus on the nature of the language used in texts, particularly on those devices which provide a structural framework to texts and those which provide the cohesion which is necessary for a text to be perceived as an organized whole.

Discourse markers

In either spoken or written discourse the 'utterer' produces not only strings of nouns, verbs, adjectives, adverbs, and the like, but, as well, makes use of forms called **discourse markers** to provide structure. One scholar who is concerned with this phenomenon of naturally occurring language use has defined discourse markers as 'sequentially dependent elements which bracket units of talk'. By this she means that these markers occur over the length of a bit of discourse, separating one 'unit of talk' from a previous one. The bits of talk are themselves defined by the markers. In English alone there are a number of such discourse markers. Not all of them have received a great deal of study and there remains much work to be done in order to reach a full understanding of what all of the markers are and how they function. Similar phenomena in other languages remain to be treated.

Two typical discourse markers in English are *well* and *y'know*. In *15)* we see an example of the use of *well* as a discourse marker.

15)

Speaker A:	Did you enjoy your trip to the mountains?
Speaker B:	Well, it rained the whole time, so we had to stay indoors and never got to do anything.

In this instance *well* serves to introduce a response that is possibly contrary to what might have been expected. It also avoids the most direct possible answer to the *yes–no* question posed by speaker A: *No!* English speakers tend to soften negative responses to such questions by using a hedge such as *well*, as seen in *16)*.

16)

Speaker C: Could you type this letter for me before you leave?
Speaker D: Well, I was really planning to get an early start on my weekend so I thought I'd leave a few minutes early.

A discourse marker such as *y'know* can be used to appeal to knowledge shared by speaker and addressee, to involve the addressee more in the interaction, to test whether the addressee does in fact share the knowledge, or a combination of these.

17)

Say, I saw Betty last week. Y'know, the woman who used to live across the street?

18)

I was driving to Flagstaff on Sunday and saw this incredible coulee on the way. Y'know, that's a sort of canyon where there's been a lot of erosion?

In *17)* the speaker apparently assumes that the addressee knows or recalls the woman in question. In *18)* the speaker assumes that the addressee does not share (or may not share) the information (what a *coulee* is) and thus uses *y'know* to bracket off the unit of talk which provides the clarification.

The long list of discourse markers in English includes such forms as *oh*, *I mean*, *anyway*, coordinating conjunctions (*and*, *but*, *or*), temporal adverbs (*then*, *now*), and others. Although speakers are not usually aware of them, they are essential and their use provides organization to discourse (especially spoken discourse).

Textual cohesion

While discourse markers bracket off units of talk and do provide some element of cohesion, there are other linguistic resources that are more typically thought of as the primary **cohesive devices** in English. Table 14.31 provides a list of some of these devices.

Table 14.31 Textual cohesion in English

(1) Reference (anaphoric): I know <u>Jane</u>. <u>She</u> drives a red car.
(2) Reference (cataphoric): <u>It</u>'s awfully dry, <u>this toast</u>.
(3) Lexical cohesion (substitution): *Speaker G*: Do you know <u>our MP</u>? *Speaker H*: I've never met <u>the smarmy creep</u>.
(4) Ellipsis: *Speaker E*: Do you speak French? *Speaker F*: No.

In examples (1), (3), and (4) in Table 14.31 there are two sentences, either uttered by one speaker or by two speakers in sequence. Cohesive devices are not limited, however, to operating between sentences. Most of these can function within one sentence, as we see in example (2). In examples (1), (2), and (3) the underlined elements are the ones which exhibit cohesion; one underlined constituent presupposes the other. The more usual type of pronominal reference in English is **anaphoric**, in which the noun or noun phrase occurs earlier in the text than the pronoun with which it is coreferential. In the less frequent **cataphoric** reference, a pronoun is coreferential with a noun or noun phrase which occurs later in the text. In both of these (which are subcategories of **endophoric** or **textual reference**) one must know (or be able to find) the coreferential noun or noun phrase in order to be able to decode the pronoun. This link between the pronoun and the constituent with which it is coreferential is the cohesive tie between parts of the same text. Similarly, in example (3) *our MP* and *the smarmy creep* refer to the same individual, and understanding the second phrase requires one to have access to the first. One phrase has been substituted for the other and the two utterances are thus linked.

In example (4) the minimal utterance in response to a *yes–no* question can only be interpreted by the speaker's knowledge that this one word replaces (or stands for) a fuller response ('*No, I don't speak French*') which, however, would probably be heard as stilted and thus inappropriate here. Another possible response would be '*No, I don't*'. This is also elliptical, since decoding it requires knowledge of the preceding utterance.

These are a few instances of cohesive devices in English. Other languages possess similar ones for the creation of texts. It is possible to observe these, as was the case with discourse markers, in written as well as spoken discourse. They are some of the most important and obvious linguistic means for connecting language and situation.

Summing up

The field of **sociolinguistics** treats the social aspects of language use. This chapter focuses on three principal types of **speech variety**: **sociolects**, **regional dialects**, and **registers**, along with a number of related phenomena. All languages have such varieties, but in many communities one variety, the **standard**, has more prestige than the others. Sociolects of a language correlate with such social factors as the socio-economic status, gender, age, and occupation of their speakers. Approaches to the study of the **social differentiation** of language proceed from different perspectives, emphasizing the **social stratification** of speech varieties or focusing on the **social networks** of speakers. There are many instances of **euphemism** in language, which result in the replacement of **taboo** items. The most casual varieties of language (often associated with younger speakers) are the **slang** varieties. Some segments of any population develop secret languages or **argots**, while **jargons** are associated with specialized professions.

Dialectology deals with regional variation in language. Usually dialects form a continuum. Mutual intelligibility diminishes cumulatively, until it eventually ceases as the distance separating the dialects increases. Hence, on linguistic grounds alone, it is impossible to establish where one language ends and another begins when one investigates languages that are closely genetically related. Dialects can differ at all levels of structure – phonology, morphology, vocabulary, and syntax. Where the differences are confined to phonology alone, we speak of **accent** rather than dialect.

In a **multilingual** country like England where English is the official language other languages have experienced, to one degree or another, a loss in their numbers of speakers. The interaction of different linguistic groups may give rise to **pidgins**, mixed languages without native speakers. **Creoles** arise when pidgins are learned as native languages.

The **components of SPEAKING** provide a model for understanding language use in **speech situations**. They also serve as a framework for the discussion of **registers**, **address terms**, and specific aspects of **discourse analysis**, such as **discourse markers** and **textual cohesion**.

Note

1   This headline contains an allusion to the contrast between Christ, 'the word-made-flesh', who was good news, according to the gospel of John, chapter 1, verse 14, and big Lomu who was bad news for the England team. Alliteration (of the sound [m]) is another stylistic feature of this headline, a common feature in newspaper sports headlines.

Sources

Underlying the discussion of the social network approach are Lesley Milroy, *Language and Social Networks* (Oxford: Blackwell, 1980, 2nd edn, 1987), Lesley Milroy, *Observing and Analysing Natural Language* (Oxford: Blackwell, 1987), and Jeremy Boissevain, *Friends of Friends: Networks, Manipulators and Coalitions* (Oxford: Blackwell, 1974). Figure 14.3 and the account of Belfast speech are from Milroy, *Language and Social Networks*. Background for the discussion of Principal Components Analysis and the later treatment of phonological variables in Newfoundland English came from a paper, 'Problems in the analysis of sociolinguistic variability: from social to linguistic groupings', presented by Sandra Clarke at the 19th Annual NWAVE conference, held at the University of Pennsylvania, October 1990. The source for the section on non-standard grammatical features, and, indeed, an underlying inspiration for sections dealing with the social stratification of English, is William Labov's article 'The logic of nonstandard English', in *Report of the Twentieth Annual Round Table Meeting on Linguistics and Language Studies*, edited by James E. Alatis, pp. 1–43 (Washington: Georgetown University Press, 1970).

General sources on language and gender are David Graddol and Joan Swann, *Gender Voices* (Oxford: Blackwell, 1989), Dennis Baron, *Grammar and Gender* (New Haven: Yale University Press, 1986), Robin Lakoff, *Talking Power: The Politics of Language* (New York: Basic Books, 1990), *The Feminist Critique of Language*, edited by Deborah Cameron (London: Routledge, 1990) and Janet Holmes, *An Introduction to Sociolinguistics* (London: Longman, 1992). Some of the terminology used in the language and gender section was adapted from Anne Bodine's article 'Sex differentiation in language', in *Language and Sex: Difference and Dominance*, edited by Barrie Thorne and Nancy Henley (Rowley, Mass.: Newbury House, 1975, pp. 130–51). The Amerindian examples in this section were taken from Mary Haas's article 'Men's and women's speech in Koasati', *Language* 20: 142–49 (1944) while data showing gender-exclusive lexical differentiation in Japanese are from Janet Holmes, *An Introduction to Sociolinguistics* (London: Longman, 1992, pp. 164–6). The notion of face is borrowed from Penelope Brown and Stephen Levinson, 'Universals in language usage: politeness phenomena', in *Questions and Politeness: Strategies in Social Interaction*, edited by E. Goody (Cambridge: Cambridge University Press, 1978, pp. 56–311).

Some concepts in the discussion of slang were derived from Penelope Eckert, *Jocks and Burnouts: Social Categories and Identities in the High School* (New York: Teachers College Press, 1989). The study of language use in a Glasgow gang is from James Patrick's book *A Glasgow Gang Observed* (London: Eyre Methuen, 1973). Slang examples in Tables 14.8 and 14.9 are from Pamela Munro, ed., *U.C.L.A. Slang: A Dictionary of Slang Words and Expressions Used at U.C.L.A.* U.C.L.A. Occasional Papers in Linguistics, number 8 (1989). The rhyming slang data come from Julian Frankly, *A Dictionary of Rhyming Slang* (London: Kegan Paul, 1960).

The examples of 'gay lingo' in Table 14.12 and some of the accompanying discussion are derived from Wayne Dynes, *Homolexis: A Historical and Cultural Lexicon of Homosexuality, Gai Saber Monograph No. 4* (1985). The discussion of 'hacker jargon' and the examples in Table 14.13 are adapted from the 'Jargon File', version 2.2.1 (15 Dec. 1990), an on-line publication. The definitions of cyberspace jargon in Table 14.14 come from Sue Schofield, *The Internet Book* (Wokingham: Addison-Wesley Publishing Co., 1994).

The account of English multilingualism (including Table 14.15) is from The Linguistic Minorities Project Report, *Linguistic Minorities in England* (London: University of London Institute of Education, 1983).

General background for the discussion of contemporary methodologies in dialectology was adapted from J.K. Chambers and Peter Trudgill, *Dialectology*, (Cambridge: Cambridge University Press, 1980) as well as Alan R. Thomas, ed., *Methods in Dialectology* (Clevedon: Multilingual Matters, 1988). The map is taken from Louise Péronnet and Paul-André Arsenault, 'Linguistic atlas of French maritime terminology: computerized maps', *Journal of English Linguistics* 22 (1): 25–9 (1990). Sources on Canadian English are J.K. Chambers's *Canadian English: Origins and Structures* (Toronto: Methuen, 1975) and Mark Orkin's *Speaking Canadian English* (Toronto: General Publishing, 1970). The account of the syntax of the dialect of Hawick in the Scottish Borders draws on Keith Brown's chapter entitled 'Double modals in Hawick Scots', in *Dialects of English: Studies in Grammatical Variation*, edited by Peter Trudgill and J.K. Chambers, pp. 74–103 (London: Longman, 1991). The source of the material (including the map in Figure 14.5) on English dialects is Martyn F. Wakelin's book *English Dialects: An Introduction* (London: The Athlone Press of the University of London, 1972).

General discussion of the nature and origins of pidgins and creoles is adapted from Peter Mühlhäusler, *Pidgin and Creole Linguistics* (Oxford: Blackwell, 1986) and Derek Bickerton's article 'The language bioprogram hypothesis', *The Behavioral and Brain Sciences* 7: 173–221 (1984). Material on Cape York Creole is derived from the article 'Cape York Creole' by Terry Crowley and Bruce Rigsby, in *Languages and their Status*, edited by Timothy Shopen, pp. 153–207 (Cambridge, Mass.: Winthrop Publishers, 1979). The map showing the distribution of some English- and French-based Creoles and pidgins is from Ian F. Hancock's article 'A survey of the pidgins and creoles of the world', in *Pidginization and Creolization of Languages*, edited by Dell Hymes, pp. 509–23 (Cambridge: Cambridge University Press, 1971) and from Ian F. Hancock's article 'Repertory of pidgin and creole languages', in *Pidgin and Creole*

Linguistics, edited by Albert Valdman (Bloomington: Indiana University Press, 1977).

The components of SPEAKING and the inspiration for the section in which they appear derive from Dell Hymes's article 'Models of the interaction of language and social life', in *Directions in Sociolinguistics: The Ethnography of Communication*, edited by J. Gumperz and D. Hymes, pp. 35–71 (New York: Holt, Rinehart & Winston, 1972). The section on register is inspired partially by M.A.K. Halliday, *Language as Social Semiotic* (London: Edward Arnold, 1978). Another source on register is Hywel Coleman, ed., *Working with Language: A Multidisciplinary Consideration of Language Use in Work Contexts* (Berlin: Mouton de Gruyter, 1989). An underlying source for the section on address terms is the article by Roger Brown and Albert Gilman, 'The pronouns of power and solidarity', in *Style in Language*, edited by Thomas A. Sebeok, pp. 253–76 (Cambridge, Mass.: MIT Press, 1960). The discussion of English terms of address also draws on Laurie Bauer's book, *Watching English Change*, pp. 141–5 (London: Longman, 1994). The discussion and examples of Thai address terms are taken from Angkab Palakornkul's work, *A Sociolinguistic Study of Pronominal Strategy in Spoken Bangkok Thai* (Dissertation: University of Texas, 1972).

Underlying the sections on text and discourse is Michael Stubbs, *Discourse Analysis: The Sociolinguistic Analysis of Natural Language* (Oxford: Basil Blackwell, 1983). Discussion of discourse markers is based on Deborah Schiffrin, *Discourse Markers* (Cambridge: Cambridge University Press, 1987). Treatment of cohesive devices is derived from M.A.K. Halliday and Ruqaiya Hasan, *Cohesion in English* (London: Longman, 1976).

Question 4 was suggested by data in W. N. Francis, *Dialectology: An Introduction* (London: Longman, 1983).

Recommended reading

Allan, Keith, and Burridge, Kate. 1991. *Euphemism and Dysphemism*. Oxford: Oxford University Press.

Chambers, J.K. and Trudgill, Peter. 1980. *Dialectology*. Cambridge: Cambridge University Press.

Coates, Jennifer. 1993. *Women, Men and Language*. 2nd edn. London: Longman.

Fasold, Ralph. 1984. *The Sociolinguistics of Society*. Oxford: Blackwell.

Fasold, Ralph. 1990. *The Sociolinguistics of Language*. Oxford: Blackwell.

King, Ruth. 1991. *Talking Gender: A Guide to Nonsexist Communication*. Toronto: Copp Clark Pitman.

Saville-Troike, Muriel. 1989. *The Ethnography of Communication: An Introduction*. 2nd edn. Oxford: Blackwell.

Questions

1. Based on your knowledge of your speech community, design a simple questionnaire (along the lines of the sample in Table 14.17) testing for particular lexical items. If you live in a rural community, you might explore items similar to those in the table. If you live in a city, look for example at names for types of buildings or houses, streets, pavements, the spaces between streets and pavements, and so on.

2. Choose a particular field of endeavour (for example, farming, computers, or weaving) and, either by using secondary sources or by interviewing people, discover and describe the unique features of its jargon.

3. Find two English speakers who grew up in areas different from you. Determine what lexical items they use for the following notions:
   a) first meal of the day (morning)
   b) mid-day meal (weekdays)
   c) main evening meal (weekdays)
   d) light evening meal (weekdays)
   e) large, formal meal (weekend)
   f) mid-morning or mid-day first meal (weekends)
   g) meal midway through an evening work shift
   h) late afternoon quick meal

   Contrast their terms with yours. Does anyone have more than one term for any one of these notions? Under what conditions do they use these different terms? Did they volunteer any other meal names besides those elicited? In what ways do your findings provide evidence for social, regional, or situational differentiation of language?

4. English exhibits considerable variation (from region to region, from speaker to speaker in the same region, and even in the speech of individuals) with respect to the pronunciation of the vowel associated with the letters *oo* in the following sets of words. Examine these three groups and determine which vowel you use. If possible, contrast your pronunciation with that of a speaker of another variety of English. In which group(s) does the pronunciation appear to be most stable (uniform)? In which is the least uniformity seen? Are there any correlations between variations in pronunciation of *oo* in these words and the regional origin of speakers?
   a) pool, fool, mood, loop, boon, doom, loose
   b) good, foot, book
   c) hoof, roof, soot, room, coop, hoop
   d) blood, flood

5. Carefully examine how your local newspaper, radio, or television uses language with respect to matters of gender. Point out any instances of gender-biased or of gender-neutral language. Pay particular attention to the coverage of sports and note to what extent the nature and amount of language used is biased or not.

6. Carefully examine how your local newspaper, radio, or television uses language with respect to matters of race. Point out any instances of race-biased or of race-neutral language. Pay particular attention to the coverage of issues of good citizenship, delinquency, and violent crime and note to what extent the nature and amount of language used is biased or not.

7. Monitor the speech in your community, and determine whether there are any sociolinguistic variables such as the (ing), (ð), and (θ) discussed in section 2.3 in this chapter. If so, how are they reflected in speech? (*Hint*: You might examine the realizations of the phonemes /t/ and /d/ in words

such as *citing* and *siding*. You could also investigate the realization of the phoneme /t/ in words like *hotel, Atkins, little, letter, let, let's, get off!*)

8. Groups of people even as small as one's family can share linguistic features which set them off from other groups and provide a measure of solidarity. Consider your own family's sociolect and point out any lexical or other features which you believe to be unique. Contrast these with similar items from the family sociolects of two other students.

9. List and classify (both semantically and morphologically) as many slang words from your community as you can. Do all groups of adolescents in a particular community or school share the same slang? How do their ways of speaking differ? How are they alike?

10. In early Modern English, there were two functioning second person pronouns: *thou* and *ye. Thou* was used by social superiors to inferiors (including parents to children) and *ye* was used by the inferior in addressing the superior. *Thou* has been lost from general use in our language. Only *ye* (in the form *you*) has survived. In view of the discussion of address terms in this chapter, what has caused this change?

11. Describe, with examples, some phonological, morphological, syntactic and lexical differences between Standard English and a non-standard dialect. You should use some of the reference items listed above under Sources.

12. Choose a contemporary English-language play or film. Transcribe and examine some dialogue, if no published version is available for you to consult. List and discuss the discourse markers used in the dialogue. Point out how they may be used to achieve temporal sequencing of events related, involvement of the addressee or audience, or interjecting the speaker's own point of view. Try to compare this fictional dialogue with real-life conversations. Show how the play or film resembles or fails to resemble naturally occurring talk.

13. Consult with a speaker of another language regarding cohesive devices in his or her language. Using reference items listed above under Sources try to determine some types of such devices used in that language. Look specifically for the two types of reference mentioned, ellipsis and substitution. Are all of these exhibited in the other language? Do they appear to work in much the same way as in English? What other devices does your consultant suggest you consider?

15

Writing and language

Michael Dobrovolsky and William O'Grady

Outside of a dog, a book is man's best friend;
inside of a dog, it's too dark to read.

🕭 Groucho

Speaking and writing are different in both origin and practice. Our ability to use language is as old as humankind, and reflects biological and cognitive modification that has occurred in the evolutionary history of our species. **Writing**, the symbolic representation of language in storable graphic form, is a comparatively recent cultural development, having occurred within the past five thousand years and only in certain parts of the world.[1] The contrast between speech and writing comes into sharper focus when we consider that spoken language is acquired without specific formal instruction, whereas writing must be taught and learned through deliberate effort. There are entire groups of people in the world today, as well as individuals in every literate society, who are unable to write. While spoken language comes naturally to human beings, writing does not.

1

TYPES OF WRITING

As different as they are, speech and writing share one major characteristic: just as spoken language shows an arbitrary link between sound and meaning, the various symbols and techniques used in written language show an arbitrary link between symbol and sound. All writing can be grouped into two basic types, called logographic and phonographic, depending on the technique of linguistic representation they use.

1.1

Logographic writing

The term **logographic** (from Greek *logos* 'word') refers to a type of writing in which symbols represent morphemes or even entire words.

Logograms

Logographic writing is the oldest type of genuine writing. Ancient Mesopotamian cuneiform inscriptions, Egyptian hieroglyphics, and primordial Chinese characters were all highly logographic in their early stages. In fact, all writing systems maintain some logographic writing. Conventional abbreviations such as &, %, £, $, and the like are logographic, as are the symbols for numerals. To a certain extent, logographic writing can be read independently of its language of origin. For example, the Arabic numbers 1, 2, 7, 10, and so on can be read in any language.

1.2
Phonographic writing

No writing system is purely logographic, however. Nor can it be, since using a separate symbol to write each word in a language is simply too cumbersome. Throughout human history, writing systems have always evolved signs that represent some aspect of pronunciation. In **phonographic writing** (from Greek *phonos* 'sound'), the symbols represent syllables or segments.

Syllabic writing

As the name suggests, **syllabic** writing employs signs to represent syllables (a set of syllabic signs is called a **syllabary**). Languages with relatively simple syllabic structures such as CV or CVC (Japanese and Cree, for example) are well suited to this type of writing, since they contain a relatively limited number of syllable types. In Japanese, the word *kakimashita* '(s/he) wrote' can be written with the five syllabic signs か ka, き ki, ま ma, し shi, and た ta: かきました. Pure syllabaries perhaps do not exist. Syllabaries are typically augmented with symbols that represent segments (see Figures 15.19 on page 607 and 15.25 on page 611).

Alphabetic writing

Alphabetic writing represents phonemic consonant and vowel segments. Unlike the International Phonetic Alphabet, which is devised expressly to represent details of pronunciation, ordinary alphabets generally ignore non-phonemic phenomena. Thus, the spelling of the English words *pan* and *nap* represents the phonemes /p/, /n/, and /æ/, but ignores consonant aspiration, vowel nasalization, stress, and other subphonemic variation. As we will see in section 4 of this chapter, some spelling systems also capture certain morphophonemic alternations.

Writing systems emerged and spread around the earth over a long period of time. The next sections trace the development of some writing systems from their pictorial origins.

2

THE HISTORY OF WRITING

It is surprising that we cannot say with certainty how a comparatively recent cultural phenomenon like writing originated. We do know that writing developed in historically recorded stages, the earliest of which involves direct representation of objects and which is sometimes called *pre-writing*.

2.1
Pre-writing

Figures and scenes depicted on cave walls and rock faces in the Americas, Africa, and Europe twelve thousand years ago or perhaps even earlier may have been forerunners of writing. Some of these petroglyphs (scenes painted on stone) may represent a type of proto-literate stage that did not evolve into a full-fledged writing system.

These drawings depict a wide range of human and animal activity, and may even have been intended for purposes of linguistic communication. Some of them were doubtless a form of religious magic to guarantee a successful hunt or other benefits. Perhaps some were purely aesthetic expression. Some illustrations, such as those depicting the phases of the moon, may have been part of some form of record keeping. Figure 15.1*a* shows a pair of elk from a rock wall drawing in Sweden dating from the Old Stone Age (early palaeolithic) period, perhaps as far back as 20,000 BC. Figure 15.1*b* shows an incised eagle bone from Le Placard, France, that dates back some thirteen thousand to fifteen thousand years. The incisions, which vary subtly, have been analysed as a record of lunar phases. Pictorial records thus link the origins of writing with the history of representative art.

Figure 15.1   *a*, Early drawing, Sweden; *b*, Le Placard eagle bone.

An even more direct connection links the origin of writing with record keeping. It has been suggested that the idea of writing had its origin in small clay tokens and counters that were used in record keeping and business transactions in the ancient Middle East. These small, fire-baked pieces of clay were apparently used for thousands of years before writing emerged. Counters representing cattle and other goods were stored on shelves or in baskets. Eventually, people began to make an impression of the tokens on soft clay tablets rather than storing and shipping the tokens themselves (Figure 15.2). This may have led to the idea that other objects and events in the world could be represented symbolically in graphic form.

Figure 15.2   Ancient Mesopotamian tokens.

2.2

Pictograms

Whatever their purpose, there is no doubt that pictures were among the precursors of the written word. Early writing systems all evolved from pictorial representations called **pictograms** or picture writing. Each pictogram was an image of the object or objects (and, in some cases, concepts) it represented, and, as far as we know, offered no clues to pronunciation. This kind of communication has been found among people throughout the ancient and modern world. Figure 15.3 is an example of Amerindian picture writing taken from a record kept by a Dakota named Lonedog; these pictures served as a kind of memory aid and not as a detailed record of events.

Figure 15.3 Amerindian pictography: a Dakota record of significant events.

Pictograms are still used today, and they reflect the memory-aid nature of this form of pre-writing. Signs indicating roadside services or information in parks are all pictographic in nature. The British Sports Council has developed a standardized set of pictograms to indicate sporting events (Figure 15.4).

Figure 15.4 Contemporary pictograms: British Sports Council signs for sporting events.

A contemporary and very sophisticated development of pictographic writing, **Blissymbolics** (originally called semantography), was developed by Charles K. Bliss. It makes use of a number of recombineable symbols that represent basic units of meaning, as Figure 15.5 illustrates.

'person'   'forward'   'building'   'visitor'

Figure 15.5   Blissymbolics.

Though Blissymbolics was intended as a means of international, cross-linguistic communication by its inventor, its primary use today is as a means of augmentative communication for non-speaking individuals. The Blissymbolics Communication Institute of Toronto sets the standard for the training and application of Blissymbols for this specialized purpose.

As we consider developments that emerge from pictographic representation, it is important to remember that pictograms are not writing in any sense of the word. They do not represent any linguistic elements such as segments, syllables, morphemes, or words, nor are they associated with rules for presenting any of these elements in sequence that parallel syntactic rules. Finally, pictograms typically lend themselves to more than one interpretation, and so provide only limited clues about their intended meaning.

3

THE EVOLUTION OF WRITING

The earliest known pictographic writing came from Sumeria, from where it spread to surrounding areas about five thousand years ago (Figure 15.6). The inherently ambiguous pictograms came to represent abstract notions by extending their use to include concepts felt to be associated with them. A pictogram of the sun could also mean 'light' or 'heat' and even 'energy', an arrow, 'to run', and a foot, 'to go', 'to stay', or 'to bring'. It is possible that by the time such symbols appear, we are encountering writing in its

'to go, move, go away'   'star, god'

'hand, fist, unit of measurement'   'fire, inflammation'

Figure 15.6   Sumerian logograms.

logographic form. Sumerian writing also combined signs to express abstract meanings. For example, a head with fire coming out of the crown indicated 'anger'.

Although its evolution was gradual, we can state with some certainty that Sumerian writing was logographic because, from a fairly early stage on, it was written in a consistent linear order that would appear to reflect the order of words in speech. We cannot say with certainty at what date pictures began to be read as words, but once this practice had taken hold, the stage was set for the evolution to phonographic writing.

3.1

Rebuses and the emergence of writing

This major development in the history of writing took place around 3000 BC with the first use of Sumerian symbols to represent sound rather than just meaning. Known as the **rebus principle**, this innovation allowed a sign to be used for any word that was pronounced like the word whose meaning it originally represented. For example, in the inscription of an economic transaction, shown in Figure 15.7, the symbol in the upper left-hand corner, originally used to represent the word GI 'reed', here represents a homophonous word with the meaning 'reimburse'.

Figure 15.7   Sumerian rebus inscription (c. 3000 BC).

Thanks to the rebus principle, concepts that could not be directly depicted by a pictogram/logogram could be represented in writing. Thus, the sign for the word *ti* 'arrow', ➤—, was also used for the word *ti* 'life', and the sign for the word *mu* 'tree', ✕, could also stand for the word *mu* 'name' and the suffix -*mu* 'my'.

3.2

Towards syllabic writing

Once the breakthrough towards phonographic writing had been made, it did not take long (in historical terms) before syllabic writing began to emerge. Within about five hundred to six hundred years, signs that clearly represent not just homophonous words, but word portions – specifically, syllables – had become well established in Sumerian writing. Typically, the Sumerians overlapped their syllabic signs in order to use them more efficiently. Thus, a word like 'kir' would be represented by the syllabic signs for 'ki' and 'ir' in sequence. Without this overlapping technique, a special sign for 'r' would have had to be employed. Figure 15.8 illustrates this with Sumerian cuneiform signs, which are discussed in more detail in the following section.

ki   +   ir   =   kir

Figure 15.8   Overlapped Sumerian syllabic signs.

Sumerian writing never developed into a pure syllabary. Logographic elements were interspersed with syllabic ones, and in addition, many syllabic signs were used to represent syllables with other pronunciations as well.

Cuneiform

Over the centuries, Sumerian writing was simplified and eventually produced with the use of a wedge-shaped stylus that was pressed into soft clay tablets. This form of writing, initiated in the fourth millennium BC, has come to be known as **cuneiform** (from Latin *cuneus* 'wedge'). In time, a change in writing practices led the cuneiform signs to be rotated ninety degrees to the left. This resulted in their bearing even less resemblance to their pictographic origins than before. Figure 15.9 illustrates this development in two forms.

	Logograms (c. 3000 BC)	Earlier cuneiform (2500–1800 BC)	Later cuneiform (800 BC)
'jar'			
'bird'			

Figure 15.9   Changes in cuneiform writing.

The cuneiform system was borrowed by the Elamites and Akkadians in the third millenium BC, a little later by the Persians, and in the second millennium

BC by the Hittites far to the north in the ancient region of Anatolia (Modern Asian Turkey).

Cuneiform writing persisted until about the first few centuries of the Christian era in some areas, and then disappeared from use, not to be rediscovered until the nineteenth century. It was first deciphered from Old Persian texts, a breakthrough that led to the deciphering of Akkadian, Sumerian, and Hittite, among other languages that employed it. This script was used for thousands of years but then was generally replaced by more efficient systems of writing employed by the Semitic peoples of the Eastern Mediterranean.

3.3

Another Middle Eastern writing system: hieroglyphics

At about the time Sumerian pictography was flourishing, a similar system of pictorial communication was in use in Egypt. The Egyptian signs have become known as **hieroglyphics** (meaning 'sacred inscriptions' in Greek). The earliest texts display about five hundred such symbols. Like Sumerian pictograms, the hieroglyphic signs at first represented objects, but later they became logographic in that they began to be associated with words.

Egyptian hieroglyphics developed into a mixed system of both word writing and phonographic writing. For example, the sign for a lute was a picture of a lute: 𓏢; this represented the word itself: *nfr*. Only the consonants of words represented by hieroglyphics are known with certainty. The Egyptians did not represent the vowels, which can only be partially reconstructed from transcriptions in Greek and other languages that were made much later. Eventually, the sign came to be disassociated from the word it represented, and thanks to the rebus principle (section 3.1) was used to transcribe other words that consisted of or included these sounds, such as the word for 'good', whose consonants were also *nfr*.

These symbols eventually came to be used to represent the consonant phonemes of words by application of what is called the **acrophonic principle** (from Greek *acros* 'extreme'): sounds are represented by pictures of objects whose pronunciation begins with the sound to be represented. In this way, the first consonant of a word-sign came to be what the sign stood for. For example, the hieroglyph for 'horned viper' 𓆑 is read logographically as f(V)t; this sign is also used to represent the phoneme /f/ in spellings such as 𓆑 *fen* 'pleasant'. As we see in section 3.4, this principle was crucial in the development of true alphabets. In Egyptian writing, however, it was only part of a system that mixed logographic and phonographic elements. Figure 15.10 shows some hieroglyphics.

| s'-j | ndtjj-j | Mn-hpr-r' |
| son-my | avenger-my | Men-heper-rē' |

Figure 15.10   Egyptian hieroglyphics (c. 2000 BC).

Hieroglyphics continued in decreasing use down to Christian times. By the second century AD, Egyptian began to be written with Greek letters, and by the third century AD, hieroglyphics had been replaced by the Greek alphabet.

3.4

The emergence of alphabets

In the Middle East, alphabetic writing was slowly emerging from mixed writing systems over a long period. Building on this tradition, the Semitic peoples of ancient Phoenicia (modern Lebanon) had devised a writing system of twenty-two consonantal signs as early as 1000 BC. This system was written horizontally, right to left, without variation in the placement of the letters, as had been common in earlier scripts. It was ultimately to lead to the development of many alphabetic writing systems, including both the Greek and Latin alphabets.

The pictorial (and eventually logographic) origins of the Phoenician alphabet are evident in a number of its symbols. The development of logograms for a stylized ox's head, throwing stick, and wavy flow of water are shown in Figure 15.11, along with the corresponding letter names.

ʔāleph   gīmel   mēm

Figure 15.11   Pictorial and logographic origins of some signs in the Phoenician alphabet.

These symbols eventually came to be used to represent the consonant phonemes of words by application of the acrophonic principle (see section 3.3). In this way, ʔaleph was used to represent the glottal stop; gīmel, a /g/; and mēm, an /m/. Some of the symbols of the Phoenician alphabet had developed from Egyptian hieroglyphics, and, as in hieroglyphic writing, vowels were not represented (see Figure 15.10).

The Phoenicians were a trading people, and their alphabetic writing spread to adjacent countries and beyond. Eventually, the Greeks acquired and adapted the Phoenician alphabet.

The Greek alphabet

The Greeks developed the Phoenician writing system into a full alphabet: each sign represented one phoneme and all phonemes were recorded by a sign. The Greeks were aware that some of the Phoenician symbols represented consonant sounds that were not found in Greek. Some of these symbols were adapted to represent Greek vowels, and other unneeded consonant signs were dropped. Figure 15.12 overleaf illustrates the evolution of the Classical Greek and ultimately the Latin alphabet from the original Phoenician consonantal signs.

Phoenician ʔāleph, as we have seen, represented a glottal stop. Since Greek had no glottal stop phoneme, the ʔāleph was employed to represent the vowel /a/ in Greek. Phoenician ⊓ (h) was used to represent the Greek vowel /e/.

Symbols			Greek			Latin	
Phoenician	Name	Phonetic value	Early	Classical	Name	Early	Monumental (Classical)
𐤀	'Aleph	'	△	A	Alpha	A	A
𐤁	Beth	B	ᗺ	B	Beta		B
𐤂	Gimel	G	ᒋ	Γ	Gamma		C
𐤃	Daleth	D	◁	Δ	Delta		D
𐤄	He	H	ᗺ	E	Epsilon	϶	E
𐤅	Waw	W	ᐟ		Digamma	�7	F
							G
𐤆	Zayin	Z	I	Ζ			
𐤇	Ḥeth	Ḥ	ᗷ	H	Ēta	ᗷ	H
𐤈	Teth	Ṭ	⊗	Θ	Theta		
𐤉	Yod	Y	ᒉ	Ι	Iota	Ι	I (J)
𐤊	Kaph	K	ᛋ	Κ	Kappa	ᛋ	K
𐤋	Lamed	L	ᒉ	Λ	Lambda	ᒉ	L
𐤌	Mem	M	ᛘ	Μ	Mu	ᛘ	M
𐤍	Nun	N	ᛀ	Ν	Nu	ᛀ	N
𐤎	Samekh	S					
𐤏	'Ayin	'	Ο	Ο	Ŏmicron	Ο	O
𐤐	Pe	P	ᒉ	Π	Pi		P
𐤑	Sade	S	ᛘ				
𐤒	Qoph	Q	Φ				Q
𐤓	Reš	R	ᛩ	Ρ	Rho		R
𐤔	Šin	SH-S	ᒉ	Σ	Sigma	ᛋ	S
𐤕	Taw	T	Χ		Tau		T
				Υ	Upsilon	V	V
				Χ	Chi		X
				Ω	Omega		Y
							Z

Figure 15.12 Evolution of the Greek and Latin alphabets. (Adapted from DeFrancis, p. 180.)

Other signs were added to the system by the Greeks, such as Φ /f/, X /x/, ψ /ps/, and Ω /ō/.

The Phoenician names for the letters (*aleph, beth, gimel, daleth*, and so on) were maintained by the Greeks (as *alpha, beta, gamma, delta*, and so on), but the pictorial origins had been lost and the names carried no other meaning.[2] The writing system itself gained its name from the first two letters of the series: alphabet.

The Roman alphabet
When Greek colonists occupied southern Italy in the eighth and seventh centuries BC, they took their alphabet with them. It was in turn taken up and modified by the Etruscan inhabitants of central Italy, a non-Latin-speaking people who were a political and cultural power before the rise of Rome. It is believed that the Romans acquired their alphabet through the Etruscans. As the Romans grew in power and influence during the following centuries, first as masters of Italy and later of Europe, the Roman alphabet spread throughout the Empire.

Under the Romans, the Greek/Etruscan alphabet was again modified, this time with some symbols influenced by the Etruscans. The Γ in Greek writing developed into both C for the phoneme /k/ and G for /g/. The oldest inscriptions also retained K for /k/ in some words, but it was generally replaced by C. Similarly, Q was retained before /u/. Roman script also employed Greek U, V, X, Y, and Z and moved Z to the end of the alphabet. The symbols Φ, Θ, ψ, and Ω were among those discarded, and H was converted back to a consonant symbol.

Some subsequent changes were made in the alphabet as it was adapted by various peoples of the Roman Empire. In English, for example, W was created from two juxtaposed V's. Spanish employs a tilde (˜) over n (ñ) to signify a palatal nasal, as in *año* /aɲo/ 'year', and French uses a cedilla under the c (ç) to indicate the dental fricative /s/, as in the spelling of *français* /frãsɛ/ 'French'.

3.5

Other developments, East and West
A great number of alphabetic systems evolved and flourished in addition to the Greek and Latin traditions. In this section, we briefly present some of these that are of historical significance or interest.

Runic writing
Germanic tribes occupying the north of Italy developed an early offshoot of the Greek/Etruscan tradition of writing into a script known as Runic writing. This system emerged shortly after the beginning of the Christian era, and its developments were eventually found as far north as Scandinavia. Runic writing persisted until the sixteenth century in some areas before giving way to the Latin alphabet.

Figure 15.13 illustrates some signs from one of the oldest known Runic inscriptions, which dates from about the third century AD. The angular style of the letters arose because the alphabet was carved in wood or stone, neither of which readily lends itself to curved lines. The script is read from right to left.

Ιↂ∫ΑΥΙ⟨ΛΉ = harigasti ['the warriors' guest']
(? epithet for the god Odin)

Figure 15.13 Runic script.

Cyrillic script

Another offshoot of the Greek script was created for the Slavic peoples in the ninth century AD. The Greek missionary brothers Constantine (Cyril) and Methodius introduced a writing system for the translation of the Bible that is now known as **Glagolitic** script. A later development, which combined adaptations of Glagolitic letters with Greek and Hebrew characters, has come to be known as the **Cyrillic** alphabet. The current Russian, Byelorussian, Ukrainian, Serbian, Macedonian, and Bulgarian alphabets, as well as those used to represent many non-Slavic languages spoken in the former Soviet Union, have evolved from this early Cyrillic script. Some examples of its development and adaptation are given in Figure 15.14, followed by a short passage in contemporary Russian Cyrillic, which is transliterated for its letter values.

From Greek	From Hebrew	Later development	Russian Cyrillic	Latin alphabet equivalent
Г			Г	G
П			П	P
Р			Р	R
Д			Д	D
	ש		Ш	SH
		Я	Я	YA

Мы все учились понемногу   mɨ vse utʃilis' ponemnogu
Чему-нибудь и как-нибудь ...   tʃemu-nibud' i kak-nibud' ...

We all pick up our education
In bits and pieces as we can ...
Pushkin, *Eugene Onegin*, 1.5

Figure 15.14   Contemporary Russian Cyrillic transliterated.

Two Semitic alphabets

Both Arabic and Hebrew are written with alphabets that descend from or are closely related to Phoenician script. Both are essentially consonant-writing systems (vowels are indicated with diacritic dots), and both are written from right to left.

The contemporary Arabic alphabet is the most widespread of all the descendents of Middle Eastern writing except the Latin alphabet. Its earliest inscription dates back to the fourth century AD. In the latter half of the seventh century, this script was used to write the sacred text of Islam, the Koran, and accompanied the rapid spread of Islam over the next centuries. It contains

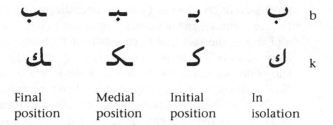

Final | Medial | Initial | In
position | position | position | isolation

Figure 15.15 Variation in two Arabic letters according to position.

Letter name	Phonetic value	Phoenician	Modern Hebrew	Modern Arabic
'Āleph	'A			
Bêth	B			
Gimel	G			
Dāleth	D			
He	H			
Wāw	V			
Zayin	Z			
Ḥēth	CH			
Ṭeth	T			
Yōdh	Y			
Kaph	K			
Lāmadh	L			
Mêm	M			
Nūn	N			
Sāmekh	S			
'Ayin	A			
Pê	P			
Ṣādê	TS			
Qōph	Q			
Rêš	R			
Šîn	SH			
Tāw	T			

Figure 15.16 The Phoenician, Hebrew and Arabic alphabets.

twenty-eight consonants (vowels are indicated by diacritics above and below the consonants), and is written from right to left. An interesting feature of this alphabet is the fact that twenty-two of its twenty-eight signs have different forms, depending on their position in (or outside) a word. Figure 15.15 above shows this variation for the forms of the letters *b* and *k* in initial, medial, and final position, as well as their forms when written in isolation.

The resemblances among the signs shown in Figure 15.16 demonstrate the clear link between Phoenician script and the Hebrew and Arabic scripts.

Other descendants of Middle Eastern systems

Early Middle Eastern scripts gave rise to Aramaic, Old Hebrew, and South Arabic syllabaries, which, in turn, led to a host of further writing systems eventually stretching across the Near East and North Africa from India to Morocco. Figure 15.17 illustrates this widespread diffusion on a time scale.

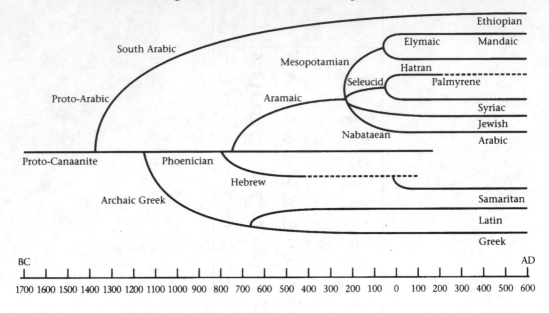

Figure 15.17 Development of writing systems (dotted lines indicate that the line of development is hypothetical). (Adapted from Senner, p. 89.)

4

SOME OTHER WRITING SYSTEMS

This section focuses on the nature and development of writing systems that originated outside the Middle East. While some of these systems emerged in response to external influences, others seem to have been entirely independent innovations.

4.1

Chinese writing

The Chinese system of writing developed out of pictograms that eventually came to represent morphemes (most of which are also words). The oldest inscriptions are the oracle texts, written on animal bones and tortoise shells and dating back to about twelve hundred BC. These include many recognizable images, such as 'sun' ○ and ☽ 'moon'. A change towards more symbolic signs began at an early date as more abstract notions were symbolized, such as ◡ 'above' and ◠ 'below'. Symbols were also combined to extend meanings metaphorically. For example, the sign for 'to tend' 牧 is composed of 牛 'cow' and 攴 'hand and whip'. 'To follow' 从 is two men in sequence, and so on. In time, the characters became more abstract. Figure 15.18 shows the historical development of the symbol for 'dog'.

Figure 15.18 Historical development of the Chinese symbol for dog'.

Calligraphy is an ancient and respected art in China, and Chinese writing exists in a number of styles. The script is usually written from left to right along a horizontal axis, although newspapers and older texts begin in the right-hand margin and are read downwards.

The units of contemporary Chinese orthography are called **characters**. Many monosyllabic words are represented in true logographic fashion by a character that consists of a single symbol. For example, the Mandarin words for 'hand' [ʃǒw] and 'horse' [mǎ] are written 手 and 馬, respectively (omitting tones). However, the overwhelming majority of the characters (one estimate is 99 per cent) consist of two parts.

The main component of a multi-element character is called the **phonetic determinative**. It provides information about the pronunciation of the corresponding morpheme. Although about four thousand different phonetic determinatives are used in Chinese writing, they represent pronunciation very imperfectly. For example, phonetic determinatives do not provide all the information needed to pronounce Chinese. Tone, which is contrastive in Chinese (see Chapter 2), is not represented at all, and many phonetic determinatives indicate only part of the morpheme's pronunciation. The determinative 敎, for instance, is used for a wide variety of words ending in *ao* without regard for whether the initial consonant is *j*, *n*, *r*, or some other element. Furthermore, due to sound changes over the last centuries, about one-third of all phonetic determinatives provide little or no useful information about current pronunciation. Finally, because Chinese has many homophones, even the most informative phonetic determinatives can be used for many different words.

Chinese characters also include a semantic component, called the **radical** or **key**, which provides clues about the morpheme's meaning. There are about two hundred different radicals in contemporary Chinese writing. Table 15.1 (overleaf) provides examples of some of the characters that can be formed by combining phonetic determinatives with radicals.

Notice that only the phonetic determinative in column A provides complete

Table 15.1 Some Chinese characters

		Phonetic determinatives			
Semantic radical		A 敖 *(áo)*	B 参 *(cān)*	C 堯 *(yáo)*	D 甫 *(fŭ)*
1	亻 'person'	傲 *(ào: 'proud')*	傪 *(cān: 'good')*	僥 *(jiăo: 'lucky')*	俌 *(fŭ: 'help')*
2	扌 'hand'	擻 *(ào: 'shake')*	搀 *(shán: 'seize')*	撓 *(náo: 'scratch')*	捕 *(bŭ: 'catch')*
3	木 'wood'	橔 *(áo: 'barge')*	椮 *(shēn: 'beam')*	橈 *(náo: 'oar')*	楠 *(fú: 'trellis')*
4	氵 'water'	潵 *(ào: 'stream')*	渗 *(shèn: 'leak')*	澆 *(jiāo: 'sprinkle')*	浦 *(pŭ: 'creek')*

information (ignoring tone) about the pronunciation of the four morphemes it represents. The other determinatives supply helpful, but incomplete, information about pronunciation. The determinative *yao* (column C), for instance, has a pronunciation that rhymes with that of the four morphemes it helps to represent.

The usefulness of the information supplied by the radicals also varies. Thus, the characters in row 1 represent morphemes whose meaning is at best indirectly associated with that of the radical ('person'), but the radicals in rows 2, 3, and 4 are much more informative. For example, the characters in row 2 all denote actions involving the hand while those in row 3 refer to things made of wood and those in row 4 all have something to do with liquids.

Although neither phonetic determinatives nor semantic radicals alone are sufficient to identify the morpheme that they represent, they are more than adequate when used in conjunction with each other. Despite its complexities – one authority has described the system as 'outsized, haphazard, inefficient, and only partially reliable' – Chinese writing provides its users with an effective way to represent the words and morphemes of the language. Moreover, the lack of efficiency in signs is offset by wide readability of the literary script among diverse peoples of differing (though related) Chinese languages. Although a speaker of Mandarin and a speaker of Cantonese may pronounce the word for 'fire' differently – [xwǒ] and [fɔ̀], respectively – they can read it from the same character (火) since Chinese writing does not directly represent a word's phonemic segments.

In recent times, the government of the People's Republic of China has introduced simplified characters (some newly invented) in an attempt to promote literacy. At the same time, a system of writing Mandarin with a modified Latin alphabet, called **pinyin**, has also been introduced. Pinyin is used as a subsidiary system for writing such things as street signs, addresses, and brand names as well as for teaching children how to pronounce characters. It is also used for word processing and other computer-related activities, including electronic mail.

4.2

Japanese writing

The writing system of modern Japanese is arguably the most complicated in the entire world. Its use requires knowledge of three distinct scripts, including a pair of syllabaries – **katakana** and **hiragana** – which were created by modifying Chinese characters. The two syllabaries are shown in Figure 15.19.

Although Japanese can be written exclusively with either syllabary, normal writing involves use of Chinese characters (called **kanji** in Japanese), in

Katakana chart

COLUMN / LINE	A	I	U	E	O
SINGLE VOWEL	ア A	イ I	ウ U	エ E	オ O
K	カ KA	キ KI	ク KU	ケ KE	コ KO
S	サ SA	シ SHI	ス SU	セ SE	ソ SO
T	タ TA	チ CHI	ツ TSU	テ TE	ト TO
N	ナ NA	ニ NI	ヌ NU	ネ NE	ノ NO
H	ハ HA	ヒ HI	フ HU	ヘ HE	ホ HO
M	マ MA	ミ MI	ム MU	メ ME	モ MO
Y	ヤ YA		ユ YU		ヨ YO
R	ラ RA	リ RI	ル RU	レ RE	ロ RO
W	ワ WA				ヲ O
N (in a coda)	ン N				

Hiragana chart

COLUMN / LINE	A	I	U	E	O
SINGLE VOWEL	あ A	い I	う U	え E	お O
K	か KA	き KI	く KU	け KE	こ KO
S	さ SA	し SHI	す SU	せ SE	そ SO
T	た TA	ち CHI	つ TSU	て TE	と TO
N	な NA	に NI	ぬ NU	ね NE	の NO
H	は HA	ひ HI	ふ HU	へ HE	ほ HO
M	ま MA	み MI	む MU	め ME	も MO
Y	や YA		ゆ YU		よ YO
R	ら RA	り RI	る RU	れ RE	ろ RO
W	わ WA				を O
N (in a coda)	ん N				

Figure 15.19 Hiragana and katakana syllabaries and their phonetic values (voicing, vowel length, and gemination are not indicated here).

addition to hiragana and katakana. Kanji symbols are typically used to represent all or part of a word's root, while affixes are represented by hiragana symbols. The phrase *in the man's car*, for example, can be written as in Figure 15.20, with the roots 'man' and 'car' represented using kanji, and the possessive morpheme *no* written in hiragana.

hito no	kuruma de
人 の	車 で
man Gen	car Loc
kanji hiragana	kanji hiragana

Figure 15.20   A phrase written in kanji/hiragana.

The katakana syllabary, whose symbols are less rounded than their hiragana counterparts, is used to write onomatopoeic words as well as words borrowed into Japanese from other languages. In addition, it is employed in advertising and in telegrams.

Finally, it should be noted that the Latin alphabet, which the Japanese call *romaji*, is also making inroads. It is not unusual to see all four writing systems used together, especially in advertising, as shown in Figure 15.21.

New Tomato

ほんのり 甘味 さらっと あと 味
(honnori   amami   saratto   ato   aji)
'Subtle sweetness and light after taste.'

———— –Hiragana
〰〰〰 –Katakana
═══ –Kanji

トマト の 新しい ジュース です
(tomato   no   atarashi   juusu   desu)
'It's a new tomato juice.'

Figure 15.21   Kanji, hiragana, katakana, and romaji in a Japanese advertisement.

Learning to read Japanese is a formidable task, in part because of the way the various scripts are intermingled and in part because of complexities in the use of kanji symbols, which can have more than one pronunciation depending on whether they are used to represent a word of Chinese or Japanese origin. (For example, Japanese has two morphemes with the meaning 'mountain' – /san/, which is of Chinese origin, and the native Japanese /yama/; both are written with the same kanji character 山.)

4.3

Korean writing

Korean was once written with Chinese characters, which had been introduced in the first centuries AD. However, Korean suffixes could not be easily represented by Chinese writing. Various devices were tried to alleviate this problem but inadequacies persisted. Finally, King Sejong (1419–1452) commissioned an alphabetic script, called **hangul**, consisting of eleven vowels and seventeen consonants that, after some modifications over the centuries, became the standard Korean writing system. An especially interesting feature of hangul is that symbols are grouped together into syllable-sized clusters rather than being arranged in a completely linear fashion. Figure 15.22 shows how a set of symbols are grouped to form words.

Hangul symbols

ㅂ	ㅜ	ㄹ	ㄱ	ㅗ	ㅣ
/p/	/u/	/l/	/k/	/o/	/i/

Grouped symbols

불　　　　고기

'fire' /pul/　　'meat' /koki/

Written form

불고기

'barbecued meat' *pulkoki*

Figure 15.22　Korean hangul.

Like Japanese, Korean also makes use of Chinese characters (called **hanja**), although in a more restricted way. Slightly more than half the vocabulary of contemporary Korean is of Chinese origin and many words of this type are written with the help of Chinese characters in newspapers and in scientific articles. However, this practice has been reduced somewhat in recent years in South Korea and it has been eliminated entirely in North Korea.

4.4

American scripts

A number of major civilizations developed on the American continents. In Mesoamerica alone more than eighteen writing systems have been discovered, among them those of the Mayans of the Yucatan and the Aztecs of Mexico. In both systems, we can see the evolution of pictograms that leaned towards phonetic word signs, just as did the Egyptian hieroglyphics illustrated in section 3.3.

Mayan symbols are called **glyphs**. Some were read as word signs (logograms). But the writing systems relied on other uses of the signs as well. The rebus principle was employed, sometimes only partially, as in the Mayan use of the sign for a smoking bundle of pine, 🮲 /taaȝ/, to represent the locative preposition /ta/. Mayan signs could be combined for their phonetic value alone in a form of syllabic writing. Glyphs that mix syllabic writing with logographic representation are also found.

Figure 15.23 Six Mayan hieroglyphics spelling 'Lord Pacal'.

Cherokee

Some American writing systems do not date back to a distant ancestor. After the colonization of North America by Europeans, a number of scripts were developed to provide native peoples with a form of written communication. In one well-known case, the Cherokee leader Sikwayi (Sequoia) devised a syllabic script (shown in Figure 15.24) of more than eighty symbols, some based on the shapes of English letters and others newly invented.

Symbol	Value	Symbol	Value	Symbol	Value	Symbol	Value	Symbol	Value
Ꭰ	a	Ꭱ	e	Ꭲ	i	Ꮎ	o	Ꮒ	u
Ꭶ	ga	Ꭷ	ge	Ᏽ	gi	Ꭺ	go	Ꭻ	gu
Ꮎ	ha	Ꭸ	he	Ꭿ	hi	Ꮁ	ho	Ꮄ	hu
Ꮃ	la	Ꮅ	le	Ꮀ	li	Ꮆ	lo	Ꮇ	lu
Ꮉ	ma	Ꮊ	me	Ꮋ	mi	Ꮋ	mo	Ꮙ	mu

Figure 15.24 Some Cherokee syllabic symbols.

Cree

Professional linguists have often played a role in the development of American scripts, as have missionaries. The syllabic script of the Cree Indians was the creation of a missionary, J. Evans, in the nineteenth century. It was employed for religious literature, and by 1861 the entire Bible appeared in the Cree syllabary. Today, in somewhat modified form, this script is used by Cree speakers across Canada.

Cree morphemes are made up of syllables that combine one of ten initial consonants with one of seven vowels; in some cases, there is also a post-vocalic consonant. The Cree writing system provides a separate symbol for each V and CV syllable. As in syllabaries in general, the symbols representing the CV syllables bear no resemblance to those representing syllables consisting of a single vowel; there is no connection, for instance, between the symbols for the syllable /ki/ Ꝑ and the syllable /i/ ∆ However, the Cree system is not wholly syllabic since consonants that occur at the end of a syllable must be represented by a separate symbol.

A striking feature of the Cree syllabary is its phonetic symbolism. The vowel in a syllable is indicated by the direction in which the symbol faces. Symbols that face 'south' (downwards on the printed page) contain /e:/; those facing 'north' (upwards) contain /i/ or /i:/; those pointing 'east' (rightwards) have /o/ or /o:/, and those looking to the 'west' (leftwards) contain /a/ or /a:/. Vowel length is indicated by a superposed dot, as in Ᵽ = /si:/.

Plains Cree, a variety of Cree spoken in Western Canada, is written with the symbols shown in Figure 15.25 (other dialects use slightly different ones).

∆	i, ī	▽	ē	▷	o, ō	◁	a
∧	pi, pī	V	pē	>	po, pō	<	pa
∩	ti, tī	U	tē	⊃	to, tō	ᒐ	ta
ᒋ	ci, cī	⌐	cē	J	co, cō	ᒐ	ca
Ꝑ	ki, kī	ᒈ	kē	ᑯ	ko, kō	ᒃ	ka
Γ	mi, mī	⌐	mē	⌐	mo, mō	L	ma
σ	ni, nī	o	nē	ᓄ	no, nō	ᑭ	na
ᒉ	si, sī	ᒉ	sē	ᒉ	so, sō	ᒉ	sa
ᒉ	yi, yī	ᒉ	yē	ᒉ	yo, yō	ᒉ	ya

Finals

ᐧ p ᐧ t ‑ c ᐠ k ᐨ m ᐢ s ᐣ n ᐧ y o w ᐦ h × hk ᐧ l ᐧ r

Figure 15.25 Western Cree syllabary.

The examples shown in Figure 15.26 illustrate the use of the Cree syllabary.

ᓂ ∧   σ ∧   ᒉ ∧

nīpi 'leaf'   nipi 'water'   sīpi 'river'

Figure 15.26 Three words in Western Cree syllabary.

Some other American scripts

The Cree syllabary, appropriately modified, is used by the Inuit of Baffin Island to represent their language, which is unrelated to Cree. A word-writing system developed by Alaskan Inuit towards the end of the nineteenth century eventually evolved into a partially syllabic system, although it did not become fully syllabic. A number of different systems are in use in different regions of Alaska, and in some, tendencies towards alphabetization are discernible.

4.5

African scripts

In the past several centuries, societies in Central Africa have also produced syllabic scripts, which have either developed through stages from pictograms to refined syllabaries or have been invented by one or several individuals. Although the idea of writing appears to have been imported into these societies, the development of the various systems was indigenous.

The first sub-Saharan African writing seems to have been that of the Vai peoples in the region of Sierra Leone and Liberia. Around 1830, a Vai man called Momalu Duwalu Bukele developed a syllabary from a system of picture communication. The new system, which grew to consist of 226 syllabic signs plus a few word signs, appears to have spawned a number of imitations throughout the area.

The writing of the Bamum people in the Cameroons was invented at the end of the nineteenth century by Njoya the Great, sultan of Foumban (c. 1880–1933). The current seventy syllabic symbols show tendencies towards alphabetization. The Bamoun case is also interesting because it illustrates how the creation of a writing system can be a political issue. Njoya is reported to have declared that 'the Muslims and Christians have their writing; the Bamoun must have theirs.' The development of a writing system for his people was seen by him as a way of resisting foreign domination.

The only sure example of alphabetic writing developed in modern times among African peoples is the Somali alphabet. The originator, acquainted with Arabic and Italian, devised an alphabet composed of nineteen consonants and ten vowels. The symbols appear to have been freely invented, but their names are based on those used for the letters of the Arabic alphabet, and are listed and recited in the same order.

4.6

Some Indian scripts

A pictorial script appears to have had an independent origin in northern India, where inscribed seals, pottery, and copper tablets dating back to the third millennium BC have been unearthed. The system seems to have consisted of about two hundred and fifty symbols such as ᛦ, Q, and ᚫ, but died away long before another writing system, seemingly derived from Semitic (see Figure 15.27), was employed in the middle of the first millennium BC to record the ancient Sanskrit language.

The date of the first appearance of Indian Sanskrit symbols cannot be ascertained, but they resemble Aramaic and appeared as a full system of writing in the edicts of Asoka (who ruled from 272 to 231 BC). They were set down in two types of writing: Kharosthi and Brahmi. The former continued

व्यवहारान्नृपः पश्येदिद्दिद्द्विर्ब्राह्मणीः सह ।
धर्मशास्त्रानुसारेण क्रोधलोभविवर्जितः ॥१॥ *a*

b ਕਿਉਕਿ ਪਰਮੇਸ਼ਰ ਨੇ ਜਗਤਨੈ ਅਜਿਹਾ ਪਿਆਰ
ਕੀਤਾ ਜੋ ਉਸਨੇ ਆਪਲ ਇਕਲੌਤਾ ਪੁੱਤ ਦਿੱਤਾ ਤਾਂ
ਹਰੇਕ ਜੋ ਉਸ ਉੱਤੇ ਨਿਹਚਾ ਕਰਦਾ ਏ ਉਹਦਾ ਨਾਸ
ਨਾ ਹੋਵੇ ਸਗੋਂ ਸਦੀਪਕ ਜੀਉਣ ਪਾਵੇ ।

തന്റെ ഏകജാതനായ പുത്രനിൽ വിശ്വ
സിക്കുന്ന ഏവനും. നശിച്ചു പോകാതെ നിത്യ *c*
ജീവൻ പ്രാപിക്കേണ്ടതിന്നു ദൈവം. അവനെ
നല്ല്വാൻ തക്കവണ്ണം. ലോകത്തെ സ്നേഹിച്ചു.

d ศาอ้อนป้ันคนฆน บ้านอยุ่ใกล้ๆป่า

Figure 15.27   *a*, Devanagari; *b*, Gurmuki; *c*, Modern Malayalam; *d*, Modern Thai.

in use until about the fifth century AD in northern India. The Brahmi script gave rise to all later varieties of Indian writing.

One of these varieties, a cursive type called the Gupta script, was later employed to write Tocharian, Saka, and Turkish manuscripts discovered in eastern Turkestan. In India, it evolved into the Devanagari script, which became the most widespread type of writing in the subcontinent and which was used to record the voluminous literature of the Sanskrit language. Inscriptions in Devanagari are found throughout Southeast Asia, Indonesia, and as far afield as the southern Philippines.

Varieties of Indian writing were carried abroad by Buddhist missionaries and influenced writing systems in Tibet and Central and Southeast Asia. The Dravidian peoples of southern India also developed a number of scripts under the influence of the northern varieties. Another ancient Indian script, called Pali, gave rise to a number of Southeast Asian writing systems, including those used for Thai and Cambodian. Figure 15.27 illustrates Devanagari and some of the many other scripts found in India and Southeast Asia.

The examples cited in this chapter only touch on the variety of writing systems past and present that scholars have investigated. The index of one standard work lists four hundred and seventy scripts. Many of these are historically related, but the number nonetheless testifies to human ingenuity and creativity in devising writing systems.

5

ENGLISH ORTHOGRAPHY

The set of conventions for representing language in written form is called an **orthography**. English employs an alphabetic orthography in which symbols are used to represent individual consonants and vowels rather than syllables or words. In this section, we will consider the nature and history of English orthography. We will then use section 5.3 to examine the relationship between writing and reading.

5.1

Irregularities

A frequently expressed complaint about English orthography is that it does not establish a one-to-one relationship between symbols and phonological segments. Table 15.2 lists some well-known examples of this.

Table 15.2   Some problems with English orthography

	Problem	Example
1.	Some letters do not represent any segment in a particular word.	through, sign, give, palm
2.	A group of two or more letters can be used to represent a single segment.	think /θ/, chip /tʃ/, ship /ʃ/, bread /e/
3.	A single letter can represent a cluster of two or more segments.	saxophone /ks/, exile /ks/ (or /gz/)
4.	The same letter can represent different segments in different words.	hot /ɒ/, bone /əʊ/, one /wʌ/
5.	The same segment can be represented by different letters in different words.	/uː/ in rule, loop, soup, chew, sue, to, two, shoe, sleuth

The following excerpt from a poem by Richard Krogh vividly illustrates the extent to which English orthography departs from the principle of one sound, one letter (one segment, one symbol).

Beware of heard, a dreadful word
That looks like beard and sounds like bird.
And dead; it's said like bed, not bead;
For goodness sake, don't call it deed!
Watch out for meat and great and threat
(They rhyme with suite and straight and debt).
A moth is not a moth in Mother,
Nor both in bother, broth in brother.

Historical factors

The relationship between symbol and segment in English orthography has not always been so indirect. In fact, the spelling system used throughout England during the Old English period provided a regular set of direct symbol–segment correspondences. The foundation for today's system, it lacked the symbols *j*, *v* and *w*, but made use of four symbols (shown in Table 15.3) that are not part of our current alphabet.

The relationship between symbol and segment in English orthography was significantly disturbed in the Middle English period, as the phonological pattern of the language began to change. To see an example of this, we need only consider the Great Vowel Shift, which dramatically altered the pronunciation of long vowels – converting /iː/ into /aɪ/, /eː/ into /iː/, /aː/ into

Table 15.3   Old English symbols not found in Modern English spelling

Symbol	Name	Segment(s) represented
æ	ash	[æ]
ð	eth	[θ] and [ð]
þ	thorn	[θ] and [ð]
ƿ	wyn	[w]

/eː/, and so on (see Chapter 8). Because Old English orthography used the same symbol for long and short vowels, complications arose when the former vowels changed. Thus, the letter *i*, which had formerly been used only to represent the phonetically similar /iː/ and /i/, ended up representing the very dissimilar /aɪ/ (the descendant of /iː/) and [ɪ] (the descendant of /i/). The end result can be seen in the spelling of *hide* and *hid*, *write* and *written*, *ride* and *ridden*, *wide* and *width*, and many other words.

Additional complications arose following the invasion of England by French-speaking Normans in the eleventh century. The use of English in official documents declined and regional orthographies developed in the absence of a national standard. To make matters worse, scribes who were trained primarily to write French and Latin, introduced a number of conventions from those languages into English spelling. Among those that have survived are the use of 'ch' rather than 'c' for /tʃ/ (*cheese*, *chin*, etc.), 'th' rather than þ (thorn) for /θ/ and /ð/ (*bath* and *they*), and 'c' rather than 's' for /s/ (*grace*, *ice*, *mice*).

Towards the end of the fifteenth century, yet another trend developed – the practice of spelling words in a manner that would reflect their etymological origin. Enduring examples of this influence are found in the spelling of the words *debt*, *doubt*, *receipt*, and *salmon* (formerly spelled *dette*, *doute*, *receite*, and *samon*), all of which were given a 'silent' consonant to make them look more like the Latin words from which they descended.

By the 1500s English orthography had become increasingly irregular and idiosyncratic, with many different spellings in use for the same word. The word *pity*, for example, could be spelled *pity*, *pyty*, *pitie*, *pytie*, *pittie*, and *pyttye*. As printing presses came into greater use and books became more widely available, the need to reform and regularize English orthography became apparent. In the late 1500s and early 1600s, a number of individuals (most notably Richard Mulcaster and Edmond Coote) formulated and published spelling rules, which were gradually adopted by printers and other literate speakers of English. While these rules retained many of the practices discussed above, they at least had the effect of stabilizing English spelling. By the 1700s, English orthography was more or less fixed.

The vast majority of the spelling conventions introduced during this period are still in use today. One of the most famous, proposed by Mulcaster in 1582, involves the use of 'silent' *e* at the end of words to indicate a preceding long (tense) vowel, as in *name*, *same*, and *mate*. Even here, though, there are complications and exceptions. In an earlier period, word-final *e* had represented [ə]. Following the loss of this sound in this position in the fourteenth century, final *e* was used quite haphazardly and was often added to words that would otherwise end in a single consonant. The *e* in the modern spelling of *have*, *done*, and *gone*, which contain lax vowels, reflects this practice and has survived even though it does not comply with Mulcaster's rule.

Obstacles to reform

Over the years, there have been numerous proposals for the reform of English orthography, including those put forward by George Bernard Shaw in Britain and Benjamin Franklin and Noah Webster in America. However, far-reaching reforms are unlikely for a variety of reasons.

For one thing, on close inspection, English spelling turns out to be much less arbitrary – and hence in less urgent need of reform – than appears to be the case at first sight. For instance, a computer analysis of seventeen thousand words which was published a generation ago in America revealed that 84 per cent of the words were spelled with regular letter-to-phoneme correspondences, and that only a mere 3 per cent of the words were spelt in a fashion that was so unpredictable that they would need to be learned by rote. The strong impression of our spelling system being chaotic is due to the fact that many high-frequency, everyday words are spelt irregularly. This is evidenced in Table 15.4. In this table, text frequency indicates the workload a word has in running text in large, representative samples of English while lexical frequency indicates the percentage of words in the lexicon that contain a particular letter–phoneme match.

Table 15.4 Spellings of /e/

Spellings of /e/	Text Frequency	Lexical Frequency	
‹e›	84%	96%	F+
‹ea›	6%	3%	F+
‹ai›	4%	1%	F+
other spellings	1%	1%	

'F+': tends to occur in high frequency words[3].

Moreover, if a programme of spelling reform were agreed on, it would require a long and difficult period of transition. As the following letter to *The Economist* by M.J. Shields illustrates, reform would not be painless even if it took place over a period of many years.

For example, in Year 1 that useless letter 'c' would be dropped to be replased either by 'k' or 's', and likewise 'x' would no longer be part of the alphabet. The only kase in which 'c' would be retained would be the 'ch' formation, which will be dealt with later. Year 2 might reform 'w' spelling, so that 'which' and 'one' would take the same konsonant, wile Year 3 might well abolish 'y' replasing it with 'i' and iear 4 might fiks the 'g-j' anomali wonse and for all.

Jenerally, then, the improvement would kontinue iear bai iear with iear 5 doing awai with useless double konsonants, and iears 6–12 or so modifaiing vowlz and the rimeining voist and unvoist konsonants. Bai iear 15 or sou, it wud fainali be posibl tu meik ius ov thi ridandant leterz 'c', 'y' and 'x' – bai now jast a memori in the maindz of ould doderers – tu replais 'ch', 'sh' and 'th' rispektivli.

Fainali, xen, after sam 20 iers ov orxogrephkl riform, we wud hev a lojikl, kohirnt speling in ius xrewawt xe Ingliy spiking werld . . .

People who knew only the reformed spelling system proposed in this letter would have difficulty reading books written in traditional orthography. Those who wished to read any of the millions of books or articles currently in print would therefore have to either learn the traditional spelling system or have the documents that interested them transliterated into the new orthography.

A third factor militating against serious orthographic reform has to do with the dialectal variation found within English. Because English is spoken in more parts of the world than any other language, it has many different dialects. Any attempt to establish an orthography based on a principle of one segment, one symbol would result in serious regional differences in spelling. For instance, speakers of say, RP, Australian and Boston English would write *far* as *fa* since they do not pronounce syllable-final [r] while the Scots, Jamaicans and most North Americans would retain the old spelling. Speakers of some dialects of Dublin, Jamaican and Newfoundland English would write both *tin* and *thin* as *tin* since they have no /t/–/θ/ distinction. Moreover, while most Scots would have identical spellings for *full* and *fool* (since these words are homophonous in their speech), speakers of English in other parts of the world would spell the words differently to reflect the fact that they pronounce them differently.

Other considerations

Even if considerations relating to practicality and dialectal variation did not rule out major reforms to our orthography, there might still be reasons for retaining at least some of the current irregular spelling conventions.

One advantage of the current system is that it often indicates derivational relationships among words. For instance, if the words *logic* and *logician* or *sign* and *signature* were spelled phonetically, it would be difficult to perceive the relationship between them since the root is pronounced differently in each case.

1)

| logic | [lɒdʒɪk] | logician | [lɒdʒɪʃən] |
| sign | [saɪn] | signature | [sɪgnɪtʃə] |

There are many other such cases where English orthography ignores differences in pronunciation, so that a morpheme can have the same or nearly the same spelling in different words, as shown in Table 15.5 on p. 618.

Examples such as these show that English orthography does not simply try to represent phonemic contrasts. In some cases at least, it ignores morphologically conditioned alternations among phonemes to provide a single representation for the variants of a morpheme. This has led some people to conclude that English orthography is a type of morphophonemic spelling

Table 15.5 Some pronunciation differences not represented by English spelling

electri<u>c</u> – electri<u>c</u>ity	[k] and [s] represented by *c*
inser<u>t</u> – inser<u>t</u>ion	[t] and [ʃ] as *t*
righ<u>t</u> – righ<u>t</u>eous	[t] and [tʃ] as *t*
bom<u>b</u> – bom<u>b</u>ard	ø and [b] as *b*
dam<u>n</u> – dam<u>n</u>ation	ø and [n] as *n*
impre<u>ss</u> – impre<u>ss</u>ion	[s] and [ʃ] as *ss*
all<u>ege</u> – all<u>ege</u>ation	[dʒ] and [g] as *g*; [e] and [ɪ] as *e*
res<u>ig</u>n – res<u>ig</u>nation	ø and [g] as *g*; [aɪ] and [ɪ] as *i*
ch<u>a</u>ste – ch<u>a</u>stity	[eɪ] and [æ] as *a*
prod<u>u</u>ce – prod<u>u</u>ctive	[juː] and [ʌ] as *u*
pl<u>ea</u>se – pl<u>ea</u>sant	[iː] and [e] as *ea*

system, in that it is more sensitive to morphophonemic factors (see Chapter 6, section 1) than to phonemic ones. Once this fact is taken into account, it is possible to see the usefulness of orthographic conventions that allow *c* to stand for either /k/ (*electric*) or /s/ (*electricity*) and *t* to represent /t/ (*react*) or /ʃ/ (*reaction*).

Morphological considerations are reflected in English orthography in other ways as well. Consider in this regard the spelling of the following words.

2)

mess	lapse
crass	dense
kiss	house
miss	mouse

Although these words all end in the phoneme /s/, this segment cannot be represented as a simple 's'. Instead, the 's' is either doubled (when immediately preceded by a lax vowel, as in the first column) or followed by an 'e' (all other cases). This reflects a general rule of English orthography, which reserves word-final 's' for inflectional suffixes (particularly, the plural and the third person singular). Thus, the single 's' is permitted in the word *laps* (the plural of *lap*) but not in *lapse*.

Conversely, a morpheme appearing as part of different words may be consistently represented in the orthography by the same letters – which facilitates its identification – even though the pronunciation may vary. For instance, both the regular plural ending and the third person singular present tense suffix are spelt morphophonemically as *-s* although they have three different phonetic realizations. They are pronounced as /-z/ as in *rules*, /s/ as in *locks* and /-ɪz/ as in *fuses*. Likewise, the regular past tense morpheme is spelt *-ed* although it is pronounced /-d/ as in *opened*, /t/ as in *bumped* and /-ɪd/ as in *wanted*.

Another example of morphological influence is found in the rule that prohibits a final 'll' in polysyllabic words – *plentiful*, *excel*, *repel*, and so on. As the following examples show, this rule is systematically suspended for two types of morphological pattern: compounds (the first column) and derivations consisting of a prefix and its base (the second column).

3)

football	unwell
spoonbill	resell
landfill	recall

Yet another morphologically influenced rule of English orthography converts a post-consonantal 'y' to an 'i' in front of a suffix.

4)

carry	carri-ed
merry	merri-ly
marry	marri-age
jetty	jetti-es
beauty	beauti-ful

The existence of conventions and practices such as these demonstrates that English orthography is much more than a system for phonemic transcription. Its intricacies can be understood only through the careful study of the history and structure of the linguistic system that it seeks to represent.

6

WRITING AND READING

The three types of writing described earlier in this chapter each represent different types of linguistic units – morphemes and words in the case of logographic systems, syllables in the case of syllabaries, and consonants and vowels in the case of alphabets. Because of these differences, each orthography places different demands on readers. We know that different parts of the brain are used for reading logographic writing systems and phonographic orthographies such as syllabaries and alphabets. Because phonological structure is largely irrelevant to logographic writing, people suffering from Broca's aphasia (see Chapter 10) typically do not lose the ability to write and read logograms. However, the use of syllabaries and alphabets can be severely disrupted by this type of brain disorder. There are reports of Japanese patients suffering from Broca's aphasia who are unable to use hiragana or katakana (the Japanese syllabaries), but retain mastery of kanji (the logographic writing system).

Further information about the relationship between language and writing systems comes from the study of the congenitally deaf. Because such people have never heard speech, they have little or no understanding of the phonological units that alphabets represent. Significantly, congenitally deaf individuals have a great deal of difficulty learning to read English. Even after many years of instruction, their reading remains poor and few attain college-level skills in this area.

The type of linguistic unit represented by an orthography also has an effect on how children with normal hearing learn to read. Each system has its own advantages and disadvantages. Children learning Chinese characters, for instance, have little difficulty understanding what each symbol represents, but it takes them many years to learn enough symbols to be able to write and read all the items in their vocabulary. (Knowledge of several thousand separate symbols is required just to read a newspaper.) Even educated people typically know only a few thousand characters and must use dictionaries for new or unfamiliar words.

This problem does not arise in syllabic and alphabetic orthographies. Because languages have far fewer syllables and phonemes than morphemes or words, the entire inventory of symbols can be learned in a year or two and then used productively to write and read new words. This is the major advantage of sound-based orthographies over word-based writing systems.

There is reason to think that children find syllabaries easier to master than alphabets. Children learning syllabaries (such as Japanese *hiragana*) are reported to have fewer reading problems than children learning alphabetic orthographies. Although at least some difficulties encountered by children learning to read English may be due to the complexity of English spelling conventions, Italian and German children learning to use their relatively regular alphabetic orthographies also have reading problems.

The advantage of syllabaries over alphabets for young readers apparently stems from the fact that children have less difficulty identifying syllables than phonemes. One study revealed that 46 per cent of four year olds and 90 per cent of six year olds can segment words into syllables. In contrast, virtually no four year olds and only about two-thirds of all six year olds can segment words into phoneme-size units. Since learning to read involves an understanding of the type of unit represented by written symbols, it is not surprising that syllabaries are generally easier for young children to learn.

Of course, it must be remembered that syllabaries may have disadvantages of other sorts. While syllabic writing is feasible for languages such as Japanese that have a relatively small number of syllable types, it would be quite impractical in English where there are dozens of different syllable structures. Ultimately, an orthography must be judged in terms of its success in representing language for the purpose of reading and writing. There is no doubt that an alphabetic orthography is superior to a syllabary for representing the phonological structure of English.

Summing up

The development of writing has been one of humanity's greatest intellectual achievements. From **pictograms**, and **logograms**, the graphic representation of language has developed through **syllabic** writing to the **alphabet**. This was achieved through the discovery that the sounds of language can be associated with arbitrary graphic symbols. Eventually, this was followed by another discovery that a fairly small number of symbols is sufficient to represent language in written form.

Many of the large number of writing systems found throughout the modern world owe their origin directly or indirectly to the Semitic writing systems of the eastern Mediterranean. As the idea of writing spread, new forms of the symbols were independently invented and sound–symbol correspondences were altered in accordance with language structures. Some writing systems derived from the Graeco-Phoenician tradition are today scarcely recognizable as such, since so little remains of the original signs. In cases where the entire system was invented, perhaps only the idea of writing is traceable to the early traditions.

In all cases, the historical line of development is clear. There seems to be no evidence of a culture that has developed an alphabet and then followed this with the development of, for example, a logographic script. But this cultural line of development does not imply that earlier forms of writing are inferior to alphabetic writing. In the case of languages such as Japanese or Cree, the syllabic writing system is as well suited to the phonological structure of the language as an alphabetic script.

Turning to English, we observe that although the orthography has numerous irregularities, nonetheless normally it observes the phonemic principle of representing the same sound consistently with the same letter (or combination of letters). Yet English spelling has the undeserved reputation of being confused and chaotic. This is largely because most of the irregularities occur in the spelling of some of the most frequently used words. In fact, where the orthography departs from the phonemic principle, usually the motivation is morphophonemic, the result of an attempt to ensure that a morpheme is spelt consistently despite alternations in its pronunciation.

Notes

1   Scholars are still not in agreement on this question. Some claim a single common origin in the Middle East for all writing systems. Others state that certain systems, for example, Mayan writing (see section 4.4), must have emerged independently.

2   Ancient Greek was represented by reversing the direction of writing at the end of each line. If the first line of a text was written right-to-left, the next line continued left-to-right, then right-to-left, and so on. This practice was typical of many old writing systems and is known as **boustrophedon** (Greek for 'as the ox turns'), since it was said to resemble the pattern made by plowing a field.

3   The statistics are from Edward Carney's book cited below and they are based on five frequency counts in four representative English language databases:

1.   Thorndike, E.L. and Lorge, I. 1944. *The Teacher's Wordbook of 30,000 Words*. New York: Teachers' College, Columbia University (derived from approximately 18 million words).

2.   The Brown Corpus of American English. (See Kucera, Henry, and Nelson, W. Francis. 1967. *Computational Analysis of Present-Day American English*. Providence, RI: Brown University Press (approximately 1 million words).)

3.   The Lancaster–Oslo–Bergen Corpus of British English. (See Johansson, S. and Hofland, K. 1989. *Frequency Analysis of English Vocabulary and Grammar*. Oxford: Clarendon Press (approximately 1 million words).)

4.   The Louvain Corpus. (*Analysis of Present-Day English Theatrical Language 1966-1972* (approximately 1 million words).)

Sources   Comprehensive surveys of the development of writing and of the world's writing systems are found in Jensen, Gelb, and DeFrancis (all cited below). The point that pure syllabaries may not exist was called to the authors' attention by Professor W. Poser of the University of Northern British Columbia (personal communication). The idea that writing may have originated in record keeping with clay tokens is taken from Schmandt-Besserat (cited below). The following figures are adapted: from Jensen, 15.1*a*, 15.3, 15.6, 15.10, 15.13, 15.26, 15.29; from Alexander Marshack, *The Roots of Civilization* (New York: McGraw-Hill, 1972), 15.1*b*; from Schmandt-Besserat, 15.2; from DeFrancis (see further references to origins of these figures therein), 15.7 (p. 76), 15.8 (p. 82), 15.12 (p. 180), 15.16 (p. 168), 15.25 (p. 127), copyright © 1989 by the University of Hawaii Press; from M.W. Green, 'Early cuneiform', in Senner (cited below), 15.9 (p. 45); from Sampson (cited below), 15.11; from Frank Moore Cross, 'The Invention and Development of the Alphabet', in Senner (cited below), 15.17 (p. 89). Figures 15.9 and 15.17 are copyright © 1989 by the University of Nebraska Press and reprinted by permission. The sport pictograms in Figure 15.4 are courtesy of the British Sports Council. Figure 15.5 is courtesy of the Blissymbolics Communication Institute, Exclusive licensee, 1982, and is derived from the symbols described in the work, *Semantography*, original copyright C.K. Bliss, 1949.

Reference to Arabic writing is from James A. Bellamy, 'The Arabic Alphabet', in Senner (cited below). John DeFrancis (University of Hawaii), Robert Fisher (University of Toronto/York University), and Brian King (University of British Columbia) all provided insightful and helpful comments (especially regarding Chinese writing), so many, in fact, that we were not able to make use of all of them here. Their views are not necessarily those reflected in the chapter. The discussion of Chinese writing is derived from DeFrancis (cited below), as is Table 15.1 (p. 107); Figure 15.18 was adopted from from Jerry Norman, *Chinese* (Cambridge: Cambridge University Press, 1988); Chinese characters were provided by Lin Zhiqiu. The presentation of Japanese writing also owes to DeFrancis, as well as to M. Shibatani, *The Languages of Japan* (Cambridge: Cambridge University Press, 1990); The hiragana and katakana charts (Figure 15.19) are adapted from Len Walsh's *Read Japanese Today* (Tokyo, Japan: Charles E. Tuttle, 1971) and reprinted by permission of the publisher; examples of Japanese writing were provided by Kazue Kanno. For a discussion of Cherokee writing, see 'Native American writing systems' by W. Walker in C. Ferguson and S. Heath (eds), *Language in the U.S.A.* (Cambridge: Cambridge University Press). Presentation of the Cree syllabary is adapted from D. Pentland, *Nēhiyawasinahikēwin: A Standard Orthography for the Cree Language* (Saskatoon: Saskatchewan Indian Cultural College, 1977). The account of sub-Saharan African writing systems draws on Pierre Alexandre, *An Introduction to Languages and Language in Africa* (London: Heineman, 1972). The examples of Northern Indian pictorial script are from John Marshall, *Mohenjo-Daro and the Indus Civilization* (London, 1931).

The discussion of the history of English spelling is based on *A History of English Spelling* by D.G. Scragg (Manchester: Manchester University Press, 1974). The data in Table 15.4 are from p. 141 of Carney (cited below). The American report on the regularities in a seventeen thousand database is by P.R. Hanna, J.S. Hanna, R.E. Hodges, and E.H. Rudorf, *Phoneme–Grapheme Correspondences as Cues to Spelling Improvement* (Washington, DC: US Department of Health, Education and Welfare, 1966). The examples of spelling rules sensitive to morphological structure come from the book by D.W. Cummings cited below. Data on children's ability to segment words into syllables and phonemes come from I.Y. Liberman, reported in Gibson and Levin (cited below). John Sören Pettersson of Uppsala University commented extensively and helpfully on the entire chapter.

Recommended reading

Carney, E. 1994. *A Survey of English Spelling*. London: Routledge.

Cummings, D.W. 1988. *American English Spelling*. Baltimore, Md.: The Johns Hopkins University Press.

DeFrancis, John. 1989. *Visible Speech: The Diverse Oneness of Writing Systems*. Honolulu: University of Hawaii Press.

Gelb, I.J. 1963. *A Study of Writing*. Chicago: University of Chicago Press.

Gibson, E. and Levin, H. 1975. *The Psychology of Reading*. Cambridge, Mass.: MIT Press.

Gleitman, L. and Rozin, P. 1977. 'The structure and acquisition of reading I: Relations between orthographies and the structures of language.' In *Toward a Psychology of Reading*. Edited by A. Reber and D. Scarborough, pp. 1–53. Hillsdale, NJ: Erlbaum.

Jensen, H. 1970. *Sign, Symbol and Script*. G. Unwin, trans. London: George Allen & Unwin.

Sampson, G. 1985. *Writing Systems: A Linguistic Introduction*. London: Hutchinson.

Schmandt-Besserat, Denise. 1989. 'Two precursors of writing: plain and complex tokens.' In *The Origins of Writing*. Edited by W.M. Senner, pp. 27–42. Lincoln, Neb.: University of Nebraska Press.

Senner, W.M., ed. 1989. *The Origins of Writing*. Lincoln, Neb.: University of Nebraska Press.

Wallace, Rex. 1989. 'The origins and development of the Latin alphabet.' In *The Origins of Writing*. Edited by W. M. Senner, pp. 121–36. Lincoln, Neb.: University of Nebraska Press.

Questions

1. Suppose you are the user of a pictographic writing system that can already represent concrete objects in a satisfactory way. Using the pictographic symbols of your system, propose ideographic extensions of these symbols to represent the following meanings.

   a) hunt   f) cook
   b) cold   g) tired
   c) fast   h) wet
   d) white   i) angry
   e) strength   j) weakness

2. Construct a syllabary for English that can be used to spell the following words. What problems do you encounter?

foe	law	shoe
Slough	slow	slowly
lee	day	daily
sue	pull	shop
ship	loop	food
lock	shock	unlock
locked	shocked	pulled
shops	locker	shod
float	splint	Schweppes

3. How does English orthography capture the morphophonemic alternations in the following words? Begin your analysis with a phonemic transcription of the forms.
   a) hymn   hymnal
   b) part   partial
   c) recite   recitation
   d) reduce   reduction
   e) design   designation
   f) critical   criticize   criticism
   g) analogue   analogous   analogy

4. After discussing the forms in question 3, consider the following forms. Does the spelling system treat all cases of allomorphic variation the same way?
   a) invade   invasion
   b) concede   concession
   c) assume   assumption
   d) profound   profundity

5. Briefly outline the advantages and disadvantages of the three major types of writing that have evolved throughout history.

16

Animal communication

Michael Dobrovolsky

As I listened from a beach-chair in the shade
To all the noises that my garden made,
It seemed to me only proper that words
Should be withheld from vegetables and birds.

❧ W. H. Auden

Communication – the passing on or exchange of information – distinguishes what is living from what is non-living in nature.[1] Communication is found even in the apparently passive world of plants; trees, for example, have been found to pass on information about advancing predators by means of chemical signals. Animals communicate among themselves and with humans so effectively that they are frequently held to use 'language'. But communication and language are not simply two words that mean the same thing. Human language is a specific way of representing the world and passing on information. From the linguist's point of view not just any communication qualifies as language as it is defined in this book.

A question which therefore interests many linguists is whether animals make use of any system of communication that genuinely resembles or approximates human language. Just as the use of communication sets what is living apart from what is non-living, the use of language is often said to set humans apart from all other animals. If animals communicate with a system that is structured like human language, then language as we know it is not the unique property of our species, and we will have to look for other ways of defining humanness. This chapter investigates the ways in which animal communication is like human language and the ways in which it is different.

1

NON-VOCAL COMMUNICATION

One of the most striking things about animal communication is the variety of means with which it is carried out. Animals communicate not only with sounds but with scent, light, ultrasound, visual signs, gestures, colour, and even electricity. From the slime mold to the giant blue whale, all animals appear to have some means of communication. Some non-vocal modes of communication are described here.

Scent   Chemically based scent communication is used by species as different as molds, insects, and mammals. Chemicals used by animals specifically for communicative purposes are called **pheremones**. A female moth signals its reproductive readiness through the release of a pheremone into the air. Only a few of these molecules need to be scented by a male moth for it to start flying zig-zag upwind towards its potential mate. Dogs and other canines leave a urine-based pheremone as an identification mark to stake out their territory, and many non-human primates have specialized scent glands for the same purpose.

Light   Probably the most well-known light user in North America is the firefly or lightning bug. This small flying beetle uses light flashes in varying patterns to signal its identity, sex, and location. Different species of these insects have different and distinguishing light patterns.

Electricity   Certain species of eels in the Amazon River basin communicate their presence and territoriality by means of electrical impulses at various frequencies. Each species signals at a specific frequency range, and the transmitting frequencies, like those of radio and television stations, do not overlap.

Colour   The colour (or colour pattern) of many animals plays an important role in their identification by members of their own species and other animals. The octopus changes colour frequently and this colouring is used for a range of messages that include territorial defence and mating readiness.

Posture   This is a common communicative device among animals. Dogs, for example, lower the front part of their bodies and extend their front legs when they are playful. They lower their whole bodies to the ground when they are submissive. Postural communication is found in both human and non-human primates as well.

Gesture   A gesture may be defined as active posturing. Humans wave their arms in recognition or farewell, dogs wave their tails in excitement, and cats flick their tails when irritated. Many birds perform elaborate gestures of raising and lowering the head or racing back and forth across the water in their mating rituals. Some fish, such as the male stickleback, perform a series of distinct movements in the water as part of their mating ritual.

Facial expressions   These are specific types of communicative gestures. When a male baboon yawns, bares its fangs, and retracts its eyebrows, it is indicating a willingness to fight. A wide and recognizable variety of facial expressions is found among chimpanzees, a number of which are shown in Figure 16.1. Experiments have shown that humans can classify the meanings of these expressions quite accurately. For example, when humans draw back the corners of their mouths into a smile, they are generally indicating co-operation. A non-human primate's smile also indicates non-aggressiveness.

Figure 16.1   Some chimpanzee facial expressions: *a*, anger; *b*, fear—anger; *c*, affection; *d*, frustration—sadness; *e*, playfulness.

2

COMMUNICATION STRUCTURE: THE STUDY OF SIGNS

Underlying the bewildering variety of communicative methods found in nature are certain common elements. An understanding of these is necessary for comparing the differences and similarities among systems of communication.

2.1

Signs

Normally, communication relies on using something to stand for something else. Words are an obvious example of this: you do not have to have a car, a sandwich, or your cousin present in order in order to talk about them – the words *car*, *sandwich*, and *cousin* stand for them instead. This same phenomenon is found in animal communication as well. Instead of fighting over territory, for example, many animals produce sounds or make gestures that threaten and intimidate intruders – the message replaces the attack. Birds utter warning calls that represent the presence of a threat. A threatening animal or human need not be seen by other birds before they take flight – the message replaces visual perception of the threat.

Each of these things that stand for other things is technically known as a **sign**. The sign is a unit of communication structure that consists of two parts: a **signifier**, be it a word, a scent, a gesture, or an electrical frequency, and something **signified** that exists in the real world, and which is mentally represented by the sign – the sign's conceptual content. The real world can be thought of as either external, mental, or emotional, and so what is signified by a sign can be as diverse as a tree, an abstract idea, a perception, or a feeling. Because their content is conceptual, all signs are associated with some **meaning**, such as 'danger', or 'item of furniture with legs and a flat top'. Individual instances of signs are called **tokens**. For example, in the sentence *The baby threw the rattle* there are five word tokens, but only four signs; *the* occurs twice as a token, but it is the same sign in both instances. Figure 16.2 illustrates these distinctions.

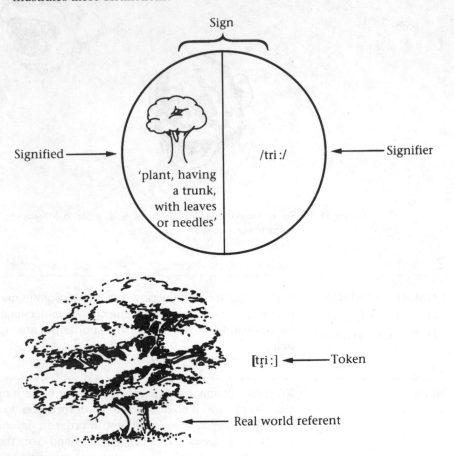

Figure 16.2   A sign.

The study of signs is known as **semiotics**. Semiotics is a field of study that links many diverse disciplines, among them linguistics, anthropology, philosophy, zoology, genetics, literary study, and computer science. An understanding of signs is essential for understanding how messages are transmitted. To understand signs better before proceeding on to analysing animal communication, the next section examines their structure in more detail.

The signifier

A signifier is that part of a sign that stimulates at least one sense organ of the receiver of a message. The phonological component of the word *tree*, represented as /tri:/ and pronounced [tɹi:] is a typical linguistic signifier. A signifier can also be a picture, a photograph, a sign language gesture, or one of the many other words for *tree* in different languages.

The signified

The signified component of the sign refers to both the real world object it represents and its conceptual content.

The first of these is the real world content of the sign, its *extension* or *referent* (Chapter 7, section 1.3) within a system of signs such as English, avian communication, or sign language. In our example, the referent is represented by a drawing since there is no room to include a real tree between the pages of this book. (Of course, the signifier [tɹi:] could also have a picture of a tree as its referent.) It is easiest to think of referents as concepts or persons or things but they may be ideas or feelings as well.

The signified component of a sign also evokes an *intension* (Chapter 7, section 1.3) to users of the system in question . A word for 'tree' evokes concepts that probably include 'plant', 'having a trunk', and 'bearing leaves or needles' in the minds of speakers of any language who are familiar with trees. Animals appear to conceptualize in terms of classes or categories as well. Certain monkeys, for example, distinguish among various types of predators on the basis of size, shape, and motion (see section 5.3)

2.2

Types of signs

Signs can be divided into three basic types, depending on (1) whether the signifier naturally resembles its referent, (2) whether the signifier is directly (causally) linked with the referent in a physical or mechanical sense, or (3) whether signifier and referent are arbitrarily associated.

Iconic signs

Iconic signs, or *icons*, always bear some resemblance to their referent (Figure 16.3). A photograph is an iconic sign; so too is a stylized silhouette of a female or a male on a toilet door. A baboon's open-mouth threat is iconic, resembling as it does the act of biting. Onomatopoeic words like *buzz*, *splat*, and *squish* in English and their counterparts in other human languages are also iconic in that they somewhat resemble what they signify.

[bʌz]

[splæt]

[skwɪʃ]

Figure 16.3   Some iconic tokens: *a*, open mouth threat by a Japanese macaque (*Macaca fustaca*); *b*, park recreation signs; *c*, onomatopoeic words in English.

Icons are widespread in the communication systems of all animals; many postures and gestures that are critical to animal communication are iconic, as are the postures and gestures used by humans. Human linguistic communication, however, does not make extensive use of iconic signs.

Indexical signs

An **indexical** sign, or *index*, fulfils its function by pointing out its referent, typically by being a partial or representative sample of it. Indexes are not arbitrary, since their presence has in some sense been caused by their referent. For this reason it is sometimes said that there is a causal link between an indexical sign and its referent. The track of an animal, for example, points to the existence of the animal by representing a part of it. The presence of smoke is an index of fire.

Most important for our discussion here is a specific kind of indexical sign called a **symptomatic** sign, or *symptom*. Symptomatic signs spontaneously convey the internal state or emotions of the sender and thus represent the sender in an indexical manner. For example, the fact that our body temperature rises when we are ill is a spontaneous reflection of our internal state. When someone steps on our foot and we cry out, the cry is a spontaneous reflection of our internal state and thus constitutes a symptomatic sign.

Since symptomatic signs are spontaneous, we do not consider them to be deliberately selected by the sender for purposes of communication. We do not choose to cry out in pain in the same way as we might, for example, decide to call our dwelling place a *house*, *home*, *dwelling*, or *residence* in the appropriate circumstances. As forms of communication, symptomatic signs are therefore used primarily by the receiver of a message to assess the internal state of the sender. Since senders do not deliberately choose to send the signal, the message is assumed to be essentially out of their control.[2]

Symbolic signs

Symbolic signs bear an arbitrary relationship to their referents and in this way are distinct from both icons and indexes. Human language is highly symbolic in that the vast majority of its signs bear no inherent resemblance or causal connection to their referents, as the words in Figure 16.4 show.

hana	=	?
mazə	=	?
talo	=	?
kum	=	?
berat	=	?

Figure 16.4   Arbitrary sound-meaning correspondence in language.

No phonological property of the words in this Figure gives you any hint as to their possible meaning. (*Hana* means 'flower' or 'nose' in Japanese, *mazə* is 'forest' in Kabardian, *talo* is 'house' in Finnish, *kum* means 'sand' in Turkish, and *berat* means 'heavy' in Indonesian.)

We encounter many other symbolic signs in everyday life. The octagonal shape of a stop sign is symbolic; it bears no inherent connection with the message it helps to communicate. The colours used in traffic signals are symbolic as well; red has no more inherent connection with the act of stopping than yellow.

Mixed signs

Signs are not always exclusively of one type or another. Symptomatic signs, for example, may have iconic properties, as when a dog opens its mouth in a threat to bite. Symbolic signs such as traffic lights are symptomatic in that they reflect the internal state of the mechanism that causes them to change colour. Still, we classify a sign according to its major property: if it resembles its referent, it is iconic; if it is linked to its referent in some causal way or represents it partially in some non-arbitrary way it is indexical (and symptomatic if it spontaneously expresses some internal state); and if its relationship to its referent is arbitrary, it is a symbol.

Signals

All signs can act as **signals** when they trigger a specific action on the part of the receiver, as do traffic lights, words in human language such as the race starter's 'Go!', or the warning calls of birds. Typically, a signal releases more energy in the receiver than it takes for the transmitter to send it. For example, the simple release of a mating pheremone into the wind by a female moth (a symptomatic sign and also a signal) can cause the male to fly as much as four miles in search of her. Signals are very common in animal communication, but only a limited subset of human linguistic activity consists of signalling.

2.3

Sign structure

No matter what their type, signs show different kinds of structure. A basic distinction is made between **graded** and **discrete** sign structure.

Graded signs

Graded signs convey their meaning by changes in degree. A good example of a gradation in communication is voice volume. The more you want to be heard, the louder you speak along an increasing scale of loudness. There are no steps or jumps from one level to the next that can be associated with a specific change in meaning.

Gradation is common in many forms of communication. The hands of most clocks move (or appear to move) in a graded manner, as does the needle of an automobile speedometer. Many animal signs, such as the barking of dogs, are graded as well. A goose has essentially one type of honk, which may become louder and faster as it takes off in flight, but does not become another kind of honk. The gradually increasing fear in the facial expression of the monkey depicted in Figure 16.5 is also a graded sign.

Figure 16.5   Some graded tokens: the facial expressions *a*, *b*, and *c* of the macaque monkey represent just three points on a continuum expressing fear. *a*, is a neutral face; *b*, expresses slight fear; and *c*, expresses extreme fear. Each expression grades into the next. The hands on the clock in *d* express minutes in a graded manner.

Discrete signs

Discrete signs (Figure 16.6) are distinguished from each other by categorical (stepwise) differences. There is no gradual transition from one sign to the next. The words of human language are good examples of discrete signs. There is no intermediate stage between the words *stop* and *go* in English except that which can be expressed by other discrete words or combinations of words, such as 'start to go'. The digital displays of watches are discrete as well, since they progress from one minute (or even second) to the next with no gradation. Traffic lights, too, are discrete signs; there is no gradual shifting from green to yellow to red.

Figure 16.6   Some discrete signs: *a*, digital time display; *b*, traffic lights.

Sign types and structure

All three types of signs – *iconic*, *indexical/symptomatic*, and *symbolic* – can be graded or discrete. A photograph is iconic and discrete, but a threatening canine's gradual baring of its fangs is iconic and graded. Morse code is symbolic and discrete, but a slowly dimming light that signals the beginning of a theatrical performance is symbolic and graded. Symptomatic signs, too, may be discrete (the traffic light again) or graded (the crying of a child or the act of blushing).

It is possible for a discrete sign to be internally graded, and even to slip over into another type by degrees. Human crying, for example, is interpreted by experimental subjects as becoming gradually more like screaming as the audible intake of breath between sobs becomes shorter and shorter. Figure 16.7 illustrates this phenomenon.

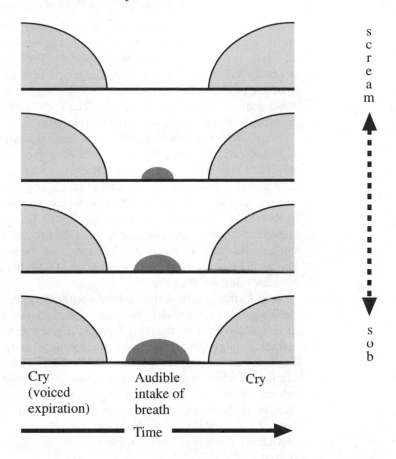

Figure 16.7 The graded continuum from sobbing to screaming (the height of the stippled and blackened areas represents the audibility of the vocalization and the width of its time); both sob and scream are discrete signs, even though each grades into the other.

At the extreme ends of the continuum, there is no difficulty interpreting the sound as one or the other, although it is difficult to say precisely when a 'sob' becomes a 'scream'. Thus we can say that 'sobbing' and 'screaming' are discrete symptomatic signs, but each of them is internally graded, and their gradations overlap. The same is true of many vocalizations in animal communication.

2.4

A view of animal communication

They're like Swiss watches ... they just react. Their genes and hormones and experience tell them what to do. They don't think about it.
> ≈ Zookeeper Ben Beck (on golden lion tamarin monkeys)

Most animal communication, it is claimed, shows little arbitrariness. It is said to be largely iconic and symptomatic and hence not deliberate or conscious in intent, nor symbolic in its sign repertory. For example, if a monkey gives a certain cry in the presence of danger, it is assumed that the monkey is spontaneously signalling its fear by vocalizing, but is not deliberately warning other group members of the danger. The vocalization is interpreted and used by other members of a troop for their own benefit.

It follows from this view of animal communication that the acquisition of communicative systems by animals was in the past assumed to be largely devoid of learning and experience. Rather, it was claimed that the systems are rather strictly limited by genetic inheritance, and in this sense radically unlike human language, the acquisition of which requires exposure to a mature system. This limitation certainly appears to be true in some cases. When raised in isolation, animals as diverse as the fox, the elephant seal, the cat, and certain monkeys develop the full range of vocalizations typical of their species. However, as we will see in section 4 of this chapter, the situation can be more complex than this.

It is further claimed that animal communication is neither conscious nor deliberate. It is not widely believed, for example, that a monkey assesses a situation and then deliberately chooses to warn group members of danger by selecting a sign from a repertoire of meaningful sound symbols at its disposal. For this reason, the term **stimulus-bound** is also used to describe animal communication, since it is often claimed that animal communication only occurs when it is triggered by exposure to a certain stimulus or for certain specific ends. Animals do not communicate about anything but the here and now. As the philosopher Bertrand Russell once noted, 'No matter how eloquently a dog may bark, it cannot tell you that its parents were poor but honest.'

With respect to structure, animal communication is said to show few traces of discrete structuring beyond the obvious fact that one group of symptomatic, graded signals may sound very different from another. Whining in dogs, for example, is clearly different from barking, but both are assumed to be symptomatic, and the two may grade into each other. Combining and recombining of discrete units of structure such as phonemes, morphemes, and words is not characteristic of the way animals communicate. Dogs do not combine whines and barks to produce novel messages.

This does not mean that animal communication consists of random emotional outbursts. Nor does it mean that animal communication does not show structure. Animal communication is both complex and organized. Evolutionary pressure has guaranteed that animal communication is optimally in tune with the survival requirements of each species. The electrical communication of Amazonian eels is an excellent means of communication in muddy waters. The danger whistle of a small, tree-dwelling primate like the galago is ideal for nocturnal communication in dense forest. Small jungle frogs in South America communicate by sticking out their long and colourful legs, ideal for sending messages in the dim and noisy jungle. But jungle frogs do not try new combinations of leg movements in order to come up with an original message, any more than the electric eel recombines frequencies in order to signal something it has never conveyed before. Animal communication appears to be limited in the messages it can convey.

But is animal communication so very unlike human language in all respects? Recent work on animal communication has often focused on its relationship to human linguistic communication. The next sections examine communication among several kinds of animals and compare it with human language.

3

THE BEES

I have no doubt that some will attempt to 'explain' the performances of the bees as the results of reflexes and instincts . . . for my part, I find it difficult to assume that such perfection and flexibility in behavior can be reached without some kind of mental processes going on in the small heads of the bees.

                    ⸱ August Krogh, *Scientific American*

3.1

The system

Forager bees display a remarkable system of communicating the location of a food source to other bees in their hive. When a food source has been discovered, the forager flies back to the hive and communicates information about it by performing special movements (which humans call *dancing*) before other members of the hive. The dancing conveys information about the location of the food source, its quality, and its distance from the hive.

Distance

Distance is conveyed by one of three different dances performed on the wall or floor of the hive (some species have only two different dances, and so may be said to have a different 'dialect'). In doing the round dance, the bee circles repeatedly. This indicates a food source within five metres or so of the hive. The sickle dance indicates a food source from five to twenty metres from the hive. It is performed by the bee dancing a curved figure-eight shape. The tail-wagging dance indicates distances further than twenty metres. In this dance, the bee wags its abdomen as it moves forwards, circles to the right back to its starting point, repeats the wagging forward motion, and circles left. The cycle then begins again.

Direction

The round dance does not communicate direction, presumably since the food source is so close to the hive. The direction of more distant food sources is indicated in the other two types of dance.

As the bee performs the sickle and tail-wagging dances, it is simultaneously indicating the direction of the food source. Bees orient themselves in flight relative to the angle of the sun. When danced on the floor of the hive, the angle of the open side of the sickle dance's figure eight or the angle of the wagging path during the tail-wagging dance indicates the direction of flight. When the dancing is performed on the vertical wall of the hive, it is apparently 'understood' that the top of the hive wall represents the current position of the sun in the sky. During the sickle dance, the angle of the open side of the figure eight relative to the hive's vertical alignment indicates the direction of flight towards the food source relative to the sun. When the bee performs the tail-wagging dance, the angle of its wagging path relative to the hive's vertical angle indicates the path of flight towards the food source relative to the sun. Figure 16.8 illustrates the dances and their manner of indicating the direction of the food source.

Figure 16.8 Bee dancing.

Quality

Quality of the food source is indicated by the intensity of the dancing and the number of repetitions of the circling movements. As the food source is depleted, the dance is performed with less vivacity.

Other factors

These messages are not communicated with perfect accuracy, nor are they the only ones involved in bee communication. Bees also leave a hive-specific pheremone trace at the site of the food source, thereby directing their fellow foragers to the precise location. The bees also carry back traces of the food source odours, which further aid other bees in the search. A complex of communicative modes operating on different channels – a **constellation** – is employed in bee communication. The use of different modalities to communicate the same information is called **redundancy**. Redundancy helps guarantee that communication will succeed in the event one or the other modalities fails or is imperfectly transmitted. All communication systems make use of redundacy, and human language is no exception. For example, the presence of allophonic features such as voicelessness and aspiration on syllable initial voiceless stops, or both length and quality differences on vowels provides redundancy that assists in decoding the signals.

3.2

Bees and humans

How does bee communication compare with human language? The three patterns that the bees dance are not obviously connected with the messages they communicate and so are symbolic in nature (though it is possible to argue that relative distance is iconically represented in that a greater distance covered by the bee in each cycle of the dance corresponds to a greater distance of the nectar source from the hive). The communication of direction is indexical when carried out on the hive floor (in the sense that it points in the direction of flight), and in this sense may be comparable to a human gesture. Bees are, however, capable of transforming this information into a symbolic representation, since they transfer the horizontal flight path to a vertical representation on the hive wall. The expression of food source quality is, in all probability, symptomatic: the more stimulated a bee is by the quality of the food source, the faster it dances.

The total communicative constellation involves other, redundant sources of communication as well, such as pheremones and food source samples. The performance even involves audience participation. During its dancing, the returning bee is expected to provide samples from the food source. If it fails to do so, it may be stung to death.

Bee communication, then, like human language, shows symbolic, indexical, and symptomatic traits, as well as interaction between sender and receiver of the messages. But there is a major difference between the two systems of communication. The topic of bee language is severely constrained. Bees communicate only about food sources. Furthermore, their potential for communication is very limited. Only certain locations of food sources can be conveyed. Bees cannot communicate the notion of up or down. They can be easily tricked into communicating the wrong direction of the food if a strong light source is placed in an incorrect position with relation to the food. They can also be tricked into giving the wrong information about distance to the food source if they are forced to walk or stop several times during their trip. This indicates that they gauge distance by time. The bees show no means of assessing varying information and communicating this fact. Their system of communication appears to be closed ended and limited to a specific number of facts about a specific type of information.

It also appears that bee language is largely innate – that is, there is very little need for a new forager bee to be exposed to the system in the presence of other bees. Foragers on their first flight perform the appropriate dances, although they refine their performance to some extent with time and exposure to other dancing. Their flight orientation to the sun is imperfect at first, but it develops within a few hours.[3]

The innateness of bee dancing has been tested by cross-breeding Austrian bees, which do not perform the sickle dance to express intermediate distance of the food source from the hive, with Italian honeybees, which do. The results of such experiments further support a genetic interpretation of bee communication. In a cross-breeding experiment, the bees that bore a physical resemblance to their Italian parent performed the sickle dance to indicate intermediate distance 98 per cent of the time. The bees that bore a physical resemblance to their Austrian parent performed the round dance to indicate intermediate distance 98 per cent of the time; they did not perform the sickle dance at all. The dance pattern used in a specific situation appears to be inherited from a certain parent along with other more obvious genetic traits.

In 1948, when the Danish physiologist August Krogh made the statement quoted at the beginning of this section, he struck at the widely accepted notion that animal behaviour was either the result of some kind of conditioning, or, in some ill-defined way, instinctive. Much has been learned since then about the enormous quantity of information imparted by genetic transfer. It is now possible to state with a fair degree of certainty that the complex and sophisticated behaviour of bees and other equally remarkable insects is in all probability largely genetically predetermined and, unlike human language, it relies very little on exposure to the mature system in order to be acquired.

4

THE BIRDS

How intelligent is a creature that can amuse himself for 15 minutes by uttering, over and over, the following sounds: uhr, uhr, uhr, Uhr, URH, URH, Wah, Wah, wah, wah, wah.

⇄ Jake Page (on his Amazon Parrot)

4.1

Bird vocalization

Birds, as Jake Page later found out, can do a lot more than utter sounds over and over. Even the parrot, which has been labelled for years as nothing but a stimulus-bound mimic, has been shown to have some capacity for meaningful labelling (although it took one test parrot four years to acquire a vocabulary of eighteen nouns). The parroting of trained birds is generally accepted to be nothing more than non-intentional response to external stimuli arrived at through repetitive conditioning. But recently it has been claimed that certain kinds of parroting have cognitive underpinning of a type shared with primates and perhaps even humans. Research on natural communication among birds has already shed light on parallels in human linguistic communication.

Bird vocalization can be divided into two types, **call** and **song**. Calls are typically short bursts of sound or simple patterns of notes. Songs are lengthy, elaborate patterns of mostly pitched sounds.

Calls

Calls serve very specific functions in the bird community. They typically warn of predators, coordinate flocking and flight activity, express aggression, and accompany nesting or feeding behaviour. The cawing of crows is a typical call. It appears to convey a generalized mobilization to possible danger. When a crow hears cawing, it flies up to a tree if it is on the ground, or flies higher in a tree – or to another tree – if it is already in one. (If there are crows in your neighbourhood, you can test this yourself, as cawing is easy to imitate.)

In some birds, individual calls are associated with specific activities; a danger call is quite different from a call given when birds are grouped in flight. A flight call is generally short, crisp, and easy to locate by other group members. The honking of geese in flight is a typical example of this sort of call. Because it is loud and easy to locate, it is well suited to enable the bird flock to stay together. The call given by small birds when larger avian predators threaten them is very different. It is typically thin and high-pitched. This kind of sound is difficult to locate, and so can be given as a warning without revealing the position of the caller. Such functional utility is typical of bird calls, and in fact, calls that serve the same communicative purpose are often remarkably similar among different species of birds.

Song

Birdsong is different from calling. Although calls are produced year round, singing is largely limited to spring, summer, and autumn. Furthermore, it is generally only male birds that sing.

The main purposes of song are, as far as we know, to announce and delimit the territory of the male and to attract a mate. Birds establish territory for breeding purposes and defend it vigorously. For instance, a male wren sings in order to proclaim its territorial rights (and at the same time listens to the singing of other birds doing the same). If it knowingly intrudes into the territory of another male, it moves silently so as to avoid detection. For, should it be detected by the owner of the territory, it is likely to be aggressively sung at. When this happens, the trespasser normally takes the hint and beats a hasty retreat. If it does not flee immediately, the singing becomes more fierce and it is accompanied by threatening posturing. Thus, the use of song enables male birds to establish and maintain their territory without constant patrolling and fighting. Moreover, once a bird has established its territory, its song serves to attract and maintain contact with a mate. It follows that birdsong is unique from species to species, and even varies to some degree from bird to bird within the same species, since its purposes require species and individual recognition.[4]

In some species, songs are nothing more than a successive repetition of calls. In others, songs consist of complex patterns of pitches – sometimes called syllables – that form longer repeated units or themes. The sometimes elaborate complexity of song structure reflects individual variation among the singers, and, as pointed out previously, serves a specific purpose. Figure 16.9 (overleaf) shows a **spectrogram** of the song of the European Robin (*Erithacus rubecula*) – a spectrogram is a visual display of the frequencies, pitch and intensity which make up a sound (see Chapter 17, section 1). Note how the different subsections of the song are distinct and recognizable. There is also some evidence that sections of a song are combined in different orders by certain birds, but there is no evidence that recombination is associated with different meanings.

Figure 16.9 Spectrogram of a robin song.

Avian dialects

There is evidence for both song and call dialects among bird species. Researchers even speak of avian *isoglosses* (lines drawn on a map to indicate shared characteristics among dialects; see Chapter 14, section 3.1) that are based on variations in the melody of song syllables or themes (see Figure 16.10). The reason for the existence of dialects is still unclear; it may be no more than a reflection of individual avian variation in song and call learning. If it is, we are led to an intriguing issue in the relationship of bird vocalization to human language – the question of how bird vocalizations are acquired.

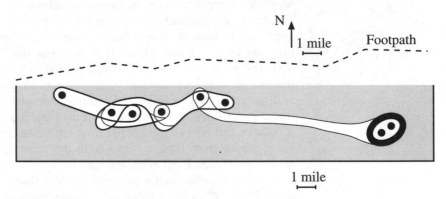

Figure 16.10 Avian isoglosses: call patterns of male Hill Mynas (the black dots indicate myna groups; the shaded area indicates forested hills and the unshaded, open plain; the heavier the black lines, the more song characteristics are shared by the group within its boundaries).

4.2

Birds and humans

The acquisition of call and song by birds shows interesting parallels with recent hypotheses about the acquisition of language by human children (see Chapter 12). Though a great deal of bird vocalization – particularly calls – appears to be innate, there is much that appears to be acquired. Studies of avian dialects have shown that birds reared in the same nest acquire different song dialects when they live in different dialect areas. It also appears to be the case that singing ability is lateralized in the left brains of birds, as is linguistic ability in humans. Still more significant for linguistic study is the fact that some birds must acquire the species-specific characteristics of their song within a certain timespan or critical period.

A number of bird species do not develop fully characteristic songs if they are deprived from hearing them during the early stages of their lives. The chaffinch (*Fringilla coelebs*) is one such bird. If chaffinches are reared in isolation, they sing, but replicate only in a general way the typical song of the species. If young chaffinches are reared away from fully developed singers, but with other young chaffinches, the entire experimental community develops an identical song. Finally, chaffinches that have been exposed to only some part of the fully developed song (those that are captured in the autumn of the first year of life) will, the following spring, develop a song that is partially typical but not completely well formed.

These experiments indicate that there are some songbirds that have both an innate and a learned component in their song. The innate component predisposes them to perform a general song that is extremely simplified. This has been called a **template** or a blueprint. Only exposure to the fully formed song of the species will enable them to produce the correct song. (Exposure to other song causes some species to imitate in this direction; other species simply do not acquire anything they are exposed to unless it is their own species-characteristic song.) Finally, it is clear that certain birds do not acquire their characteristic song in a brief span of time, but that several seasons of exposure are required. The evidence from songbird studies, while not transferable directly to humans, gives strong support to the idea that a combination of innate and learned components is one way that the acquisition of complex behaviour takes place in nature.

5

NON-HUMAN PRIMATES

Some animals share qualities of both man and the four-footed beasts, for example, the ape, the monkey, and the baboon.

Aristotle, *On Animals*

Fascination with non-human primates goes far back in human history. Their social behaviour has long been seen as an amusing (and sometimes instructive) parody of human behaviour. Since the recent establishment of the fact that we are closely related genetically to these animals – some 99 per cent of our genetic matter is shared with chimpanzees and gorillas – the resemblance of their behavioural, social, and communicative traits to ours has been seen as more than an amusing counterpart to human activity. Recently, the question of our shared cognitive, and especially linguistic, ability has become more important; it is thought that a better understanding of non-human primates may shed light on the evolution of human social and cognitive abilities.

Primates form a large class of mammals, which range from the tiny Tarsier to the imposing Mountain Gorilla. Among the non-human primates, some are nocturnal, some diurnal in their activity cycle. Some are solitary, some form part of complex social groups. Many are tree-dwelling, and many are ground-dwelling. Some are quadrupeds, and some show periods of bipedal locomotion. Figure 16.11 shows one widely accepted classification of the primates.

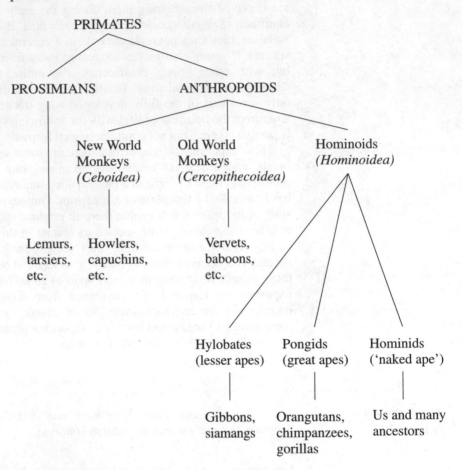

Figure 16.11 The primates.

The prosimians are an evolutionarily early group found on the island of Malagasy, in sub-Saharan Africa, and in Southeast Asia. New World Monkeys range from Mexico through South America. Among them are the only primates with prehensile (grasping) tails. Old World Monkeys include the many tree- and ground-dwelling species of Africa and the Far East. The larger non-human primates – baboons, chimpanzees, and gorillas – are not native to North or South America. Baboons, large, mainly ground-dwelling primates, are found from central to northern Africa. They show a high degree of social organization, intelligence, and aggressiveness. The hominoids include the agile gibbons, solitary orangutans (both found only in Southeast Asia), the large but peaceful gorillas, chimpanzees, and humans.

The validity of studies of communication among captive primates has been criticized because the animals' social existence is highly limited and compromised in zoos. Studies of non-human primate communication have largely left the zoo and laboratory and moved into the animals' natural habitat. While careful observation of non-human primate communication is still the basis of this work, the use of playback experiments, in which tape recordings of natural calls are played back over hidden loudspeakers, has led to a greater understanding of the communicative systems of these animals.

In the next section, we first turn our attention to non-human primate communication in the wild. It is there that we can gain an initial understanding of how forms of non-human primate communication resemble or differ from our own in terms of function and structure.

5.1
Some functions of non-human primate communication

Although the societal existence of even the most gregarious non-human primate is relatively simple when compared to that of humans, primates communicate for many different reasons.

Typical non-human primate communication serves to mark and announce territory, to warn other group members of danger, to seek or maintain contact with a mate or other members of the species, and to interact with members of the troop or species in various ways we can call 'socializing'. Socializing vocalizations are particularly important in mother–child bonding and in primate groups with a complex and hierarchical social structure. In these groups, it is important to know which members have a higher or lower rank so that group members can behave accordingly in their presence. Vocalization is a key factor in maintaining this behaviour.

As we briefly survey some aspects of the structure of non-human primate communicative systems, we will also refer to the ways in which structure and function are linked.

5.2
Prosimian communication

Prosimian communication shows a small repertoire of sounds that are patterned into discrete groups. The lemur (*Lemur catta*) of Malagasy is a typical prosimian with respect to its vocal communication system. It has been described as making essentially two types of vocalization, noises and calls, each of which shows some grading. The vocalizations appear to be symptomatic. They are classified in Table 16.1 (overleaf); quasi-phonetic descriptions like *spat* should be interpreted as onomatopoeic.

Each graded set of sounds is used in a circumscribed range of situations. The calls, in particular, are limited to threat or fear encounters. They seem to form a graded series, ranging from the *light spat* to the *bark* in intensity.

A small repertoire of distinct vocalizations is the norm among prosimians. The slow loris (*Nycticebus coucang*), an Asian prosimian, is reported to have no more than five calls.

Table 16.1 Lemur vocalization

	Noises		Calls	
Sound	Context	Sound	Context	
Single click	in response to strange objects	Light spat (yip)	when driving off threatening inferiors	
Clicks, grunts	during locomotion, or for friendly greeting	Spat	when crowded or handled roughly	
Purr	while grooming	Bark	when startled	

5.3

Monkeys

The study of communication among the many varieties of New and Old World Monkeys is too vast for this chapter. An oversimplified picture reflects what most researchers agree is primarily a symptomatic system, but one that shows a larger number of signs, with more gradation among them, than does the communication of prosimians.

One study of the Bonnet Macaque (*Macaca radiata*), a South Asian monkey, presents a system of twenty-five different basic patterns that are used in various social interactions, including contact, agonistic encounters, foraging, greeting, sexual contact, and alarm giving. These vocalizations are determined by correlating observation with spectrographic analysis; descriptive labels are also given to the vocalizations, such as *whoo*, *rattle*, *growl*, *whistle*, and *bark*. These basic patterns are described as grading into each other. It is also claimed that they occur in combinations. There is no evidence, however, that these recombinations mean anything novel when they occur.

The communication systems of many monkeys appear to be genetically determined. This has been established by raising newborns in isolation. However, this statement cannot be made for all monkeys. For some monkeys, input from the adult system appears to be required. The study of one small monkey has suggested that not all monkey vocalizations are symptomatic, and that experience and learning can play a role in the acquisition of the communicative system.

The East African vervet monkey (*Cercopithecus aethiops*) is said to have three distinctive and arbitrary calls that announce the presence of either eagles, snakes, or large mammals posing a threat. These calls are associated with different responses by the monkeys. When they hear the eagle call, the monkeys look up or run into the bushes. The snake call causes them to look down at the ground near them. The mammal alarm sees them run up into the trees, or climb higher in a tree if they are already in one.

These findings, which appear to have been well established by experimentation since they were first reported in 1967, suggest that not all non-human primates rely strictly on symptomatic signals to communicate or to trigger behaviour in other monkeys. It is claimed rather that the vervets assess the potential danger situation and then choose a specific call with a clearly defined referent to announce the danger. Furthermore, each call is a vocalization signifier that is arbitrarily linked with its referent. Other monkeys respond appropriately to the calls without necessarily observing the danger themselves. All this taken together suggests a cognitive ability for classification of objects in the world and an ability to link this classification system to arbitrary sounds for purposes of intentional communication (see Figure 16.12, on the next page).

The vervet may not be an isolated case. Goeldi's Monkey (*Callimico goeldii*), found in South America, is cited as having five different alarm calls, three of which are used when terrestrial predators approach, and two of which have been heard in the presence of large birds. Such observations support the claim that monkeys have the cognitive capacity to associate perceptual categories with vocalizations.

The acquisition of these signals among vervets is interesting. Infant vervets appear to distinguish innately among broad classes of mammals, snakes, and birds, but they also give the 'eagle call' when other birds appear and the 'leopard call' when other terrestrial mammals appear. Adults distinguish between leopards and less dangerous mammals, and eagles and less dangerous birds (as well as between snakes and sticks), and it is claimed that this ability must be perfected through experience. This once again suggests that a mixture of innate components and learning is typical of the way communication systems are naturally acquired.

5.4

Gibbons, orangutans, and chimpanzees

Since the higher primates are close genetic relatives of humans, it is natural to expect their vocal communication to resemble that of humans. Perhaps surprisingly, communication among the higher primates does not show much indication of discrete vocal signs that could be interpreted as resembling human words. Rather, the communication systems of these animals are made up of groups of graded vocal signs.

Gibbons and orangutans

Gibbons display an interesting form of vocal interaction known as duetting. **Duetting**, the interchange of calls in a patterned manner between two members of a species, is found among certain birds, bats, and even antelopes. Duetting is, however, atypical of primate communication – among the hominoids, only gibbons perform it. Recent playback experiments show that duetting among gibbons serves to maintain spacing among territories much as does birdsong (see section 4.1). Playback of duetting within a gibbon's territory will cause it to approach the apparent source of the vocalizations, possibly with the intent of driving the intruders out. Playback of singing and duetting from outside a group's territory only infrequently evokes a response. Recognition of individuals does not appear to play a role in these vocalizations.

Unlike gibbons, which live in family groups, orangutans largely keep to themselves (except for mother–child pairs). Among the solitary forest males, loud calls serve a territorial and spacing function. These calls also identify the

Figure 16.12 Responses of vervet monkeys to specific predators.

individuals who produce them. High-ranking males approach calls, presumably to confront the intruder, while low-ranking males stay away from areas where they hear the calls of high-ranking males. These calls are, in other words, indexes, which stand in for the individual animals themselves, and orangutans must identify and assess each of these calls before acting on them.

Chimpanzees

Chimpanzees vocalize with a number of graded calls. As many as sixteen types have been reported. Some of these appear to show rather specific referents. Chimps typically hoot to signal location (a sound that carries well in dense forest). Hooting is also used in greeting or when chimps are excited about something. Another typical vocalization is known as rough grunting and is given in the presence of a favourite food source. A recent experiment has led to the claim that transmission of signs from one generation to the next plays a role in the acquisition of certain signs among chimpanzees. (For more on tradition, see section 7.1.)

'Language' in the wild

Especially among highly socialized species, non-human primate vocalizations all show a great deal of variation. There is every indication that their vocalizations form part of a constellation of redundant communicative acts including gesture, posture, gaze (eye 'pointing'), and the expression of affect, all of which must be interpreted by other troop members. The obvious complexity of communication systems among these animals suggests that the level of mental activity devoted to communicative behaviour is quite high.

Despite the high degree of intelligence and social organization these animals demonstrate, there is very little evidence for arbitrary relationships between sound and meaning among apes. Even more significantly, there is no evidence of recombining various sections of a message to form new messages. Nothing that parallels the phonemic or morphological recombination of human language has been discovered in the natural communication systems of non-human primates.

It is possible that the lack of parallels with human linguistic communication in species closely related to our own may be due to the nature of their social organization. The small groups or family units typical of chimpanzees and gorillas living in a food-rich environment may not have required the development of any other mode of communication. What has evolved is suited to their needs. This does not mean, however, that our near-relatives do not possess any of the cognitive abilities necessary for using a system of communication akin to human language. There is some evidence, for example, of left hemisphere development of the type associated with human linguistic ability. A number of recent experiments with non-human primates have attempted to determine the extent – if any – of their linguistic abilities.

6

TESTING NON-HUMAN PRIMATES FOR LINGUISTIC ABILITY

Much attention has been paid in recent years to non-human primates who communicate with humans through the use of sign language.

Controlled testing of the possible shared linguistic abilities of non-human primates and humans goes back to 1948 when two psychologists attempted to train Viki, a young chimpanzee, to say meaningful words in English. With great effort, Viki learned to approximate the pronunciations of a few words like *cup* and *papa* over a period of fourteen months. Unfortunately, the experiment was doomed to failure from the start, since the vocal fold structure and supralaryngeal anatomy of the chimpanzee is unsuited for producing human sounds.

Chimpanzee vocal folds are fatty and less muscular than those of humans, and the neurological pathways between the brain and vocal folds are less developed than in humans. The chimpanzee's epiglottis extends well up into the throat cavity, which lessens the range of sounds it can produce. Finally, the whole larynx–tongue linkage rests higher in the chimpanzee throat, which results in limitations on its human-like sound production as well. In short, the chimpanzee is unsuited for human speech, and concentrating effort on teaching it to articulate words was distracting from the more provocative question: to what extent is the chimp mentally capable of linguistic behaviour?

6.1

Some experiments

An experiment conducted from 1965 to 1972 by Allen and Beatrice Gardner with a young female chimpanzee named Washoe created a new perspective on non-human primate linguistic abilities. The Gardners attempted to raise Washoe much as a human child would be raised, and to teach her American Sign Language (ASL), on the assumption that it was a genuinely linguistic form of communication (of which there is little doubt). Given the known manual dexterity of chimpanzees, it was felt that sign language might provide a window on chimpanzee linguistic abilities.

Washoe

The Gardners' reports claim that Washoe communicates intentionally with arbitrary signs in a creative manner, and thus shows the rudiments of human linguistic ability. Washoe learned to produce approximately one hundred and thirty signs over a period of three years. (She recognized many more.) Most significantly, it is claimed that Washoe spontaneously combined these signs to form novel utterances. She is reported to have signed WATER BIRD (in this chapter, signs are indicated by small capital letters) on seeing ducks. Washoe also is said to have spontaneously produced BABY IN MY CUP when her toy doll was placed in her drinking cup and she was asked WHAT THAT?

Washoe was the first, but not the only chimpanzee to be taught sign language. The results have suggested to some linguists that chimpanzees show greater ability to associate arbitrary tokens with referents than was believed earlier, and that they demonstrate rudimentary syntactic behaviour.

Other chimps, gorillas, and an orangutan that have been taught ASL since the pioneering Washoe experiment are reported to have performed even better.

Nim

Still other experiments in teaching chimpanzees sign language have produced contradictory results. The achievements of a chimpanzee named Nim have been interpreted by his teachers as consisting of frequent repetitions of a small number of all-purpose signs (NIM, ME, YOU, EAT, DRINK, MORE, and GIVE) that were largely appropriate to any context. These signs are said to have made up almost 50 per cent of Nim's production. Furthermore, there are no reports of his engaging in creative combining of signs.

6.2

Non-signing experiments

Much of the criticism levelled at Washoe's performance centred on the relative informality of her training and claims that ASL is a loose communicative system that does not require a strict adherence to syntactic rules. Two very different experiments with chimpanzees attempted to forestall such criticism.

Lana

A chimpanzee called Lana was trained to fulfil her needs for food, fresh air, grooming, and entertainment (in the form of slide shows) by requesting these from a computer-controlled apparatus. Communication with the computer was carried out by means of a simple rule-governed language of nine arbitrary symbols. The symbols were on buttons that lit up and activated the computer when pressed. Any deviation from the syntactic rule system invented for the experiment failed to get the desired responses from the computer. Human experimenters communicated directly with the chimpanzee through use of the same symbols. Lana learned to label and request food and other amenities through the computer. The experiment with Lana was criticized because she was said to have learned simple reflex associations among symbol, sequence, and reward. There was no evidence that she had acquired the rules underlying the sequences, and so could not be said to have displayed linguistic abilities.

Sarah

Another now classic experiment involved training a young female chimp named Sarah to manipulate arbitrary plastic symbols in a predetermined manner in order to obtain rewards. Sarah had to learn to use word order correctly, since only the order shown in Figure 16.13 would obtain a banana.

Figure 16.13   Arbitrary symbols used in experiments with the chimpanzee Sarah.

She also seemed to show sensitivity to more abstract words like *if/then* in sentences like that shown in Figure 16.14.

Figure 16.14 A 'sentence' understood by Sarah.

But was Sarah learning aspects of human language or was she, too, trained? Humans who are taught similar skills perform them as well as Sarah but find it difficult to translate them into human language. They approach the exercise of moving plastic symbols around to obtain a reward as a puzzle that is not necessarily associated with language. It has been suggested that Sarah was performing the same kind of puzzle solving and not demonstrating human-like linguistic capacities.

These studies have led to a resurgence of interest in human–animal communication. Language-using dogs, cats, pigs, and even turtles have been reported for thousands of years. The basis of much of the current criticism of all of these experiments rests on the performance of a horse in Germany at the turn of this century.

6.3	
The Clever Hans controversy	*When I play with my cat, who is to say that my cat is not playing with me?* ❧ Michel de Montaigne, *Essays*

In 1904, a Berlin school teacher named Wilhelm von Osten claimed to possess a horse that showed evidence of a human-like capacity to think. His horse, Clever Hans (*der kluge Hans*), could supposedly calculate and convey messages by tapping out numbers or numbered letters of the alphabet with a front hoof or by nodding his head.

Experimentation by a sceptical scientist, Oskar Pfungst, eventually showed that Clever Hans was not so much a creative thinker as a careful observer. The horse perceived cues that indicated that he had performed correctly. For example, van Osten involuntarily moved his head very slightly when a correct answer had been reached. This movement was outside the normal perceptual range of human observers (less than five millimetres), but the horse had learned to associate it with the correct answer. When observers did not know the answer to a question, or when Clever Hans was blindfolded, he failed to perform his miracles.

Clever Hans's performance resulted from **dressage**, a type of interaction between trainer and animal that depends on the animal's interpreting subtle cues given by the trainer. The Clever Hans phenomenon is an excellent example of dressage, which need not involve conscious communication on the part of humans. The highly developed perceptual ability displayed by Clever Hans is common to many animals. Many scientists believe that chimpanzees and gorillas that use sign language and perform other language-like tasks are demonstrating nothing more than the Clever Hans phenomenon.

The position is explained as follows. Human trainers want very much for their animal charges to succeed. This desire is translated into involuntary actions, which can be seized on by the animal due to its keen perceptual abilities; it is these cues that determine the animal's performance. A typical example of this is pointed out in Washoe's signing of BABY IN MY CUP which has been recorded on film (*First Signs of Washoe*). A careful examination of this interchange shows that the human repeatedly holds out the object to be signed and then points rapidly at the cup. Probably none of this cueing was intentional on the human's part.

Some so-called linguistic activity may be the result of factors other than the Clever Hans effect. Some reports of creative signing, such as Washoe's WATER BIRD, are dismissed as reflex signing that shows no intention of forming combinations on the part of the chimp. Reports of the gorilla Koko's displays of wit (she occasionally produces the opposite sign of the one requested, such as UP for DOWN) are also considered to be exaggerated or simply wishful thinking by researchers.

Some reports of linguistic behaviour are attributed to inaccurate or non-systematic observing. (For example, if Washoe answered 'WHAT'S THAT' with any noun sign, the answer was considered correct.) Other reports are attributed to overoptimistic interpretation of signs. (Koko is reported to intentionally produce 'rhyming' signs – those that are very similar to the one asked for or expected.) In short, those who do not view chimpanzee signing and symbol manipulation as linguistically relevant claim that this behaviour is more simply explained as arising from straightforward response–reward association and/or from dressage, and not a reflection of linguistic competence. As one researcher noted, training two pigeons to bat a ping-pong ball across a net does not mean that the birds know the rules of ping-pong.

6.4

The great ape debate

We believe that . . . there is no basis to conclude that signing apes acquired linguistic skills.

                 ❧ Mark S. Seidenberg and Laura Petitto

When these projects [Washoe, Lana, Sarah, and Nim] are taken together, it can be seen that chimpanzees are within the range of language behavior of humans and therefore have the capacity for language.

                 ❧ Roger Fouts

Researchers involved with the chimpanzees and gorillas who are being taught to sign attest to the emotional bonds they form with them, and also emphasize that in using human language, such bonds are a prerequisite to normal communication. They strongly insist that apes communicate spontaneously and creatively with humans. Roger Fouts, who has spent many years in close contact with Washoe and other chimpanzees, puts the case this way.

I reject the notion that there is some ultimate cut-and-dried criterion that distinguishes language from all other social and cognitive behaviors, or that distinguishes human communication and thought from that of all other species.

It is important to emphasize that most researchers sympathetic to the idea that apes show human linguistic abilities employ a broader definition of language than many of their critics. For these researchers, language use includes socialization and the use of communicative constellations.

For many linguists critical of these projects, a definition of language that rests on its social or functional aspects is unacceptable. In much current linguistic thinking, language is viewed as independent of the purposes it serves. This view, sometimes called the *linguistic autonomy hypothesis*, equates language with grammar – the 'mental system that allows humans to form and interpret the words and sentences of their language', to quote from Chapter 1 of this text. It follows from this definition that linguistic ability in non-human primates can only be claimed to exist if the animals show, at the very least, spontaneous and intentional symbolic signs that are manipulated in a rule-governed manner.

Symbol use

All researchers who support the claim that non-human primates can employ intentional symbolic communication deny that cueing is a major factor in the apes' abilities, although most admit that it might be present on occasion. In order to refute charges of the Clever Hans effect, researchers employ a strict form of experimentation.

Primate sign language researchers try to avoid cueing by the use of a **double-blind test**. In this test, the ape is shown objects or pictures of objects that are invisible to a second human researcher. The ape's signing is then recorded by this researcher and the record is interpreted by a third researcher who has not seen the signing. In this way, unintentional cueing is said to be avoided.

Critics of this research claim that even double-blind tests can be affected by human–animal interaction. First, the apes must be taught to perform the task. During this process they may be conditioned to provide certain responses. Second, it is difficult to avoid any human–animal interaction during these tests, and this could lead to subliminal cueing. As we have also seen, many claims for symbolic behaviour on any ape's part have been dismissed as stimulus–response conditioning – the mere aping of behaviour in order to obtain a reward. We still have no way of knowing whether Washoe's use of a sign sequence like TIME-EAT indicates that she has a concept of time.

Ongoing work with two chimpanzees named Sherman and Austin has led to their exchanging signed information about classes of objects such as 'tool' and 'food'. These experiments are claimed to have circumvented any reliance on the Clever Hans effect and shown that signing apes can communicate about whole referential classes of items rather than be bound to simple stimulus–response association with individual items such as 'banana' and 'ice cream'.

Careful control of experiments has convinced some linguists that limited symbol use has been exhibited by some apes, perhaps even up to the level of a two-year-old human child. But some linguists who allow that a level of symbolic signing has been achieved have also denied this is a critical feature for defining language. Rather, rule-governed, creative symbol combinations and syntactic behaviour are said to be the critical features.

Creative signing?

A feature of language that sets it apart from most animal communication is its creativity – the fact that humans can use language to create novel messages. Sign researchers claim that such creativity is present in the many instances of novel combinations signed by the animals.

An early and famous instance of alleged creative signing was Washoe's WATER BIRD (referred to in section 6.3), which she signed on seeing a duck in the water for the first time. Such alleged compound signing behaviour has been noted in various signing apes. Some of the gorilla Koko's novel combinations are provided in Table 16.2.

Table 16.2   Some sign combinations produced by Koko

Compound	Referent
MILK CANDY	rich tapioca pudding
FRUIT LOLLIPOP	frozen banana
PICK FACE	tweezers
BLANKET WHITE COLD	rabbit-fur cape
NOSE FAKE	mask
POTATO APPLE FRUIT	pineapple

Critics say either that such combinations are accidental or that the ape produces the two signs independently of each other and thus does not display true compounding. There is no doubt that Washoe signed both WATER in the presence of water, and BIRD in the presence of the bird, but there is no consistent indication from her other output that she has a rule of compound formation.

It has been claimed that in more recent and carefully controlled experiments with a pygmy chimpanzee (*Pan pansicus*) named Kanzi, statistically significant differences in the spontaneous ordering of symbols has been observed. The conclusion that has been drawn from this is that Kanzi has exhibited a form of grammatical rule. For example, Kanzi frequently used combinations of signs that link two actions, such as CHASE HIDE, TICKLE SLAP, and GRAB SLAP. In fifty-four out of eighty-four cases, the first sign corresponded to the invitation to play and the second to the type of play requested.

Is there syntax?

Claims for syntactic behaviour among signing apes have also been made. Even though it has been claimed that the general (though loose) syntax of ASL is copied by the apes, reports on the signing chimp Nim (section 6.1) showed that the animal had no consistent word order patterning. In fact, Nim's syntactic output was structurally incoherent. His longest sentence is reported as GIVE ORANGE ME GIVE EAT ORANGE ME EAT ORANGE GIVE ME EAT ORANGE GIVE ME YOU.

Koko is said to have developed her own word order in noun phrases – the adjective consistently follows the noun it modifies. It is difficult to prove claims for syntactic behaviour in animal signing, because (all) signing forms constellations with facial expression and gestures and so may be said to reduce the need for rigorous syntax. Koko, for example, can sign a meaning like 'I love Coca-Cola' by hugging herself (the sign for *love*) while signing Coca-Cola at the same time with her hands.

In spite of what is now widely considered to be the disappointment of the earlier studies (possibly because they expected too much), some controlled experimentation continues. Recently, the pygmy chimpanzee Kanzi is reported to have produced significant (though not wholly consistent) differences in the placement of animate agents in sign combinations. When another chimpanzee named Matata was grabbed, Kanzi produced GRAB MATATA, but when Matata performed an action such as biting, Kanzi produced MATATA BITE.

Lingering doubts

As we have seen, supporters of language use among apes have not yet proved to the satisfaction of all their critics that genuine symbolic behaviour is occurring, much less anything resembling rule-governed creativity in compounding or syntactic patterning.

Researchers who see the results of ape studies as positive evidence for linguistic ability in these animals claim that their opponents keep raising the stakes every time a chimp or a gorilla accomplishes something that could be interpreted as linguistic behaviour. Possible evidence of symbol use or creative signing as evidence of linguistic ability is dismissed by these opponents as unsurprising or irrelevant.[5] Supporters of ape studies note that such critics are motivated by a long tradition of viewing animals as 'organic machines' that are locked into specific behavioural and communicative repertoires by their genetic inheritance, and that can therefore only respond automatically to a given situation with a narrow range of signs. Their own view, they claim, is at once more ancient and more modern in granting animals a certain as yet unknown degree of intentionality and cognitive ability in their behaviour.

In general, recent experiments have established more convincingly than earlier ape studies that symbol use and referential behaviour form part of the cognitive makeup of some non-human primates. Taken together with naturalistic studies, they help circumvent the claim that all evidence of symbol use among non-human primates is caused by the Clever Hans phenomenon.

Nonetheless, questions about creative sign combination and syntactic use still remain. Kanzi's alleged rules have been equated with those of a two-year-old child. But the major difference between a chimpanzee and a child at that point in their lives is that the elementary grammar of a two year old is the first hint of a full system that is rapidly developing and that will be in place in a matter of a few more years. While Kanzi's communicative behaviour constitutes interesting evidence for a chimpanzee's awareness of the world, it does not unequivocally imply a system of grammar. It has been noted, for example, that Kanzi's 'rules' are often bound up with a natural order of action or relationships (as when the sign GRAB precedes the sign SLAP).

The apparent lack of rule-governed behaviour among signing apes (especially in the realm of syntax) remains to critics of these experiments the linguistic hurdle that the animals have not overcome. It is certain that apes do not show syntactic behaviour to any degree that humans do (for example, embedding is completely lacking) and many linguists claim that without such behaviour, the apes cannot be said to be using language. Syntax, in the strict linguistic sense, provides a system of rules capable of producing a sentence of potentially infinite length (even though in practice this is never required). There is no evidence that primates have shown this ability.

6.5

Implications

Critics of the ape studies have at this time carried the day. Funding sources for ape–human research have dried up, and most of the subjects have lost their privileged relationships with humans and been returned to zoos. But the severe reaction to the apparent failure of ape–human linguistic communication research has had positive effects on the field as well. Recent trends – the number of experiments on animal cognition in the wild, and the more carefully controlled experiments with apes like Kanzi – are leading us slowly closer to new ideas on this age-old issue.

The real significance of these experiments in ape–human linguistic communication goes far beyond popular enthusiasm about what an ape might say to us if it could talk. It has often been pointed out that an animal's view of the world must be totally unlike our own. It is perhaps not surprising that apes appear to communicate largely about their fundamental emotions and such basic needs as food and play.

In time, this research may help illuminate what is truly unique about human linguistic ability. As we have seen, many linguists claim that there is no connection between the communicative behaviour of non-human primates and the complex structures of human language. The opposing view claims that the capacity for true grammatical activity can be found in non-human primates. This implies that what we call language reflects a cognitive difference in *degree* and not in *kind* between humans and these animals. The optimistic view is that such research may ultimately shed light on the evolutionary origins of our species and its language use by demonstrating the degree of shared cognitive abilities between ourselves and our nearest genetic relatives.

7

COMPARING COMMUNICATION SYSTEMS: DESIGN FEATURES

Throughout this chapter, we have emphasized the distinction between communication and language. In this final section, we will compare human linguistic communication with what we have learned about systems of animal communication.

7.1

The features

Differences and similarities between human language and natural animal communication systems can be highlighted by comparing essential characteristics of the systems. These characteristics are called **design features**, and are set up (perhaps unfairly) with reference to human language. Since this book emphasizes the essentially mental nature of linguistic ability, the design features that follow do not include the traditional reference to vocal–auditory transmission. What is emphasized is the nature of the semantic and organizational structuring of each system. These design features represent an adaptation of those of Charles Hockett and W.H. Thorpe, as noted at the end of this chapter, and are summarized in Tables 16.3 and 16.4.

1. Interchangeability *All members of the species can send and receive messages.*

This is obviously true of human language. It is not the case with bee dancing (performed only by foragers) or birdsong (performed only by males). Non-human primate vocalizations appear to be interchangeable.

2. Feedback *Users of the system are aware of what they are transmitting.*

Humans monitor their linguistic output and correct it. It is debatable whether bees do so when they dance, or whether birds monitor their calls. It is not known if birds monitor their song; it is likely that they do.

3. Specialization *The communication system serves no other function but to communicate.*

Human language represents reality – both external (real world) and internal (states, beliefs) – symbolically in the mind. Manifested as speech, language serves uniquely as a communicative system. Bee dancing and birdsong also appear to be specialized communicative activity. Alarm calls of any species may be symptomatic but at the same time are specialized for different types of predators. Symptomatic tokens, on the other hand, are unspecialized. Crying is a symptomatic sign that may be interpreted by someone else and thus function communicatively, but its primary purpose is physiological (the clearing of foreign matter from the eye, the release of emotional tension). If animal communication is primarily symptomatic – a claim which is hotly disputed by specialists in animal communication – then it would not qualify as a specialized communicative system.

4. Semanticity   *The system conveys meaning through a set of fixed relationships among signifiers, referents, and meanings.*

Human language conveys meaning through arbitrary symbols. Bee dancing conveys meaning, but within a very limited range, as do bird calls and song. The range of meaning is broader and more subtle in non-human primate vocalizations. Although we cannot claim to know the minds of such near relations as chimpanzees and gorillas, it appears that the range of meanings suggested by their behaviour in the wild does not approach the vastness of human semanticity (see feature 8).

5. Arbitrariness   *There is no natural or inherent connection between a token and its referent.*

This is true of human language, with the possible exception of a few onomatopoeic terms. Bee dancing may shows arbitrariness in that there may be no connection between the form of the dance and the distance from the hive. Expressions of food source quality and direction are not arbitrary, however. Many bird calls are highly suited for their purpose, such as danger calls which are difficult to locate, and in this sense are not arbitrary. Most non human primate vocalization appears to be equally adaptive. Arbitrariness has, however, been claimed for vervet monkey alarm calls.

6. Discreteness   *The communication system consists of isolatable, repeatable units.*

Human language shows distinctive features, phonemes, syllables, morphemes, words, and still larger combinations. There are two (three, in some dialects) discrete types of bee dances, but these dances are not combined in various ways to produce novel messages. There is some evidence for subunits in birdsong. They are also present in primate call systems.

7. Displacement   *Users of the system are able to refer to events remote in space and time.*

Bee dancing shows displacement. No evidence for displacement is found in bird calls or songs. Baboons occasionally produce threat and fight vocalizations long after an aggressive encounter, but there is no evidence that this is reflecting displacement; it probably reflects a slow winding down of the animal's affective state. Among apes, it is not yet clear whether to some degree displacement is a feature of either their communication in the wild or the systems they have learned from humans. Non-human primates do not appear to communicate about imaginary pasts or futures, which humans are able to do with language.

8. Productivity   *New messages on any topic can be produced at any time.*

This is obviously true of human language. Bees show limited productivity. Bird calls show none. Birdsong shows evidence of recombination (the songs of laughing gulls are well documented in this respect) but it is doubtful whether these recombinations transmit novel messages. This is also true of recombination in the calls of certain monkeys, such as macaques.

9. Duality of patterning   *Meaningless units (phonemes) are combined to form arbitrary signs. These signs in turn can be recombined to form new, meaningful larger units.*

In human language, phonemes can be combined in various ways to create different symbolic tokens: *spot*, *tops*, *opts*, and *pots*. These tokens in turn can be combined in meaningful ways: *Spot the tops of the pots*.

There is no evidence of this type of patterning in any known animal communication system.

10. Tradition   *At least certain aspects of the system must be transmitted from an experienced user to a learner.*

This is obviously a factor in the acquisition of human language. It is possibly present in a very limited way in bee communication, and it is definitely present in the acquisition of birdsong for some species. As noted in section 5.3, there is some recent evidence for a degree of tradition among chimpanzees.

11. Prevarication   *The system enables the users to talk nonsense or to lie.*

Undoubtedly, this property is found in human language. There are specialized mimics among birds, fishes, and even insects. A few examples of animal deception have been noted among the arctic fox and among vervets, but it is not clear whether this is normal species-specific behaviour or the acts of a few isolated individuals. The question of intentionality is crucial here. Current work with birds suggests that some species learn as many songs as possible and use this repertoire to maintain territorial advantage by 'impersonating' other species. This may well be purely genetically determined behaviour, but, in any event, it is highly complex.

12. Learnability   *A user of the system can learn other variants.*

Humans can learn a number of different languages. Bees are limited to their own genetically specified dialect. Bird calls are apparently limited in this same way. As noted previously, some birds learn songs of other species, but this may well be simply mimicry. Non-human primates seem restricted to their own systems.

13. Reflexiveness   *The ability to use the communication system to discuss the system itself.*

No evidence exists that any other species writes grammars or linguistics textbooks.

Tables 16.3 and 16.4 summarize this survey of design features.

Table 16.3 Summary of design features for bees and birds

Design feature	Bees	Birds
1. Interchangeability	no; foragers only	no; only males sing
2. Feedback	?	?
3. Specialization	yes	yes
4. Semanticity	yes, very limited	yes, limited
5. Arbitrariness	yes, for expressing distance	yes, though highly adaptive
6. Discreteness	in a limited way	yes, in song
7. Displacement	yes	no
8. Productivity	yes, very limited	possibly
9. Duality of patterning	no	no
10. Tradition	possibly, but highly limited	yes, limited
11. Prevarication	no	possibly
12. Learnability	no	possibly
13. Reflexiveness	no	no

Table 16.4 Summary of design features for non-human primates and humans

Design feature	Non-human primates	Humans
1. Interchangeability	yes	yes
2. Feedback	probably	yes
3. Specialization	in part	yes
4. Semanticity	yes	yes
5. Arbitrariness	limited confirmation; selectively adaptive	yes
6. Discreteness	in call systems	yes
7. Displacement	no	yes
8. Productivity	possibly	yes
9. Duality of patterning	no	yes
10. Tradition	possibly	yes
11. Prevarication	possibly	yes!
12. Learnability	no	yes
13. Reflexiveness	no current evidence	yes

Summing up

This brief overview of animal communication systems emphasizes that human language is one communication system among the many that life forms on this planet employ.

Communication can be described with reference to the **sign**, which is composed of two components, a **signifier** and that which is **signified**. Tokens may be **iconic**, **symbolic**, or **indexical** (the latter including the **symptomatic** token), and structured as **graded** or **discrete** types. Most animal communication has traditionally been viewed as symptomatic, though studies of communication among birds and bees suggest symbolic signs are used. A significant innate component may interact with some exposure to the communication system, especially among birds. Non-human primate communication consists of graded series of vocalizations and appears to show little arbitrariness, though some has been reported for the alarm calls of several monkeys.

Experiments with non-human primates have created controversy over whether chimpanzees and gorillas have shown symbolic behaviour and a capacity for linguistic behaviour. Many researchers have dismissed the work as an example of **dressage** or the Clever Hans phenomenon.

Human language and systems of animal communication share certain **design features**. Humans, however, lack many of the communicative skills that animals possess. We are hopelessly inadequate at following scent trails, a feat that prosimians accomplish with ease; we cannot change colour for communicative purposes with the facility of an octopus; and we are not as gifted as horses and many other mammals at assessing and interpreting subtle body gestures. Humans do possess an ability to symbolize which far exceeds that of chimpanzees and gorillas (our nearest genetic relatives), even allowing for the most generous interpretation possible of recent experiments. Human language is also more flexible and productive in manipulating these symbols than any known animal communication system. Language is as suited for and as much a part of human life patterns as the communication systems of our fellow creatures are for their modes of existence.

Notes

1 Communication since the industrial revolution increasingly involves non-organic life. Machines pass information to humans (for example, car speedometers, geiger counters, toasters), and among themselves (for example, computers, communication satellites). Still, non-living communicators have been designed by humans and use principles of communication based on living models.

2 Among humans, this fact about symptomatic signs can be turned on its head and symptoms such as tears or laughter can be feigned. The result is deception, trickery, or lying.

3 The bees are not perfect genetic machines, however. The fact that there are dancers that communicate more (or less) effectively than others shows the existence of varying ability among individuals.

4 You might wonder how song serves to establish and maintain territory. A recognized song is an indication to a bird that a certain amount of territory is occupied and that to stray onto that territory could provoke an attack. A recent hypothesis suggests that song also intimidates other males by disturbing their foraging patterns, since, again, hearing a song might lead a bird to think it was in another's territory and might have to flee or fight. Field studies support this hypothesis; they show that there is less singing among birds that co-exist in a forage-rich environment, where there is less competition for food resources (E.S. Morton, 'Grading, discreteness, redundancy, and motivation-structure rules' in Kroodsma *et al.*, eds, vol. 1, pp. 183–212, cited in 'Picture credits').

5 For example, the relevance of all non-syntactic communicative behaviour by

non-human primates has recently been dismissed with these words: 'virtually all of the nonsyntactic component of language predated the emergence of our species' (Derek Bickerton, review of E. Sue Savage-Rumbaugh, 1986, 'Ape Language: from conditioned response to symbol', *International Journal of Primatology* 8(3): 293–98).

Picture credits

Chimpanzee facial expressions in Figure 16.1 and question 3, and monkey facial expressions in Figure 16.5 are adapted from S. Chevalier-Skolnikoff's 'Facial expression and emotion in nonhuman primates', in *Darwin and Facial Expression*, edited by P. Ekman, pp. 11–90 (New York: Academic Press, 1973). The baboon open-mouth threat in Figure 16.3 is adapted from a photograph in K.R.L. Hall and I. DeVore's 'Baboon social behavior', in *Primate Behavior*, edited by I. DeVore, pp. 53–110 (New York: Holt, Rinehart & Winston, 1965); park information signs in Figure 16.3 are courtesy of Alberta Provincial Parks. Figure 16.7 is adapted from D. Todt's 'Serial calling as a mediator of interaction processes: crying', in *Primate Vocal Communication*, edited by D. Todt, D.P. Goedeking, and D. Symmes, pp. 88–107 (Berlin: Springer-Verlag). Bee dancing (Figure 16.8) is adapted from K. von Frisch's *The Dance Language and Orientation of Bees*, p. 57 (cited in sources) and reprinted by permission. The spectrogram of the robin song (Figure 16.9) is from *Bird-Song* by W.H. Thorpe (cited in sources), copyrighted and reprinted with the permission of Cambridge University Press. Avian isoglosses in Figure 16.10 are from Paul Mundinger's 'Microgeographic and macrogeographic variation in acquired vocalizations of birds', in *Acoustic Communication in Birds 2*, edited by D.E. Kroodsma, E.H. Miller, and H. Ouellet, pp. 147–208 (New York: Academic Press, 1982) and reprinted by permission. Figure 16.12 illustrating the response of vervet monkeys to predators is taken from *Animal Language* by Michael Bright with the permission of BBC Enterprises Ltd (cited in sources). Tokens used in the Sarah experiments (Figures 16.13 and 16.14) are taken from D. Premack and A.J. Premack, as cited on p. 179 in E. Linden's *Apes, Men, and Language* (London: Penguin Books, 1976).

Sources

The theory of semiotics outlined in this chapter is drawn from several recent works on semiotics, including T. Sebeok's *Contributions to the Doctrine of Signs, Studies in Semiotics 5* (Bloomington: Indiana University Press 1976), *I Think I Am a Verb* (New York: Plenum Press, 1986), and U. Eco's *Semiotics and the Philosophy of Language* (Bloomington: Indiana University Press, 1984). Bee communication is drawn from K. von Frisch's 'Dialects in the language of the bees', *Scientific American* 202(2): 78–87 (1962) and his work *The Dance Language and Orientation of Bees*, translated by C.E. Chadwick (Cambridge, Mass.: Harvard University Press, 1967). Bird vocalization is based largely on W.H. Thorpe's *Bird-Song* (Cambridge: Cambridge University Press, 1961). The report on the wren's song draws on *The Reader's Digest Book of British Birds* (London: Hodder & Stoughton, 3rd edn, 1980). Jake Page's parrot is reported in *Science* (1982). Lemur vocalizations in Table 16.1 are drawn from A. Jolly's *Lemur Behavior* (Chicago: University of Chicago Press, 1966). Vervet communication is drawn from R.M. Seyfarth and D.L. Cheney's 'How monkeys see the world', edited by Snowden *et al.* (cited below). Creative signing by Koko is reported in F. Patterson and E. Linden's work *The Education of Koko* (New York: Holt, Rinehart & Winston, 1981). The reference to cultural transmission of signs among chimpanzees is drawn from Michael Tomasello's 'Cultural transmission in the tool use and communicatory signaling of chimpanzees?', in Parker and Gibson (cited below), pp. 274–311; some of the material on invented rules by the pygmy chimpanzee Kanzi is drawn from Patricia Marks Greenfield and E. Sue Savage-Rumbaugh, 'Grammatical combination in *pan paniscus*', also in Parker and Gibson, pp. 540-76; this volume contains a number of other articles relevant to the question of non-human primate cognitive and linguistic abilities. Some exercise material is drawn from various articles in *How Animals Communicate*, edited by Thomas A. Sebeok (Bloomington: Indiana University Press, 1977).

Recommended reading   Bright, Michael. 1984. *Animal Language*. London: British Broadcasting Corporation.

Cheney, Dorothy L. and Seyfarth, Robert M. 1991. *How Monkeys See the World*. Chicago: University of Chicago Press.

de Luce, Judith, and Wilder, Hugh T. eds. 1983. *Language in Primates: Perspectives and Implications*. New York: Springer-Verlag.

Hockett, Charles. 1960. 'The origin of speech.' *Scientific American* 203(3): 88–96.

Lieberman, Philip. 1984. *The Biology and Evolution of Language*. Cambridge, Mass.: Harvard University Press.

Parker, Sue Taylor and Gibson, Kathleen Rita. 1990. *'Language' and Intelligence in Monkeys and Apes: Comparative Developmental Perspectives*. Cambridge: Cambridge University Press.

Sebeok, Thomas A. and Umiker-Sebeok, Jean. 1980. *Speaking of Apes*. New York: Plenum Press.

Sebeok, Thomas A. and Rosenthal, Robert.eds. 1981. *The Clever Hans Phenomenon: Communication with Horses, Whales, Apes, and People*. Annals of the New York Academy of Sciences 364. New York: The New York Academy of Sciences.

Snowden, C.T., Brown, C.T. and Petersen, M.T. eds. 1982. *Primate Communication*. Cambridge: Cambridge University Press.

Thorpe, W.H. 1974. *Animal Nature and Human Nature*. Garden City, NY: Doubleday.

Questions

1. The following signs are all symptomatic.
   (1) Dogs wag their tails when happy, cats flick their tails when irritated.
   (2) An octopus, when showing aggressive behaviour, becomes bright red.
   (3) The Canada goose shows aggressive intentions by opening its mouth, coiling its neck, and directing its head towards an opponent. When it is unlikely to attack, its mouth is closed, its neck is horizontally extended, and its head is directed away from an opponent.
   (4) Tree leaves change colour in autumn.
   (5) The presence of stratocumulus clouds accompanies good weather.

   a) Why is this designation appropriate in each case?
   b) State which of these signs are, in addition to being symptomatic, primarily *iconic*, which are primarily *symbolic*, and which are primarily *indexical*.

2. Find two examples each of *iconic, symbolic*, and *indexical* signs you encounter in the course of a day. Is it possible to classify unambiguously each sign as to type? If not, state why in each case.

3. What do the following chimpanzee facial expressions convey? Using a mirror, try to imitate the facial expressions; does this make it easier for you to label them? What characteristics of the signs lead you to your conclusion in each case? (*Answers are given at the bottom of this page.*)

4. Observe an animal in a zoo or at home for at least one half hour. Try to discover at least three unambiguous signs the animal employs to communicate. Describe each one in terms of both *signifier* and *signified*. (A good way to do this is to note carefully the context in which the sign is given, who it is addressed to, and what the receiver's response is to the communication.)

5. Add two columns to the list of design features presented in Tables 16.3 and 16.4. For one column, take the perspective of a researcher who believes that apes show true linguistic ability in their signing, and fill in the column from this point of view. Fill in the other column from the perspective of a researcher who does not believe such ability has been shown. Be sure to comment on each design feature.

6. Now that you have been exposed to both sides of the ape language issue, summarize your own conclusions about it. Do you believe that human language is different in degree or in kind from the communicative behaviour of the great apes? Why?

Answers top question 3: *a* submission; *b* excitement, perhaps affections; *c* desiring, perhaps mixed with frustration.

17

Computational linguistics

Judith Klavans

How comes it that human beings, whose contacts with the world are brief and personal and limited, are nevertheless able to know so much as they do know?

❧ Bertrand Russell

Imagine that you have a robot, but the robot does not talk or understand language. It is your job to program the robot to speak English (or any other language), and to program it to understand what you say to it. One of the central questions in computational linguistics is this: what would a computer program have to contain to enable the computer or the robot to analyse, understand, and create sentences and paragraphs correctly? These sentences could be either spoken or written. This is something that we humans achieve effortlessly. However, consider the amount and type of information that a computer would have to know about language in order to understand a simple sentence like this:

1)

The essay reads well and provides strong arguments.

First, the computer would have to understand the meaning and use of each of the words. For example, the computer would need to know that when the determiner *the* is used, this indicates a specific essay. The determiner *a* or *an* would indicate that it is the class of items or entities known as *essays* which read easily; this is the kind of usage found in a sentence like *An apple a day keeps the doctor away.* Since the subject of the sentence, *essay*, is a singular noun, then the computer would have to know that the verb must be singular, in order to avoid sentences like **The essay read well.* But this is only true in the present tense, since in the past, the verb *read* would serve both for singular or plural, as in *Yesterday's essay read well/Yesterday's essays read well.* This is because *read is* an irregular verb, with homophonous verb forms, as discussed in Chapter 4 on morphology, and Chapter 7 on semantics.

In addition to this grammatical knowledge about *the* and about agreement between subject and verb, there is a great deal of other information people have about sentence *1)*. For example, we know that essays are written and thus are likely to be read, essays are likely to contain arguments. This is called **real world knowledge** as distinct from *grammatical knowledge*. For example, although telephone messages are written, and are likely to be read, they are unlikely to contain arguments. Furthermore, when analysed carefully, the verb *read* has several uses. One is the transitive use, in which the subject is the Agent, i.e., the entity that performs the action, as in *The professor read forty essays.* The other is the intransitive use in which the subject of the sentence, in this case *essay*, is the Theme, i.e., the entity undergoing the action. In sentence *1)*, the Agent is not explicit; we do not know who is doing the reading. These two ways of using the verb *read* are related, but their interpretation is quite different. Finally, the word *strong*, like many adjectives, has many different meanings in context. The most common use of *strong* is to mean *powerful* as in *strong muscles*; another common use is found in *strong odour.* The interpretation of the word *strong* depends on the noun *argument*, relating to the fact that *arguments* have a gradation of effectiveness, measured from *weak* or *unconvincing* to *strong* or *persuasive.*

What sort of knowledge about pronunciation would a computer need to know to utter this sentence? The rules of pronunciation, like the rules of grammar, are different for each language. They are likely to vary within the same language depending on many factors. For example, the vowel in *the* when preceding a consonant is pronounced as a schwa /ə/ (see Chapter 2), whereas when preceding a vowel, it is pronounced as /i:/. English speakers know that the letter *e* in *the* is to be pronounced differently depending on the initial phoneme in the word that follows. But this is not true for every word ending in the sound /i:/. For example, the word *we* or *flea* does not change pronounciation so drastically according to the word that follows, although there is always some adjustment in spoken language. Another fact of pronunciation concerns the verb *read*, is this present or past tense? Of course, there is more to pronunciation than just converting letters to sounds, as shown in Chapters 2 and 3, and in later sections of this chapter.

These examples are sufficient to illustrate the quantity and variety of information that humans know about language. We take this knowledge for granted. Until we try to write computer programs to understand or generate even the most simple sentences, there is no need to pick apart the knowledge about language that we possess. However, computers are only as capable as the humans that program them, so it is the task of the computational linguist to spell out this knowledge for the computer. This is a major undertaking, involving all aspects of knowledge of language.

Computational linguistics is a relatively new discipline that lies in the intersection of the fields of linguistics and computer science. It is but one of many new hybrid disciplines involving computers that require computational expertise as well as a background in another field. The term *computational linguistics* covers many subfields. It sometimes refers to the use of computers as a tool to understand or implement linguistic theories. This means that linguists and computer scientists can gain a better understanding of the scientific and research questions by using computers. On the other hand, the term is sometimes used to refer to working systems or applications in which linguistic knowledge is needed. In this case, the questions and issues are usually ones of software engineering as well as of theory.

This chapter is organized around subfields of linguistics that are discussed in other chapters in this book: phonetics and phonology, morphology, syntax, and semantics. There is also a section on computational lexicology and text or corpus analysis. The first part of the chapter shows how each *linguistic* subfield is used as the basis for a *computational linguistic* subfield. The second part of the chapter shows some ways in which these various subsystems are combined to create computer systems that use language.

1

COMPUTATIONAL PHONETICS AND PHONOLOGY

1.1

The talking machine: speech synthesis

At the 1939 World's Fair in New York, a device called a vocoder was displayed. The machine, developed by scientists at Bell Laboratories, reconstructed the human voice by producing a sound source which was then modified by a set of filters. The values for the filters were derived from the analysis of human speech. The vocoder system consisted of a source of random noise for unvoiced sound, an oscillator to give voicing, a way to control resonance, and some switches to control the energy level. This was to simulate the vowel sounds and fricatives (see Chapter 2). Then there were controls for the stop consonants /p, b/, /t, d/, and /k, g/. An amplifier then converted the modified source signal into sound that resembled the human speech it was originally modelled after.

The vocoder was nicknamed the Talking Machine. It was a crude device, but it demonstrated that good speech synthesis could indeed be achieved, given the right values for the major frequencies, and the right methods of concatenating and modifying adjacent values. Early systems used different technology from that used today, but the principles remain the same. The goal is to replicate the wave forms that correctly reflect those of human speech in order to produce speech which, at the very least, will be intelligible and aesthetically pleasing and, in the ultimate, could not be distinguished from the speech of a human being.

Chapter 2 gave a summary of articulatory phonetics, that is, how sounds are made when humans speak. Chapter 3 covered some aspects of sound systems. Speech recognition and speech synthesis rely on a detailed knowledge of acoustic phonetics as well as articulatory phonetics, although there are correlations between the acoustic and articulatory properties of sounds. Acoustic phonetics is the study of the structure of the wave forms that constitute speech. As explained in Chapter 2, the lungs push a stream of air through the trachea. The airstream is modified first at the glottis and then by the tongue and lips.

Each sound can be broken down into its fundamental wave forms, as shown in Figure 17.1. The figure shows a spectrographic analysis or

Figure 17.1   A spectrogram of the words *heed, hid, head, had, hod, hawed hood,* and *who'd.*

spectrogram of the words *heed, hid, head, had, hod, hawed, hood,* and *who'd* as spoken by a British speaker. The diagrams give a visual representation of the duration of the utterance on the horizontal axis, and the different frequencies in the wave form on the vertical axis. The main frequencies, or **formants**, show up because they have more intensity than other frequencies. Note the different locations of the formants along the frequency dimension for the different vowels. The sound /h/ is only slightly visible as fuzzy lines across the spectrum because /h/ is a voiceless fricative with little or no glottal constriction (see Chapter 2). The acoustic effect is weak 'white noise' resembling fuzz or static. The /d/ is a stop, so there is just a low-frequency 'voice bar' resulting from the vibrations in the glottis, but there are no vowel formants for the period of closure since the airflow is blocked. This shows up as blank space on the spectrogram. For speech synthesis, the first three formants are the most critical for identifying different vowels. The others add some refinement to the sound, but they do not determine intelligibility or naturalness with the same significance as the first three formants.

Since different vowels are composed of different frequencies, in theory the task of the speech synthesizer is simply to replicate those vowel sounds, put in a few consonants, and string them together just as letters are strung together to make words and sentences. Unfortunately, the matter is not so simple, since sounds are not fixed; rather, they vary according to the segments that surround them. Effects occur on adjacent segments and across groupings, sometimes as far as six phonemes away. For example, Figure 17. 2 shows the same phonetic vowel [æ], but notice the rises and slumps in the formants. The figure shows how adjacent consonants can modify vowels. Similarly, vowels modify consonants. Nasal sounds modify larger chunks of surrounding phonemes. On top of these local changes, there are changes to entire phrases based on suprasegmental features such as stress and intonation (see Chapter 2.)

Figure 17.2   The modification of vowel formant caused by adjacent consonants.

Many steps are involved in achieving speech synthesis, and there are many different choices in ordering these steps. The text to be spoken has to be analysed syntactically, semantically, and orthographically. Pronunciations for exceptional words such as *have* /hæv/ or *four* /fɔː/ (or /fɔə/) must be found. These words do not follow the predictable phonological rules of English: *have* does not rhyme with *nave* or *rave*, and *four* does not rhyme with *sour* or *glamour*. Contrastive sounds need to be assigned based on the letters and other information about the word. After the correct phoneme is chosen, a system must look at the environment to see which allophone of the phoneme to choose. For example, to return to Figure 17.2, if the system were trying to pronounce *bab* /bæb/, the vowel /æ/ corresponding to the labial onset and labial offset would be chosen, since labials tend to lower adjacent formants.

A syntactic analysis of a sentence permits a system to identify words that might go together for phrasing. This is particularly important for noun compounds in English. As many as six nouns can be strung together, and the pronunciation of the compound can change the listener's interpretation of the meaning. For example, the phrase *Mississippi mud pie* could have two interpretations, depending on the syntax of the phrase. The most likely interpretation is shown in Figure 17.3, where the mud pie is Mississippi style.

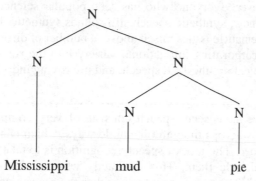

Figure 17.3   The role of syntax in disambiguation: one syntactic analysis of an ambiguous phrase.

Alternatively, the pie could be made of mud from Mississippi, in which case the syntax of the phrase is different, as shown in Figure 17.4, and so is the pronunciation. Syntactic analysis can also determine the part of speech for noun/verb pairs that are spelled the same but pronounced differently, such as the verb *record* /rɪkɔːd/ and the noun *record* /rékɔːd/.

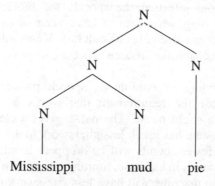

Figure 17.4   The role of syntax in disambiguation: an alternative syntactic analysis of an ambiguous phrase.

Also, parenthetical structures will be identified, as in these sentences:

2)

Here are the apples, as you can see.

3)

He said, although I don't believe it, that he was a good driver.

Parentheticals are typically pronounced at a lower pitch and loudness. When pronounced with main phrase intonation, they are difficult to understand. Finally, a semantic analysis of a sentence, and of a text, gives an idea of focus and stress. These features must be translated into duration (length), pitch, and loudness in order for synthetic speech to sound completely natural.

Given advances in computer technology, along with advances in electronics and acoustics, intelligible speech synthesis has already been achieved. However, everyone who has seen popular science fiction films knows that even now, synthetic speech still sounds synthetic. In addition to the syntactic and semantic issues raised above, a number of difficult problems remain, such as incorporating intonational variety into the rules to eliminate the droning quality of synthesized speech, and improving individual sounds.

1.2

The listening machine: speech recognition

As we have seen, speech consists of very complex wave forms changing rapidly across time and in subtle ways, which can affect the perception of a message. The task of speech recognition is to take these wave forms as input and decode them. This is exactly what we humans do when listening to speech. The wave form that reaches the ear is a continuous stream of sound; we segment the sound into words, phrases, and meaningful units so we can determine the meaning of the utterance. The task of a speech recognition system is to teach a computer to understand speech, whether the system models human mechanisms or not.

Even though human beings have no trouble decoding speech wave forms, computers do. The problems are immense. First of all, as shown in Chapter 2, speech sounds are modified by adjacent sounds in natural speech. The faster and more informal the speech, the more sounds are merged and dropped. Guessing what sounds have been dropped based on faulty and limited input is an extremely difficult task. Knowledge of context, of syntactic structure, of probabilities of occurrence are helpful, but the problem is still not solved.

Since decoding of continuous speech presents such problems, some systems impose the requirement that words be pronounced slowly, and separated by a slight pause. The pause gives a clear cue that the word has ended, so a system has much less guesswork to do. Also, if the speech is said more slowly, fewer sounds will be dropped. In addition to the constraint of pronouncing words in isolation, limiting a system in its vocabulary means that the recognition machine will have less guesswork to do. Finally, yet another way to reduce the guesswork is to require that an individual user 'train' the system to be tailored to her or his voice alone. Anyone who is skilled at recognizing voices can attest to the fact that no two people sound alike. The purpose of 'training' a computer is to familiarize it with the unique and distinguishing features of the user's voice.

Another very difficult problem for speech recognition is what is called the 'cocktail party effect', such as that of being in a crowded room. Even though there is much noise from other people, from music, or from the street, humans manage to filter out the background noise and pick out a particular sound or conversation to listen to. Everyone has had the experience of not hearing a sound, such as a leaking tap, until someone points out the sound, and the annoying sound then becomes the only one to be heard. Whatever mechanisms were used to suppress the noise of the tap were deactivated when brought to the listener's attention. Computer recognition systems cannot distinguish the speech signal from the noise, so they perform poorly in noisy environments. Thus, another condition – a reasonably quiet environment – must be imposed on systems in order for them to function adequately.

Each of these constraints can be imposed to result in more reliable systems, but the overall research problem still remains; how can humans be so adept at decoding speech yet computers cannot be easily taught to do so?

2

COMPUTATIONAL MORPHOLOGY

Morphology is the study of the internal structure of words, covering such topics as affixation, compounding, and infixation (see Chapter 4). Most research in computational morphology arose as a by-product of developing natural language-processing systems. Looking up words in a computational dictionary for these systems turned out to be more complicated than met the eye, precisely because of morphological processes that can conceal the base word. For example, if a dictionary has the word *book*, the word *books* would not be found by a simple search. Unless a system is explicitly told that *book* is related to *books* by a productive and regular rule of inflectional morphology, it would not be able to infer that those words are related. Thus, a program needs to include the rule of pluralization in English as well as other rules in order to recognize or generate the morphological permutations of words.

2.1

Morphological processes

Most morphologically conditioned changes in written English involve spelling, with some changes in stems, and some truncation rules. Examples are *stop/stopped*, *sing/sang*, and *tolerate/tolerant*. In general, morphological variations in English are not as opaque as in other languages. Some languages, such as German, have very productive compounding whereas others have infixation and reduplication, or complex stem changes. Words altered by morphological processes cannot be easily recognized by a natural language processor unless they are properly related to their bases for lexical lookup.

Implementing morphological processes: method one

Broadly speaking, there are two approaches to computational morphology. Historically, the first was called a **stemming** or **stripping algorithm**. An algorithm is a set of rules for solving a problem; the term was first used in mathematics to describe the rules for solving mathematical problems. Since algorithmic procedures usually involve a sequence of repeated steps, the term is naturally suited to computer programs in general, and to programs for computational linguistics in particular. In the stemming or stripping algorithm, affixes are recursively stripped off the beginnings and ends of words, and base forms are proposed. If the base form is found in the base-form dictionary, then the word is analyzable. Successful analyses provide information about the internal structure of the words as well as whatever other information is produced by the rule for a given affix, such as part of speech change, inherent semantic changes (e.g., *-ess* is + feminine), or other information (e.g., abstract, Latinate, singular, plural). Most of these systems are sensitive to constraints on affix ordering such as described in the chapter on morphology. Inflectional affixes occur outside derivational affixes, and there may be some derivational affixes that occur outside other derivational affixes.

Two different types of dictionaries are possible with the stemming method: word based and stem based. A word-based system has a dictionary with words only. For word generation, all input to morphological rules must be well-formed words, and all output will be well-formed words. For word analysis, all proposed bases will be words. The word-based system has proved to be very useful for projects that use large machine-readable dictionaries, since dictionaries list words not stems. A machine-readable dictionary is a dictionary that appears in computer form, such as that available in spelling checkers or thesauruses. Machine-readable dictionaries have definitions, pronunciations, etymologies, and other information, not just the spelling or synonyms. (See section 4 for more on machine-readable dictionaries.) The stem-based dictionary is somewhat more complex to build, since there are no on-line dictionaries of word stems.

Table 17.1 presents an example of the type of analyses given by a word-based stemming system. To analyse *conceptualize* as an infinitive verb (V form(inf)), first *conceptual* must be analysed as an adjective (Adj). This would be done by a rule stating that the suffix *-ize* can attach to certain adjectives to create verbs. *Conceptual* can be analysed as an adjective if *concept* can first be analysed as a singular noun (N num(sg)). This would be done by a rule for *-ual* stating that the suffix *-ual* can attach to certain nouns to create adjectives. *Concept* is stored in the dictionary as a singular noun, so this lexical lookup serves as the final step of the analysis. The analyses shown here actually result from recursive calls to the morphological rules. Each rule has conditions that restrict its operation. In this example, the *-ual* rule states that the base must be a singular noun. The condition for the *-ize* rule is that the base is normally an adjective (but cf. terrorize, hospitalize where in each case the base, namely terror and hospital, is a noun). Since each condition is met, an analysis is possible. The word *conceptualize* is deemed a well-formed infinitive verb.

Table 17.1   Input word: conceptualize

Analysis	Part of speech	Features
concept	N	num(sg)
-ual	Adj	
-ize	V	form(inf)

How would the system analyse a more complex form? Consider the analyses in Table 17. 2 of the word *conceptualizations*, which is based on the previous example. In this example, the *suffix -ation* attaches to infinitival verbs. Notice that when *-ations* attaches to *conceptualize*, there is a spelling change. If no spelling rules were written, then the word *conceptualizeations would be allowed by the system. Finally, the plural marker *-s* is attached at the outside of the noun. For the plural suffix *-s*, there is no change in the part of speech, but only in the number feature of the word from singular to plural. Observe that these examples illustrate a word-based system. Both the dictionary entry, in this case *concept*, and the complex words *conceptualize* and *conceptualizations* are well-formed words of English.

Table 17.2   Input word: conceptualizations

Analysis	Part of speech	Features
concept	N	num(sg)
-ual	Adj	
-ize	V	form(inf)
-ation	N	num(sg)
-s	N	num(pl)

How would this system differ if it were stem-based? For this example, the morpheme *-cept* might be listed in a stem dictionary, due to its presence in other words in English, such as *reception*, *conception*, *inception*, and *perception*. Since *-ceive* and *-cept* are related in a regular way, this relationship might also be given in the stem dictionary, or the words could be related by rule. Consider again *conceptualizations*, analysed down to a stem in Table 17.3.

Table 17.3   Input word: conceptualizations

Analysis	Part of speech	Features
con		
-cept	N	num(sg)
-ual	Adj	
-ize	V	form(inf)
-ation	N	num(sg)
-s	N	num(pl)

In this example, the prefix *con-* attaches to *-cept*. The point was made earlier that a word-based morphology system can use an ordinary dictionary as its lexicon, but no such convenience exists for a stem-based system. In order for stem-based morphology to get wide coverage, a large dictionary of stems is required. (More on this topic is found in the section on computational lexicology later in this chapter.)

Morphological processes: method two

The other common approach to computational morphology, the two-level approach, is fundamentally different from the stemming approach. This results in basic differences in computational properties. Both systems contain a lexicon or dictionary, although two-level morphology *requires* a stem-based lexicon. Both systems have rules, but the rules are very different. In two-level morphology, the rules define correspondences between surface and lexical representations; they specify if a correspondence is restricted to, required by, or prohibited by a particular environment. *Lexical* roughly corresponds to *underlying*, whereas *surface* usually means *orthographic* but sometimes *phonemic*. In Figure 17.5, the lexical representation of *try* followed by the +*s* is compared with a surface representation *tries*.

Figure 17.5 Lexical and surface representations.

Lexical and surface representations are compared using a special kind of rule system called finite-state transducer. Simply put, the rules would decide whether the lexical *y* could correspond to the surface *i* based on information the rules have already seen. The rules that compare lexical and surface form move from left to right, so when a successful correspondence is made, the rule moves along. One of the claimed strengths of this method is that, since the procedure moves from left to right, it accurately reflects the way that people process words. Since people hear and read English from left to right (i.e., the beginning of the word is heard before the end), a system that incorporates this directionality might be an actual model of performance. Furthermore, since the two-level system processes from left to right for morphological analysis, it can be easily reversed and function from right to left for morphological generation. The primary drawback of the two-level system is that it requires a specialized stem dictionary, complete with restrictions on the stems so that not all affixes attach without restrictions. For example, a dictionary would need to include -*cept* or -*mit* (for *transmit*, *submit*, *permit*, and so on).

2.2

Some problems in computational morphology

Compounding is a particularly thorny problem since it tends to be so productive that compounds are often not listed in a dictionary. The word *bookworm*, for example, does not appear in Webster's Seventh New Collegiate Dictionary which is a standard reference work in American

English. A good morphological analyser should be able to analyse *bookworm* as shown in Table 17.4. However, what about a word like *accordion*?

Table 17.4 Input word: bookworm

Analysis	Part of speech	Features
book	N	num(sg)
worm	N	num(sg)

The analysis in Table 17.5 shows *accordion* to be composed of the noun *accord* plus the noun *ion*. This is obviously incorrect because *accordion* is not a compound analogous to *bookworm*. Since *accordion* does not ever have this analysis, it might be marked as an exception to morphological decomposition.

Table 17.5 Input word: accordion

Analysis	Part of speech	Features
accord	N	num(sg)
ion	N	num(sg)

A related problem arises due to overenthusiastic rule application. Table 17.6 presents an analysis of *really*. Here *really* is analysed as [*re-*[*ally-*verb]verb], meaning 'to ally oneself with someone again'.

Table 17.6 Input word: really

Analysis	Part of speech	Features
re-		
ally	V	form(inf)

This analysis is correct, although highly improbable. Cases like that of *re-* in *really* bring up a difficult issue. Should a word like *really* be specially marked in the dictionary as a non-analysable word, an exception to the rules that would apply to regular formations like *reapply, redo*, and *reduplicate*? Or should the rules be allowed to apply freely? What about a word like *resent*, which could either be [re-[sent$_{verb}$]$_{verb}$] as in *He didn't get my letter, so I resent it* and [resent$_{verb}$] as in *Did he resent that nasty comment?* The spelling of this word is truly ambiguous, so a decision about its analysability requires knowledge of syntactic and semantic features in the sentence and context. Usually the decision is driven by practical concerns. A system that is designed to implement a theory, but that does not need to perform well on a task that applies the theory, would probably allow the rules to apply freely. A system that needs to perform accurately on large texts would probably mark *really* and *resent* as non-analysable words, even though strictly speaking they are not.

3

COMPUTATIONAL SYNTAX

Research in computational syntax arose from two sources. One was the practical motivation resulting from attempts to build working systems to analyse and generate language. Some of these systems, such as machine translation and database query systems, are discussed in section 6. The other source was a desire on the part of theoretical linguists to use the computer as a tool to demonstrate that a particular theory is internally consistent. In this case, less value was given to efficiency or broad coverage since this was not the goal. The emphasis was instead on theory testing and on formal issues in natural language analysis. Ideally, builders of practical systems should take more advantage of theoretical insights, and linguistic theoreticians should pay more attention to practical problems. This has been the case in recent research on parsing, although this is a fairly new friendship.

3.1

Natural language analysis

Parsers and grammars

Chapter 5 showed how sentences can be analysed by rules into substructures such as noun phrases, verb phrases, prepositional phrases, and so on, as shown in Figure 17.6. Given a system of rules, an analyser will be able to break up and organize a sentence into its substructures. A **grammar** can be viewed as the set of rules that define a language. These rules can be of different shapes or formats, which give them different properties. A **parser** is the machine or engine that is responsible for applying the rules. A parser can have different strategies for applying rules. Chapter 5 showed how the rules for sentence

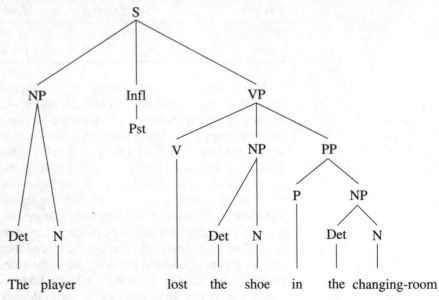

Figure 17.6　A syntactic analysis done by a parser.

structure differ between languages. These differences are reflected in the grammars for these languages, although the parser that drives the grammars can remain constant. (Recall the discussion of the role of parsers in language processing in Chapter 11, section 2.3.)

Determinism vs non-determinism

Any time a syntactic parser can produce more than one analysis of the input sentence, the problem of backtracking is raised. For example, if the beginning of the sentence in Figure 17.7 is read word by word, there is more than one possible ending. In choice (a), the word *you* is the object of the main verb *see*. For (b) the word *that* has been left out, as is permitted in English, so the word *you* is the subject of the clause *you have finished*. If the parser follows path (a), and if that path turns out to be the wrong one, how can the situation be rectified to get the right analysis? Or can choices be controlled so that a parser never has to undergo the time-consuming task of going back and starting over? (See also the discussion of garden path sentences in Chapter 11, section 2.3.)

Figure 17.7 Deterministic and non-deterministic parsing.

The term **non-deterministic** may refer to going back or backtracking if the first analysis turns out to be impossible. It may also mean following multiple paths in parallel, meaning that both analyses are built at the same time but on separate channels. By contrast, the term **deterministic** means that the parser has to stick to the path it has chosen. There have been many proposals about controlling the backtracking of parsers. The problem is a serious one since the number of alternatives increases as the coverage of a system increases. The result is that as an analyser improves, it also becomes more and more cumbersome because each time it is presented with more and more options.

Top-down vs bottom-up parsing

Consider the following phrase structure rules for English (introduced in chapter 5, section 1.2):

4)

a) S → NP Infl VP
b) NP → (Det) (AdjP) N (PP)
c) VP → V (NP) (PP)
d) PP → P NP

There are two ways to build an analysis of a sentence, using just these rules. This section illustrates the principles of what is called *top-down* and *bottom-*

up parsing. Working systems may not be built to function exactly like this, but the principles are the same.

In addition to the rules in *4)*, we also need to give some lexical items, or **terminal nodes**, for each category or **non-terminal**.

5)

N → Curly
Infl → Pst
V → sat
P → on
Det → the
N → grass

Generally speaking, a non-terminal is not a word in the language. Rather, it is a category or a phrase, such as N or NP. A terminal can be thought of as a word (although sometimes a terminal is a part of a word or several words). In top-down parsing, the analyser always starts with the topmost node, in this case S, and finds a way to expand it. The only rule in the set in *4)* for S is shown in Figure 17.8. Both NP and VP are non-terminal nodes.

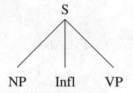

Figure 17.8 Top-down parsing: first step starts with S node.

The next rule to apply is the NP expansion rule and then the VP expansion rule. The results are shown in Figure 17.9. Although N is a non-terminal, it has no expansions, so the next rule to apply would be the VP rule. If the subject of the sentence had been the *batter*, then the NP would have been expanded to Det and N. This process continues until no more expansions could apply, and until all the lexical items or words in *5)* occur in the correct position to match the input sentence *Curly sat on the grass*. Top-down parsers suggest a hypothesis that a proposed structure is correct until proven otherwise.

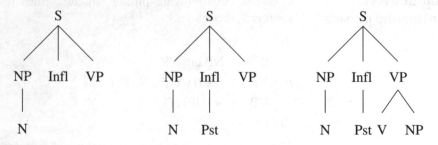

Figure 17.9 Top-down parsing: next step NP, Infl and VP expansion.

In contrast, bottom-up parsers take the terminals (words) of a sentence one by one, replace the terminals with proposed non-terminal or category labels, and then reduce the strings of categories to permissible structures. For the same example, the analysis would be built as follows; first the word *Curly* would be assigned the category N; then *sat* would be assigned to V, and so on. The partial analysis up to this point is shown in Figure 17.10.

Figure 17.10 Bottom-up parsers start by replacing category labels with words.

None of the rules in *4)* permit the combination of N and V; none permit V and P or P and Det to combine. But the NP rule does combine Det and N to build up a structure, as shown in Figure 17.11. This continues until the structure of a sentence is built. It has been proposed that the building of the structure from the terminal nodes up to the topmost S node from left to right reflects the way human beings process sentences more accurately than the top-down approach, but this is a controversial issue.

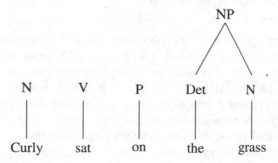

Figure 17.11 Bottom-up parsers: next step is to group words into permissible constituents.

Generative capacity

The term *generative* in this context refers to formal properties of grammars as mathematical systems. It does not refer to language generation, which is discussed below. Recall that a grammar consists of a set of rules that describe a language. Assume also some finite set of symbols, V, the vocabulary of a language. For English, examples of V would be:

6)

V_L = [player, shoe, child, lost, a . . .]

In the vocabulary V are other symbols and categories, such as N and Det. Formally, a language *L* over *V* is a finite set of strings of symbols taken from V. Informally, a language consists of strings from the vocabulary. Of course, a sentence is more than just a string of words, as shown in Chapter 5. Furthermore, the set of strings is greater than the set of well-formed sentences, as sentences 7) to 9) show. Even though the vocabulary V may be a finite list, the language L may be finite or infinite. This is because of recursion, a very powerful property of natural languages. (Chapter 5 contains a discussion of recursive rules.) The application of a finite number of recursive rules results in languages that can contain an infinite number of well-formed strings.

The following sentences consist of vocabulary from the set in 6). While 7) is a well-formed sentence in English, 8) and 9) are not.

7)

A child lost a shoe.

8)

*child shoe a.

9)

*Lost a shoe a child

Although 9) is not in the language L for English it could be found in the language L for Spanish, given a parallel set of vocabulary.

10)

Perdio un zapato un niño.
lost   a   shoe   a   child

The grammar of English would give a correct description of 7), but not 8) or 9). On the other hand, the grammar of Spanish would allow both 7) and 9), but not 8). The goal of an implemented grammar is exactly the same. An **implementation** is simply a practical system. The grammar rules are programmed into a computer, and the computer program then decides if the string is permitted in the language. If the string is permitted, it then has the task of giving the sentence the correct description.

Natural languages (as opposed to computer languages) are highly complex, so discovering the correct grammar for a given language is an extremely difficult task. The complexity and subtlety of natural languages continue to present a challenge to linguists. There are many competing theories of what the 'correct' grammar of natural languages will be like. Even the grammar for English, a very well-studied natural language, is not at all well understood. One issue that all theories agree upon, however, is that a grammar should have certain properties. Grammars should give a correct description of the following:

A.   The strings of a language L
B.   The structures corresponding to the strings in L

Property A is called **weak generative capacity**. Property B is called **strong generative capacity**. (Generative here does not mean 'create' but rather 'describe'.)

To explain, Figure 17.6 on page 676 shows an analysis in which the first two words *the* and *player* are joined into a noun phrase (NP); Infl is dominated by S. The verb phrase (VP) is described by the grammar as consisting of a verb (V), followed by a noun phrase (NP), followed by a preposition phrase (PP). These three constituents are immediately dominated by the VP node. What if a different grammar were to claim a different structure for this sentence? Consider the structure in Figure 17.12. This analysis makes different claims about the structure of the sentence, but the actual string of words stays the same. The tree in Figure 17.12 has two levels of verb phrase. One is VP^1, which dominates the predicate of the sentence (everything in the sentence, except the subject and Infl). The other is VP^0, which dominates only the main verb and the direct object. The grammar generating the structure in Figure 17.12 differs in strong generative capacity from the grammar for Figure 17.6. However, both grammars may have the same weak generative capacity since they both have the ability to describe the string *The player lost a shoe in the changing room.*

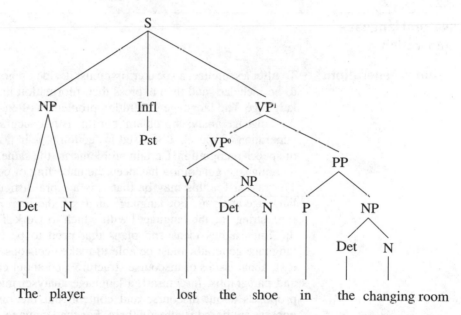

Figure 17.12   Difference in generative capacity (contrast with Figure 17.6).

Role of syntax and semantics

The preceding section dealt with syntactic analysers, but it is important to note that the division between what should be handled by the syntactic component of a system and what is properly in the semantic component is a matter of great debate. For example, some systems might claim that selection of prepositions by verbs, often considered a syntactic property, is actually dependent on the semantic category of the verb. For example, not all verbs can take the instrumental, as in the reading of *11)* in which *the stick* was used to hit the dog.

11)

He hit the dog with a stick.

If a different verb is substituted for *hit*, would the sentence be semantically or syntactically ill-formed?

12)

?He told his story with a stick.

Some systems assume that a syntactic analysis precedes a semantic one, and that the semantics should be applied to the output of syntactic analyses. This is the position of the earliest transformational models, which was incorporated into many computational systems. Some systems perform syntactic and semantic analyses hand-in-hand. Other systems ignore the syntactic, viewing it as a second-step derivative from semantic analyses.

3.2

Natural language generation

What is generation?

To utter a sentence, a speaker first must decide on goals, plan the information to be included, and then express that information in a sentence of his or her language. The language generation problem is often viewed as the reverse of the language analysis problem, but this is not accurate. In the same way, the generation of speech, discussed in section 6, is in no way simply the reverse of speech recognition. Certain problems are the same, but many are not.

Language generation has been the underling of computational linguistics. The reason for this may be that it is a more difficult area to work in than language analysis. For language analysis, the linguist is given a set of data (i.e., strings of the language) with which to work. For language generation, the linguist has ideas and plans that need to be turned into language. A language generator must be able to make decisions about the content of the text, about issues of discourse structure, and about cohesion of the sentences and paragraphs. In contrast, a language analyser might be invoked to make proposals about discourse and content, but the raw material upon which guesses are based is already there. For the language generator, only concepts and ideas are available to work with. Choices of words (lexical items) and syntactic structures are part of decisions to be made in building a text.

As with syntactic analysers, there are two approaches to generation: top-down and bottom-up. In the top-down approach, first a very high-level structure of the output text is determined, along with very abstract expressions of meaning and goal. Then lower levels are filled in progressively. Subsections are determined, and examples of the verbs with their subjects and objects, if any, are proposed. This is refined, until the pre-final stage when lexical items are chosen from the dictionary. When all sentences have been decided upon, and when all lexical items have been inserted, there is a component to 'smooth' and provide low-level coherence to the text. This component makes sure that pronouns are used correctly, for example, and that connecting phrases such as *in the preceding paragraph* or *on the other hand* are used correctly. In contrast, the bottom-up approach builds sentences from complex lexical items. First, words to achieve the goals are hypothesized. Then sentences are composed, and finally high-level paragraph and text coherence principles are applied.

The generation lexicon

The lexicon is just one link in many difficult steps involved in generating natural and cohesive text for an underlying set of goals and plans. Imagine that you have determined an underlying message, plan, or goal. In order to figure out how to translate the underlying message into some actual words in a language, your generation system will have to determine such matters as what verbs to pick and how to pick the subjects and objects, if any, for those verbs.

Suppose you want to express how fast time is going by in your life. You might use the verb *elapse*. *Elapse* is said to be a one-place predicate or a one-place verb. It is intransitive, so it takes just one **argument**, the subject. (The term *argument* here refers to grammatical dependents of a verb.) If you want to talk about tennis, you need to describe the action. You might use the verb *hit*. *Hit* is transitive; it takes two arguments. *Hit* is also often used with an instrumental, a phrase that tells what the subject hit *with*, as in *with a stick* in sentence *11)*. In this case, *hit* can take three arguments. Finally, a verb like *give* takes a subject, object, and indirect object, and those three arguments can be expressed as a subject, object, and a recipient, indicated by *to* as in *13)*. Alternatively, *give* can undergo what is called Dative Movement, as in *14)*, in which case the indirect object *dog* appears next to the verb and is not preceded by the preposition *to*.

13)

He gave a stick to the dog.

14)

He gave the dog a stick.

Often verbs with very close meanings take different numbers of arguments and in different order. For example, *give* can also mean *donate*, but *donate* does not permit the same alternations as *give*.

15)

He donated a stick to the dog.

16)

*He donated the dog a stick.

A system must be capable of deciding what the meaning to be conveyed is, and then it must be capable of picking very similar words to express that meaning. The lexicon or dictionary must supply items to instantiate the link between meaning and words.

The design and content of the generation lexicon is one of the most difficult areas in language generation. The lexicon needs to contain many different types of information, such as syntactic facts about verbs, facts about usage and focus, and facts about types of modifiers. Building lexicons for generation is one of the goals of computational lexicology, as discussed in the following section.

4

COMPUTATIONAL LEXICOLOGY

Since phrases, sentences, and paragraphs are composed of words, computer systems need to contain detailed information about words. The section on morphology dealt with the structure and analyses of word forms, but there is more to know about words than this.

Computational linguists are realizing that an analyser or generator is only as good as its dictionary or lexicon. The lexicon is the repository of whatever information a particular system needs. The individual words in the lexicon are called lexical items. Chapter 5 shows how lexical insertion occurs in syntactic structure. For example, in order for a bare structure such as Figure 17.13 to be 'filled out' with real words, a program would need to have a match between a word marked Det in the lexicon and the slot in the tree requiring a Det.

Figure 17.13   Bare structure available for lexical insertion.

The same goes for any part of speech, such as noun, verb, or adjective. Given the items in 5), a valid match for Figure 17.13 would be Figure 17.14.

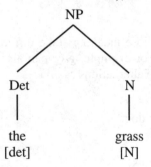

Figure 17.14   A valid match of slots in the syntactic tree with words in the lexicon.

Figure 17.15 would not be a valid match. Notice that the preposition *on* occurs under the determiner node, and the verb *sat* occurs under the noun node. At the very least, the condition of matching part of speech has to be met.

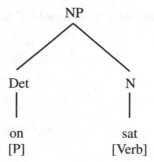

Figure 17.15   An invalid match of slots in the syntactic tree with words in the lexicon.

As the examples below illustrate a computer program would need to know more than just the part of speech to analyse or generate a sentence correctly. Subcategorization, that is, the number and type of arguments a verb can take, must be considered (see Chapter 5). Knowledge of thematic roles, such as agent, patient, and goal, is also needed (see Chapter 7, section 3.2). A syntactic analyser would also need to know what kinds of complements a verb can take (see Chapter 5, section 2.1).

17)
I decided to go.

18)
*I decided him to go.

19)
*I persuaded to go.

20)
I persuaded him to go.

The verb *decide* can take the infinitive *to go* as in *17)* but it cannot take an NP object and then the infinitive, as in *18)*. The verb *persuade* is the opposite. It cannot take the infinitive *to go* as in *19)*, but it must have an NP object before the infinitive, as in *20)*.

The lexicon needs to know about the kinds of structures in which words can appear, about the semantics of surrounding words, and about the style of the text. For example, sentence *21)* is strange in meaning, but the structure is fine.

21)
I broke the concept.

The verb *break* is transitive and so can take an object, but the problem here is the type of noun; *concept* is [+ abstract], but *break* requires a [+ concrete] noun. Only concrete objects are breakable, unless the meaning is metaphorical as in *The disease broke his will to live*. (See Chapter 7 for a fuller discussion of semantics.)

What does a computational lexicon look like? So far the list of information includes:

22)
Lexical Entry
1. Part of speech
2. Sense number
3. Subcategorization
4. Semantic properties

Keeping in mind that a computational lexicon has to contain as much information as possible in order to correctly analyse and generate phrases, sentences, and text, the following are also needed:

22) (continued)
5. Pronunciation
6. Context and style
7. Etymology
8. Usage (e.g., taboos)
9. Spelling (including abbreviations)

The task of collecting all the important information for every existing word in the English language is awesome. In addition, given that the kind of information needed cannot be found in conventional dictionaries, how are computational lexicons built?

There are several approaches. One is to hand-build a lexicon specifying only those features that a given system needs and using only the lexical items that are most likely to occur. For example, assume that an analyser is reading the *Financial Times* or the *Wall Street Journal*, and assume that the sentence to be analysed is *His interest is high this month*. If the analyser is to assign a meaning to this sentence, it has to know at least the information below.

Word: interest 1
1. Part of speech: Noun
2. Inherent semantic features: [+ concrete], . . .
3. Context: Financial

In just this usage, there is no reason to know about the abstract meaning of *interest* as 'attention' or 'concern'. The lexical entry for this other sense would include the information below.

Word: interest 2
1. Part of speech: Noun
2. Inherent semantic features: [+ abstract], . . .
3. Context: emotional

Most words have many different senses, and sometimes the different senses have very different grammatical behaviour. Every time a new word is added to the lexicon, if a new feature is also added, then the dictionary builder has to go back through the lexicon and modify every word to match the new expanded word. When *interest-2* was added to the dictionary, new features had to be added, namely that *interest-1* does not have a context 'Emotional' and that *interest-2* does not have a context 'Financial'. One of the major challenges in building computational dictionaries is extensibility. The problem is how to add new information, and modify old information, without starting over each time.

Another option in building large lexicons is to use two resources: the power of the computer and the data of machine-readable dictionaries. A machine-readable dictionary (MRD) is a conventional dictionary, but it is in machine-readable form (i.e., on the computer) rather than on the bookshelf. (An example is the Longman Dictionary of Contemporary English which has been widely used for computational purposes.) MRDs are useful in building large lexicons because the computer can be used to examine and analyse automatically information that has already been organized by lexicographers, the writers of dictionaries. Unfortunately, the type of information that is needed by a computational dictionary is not always easy to find in a conventional dictionary. However, with some clever approaches to exploiting the hidden information in conventional MRDs, it appears that many important facts can be pulled out and put into a computational lexicon. This work is at a fairly early stage, so it is uncertain how far it can be pushed, but it is an important line of research in computational linguistics.

For example, the knowledge that a word has a sense that is [+ human] is needed in a computational lexicon for both syntactic and semantic reasons. Webster's Seventh New Collegiate Dictionary, which has about seventy thousand headwords, has just over a thousand nouns that are defined in terms of the word *person*. Some examples are given below:

> *accessory*
> a *person* not actually or constructively present but contributing as an assistant or instigator to the commission of an offence – called also accessory before the fact

> *acquaintance*
> a *person* whom one knows but who is not a particularly close friend

> *intellectual*
> a very intelligent or intellectual *person*

> *scatterbrain*
> a giddy heedless *person*: FLIBBERTIGIBBET

> *unbeliever*
> one that does not believe; an incredulous *person*: DOUBTER, SCEPTIC

Notice that each word can have other senses. *Accessory*, for example, can mean an object or device that is not essential but that enhances the main object. A program has been written to extract these words. The headwords are then marked [+human], and synonyms such as *flibbertigibbet*, *doubter*, and *sceptic* can also be marked as [+ human] in one sense.

Although this approach is appealing, caution is in order. In the first place, lexicographers are people, and dictionaries are huge undertakings written by many different contributors. Therefore, there is less internal consistency than would be ideal. Finally, and most seriously, there is the problem that most words have more than one sense. Keeping track of which senses have which features is not an easy task. Furthermore, the decision on what is a sense is also not clear-cut. The problem of extensibility enters into play again. Even with all these restrictions, however, using machine-readable dictionaries as a resource for constructing large lexicons looks very promising.

Another approach to building large lexicons for natural language analysis and generation is **corpus analysis**. The larger the corpus, or collection of texts, the more useful it is, since the chances of covering the language as it actually is used increase. In addition to size, a good corpus should include a wide variety of types of writing, such as newspapers, textbooks, popular writing, fiction, and technical material. As an example of the way large corpora (the plural of corpus) are useful, consider the verb of movement *flounce*. The definitions given for the verb in Webster's Seventh New Collegiate Dictionary are:

> *flounce 1*
> to move with exaggerated, jerky motions
> to go with sudden determination
> to trim with flounces

These definitions tell nothing about likely subjects. Looking at corpus data will yield this information. From a large corpus, about twenty occurrences of the verb *flounce* were extracted. Thirteen had subjects that were female, as in sentences *23)* and *24)*.

23)

Carol flounced out to the kitchen for an apron.

24)

She flounced off with a following of hens behind her.

Four had subjects that were clothing:

25)

The white cashmere dressing-gown flounced around her.

One had *horses* as the subject, and the other subjects were pronouns. The point is that, given a good parser, it would be possible to extract automatically all the subjects of a given verb, and then to look for properties of those subjects. For *flounce*, that information would appear in the lexicon as:

Word: flounce 1

1. Part of speech: Verb
2. Subcategorization: Intransitive
3. Semantic properties: female human subject

Word: flounce 2

1. Part of speech: Verb
2. Subcategorization: Intransitive
3. Semantic properties: clothing subject

Using computers to extract linguistically useful information from dictionaries and texts for the purpose of constructing large lexicons is a new field within computational linguistics. The use of statistical methods to analyse language has seen great advances in recent years, giving promise in providing a solution to the difficult but fundamental problem of building computational lexicons out of already existing resources. At this point, clever programs give large and comprehensive lists of words and phrases with a potential characteristic, but human judgements are still necessary. If the computer is viewed as a tool to be used in collecting lists of words, then the endeavour is successful. If the goal is to view the computer as the only tool, and to eliminate the human judge, then computational lexicon builders still have a long way to go.

5

COMPUTATIONAL SEMANTICS

So far in this chapter, we have focused on structure: the structure of sentences and words. However, in order to understand what a word, sentence, or text means, a computer program has to know the semantics of words, sentences, and text. This section treats briefly some of the semantic representations and processes that have been proposed in computational linguistics.

Semantic issues were touched on in the preceding section. The lexical item contains a field for semantic information, including such information as what kind of semantic features a verb requires for its subject or which thematic roles a verb requires or permits. The semantic fields for the two senses of *flounce* are:

Word: flounce 1
Semantic restrictions: female human subject

Word: flounce 2
Semantic restrictions: clothing subject

Although the semantics of words is an important component of any language system, there is yet a broader issue: the semantics of sentences and paragraphs.

Two approaches to semantics and language analysis have been proposed: syntactically based systems and semantically based systems. Considering for

Figure 17.16 Syntactically based systems.

the moment the analysis of sentences, in the first approach the sentence is assigned a syntactic analysis, much in the way outlined in Chapter 5 and earlier in this chapter. A semantic representation is built after the syntactic analysis is performed (see Figure 17.16). The problems arise in getting from one representation to the other. This is sometimes called the mapping problem. However, in the semantically based system, first a semantic representation is built. Sometimes there is no syntactic analysis at all (see Figure 17.17). Consider a response to the question *Who got the coffee today?*

26)
The new student went.

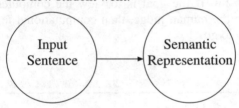

Figure 17.17 Semantically based systems.

A syntactic analysis of the sentence would show that *the new student* is the first NP directly dominated by S (see Figure 17.18). From there, the parser might guess that the subject is *the new student*. This is often true in English, although it is not always the case. Still, nothing is said about the fact that the subject is the actor (i.e., the one who performs the action) with a verb like *go*.

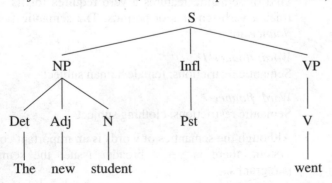

Figure 17.18 Assigning the sentence a syntactic analysis first.

Compare this to the intransitive version of the verb *open*.

27)

The door opened.

In this case, the subject *door* is not performing an action. Something or someone opened the door. A syntactically based system obtains this knowledge about a sentence after a structure is built.

In contrast, a semantically based system builds a semantic representation first. For sentence *26)*, it might look something like the one in Figure 17.19.

```
Go —    Actor
             NP
Went      the new student
```

Figure 17.19 Building the semantic representation first.

The word order is not represented, but the underlying semantic information is captured. The semantic representation of related sentences might be the same.

28)

It was the new student who went.

The mapping into the various syntactic forms of what is basically the same sentence occurs after the semantic representation is decided upon. Semantically based systems have been used for text and discourse analysis, such as for understanding stories.

Both approaches still need to accomplish the same goal, namely that of assigning word meaning, sentence meaning, and text meaning. The problem of semantic representation will not be covered here. However, it must be mentioned that determining matters like reference, as in *29)*, and scope, as in *30)* to *32)*, are part of what needs to be achieved.

29)

Chris wants to marry an Australian.

30)

Pregnant women and children get out first.

31)

Ripe apples and peaches make a good fruit salad.

32)

Every person speaks two languages.

For *29)*, is this a specific Australian or would any Australian at all do? For *30)*, what is the scope of *pregnant*? Is it *pregnant women and pregnant children*? This is unlikely. But in *31)*, the likely interpretation is *ripe apples and ripe peaches*. Finally, in *32)*, does every person speak the same two languages? Or different languages?

5.1

Pragmatics

The word *meaning* itself has many meanings. In addition to word meaning, logic, paragraph meaning and so on, it has also been loosely applied to the field of **pragmatics**. Pragmatics (as we saw in Chapter 7) is the study of how language is used in communication. Consider the following telephone conversation.

33)

Caller: Is George at home?
Answer: Yes.

This dialogue is amusing because the answerer has broken some basic conversational principles. The caller is not really asking the literal question *Is George at home?* although the semantic analysis of the sentence would indicate that this is a request for information about whether or not George is at home. The syntactic form of the question requires the answers *yes* or *no* but nothing else. The dialogue in *34)* does not have the amusing quality of *33)*.

34)

Caller: Are you tired?
Answer: Yes.

Conversational principles require that an answer be as informative as possible. This is not the case in *33)*, which violates the maxim of quantity (see Chapter 7, section 4.4).

Another example of conversational principles is illustrated in *35)* and *36)*.

35)

Sue got on the horse and rode into the sunset.

36)

Sue rode into the sunset and got on the horse.

Why is *36)* strange? The coordinating conjunction *and* should just be a simple joining of two like parts. The nouns from *31)*, for example, could be reversed with no strange result (the scope problem remains unsolved, however):

37)

Ripe peaches and apples make a good fruit salad.

The reason for the problem in *36)* is that the word *and is* often given a temporal interpretation. This may not be part of the meaning of *and* but rather a matter of how it is used.

Whether pragmatics is a subfield of semantics is controversial, but there is no disagreement on the fact that knowledge of pragmatic principles is necessary to understanding and generating language.

6

PRACTICAL APPLICATIONS OF COMPUTATIONAL LINGUISTICS

The previous sections of this chapter have shown how the use of computers has forced linguists to formulate rigorous statements of theory and facts, because all of the implicit knowledge that humans have about language has to be made explicit. Theories become testable in a concrete way. Implementations of practical systems tend to force researchers (and students) to understand a particular language process in very detailed terms. Since related skills are needed both for linguistic analysis and for programming, the field of computational linguistics has flourished. This section discusses some specific types of computer systems that involve using linguistically sophisticated programs.

An **application** can be defined as the use to which a program or set of programs is put, for example, a payroll application, an airline reservation application, or a word-processing application. Most early applications in computational linguistics fell into three categories: indexing and concordances, machine translation, and information retrieval. Other applications included speech synthesis and recognition and database applications.

6.1

Indexing and concordances

Indexing means finding, identifying, and usually counting all occurrences of a certain word in large texts. This application of computers to language study does exactly what computers are best at doing: locating a word, recording the location by line or sentence number, and counting how many times it appears. The examples of the use of the word *flounce* in the lexicology section were extracted from text using an indexing program. The program searched text on the computer to find any occurrence of the string *flounce*, *flouncing*, *flounced*, or *flounces*. When the string was found, the computer program took out the sentence and saved it in a separate file. A tally was kept of each time a targeted word was found.

A concordance tells which words occur near other words. Concordance and indexing programs are used widely in literary analysis and lexicography. Some authors seem to favour using certain words in the context of other words. Concordance programs can find these relationships. A concordance program could tell, for example, how many times the word *she* occurred next to *flounce*.

Perhaps the most widely used word count was performed by Henry Kučera and Nelson Francis in the early 1960s on a corpus of one million words. The corpus is referred to as the Brown corpus since the work was completed at Brown University in America. Kučera and Francis took fifteen different texts and wrote a program to count the number of times each word appeared. The ten most frequent words of American English, according to this corpus, are:

the	69,971
of	36,411
and	28,852
to	26,149
a	23,237

in	21,341
that	10,595
is	10,099
was	9,816
he	9,543

The numbers after the words indicate how many times they appeared in the one million words. Word frequency lists derived from these data have been useful to psycholinguists who need to pay attention to frequency when designing experiments.

These early applications are still very useful, but they are not linguistic in nature. They used the power of the computer to count and categorize words, so the results were of use to the linguist, but they did not rely on any linguistic knowledge. For example, to find *flounce*, the related words *flounced*, *flounces*, *flouncing* also had to be looked for. Early systems were not endowed with morphological knowledge, so they could look only for the exact string given. The program could not figure out that *flounce* and *flouncing* were related forms. Furthermore, all occurrences of the strings *flounce*, *flounces*, and so on were pulled out, without regard to part of speech. Since the goal was to look at subjects of verbs, it was necessary to distinguish between the verb *flounce* and the noun *flounce* as in *The women always flounce out* and *The chair had a lacy flounce around the bottom*. Notice the implications of this; two of the top ten most frequent words listed above are forms of the verb *be*, but since the system counts only strings, the forms *is* and *was* are counted separately. The inability of early systems to relate words had other problems. For example:

Minute	53
Min	5
Min.	1
Min.	

are probably all variations of the word *minute* in the corpus, although this would have to be verified by checking the original text. The count of *minute* is 53, but it really should be 60. (Note, however, that there is a possible complication: some of the occurrences of *minute* may be examples of the noun *minute* meaning 'memorandum' rather than 60 seconds, or the unrelated, differently pronounced adjective *minute* [maɪnjúːt] meaning 'very small', or it could be an abbreviation of *minister, ministry, minimum* or *minim* (a fluid measure roughly equivalent to a drop). We cannot be sure.)

On this side of the Atlantic, the Lancaster–Oslo/Bergen corpus was designed to replicate as closely as possible the Brown corpus, the only difference being that this corpus contains British rather than American English texts.

In recent years, the value of corpora as sources of data for lexicography has been fully recognized by a number of major British publishers of dictionaries. Collins sponsored researchers at Birmingham University to set up a large computer corpus which was used as a data-source for the Collins Cobuild Dictionary. Not long afterwards, two other major publishers, Longman Group (now Addison Wesley Longman) and Oxford University Press, set up similar projects – with one new major ingredient added: large samples of spoken English. Longman sponsored a 25-million word corpus which was compiled with the collaboration of Lancaster University. More recently, a consortium including the universities of Oxford and Lancaster, the British Library as well as several major publishers (Addison Wesley Longman, Chambers and Oxford University Press) has produced a 100-million word National Corpus of British English. The inclusion of spoken English in these two corpora is a step in the right direction. Spoken language differs significantly from written language. So, collecting material from both is essential if lexicographers are going to show usage in both written and spoken English.

Most current concordance and indexing programs have solved some of the easier problems such as abbreviations. Much larger bodies of texts are being used to overcome some of the problems of sparse and limited data, and more sophisticated statistical techniques are being utilized. But most of the harder problems still remain. First of all, some morphological knowledge is needed in order to relate various forms of the same word to just one base word. Second, syntactic knowledge is needed in order to establish precisely the part of speech of the word in the sentences and in order to determine the arguments of the verbs, such as subject and object. Finally, semantic knowledge is needed to know the thematic roles of the arguments and to know which meaning of a word is intended.

6.2

Information access and retrieval

The Internet and the World Wide Web have created a growing body of text and images that can now be searched by anyone with access to a computer and modem. Furthermore, there are dozens of freely available search systems or engines for roaming through titles, articles, captions, and other sections of texts. However, anyone who has ever tried to search for articles on a particular topic has had the frustrating experience of having to wade through masses of irrelevant material to find what was wanted. For example, when the word *morphology* was searched in the Library Index of Book Titles, the following titles were among those returned:

> *Principles of Polymer Morphology*
> *Image Analysis and Mathematical Morphology*
> *Drainage Basin Morphology*
> *French Morphology*

If a linguistically sophisticated program had been used to retrieve these titles, it is likely that they would have been divided according to the semantic subject field. Thus a chemist would not get titles on French, just as a linguist would not get titles on chemistry.

What linguistic expertise could an information retrieval system use? Again, as with indexing and concordance, the three critical sub-areas are computational morphology, syntax, and semantics. For example, someone wanting to know about the theory of *light* might want to find all references to the word *light* in an encyclopedia. Searching for the string *light* anywhere in the text might give *lightening*, *enlightenment*, and *lighthearted*, but also *delight* and *candlelight*. On the other hand, if the user searches only for *light* surrounded by blanks, then words like *lighting* or *lights* would be missed. The user might want to find synonyms or related words, such as *colourless* or *clear* for the adjective, or *illuminate* for the verb. Without a parser and semantics, there is no clue about the nature of the word *light* when it is found in the text. The problem appears simplistic, but it is far more complex than meets the eye.

6.3

Machine translation

The purpose of a machine translation system is the same as that of any translation system: taking text written or spoken in one language and writing or speaking it in another (see Figure 17.20). Translation poses challenging problems both for the human translator and for the machine attempting to do what the human does. Projects in machine translation in the 1940s and 1950s spawned much of the early research in computational linguistics. Consider the written case first, and think of a single institution like the United Nations. Every day millions of words need to be translated from one language to another. Add to that other political and scientific institutions, plus businesses and publishers. This results in an overwhelming need for help in translation since the process, when done correctly, is time-consuming and mentally demanding. Since computers are suited to tasks requiring memory, it would seem that, with careful programming, the problem of translating by computer could be solved.

Figure 17.20 Machine translation.

This was the thinking of computer scientists and linguists, but the problems turned out to be far more difficult than was imagined. Much government money was poured into the machine translation task from the late 1940s to the early 1960s, but results were slow to emerge due to the complexity of unforeseen problems. The subtlety of language, the nuances and lack of precision, caused problems because computers are suited to mathematical computation where subtleties do not prevail. Funding agencies became disillusioned, and although most researchers were still hopeful, they were humbled by the difficulties encountered in early years.

Researchers are now more realistic about their goals. Rather than attempting to build full-fledged machine translation systems that automatically convert a text from one language to another, some projects are aiming towards machine-assisted translation. In these projects, the computer is viewed as a tool to aid the translator. The computer makes suggestions, but the human translator makes final decisions. Another simplification is to aim the translation at a specific subject area; this way, word ambiguities are reduced to a minimum. For example, in the financial domain, the word *vehicle* is probably an investment device, but in the automobile domain, *vehicle* is most likely a device for driving. Yet other projects are developing ways to take texts and pass them through a preprocessor. A preprocessor is a system that looks at sentences and picks out which ones might present problems. The computer can identify the problem, and then ask the original writer to clarify. Take the following example:

38)

Many elephants smell.

Since this sentence could be confusing (because the verb *smell* is ambiguous – is the intended interpretation that many elephants stink or that many elephants are capable of perceiving odours?) it might be sent back to the writer to be clarified.

Machine translation applications encompass many aspects of computational linguistics. For this reason, the venture is one of the more challenging to researchers. In addition, the notion of a machine that is capable or nearly capable of mimicking a very complex and subtle human activity constitutes an intriguing enterprise. The source language needs to be analysed syntactically and semantically. Lexical items need to be matched. This is a particularly difficult task. Not only do words in one language often not exist in another, but sometimes several words are used for one. One example involves the German words *essen* and *fressen*. Both words mean *eat* in English, but the verb *essen* is used for humans, whereas *fressen* is used for animals. If the system made the mistake of using *fressen* for people, it would be an insult. An example from Spanish concerns a missing word, as shown in *39)* and *40)*. Sentence *41)* gives the word-by-word translation of the Spanish in *40)*.

39)

The elephants slept but did not snore.

40)

Los elefantes durmieron pero no roncaron.

41)

*The elephants slept but not snored.

The word-by-word translation in *41)* is not English. What's wrong? In English, if the subject of a negative sentence is omitted, then the properly inflected form of the verb *do* needs to be inserted. Since *39)* is in the past tense, the correct form is *did* (subject–verb number agreement does no apply in the past tense). There is no word for *did* in the Spanish version of the same sentence. Just as the human translator has to know this fact, so does the machine translation system. If the input language were Spanish and the input sentence were *40)*, then the English generation system would need to know to insert the verb *do*, properly inflected, and not to inflect the main verb. The difficulties increase with languages that are fundamentally different in nature, such as English and Japanese, or Spanish and Finnish, or French and Chinese.

If the machine translation system is required to take spoken language as input and give spoken language as output, then the system, now called a speech-to-speech translation system, becomes even more complex, as shown in Figure 17.21.

Figure 17.21 Modelling a speech-to-speech translation system.

6.4

Speech recognition

A speech recognition system takes spoken language as input and understands it (see Figure 17.22). The result could be the written text of what was said, or it could be orders to another machine. For example, a smart typewriter equipped with a recognition device will take orders to delete a line. The typewriter follows orders, but the words *delete line* will not be written. Speech recognition is a process that humans perform effortlessly, but teaching computers to recognize speech has turned out to be more difficult than was originally thought. Some of the linguistic problems involved were outlined in the sections on computational phonetics and phonology.

Figure 17.22 Modelling a speech recognition system.

What are some applications that would benefit from a speech recognition system? One that has been explored is in the area of medical record keeping. Writing down details of examinations is time-consuming; often doctors leave out critical information due to these time pressures. With a speech recognition system, the doctor would simply talk while doing an examination. The speech would automatically and instantly be translated into text, which could be printed out immediately. In this way, the doctor could examine the report with the patient there to make sure everything has been covered. Medical terminology is fairly controlled, so the computer would have an advantage in guessing words. Also, a speech recognition system would allow the doctor to use both hands while speaking. Medical records could immediately go into a central library, which could be referred to by researchers studying symptoms and diagnoses. Last but not least, no one would ever have to struggle to read the doctor's illegible handwriting!

Such a system would have to be absolutely perfect. However, it is easier to correct an error in a report than to write one. Other applications that have been explored include quality control devices for inspecting assembly lines. For example, a worker would be able to say words like *pass* or *fail*, and the machine would then know whether to accept the part or refuse it. Already, simple speech recognition is used by telephone carriers, e.g., say 'operator' to get an operator. A very important application of speech recognition is in developing aids for the physically disabled. These include devices such as voice-operated appliances, machines, and tools. Applications such as these have great promise.

6.5

Speech synthesis

A speech synthesis system has the opposite goal from a speech recognition system (see Figure 17.23). Applications for speech synthesis systems abound. One of the most important uses is 'reading' to the visually impaired. Previously this required a human either to do the actual reading or to pre-record books and other material. This is not only expensive but also limiting, since what the person wants or needs to read may not be available on tape. Another important application is as a talking aid for the vocally handicapped. Communication boards and talking typewriters show the need for converting text to spoken language.

Figure 17.23 A speech synthesis system.

Yet another fairly common application is in an area called *database query*. A database is a large source of information, such as bank records, billing records, airline timetables, and theatre and film schedules. Imagine wanting to find out about ticket availability for the theatre, cinema, or other cultural events. This information is constantly changing as people buy tickets and as agencies release tickets. When you call, the text-to-speech machine can read the information aloud directly out of the database. No one has had to record it, which is time-consuming and expensive. Furthermore, the information is completely up-to-date. Such systems already exist on the Internet, e.g., for tracking packages, so if this were hooked up to a speech synthesizer, the results could simply be read aloud. Other applications include use in machine translation systems, for robots, for expert systems, and for novel medical applications.

Summing up

This chapter has covered the relatively new field of **computational linguistics**, which is the application of computers to the study of linguistic problems. There are two goals in computational linguistics. One is to use the computer as a tool to build programs that model a particular linguistic theory or approach. For this goal, the computer becomes a testing ground for the theory. The other goal is to build working systems that use linguistic information. The chapter covers the fields of computational phonetics and phonology, morphology, syntax, lexicology, and semantics and pragmatics. A section on **applications** presents some of the devices that have incorporated linguistic tools, such as *machine translation* systems and *reading machines* for the visually impaired.

Recommended reading

Allen, James. 1995. *Natural Language Understanding*. Menlo Park, California: Benjamin/Cummings (2nd edn.)

Grishman, Ralph. 1986. *Computational Linguistics: An Introduction. Cambridge University Studies in Natural Language Processing*. Cambridge: Cambridge University Press.

King, Margaret. ed. 1983. *Parsing Natural Language*. London: Academic Press/ Harcourt Brace Jovanovich.

Klatt, Dennis. 1987. 'Review of text-to-speech conversion for English.' *Journal of the Acoustical Society of America*. 82: 3.

Leech, Geoffrey and Fligelstone, Steven. 1992. 'Computers and corpus analysis.' In C. Butler, *Computers and Written Texts*. Oxford: Blackwell.

Levinson, Stephen E. and Liberman, Mark Y. 1981. 'Speech recognition by Computer.' *Scientific American* 224 (4): 56–77.

Pullman, Steve. 1997. *Computational Linguistics*. Cambridge: Cambridge University Press.

Questions

1. What kinds of problems might a computer have with these sentences?
    a) Sue bought red apples and plums.
    b) It was a large animal house.
    c) Susan baked in kitchen.
    d) Susan baked in the sun.
    e) Susan baked.

2. What are the main uses of a text-to-speech system? What information does a computer need to know in order to pronounce these sentences in informal style?
    a) What are you doing tonight?
    b) The woman was delighted.
    c) The article misled me.

d) That's a new car, isn't it?

e) It was a tough exam, although I did well.

f) Can't you sing better?

3. What rules are necessary for a computer program to analyse these words? (*Hint*: First identify the prefixes and suffixes. Refer to the chapter on morphology if necessary especially sections 1.2 and 2.)

a) kindness

b) kindly

c) kindnesses

d) nationalism

e) countability

f) non-transformational

g) reusable

h) resent

4. What different structures might a syntactic analyser propose for the following ambiguous sentences?

a) She saw the man with a telescope.

b) Watch dogs bark.

c) Broadcast programs like 60 Minutes.

d) Ten rickshaws were reported stolen by the Delhi police.

5. Think of a word that has many different meanings, such as *bank* or *interest*. Then give information about that word using the categories in section 17.4. Give at least two senses for each part of speech. The following example has one sense for the noun part of speech, and two senses for the verb part of speech.

Word: Bank

a) *Part of speech*: Noun

b) *Sense number*: 1

c) *Semantic restrictions*: of a river

d) *Pronunciation*: /bæŋk/

e) *Context and style*: normal

f) *Example*: The bank of the river was grassy.

Word: Bank

a) *Part of speech*: Verb

b) *Sense number*: 1

c) *Subcategorization*: transitive, requires the preposition *on*

d) *Semantic restrictions*: object of preposition is either a person or a thing

e) *Pronunciation*: /bæŋk/

f) *Context and style*: normal

g) *Example*: I can't bank on him to do it.

Word: Bank

a) *Part of speech*: Verb

b) *Sense number*: 2

    c) *Subcategorization*: transitive
    d) *Semantic restrictions*: object is money
    e) *Pronunciation*: /bæŋk/
    f) *Context and style*: normal
    g) *Example*: She banks her money at the local branch.

6. Give three examples of computational linguistics applications. How can these systems improve the quality of life for people with physical disabilities?

7. The use of the Internet and the World Wide Web has changed the way people access information. In the context of requesting information from an electronic source:

    a. List three cases where linguistic information would help you to find your way around the Net. For example, if you are looking for information on *barristers* and *solicitors*, it would help in your search to know that the American equivalent is *attorney*.

    b. List three cases where linguistic ambiguity will hurt you in searching for information electronically. For example, in looking for articles on the word *bank*, you will find articles on rivers and financial institutions.

What are some words and phrases that would give you problems? Explain for each example what the problem is, and how you could solve it.

Glossary

Ablaut A vowel alternation that marks a grammatical contrast (e.g., *mouse/mice*).

Absolute universals Patterns or traits that occur in all languages.

Absolutive In some languages the case associated with both the direct object of a transitive verb and the subject of an intransitive verb. (*See also* **Ergative**.)

Abstract representation A representation that is to a greater or lesser degree distinct from its phonetic realization.

Accent Differences between spoken varieties of the same language that are restricted to pronunciation.

Accidental gaps Non-occurring but possible forms of a language (e.g., in English, *blork*).

Acoustic phonetics An approach to phonetics that is concerned with measuring and analysing the physical properties of sound waves produced when we speak.

Acquired agraphia *See* **Acquired dysgraphia**.

Acquired alexia *See* **Acquired dyslexia**.

Acquired dysgraphia The impairment of writing ability in patients who previously possessed normal writing ability (also called **acquired agraphia**).

Acquired dyslexia The impairment of reading ability in patients who previously possessed normal reading ability (also called **acquired alexia**).

Acrolect A creole variety that is relatively similar to the standard language from which it arose. (*See also* **Basilect** and **Mesolect**.)

Acronym A word that is formed by taking the initial letters of (some of or all) the words in a phrase or title and pronouncing them as a word (e.g., *NATO* for *North Atlantic Treaty Organization*).

Acrophonic principle The representation of sounds by pictures of objects whose pronunciation begins with the sound to be represented (e.g., the sound [b] might be represented by a picture of a bird).

Active sentence A sentence in which the NP with the agent role is the subject (e.g., *Helen painted the room*).

Address terms The various forms that are used to address people, indicating something of one's relationship to the individual addressed (e.g., in English, *Ms Callaghan, Professor Van Haar, Betty*).

Adjective (A) A lexical category that designates a property that is applicable to the entities named by nouns, can often take comparative and superlative endings in English, and functions as the head of an adjective phrase (e.g., *red, obese, hearty*).

Adstratum influence   The mutual influence of two equally dominant languages on each other (e.g., the influence of English and French on each other in Montreal).

Adverb (Adv)   A lexical category that typically names properties that can be applied to the actions designated by verbs (e.g., *quickly*, *fearfully*).

Affix   A morpheme that does not belong to a lexical category and is always bound (e.g., *-ing*, *un-*).

Affricates   Non-continuant consonants that show a slow release of the closure (e.g., tʃ, dʒ]).

Affrication   A process in which palatalized stops become affricates.

Agent   The thematic role of the doer of the action designated by the verb (e.g., *Marilyn* in *Marilyn fed the dolphin*).

Agglutinating languages   Languages in which words typically contain several morphemes, of which usually only one is a lexical category. The others are clearly identifiable affixes, each of which typically encodes a single grammatical contrast.

Agrammatism   An aphasic disturbance characterized by the omission of function words and inflectional affixes and by syntactic comprehension deficits.

Agreement   The result of one category being inflected to mark properties of another (e.g., the verb marked for the person and/or the number of the subject).

Allomorphs   Variants of a morpheme (e.g., [-s], [-z], and [-ɪz] are allomorphs of the English plural morpheme).

Allophones   Variants of a phoneme, usually in complementary distribution and phonetically similar (e.g., voiced and voiceless /l/ in English).

Alphabetic writing   A type of writing in which symbols represent consonant and vowel segments.

Alveolar ridge   The small ridge that protrudes from just behind the upper front teeth.

Alveopalatal (area)   *See* **Palato-alveolar**.

Ambisyllabicity   The simultaneous presence of a segment in two adjoining syllables.

Amelioration   The process in which the meaning of a word becomes more favourable (e.g., *pretty* used to mean 'tricky, sly, cunning').

Amerind   The group into which all the Amerindian languages (except for Na-Dené and Eskimo-Aleut stocks) have been placed, according to one controversial classification system.

Amerindian languages   Languages spoken by the aboriginal peoples of North, South, and Central America.

Analogy   A source of language change that involves the generalization of a regularity on the basis of the inference that if elements are alike in some respects, they should be alike in others as well (e.g., *bring* becoming *brung* by analogy with *ring/rung*).

Analytic languages   *See* **Isolating languages**.

Anaphoric reference   The use of a pronoun that refers to an NP earlier in the discourse (e.g., *Hilary ate her dinner*).

Angular gyrus   An area of the brain that plays an important role in reading.

Animate   A noun class category in some languages, comparable to masculine and feminine nouns in some European languages (e.g., both *duck* and *pipe* are animate nouns in Cree).

Antecedent   The element that determines the interpretation of a pronoun (e.g., *Jeremy* in *Jeremy looked at himself in the mirror*).

Anterior   A place feature that characterizes sounds articulated in front of the palato-alveolar region.

Antonyms   Words or phrases that are opposites with respect to some component of their meaning (e.g., *big* and *small*).

Aphasia   A language deficit caused by damage to the brain.

Apical   An apical sound is articulated with the tip of the tongue.

Apocope   The deletion of a word-final vowel (e.g., *name* used to be pronounced with a word-final schwa).

Approximant (Frictionless continuant)   A sound produced by bringing the articulators close together while at the same time leaving a sufficiently large gap between them through which air escapes without causing audible turbulence.

Archaism   A lexical item that was previously widely used but has survived only in a limited area (e.g., *bairn* 'child' from Old English *bearn* only survives in Scotland and northeast England).

Areal classification   An approach to language classification that identifies characteristics shared by languages which are in geographical contact.

Argot   A secret language associated with social groups whose members wish to conceal some aspect of their communication from non-members.

Argument   A NP which is syntactically a grammatical dependent of a verb and about which semantically the verb says something.

Articulatory phonetics   An approach to phonetics that studies the physiological mechanisms of speech production.

Arytenoids   Two small cartilages in the larynx that are attached to the posterior ends of the vocal folds, enabling the vocal folds to be drawn together or apart.

Aspiration   The lag in the onset of vocalic voicing, accompanied by the release of air, that is heard after the release of certain stops in English (e.g., the first sound of *top* is aspirated).

Assimilation   The influence of one segment on another, resulting in a sound becoming more like a nearby sound in terms of one or more of its phonetic characteristics (e.g., in English, unrounded consonants like /t/ or /k/ become rounded when they are followed by a round vowel like /uː/ or /ʊ/ as is *Cooper took two cool cooks*).

Association line   A line linking a symbol that represents a sound segment with a symbol that represents a tone or feature.

Audiolingualism   A method of L2 teaching that emphasizes memorization and pattern drills, based on the behaviourist notion that L2 learning is a mechanistic process of habit formation.

Autopsy studies   Studies based on post-mortem examination.

Autosegmental (notation)   A type of notation that links segments with tones or features by association lines.

Auxiliary verb   A functional category that serves as the specifier of a verb (e.g., *was* in *was talking*).

Back   A dorsal feature that characterizes sounds articulated behind the palatal region in the oral cavity.

Back (of the tongue)   The part of the tongue that is hindmost but still lies in the mouth.

Back vowel   A vowel that is made with the tongue positioned in the back of the oral cavity (e.g., the vowel sounds in *hoot* and *board*).

Backformation   A word formation process that creates a new word by removing a real or supposed affix from another word in the language (e.g., *edit* came from *editor* through the removal of *-or*).

Base   The form to which an affix is added (e.g., *book* is the base for the affix *-s* in *books*, *modernize* is the base for the affix *-ed* in *modernized*).

Basilect   A creole variety that shows the least influence from the standard language from which it arose. (*See also* **Acrolect** and **Mesolect**.)

Bilabials   Sounds involving both lips (e.g., the first sound of *bones*).

Bilingual   A person or community with a mastery of two languages.

Binyan   A morphological class of verbs in a Semitic language characterized by a particular sequence of skeletal positions on which the actual consonant and vowel segments are mapped (e.g., CVCVCV represents 'past tense/completed action' in Arabic). (*See also* **Templatic morphology**.)

Blade (of the tongue)   The area of the tongue just behind the tip.

Blend   A word that is created from parts of two already existing items (e.g., *brunch* from *breakfast* and *lunch*).

Blissymbolics   A contemporary development of pictographic writing that uses a number of recombinable symbols representing basic units of meaning, primarily used for non-speaking individuals.

Body (of the tongue)   The main mass of the tongue.

Borrowing   A source of language change that involves adopting aspects of one language into another.

Bound morpheme   A morpheme that must be attached to another element (e.g., the past tense marker *-ed*).

Bounded foot   A unit of metrical representation that consists of a stressed syllable and no more than one unstressed syllable.

Boustrophedon   The practice of reversing the direction of writing at the end of each line, typical of many old writing systems.

Broca's aphasia   A non-fluent aphasia in which the speech is very halting, there are numerous phonemic errors, and there is a lack of intonation.

Broca's area   The area of the left frontal lobe that plays an important role in language production.

C-command   A syntactic notion that is involved in pronoun interpretation and is formulated as: NP_a c-commands NP_b if the first category above NP_a contains NP_b.

Call   In avian communication, short bursts of sound or simple patterns of notes, typically used as warning or other group-related signals.

Caregiver speech *See* **Motherese**.

Case A morphological category that encodes information about an element's grammatical role (subject, direct object, and so on) (e.g., the contrast between *he* and *him*).

Case Filter, the The requirement that every NP in a grammatical sentence be in a position to which case can be assigned by the Case Rules.

Cataphoric reference The use of a pronoun that refers to an NP later in the discourse.

Central sulcus The sulcus that extends from the top of the cerebral cortex to the lateral fissure (also called the fissure of Rolando).

Cerebral blood flow study A technique for observing cognitive activity in the brain that uses a radio-isotope detector to produce images of how much blood is going to particular parts of the brain.

Cerebral cortex The grey wrinkled mass that sits like a cap over the rest of the brain and is the seat of cognitive functioning.

Cerebral hemispheres The left and right halves of the cerebrum, separated by the longitudinal fissure.

Cerebro-vascular accident *See* **Stroke**.

Characters The units of contemporary Chinese orthography, most of which consist of two parts, a phonetic **determinative** and a **radical**.

Class A group of sounds that shares certain phonetic properties (e.g., all voiced sounds).

Class node A label that represents each feature grouping in the feature hierarchy (also called simply a **node**).

Clipping A word formation process that shortens a polysyllabic word by deleting one or more syllables (e.g., *prof* from *professor*).

Clitic A phonologically deficient word-like form (like *'ve* in *I've done it*) that must be attached to some word because it cannot occur in isolation.

Closed syllable A syllable with a coda (e.g., both syllables in *camping*).

Co-articulation Extension of articulatory gestures used in the prediction of one sound to adjacent sounds.

Co-operative Principle, the The general overarching guideline thought to underlie conversational interactions: Make your contribution appropriate to the conversation.

Coda (C) The elements that follow the nucleus in the same syllable (e.g., [rf] in *surfboard*).

Cognates Words of different languages that have descended from a common source, as shown by systematic phonetic correspondences (e.g., English *father* and German *Vater*).

Cognitive development The emergence of the various mental abilities (such as language) that make up the human intellect.

Cohesive devices Linguistic resources used to provide the cohesion that is necessary for discourse to be perceived as an organized whole.

Cohort model This is a model which claims that in word comprehension, words are analysed by hearers from beginning to end.

Coinage *See* **Word manufacture**.

Communication strategies   Strategies used by L2 learners when they are lacking the necessary linguistic knowledge to say what they want to communicate (e.g., paraphrasing).

Communicative competence   A speaker's underlying knowledge of the linguistic system and the norms for the appropriate socio-cultural use of language in particular speech situations.

Communicative language teaching   Any L2 teaching method that is communicative in design, emphasizing functional language in the attempt to attain the goal of communicative competence.

Comparative reconstruction   The reconstruction of properties of a parent language through comparison of its descendant languages.

Compensatory lengthening   The increment in the duration of a vowel when its neighbour is deleted or realized as a non-syllabic glide.

Complement clause   A sentence-like construction that is embedded within a larger structure (e.g., *that his car had been stolen* in *Jerry told Mary that his car had been stolen*).

Complement   The element or elements for which a head is subcategorized and which provide information about entities and locations whose existence is implied by the meaning of the head (e.g., *the book* in *bought the book*). (*See also* **Direct object**.)

Complementary distribution   Variants of a phoneme that never occur in the same phonetic environment are in complementary distribution.

Complementizer (C)   A functional category that takes an S complement, forming a CP (complementizer phrase) (e.g., w*hether* in *I wonder whether Lorna has left*).

Complex word   A word that contains two or more morphemes (e.g., *theorize, unemployment*).

Componential analysis   The representation of a word's intension in terms of smaller semantic components called features.

Compound level   The metrical level on which the stress patterning of compounds is represented.

Compounding   The combination of lexical categories (N, V, A, or P) to form a larger word (e.g., *fire + engine*).

Computational linguistics   The term refers either to the use of computers as a tool to understand/implement linguistic theories or to working computer systems which require linguistic knowledge.

Computerized Axial Tomography   A technique for observing the living brain that uses a narrow beam of X-rays to create brain images which take the form of a series of brain slices (also called **CT scanning**).

Concordance   This shows which words occur in the neighbourhood of certain other words in a corpus.

Conjugation   The set of inflected forms associated with a verb (also called a **verbal paradigm**).

Conjunction   A functional category that joins together two or more categories of the same type, forming a coordinate structure (e.g., *and* in *a man and his dog*).

Connotation   The set of associations that a word's use can evoke (e.g., *winter* evokes short days and long nights, snow, bare trees, etc.). (*See also* **Denotation**.)

Conservative language   A language whose forms have stayed relatively close to those of the proto-language.

Consonant deletion   A phonetic process that elides a consonant (e.g., the deletion of [θ] in *fifths*).

Consonant weakening   A process that weakens a consonant, usually between vowels, according to the scale of consonantal strength.

Consonantal   A major class feature that characterizes sounds produced with a major obstruction in the vocal tract.

Consonantal strength   The relative placement of a consonant on a scale of consonantal strength.

Consonants   Sounds produced by partially or totally obstructing the vocal tract that are (normally) used at the periphery of the syllable (in the onset or coda).

Constellation   A complex of communicative modes operating on different channels.

Constituent   One or more words that occur together as a syntactic unit (e.g., *the apple* in *The apple fell onto the floor*). (*See also* **Coordination test**, **Substitution test**, and **Movement test**.)

Constricted Glottis ([CG])   A laryngeal feature that characterizes sounds made with the glottis closed (in English, only [?]).

Continuant   A manner feature that characterizes sounds made with free or nearly free airflow through the oral cavity: vowels, fricatives, glides, and liquids.

Continuants   Sounds that are produced with a continuous airflow through the mouth.

Contour tones   Moving pitches on a single segment that signal meaning differences.

Contradiction   A relationship between sentences wherein the truth of one sentence requires the falsity of another sentence (e.g., *Raymond is married* contradicts *Raymond is a bachelor*).

Contralateral   The control of the right side of the body by the left side of the brain and vice versa.

Contrast   Segments are said to contrast when their presence alone may distinguish forms with different meanings from each other (e.g., [s] and [z] in the words *sip* and *zip*).

Conversational implicature   Information that is conveyed through inference but is not actually said.

Conversion   A word formation process that assigns an already existing word to a new syntactic category (also called **zero derivation**) (e.g., *nurse* (V) from *nurse* (N)).

Coordinate Structure Constraint, the   A constraint on transformations that does not allow an element to be removed from a coordinate structure.

Coordinate structure   A phrase that is formed by joining two (or more) categories of the same type with a conjunction such as *and* or *or* (e.g., *those men and that woman*).

Degenerate foot   A metrical foot that consists of only a head, also called a minimal foot.

Degree word (Deg)   A functional category that serves as the specifier of a preposition or an adjective (e.g., *quite* in *quite tired*; *very* in *very near the house*).

Deictics   Forms whose use and interpretation depend on the location of the speaker and/or addressee within a particular setting (e.g., *this/that, here/ there*).

Delayed release   A manner feature that characterizes all and only affricate consonants.

Deletion   A process that removes a segment from certain phonetic contexts (e.g., the pronunciation of *fifths* as [fɪfs]).

Denasalization   A common substitution process in child language acquisition that involves the replacement of a nasal stop by a non-nasal counterpart (e.g., *come* is pronounced [kʌb]).

Denotation   The set of entities to which a word or expression refers (also called its **referents** or **extension**).

Dentals   Sounds made with the tongue placed against or near the teeth.

Derivation   A process that forms a word with a meaning and/or category distinct from that of its base through the addition of an affix (e.g., the formation of *helper* (N) from *help* (V)).

Derived (phonology)   Resulting from the application of phonological rules to underlying representations.

Descriptive   A characteristic of linguistic research that seeks to describe human linguistic ability and knowledge, not to prescribe one system in preference to another. (See *also* **Prescriptive**.)

Design features   Characteristics of human language that are used to compare animal communication systems with human language.

Determiner (Det)   A functional category that serves as the specifier of a noun (e.g., *a, the, these*).

Deterministic (parser)   Refers to a parser that is obliged to stick to the original analysis that is proposed and is forbidden to backtrack even when new information casts doubt on the initial analysis. (See also **Parser**.)

Developmental errors   Errors that occur in L1 language acquisition or L2 learning that result from the manner in which the language acquisition mechanisms operate (e.g., *goed* results from overgeneralization).

Developmental sequences   The stages of linguistic development that are relatively invariant across language learners.

Devoicing   Voicing assimilation in which a sound becomes voiceless because of a nearby voiceless sound (e.g., the *l* in *place* is devoiced because of the voiceless stop preceding it).

Diacritic   A mark added to a phonetic symbol to alter its value in some way (e.g., a circle under a symbol to indicate voicelessness).

Dialect continuum   A situation where dialect boundaries are not marked by clearly but where instead the differentiation of dialects increases cumulatively.

Dialectology   The study of linguistic variation in terms of the geographical distribution of speakers.

Diaphragm   The large sheet of muscle that separates the chest cavity from the abdomen and helps to maintain the air pressure necessary for speech production.

Diary study   A type of naturalistic investigation in which a researcher (often a parent) keeps daily notes on a child's linguistic progress.

Dichotic listening   A technique in which stimuli (either linguistic or non-linguistic) are presented through headphones to the left and right ears to determine the lateralization of various cognitive functions.

Diphthong   A vowel that shows a noticeable change in quality during its production (e.g., the vowel sounds in *house* and *ride*).

Diphthongization   A process in which a monophthong becomes a diphthong (e.g., [i:] became [əɪ] during the Great English Vowel Shift – which subsequently became [aɪ]).

Direct method   A method of L2 teaching that is based on the belief that an adult L2 learner can learn language in the same manner as a child and therefore involves no grammar instruction but rather concentrates on communicating.

Direct object   The NP complement of a verb (e.g., *a fish* in *Judy caught a fish*).

Discourse   A set of utterances produced by a speaker.

Discourse analysis   The field that deals with the organization of texts, including ways in which parts of texts are connected and the devices used for achieving textual structure.

Discourse markers   Markers that occur over the length of a bit of discourse, separating one 'unit of talk' from a previous one (e.g., *well*, *y'know*).

Discrete sign   A sign that is distinguished from other signs by stepwise differences (e.g., voiced and voiceless phonemes, the numbers of a digital clock).

Dissimilation   A process whereby one segment becomes less like another segment in its environment (e.g., *anma* 'soul' in Latin became *alma* in Spanish).

Distinctive   *See* **Contrast**.

Distinctive feature   A feature that is able to signal a difference in meaning by changing its plus or minus value (e.g., the feature [voice] in the words *peer* and *beer*).

Dorsal features   Features that represent placement of the body of the tongue.

Dorsum (of the tongue)   The body and back of the tongue.

Double-blind test   A type of test in which the experimenter is prevented from seeing the stimulus in order to avoid cueing particular behaviours.

Downdrift   The maintenance of a distinction among the pitch registers of an utterance even as the overall pitch of the utterance falls.

Dressage   A type of interaction between trainer and animal that depends on the animal's interpreting subtle cues given by the trainer.

Duetting   The interchange of calls in a patterned manner between two members of a species.

Dysprosody   The lack of sentence intonation, a common characteristic of the speech of Broca's aphasics.

Enclitic   A clitic attached to the end of a preceding word (e.g., *'s* as in *She's here*. (*See also* **Clitic.**)

Endocentric compound   A compound whose rightmost component (in English) identifies the general class to which the meaning of the entire word belongs (e.g., *kettledrum* is a type of drum). (*See also* **Exocentric compound.**)

Endophoric reference   The use of a pronoun to refer to a noun phrase in the discourse (also called **textual reference**).

Entailment   A relation between sentences in which the truth of one sentence necessarily implies the truth of another (e.g., *Shaun is Louise's husband* entails the sentence *Louise is married*).

Environment   The phonetic context in which a sound occurs.

Epenthesis   A process that inserts a segment into a particular environment (e.g., the insertion of a schwa in the pronunciation of *athlete* as [æθəliːt]).

Ergative   The case associated with the subject of a transitive verb (but not that of an intransitive verb).

Euphemism   A term that is used to avoid an expression that may be seen as offensive (e.g., *Your son has severe, general learning difficulties* instead of *Your son is very thick*; *perspire* instead of *sweat*).

Exclusive   A person contrast in some languages that indicates that the addressee is to be excluded in the interpretation of the first person plural morpheme. (*See also* **Inclusive.**)

Exocentric compound   A compound whose meaning does not follow from the meaning of its parts (e.g., *redneck*, since it is not a type of neck).

Experimental approach   An approach to investigating child language in which researchers make use of specially designed tasks to elicit linguistic activity relevant to a particular phenomenon.

Extension   The set of entities to which a word or expression refers (also called its **denotation** or **referents**).

Extrametrical syllable   A syllable that falls outside the effects of stress rules.

Face   Face-saving language and behaviour maintains the other person's reputation, dignity, credibility, and the like, while face-threatening behaviour does the reverse.

Feature (phonetic)   The smallest unit of analysis of phonological structure, combinations of which make up segments (e.g., [nasal], [continuant]).

Feature hierarchy   A hierarchical representation of how features are related to each other.

Features (semantic)   The semantic components that make up a word's intension.

Feeding (order)   Rules are said to be in a feeding relationship if the application of one rule is necessary for the creation of the circumstances in which another rule is able to apply.

Fissure   A relatively deep sulcus of the cerebral cortex. (*See also* **Sulci**.)

Flap   A sound commonly identified with *r* and produced when the tongue tip strikes the alveolar ridge as it passes across it (e.g., in North American English, the medial consonant in *bitter* and *bidder*).

Flapping   An assimilation process in which a dental or alveolar stop ([–continuant]) changes to a flap ([+continuant]) in the environment of other continuants.

Fluent aphasia   The aphasia that occurs due to damage to parts of the left cortex behind the central sulcus, resulting in fluent speech but great difficulty selecting, organizing, and monitoring language production (also called **sensory aphasia**).

Folk etymology   Reanalysis of a word that is based on an incorrect historical analysis and does not usually involve a conscious or detailed study of the word on the part of the speaker (e.g., *hamburger* being reanalysed into two morphemes, *ham* and *burger*.)

Foot level   The level of metrical representation that is below the word level.

Foreigner talk   The type of speech that is typically addressed to second language learners, characterized by such properties as simple word order and more common vocabulary items (also called **teacher talk**).

Formants   The principal concentrations of bands of energy in a speech sound (particularly in a vowel) which give it its peculiar auditory quality. (*See also* **Spectrogram**.)

Fossilization   If the interlanguage grammar gets stuck in a rut, and stops approximating to the grammar of the target language it is said to have fossilized.

Free form   An element that can occur in isolation and/or whose position with respect to neighbouring elements is not entirely fixed.

Free morpheme   A morpheme that can be a word by itself (e.g., *fear*).

Free variation   Sounds are in free variation when they do not contrast, can occur in identical phonetic environments, and are phonetically similar.

Frication   The weakening of a stop to a fricative (e.g., [d] becoming [ð]).

Fricatives   Consonants produced with a continuous airflow through the mouth, accompanied by a continuous audible noise (e.g., [f], [ʃ]).

Frictionless continuant   *See* **Approximant**.

Front vowel   A vowel that is made with the tongue positioned in the front of the oral cavity (e.g., the vowel sounds in *seal* and *bat*).

Frontal lobe   The lobe of the brain that lies in front of the central sulcus and in which Broca's area is located.

Fronting   A common substitution process in child language acquisition that involves the moving forward of a sound's place of articulation (e.g., *cheese* pronounced as [tsi:z]).

Full reduplication   A morphological process that duplicates the entire word (e.g., in Malay, *anak* 'child'/*anakanak* 'various children').

Function words   Words such as determiners and conjunctions that are lacking in the speech of Broca's aphasics, resulting in telegraphic speech.

Functional analysis   An approach to syntactic analysis that attempts to understand syntactic phenomena in terms of their communicative function.

Functional category   A word-level syntactic category whose members are harder to define and paraphrase than those of lexical categories (e.g., auxiliary verbs, conjunctions, determiners, and degree words) (also called **non-lexical category**).

Fusion   The process by which words develop into affixes over time.

Fusional languages   Languages in which words typically consist of several morphemes and the morphemes that are affixes often mark several grammatical categories simultaneously (e.g., Russian).

Fuzzy concepts   Concepts that do not have clear-cut boundaries to distinguish them from other concepts (e.g., the concept 'poor').

Garden path sentence   An awkward sentence that misleads the syntactic parser and takes it down the garden path to the wrong analysis.

Gender-exclusive differentiation   The situation in certain societies characterized by radically different speech varieties used by men and women.

Gender-variable differentiation   The relative frequency with which men and women use certain features of language.

Genetic classification   The categorization of languages according to the ancestor languages from which they developed.

Genetically related languages   Languages that have descended from a common parent (e.g., German and Italian have both descended from Indo-European).

Given information   Knowledge that the speaker assumes is available to the addressee at the time of the utterance, either because it is shared by both or because it has already been introduced into the discourse (also called **old information**).

Glagolitic script   A script that was introduced in Slavic-speaking areas in the ninth century AD for the translation of the Bible.

Glide strengthening   The strengthening of a glide to an affricate (e.g., [j] becoming [dʒ]).

Glides   Sounds that are produced with an articulation like that of a vowel, but move quickly to another articulation (e.g., [j], [w]).

Gliding   A common substitution process in child language acquisition which involves the replacement of a liquid by a glide (e.g., *play* is pronounced [pweɪ]).

Global aphasia   The most severe form of aphasia, in which the patient is completely mute.

Glottals   Sounds produced by using the vocal folds as the primary articulators (e.g., [h], [ʔ]).

Glottis   The space between the vocal folds.

Graded sign   A sign that conveys its meaning by changes in degree (e.g., voice volume, a blush).

Grammar   The mental system of rules and categories that allows humans to form and interpret the words and sentences of their language.

Grammar-translation method   A method of L2 teaching that emphasizes reading, writing, translation, and the conscious learning of grammatical rules, its primary goal being to develop a literary mastery of the target language.

Grammatical   The status of a sentence that speakers judge to be a possible sentence of their language.

Grammaticized concepts   Concepts that are expressed as affixes or non-lexical categories (e.g., the concept of 'obligation' as expressed by the auxiliary verb *must*).

Grimm's Law   The consonant shifts that took place between Proto-Indo-European and Proto-Germanic.

Gyri   The areas where the cerebral cortex is folded out (singular: *gyrus*).

Hangul   The alphabetic script used to represent Korean, the symbols of which are grouped to represent the syllables of individual morphemes.

Head (of a foot)   The stressed element of a metrical foot.

Head (of a phrase)   The word around which a phrasal category is built (e.g., V, N, A, P).

Head (of a word)   The morpheme that determines the category of the entire word (e.g., *green* in *greenfly*).

Heavy syllable   A syllable with a rhyme containing a long vowel, or a short vowel followed by at least one consonant, has two moras and is said to be heavy. (*See also* **Syllable weight**.)

Hieroglyphics   An Egyptian pictorial writing system, which later developed into a mixed writing system.

High   A dorsal feature that characterizes sounds produced with the tongue body raised.

High vowel   A vowel that is made with the tongue raised (e.g., the vowel sounds in *beat* and *lose*).

Hiragana   The Japanese syllabary that is used in conjunction with katakana and kanji to write Japanese.

Historical linguistics   The linguistic discipline that is concerned with the description and the explanation of language change.

Holophrases   Utterances produced by children in which one word expresses the type of meaning that would be associated with an entire sentence in adult speech (e.g., *up* used to mean 'Pick me up').

Homophony   The situation in which a single form has two or more entirely distinct meanings (e.g., *club* 'a social organization'; *club* 'a blunt weapon').

Hypercorrection   A source of language change that occurs when a speaker who is attempting to speak another language or dialect overgeneralizes particular rules.

Iambic   A bounded, right-headed metrical foot (e.g., *collect*).

Iconic sign   A sign that bears some resemblance to its referent (e.g., a picture of a woman on a washroom door).

Immersion   A method of teaching a second language to children in which students are taught most of their courses and school activities in the target language.

Implicational universals   A universal of language which specifies that the presence of one trait implies the presence of another (but not vice versa).

Inanimate   A noun class category in some languages (such as Cree), comparable to masculine and feminine nouns in some European languages. (*See also* **Animate**.)

Inclusive   A person contrast in some languages that indicates that the addressee is to be included in the interpretation of the first person plural morpheme. (*See also* **Exclusive**.)

Incorporation   The combination of a word (usually a noun) with a verb to form a compound verb.

Indexical sign   A sign that fulfils its function by pointing out its referent, typically by being a partial sample of it (e.g., the track of an animal).

Indirect negative evidence   The assumption that non-occurring structures in the linguistic environment are ungrammatical. (*See also* **Negative evidence**.)

Infix   An affix that occurs within a base.

INFL (Inflection)   The node that appears directly under S in a phrase structure tree and dominates tense as well as other verbal inflection (i.e., person and number); the constituents of INFL take part in subject–verb agreement. **INFL** is often abbreviated to **I**.

Inflection   The modification of a word's form to indicate the grammatical subclass to which it belongs (e.g., the -*s* in *books* marks the plural subclass).

Instrumental motivation   The desire to achieve proficiency in a new language for utilitarian reasons, such as job promotion.

Integrative motivation   The desire to achieve proficiency in a new language in order to participate in the social life of the language community.

Intension   An expression's inherent sense; the concepts that it evokes.

Interactional sociolinguistics   Sociolinguistic research that is mainly concerned with the language used in speech situations.

Intercostals   The muscles between the ribs that help to maintain the air pressure necessary for speech production.

Interdentals   Sounds made with the tongue placed between the teeth (e.g., [θ], [ð]).

Interfaces   The ways in which components of a grammar (such as phonology and syntax) are related to each other.

Interference   *See* **Transfer.**

Interlanguage   The interim grammatical system that an L2 learner is using at a particular period in his or her acquisition of a second language.

Internal reconstruction   The reconstruction of a proto-language that relies on the analysis of morphophonemic variation within a single language.

International Phonetic Alphabet (IPA)   The universal system for transcribing the sounds of speech, which has been developing since 1888. The latest version appeared in 1989.

Intonation   Pitch movement in spoken utterances that is not related to differences in word meaning.

Intransitive verb   A verb that does not take a direct object (e.g., *sleep*).

Inversion   A transformation that moves Aux from its position within the VP to a position to the left of the subject, formulated as: Move Aux to C.

Island A constituent that does not permit extraction of a component part (e.g., a coordinated phrase like *Dave and Pam*).

Isogloss Line drawn on a dialect map to represent boundaries between dialects.

Isolate A language that is not known to be related to any other living language (e.g., Basque, Kutenai).

Isolating languages Languages whose words typically consist of only one morpheme (also called **analytic languages**) (e.g., Mandarin).

Jargon Vocabulary peculiar to some field (also called **occupational sociolect**).

Jargonaphasia A symptom of severe cases of Wernicke's aphasia in which the speech contains very few real words of the language.

Kanji The Japanese word for the Chinese characters used to write Japanese.

Katakana The Japanese syllabary that is used in conjunction with hiragana and kanji to write Japanese.

Key *See* **Radical**.

Labial A place feature that characterizes sounds articulated with one or both lips.

Labials Sounds made with closure or near closure of the lips (e.g., the initial sounds of *pan*, *ban* and *man*).

Labiodentals Sounds involving the lower lip and upper teeth (e.g., the initial sounds of *freedom* and *vintage*).

Labiovelars Sounds made with the tongue raised near the velum and the lips rounded at the same time (e.g., the initial sound of *wound*).

Laminal A laminal sound is articulated with the blade of the tongue.

Language bioprogram hypothesis The hypothesis that similarities among creoles reflect linguistic universals both in terms of first language acquisition and with respect to processes and structures which are innate.

Language contact A source of language change that involves the speakers of one language frequently interacting with the speakers of another language.

Laryngeal features Features that represent voicing states.

Laryngeal node The node of the feature hierarchy from which branch out the features that capture voicing states.

Larynx The boxlike structure located in the throat through which air passes during speech production, commonly known as the voicebox.

Lateral A manner feature that characterizes all and only varieties of *l*.

Lateral fissure The fissure that separates the temporal lobe from the frontal and parietal lobes.

Lateral fricative A lateral sound made with a narrow enough closure to be classified as a fricative.

Lateralization The unilateral control of cognitive functions by either the left or the right side of the brain (e.g., language is lateralized to the left hemisphere in most people).

Laterals Sounds made with the sides of the tongue lowered (e.g., varieties of *l*).

Latinate Refers to English morphemes of classical origin the majority of which are from Latin. Many such morphemes have been borrowed indirectly through French or some other Romance language descended from Latin.

Lax vowel A vowel that is made with a placement of the tongue that results in relatively less vocal tract constriction (e.g., the vowel sounds in *hit*, and *but*).

Learning strategies The ways in which language learners process language input and develop linguistic knowledge.

Left-headed unbounded foot An unbounded metrical foot in which the head is located over the leftmost syllable (e.g., *promise*).

Length The auditory property of a sound that enables us to place it on a scale that ranges from short to long.

Lesion Severe damage to the brain.

Lexical ambiguity The result of homophony or polysemy in that a single form has two or more meanings, either related or not.

Lexical category The word-level syntactic categories noun (N), verb (V), adjective (A), and preposition (P).

Lexical diffusion Linguistic change that first manifests itself in a few words and then gradually spreads through the vocabulary of the language.

Lexical gaps Gaps in the lexicon that result from technological innovation or contact with another culture.

Lexicalization The process whereby concepts are encoded in the words of a language (e.g., the concepts of 'motion' and 'manner' are both encoded by the word *roll*).

Lexicon A speaker's mental dictionary, which contains information about the syntactic properties, meaning, and phonological representation of a language's words.

Light syllable A syllable whose rhyme contains a lone, short vowel has one mora and is said to be light. (*See also* **Syllable weight**.)

Lingua franca A third language that is used when speakers of two or more different languages come into contact and are not fully conversant with each other's languages.

Linguistic competence Speakers' ability to produce and understand an unlimited number of utterances, including many that are novel.

Linguistic typology An approach to language classification that classifies languages according to their structural characteristics without regard for genetic relationships.

Linguistic universals Structural characteristics that occur across the languages of the world.

Linguistics The discipline that studies the nature and use of language.

Lobes Substructures of the cerebral hemispheres that appear to have distinct responsibilities (e.g., frontal lobe, temporal lobe).

Logographic writing A type of writing in which symbols represent morphemes or even entire words.

Longitudinal fissure The fissure that extends from the front of the brain to the back and separates the left and right cerebral hemispheres.

Loudness   The auditory property of a sound that enables us to place it on a scale that ranges from soft to loud.

Low   A dorsal feature that characterizes vowels made with the tongue body distinctly lowered from a central position in the oral cavity.

Low vowel   A vowel that is made with the tongue lowered (e.g., the vowel sounds in the words *cat* and *tar*

Machine translation   Translating from one language, such as English, to another language, such as French, using a computer.

Machine-readable dictionary   A dictionary that appears in computer form, such as that found in spelling checkers and thesauruses.

Major class features   Features that represent the classes consonant, obstruent, nasal, liquid, glide, and vowel.

Majority rules strategy   A secondary strategy used to reconstruct proto-forms that stipulates that the segment found in the majority of cognates should be assumed to be the proto-form. (*See also* **Phonetic plausibility strategy**.)

Manner features   Features that represent manner of articulation.

Manner node   The node of the feature hierarchy from which branch out the features that relate to manner of articulation.

Manners of articulation   The various configurations produced by positioning the lips, tongue, velum, and glottis in different ways (e.g., nasal, fricative, liquid).

Marked traits   Those characteristics that are considered to be more complex and/or universally rarer in languages.

Markedness Differential Hypothesis   This hypothesis investigates the assumption that the degree of markedness plays a role in second language acquisition by comparing the relative markedness of structures in the L1 and the L2.

Markedness theory   A theory that classifies traits or patterns of languages as marked (those that are considered to be more complex and/or universally rarer) and unmarked (those that are considered to be less complex and/or universally more common).

Matrix   An array of features that represents a segment.

Matrix clause   The larger phrase in which a complement clause occurs.

Maxim of Manner   A principle that is thought to underlie the efficient use of language and is formulated as: Avoid ambiguity and obscurity; be brief and orderly.

Maxim of Quality   A principle that is thought to underlie the efficient use of language and is formulated as: Try to make your contribution one that is true. (Do not say things that are false or for which you lack adequate evidence.)

Maxim of Quantity   A principle that is thought to underlie the efficient use of language and is formulated as: Do not make your contribution more or less informative than required.

Maxim of Relation   A principle that is thought to underlie the efficient use of language and is formulated as: Be relevant.

Maxims   The specific principles that ensure that conversational interactions satisfy the Co-operative Principle.

Meaning   The message or content that a sign conveys.

Merger   A change in a phonological system in which two or more phonemes collapse into one, thereby reducing the number of phonemes in that language.

Mesolect   A creole variety that sits between an acrolect and a basilect in terms of the amount of influence from the standard language.

Metacognitive strategies   Learning strategies that are used consciously and deliberately in L2 learning.

Metaphor   The understanding of one concept in terms of another, sometimes responsible for language change (e.g., 'argument' understood in terms of 'war': *She annihilated him in the debate*).

Metathesis   A process that reorders a sequence of segments (e.g., West Saxon *a[ks]ian* became *ask*; Old English *brid* became *bird*).

Metrical feet   Units of metrical structure consisting of a stressed syllable and one or more associated unstressed syllables.

Metrics   The study of stress placement.

Mid vowel   A vowel that is made with the tongue neither raised nor lowered (e.g., the vowel sound in *set*).

Minimal foot   *See* **Degenerate foot**.

Modified input   Simplified speech directed at non-native speakers. (*See also* **Foreigner talk**.)

Modifier   An optional element that describes a property of a head (e.g., *blue* in *that blue car*; *that Gloria likes* in *the car that Gloria likes*).

Module (psycholinguistics)   A unit of processing that is relatively autonomous from other processing units.

Mora   This is the minimal rhythmic unit; it belongs to the rhyme constituent of the syllable. (*See also* **Syllable weight**.)

Morpheme   The smallest unit of language that carries information about meaning or function (e.g., *books* consists of the two morphemes *book* + *s*).

Morphology   The system of categories and rules involved in word formation and interpretation.

Morphophonemic rules   Rules that account for alternations among allomorphs.

Motherese   The type of speech that is typically addressed by mothers or other adults to young children (also called **caregiver speech**).

Motor aphasia   *See* **Non-fluent aphasia**.

Movement test   A test used to determine if a group of words is a constituent by moving them as a single unit to a different position within the sentence.

Murmur   The glottal state that produces voiced sounds with the vocal folds relaxed enough to allow enough air to escape to produce a simultaneous whispery effect (also called **whispery voice**).

Mutual intelligibility   The criterion that is sometimes used to distinguish between language and dialect: mutually intelligible varieties of a language can be understood by speakers of each variety and are therefore dialects of the same language.

Nasal   A manner feature that characterizes any sound made with the velum lowered.

Nasalization   The nasalizing effect that a nasal consonant can have on an adjacent vowel.

Nasals   Sounds produced by lowering the velum, allowing air to pass through the nasal passages.

Native speaker   One who has acquired a language as a child in a natural setting.

Nativism   The view that certain grammatical knowledge is inborn.

Natural class   A class of sounds that shares a feature or features (e.g., voiced stops).

Naturalistic approach   An approach to investigating child language in which researchers observe and record children's spontaneous verbal behaviour.

Naturalness   A criterion that guides language reconstruction by determining whether or not changes are natural.

Negative evidence   Clues about grammaticality gleaned by language learners on the basis of what is missing or ungrammatical in the data available to them. (*See also* **Positive evidence**.)

Neologism   A lexical innovation (e.g., *fishocracy* in Newfoundland English).

Neurons   The basic information-processing units of the nervous system, also called nerve cells.

Neuroscience   The scientific study of the brain.

New information   Knowledge that is introduced into the discourse for the first time.

No-naming   The practice of avoiding address terms when participants are unsure which term to use.

Node   *See* **Class node**.

Nominal paradigm   The set of related forms associated with a noun (also called a **declension**).

Non-fluent aphasia   Aphasia that results from damage to parts of the brain in front of the central sulcus and that is characterized by slow, effortful speech production (also called **motor aphasia**).

Non-lexical category   *See* **Functional category**.

Non-terminal intonation contour   Rising or level intonation at the end of an utterance, often signalling that the utterance is incomplete.

Noun (N)   A lexical category that typically names entities, can usually be inflected for number and possession (in English), and functions as the head of a noun phrase (e.g., *key*, *Bob*, *perception*).

NP Movement   A transformation that moves a noun phrase into the subject position.

Nucleus (N)   A vocalic element that forms the core of a syllable (e.g., the vowel [æ] is the nucleus of the first syllable of *Patrick*).

Null Subjects (Pronoun drop parameter)   If a language allows Null Subjects, a subject noun phrase may be omitted without rendering the sentence ungrammatical.

Number   The morphological category that expresses contrasts involving countable quantities (e.g., in English, the two-way distinction between singular and plural).

Object permanence A developmental milestone characterized by the ability to recognize that objects have an existence independent of one's interaction with them.

Oblique NP A noun phrase that combines with a preposition.

Obstruent Any non-sonorant consonant: fricatives, affricates, oral stops.

Obviative A verb form used in some languages to indicate that the entity referred to by the verb is not the entity previously chosen as the focus of the conversation. (*See also* **Proximate**.)

Occipital lobe The area of the brain to the rear of the angular gyrus in which the visual cortex is located.

Old information *See* **Given information**.

Onomatopoeic words Words that have been created to sound like the thing that they name (e.g., *plop*, *hiss*).

Onset Within a syllable, the longest sequence of consonants to the left of each nucleus that does not violate the phonotactic constraints of the language in question (e.g., [st] forms the onset of the second syllable in *hamster*).

Opposition *See* **Contrast**.

Oral sounds Sounds produced with the velum raised and the airflow through the nasal passage cut off.

Orthography A set of conventions for representing language in written form.

Overextension A developmental phenomenon in which the meaning of the child's word is more general or inclusive than that of the corresponding adult form (e.g., *daddy* used to refer to any adult male).

Overgeneralization A developmental phenomenon that results from the overly broad application of a rule (e.g., *falled* instead of *fell*).

Palatalization The effect that front vowels and the palatal glide [j] typically have on velar, alveolar, and dental stops, making their place of articulation more palatal (e.g.,the first sound of *keep* is palatalized).

Palatals Sounds produced with the tongue on or near the palate (e.g., [j]).

Palate The highest part of the roof of the mouth.

Palato-alveolar (area) The area just behind the alveolar ridge where the roof of the mouth rises sharply (also called **alveopalatal**).

Paragraphia An error in writing associated with a linguistic deficit.

Parameter The set of alternatives for a particular phenomenon made available by Universal Grammar to individual languages.

Paraphrases Two sentences that have the same basic meaning (e.g., *'Faust' was written by Goethe* is a paraphrase of *Goethe wrote 'Faust'*).

Parietal lobe The lobe of the brain that lies behind the central sulcus and above the temporal lobe.

Parser A device that provides a grammatical analysis – complete with appropriate labels – of an input string (e.g., a sentence, phrase, etc.).

Parsing The aspect of sentence comprehension (in reading or listening) involving the analysis of the meanings of its words and through the analysis of its syntactic structure.

Partial reduplication   A morphological process that duplicates part of the base to which it applies (e.g., in Tagalog, *takbuh* 'run' and *tatakbuh* 'will run').

Partial suppletion   A morphological process that marks a grammatical contrast by replacing part of a morpheme (e.g., *think/thought*).

Passive sentence   A sentence in which the noun phrase bearing the theme role is encoded as subject (e.g., *The report was prepared by the committee members*).

Pejoration   The process in which the meaning of a word becomes less favourable (e.g., *wench* used to mean simply 'girl').

Penultimate (syllable)   The syllable before the very last one in a word.

Person   A morphological category that typically distinguishes among the first person (the speaker), the second person (the addressee), and the third person (anyone else) (e.g., in English, the difference between *I*, *you*, and *she/he/it*).

Pharyngeals   Sounds made through the modification of airflow in the pharynx by retracting the tongue or constricting the pharynx.

Pharynx   The area of the throat between the uvula and the larynx.

Pheremones   Chemicals used by animals specifically for communicative purposes.

Phone   Any sound used in human language (also called a **speech sound**).

Phoneme   The phonological unit into which predictable variants of non-contrastive segments are grouped (e.g., in English, [l] and [ļ] belong to the phoneme /l/).

Phonemic paraphasia   Speech errors that result from phonemic substitutions and omissions (e.g., *spoon* may be pronounced as *poon*).

Phonetic determinative   The part of a Chinese character that provides information about the pronunciation of the corresponding morpheme.

Phonetic plausibility strategy   The primary strategy used to reconstruct proto-forms; it requires any sound changes posited to be phonetically plausible. (*See also* **Majority rules strategy**.)

Phonetic sound change   A sound change that results in a new allophone of an already existing phoneme.

Phonetically conditioned sound change   Sound change that begins as subtle alterations in the sound pattern of a language in particular phonetic environments.

Phonetics   The branch of linguistics that examines the inventory and structure of the sounds of language.

Phonographic writing   A type of writing in which symbols represent syllables or segments.

Phonological change   A sound change that results in the addition, elimination, or rearrangement of phonemes (e.g., splits, mergers).

Phonological dyslexia   A type of acquired dyslexia in which the patient seems to have lost the ability to use spelling-to-sound rules and can only read words that he or she has seen before.

Phonological rules   Rules that derive phonetic representations from underlying representations, accounting for alternations among allophones.

Phonological skeleton   *See* **Skeleton**.

Phonology   The component of a grammar made up of the elements and principles that determine how sounds pattern in a language.

Phonotactics   The set of constraints on how sequences of segments pattern.

Phrase level   The metrical level on which the stress patterning of phrases is represented.

Phrase   One or more words that are built around a 'skeleton' consisting of two levels, a phrase level and a word level, and act as a syntactic unit (e.g., *the apple*, *Bob*, *hurried to class*).

Phrase structure rule   A rule of grammar that states the composition of a phrase (e.g., XP → (Specifier) X).

Phyla   The groups into which purportedly related Amerindian language stocks are placed (also called **superstocks**).

Pictograms   Pictorial representations of objects or events.

Pidgin   A speech variety that develops when speakers of two or more different languages come into contact and do not know each other's languages.

Pinyin   The system of writing Mandarin with a modified Latin alphabet, used for such things as street signs and brand names.

Pitch   The auditory property of a sound that enables us to place it on a scale that ranges from low to high.

Place features   Features that represent place of articulation.

Place node   The node of the feature hierarchy from which branch out the major place features.

Places of articulation   The points at which the airstream can be modified to produce different sounds.

Plural   A contrast associated with the morphological category of number and associated with nouns that refer to a group.

Politeness formulas   Ways in which requests or commands are made less direct (e.g., *Could you shut the door?* instead of *Shut the door!*).

Polysemy   The situation in which a word has two or more related meanings (e.g., *bright* 'intelligent', *bright* 'shining').

Polysynthetic languages   Languages in which single words can consist of long strings of lexical categories and affixes, often expressing the meaning of an entire sentence in English (e.g., Inuktitut).

Positive evidence   Evidence obtained by language learners from well-formed utterances to which they are actually exposed. (*See also* **Negative evidence**.)

Postposition   A P that occurs after its complement.

Pragmatics   The study of various factors involved in appropriate use and understanding of language, such as the following: the speaker's intentions and how they are surmised by the addressee, the speaker's and addressee's background attitudes and beliefs, their understanding of the context in which the utterance is made, and their knowledge of how language can be used for a variety of purposes.

Prefix   An affix that is attached to the front of its base (e.g., *re-* in *replay*).

Preposition (P)   A lexical category that functions as the head of a prepositional phrase and occurs before its complement (e.g., *into*, *with*, *for*).

Prescriptive   A characteristic of certain non-linguistic approaches to grammar in that they seek to prescribe one system in preference to another. (*See also* **Descriptive**.)

Presupposition   The assumption or belief implied by the use of a particular word or structure.

Primary stress   The most prominent stress of a word.

Principal Components Analysis   A highly quantitative approach to sociolinguistic research, using statistical techniques that allow the investigator to examine a large number of linguistic variants.

Principle A   The principle that constrains the interpretation of reflexive pronouns and is formulated as: A reflexive pronoun must have an antecedent that c-commands it.

Principle B   The principle that constrains the interpretation of pronominals and is formulated as: A pronominal must not have an antecedent that c-commands it.

Principle of Compositionality, the   A principle underlying sentence interpretation that is formulated as: The meaning of a sentence is determined by the meaning of its component parts and the manner in which they are arranged in syntactic structure.

Processes   Articulatory adjustments that occur during the production of speech (e.g., deletion, epenthesis, assimilation).

Proclitic   A clitic attached to the beginning of a following word (e.g., *l'* 'the' in *l'ami* 'the friend' French . (*See also* **Clitic**.)

Productivity   The relative freedom with which affixes can combine with bases of the appropriate category.

Progressive assimilation   Assimilation in which a sound influences a following segment (e.g., liquid–glide devoicing).

Pronominal   A pronoun whose interpretation may, but does not have to be, determined by an antecedent in the same sentence (e.g., *he*, *her*).

Pronoun   A word whose interpretation can be determined by another element (an antecedent) in the same sentence (e.g., *him*, *she*, *themselves*, *herself*).

Pronoun drop parameter   *See* **Null Subjects**.

Prosodic morphology   A theory that highlights the ways in which prosodic units condition morphological processes.

Prosodic properties   *See* **Suprasegmental properties**.

Proto-forms   Forms of a proto-language, written with a preceding asterisk to indicate their hypothetical character.

Proto-Indo-European   The proto-language from which evolved most of the languages of Europe, Persia (Iran), and the northern part of India.

Proto-language   A language reconstructed through the methods of historical linguistics.

Prototypes   The best exemplars of a concept (e.g., robins or magpies are prototypes of the concept 'bird').

Proximate   A verb form used in some languages to indicate that the subject of the verb has been chosen as the focus of the conversation and any further use of which (without an overt subject) indicates a reference to that focused entity. (*See also* **Obviative**.)

Radical   The part of a Chinese character that provides clues about the morpheme's meaning (also called a **key**).

Reading   The interpretation for a particular utterance.

Real world knowledge   Facts people know about the world (e.g., that cats do not laugh and rocks do not sleep) as opposed to specifically linguistic knowledge.

Reanalysis   A source of language change that involves an attempt to attribute a compound or root + affix structure to a word that formerly was not broken down into component morphemes (e.g., *ham + burger*).

Rebus principle   The extension of a sign to any word that is pronounced like the word whose meaning the sign represented initially.

Received Pronunciation (RP)   The prestigious accent of British English which is based on the upper-class speech of the southeast of England, but is generally regarded as regionally neutral.

Reduced   A dorsal feature that characterizes only schwa.

Reduced vowel   An (unstressed) vowel produced with the highest point of the tongue in central region of the mouth so that it sounds like [ə],[ʉ] or [ɨ]. (*See also* **Schwa**.)

Reduplication   A morphological process that duplicates all or part of the base to which it applies. (*See also* **Partial reduplication** and **Full reduplication**.)

Referents   The set of entities to which a word or expression refers (also called its **denotation** or **extension**).

Reflexive pronoun   A pronoun that must have a c-commanding antecedent (e.g., *himself, herself*).

Regional dialect   A speech variety spoken in a particular geographical area (e.g., Newfoundland English).

Register   A speech variety appropriate to a particular speech situation (e.g., formal vs casual).

Register tones   Level tones that signal meaning differences.

Regressive assimilation   Assimilation in which a sound influences a preceding segment (e.g., in fast casual speech, the final alveolar *t* of *that* may become [p] in anticipation of the labial *p* at the start of the next word in the phrase *that pen* [ðæp pen]) .

Related languages   Languages that developed historically from the same ancestor language.

Relational analysis   An approach to syntactic analysis in which syntactic phenomena are described in terms of grammatical relations such as subject and direct object.

Relative clause   A CP-sized modifier that provides information about the noun (e.g., *that Pat wants* in *the job that Pat wants*).

Relevance   In the theory of pragmatics called Relevance Theory, an utterance is said to be *relevant* if it interacts with a particular context by having implications that yield fresh information, refute some belief, or give support to a proposition that is still being entertained.

Relexification   The hypothesis that creoles are largely re-formed over time through the replacement of lexical items, retaining the grammar of the pidgins from which they developed.

Replacement   A morphological process that substitutes one non-morphemic segment in a word by another (e.g., *sing/sang*).

Representations   Graphic presentations of feature changes.

Retroflex   The *r* made by either curling the tongue tip back into the mouth or by bunching the tongue upwards and back in the mouth.

Rhotacism   A type of weakening that typically involves the change of [z] to [r].

Rhotacization   A vowel articulation with *r*-colouring.

Rhyme (R)   The nucleus and the coda of a syllable (e.g., [u:ts] in the word *boots*).

Right ear advantage   The phenomenon in which people with language in the left hemisphere hear speech louder and clearer with the right ear.

Right-headed unbounded foot   An unbounded metrical foot in which the head is located over the rightmost syllable (e.g., *collect*).

Root (of a word)   The morpheme in a word that carries the major component of the word's meaning and belongs to a lexical category (e.g., *collect* in the word *collections*).

Root (of the tongue)   The part of the tongue that is contained in the upper part of the throat.

Root node   The highest node of the feature hierarchy.

Round   A place feature that characterizes sounds made by protruding the lips (e.g., [ɔ], [w]).

Rounded (sounds)   Sounds made with the lips protruding (e.g., [u:], [ø], [ɔ]).

S Rule, the   The phrase structure rule that states the composition of a sentence: S → NP Infl VP.

Schwa   The lax vowel that is characterized by briefer duration than any of the other vowels (also called a **reduced vowel**) (e.g., the underlined vowels in *amid*, *banana*, *police*, *suppose*).

Second language acquisition (SLA)   The acquisition of proficiency in a language that is not one's first language.

Secondary stress   The second most prominent stress of a word.

Segmental change   Sound change that involves the simplification of a complex consonant (e.g., deaffrication).

Segments   Individual speech sounds.

Semantic broadening   The process in which the meaning of a word becomes more inclusive than its earlier form (e.g., *barn* used to mean 'a place to store barley').

Semantic decomposition   *See* **Componential analysis**.

Semantic narrowing   The process in which the meaning of a word becomes less inclusive than its earlier form (e.g., *meat* used to mean 'any type of food').

Semantic shift   The process in which a word loses its former meaning, taking on a new, often related, meaning (e.g., *immoral* used to mean 'not customary').

Semantics   The study of meaning in human language.

Semiotics   The study of signs.

Sensory aphasia   *See* **Fluent aphasia**.

Sequential change   Sound change that involves sequences of segments (e.g., assimilation).

Shift   A change in a phonological system in which a series of phonemes is systematically modified so that their organization with respect to each other is altered (e.g., the Great English Vowel Shift).

Sibilants   *See* **Stridents**.

Sign   A unit of communication structure that consists of two parts: a signifier and something signified.

Signal   A sign that triggers a specific action on the part of the receiver (e.g., traffic lights).

Signified   The real world object that a sign represents, as well as the sign's conceptual content.

Signifier   That part of a sign that stimulates at least one sense organ of the receiver of a message.

Simple vowels   Vowels that do not show a noticeable change in quality during their production (also called **monophthongs**) (e.g., the vowel sounds of *cab* and *get*).

Simple word   A word that consists of a single morpheme (e.g., *horse*).

Singular   A contrast associated with the morphological category of number and associated with nouns that refer to a single entity.

Skeleton (CV-tier)   A sequence of timing positions mediating between syllable structure and segmental structure.

Slang   Informal or faddish usages of language.

Social network analysis   An approach to sociolinguistic research in which the researcher is a participant-observer of a social group and interprets linguistic variation in terms of the kinds and densities of relationships experienced by speakers.

Social stratification   The differentiation of language varieties along the vertical continuum of socio-economic status.

Sociolect   A speech variety spoken by a group of people who share a particular social characteristic such as socio-economic class, ethnicity, or age.

Sociolinguistics   The study of the social aspects of language.

Song   In avian communication, lengthy elaborate patterns of mostly pitched sounds.

Sonorant   A major class feature that characterizes all and only the 'singables': vowels, glides, liquids, and nasals.

Sonority   The relative loudness of a sound; it correlates with the degree of openness of the vocal tract involved in its production.

Sound shift   The systematic modification of a series of phonemes (e.g., Grimm's Law).

Specifier   A word that helps to make more precise the meaning of the head of the phrase and that occurs immediately beneath XP (e.g., *will* in *will leave*).

Spectrogram   A visible image of the acoustic properties of speech sounds which shows their frequencies, duration, and intensity.

Spectrograph   An instrument that produces spectrograms.

Speech community   A group whose members share both a particular language or variety of language and the norms for its appropriate use in social context.

Speech recognition   The simulation of the process of decoding the speech signal; it is an essential first step in understanding speech.

Speech situation   A social situation in which there is appropriate use of language.

Speech sound   *See* **Phone**.

Speech synthesis   The simulation of speech production by computer.

Speech variety   The language or form of language used by any group of speakers.

Spelling pronunciation   A source of language change whereby a new pronunciation arises that reflects more closely the spelling of the word (e.g., *often* pronounced as [ɒftən] rather than [ɒfən]).

Split   A situation in which allophones of the same phoneme come to contrast with each other due to the loss of the conditioning environment, resulting in one or more new phonemes.

Split brain experiments   Studies that investigate the effects of surgically severing the corpus callosum.

Spoonerism   A slip of the tongue involving the transposition of the initial sounds of words in an utterance.

Spread Glottis ([SG])   A laryngeal feature that distinguishes unaspirated from aspirated sounds.

Standard language   The superposed variety of a language that is employed by the government and media, used and taught in educational institutions, and is the main or only written variety.

Stem   The base to which an inflectional affix is added (e.g., *modification* is the stem for -*s* in the word *modifications*).

Stimulus-bound communication   Communication that only occurs when it is triggered by exposure to a certain stimulus or for certain specific ends (e.g., the warning call of a bird).

Stocks   The groups into which purportedly related Amerindian language families have been placed.

Stopping   A common substitution process in child language acquisition that involves the replacement of a fricative by a corresponding stop (e.g., *zebra* is pronounced [di:brə]).

Stops   Sounds made with a complete and momentary closure of airflow through the vocal tract (e.g., the initial sounds of *pleasure* and *grab*).

Strategies   The mental processes used by language learners in forming and testing hypotheses about linguistic input and in using linguistic knowledge in communicative situations.

Stray syllable adjunction   The process whereby extrametrical syllables are joined to the metrical foot after stress placement.

Stress clash   A configuration of stresses in which two stresses stand immediately next to each other on one level (first cycle) and also have corresponding stresses on the level below.

Stressed vowels   Vowels that are perceived as relatively more prominent due to the combined effects of pitch, loudness, and length.

Strident   A place feature that acoustically characterizes the 'noisy' fricatives and affricates (in English, [s z ʃ ʒ tʃ dʒ]) (also called **sibilants**).

Stroke   A haemorrhage in the brain or the blockage or rupture of an artery, causing brain damage (also called a **cerebro-vascular accident**).

Structurally ambiguous   The relation between phrases or sentences in which the meanings of their component words can be combined in more than one way (e.g., *fast cars and motorcyles*).

Subcategorization   The classification of words in terms of their complement options (e.g., the verb *devour* is subcategorized for a complement NP).

Subject   The NP occurring immediately under S (e.g., *Irene* in *Irene is a tailor*).

Subject Constraint, the   A constraint on transformations that prevents elements from being removed from a subject phrase.

Subset Principle, the   The initial or default setting of a parameter will correspond to the most restrictive option (i.e., the option that permits the fewest patterns).

Substitution   A type of auditorily based change involving the replacement of one segment with another similar segment (e.g., in the history of English [f] replaced [x] in some words).

Substitution test   A test used to determine if a group of words is a constituent by replacing them with a single word.

Substratum influence   The influence of a politically or culturally non-dominant language on a dominant language in the area (e.g., the borrowing of words into English from Amerindian languages).

Succeeds   Rapid, jerky movements of the eyes used in reading or searching for an object.

Suffix   An affix that is attached to the end of its base (e.g., *-ly* in *quickly*).

Sulci   The areas where the cerebral cortex is folded in (singular: sulcus).

Superstratum influence   The influence of a politically or culturally dominant language on another language in the area (e.g., the effects of Norman-French on English) during the Middle English period.

Suppletion   A morphological process that marks a grammatical contrast by replacing a morpheme with an entirely different morpheme (e.g., *be/was*).

Suprasegmental properties   Those properties of sounds that form part of their makeup no matter what their place or manner of articulation: pitch, loudness, and length (also called **prosodic properties**).

Surface dyslexia   A type of acquired dyslexia in which the patient seems unable to recognize words as wholes, but must process all words through a set of spelling-to-sound rules (e.g., *yacht* would be pronounced /jætʃt/).

Surface structure The structure that results from the application of whatever transformations are appropriate for the sentence in question.

Syllabary A set of syllabic signs used for representing a language.

Syllabic liquids Liquids that function as syllabic nuclei (e.g., the *l* in *bottle*).

Syllabic nasals Nasals that function as syllabic nuclei (e.g., the *n* in *button*).

Syllabic writing A type of writing in which each symbol represents a syllable.

Syllable A unit of linguistic structure that consists of a syllabic element and any segments that are associated with it. (*See also* **Onset, Nucleus, Coda, Mora.**)

Syllable weight A syllable with one mora is *light* and a syllable with two moras is *heavy*. (See **Mora**.)

Symbolic sign A sign that bears an arbitrary relationship to its referent (e.g., non-onomatopoeic words, a stop sign).

Syncope The deletion of a word-internal vowel (e.g., the deletion of the schwa in *police* so that it is pronounced [pli:s].

Synonyms Words or expressions that have the same meanings in some or all contexts (e.g., *buy* and *purchase*).

Syntactic category The category into which an element is placed depending on the type of meaning that it expresses, the type of affixes it takes, and the type of structure in which it occurs (includes both lexical and functional categories).

Syntax The system of rules and categories that underlies sentence formation in human language.

Synthetic languages Languages that are agglutinating or fusional.

Systematic gaps Gaps in the occurring syllable structures of a language that result from the exclusion of certain sequences (e.g., *pfordv* in English).

Systematic phonetic correspondences Sound correspondences between two or more related languages that are consistent throughout the vocabularies of those languages.

Taboo Expressions that are seen as offensive and are therefore often euphemized.

Target language (language pedagogy) The language that an L2 learner is learning.

Target language (translation) The language into which a text in the source language is translated.

Teacher talk *See* **Foreigner talk**.

Telegraphic speech Speech lacking functional categories and bound morphemes.

Telegraphic stage The stage in child language acquisition in which children's utterances are generally longer than two words but lack bound morphemes and most non-lexical categories.

Template The innate blueprint of birdsong that predisposes birds to perform a general song that is extremely simplified.

Template   *See* **Templatic morphology**.

Templatic morphology   An approach to morphology in which skeletal positions of the CV-tier provide a template or mould which is then filled by the actual consonant and vowel sounds that realize that form. (*See also* **Binyan**.)

Temporal lobe   The lobe of the brain that lies beneath the lateral fissure and in which Wernicke's area is located.

Tense (feature)   A dorsal feature that captures the tense-lax distinction among vowels.

Tense (verb)   A morphological category that encodes the time of a situation with reference to the moment of speaking (e.g., in English, the two-way contrast between past and non-past).

Tense vowel   A vowel that is made with a placement of the tongue that results in relatively greater vocal tract constriction (e.g., the vowel sounds in *heat* and *boat*).

Terminal (intonation) contour   Falling intonation at the end of an utterance, signalling that the utterance is complete.

Text   The written version of any utterance or body of discourse.

Textual reference   *See* **Endophoric reference**.

Thematic role   The part played by a particular entity in an event (e.g., agent, theme, source, goal, location).

Theme   The thematic role of the entity directly affected by the action designated by the verb (e.g., *the ball* in *Tom caught the ball*).

Thyroid cartilage   The cartilage that forms the main portion of the larynx, spreading outwards like the head of a plough.

Tiers   Levels on the feature hierarchy that reflect the nodes' and features' relation to each other.

Tip (of the tongue)   The narrow area at the front of the tongue.

Token   An individual instance of a sign.

Tone language   A language in which differences in word meaning and/or grammatical contrasts are signalled by differences in pitch.

Tone   Pitch movement in spoken utterances that is related to differences in word meaning.

Top-down processing   A type of processing using a set of expectations to guide phonetic processing and word recognition.

Topic   What a sentence or group of sentences is about.

Trace   The empty element, marked by the symbol *e*, that is left in syntactic structure after an element has been moved.

Trachea   The tube below the larynx through which air travels when it leaves the lungs; commonly known as the windpipe.

Transfer   A process whereby a property or rule of the learner's first language is carried over to the interlanguage grammar.

Transfer error   An error reflecting the carry over of a characteristic of the first language to the interlanguage.

Transformation   A type of syntactic rule that can move an element from one position to another.

Transformational syntax   A widely accepted approach to syntactic analysis in which syntactic phenomena are described in terms of phrase structure rules (which generate deep structures) and transformations (which generate surface structures).

Transitional constructions   The structures characteristic of different stages in the developmental sequence during L2 acquisition.

Transitive verb   A verb that takes a direct object (e.g., *hit*).

Tree structure   A diagram that represents the details of a word's or phrase's internal structure.

Trill   An *r*-like sound that is made by passing air over the raised tongue tip, allowing it to vibrate.

Trochaic (foot)   A bounded, left-headed metrical foot (e.g. *tender*, *drawer*, *sailor* etc.).

Truth conditions   The circumstances in which a sentence is true.

Typological plausibility   A criterion that guides language reconstruction by referring to universals or existing properties of language.

Umlaut   The effect that a vowel (or sometimes a glide) in one syllable can have on the vowel of another (usually preceding) syllable.

Unbounded foot   A metrical foot consisting of a head and any number of unstressed syllables.

Underextension   A developmental phenomenon in which a child uses a lexical item to denote only a subset of the items that it denotes in adult speech (e.g., *car* used to refer to only moving cars).

Underlying   The unpredictable features of a phonemic segment are basic or underlying.

Underspecification (phonological)   Partial specification of segments, using the minimal number of features required to distinguish them phonologically.

Universal Grammar   The system of categories, mechanisms, and constraints shared by all human languages and considered to be innate.

Universal tendencies   Patterns or traits that occur in most languages.

Unmarked traits   Those characteristics of language that are considered to be less complex and/or universally more common in languages.

Utterance   Any bit of talk produced by a speaker that is distinct from other bits of talk in a speech situation.

Uvula   The small fleshy flap of tissue that hangs down from the velum.

Uvulars   Sounds made with the tongue near or touching the uvula (e.g., [q], [N]).

Velars   Sounds made with the tongue touching or near the velum (e.g., [ŋ], [k]).

Velum   The soft area towards the rear of the roof of the mouth.

Verb (V)   A lexical category that typically designates actions, sensations, and states, can usually be inflected for tense, and functions as the head of a verb phrase (e.g., *see*, *feel*, *remain*).

Verbal hedges   Words or phrases that make statements less assertive (e.g., *maybe*, *sort of*).

Verbal paradigm   The set of inflected forms associated with a verb (also called a **conjugation**).

Vocal cords   *See* **Vocal folds**.

Vocal folds   A set of muscles inside the larynx that may be positioned in various ways to produce different glottal states (also called **vocal cords**).

Vocal tract   The oral cavity, nasal cavity, and pharynx.

Vocalic   A major class feature that characterizes vowels and liquids.

Voice   A laryngeal feature that distinguishes between voiced and voiceless sounds.

Voiced   The glottal state in which the vocal folds are brought close together, but not tightly closed, causing them to vibrate as air passes between them (e.g., [e], [z], [m] are voiced).

Voiceless   The glottal state in which the vocal folds are pulled apart, allowing air to pass directly through the glottis (e.g., [t], [s], [f] are voiceless).

Voicing assimilation   Assimilation in which one segment becomes more like a nearby segment in terms of voicing (e.g., liquid–glide devoicing).

Voicing   Voicing assimilation in which a sound becomes voiced because of a nearby voiced sound.

Vowel reduction   A process that reduces a full vowel, typically unstressed, to a schwa.

Vowels   Sounds that are produced with little obstruction in the vocal tract and that are generally voiced.

Weakening (phonetic)   A process that weakens a segment according to a particular scale of strength.

Weakening (semantic)   The process in which the meaning of a word weakens (e.g., *soon* used to mean 'immediately' but now means 'in the near future').

Wernicke's aphasia   The aphasia that results in fluent but nonsensical speech, sometimes characterized by **jargonaphasia**.

***Wh* Movement**   A transformation that moves a *wh* phrase to the beginning of the sentence: Move a wh phrase to the specifier position under CP.

***Wh* question**   A sentence that begins with a *wh* word (e.g., *Who did you see?*).

Whisper   The glottal state in which the vocal folds are adjusted so that the front portions are pulled close together, while the back portions are apart.

Whispery voice   *See* **Murmur**.

Word level   A level of metrical representation above the foot level.

Word manufacture   The creation of a word from scratch (also called coinage) (e.g., *Kodak*).

Word-based morphology   Morphology in which most complex words are formed from a root that can itself be a word.

Words   The smallest free forms found in language.

Writing   The symbolic representation of language in storable graphic form.

Zero derivation   *See* **Conversion**.

Language index

Subject Index